MELVILLE
in the
SOUTH SEAS

By CHARLES ROBERTS ANDERSON

HERMAN MELVILLE, *with his cigar and his Spanish eyes,* talks *Typee and Omoo, just as you find the flow of his delightful mind on paper. Those who have only read his books know the man—those who have only seen the man have a fair idea of his books.* (N. P. Willis *in the New York* Home Journal, *October 13, 1849.*)

NEW YORK

DOVER PUBLICATIONS, INC.

TO

EUGENIA BLOUNT ANDERSON

Published in Canada by General Publishing Company, Ltd., 30 Lesmill Road, Don Mills, Toronto, Ontario.
Published in the United Kingdom by Constable and Company, Ltd., 10 Orange Street, London W. C. 2.

This Dover edition, first published in 1966, is a revised republication of the work first published by Columbia University Press in 1939.
A grant to assist in the publication of the first edition of this volume was awarded by the American Council of Learned Societies from a fund provided by the Carnegie Corporation of New York.

Library of Congress Catalog Card Number: 66-17122

Manufactured in the United States of America
Dover Publications, Inc.
180 Varick Street
New York, N. Y. 10014

PREFACE TO THE DOVER EDITION

ERMAN MELVILLE'S career as a novelist came into being through the fortunate conjunction of a brilliant talent and a sequence of experiences remarkable enough to furnish the writer of fictions with abundant materials ready-to-hand. The most dramatic were Melville's four years in the South Seas—which included his outward-bound voyage on a whaler, his adventures among the romantic primitives of Polynesia, and his return home on an American man-of-war. Without these experiences, which formed the staple of half-a-dozen novels, the very idea of authorship might never have occurred to him. Many other young men in the mid-nineteenth century were having similar experiences, of course, and Melville like them might have remained inarticulate had it not been for an innate urge to expression. A potential artist was confronted with compelling materials. It was the reaction of this sensitive intelligence to a strange new world that produced in rapid succession *Typee, Omoo, Mardi, White-Jacket, Moby-Dick* (between 1846 and 1851) and "The Encantadas" a few years later.

These fictions, insofar as they relate to the Pacific, are the subject of the present study. At the time of its first publication scarcely a single authenticated fact had been turned up by previous biographers for the years 1841-1845—the most important period of Melville's life, since it furnished the experiencess drawn on for the bulk of his writings. In fact, none of the impressive shelf of scholarly and critical works now available had appeared by 1939, the only one of any interest to serious students being Raymond Weaver's *Herman Melville, Mariner and Mystic* (1921). This was followed by John Freeman's short biography in the "English Men of Letters" series (1926), and Lewis Mumford's popular appreciative volume (1929). For Melville's four-year residence in the

South Seas all of them merely transcribed his novels as auto-biography, filling in the background with a history of whaling and a general account of missionaries and colonizers in Polynesia. It is true that Melville is one of those special creators, like Mark Twain and Ernest Hemingway, whose novels play close to the line of his personal experiences; but it is a very dubious procedure to read the fictions as fact. For the literary student the only valid approach is the opposite one: to establish the autobiographical record as fully as possible and then to study the fictions in their relation to that, departures and differences being the chief matters of interest.

The present writer's chance examination of the official records covering Melville's brief service in the American Navy revealed the rather surprising fact that no previous biographers had consulted this obvious source material. The routine facts furnished by log books, muster rolls, squadron letters, and other official documents were richly supplemented by the discovery of an anonymous and discursive journal—all dealing with Melville's homeward-bound voyage in the frigate *United States*. (These manuscripts are in the Naval Records and Library, Washington, D. C., except in a few instances as noted. They are described in detail and the most important ones reproduced in my *Journal of a Cruise to the Pacific Ocean, 1842-1844, in the Frigate United States; with Notes on Herman Melville,* Duke University Press, 1937.) They provided a great wealth of new biographical data for this period of fourteen months, and more importantly the opportunity of seeing at first hand actual scenes and characters later embodied in *White-Jacket*.

The discovery of these new naval manuscripts led to a search for records of Melville's first two and a half years in the South Seas, as whaleman and rover. The first task was to read everything in print about him, then to comb again the known repositories of Melvilleiana in the Widener Library at Harvard and in the Duyck-inck and Gansevoort-Lansing Collections at the New York Public Library. But the great mass of new biographical material came from previously unknown manuscripts and documents in widely scattered institutions from Paris to Sydney, Australia. (The range of these sources is indicated in the paragraph of acknowledgements below. The adventures enjoyed during this research are recorded in my essay, "The Romance of Scholarship: Tracking Melville in the South Seas," published in *The Colophon*, Spring 1938.) Finally, the search was extended to the contemporary literature of travel, Pacific explorations, and Polynesian ethnology. From these sources was gleaned a large body of material related to *Typee* and *Omoo*, also in lesser degree to *Mardi*, *Moby-Dick*, and "The Encantadas." The most important result of all this was that it enabled me to indicate for the first time the three strands out of which Melville composed these novels: direct transcriptions from his life, borrowings from his reading transmuted into the stuff of fiction, and best of all, those parts of his books which were clearly imaginative creations. These are some of the ways in which *Melville in the South Seas* pioneered the great flood of scholarly and critical studies that have appeared since 1939.

Several mechanical matters call for a word of explanation. All references to Melville's works throughout the present volume are to the standard edition by Constable & Company, London (1922-1924), unless otherwise indicated. For the sake of uniformity I have followed the *Century Dictionary and Atlas* for proper names, and the French spelling of Polynesian words (standard in the nineteenth century), with two exceptions: I have retained Melville's from "Typee" and the more popular "Papeete," instead of "Taipi" and "Papéiti." To avoid confusion I have used quotation marks for fictitious ships ("Pequod") to differentiate them from actual ships (*Acushnet*). The list of works at the back, preceding the index, is merely a key to the abbreviations used in the notes, and is not intended in any sense as a bibliography. Finally, the map that follows this Preface I have drawn as a chart of Melville's South Sea wanderings. The route outward-bound (. . . . .) was established by conjecture from half-a-dozen documented points on his itinerary; the route homeward-bound ($\rightarrow$ $\rightarrow$) was taken from the Log Book of the frigate *United States*.

For research aid I would like to thank the curators and librarians of the following institutions: the British Museum, Duke

University Library, Houghton and Widener Libraries at Harvard, Historical Society of Delaware, Library of Congress, Ministère de la Marine (Paris), Mitchell Library (Sydney, Australia), Naval Records and Library (Washington), New York Public Library, Old Dartmouth Historical Society (New Bedford, Massachusetts), Public Library of New South Wales (Australia), University of Hawaii Library, Whaling Museum (New Bedford, Massachusetts). For assistance in the discovery of new source material in private hands: Robert S. Forsythe of the Newberry Library, Nelson Gaskill of Washington, D. C., and Carroll A. Wilson of New York. Acknowledgement is made to Doubleday and Company for permission to quote from Raymond Weaver's *Herman Melville* and to Harcourt, Brace and Company to quote from Lewis Mumford's *Herman Melville.*

Finally, I am grateful to the Columbia University Press, publishers of the original edition of *Melville in the South Seas* (1939), for allowing this work to be republished. The Dover edition differs from the first only in that the present Preface has been substituted for a considerably longer Preface and Introduction, which seemed timely a quarter-century ago but have no relevance today. Of course, the notes pertaining to the deleted Preface and Introduction have also been omitted. Otherwise the text has not been altered.

CHARLES R. ANDERSON

Johns Hopkins University
December, 1965

TABLE OF CONTENTS

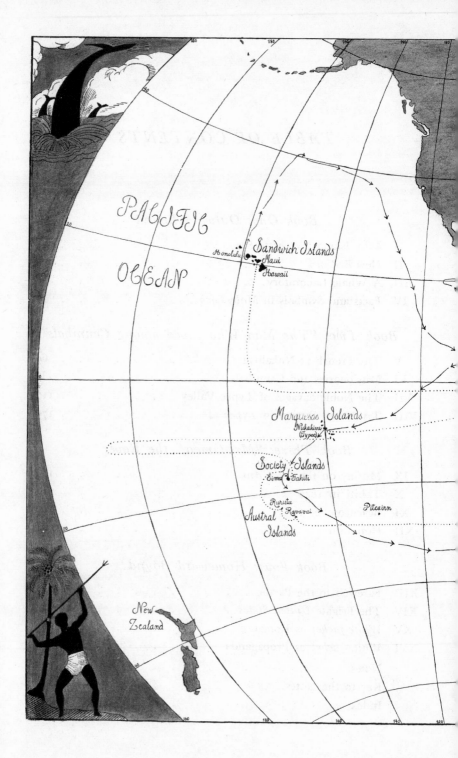

MELVILLE
South Sea Routes
Outward Bound ......
Homeward Bound →
ERA

ATLANTIC

OCEAN

NORTH

AMERICA

Boston
New Bedford

Mazatlan

Cape Verde
Islands

Galapagos
Islands

Santa

Lima
Callao

SOUTH

AMERICA

Rio de Janeiro

Coquimbo

Valparaiso

Cape
Horn

BOOK ONE

OUTWARD BOUND

CHAPTER I

WHY ISHMAEL WENT TO SEA

CALL me Ishmael. Some years ago—never mind how long precisely—having little or no money in my purse, and nothing particular to interest me on shore, I thought I would sail about a little and see the watery part of the world. It is a way I have of driving off the spleen, and regulating the circulation. Whenever I find myself growing grim about the mouth; whenever it is a damp, drizzly November in my soul; whenever I find myself involuntarily pausing before coffin warehouses, and bringing up the rear of every funeral I meet; and especially whenever my hypos get such an upper hand of me, that it requires a strong moral principle to prevent me from deliberately stepping into the street, and methodically knocking people's hats off—then, I account it high time to get to sea as soon as I can. This is my substitute for pistol and ball. With a philosophical flourish Cato throws himself upon his sword; I quietly take to the ship.[1]

WITH these words Herman Melville launched his leviathan *Moby-Dick,* on the full tide of his literary popularity in the fall of 1851. But whether any such dramatic mood actually drove him to sea in the bitter January of a decade before is an entirely different matter. Since most students of Melville have concerned themselves with analyzing his motives—and since many of them have been fascinated, in spite of themselves, with his theatrical pose—it seems pertinent now to collect whatever facts are available to explain why the "son of a gentleman," as Melville himself phrases it in *Redburn,* "ran away to sea."

Arthur Stedman, the friend of Melville's old age, was apparently the first to suggest one of the most persistent of the many explanations that have been ventured. Writing for a forgetful public at the time of Melville's death, he said: "It is more than probable that the publication of Dana's Two Years Before the Mast,' in 1840, influenced him to follow the sea as a vocation, and to ship for Liverpool as cabin boy." [2] But here the chronology is plainly confused, for it was in June, 1837, that Melville had first gone to sea, with England as his destination. In his next biographical sketch Stedman corrected this error, but he now applied the same motivation to Melville's second voyage, saying this time that the reading of *Two Years Before the Mast* "revived the spirit of adventure in Melville's breast." ³ His most recent biographer is still favorable to this suggestion: "One has no proof that Melville read Dana's book as soon as it came out; but . . . the chances are that [it] gave Melville just the fillip he needed to determine on a wider, farther jaunt into the South Seas." ⁴ This hypothesis was rejected unceremoniously some years ago, however, by Melville's first biographer, who concluded sensibly: "That the reading of Dana's book should have filled his head with a mere adolescent longing for brine-drenched locomotion and sent him gallantly off to sea is a surmise more remarkable for simplicity than insight." ⁵ The matter should have been allowed to rest there. It is true that *Two Years Before the Mast* did start a vogue of seafaring for gentlemen's sons in the 1840's and 1850's. But it is extremely doubtful that Melville was so influenced, for the famous volume was not published until October 6, 1840.⁶ To assume that he arrived in New Bedford at the end of December, 1840, with a carpetbag under one arm and a copy of Dana's book—just two and a half months off the press—tucked under the other is unconvincing, though picturesque.

This explanation has given place to others, equally romantic. In summing up the evidence of "Why Ishmael Went to Sea," one critic concluded:

He had tried alternating school with a job clerking in the New York State Bank; losing that job, for he was never good at mathematics, he had then tried clerking in his brother's shop, with no better success; then he tried haying on his uncle's farm; then teaching—for one term. He had failed at everything. Going to sea was his "substitute for pistol and ball." ⁷

These are set forth as the motives that inspired Melville with the romance of forecastle life in 1837. But they are applied equally to the second venture in 1841, when he "knew already what it was like; he fled to it merely as an escape from a greater evil." And they seem to fill out the less specific explanation that Melville himself gives on the opening page of *Redburn*:

Sad disappointments in several plans which I had sketched for my future life; the necessity of doing something for myself, united to a naturally roving disposition, had now conspired within me, to send me to sea as a sailor.[8]

The added phrase that this was his "substitute for pistol and ball," however, merely carries the discussion back to Melville's artistic flourish in setting the dominant tone for *Moby-Dick*. Even his most conservative biographer, apparently accepting this flight-from-suicide as autobiographical, hints at an equally dramatic mood compelling Ishmael to sea, in spite of his confession that the actual reasons are unknown:

Just what specific circumstances were the occasion of Melville's escape into whaling will probably never be known: what burst of demoniac impulse, either of anger, or envy, or spite; what gnawing discontent; what passionate disappointment; what crucifixion of affection; what blind impetuosity; what sinister design. But in the light of his writings and the known facts of his life it seems likely that his desperate transit was made in the mid-winter of his discontent.[9]

Speculating on the emotional despair and spiritual crises of a clinical patient when there are no facts in the record, however, is unsatisfactory, and may even prove misleading if adopted as a persistent attitude of approach.

One piece of evidence has been brought forward which has a convincing ring. The discoverer derives his clue from Melville himself, who speculated in *Moby-Dick*:

Though I cannot tell why it was exactly that those stage managers, the Fates, put me down for this shabby part of a whaling voyage, when others were set down for magnificent parts in high tragedies, and short and easy parts in genteel comedies, and jolly parts in farces— . . . I think I can see a little into the springs and motives which [were] cunningly presented to me under various disguises. . . .

Chief among these motives was the overwhelming idea of the great whale himself. Such a portentous and mysterious monster roused all my curiosity. Then the wild and distant seas where he rolled his island bulk; the undeliverable, nameless perils of the whale; these, with all the attending marvels of a thousand Patagonian sights and sounds, helped to sway me to my wish. With other men, perhaps, such things would not have been inducements; but as for me, I am tormented with an everlasting itch for things remote. I love to sail forbidden seas, and land on barbarous coasts. . . .

By reason of these things, then, the whaling voyage was welcome; the great flood-gates of the wonder-world swung open, and in the wild conceits that swayed me to my purpose, two and two there floated into my inmost soul, endless processions of the whale, and, midmost of them all, one grand hooded phantom, like a snow hill in the air.[10]

The investigator then raises the question: How did Melville know of the existence of a great White Whale before he went to the Pacific? This question he answers himself: Melville must have read "Mocha-Dick; or, the White Whale of the Pacific (a leaf from a Manuscript Journal)," published by John M. Reynolds in the *Knickerbocker Magazine* for May, 1839. When it is remembered that Melville was contributing juvenilia to the periodical press in this very year, it does not seem improbable that such an exciting true story, published in a household journal, should have come under his eye. Here his imagination could well have been kindled by reading of the exploits and final death of this White Whale, the victor in a hundred fights with whaleboats, whose renown among whalemen was so universal that the customary salutation between passing ships in the Pacific was: "Any news of Mocha Dick?" So striking, indeed, is the resemblance between this leviathan of fact and the White Whale of Melville's fiction, that one is inclined to give some consideration to the twofold claim:

That Reynolds, by writing his "Mocha-Dick, the White Whale of the Pacific (a leaf from my Journal [*sic*])," did Melville, the youthful school teacher and embryo journalist of Albany, a great service I must affirm, for it furnished him with the grand idea for his *chef d'œuvre* "Moby-Dick," and, I feel sure, determined him to voyage the wonder world on a whaler in search of "the one grand hooded phantom." [11]

In addition to the influences of early reading and economic frustration, much has been made of the possibility of a spiritual turmoil induced by an unhappy family situation—a theory substantiated, if at all, by *Pierre*—as the goad which drove Melville in a "headlong retreat from all havens astern." It is, indeed, to Melville's family that we now turn for motives; but, rather than goads to escape, we find instead allurements held out, however unconsciously. In this connection, it is interesting to note that on his first voyage before the mast (the family telling his friends that he had gone "abroad") he took along his cherished copy of Allan Melville's guidebook to Liverpool, his only port of debarkation, and with filial devotion retraced his father's footsteps of thirty years before.[12] Again, Melville furnishes the clue for his second voyage when he says: "I love to sail forbidden seas, and land on barbarous coasts." What could this inland boy have known of forbidden seas and barbarous coasts before he found out from his own experience? In relating "How Wellingborough Redburn's Taste for the Sea Was Born and Bred in Him," and how the vision of foreign travel hung over his boyhood like an enchantment, he gives a partial answer to this question. For Herman Melville did not set the precedent in his family of going to sea: at least one of his seafaring kinsmen he mentions himself, with enthusiasm:

. . . an uncle of mine, an old sea-captain, with white hair, . . . used to sail to a place called Archangel in Russia, and . . . used to tell me that he was with Captain Langsdorff, when Captain Langsdorff crossed over by land from the sea of Okotsk in Asia to St. Petersburgh, drawn by large dogs in a sled. . . . He was the very first sea-captain I had ever seen, and his white hair and fine handsome florid face made so strong an impression upon me, that I have never forgotten him, though I only saw him during this one visit of his to New York, for he was lost in the White Sea some years after.[13]

This uncle was Captain John DeWolf II. He was not, however, lost in the White Sea; and, if Melville's testimony in *Moby-Dick* is to be credited, he did see him afterwards—perhaps many times.[14] For Captain DeWolf retired from the sea in 1827, at the age of forty-eight, and lived thereafter (until his death in 1872) at Brighton, Massachusetts, and later at Dorchester, near Boston, where Herman certainly must have seen him on boyhood visits to his Melville relatives—and where he testifies to a conversation with him concerning whales, previous to the publication of *Moby-Dick*.[15] DeWolf had been, in fact, closely associated with G. H. von Langsdorff, the naturalist of A. J. von Krusenstern's expedition of discovery. He met the scientist at Norfolk Sound on the northwest coast of America in 1805, just after the latter's visit to the islands of the South Seas. The two became fast friends, spending the next six months together in winter quarters, and most of the following two years as companions in travel and adventure. Captain DeWolf later testified to this friendship by naming his only son John Lansdorff [*sic*] DeWolf. In Langsdorff's account of the expedition—which mentions DeWolf affectionately many times —among the most fascinating passages are the hundred pages given over to the Marquesas Islands, the Russian explorers having spent ten days of fruitful investigaton at Nukahiva, May 7–17, 1804.[16] That Melville had read Langsdorff by 1851, he assures us in *Moby-Dick*. It seems quite reasonable to assume that the family interest in this volume should have brought it to his attention before he went to sea in 1841 (it had been translated into English in 1813), and, even more so, that Uncle John DeWolf should have discoursed upon the charms of Polynesia, as he had heard of them from his friend Langsdorff, at many a family gathering. Such "Patagonian sights and sounds" would not have fallen lightly on the romantic imagination of one whose boyhood was haunted by visions of forbidden seas and barbarous coasts. There is certainly more than mere coincidence in the fact that Melville picked Nuka-hiva as his first point of debarkation in the South Seas, when he could have deserted at half-a-dozen previous ports.

Another seafaring kinsman was much more intimately connected with Melville's youth. In the village of Gansevoort, Saratoga County, New York, Leonard Herman Gansevoort, the uncle for whom Herman Melville was named, had established himself after the War of 1812. Although this uncle had died when Melville was a baby, he had left a son, Guert Gansevoort, who, in spite of being seven years Melville's senior, must have felt particularly close to his young cousin.[17] It was in this home, only forty miles from his native Albany, that Melville spent most of his summers between 1830 and 1840.[18] His cousin, however, was in the United States navy throughout Melville's youth—as a midshipman from 1823 to 1837 and as a lieutenant thereafter—so that they could have been thrown together only during Guert's leaves of absence.[19] As a boy of twelve years he went to the Mediterranean on his first cruise, 1824–1827, but on his return, because of his extreme youth, he was granted indefinite leave to attend school—probably at the Albany Academy, where Melville himself was enrolled three years later. But this schooling was brief. In October, 1828, the young midshipman sailed on his second cruise, this time in the United States Ship *St. Louis,* round Cape Horn to the west coast of South America and as far north as Mazatlán, Mexico. Although his ship did not at any time penetrate farther into the Pacific, nevertheless he must have brought home rich tales of Spanish-American life when he returned to New York in December, 1831. For the next year and a half, apparently, he was on continuous leave of absence at Albany, probably completing his irregular education. During the next five years, two and a half were spent also at Albany on leave, and for the rest he was stationed nearby at the navy yards in New York and Norfolk.

Thus, in addition to one year during Melville's boyhood, this naval cousin was on leave of absence, either at Gansevoort or at school in Albany, for more than half the period of Melville's adolescence, 1831 to 1838. One of the longest of these periods was just subsequent to Guert's most interesting cruise, round Cape Horn to the Pacific; another included the weeks just prior to Melville's own first voyage.[20] It is inconceivable that these two young cousins could have failed to enjoy frequent meetings—and even a certain degree of intimacy—during these years. And although young Gansevoort had visited none of the South Sea ports, and hence could bear no tidings of island nymphs and noble cannibals, he could at least have brought the romance of the sea and of distant lands to Melville's eager ears. Besides, he had set a precedent in the Gansevoort-Melville family for the son of a gentleman to go away to sea, albeit not in the shabby business of whaling.

Another cousin, Thomas Wilson Melville, was a midshipman in

the United States navy, and in this instance the evidence of influence is far more direct. After a residence of over twenty years
in France, Thomas Melville, the older brother of Herman's father,
had returned to America and served in the War of 1812 with the
rank of major. In 1816, he had moved with his French wife and
six children to Pittsfield, Massachusetts,[21] where he purchased a
mansion known as Broadhall, "built by Henry Van Schaack, in
1781, with extraordinary care and liberal expenditure, and . . .
for many years much the best-built edifice in the town." [22] It was
here that young Herman Melville had visited, in all probability,
while a schoolboy in Albany, only thirty miles away. And, from
the sketch of this uncle which he contributed to *The History of
Pittsfield*, we know that he lived here as a member of his uncle's
family during the entire year preceding his first trip to sea.[23] The
most interesting member of the household during this year was,
undoubtedly, his cousin Pierre Francois Henry Thomas Wilson
Melville, who was thirteen years his senior, having been born
in Paris in 1806.

Thomas Melville, as he was usually called, had been a midshipman in the United States Navy since 1826, had resigned on June 3,
1834, and had returned home, probably because of ill-health.[24]
Here again, then, Herman Melville's ears must have burned with
tales of the sea and of distant lands. "By the late October fire, on
the great hearth of the capacious kitchen of the old farm-mansion,"
he has recorded, his uncle, with the air of an eighteenth-century
French gentleman, would indulge in reveries of his life in Paris.[25]
And on other occasions, one would imagine, the ex-midshipman
must have held his family audience spellbound with his own reminiscences. For, among other places, his far wanderings had taken
him to the Marquesas Islands, where his ship, the *Vincennes*, had
remained for more than two weeks at Nukahiva, July 27–August
13, 1829; and the crew had even passed a day in Typee Valley—
where Herman Melville later lived in "indulgent captivity"! Just
what personal experiences Thomas Melville recounted, if these
fireside conversations did take place, will probably never be
known; but a fairly close approximation to the general tone of

his observations can be had from the manuscript journal of Thomas Melville's commander, Captain William Bolton Finch.[26]

From these journal jottings we learn that the natives of Nuka-hiva (Taiohaë) Bay were at war with the Typees (Taïpis), who, they said, had stolen seven persons from their valley to sacrifice on the occasion of the death of one of their own chiefs: "They represented the Typees as a very bad people, that they ate men, and are otherwise ferocious and treacherous, and urged me to join in a war against them." Captain Finch gave them a peace talk and then paid a visit to Typee Bay, where the natives in similar manner assured him that the "Happahs" and "Noohevans" were themselves bad neighbors. Again he urged peace, in the interest of trade and of their own welfare, but was not sure of the persuasive power of his logic, concluding: "I doubt if the Natives will be at peace for any time." [27] Before leaving the Marquesas, Captain Finch made some parting reflections:

It appears to me that nothing is required to be done at Noohevah [sic] but to overcome wars and occasional sacrifices, to render the inhabitants a most estimable people; happy they certainly are—well fed, well clad, and amply accommodated for the climate. I have never witnessed more attention bestowed on females and children anywhere than at Noohevah. They are decidedly beautiful, and unquestionably a higher order and more noble race of people than those of the Georgian and Society groupes [sic]. . . .

[But he added:] The Noohevans have, probably, never seen an American or European woman—and they absolutely suppose that all our objects in visiting them are secondary to the enjoyment of female favours.[28]

Quitting this primitive group, the *Vincennes* next visited the Society Islands, remaining at Tahiti from August 17 to September 13, 1829. (It will be remembered that Herman Melville followed exactly this same route, thirteen years later.) Here Captain Finch found an entirely different situation, for civilization had been struggling with barbarism in these islands for thirty years and there was less to evoke eloquent comments in his journal. Although he visited the native queen, Pomaré, then a young girl of about seventeen (but later to become famous in fiction and in fact), his only comment was that the royal family was not only powerless but was the most lewd and licentious of all the population. His final observation was:

That great advantages to the civilized world (which has to traverse and often touch at these ports) has been produced [by the work of the missionaries], is without question; but whether the people are better off than heretofore, in a temporal point of view, I cannot but doubt.[29]

From the Society Islands the *Vincennes* made her way to the Sandwich Islands, where she remained from October 2 to November 24, 1829. Here, especially at Honolulu, an apparently flourishing outpost of the Western world invited investigation, but also gave the feeling of being back in civilization. (From this port Herman Melville shipped for home in 1843, so that the further cruising of the *Vincennes*—to Manila, Canton, and home by way of the Cape of Good Hope—is of little present interest.)

How exactly Herman Melville's route through the South Seas was charted for him by the *Vincennes!* Cousin Thomas, the midshipman, may have even marked it off for him on the map: Nukahiva (and Typee), Tahiti, Honolulu. Even the tone of *Typee* and *Omoo* was set for him: the unspoiled beauty of the Marquesans, the havoc wrought by the missionaries in the Society Islands, the half-civilization of Hawaii—if a midshipman's observations were anything like those of his captain. In all probability, if there was any discrepancy Thomas Melville's reminiscences were the more altiloquent of the two.

No wonder, then, that we find Melville soliloquizing in *Typee* as his ship approaches the Marquesas:

The Marquesas! What strange visions of outlandish things does the very name spirit up! Lovely houris—cannibal banquets—groves of cocoanuts—coral reefs—tattooed chiefs—and bamboo temples; sunny valleys planted with bread-fruit trees—carved canoes dancing on the flashing blue waters—savage woodlands guarded by horrible idols—*heathenish rites and human sacrifices.*[30]

What but the vision conjured up in his head six years before by a young midshipman just back from the South Seas, regaling a wide-eyed family circle with an account of his outlandish experiences? These, then, we may conjecture, were the sugarplums—and the candy-cannibals—that danced in Herman Melville's head when in late December of 1840 he stuffed a shirt or two into his old carpetbag and started for Cape Horn and the Pacific. And perhaps the added phantom of "Mocha-Dick" swimming in the background of his imagination made him willing to enter even the shabby business of whaling in order to secure his transportation.

For the obdurate it may be added that the cruise of the *Vincennes* was written up in two stout volumes by C. S. Stewart, the chaplain of the ship. This highly interesting work, *A Visit to the South Seas, in the U. S. Ship Vincennes, during the Years 1829 and 1830,* is specifically mentioned in *Typee* as one of the two general narratives of the Marquesas that claim particular notice, and the only one that Melville admits being acquainted with. The literary use that Melville made of Stewart's volumes will be the inquiry of subsequent chapters.[31]

Despair, frustration, and anguish of spirit there may have been that sent Melville to seek a ship in New Bedford in 1840, just as a drive to escape may lie behind even those human actions that seem to have a more positive explanation. To speculate upon such springs and motives is interesting, and Melville was as busy as his biographers have been in trying to unravel the tangled skein of his adolescent longings and defeats. But mere conjecture, in the absence of reliable evidence, is futile. On the other hand, the facts that specified his channel of escape are more tangible, simple, and commonplace; and they permit us, now, to recast him in a more normal role than that of a twenty-one-year-old misanthrope, fleeing from suicidal promptings in a quest for happiness over the rim of the world.

CHAPTER II

NEW BEDFORD

ON SATURDAY night, December 26, 1840, it must have been, Herman Melville arrived in New Bedford. For it was on the following morning that he attended the picturesque church service celebrated in *Moby-Dick* (and Sunday, December 27, was the only available Sabbath just previous to his known sailing date, January 3, 1841). According to Ishmael: "In . . . New Bedford there stands a Whaleman's Chapel, and few are the moody fishermen, shortly bound for the Indian Ocean or Pacific, who fail to make a Sunday visit to the spot. I am sure that I did not." [1] This Seamen's Bethel had been built in 1830 by the newly organized New Bedford Port Society, and it still stands today, with a bronze tablet memorializing its most important visitor:

SEAMEN'S BETHEL
THE "WHALEMAN'S CHAPEL"
OF MELVILLE'S "MOBY-DICK"

*   *   *

1830–1930 [2]

Before the service began, Melville says, he occupied himself by "steadfastly eyeing several marble tablets, with black borders, masoned into the wall on either side the pulpit"; and, speculating on the possibility of a watery grave suggested by the desolation of "black-bordered marbles which cover no ashes," he concluded with the cheerless sentiment that "Faith, like a jackal, feeds among the tombs, and even from these dead doubts she gathers her most vital hope." Three of these epitaphs he records in *Moby-Dick*, though not pretending to quote. It is noteworthy that, improvising thus from memory, he preserved so accurately the flavor of the originals, which still remain on the walls of the Bethel. One speci-

men from each, the fictitious and the real, will serve to show this
fidelity of tone if not of fact. In *Moby-Dick* one reads:

SACRED
To the Memory
of
JOHN TALBOT,
Who, at the age of eighteen, was lost overboard,
Near the Isle of Desolation, off Patagonia,
November 1st, 1836.
THIS TABLET
Is erected to his memory
BY HIS SISTER.[3]

Compare with this one of the original tablets:

The crew of the Hibernia
erected this token of respect
to their shipmate
DANIEL H. SHIRES
of
New York
Aged 22 Years
Who was lost overboard
August 11, 1835
Near Tristan l' Cunha

*   *   *

Suddenly the shaft of death
Flew to stop his vital breath;
Sunk him to his coral bed,
Till the sea gives up its dead
Cherish'd be his memory pure,
While this marble shall endure.[4]

In Melville's other two recordings, the hand of the dramatist busy
at his preparation is more discernible, for one memorializes "the
Boat's Crews of the Ship Eliza, who were towed out of sight by a
Whale, on the Off-shore Ground in the Pacific" and the other
"Captain Ezekiel Hardy, who in the bows of his boat was killed by
a Sperm Whale on the coast of Japan." There are no actual inscriptions in the Seamen's Bethel quite so appropriate to the purposes of the author of *Moby-Dick*.

Another detail of the interior, as Melville describes it, was far more calculated to catch the visitor's attention; but, apparently, it was not a faithful reproduction of what Ishmael saw at New Bedford. This was the pulpit. In 1930, on the occasion of the dedication of the tablet which connects Melville's name with this now famous little chapel, the orator remarked:

Moby Dick is fiction of course. Accurate in certain details, such as the description of the cenotaphs on the Bethel walls, it is invention elsewhere. The pulpit was at this time [1840] in the east end of the meeting house and it was *not* as described by Melville with respect to the representation of the bow of a ship, the side ladder and the main ropes. I had this many years ago from one who attended the Bethel at the period.[5]

What, then, was the unique original of the pulpit that Melville describes?

Like most old-fashioned pulpits, it was a very lofty one, and since a regular stairs to such a height would, by its long angle with the floor, seriously contract the already small area of the chapel, the architect, it seemed, had acted upon the hint of Father Mapple, and finished the pulpit without a stairs, substituting a perpendicular side ladder, like those used in mounting a ship from a boat at sea. . . .

Nor was the pulpit itself without a trace of the same sea-taste that had achieved the ladder. . . . Its panelled front was in the likeness of a ship's bluff bows, and the Holy Bible rested on a projecting piece of scroll work, fashioned after a ship's fiddle-headed beak.[6]

A suggestion to set Melville's imagination at work fashioning this nautical pulpit he could have found in Colonel Joseph C. Hart's *Miriam Coffin or The Whale-Fisherman,* a more or less true story which he cites in the "Extracts" prefacing *Moby-Dick:*

If any of our readers should feel curious to see the style of building that prevailed one hundred years ago in the town which has since assumed the name of Nantucket, let him now pay a visit to Siasconset, and enter its dwellings. . . . He will there see how, of old, every inch of room was economized, and how sleeping chambers were scaled by perpendicular step-ladders, like those used to descend to the pent-up cabin of a fishing smack, or to clamber up the sides of a merchantman;—and how the best and most spacious room in the house is finished like the cabin

of a ship, with projecting beams, whose corners are beaded and ornamented with rude carving.[7]

Wherever Melville got the suggestion, he put it to characteristic
use; for, when the chaplain enters, this fantastic pulpit becomes a
spiritual symbol rather than a mere sailor's extravaganza:

Halting for an instant at the foot of the ladder, and with both hands
grasping the ornamental knobs of the man-ropes, Father Mapple cast
a look upward, and then with a true sailor-like but still reverential
dexterity, hand over hand, mounted the steps as if ascending the main-
top of his vessel. . . . [But] I was not prepared to see [him] after gaining the height, slowly turn round, and stooping over the pulpit, deliberately drag up the ladder step by step, till the whole was deposited
within, leaving him impregnable in his little Quebec.

I pondered some time without fully comprehending the reason for
this. Father Mapple enjoyed such a wide reputation for sincerity and
sanctity, that I could not suspect him of courting notoriety by any mere
tricks of the stage. No, thought I, there must be some sober reason for
this thing; furthermore, it must symbolize something unseen. Can it
be, then, that by that act of physical isolation, he signifies his spiritual
withdrawal for the time, from all outward worldly ties and connexions?

Then on the full tide of his metaphor—that makes a strange
christening for the pagan "Pequod"—Melville rises to his symbolic
peroration:

What could be more full of meaning?—for the pulpit is ever this
earth's foremost part; all the rest comes in its rear; the pulpit leads the
world. . . . Yes, the world's a ship on its passage out, and not a voyage
complete; and the pulpit is its prow.[8]

"Father Mapple," this chaplain that Melville has undertaken to
immortalize, next challenges the attention of the analyst, for the
sermon that he preaches from his isolated perch marks him as an
evangelist no less than an anchorite. His dual personality is attributable, undoubtedly, to the circumstance that Melville drew
from two separate models. The Reverend Enoch Mudge was actually the Bethel chaplain at the time of Melville's visit. One authority records that he was valued as a man of exceptional appeal in
the pulpit, but even more as the first organizer of religious work
among the sailors: "He ranged along the water front talking with

youth wandering about seeking chances to ship, friendless and lonesome, and urged them to attendance at the Bethel services." [9] He was at the ripe age of sixty-five when Melville heard him, and in 1844, after twelve years of service in New Bedford, he resigned. In him Melville must have found the quality of mellow and benign spirituality with which he clothes his stage figure. But for the sailor-like and evangelical qualities, which make up the substance of Father Mapple's character, he went to another source. The same authority who denies the reality of the nautical pulpit adds: "Nor does the description of Father Mapple conform precisely to Chaplain Mudge. It is said to be a composite of Father Mudge, and Father Taylor of Boston, whom Melville knew. But there is no question but Melville reflected the spirit of the old chapel and of the first chaplain." [10]

"Father" Edward Taylor, who was famous for his work among seamen, had come down from Boston and preached the sermon at the dedication of the Seamen's Bethel in New Bedford in 1832. The local newspaper recorded at the time: "Mr. Taylor has been a sailor, and he speaks from experience and from the heart. He lays no stress on technical theology, nor on creeds and dogmas of faith, but is both catholic and evangelical." [11] Such, then, were the models from whom Melville drew his description:

I had not been seated very long ere a man of a certain venerable robustness entered. . . . Yes, it was the famous Father Mapple, so called by the whalemen, among whom he was a very great favorite. He had been a sailor and a harpooneer in his youth, but for many years past had dedicated his life to the ministry. At the time I now write of, Father Mapple was in the hardy winter of a healthy old age; that sort of old age which seems merging into a second flowering youth, for among all the fissures of his wrinkles, there shone certain mild gleams of a newly developing bloom—the spring verdure peeping forth even beneath February's snow. No one having previously heard his history, could for the first time behold Father Mapple without the utmost interest, because there were certain engrafted clerical peculiarities about him, imputable to that adventurous maritime life he had led.[12]

Fortunately, there has survived a vivid picture of the original "Father" Taylor of Boston, the famous Bethel chaplain who attracted the attention of Emerson, Webster, Theodore Parker, Jenny Lind, Harriet Martineau, and other celebrities. Charles Dickens, with a reporter's eye for the picturesque, sketched him in action in his pulpit and added him to the collection of native specimens he has preserved in his *American Notes:*

The only preacher I heard in Boston was Mr. Taylor, who addresses himself peculiarly to seamen, and who was once a mariner himself. I found his chapel down among the shipping, in one of the narrow, old, waterside streets, with a gay blue flag waving freely from its roof. . . . The preacher already sat in the pulpit, which was raised on pillars, and ornamented behind him with painted drapery of a lively and somewhat theatrical appearance. He looked a weather-beaten hard-featured man, of about six or eight-and-fifty; with deep lines graven as it were into his face, dark hair, and a stern, keen eye. Yet the general character of his countenance was pleasant and agreeable. The service commenced with a hymn, to which succeeded an extemporary prayer. . . . That done he opened his discourse, taking for his text a passage from the Song of Solomon . . . : "Who is this coming up from the wilderness, leaning on the arm of her Beloved!"

He handled his text in all kinds of ways, and twisted it into all manner of shapes; but always ingeniously, and with a rude eloquence, well adapted to the comprehension of his hearers. Indeed if I be not mistaken, he studied their sympathies and understandings much more than the display of his own powers. His imagery was all drawn from the sea, and from the incidents of a seaman's life; and was often remarkably good. He spoke to them of "that glorious man, Lord Nelson," and of Collingwood. . . . Sometimes, when much excited with his subject, he had an odd way . . . of taking his great quarto Bible under his arm and pacing up and down the pulpit with it; looking steadily down, meantime, into the midst of the congregation, . . . and pursued his discourse after this manner:

"Who are these—who are they—who are these fellows? where do they come from? Where are they going to?—Come from! What's the answer?" —leaning out of the pulpit, and pointing downward with his right hand: "From below!"—starting back again, and looking at the sailors before him: "From below, my brethren. From under the hatches of sin, battened down above you by the Evil One. That's where you came from!"—a walk up and down the pulpit: "and where are you going"— stopping abruptly: "where are you going? Aloft!"—very softly, and pointing upward: "Aloft!"—louder: "Aloft!"—louder still: "That's where you are going—with a fair wind—all taut and trim, steering direct for Heaven in its glory, where there are no storms or foul weather, and where the wicked cease from troubling, and the weary are at rest."— Another walk: "That's where you're going to, my friends. That's it. That's the place. That's the port. That's the haven. It's a blessed harbour—still water there, in all changes of the winds and tides; no driving ashore upon the rocks, or slipping your cables and running out to sea, there: Peace—Peace—Peace—all peace!"—Another walk, and patting the Bible under his left arm: "What! These fellows are coming from the wilderness, are they? Yes. From the dreary, blighted wilderness of Iniquity, whose only crop is Death. But do they lean upon anything—do they lean upon nothing, these poor seamen?"—Three raps upon the Bible: "Oh yes.—Yes.—They lean upon the arm of their Beloved"— three more raps: "upon the arm of their Beloved"—three more, and a walk: "Pilot, guiding-star, and compass, all in one, to all hands—here it is"—three more: "Here it is. They can do their seaman's duty manfully, and be easy in their minds in the utmost peril and danger, with this"—two more: "They can come, even these poor fellows can come, from the wilderness leaning on the arm of their Beloved, and go up— up—up!"—raising his hand higher, and higher, at every repetition of the word, so that he stood with it at last stretched above his head, regarding them in a strange, rapt manner, and pressing the book triumphantly to his breast. . . .[13]

Whether Melville actually ran across this graphic portrayal and appropriated it to his purposes, or whether he drew from more personal observation of "Father" Taylor, this account lends plausibility to the sermon on Jonah and the Whale in *Moby-Dick*. Melville, however, may be suspected of touching up his original:

Father Mapple rose, and in a mild voice of unassuming authority ordered the scattered people to condense. "Starboard gangway, there! side away to larboard—larboard gangway to starboard! Midships! midships!"

There was a low rumbling of heavy sea-boots among the benches, and a still slighter shuffling of women's shoes, and all was quiet again, and every eye on the preacher.

He paused a little; then kneeling in the pulpit's bows, folded his large brown hands across his chest, uplifted his closed eyes, and offered a prayer so deeply devout that he seemed kneeling and praying at the bottom of the sea.

This ended, in prolonged solemn tones, like the continual tolling of a bell in a ship that is foundering at sea in a fog—in such tones he com-

s business. The Nantucket whaleman, when with his family
siter there. He touches at foreign ports merely to procure
enable him to prosecute his voyage; he touches at home
g enough to prepare for a new voyage. He is in the bosom
y weeks, on the bosom of the ocean years.18

by-Dick Melville concludes his chapter on Nantucket
sage which, however transformed by his magic, strongly
lacy's description as its humble original:

have these naked Nantucketers, these sea hermits, issuing
nt-hill in the sea, overrun and conquered the watery world
ny Alexanders; parcelling out among them the Atlantic,
Indian Oceans, as the three pirate powers did Poland. Let
d Mexico to Texas, and pile Cuba upon Canada; let the
rswarm all India, and hang out their blazing banner from
vo-thirds of this terraqueous globe are the Nantucketer's.
is his; he owns it, as Emperors own empires; other seamen
a right of way through it. Merchant ships are but extension
med ones but floating forts; even pirates and privateers,
owing the sea as highwaymen the road, they but plunder
other fragments of the land like themselves, without seek-
v their living from the bottomless deep itself. The Nan-
alone resides and riots on the sea; he alone, in Bible lan-
down to it in ships; to and fro ploughing it as his own
tation. *There* is his home; *there* lies his business, which a
d would not interrupt, though it overwhelmed all the mil-
ina. He lives on the sea, as prairie cocks in the prairie; he
g the waves, he climbs them as chamois hunters climb the
ears he knows not the land; so that when he comes to it at
s like another world, more strangely than the moon would
sman. With the landless gull, that at sunset folds her wings
d to sleep between billows; so, at nightfall, the Nantucketer,
of land, furls his sails, and lays him to his rest, while under
ow rush herds of walruses and whales.19

is sea career was over Melville certainly knew the true
er—who may or may not have conformed to his idealiza-
personal acquaintance as well as from literary repute.
as the records show, the week, more or less, prior to his
41 was spent not at Nantucket, but at New Bedford.
ary 3, 1841—on Christmas Day, according to *Moby-Dick*

---

menced reading the following hymn; but changing his manner toward
the concluding stanzas, burst forth with a pealing exultation and joy:—

> "The ribs and terrors in the whale
>   Arched over me a dismal gloom,
>   While all God's sun-lit waves rolled by,
>   And left me deepening down to doom. . . .
>
> "In black distress, I called my God,
>   When I could scarce believe him mine,
>   He bowed his ear to my complaints—
>   No more the whale did me confine." . . .14

Then follows the much-quoted sermon on the text: "And God
had prepared a great fish to swallow up Jonah." This discourse, a
masterly combination of scriptural whaling lore, social criticism,
and dramatic preparation, though not beyond the possible reach
of Father Edward Taylor's pulpit abilities, was, in all likelihood,
fabricated out of whole cloth. But the moral of "Father Mapple's"
parable, and his benediction, are so indisputably in character with
the chaplain in Dickens's thumbnail sketch that one cannot help
suspecting a literary influence:

There now came a lull in his look, as he silently turned over the
leaves of the Book once more; and, at last, standing motionless, with
closed eyes, for the moment, seemed communing with God and himself.
But again he leaned over toward the people, and bowing his head
lowly, with an aspect of the deepest yet manliest humility, he spake
these words:—
"Shipmates, God has laid but one hand upon you; both his hands
press upon me. I have read ye by what murky light may be mine the
lesson that Jonah teaches to all sinners; and therefore to ye, and still
more to me, for I am a greater sinner than ye. And now how gladly
would I come down from this mast-head and sit on the hatches there
where you sit, and listen as you listen, while some one of you reads *me*
that other and more awful lesson which Jonah teaches to *me*, as a pilot
of the living God. How being an anointed pilot-prophet, or speaker of
true things, and bidden by the Lord to sound those unwelcome truths
in the ears of a wicked Ninevah, Jonah, appalled at the hostility he
should raise, fled from his mission, and sought to escape his duty and
his God by taking ship at Joppa. But God is everywhere; Tarshish he
never reached. As we have seen, God came upon him in the whale, and

swallowed him down to living gulfs of doom, and with swift slantings tore him along 'into the midst of the seas,' where the eddying depths sucked him ten thousand fathoms down, and 'the weeds were wrapped about his head,' and all the watery world of woe bowled over him. Yet even then, beyond the reach of any plummet—'out of the belly of hell'—when the whale grounded upon the ocean's utmost bones, even then, God heard the engulphed, repenting prophet when he cried. Then God spake unto the fish; and from the shuddering cold and blackness of the sea, the whale came breeching up toward the warm and pleasant sun, and all the delights of air and earth; and 'vomited out Jonah upon the dry land;' when the word of the Lord came a second time; and Jonah, bruised and beaten—his ears, like two sea-shells, still multitudinously murmuring of the ocean—Jonah did the Almighty's bidding. And what was that, shipmates? To preach the Truth to the face of Falsehood! That was it!

"This, shipmates, this is that other lesson; and woe to that pilot of the living God who slights it. Woe to him whom this world charms from Gospel duty! Woe to him who seeks to pour oil upon the waters when God has brewed them into a gale!" . . .

He drooped and fell away from himself for a moment; then lifting his face to them again, showed a deep joy in his eyes, as he cried out with a heavenly enthusiasm,—"But oh! shipmates! on the starboard hand of every woe, there is a sure delight; and higher the top of that delight, than the bottom of the woe is deep. Is not the main-truck higher than the kelson is low? Delight is to him—a far, far upward, and inward delight—who against the proud gods and commodores of this earth, ever stands forth his own inexorable self. Delight is to him whose strong arms yet support him, when the ship of this base treacherous world has gone down beneath him. Delight is to him, who gives no quarter in the truth, and kills, burns, and destroys all sin though he pluck it out from under the robes of Senators and Judges. Delight,—topgallant delight is to him, who acknowledges no law or lord, but the Lord his God, and is only a patriot to heaven. Delight is to him, whom all the waves of the billows of the seas of the boisterous mob can never shake from this sure Keel of the Ages." . . .[15]

After this baptism in spiritual brine, Melville and his cannibal friend Queequeg left New Bedford the next day on a little packet-schooner for Nantucket, according to the record of *Moby-Dick*. It was from this latter and more historically famous place, he says, that they took passage on the "Pequod"; but Melville in reality

—Melville sailed in the *Acushnet* from Fairhaven, just across the river from New Bedford, Massachusetts, on a whaling voyage to the Pacific.²⁰ According to the certificate of registration in the United States Customs House at New Bedford, this sturdy new whaler was built at Rochester, Massachusetts, in 1840, being completed on December 30 of that year. (In *Moby-Dick,* on the other hand, the "Pequod" is described as "long seasoned and weather-stained" from "more than half a century" of whaling, and grotesquely ornamented with the barbaric trophies of many a distant voyage.) She had a tonnage of 358 and boasted two decks and three masts; she measured 104 ft. 8 in. in length, 27 ft. 10 in. in width, and 13 ft. 11 in. in depth. Melvin O. Bradford, Philemon Fuller, Valentine Pease, and fifteen others—"Peleg," "Bildad," and "a number of old annuitants," says Melville—were the owners. Pease was also the captain under whom Melville sailed, though it is hard to say just how far he served as the model for the fantastic Captain Ahab of *Moby-Dick.*

The official crew list of the *Acushnet,* dated December 30, 1840 (with one addition on January 2, 1841), contains the names of twenty-six men in addition to the captain. Of these, four were Portuguese, one a Scotchman, and one an Englishman. The rest, including three Negroes, were native-born Americans, with common American names. This ghostly crew, meaningless when mere names, take on flesh and blood and bone when placed side by side (in square brackets) with the manuscript memoranda that Melville has left us of the subsequent fates of his whaling companions:

What became of the ship's company on the whale-ship "Acushnet," according to Hubbard [Henry F. Hubard] who came back home in her (more than a four years' voyage) and visited me in Pittsfield in 1850.

Captain Pease—returned & lives in asylum at the Vinyard. [Valentine Pease, Jr.]

Raymond, 1st mate—had a fight with the Captain & went ashore at Payta. [Frederic R. Raymond]

Hall, 2nd Mate—came home & went to California. [John Hall]

3rd Mate, Portuguese, went ashore at Payta. [George W. Gahan]

Boatswain, either ran away or killed at Ropo [Roa-pua] one of the Marquesas. [Martin Brown]

Smith, went ashore at Santa, coast of Peru, afterwards committed suicide at Mobile. [David or Daniel Smith]

Barney, boatswain, came home. [Wilson Barnard]

Carpenter, went ashore at Mowee [Maui, Sandwich Islands] half dead with disreputable disease. [Henry Harmer]

Tom Johnson, black, went ashore at Mowee, half dead (ditto) & died at hospital. [Thomas Johnson]

The Czar. [?]

Reed, mulatto—came home. [Enoch Read]

Blacksmith, ran away at San Francisco. [?]

Blackus, little black, ditto. [?]

Bill Green, after several attempts to run away, came home in the end. [Carlos W. Green]

The Irishman, ran away, coast of Columbia. [?]

Wright, went ashore half dead at the Marquesas. [John Wright]

Jack Adams and *Jo Portuguese* came home. [John Adams, Joseph Luis]

The Old Cook, came home. [William Maiden]

Haynes, ran away aboard of a Sidney [*sic*] ship. [?]

Little Jack, came home. [?]

Grant, young fellow, went ashore half dead, spitting blood, at Oahu. [Henry Grant]

Murray, went ashore, shunning fight, at Rio Janeiro. [Robart Mury]

The Cooper, came home. [?] [21]

Of the twenty-five men on Melville's list, all but seven have thus been identified. And even these (the seven remaining entries on the official crew list are Stedman, Eliot, Broadrick, Wolcut, White, Williams, and Banne) likewise bear names too unromantic to fit the stage figures who make up the crew of Melville's "Pequod." However dramatic the careers listed above, they did not satisfy the romantic needs of the author of *Moby-Dick,* who chose rather to fill his ship with picturesque creations, such as the harpooners: Queequeg, the Maori chieftain; Tashtego, the full-blooded American Indian; Daggoo, the African savage; and Fedallah, the Parsee, with his mythical boat's crew of Manilla-men. As for the crew itself, says Melville, about one half of them were foreign-born, a set of "mongrel renegades, and castaways, and cannibals." [22] As the drama of *Moby-Dick* really begins to unfold itself, moreover, all effort to maintain even probability is dropped; and in one scene, cast fittingly in dramatic form, Melville ransacks the entire nautical world for his crew: five Nantucket sailors, and one each from Long Island, England, Belfast, Spain, France, Portugal, Holland, Denmark, the Isle of Man, the Azores, St. Jago, Lascar, Malta, Sicily, China, Tahiti, and Iceland.[23] It will be remembered that on the crew list of the *Acushnet* only six were listed as foreign-born, four from Portugal and two from Great Britain. It is apparent, then, that for the *dramatis personæ* of *Moby-Dick* Melville drew more heavily on his imagination than on his memory, although some slight basis in fact for such a cosmopolitan crew may be discovered in his remark, made elsewhere: "A sailor's name as it appears on a crew-list is not always his real name, nor in every instance does it indicate his country." [24]

There were two members of the "Pequod's" crew, however, who enjoyed the distinction of a factual as well as a fictional existence. (Naturally, they were not included in Melville's memoranda.) One, Richard T. Greene, a dark-skinned, black-haired young man from Rochester, New York, came to be celebrated as "Toby," the companion of Melville's adventures in *Typee*. The other, listed as number twenty, saved this whaling voyage from the oblivion that has swallowed up hundreds like it: "Herman Melville/Place of Birth, New York/Place of Residence, Fairhaven/Citizen of U. S./ Age 21/Height 5′ 9½″/Complexion, dark/Hair, brown." [25] With this crew, normal in all respects save that in addition to mortal harpoons it carried an immortal pen, the *Acushnet* set sail on its maiden voyage, January 3, 1841.

CHAPTER III

A WHALE LABORATORY

UNFORTUNATELY, since the logbook of the *Acushnet* for 1841–1845 has not yet been found, little is known of this cruise from official records. Indeed, a search for the facts behind *Moby-Dick* would perhaps be as misguided as it would be futile. Biographers and critics have in general contented themselves with an examination of the style of the book and an interpretation of its symbolism. As others have pointed out, Melville undoubtedly went to Sir Thomas Browne, Rabelais, and many others as his masters, and he may have drawn even his original inspiration and theme, as has been suggested, from the brief narrative of John Reynolds, "Mocha Dick or the White Whale of the Pacific," published in 1839.[1] It is interesting to discover in this connection that, although the white whale itself has usually been treated as symbolical rather than real, there is at least one account of the actual capture of a white whale, which lends probability to Melville's supposedly fanciful creation:

As a whaler, the Platina won considerable fame by taking the only pure white whale that was ever captured. One hot day in August, 1902, the old bark, under command of Captain Thomas McKenzie, of New Bedford, was rolling along in the lazy swell of the Atlantic in about 35 north latitude and 53 west longitude, her voyage half over, when whales were sighted. Three boats were lowered, which made for a large sperm whale. The whale sounded and was down a long time. When he came up, he was near the vessel. Captain McKenzie, who was at the masthead on the bark, saw that it was a pure white whale; the first he had ever seen in his thirty years whaling experience. The men in the boats were, fortunately, not aware of the fact, for sailors have a superstitious dread of white whales. . . .

Sperm whales of great age have been taken that were spotted with white, and with the under part of their heads entirely white, but the

Platina's whale was pure white from head to tail. Captain McKenzie, from his lofty station, could see the whale under water nearly half a mile away.

One may follow all the works of fiction and histories of whaling and he will not find of [*sic*] any white whale having been killed by a whaleman, excepting in Herman Melville's novel, "Moby Dick." To the mate of the bark Platina, Andrew W. West, therefore, belongs the honor of having killed the only pure white sperm whale evei caught.[2]

The present study, however, is more concerned with Melville's technique of composition than with vague resemblances of style, or with possible inspirations and confirmations of his subject matter. A brief glimpse into his whale laboratory, therefore, should prove instructive, not so much for the purpose of discovering literary sources as for the opportunity of watching the composer at his work. With the scholarly display of a serious antiquarian and cetologist, Melville lists in the "Extracts" that preface *Moby-Dick* no less than fourscore authorities—scientific, historical, and literary —upon which he drew, remarking subsequently: "Nor have I been at all sparing of historical whale-research when it has seemed needed." [3] For specimens of this research, it will be sufficient to examine two whaling chronicles, which he cites in the text as well as in the "Extracts."

J. Ross Browne's *Etchings of a Whaling Cruise* could not have failed to attract Melville's attention and approval, for, in addition to its reliable information, it strikes a congenial note in the preface: a plea to better the condition of seamen in the whale fishery as Dana's book had done for the merchant marine. This theme of reform runs throughout the volume in a series of grievances and complaints which sounds the burden of *Typee, Omoo,* and *White-Jacket,* as well as *Moby-Dick.* For example, Browne, who sailed from Fairhaven, July 19, 1842, on a whaling cruise to the Pacific in the *Styx,* recounts an occasion when his captain had fleeced some South Sea natives of a boatload of wood; and with the indignation of *Typee* he declares:

It is treatment like this that renders the natives treacherous and hostile. There has been more done to destroy the friendly feelings of the inhabitants of islands in the Indian and Pacific Oceans towards Americans, by the meanness and rascality of whaling captains, than all the missionaries and embassies from the United States can ever atone for.⁴

Mistreatment of the sailors themselves he condemns with equal vigor in a passage which brings to mind the first part of *Omoo:*

While visiting the ports [of the Pacific] for the purpose of recruiting, the crews of whale ships are often found in a state of lax discipline; both captains and crew take this opportunity to lay their complaints before the consuls, who are much troubled with them, and frequently at a loss to understand and pass upon the merits of the case. The crews usually complain of bad provisions, short allowance, and bad usage; in some cases, I have heard them assert that they felt their lives in danger from the outrageous conduct of the captain; and in one instance even the officers joined in the complaint. The captain, on the other hand, believed that there was a conspiracy on foot to poison him.

Many Americans are found on the different islands, who have been turned ashore from whale ships, or left because they have broken their liberty a single time, near the end of the voyage.⁵

At Zanzibar the difficulties on board Browne's ship came to a head. Driven to desperation by hard fare and brutal treatment, the seamen decided to desert in a body. The mutiny was poorly planned, however, and the captain succeeded in starving his oppressed crew into submission, although Browne, with the aid of the American consul, procured a substitute and left the ship on June 1, 1843.⁶ These extracts, which read like passages culled from the darker pages of *Typee* and *Omoo,* lend color to Melville's extraordinary recital of similar experiences; and, even if they did not serve as actual sources for him in writing, they at least prompted his memory and fired his resentment. In a digression of some ten pages, mixed with these complaints against the whale fishery, Melville might also have found the theme of his *White-Jacket* anticipated:

It is a disgrace to the American flag that the barbarous system of flogging, now permitted in our vessels, has not long since been abolished. A glorious navy is ours; a glorious whaling fleet have we when such a system is suffered to exist. What a spectacle of Republican perfection we present to the world!

. . . We have now a naval aristocracy the most arrogant and despotic, perhaps, in the world. We have a whaling marine in which cruelty and despotism are fostered with special care. . . .

[And he concludes:] There is no class of men in the world who are so unfairly dealt with, so oppressed, so degraded, as the seamen who man the vessels engaged in the American whale fishery.[7]

Etchings of a Whaling Cruise, moreover, furnishes matter more pertinent to the actual text of *Moby-Dick* than this mere similarity of purpose and attitude. In this volume Melville must have found much whale-lore—history, anatomy, and anecdote—that was admirably suited to his needs. For example, the yarn of the murdered sailor, which Browne relates under the caption of "Bob Grimsley's Ghost," may have been the germ of Melville's *"Town-Ho's* Story," for both are concerned with a deadly feud between a mate and a seaman, resulting in a near-mutiny, and both are prefaced by a description of a "gam" on shipboard—a get-together between the crews of two ships that pass each other at sea.[8] Further, the constant bickering and frequent rows between the captain and the first mate on board the *Styx* parallel the running feud that Melville describes between Captain Ahab and Starbuck; indeed, the episodes actually ended similarly on both ships, for Browne's captain put his mate ashore at one of the Seychelles Islands for refusing to submit to his tyranny, whereas the mate of the *Acushnet* had a fight with his captain and went ashore at Payta, Peru, as Melville himself records, though he does not bring the quarrel to this climax in *Moby-Dick.*[9]

Again, more specifically, Browne's description of "cutting in and trying out"—the process of extracting the oil from the whale's blubber—corroborates Melville's and gives proof, if any be needed, that he was writing authentically of the technique of whaling.[10] For such facts, of course, Melville had no reason to resort to printed authorities. But there are several scenes sketched in this connection that show a striking similarity between the two authors. Browne, for example, gives a picture of the crew feasting at night, while the oil is being "tried out":

About the middle of the watch they get up the bread kid, and, after dipping a few biscuit in salt water, heave them into a strainer, and boil them in the oil. It is difficult to form any idea of the luxury of this delicious mode of cooking on a long night-watch. Sometimes, when on friendly terms with the steward, they make fritters of the brains of the whale mixed with flour, and cook them in the oil. These are considered a most sumptuous delicacy. Certain portions of the whale's flesh are also eaten with relish, though, to my thinking, not a very great luxury, being coarse and strong. . . . [But he confesses] I have eaten whale-flesh at sea with as much relish as I ever ate roast-beef ashore.[11]

Melville shows an equal interest in "The Whale As a Dish." When the second mate indulges his "unprejudiced" appetite in a supper of steak cut from the small of the whale, Melville stops to comment:

That mortal man should feed upon the creature that feeds his lamp, and, like Stubb, eat him by his own light, as you may say; this seems so outlandish a thing that one must needs go a little into the history and philosophy of it. . . .

The fact is, that among his hunters at least, the whale would by all hands be considered a noble dish, were there not so much of him; but when you come to sit down before a meat-pie nearly one hundred feet long, it takes away your appetite. Only the most unprejudiced of men like Stubb, nowadays partake of cooked whales.

. . . But the spermaceti itself, how bland and creamy that is; like the transparent, half jellied, white meat of a cocoa-nut in the third month of its growth, yet far too rich to supply a substitute for butter. Nevertheless, many whalemen have a method of absorbing it into some other substance, and then partaking of it. In the long try-watches of the night it is a common thing for the seamen to dip their ship-biscuit into the huge oil-pots and let them fry there awhile. Many a good supper have I thus made.

[Then follows the final delicacy.] In the case of a small Sperm Whale the brains are accounted a fine dish. The casket of the skull is broken into with an axe, and the two plump, whitish lobes being withdrawn (precisely resembling two large puddings), they are then mixed with flour, and cooked into a most delectable mess, in flavor somewhat resembling calf's head, which is quite a dish among some epicures; and every one knows that some young bucks among the epicures, by continually dining upon calves' brains, by and by get to have a little brains of their own, so as to be able to tell a calf's head from their own heads; which, indeed, requires uncommon discrimination.[12]

The only noticeable difference between the two accounts is a difference in attitude, Browne being the more straightforward and unblushing epicure. Perhaps the Gansevoort–Melville palate gagged at the public confession of a relish for whale steak; and perhaps the philosopher of 1851 could not forego a sly thrust at the epicure of 1841, so forcefully recalled to his mind by Browne's description.

A second scene on this same night reveals a more significant debt that Melville owed to *Etchings of a Whaling Cruise*. Browne's account follows:

A "trying-out" scene is the most stirring part of the whaling business, and certainly the most disagreeable. . . . We will now imagine the works in full operation at night. Dense clouds of lurid smoke are curling up to the tops, shrouding the rigging from the view. The oil is hissing in the try-pots. Half a dozen of the crew are sitting on the windlass, their rough, weather-beaten faces shining in the red glare of the fires, all clothed in greasy duck, and forming about as savage a looking group as ever was sketched by the pencil of Salvator Rosa. The cooper and one of the mates are raking up the fires with long bars of wood or iron. The decks, bulwarks, railing, try-works, and windlass are covered with oil and slime of black-skin, glistening with the red glare from the try-works. Slowly and doggedly the vessel is pitching her way through the rough seas, looking as if enveloped in flames. . . . The idlers . . . entertain themselves spinning yarns, singing songs, etc., and calculating the time by the moon.

. . . A trying-out scene has something peculiarly wild and savage in it; a kind of indescribable uncouthness, which renders it difficult to describe with anything like accuracy. There is a murderous appearance about the blood-stained decks, and the huge masses of flesh and blubber lying here and there, and a ferocity in the looks of the men, heightened by the red, fierce glare of the fires, which inspire in the mind of the novice feelings of mingled disgust and awe. But one soon becomes accustomed to such scenes and regards them with the indifference of a veteran in the field of battle. I know of nothing to which this part of the whaling business can be more appropriately compared than to Dante's pictures of the infernal regions. It requires but little stretch of the imagination to suppose the smoke, the hissing boilers, the savage-looking crew, and the waves of flame that burst now and then from the flues of the furnace, part of the paraphernalia of a scene in the lower regions.[13]

Here, again, in his workshop—reading Melville evidently found the inspiration for one of his most brilliant passages. For this unpretentious sailor's memorandum reads strikingly like the rough draft of the unforgettable chapter in which Melville likens the

"Pequod" to a fire ship at sea; but if Browne's picture gave the cue, it was Melville's magic that wrought the transformation from the merely pictorial to the dramatic:

By midnight the works were in full operation. We were clear from the carcase; sail had been made; the wind was freshening; the wild ocean darkness was intense. But that darkness was licked up by the fierce flames, which at intervals forked forth from the sooty flues, and illuminated every lofty rope in the rigging, as with the famed Greek fire. The burning ship drove on, as if remorselessly commissioned to some vengeful deed. So the pitch and sulphur-freighted brigs of the bold Hydriote, Canaris, issuing from their midnight harbours, with broad sheets of flame for sails, bore down upon the Turkish frigates, and folded them in conflagrations. . . . Like a plethoric burning martyr, or a self-consuming misanthrope, once ignited, the whale supplies his own fuel and burns by his own body. Would that he consumed his own smoke! for his smoke is horrible to inhale, and inhale it you must, and not only that, but you must live in it for the time. It has an unspeakable, wild, Hindoo odour about it, such as may lurk in the vicinity of funereal pyres. It smells like the left wing of the day of judgment; it is an argument for the pit. . . .

The hatch, removed from the top of the works, now afforded a wide hearth in front of them. Standing on this were the Tartarean shapes of the pagan harpooneers, always the whale-ship's stokers. With huge pronged poles they pitched hissing masses of blubber into the scalding pots, or stirred up the fires beneath, till the snaky flames darted, curling, out of the doors to catch them by the feet. The smoke rolled away in sullen heaps. To every pitch of the ship there was a pitch of the boiling oil, which seemed all eagerness to leap into their faces. Opposite the mouth of the works, on the further side of the wide wooden hearth, was the windlass. This served for a sea-sofa. Here lounged the watch, when not otherwise employed, looking into the red heat of the fire, till their eyes felt scorched in their heads. Their tawny features, now all begrimed with smoke and sweat, their matted beards, and the contrasting barbaric brilliancy of their teeth, all these were strangely revealed in the capricious emblazonings of the works. As they narrated to each other their unholy adventures, their tales of terror told in words of mirth; as their uncivilized laughter forked upward out of them, like the flames from the furnace; as to and fro, in their front, the harpooneers wildly gesticulated with their huge pronged forks and dippers; as the wind howled on, and the sea leaped, and the ship groaned and dived, and yet steadfastly shot her red hell further and further into the blackness of the sea and the night, and scornfully champed the white bone in her mouth, and viciously spat round her on all sides; then the rushing *Pequod*, freighted with savages, and laden with fire, and burning a corpse, and plunging into that blackness of darkness, seemed the material counterpart of her monomaniac commander's soul.[14]

Certainly no one, not even Browne himself could carp at an appropriation handled in such a masterly manner. But it is such dramatic passages as these, tacitly presented as autobiography, that have misled Melville's biographers. For it was at the conclusion of this scene that Melville declared: "Uppermost [in my mind] was the impression, that whatever swift, rushing thing I stood on was not 'so much bound to any haven ahead as rushing from all havens astern"—a declaration frequently quoted as the true explanation of "Why Ishmael Went to Sea." [15]

Finally, the portrait that Browne draws of his tyrannical captain may have served in some measure as the prototype of Melville's mad commander, Ahab. In both instances, the authors had their curiosity aroused by the rapturous, awe-stricken terms in which the owners of the two ships had spoken of their captains; and, in both instances, these same captains prolonged the suspense by failing to appear on deck until the ships were well at sea. When finally revealed, the commander of the *Styx* was at least imposing enough to have struck fire from Melville's imagination as he read:

Picture to yourself a man . . . [of] cold blue eyes, and a shrewd, repulsive expression of countenance; of a lean and muscular figure, rather taller than the ordinary standard, with ill-made, wiry limbs, and you have a pretty correct idea of Captain A——. . . . When he gave orders, it was in a sharp, harsh voice, with a vulgar, nasal twang, and in such a manner as plainly betokened that he considered us all slaves of the lowest cast, unworthy of the least respect, and himself our august master.

To readers of *Moby-Dick*, the figure that Melville has created of moody, stricken Ahab—who "looked like a man cut away from the stake, when the fire has overrunningly wasted all the limbs without consuming them," and who "stood before them with a crucifixion in his face, in all the nameless regal overbearing dignity of some mighty woe"—is distinctly reminiscent of "Captain A–" in more than the provocative initial.[16] And the latter's speech to his crew, in which he lays down the program of his despotism, brings to mind the stirring scene when Ahab musters his crew and in a fiery speech pledges them to the fulfillment of his mad vengeance against Moby-Dick.[17] Perhaps the whaling world had many overbearing masters who might have served as models for Melville, but the captain of the *Styx* is at least a fair specimen of what he had to draw from, though Ahab himself towers above them all by reason of the monomaniacal obsession that motivates his tyranny.

Sometimes in the composition of *Moby-Dick* Melville worked even closer to his originals than has been demonstrated thus far. "I know of only four published outlines of the great Sperm Whale," he says, and of these "by great odds, Beale's is the best." Thomas Beale's *Natural History of the Sperm Whale* is undoubtedly the handbook that Melville found most useful in his "historical whale-research." Here he found an ample sketch of the whaling industry from its inception with numerous quotations from the older chroniclers, a detailed anatomy and an authoritative natural history of the sperm whale, and a full account of the art of whaling as demonstrated on a typical voyage. A single sample—on the history, nature, and uses of ambergris—will indicate how adequate Melville found this source-book, and how directly he gathered his materials from it:

Although ambergris, even during the sixteenth century, appeared to be much valued as a mercantile commodity by the English, it is curious that we knew nothing of its source, and very little of the use which was made of it in other countries. . . .

In 1791, the attention of government was drawn to this subject, in order to discover if it could be more frequently found. . . . Captain Coffin was examined at the bar of the House of Commons on the subject, and stated that he had lately brought home 362 ounces, troy, of this costly substance, which he had found in the anus of a *female* sperm whale that he had captured off the coast of Guinea, and which he stated was very bony and sickly. . . .

"The use of ambergris," says Brande [Brande's *Manual of Chemistry*, p. 594], "in Europe is now nearly confined to perfumery. . . . Our perfumers add it to scented pastiles, candles, balls, bottles, gloves, and hair powder; and its essence is mixed with pomatum for the face and hands. . . . In Asia and part of Africa, . . . considerable use is also made of it in cooking. . . . A great quantity of it is also constantly brought by the pilgrims who travel to Mecca, probably to offer it there . . . in the same manner as frankincense is used in Catholic countries. . . ."

Ambergris appears to be nothing but the hardened fæces of the spermaceti whale, which is pretty well proved from its being mixed so intimately with the refuse of its food (the squids' beaks). . . .

[Quoting from Sir Thomas Browne:] . . . "in vain it was to rake for ambergris in the paunch of this leviathan, . . . insufferable fetor denying that inquiry; and yet if, as Paracelsus encourageth, ordure makes the best musk, and from the most feted substances may be drawn the most oderiferous essences, all that had not Vespasian's nose might boldly swear here was a substance for such extractions." [18]

Compare Melville:

Now this ambergris is a very curious substance, and so important as an article of commerce, that in 1791 a certain Nantucket-born Captain Coffin was examined at the bar of the English House of Commons on that subject. For at that time, and indeed until a comparatively late day, the precise origin of ambergris remained, like amber itself, a problem to the learned; . . . ambergris is soft, waxy, and so highly fragrant and spicy, that it is largely used in perfumery, in pastiles, precious candles, hair-powders, and pomatum. The Turks use it in cooking, and also carry it to Mecca, for the same purpose that frankincense is carried to St. Peter's in Rome. . . .

Who would think, then, that such fine ladies and gentlemen should regale themselves with an essence found in the inglorious bowels of a sick whale! Yet so it is. . . .

I have forgotten to say that there were found in this ambergris certain hard, round, bony plates, which at first Stubb thought might be sailors' trowsers buttons; but it afterwards turned out that they were nothing more than pieces of small squid bones embalmed in that manner.

Now that the incorruption of this most fragrant ambergris should be found in the heart of such decay; is this nothing? Bethink thee of that saying of St. Paul in Corinthians, about corruption and incorruption; how that we are sown in dishonour, but raised in glory. And likewise call to mind that saying of Paracelsus about what it is that maketh the best musk. [19]

The various refinements and recastings by which Melville fused these isolated fragments of raw material into a more disciplined unity are alone sufficient to stamp the finished product as his own;

but he was not content with the mere facts and figures of perfumery. He used this borrowed account of ambergris to refute the
odious stigma that "whalemen [can] be recognised, as the people
of the middle ages affected to detect a Jew in the company, by the
nose"; and, growing eloquent, he declares that, for fragrance, a
sperm whale can be likened to "a musk-scented lady [who] rustles
her dress in a warm parlor" or to "that famous elephant, with
jewelled tusks, and redolent with myrrh, which was led out of an
Indian town to do honour to Alexander the Great."

This glimpse into Melville's workshop, however, pretends to
show no more than the fingers and thumbs of the compositor turning the pages of his copy, the amateur cetologist poring over his
authorities. The magic that transforms these inert elements into
the living drama of *Moby-Dick*—"the hell-fire in which the whole
book is broiled"—is another matter. To the philosopher and the
psychologist must be left the task of investigating the sources consulted by the searching eyes of Melville when they were turned
inward to the microcosm of his own mind or outward to the
macrocosm of moral symbols through which Moby-Dick ploughs
his way.

CHAPTER IV

FACTS AND SYMBOLS IN "MOBY-DICK"

O RETURN from the author's whale laboratory of 1851 to the actual voyage of the *Acushnet* in 1841–1845, we find that the route given by Melville in *Moby-Dick* is just as fanciful and unrelated to actuality as almost everything else in this wild, beautiful romance. The "Pequod," according to Melville, went first to the cruising grounds off the Azores, the Cape de Verde Islands, and St. Helena, consuming many weeks in this fruitless search for whales; then she turned eastward round the Cape of Good Hope and made her way north from the Crozetts across the Indian Ocean; next, she passed through the Straits of Sunda, between Sumatra and Java Head, into the Pacific; finally, leaving Formosa and the Bashee Isles behind, she entered the Japanese Sea, where Ahab in a frenzy broke the quadrant, leaving the "Pequod" to be hurried to her doom in uncharted waters.[1]

There is fragmentary evidence, however, from which the actual route of the *Acushnet* can be charted in its general outlines. In *Omoo* Melville speaks of having touched at Rio de Janeiro, outward bound; and, more definitely, he refers in *Typee* to "our forty days beating about that horrid headland, . . . outward bound, and off the pitch of Cape Horn."[2] These incidental references, untouched by the dramatic purposes that mapped the course in *Moby-Dick*, are naturally more to be relied upon. Moreover, we do not have to depend upon Melville's own contradictory accounts. The fortunate survival of an affidavit made by the captain of the *Acushnet* before the American consul at the Sandwich Islands in June, 1843, enables us to track this despotic commander through the Pacific—how fittingly!—by his own testimony as to desertions from his ship.[3]

[47]

This meager document—the one surviving ship's record, so far as is known, of the most famous whaling voyage ever made—contains as much and as pertinent information as half-a-dozen lines could well contain. Among other functions, it gives an outline of reality to the voyage of the ghost-ship *Acushnet*. The earliest glimpse shows her touching at Santa, Peru, on June 30, 1841, just six months out from home, probably her first port in the Pacific after rounding Cape Horn.[4] It would have been impossible to reach Peru in a sailing ship by way of the Cape of Good Hope and across the Pacific Ocean (the route given in *Moby-Dick*) in six months, even without reckoning the time that normally would have been spent in cruising for whales.[5] According to J. Ross Browne, the usual length of such a voyage was twelve months. One of the two possible routes to the Pacific for whalers was to leave the United States in the early autumn and proceed by way of the Cape of Good Hope, arriving in time to meet the season at New Zealand in March and at the Society Islands in June; then it was customary to recruit at some port in Peru in October, so as to be ready to take up the season on the "Off-Shore Ground," near the Galapagos Islands, in November.[6] It is worthy of note that the route Melville ascribes to the "Pequod" is strikingly similar to that taken by Browne in the *Styx;* and, if Melville ever took the shadowy voyage described in *Moby-Dick,* no record of it survives save the vicarious one he might have found in *Etchings of a Whaling Cruise.* The second route outlined by Browne was for ships leaving the United States in the winter or spring to proceed round Cape Horn, reach Peru in time to recruit before November, and then spend one to three months on the Off-Shore Ground.[7] It is apparent, then, that the *Acushnet* took this the more usual route—a voyage that required almost four months of steady sailing in a fast ship—recruiting at Santa, Peru, on June 30, 1841, before the fall Season-on-the-Line.

Another contemporary memorandum survives to give us a second glimpse of the *Acushnet* while Melville was still on board. In *Mardi,* while citing instances of ships that have been attacked by swordfish, Melville relates such an accident as happening to the

Rousseau, of Nantucket, and remarks in an aside: "This ship I met with at sea, shortly after the disaster." [8] He seemed, here, to be stepping so deliberately out of the context of his romance that this reference was taken as a clue to an actual meeting. And, surely enough, the Log Book of the *Rousseau,* a whaleship from New Bedford, though containing no mention of the swordfish incident, does record, under the caption of CRUISING ABOUT THE GALLAPAGOS [*sic*] ISLANDS:

Remarks on board, Wednesday November 3rd [1841] . . . Ships in sight . . . spoke Ship Acushnet of Fairhaven, 10 [11] months out, 700 [barrels of oil]. Lat. 00.40 S.; Long. 91.56 W. Land 5 miles.[9]

The land in sight was Albemarle Island, the largest and western-most of the Galapagos archipelago.

This fragment of information, recorded in the unprejudiced routine business of whaling, is sufficient to give a basis of reality to Melville's visit to the Galapagos Islands, so effectively preserved in the descriptive sketches entitled "The Encantadas." If the testi-mony of these essays is to be credited, Melville had visited this group in the preceding May, before touching at Peru:

Some months before my first stepping ashore upon the group, my ship was cruising in its close vicinity. One noon we found ourselves off the South Head of Albemarle, and not very far from the land. . . . A boat's crew was sent ashore, with orders to . . . bring back whatever tortoises they could conveniently transport.
  . . . [At this time] We had been abroad upon the waters for five long months.[10]

But it was in the fall and winter of 1841–1842 that Melville's ship did her most extensive cruising about the Galapagos Islands; and it was during this time that he undoubtedly went ashore on several islands in the group, because it was customary, during the whaling season, for ships to send their crews on expeditions to secure tor-toises as well as the usual refreshments of wood and water, and sometimes even on overnight excursions inland to secure fowl.

These barren volcanic isles, then, were the first taste that Mel-ville had of Pacific lands—far different from the island paradises which had filled the imagination of Ishmael embarking at New Bedford. They were so striking in their desolation, in fact, as to call for separate and special treatment when he later brought them into their first literary prominence. How many days Melville spent on shore at the Galapagos is not known, but he certainly gave his descriptions the coherence and richness of detail that only an eye-witness could have commanded. In accordance with his habitual literary technique, however, he did not rely solely upon his own observations in writing "The Encantadas." His indebtedness to several contemporary travel writers—notably, David Porter and James Colnett, both of whom he cites in a footnote—has already been pointed out. To these may be added one more commentator on the Galapagos Islands, whom Melville failed to include in the "only three eye-witness authorities worth mentioning touching the Enchanted Isles," but whom he undoubtedly consulted.

In the ship's library of the frigate *United States* during the first year of Melville's residence on board (1843–1844, homeward bound), there was a four-volume set entitled *Narrative of the Surveying Voyages of His Majesty's Ships Adventure and Beagle.* The third volume of this now famous work was written by the celebrated Charles Darwin. In the *Beagle,* as naturalist, he had visited the Galapagos Islands in October, 1835, just six years before Melville was there; and his engaging accounts of the flora and fauna of the group certainly must have aided Melville in organizing and classifying his own observations. More specifically, Darwin's general impression of the islands must have appealed strongly to his literary interest. Writing of Chatham Island, the scientist says in his *Journal and Remarks:*

The day, on which I visited the little craters, was glowing hot, and the scrambling over the rough surface, and through the intricate thickets, was very fatiguing; but I was well repaid by the Cyclopian [*sic*] scene. In my walk I met two large tortoises, each of which must have weighed at least two hundred pounds. One was eating a piece of cactus, and when I approached, it looked at me, and then quietly walked away: the other gave a deep hiss and drew in its head. These huge reptiles, surrounded by the black lava, the leafless shrubs, and the large cacti, appeared to my fancy like some antediluvian animals.[12]

Robert Fitzroy, captain of the *Beagle* and author of the first two volumes, records a similar impression:

> This part of the island is low, and very rugged. We landed upon black, dismal-looking heaps of broken lava, forming a shore fit for Pandemonium. Innumerable crabs and hideous iguanas started in every direction as we scrambled from rock to rock. Few animals are uglier than these iguanas; they are lizard-shaped, about three feet in length; of a dirty black colour; with a great mouth, and a pouch hanging under it; a kind of horny mane upon the neck and back; and long claws and tail. . . . [There] were prickly pears, and a kind of gum-tree: how their roots are able to penetrate, or derive nourishment from the hard lava, it is hard to say; for earth there is scarcely any. . . . This first excursion had no tendency to raise our ideas of the Galapagos Islands. [And, writing of Albemarle Island, he adds:] Passing a low projecting point, our eyes and imagination were engrossed by the strange wildness of the view; for in such a place Vulcan might have worked. Amidst the most confusedly heaped masses of lava, black and barren, as if hardly yet cooled, innumerable craters (or fumeroles) showed their very regular, even artificial looking heaps. It was like immense iron works, on a Cyclopian [*sic*] scale! [13]

Pandemonium, antediluvian and Cyclopean scenes, where Vulcan might have worked! [14] These words must have fixed themselves in Melville's memory, for, when he came to set the dominant mood of his "Encantadas," he conjured up such images for the "Plutonian sight" he wished to set before his readers:

> It is to be doubted whether any spot of earth can, in desolateness, furnish a parallel to this group. . . .
> Another feature in these isles is their emphatic uninhabitableness . . . the Encantadas refuse to harbour even the outcasts of the beasts. Man and wolf alike disown them. Little but reptile life is here found:— tortoises, lizards, immense spiders, snakes, and the strangest anomaly of outlandish Nature, the *aguana*. . . .
> In many places the coast is rock-bound, or more properly, clinker-bound; tumbled masses of blackish or greenish stuff like the dross of an iron-furnace, forming dark clefts and caves here and there. . . . On the oppressive, clouded days such as are peculiar to this part of the watery Equator, the dark vitrified masses, many of which raise themselves among white whirlpools and breakers in detached and perilous places off the shore, present a most Plutonian sight. In no world but a fallen one could such lands exist.[15]

Melville's experiences in the Galapagos Islands—probably falling somewhere between November, 1841, and February, 1842—
were slight, however, in comparison with his subsequent visits to
other and more enchanting Pacific groups. What waters the *Acushnet* sailed during the next six months cannot be said with certainty, though, according to Melville, she was continually at sea.[16]
Upon leaving the Off-Shore Ground, whalemen usually took one
of two routes. The first was to proceed directly to the Marquesas
and then to run west along the Equator as far as the coast of Japan,
returning to the Sandwich Islands in time to recruit again for a new
fall Season-on-the-Line. The second was to proceed directly to the
neighborhood of the Sandwich Islands, remain there during February, March, and April, then drop down to 30° south latitude, and
cruise along that parallel between 165° and 145° west longitude—
south of the Society and Marquesas groups—and thence back to
the Sandwich Islands in time to recruit as before.[17] If Melville ever
made his much-talked-of trip to the coast of Japan, it must have
been during these six months. But it is much more likely that the
Acushnet followed the second of these two routes, for that is the
only one which could have brought her to the Marquesas Islands in
July, 1842, when, according to Captain Pease's affidavit, Richard
T. Greene and Herman Melville deserted. These eighteen months
outward-bound, then, were substantially the whole of Melville's
experience in the whale fishery, for his two later cruises on whalers
—from the Marquesas to Tahiti and from there to Honolulu—
were too brief to be considered as more than mere voyages for
transportation. What factual autobiography went into the composition of *Moby-Dick* must have come from this still obscure prelude
to his South Sea island adventures. In one of his accounts, *Typee,*
Melville brings his residence on board the *Acushnet* to an end by
desertion at the Marquesas, in accordance with the actual facts.
This was an appropriate introduction to a romantic adventure
among savages; but it did not form an equally appropriate conclusion to a stirring drama of life on board a whaler. For the final
curtain in *Moby-Dick*, therefore, he departed sharply from auto-

biographical fact and invented a last act that challenges investigation, as he well knew it would.

The inexorable feud between Captain Ahab and Moby-Dick, steadily built up through more than five hundred pages, demanded a sudden and overwhelming catastrophe suitable to high tragedy. An immortal whale, invested with Olympian meaning, could not succumb to a man-made "Pequod" freighted with mortals, however heroic their enmity. Nemesis, swift and sure, must overtake the insolence of a mortal antagonist who dared set himself against the machinery of an inimical world, must justify the ways of a great White Whale—the *deus ex machina*—to puny, inquisitive man. Early in the unfolding of his drama, anticipating the unbelief of his readers, Melville steps out of his narrative to hold up an affidavit for the querulous:

I do not know where I can find a better place than just here, to make mention of one or two . . . things, which to me seem important, as in printed form establishing in all respects the reasonableness of the whole story of the White Whale, more especially the catastrophe. For this is one of those disheartening instances where truth requires full as much bolstering as error. . . .

But fortunately the special point I here seek can be established upon testimony entirely independent of my own. That point is this: The sperm whale is in some cases sufficiently powerful, knowing, and judiciously malicious, as with direct aforethought to stave in, utterly destroy, and sink a large ship; and what is more, the sperm whale *has* done it.[18]

He then brings to the stand four witnesses whose sworn evidence bolsters up the truth of his catastrophe in *Moby-Dick*. Two of them testify merely to the power of the whale to incommode a ship's progress by an accidental collision: the anecdote of Captain DeWolf's ship, en route to Ochotsh in Krusenstern's expedition, and that of "Commodore J— then [about 1830] commanding an American sloop-of-war," en route from Honolulu to Valparaiso.[19] The first of these he further substantiates by saying that Captain DeWolf, his uncle, confirmed the incident in a personal interview; the second may gain additional validity when it is pointed out that "Commodore J—" was in all probability Commodore Thomas ap

Catesby Jones, who commanded the *Peacock* on an expedition to the Sandwich Islands in 1825, and who was later Melville's commander on board the frigate *United States,* where he may have heard the story.

The other two testimonials are even more to the point. The ship *Union* of Nantucket, declares Melville, was totally destroyed by a whale's attack off the Azores in 1807, "but the authentic particulars of this catastrophe I have never chanced to encounter." [20] Lapse of memory must have been responsible for this disclaimer of accurate knowledge, for he certainly must have read the full account of it in Obed Macy's volume, which he elsewhere cites as an authority that he had consulted.[21] The fourth was the star witness, whose testimony Melville gives in detail:

> In the year 1820 the ship *Essex,* Captain Pollard, of Nantucket, was cruising in the Pacific Ocean. One day she saw spouts, lowered her boats, and gave chase to a shoal of sperm whales. Ere long, several of the whales were wounded; when, suddenly, a very large whale escaping from the boats, issued from the shoal, and bore directly down upon the ship. Dashing his forehead against her hull, he so stove her in, that in less than "ten minutes" she settled down and fell over. Not a surviving plank of her has been seen since. . . . I have seen Owen Chace [*sic*], who was chief mate of the *Essex* at the time of the tragedy; I have read his plain and faithful narrative; I have conversed with his son; and all this within a few miles of the scene of the catastrophe.[22]

He then quotes several passages from Owen Chase's published account, witnessing the deliberate malice of this whale.[23] Whether Melville actually heard the story from Owen Chase and his son "within a few miles of the scene of the catastrophe [latitude 00°.40′ south, longitude 119° west—about midway between the Galapagos and Marquesas Islands]" is not known; but it is certain that he owned a copy of Chase's *Narrative,* with marginalia in his own handwriting.[24]

The account of the sinking of the *Essex* has long been recognized as the chief source from which Melville borrowed the catastrophe which concludes *Moby-Dick.* But there is another story of a malicious whale that attacked and sank a ship, which may have served as a model for the catastrophe—and, in broad outline, for the

entire plot—of *Moby-Dick*. Although Melville does not cite Joseph
Hart's *Miriam Coffin, or The Whale-Fishermen* as one of the witnesses in his affidavit, he does quote from it (in the prefatory "Extracts" that are designed to give an air of authenticity to his wild
tale) the following vivid sentences: "Suddenly a mighty mass
emerged from the water, and shot up perpendicularly into the air.
It was the whale." And this is culled from the passage in *Miriam
Coffin* that was most appropriate to the author of *Moby-Dick*, as
will be seen. The whaling voyage in Joseph Hart's story occupies
only two chapters, but it holds a genuine interest for the student of
Melville. In the first place, the mate of the "Grampus" is named
Starbuck, the very name that Melville gives to the mate of his
"Pequod." Again, before the ship sails for the Pacific, a half-breed
squaw on Nantucket prophesies that Starbuck is to die in a whale's
jaws; whereas in *Moby-Dick*, it will be remembered, Melville is
told on the day when he signs the ship's articles that "the old squaw
Tistig, at Gayhead, said that the name [of Ahab] would somehow
prove prophetic." But it is in the climax of *Miriam Coffin* that we
find the most pertinent analogy. Near the Galapagos the boats
lower after a school of whales. Starbuck, in spite of evil premoni-
tions, enters a boat which ignores the school and sets out after the
leader, a monster of "prodigious size." After leading them a tire-
some chase, the whale sounds, only to come up under the boat
and stave it in with his thrashing tail. In the consummation of this
disaster Starbuck is thrown into the whale's jaws, where he perishes,
in fulfillment of the prophecy. The sequel is worth quoting entire:

> The unfortunate crew were rescued in time to witness the last agonies
> of the desperate whale, which, like Samson crushing the temple in his
> might, dealt death and destruction on all sides, while he himself was
> overwhelmed in the general ruin.
> The animal, blind with rage, and feeling the sting of the death-wound
> in his heart, whirled round the ship, in irregular circles, for a short
> time, and then descended. The crews lay upon their oars, watching
> where he would next appear, while the ship was hove to, to await the
> result.
> Suddenly a mighty mass emerged from the water, and shot up per-
> pendicularly, with inconceivable velocity, into the air. It was the whale;

—and the last effort was his last expiring throe!—He fell dead;—but in his descent, he pitched headlong across the bows of the Grampus, and, in one fell swoop, carried away the entire fore-part of the vessel!

The crew escaped, by throwing themselves into boats alongside, and rowing quickly off. The gallant ship instantly filled with water, and settled away from their sight.[25]

Thus, in *Miriam Coffin* Melville found an account of a whaling voyage brought to a sudden conclusion when a whale of prodigious size turns on the ship and sends her to the bottom, though the catastrophe here, it is true, is attributed to accident rather than malice; and he found a drama heightened by coupling the disaster with the fulfillment of a prophecy. That he was acquainted with this volume we know from his own acknowledgement. It is more than likely, therefore, that *Moby-Dick* owes a real debt to *Miriam Coffin*.[26]

Whatever sources Melville may have drawn upon in the composition of his catastrophe, he wrought a superb transformation in the recasting of his material. On the third day of "The Chase" the inevitable tragedy closes in:

The boats had not gone very far, when by a signal from the mast-heads—a downward-pointed arm, Ahab knew that the whale had sounded; but intending to be near him at the next rising, he held on his way a little sideways from the vessel; the becharmed crew maintaining the profoundest silence, as the head-beat waves hammered and hammered against the opposing bow. . . .

Suddenly the waters around them slowly swelled in broad circles; then quickly upheaved, as if sideways sliding from a submerged berg of ice, swiftly rising to the surface. A low rumbling sound was heard; a subterraneous hum; and then all held their breaths; as bedraggled with trailing ropes, and harpoons, and lances, a vast form shot lengthwise, but obliquely, from the sea. Shrouded in a thin drooping veil of mist, it hovered for a moment in the rainbowed air; and then fell swamping back into the deep. Crushed thirty feet upward, the waters flashed for an instant like heaps of fountains, then brokenly sank in a shower of flakes, leaving the circling surface creamed like new milk round the marble trunk of the whale.

"Give way!" cried Ahab to the oarsmen, and the boats darted forward to the attack; but maddened by yesterday's fresh irons that corroded in him, Moby-Dick seemed combinedly possessed by all the angels that fell from heaven. The wide tiers of welded tendons overspreading his broad white forehead, beneath the transparent skin, looked knitted together; as head on, he came churning his tail among the boats; and once more flailed them apart; spilling out the irons and lances from the two mates' boats, and dashing in one side of the upper part of their bows, but leaving Ahab's almost without a scar. . . . "Away, mates, to the ship! those boats are useless now; repair them if ye can in time, and return to me; if not, Ahab is enough to die—Down, men! the first thing that but offers to jump from this boat I stand in, that thing I harpoon. Ye are not other men, but my arms and my legs; and so obey me.— Where's the whale? gone down again?" . . .

At length . . . Ahab was fairly within the smoky mountain mist, which, thrown off from the whale's spout, curled round his great Monadnock hump; he was even thus close to him; when, with body arched back, and both arms lengthwise high-lifted to the poise, he darted his fierce iron, and his far fiercer curse, into the hated whale. As both steel and curse sank to the socket, as if sucked into a morass, Moby-Dick sideways writhed; spasmodically rolled his nigh flank against the bow, and, without staving a hole in it, so suddenly canted the boat over, that had it not been for the elevated part of the gunwale to which he then clung, Ahab would once more have been tossed into the sea. . . . But when Ahab cried out to the steersman to take new turns with the line, and hold it so; and commanded the crew to turn round on their seats, and tow the boat up to the mark; the moment the treacherous line felt that double strain and tug, it snapped in the empty air!

"What breaks in me? Some sinew cracks!—'tis whole again; oars! oars! Burst in upon him!"

Hearing the tremendous rush of the sea-crashing boat, the whale wheeled round to present his blank forehead at bay; but in that evolution, catching sight of the nearing black hull of the ship; seemingly seeing in it the source of all his persecutions; bethinking it—it may be— a larger and nobler foe; of a sudden, he bore down upon its advancing prow, smiting his jaws amid fiery showers of foam. . . .

"The whale! The ship!" cried the cringing oarsmen.

"Oars! oars! Slope downward to thy depths, O sea, that ere it be forever too late, Ahab may slide this last, last time upon his mark! I see: the ship! the ship! Dash on, my men! will ye not save my ship?"

But as the oarsmen violently forced their boat through the sledge-hammering seas, the before whale-smitten bow-ends of two planks burst through, and in an instant almost the temporarily disabled boat lay nearly level with the waves; its half-wading, splashing crew trying hard to stop the gap and bale out the pouring water.

Meantime, for that one beholding instant, . . . Starbuck and Stubb, standing upon the bowsprit . . . , caught sight of the down-coming monster. . . .

"The whale, the whale! Up helm, up helm! Oh, all ye sweet powers of air, now hug me close! . . . Steady! helmsman, steady. Nay, nay! Up helm again! He turns to meet us! Oh, his unappeasable brow drives on toward one, whose duty tells him he cannot depart. My God, stand by me now!" . . .

From the ship's bows, nearly all the seamen now hung inactive; hammers, bits of plank, lances, and harpoons, mechanically retained in their hands, just as they had darted from their various employments; all their enchanted eyes intent upon the whale, which from side to side strangely vibrating his predestinating head, sent a broad band of overspreading semicircular foam before him as he rushed. Retribution, swift vengeance, eternal malice were in his whole aspect, and spite of all that mortal man could do, the solid white buttress of his forehead smote the ship's starboard bow, till men and timbers reeled. Some fell flat upon their faces. Like dislodged trunks, the heads of the harpooneers aloft shook on their bull-like necks. Through the breach, they heard the waters pour, as mountain torrents down a flume. . . .

Diving beneath the settling ship, the whale ran quivering along its keel; but turning under water, swiftly shot to the surface again, far off the other bow, but within a few yards of Ahab's boat, where, for a time, he lay quiescent. . . .

For an instant, the tranced boat's crew stood still; then turned. "The ship? Great God, where is the ship?" Soon they through dim, bewildering mediums saw her sidelong fading phantom, as in the gaseous Fata Morgana; only the uppermost masts out of water; while fixed by infatuation, or fidelity, or fate, to their once lofty perches, the pagan harpooneers still maintained their sinking look-outs on the sea. And now, concentric circles seized the lone boat itself, and all its crew, and each floating oar, and every lance-pole, and spinning, animate and inanimate, all round and round in one vortex, carried the smallest chip of the *Pequod* out of sight.[27]

There remains a sequel, one of the most curious coincidences in all literary history. In the midsummer of 1851 Melville was pushing *Moby-Dick* through the press and at the same time writing the final chapters, just one jump ahead of the printer. On June 29, 1851, he wrote to Hawthorne:

FACTS AND SYMBOLS IN "MOBY-DICK"

The *Whale* is only half through the press. . . . Shall I send you a fin of the *Whale* by way of a specimen mouthful? The tail is not yet cooked, though the hell-fire in which the whole book is broiled might not unreasonably have cooked it ere this. [And on July 24, 1851, he added:] But I was talking about the *Whale*. As the fishermen say, "he's in his flurry" when I left him some three weeks ago. I'm going to take him by his jaw, however, before long, and finish him up in some fashion or other.[28]

It is not known exactly how many more weeks passed before Melville hit upon the plan of cooking his tale by letting Moby-Dick send the "Pequod" to the bottom. But less than a month after this last letter to Hawthorne—even as Melville was writing the powerful closing scenes in which the vortex "carried the smallest chip of the *Pequod* out of sight"—on August 20, 1851, an actual malignant whale carried an actual whaleship to the bottom near the Off-Shore Ground, not far from the scene of the *Essex* disaster. The catastrophe was written up in the *Panama Herald*:

THRILLING ACCOUNT *of the Destruction of a Whale Ship by a Sperm Whale—Sinking of the Ship—Loss of two of the Boats and Miraculous Escape of the Crew.*—We have just received the following thrilling account of the destruction of the Whale Ship *Ann Alexander,* Capt. John S. Deblois, of New Bedford, by a large Sperm Whale, from the lips of the Captain, himself, who arrived in this city from Paita on Sunday last, in the Schooner Providence [Captain Starbuck]. It is one of the most remarkable events on record, and will be read with deep interest throughout the whole commercial and civilized world, where, it may be made known. A similar circumstance has never been known to occur but once in the whole history of whale-fishing, and that was the destruction of the Ship *Essex,* some twenty or twenty-five years ago. . . . We proceed to the narrative as furnished us by Capt. Deblois, and which is fully authenticated by nine of the crew in a protest under the seal of the U. States Consul, Alex. Runen, Jr. at Paita.

The Ship *Ann Alexander,* Capt. John S. Deblois, sailed from New Bedford, Mass., June 1st, 1850, for a cruise in the South Pacific for sperm whale. . . .

On the 20th of August last, she reached what is well known as the "Off-Shore-Ground," in Lat. 5°50′ South, Long. 102° West. In the morning of that day, at about 9 o'clock, whales were discovered in the neighborhood and about noon, the same day, they succeeded in making fast to one. Two boats had gone after the whales—the larboard and the starboard, the former commanded by the first mate, and the latter by Capt. Deblois. The whale which they had struck, was harpooned by the larboard boat. After running some time, the whale turned upon the boat and rushing at it with tremendous violence, lifted open its enormous jaws and taking the boat in, actually crushed it into fragments as small as a common sized chair! Capt. Deblois immediately struck for the scene of the disaster with the starboard boat, and succeeded against all expectation in rescuing the whole of the crew of the demolished boat—nine in number! How they escaped from instant death when the whale rushed upon them with such violence and seized their boat in his ponderous jaws, is a mystery known only to "Him who holds the waves as in the hollow of his hands."

There were now eighteen men in the starboard boat, consisting of the Captain, the first mate and the crews of both boats. The frightful disaster had been witnessed from the ship and the waist-boat was called into readiness and sent to their relief. The distance from the ship was about six miles. As soon as the waist-boat arrived, the crews were divided, and it was determined to pursue the same whale, and make another attack upon him. Accordingly they separated and proceeded at some distance from each other, as is usual on such occasions, after the whale. In a short time, they came up to him and prepared to give him battle.— The waist-boat commanded by the first mate, was in advance. As soon as the whale perceived the demonstration being made upon him, he turned his course, suddenly, and making a tremendous dash at this boat, seized it with his wide spread jaws, and crushed [it] into atoms, allowing the men barely time to escape his vengeance by throwing themselves into the ocean.

Capt. Deblois, again seeing the perilous condition of his men, at the risk of meeting the same fate, directed his boat to hasten to their rescue, and in a short time, succeeded in saving them all from a death, little less horrible than that from which they had, twice, so miraculously escaped. He then ordered the boat to put for the ship as speedily as possible, and no sooner had the order been given than they discovered the monster of the deep mak[ing] towards them with his jaws widely extended! Escape from death now seemed totally out of the question. They were six or seven miles from the ship—no aid even there to afford them necessary relief, and the whale, maddened by the wounds of the harpoon and lances which had been thrown into him, and seemingly gloating with the prospect of speedy revenge, within a few cables length! Fortunately, the monster came up and passed them at a short distance. The boat then made her way to the ship and they all got on board in safety.

After reaching the ship a boat was despatched for the oars of the demolished boats, and it was determined to pursue the whale with the ship. As soon as the boat returned with the oars, sail was set, and the ship proceeded after the whale. In a short time she overtook him, and a lance was thrown into his head. The ship passed on by him, and immediately after, they discovered that the whale was making for the ship! As he came up near her, they hauled on the wind, and suffered the monster to pass her. After he had fairly passed, they kept off to overtake and attack him again. When the ship had reached within about fifty rods of him, they discovered that the whale had settled down deep below the surface of the water, and as it was near sundown, they concluded to give up the pursuit.

Capt. Deblois was at this time standing in the nigh-heads [knight-heads] on the larboard bow, with craft in hand ready to strike the monster a deadly blow should he appear, the ship moving about five knots, when working on the side of the ship, he discovered the whale rushing towards her at the rate of fifteen knots! *In an instant the monster struck the ship with tremendous violence shaking her from stem to stern.* She quivered under the violence of the shock, as if she had struck upon a rock! Capt. Deblois immediately descended into the forecastle and there to his horror, discovered that the monster had struck the ship about two feet from the keel, abreast the foremast, knocking a great hole entirely through her bottom, through which the water roared and rushed in impetuously! . . . The ship was then sinking very rapidly. The Captain went into the cabin, where he found three feet of water; he however, succeed[ed] in procuring a chronometer, sextant and chart. . . . He then came upon deck, ordered all hands into the boats an[d] was the last, himself, to leave the ship, *which he did by throwing himself into the sea and swimming to the nearest boat!* [On the second day following, the captain and crew were rescued by the ship *Nantucket* and safely carried to Paita, Peru.] [29]

At first blush it would seem that this remarkable piece of news might have come in the nick of time to be put to dramatic use by the author who was casting about for just such a finale. The account in the *Panama Herald* first reached the United States on November 4, and *Moby-Dick* did not issue from the press of Harper & Brothers, New York, until November 19, 1851.[30] But *Moby-Dick* must have been completed fully a month before, for the English edition appeared on October 18, and, though it omits the "Epilogue" in which Melville tells of his own rescue, it does contain the final chapter of the catastrophe.[31] Thus the news of the sinking of the *Ann Alexander* by a whale reached America too late to have served as a source for the author of *Moby-Dick,* though, if he could, he would undoubtedly have made good use of its thrilling details to fill in his own rather meager close-up of the whale's actual attack. His alert literary adviser, Evert Duyckinck, sent him the account from the *Panama Herald* as soon as it arrived, and Melville replied, characteristically, on November 7:

> Your letter received last night had a sort of stunning effect on me. For some days past being engaged in the woods with axe, wedge, and [——], the Whale had almost completely slipped me for the time (and I was the merrier for it) when Crash! comes Moby-Dick himself (as you justly say) and reminds me of what I have been about for part of the last year or two. It is really and truly a surprising coincidence, to say the least. I make no doubt it *is* Moby-Dick himself, for there is no account of his capture after the sad fate of the Pequod about fourteen [*sic*] years ago—
>
> Ye Gods! What a Commentator is this Ann Alexander whale. What he has to say is short and pithy but very much to the point. I wonder if my evil art has raised this monster.[32]

Duyckinck also called public attention to this news story in his long and favorable review of *Moby-Dick,* holding it up as confirmatory evidence for any readers who might find Melville's catastrophe outlandish.[33] And although this firsthand testimony to the sperm whale's death-dealing malignity was copied far and wide in contemporary periodicals, many reviewers continued to be incredulous of the climax of *Moby-Dick.*[34]

A second fatal coincidence came in the wake of *Moby-Dick.* If Melville's evil art raised this monster, it may also be charged with sinking the ship that had served as a model for the "Pequod." For before the year was out, the *Whalemen's Shipping List* recorded another catastrophe that certainly must have staggered the author of so much black magic:

> Brig Wyandott, Bush, from Arctic Ocean, arrived at Honolulu Oct. 2, bringing the Captain and crew of the ship Acushnet, Bradley, of Fairhaven, and a part of the cargo from the ship. The Acushnet was wrecked

August 16th [1851] on St Lawrence Island. The ship was a total loss. Crew saved. The A[cushnet] had 1300 bbls. oil, 250 of which was saved by the Wyandott.[35]

Melville's comment on this demonic fatality has not been discovered.

These, then, are all the available pertinent facts that preceded, and followed, the composition of *Moby-Dick*. They are few enough, but their very paucity is an intimation of how large a part of this magnificent tale of the sea must have been spun out of the author's imagination. It is this supersensory part of the book, moreover, which has chiefly attracted the attention of commentators. Scarcely a student of *Moby-Dick* has been able to deny himself the indulgence of a personal interpretation of its symbolism and even an explanation of its allegory. Yet this has been done in the face of Melville's insistence, perhaps only half serious, upon the substantial reality of his masterpiece:

So ignorant are most landsmen of some of the plainest and most palpable wonders of the world, that without some hints touching the plain facts, historical and otherwise, of the fishery, they might scout at Moby-Dick as a monstrous fable, or still worse and more detestable, a hideous and intolerable allegory.[36]

One of the most common interpretations has been that Ahab's feud with Moby-Dick represents man's heroic and eternal struggle against an indifferent, even hostile, nature.[37] An equally common one is that this struggle was between man and moral evil. One of the most elaborate expositions of this allegorical meaning, which the critic feels that Melville was partly conscious of while writing, calls *Moby-Dick:*

. . . a parable on the mystery of evil and the accidental malice of the universe. The white whale stands for the brute energies of existence, blind, fatal, overpowering, while Ahab is the spirit of man, small and feeble, but purposive, that pits its puniness against this might, and its purpose against the blank senselessness of power.[38]

A more complicated symbolical interpretation holds that all the characters, major and minor, represent abstractions, such as Fate, Revenge, and Blasphemy.[39] Finally, the psychologically-minded critics have found fertile ground in the symbolism of *Moby-Dick* to probe for the spiritual disillusionment and tragedy of its author.[40] One, feeling that such an elemental embodiment of malice deserves an imposing ancestry at least in folk story, suggests that Melville was reviving in his whale hunt the epic of Beowulf.[41] And another has gone so far as to find portrayed in Ahab's feud with the White Whale the universal inner struggle of man's dual ego—the blood-being of the white race, hunted by its own mental consciousness.[42]

Like all large poetic efforts, *Moby-Dick* will perhaps remain a mirror for its readers. Whatever particular hidden meanings Melville may have wrought, consciously or otherwise, into the fabric of his broad canvas, he has left no chart to guide the explorer. Evidently Hawthorne, to whom fittingly the book was dedicated, assumed that there was a "part-and-parcel allegoricalness" to the whole in Melville's mind; but his intimation of this in his acknowledgement to Melville is unfortunately lost, though from a letter to Duyckinck we know that he found richness and depth of meaning in *Moby-Dick:* "What a book Melville has written! It gives me an idea of much greater power than his preceding ones." [43] Mrs. Hawthorne, also, in a letter to Melville on December 29, 1851, outlined his symbolical meanings for him more specifically; and his reply, in which he may be guilty of some posing, is his only surviving explicit reference to whatever of "monstrous fable" and "hideous and intolerable allegory" he himself found, with her aid, in his own creation:

[January 8, 1852]
. . . I have hunted up the finest Bath [stationery] I could find, gilt-edged and stamped, whereon to indite my humble acknowledgement of your highly flattering letter. . . . It really amazed me that you should find any satisfaction in that book. It is true that some *men* have said they were pleased with it, but you are the only *woman*. . . . But, then, since you, with your spiritualizing nature, see more things than other people, and by the same process, refine all you see, so that they are not the same things that other people see, but things, which while you think you but humbly discover them, you do in fact create them for yourself— therefore, upon the whole, I do not so much marvel at your expressions

concerning Moby Dick. At any rate, your allusion for example to the "Spirit Spout" first showed to me that there was a subtle significance in that thing—but I did not, in that case, *mean* it. I had some vague idea while writing it, that the whole book was susceptible of an allegorical construction, and also that *parts* of it were—but the speciality of many of the particular subordinate allegories, were [*sic*] first revealed to me, after reading Mr. Hawthorne's letter which, without citing any particular examples, yet intimated the part-and-parcel allegoricalness of the whole. But, my Dear Lady, I shall not again send you a bowl of salt water. The next chalice I shall commend will be a rural bowl of milk. . . .[44]

Perhaps the matter should be allowed to rest in Melville's own ambiguous words.

What this "rural bowl of milk" was to be is not manifest. Only in bitterest irony could it have been applied to *Pierre,* which was making at the time, and which is, therefore, the only chronological possibility. But, harking back ten years to the summer of 1842 at the Marquesas, we find that Melville did in fact turn away in surfeit from a bowl of salt water to what he then hoped would be a chalice of the milk of the cocoa-palm, in the cannibal paradise that Ishmael had cherished in his adolescent imagination.[45]

BOOK TWO

"THE MAN WHO LIVED
AMONG CANNIBALS"

CHAPTER V

THE FRENCH AT NUKAHIVA

SIX months at sea! Yes, reader, as I live, six months out of sight of land; cruising after the sperm whale beneath the scorching sun of the Line [some twenty
degrees to the westward of the Galapagos], and tossed on the billows of the wide-
rolling Pacific—the sky above, the sea around, and nothing else! Weeks and
weeks ago our fresh provisions were all exhausted. There is not a sweet potato
left; not a single yam. Those glorious bunches of bananas which once decorated
our stern and quarter-deck have, alas, disappeared! and the delicious oranges
which hung suspended from our tops and stays—they, too, are gone! Yes, they
are all departed, and there is nothing left us but salt-horse and sea-biscuit. . . .
   Poor old ship! . . . for six months she has been rolling and pitching about,
never for one moment at rest. But courage, old lass, I hope to see thee soon
within a biscuit's toss of the merry land, riding snugly at anchor in some green
cove, and sheltered from the boisterous winds.

                    *   *   *

   "Hurrah, my lads! It's a settled thing; next week we shape our course to the
Marquesas!" . . .[1]

T HUS in *Typee* Melville brings his whaling voyage to a close,
       when the "Dolly" (another sobriquet for the *Acushnet*)
       at last comes to anchor at Nukahiva, one of the Marquesas
Islands, "fifteen months out" from home.[2] This would have been
about the first of April, 1842. Elsewhere, however, he says that
when he arrived at these islands "in the summer of 1842 . . . the
French had then held possession of them for several weeks."[3] The
historical facts are that Rear-Admiral Dupetit-Thouars, commanding *La Reine Blanche* and a squadron of men-of-war, had taken
possession of the Marquesas Islands for France in a triumphant
progress through the group, beginning at Tauata, May 1, 1842, and
ending at Anna Maria Bay (Taiohaë), Nukahiva, on June 2.[4] "Several weeks" after this would place Melville's arrival at least as late
as the end of June, instead of the first of April. One would naturally

be inclined to trust such cited and verifiable historical events rather than the rough calculation of months in round numbers from memory. And the fortunate survival of the affidavit certifying to Melville's desertion, already mentioned,[5] confirms this judgment and, beyond dispute, establishes the date of his arrival as some time shortly before July 9, 1842.

As will appear in the subsequent itinerary of Melville's year of roving in the South Seas, a significant conclusion hangs upon this date. For, taken in conjunction with a second terminal date (which will be established in a later chapter), it narrows the limits of his "four months residence in Typee Valley" to a bare four weeks, or a possible eight weeks at the utmost—a brief space indeed to compass all the multitudinous events recorded in *Typee!* It was a convenient lapse of memory that made up this discrepancy of three months by placing his desertion at the Marquesas Islands fifteen instead of eighteen months out from home. Although Melville assures us that "No journal was kept by the author during his wanderings in the South Seas," [6] he was capable of remembering dates with precision, as will be seen, except when it served his purposes to confuse them. In both *Typee* and *Omoo* he dates his subsequent rovings by two such conflicting sets of data; but, with the aid of a number of recently discovered documents, a reasonably reliable chronology can now be established for this year of dark adventuring.

Undoubtedly, Midshipman Thomas Wilson Melville had filled his cousin's head with romantic descriptions of the scenery that had enchanted his young eyes when the *Vincennes* dropped anchor at Nukahiva twelve years before. And Herman Melville seems to be remembering such when, in reference to the Marquesas, he speaks of the "vague accounts we sometimes have of their beauty," from which "many people are apt to picture to themselves enamelled and softly swelling plains, shaded over with delicious groves, and watered by purling brooks." [7] Moreover, there is every reason to suppose that before his own arrival Melville was also familiar with the lavish and detailed description of Anna Maria Bay contained in Stewart's official volumes on the cruise of the *Vincennes:*

Picture to yourself a smooth basin eight or nine miles in circumference, stretching in a circular form from the narrow passage between the sentinels [twin islets on either side of the entrance to the harbor], about three miles inland, and terminating at that distance, in a curving beach of sand, three fourths of a mile or more in length. This beach is the front of a valley of the same width, which rises gradually for a couple of miles, and then branching into three or four others more narrow and steep, suddenly terminates on every side in the abrupt acclivities and precipices of a range of lofty mountains which encloses the whole, and descends on either side, to the sentinels at the entrance, in bold promontories of rock, thinly covered with a green sward.

From the beach in the centre, luxuriant groves spread thickly and widely among bright unwooded hills, and velvet-like lawns, through the valleys behind, and up the lower hills skirting them, to the highest elevations. At the head of the principal valley, a gigantic pyramid of rock presents an object strikingly unique in its form and position: on the right, and behind it, a perpendicular basaltic wall of several hundred feet crowns the summit of the loftiest mountain, and opposite on the left, an immense projecting cliff of gray stone—mantled with trees, and richly hanging parasitical plants—seems ready, momentarily to leap from the face of the precipice against which it stands, to the bosom of the green valley below. Innumerable sharp ridges and deep glens intersect the whole—down which the mountain streams tumble and foam in rapids and cascades, gleaming in their dark channels like streams of silver on the eye.

The valleys are so thickly covered with trees, that few of the habitations of the natives are seen. Three or four occupy the open summit of some of the nearest hills—the bleached thatch of others here and there peeps through the heavy foliage embowering them, and one or two are discerned, hanging like birds' nests, high in the solitudes of the mountain forests.[8]

In *Typee* Melville acknowledges his indebtedness to Stewart as the chief authority on whom he drew. How closely he followed his guide will appear from his own description of Anna Maria Bay— to which he carelessly gives the name applied to the whole island:

The bay of Nukuheva [sic], in which we were then lying, is an expanse of water not unlike in figure the space included within the limits of a horse-shoe. It is, perhaps, nine miles in circumference. You approach it from the sea by a narrow entrance, flanked on either side by two small twin islets which soar conically to the height of some five hundred feet.

From these the shore recedes on both hands, and describes a deep semi-circle.

From the verge of the water the land rises uniformly on all sides, with green and sloping acclivities, until from gently rolling hillsides and moderate elevations it insensibly swells into lofty and majestic heights, whose blue outlines, ranged all around, close in the view. The beautiful aspect of the shore is heightened by deep and romantic glens, which come down to it at almost equal distances, all apparently radiating from a common centre, and the upper extremities of which are lost to the eye beneath the shadow of the mountains. Down each of these little valleys flows a clear stream, here and there assuming the form of a slender cascade, then stealing along until it bursts upon the sight again in larger and more noisy waterfalls, and at last demurely wanders along to the sea.

The houses of the natives, constructed of the yellow bamboo, tastefully twisted together in a kind of wicker-work, and thatched with the long tapering leaves of the palmetto, are scattered irregularly along these valleys beneath the shady branches of the cocoa-nut trees.

Nothing can exceed the imposing scenery of this bay. Viewed from our ship as she lay at anchor in the middle of the harbour, it presented the appearance of a vast natural amphitheatre in decay, and overgrown with vines, the deep glens that furrowed its sides appearing like enormous fissures caused by the ravages of time. Very often when lost in admiration at its beauty, I have experienced a pang of regret that a scene so enchanting should be hidden from the world in these remote seas, and seldom meet the eyes of devoted lovers of nature.[9]

At any rate, Stewart's description, if it did not furnish a source for *Typee,* confirms a picture that might otherwise be thought romantically overdrawn.

Sunny valleys, groves of cocoanuts, and bamboo temples, however, were not the only visions conjured up in Melville's imagination at the mere mention of the Marquesas. His list of South Sea island delights is headed by "lovely houris!" It has already been pointed out that his Uncle DeWolf's anecdotes drawn from Langsdorff's visit to Nukahiva in 1804 had served, in all likelihood, as one of the inspirations for his own jaunt to the South Seas; and if, as is quite probable, he had read Langsdorff's account of this famous expedition, he was prepared in advance for a glamorous

scene of welcome from a bevy of island-nymphs, such as the one
described by the Russian naturalist:

A number of the islanders a short time after came from the opposite
shore of the harbour, which was to the north-west, and swam to the
place where we were anchored, a distance of three miles. At first we
could only see a shoal of black-haired heads just above the water; but in
a short time we had the extraordinary spectacle presented us of some
hundred men, women, girls, and boys, all swimming about the ship,
having in their hands cocoa-nuts, bread-fruit, and bananas, which they
had brought to sell.

. . . The young girls and women were not more clothed than the
men, and were collected in even greater numbers; they were above all
loud and noisy, and, according to our European ideas, immodest. They
burst into a loud laugh at the most trifling things; and as we did not
understand a word of the many comic effusions addressed to us, their
oratory was illustrated with pantomimic gestures, by which we were
sufficiently given to understand that they were making us the most liberal and unreserved offers of their charms. The men who were with them
did not show the slightest symptoms of jealousy, but rather seemed
pleased and flattered when a wife, a daughter, or a sister, attracted our
particular attention. . . . Suffice it, that the beauties of the island were
so extremely importunate to be permitted to come on board, and urged
their importunities with so much noise, that, merely for the sake of
getting rid of them, and being left quiet awhile, we were obliged to
grant some of them free access to the ship.

These graces appeared in general with all their charms exposed; for
though they never left the land without at least so much clothing as a
large green leaf, yet this light covering was generally lost by swimming
any length of way. By a few only were the leafy aprons preserved, and
luckily for them we had no sheep or goats on board; since they might,
perhaps, have been no less eager to feast upon them, than we were to
feast upon the bananas, cocoa-nuts, and bread-fruit, which the lovely
creatures brought in their hands. We are told by Captain Wilson, in
the account of his missionary voyage to the South Sea, in the ship Duff,
that an adventure of this kind happened to some visitors who came to
pay their respects to himself and his crew. "The knavish goats," he says,
"were guilty of a very great offence, with regard to the poor young
maidens, for they would not leave them even the little clothing they
had: they flocked round them to get at the green leaves, till most of them
were left entirely in their native beauty."

But however prodigal of their favours, and however ready to follow any sailor that held out a hand to them, the fair sex were still not without a certain degree of modesty. They seemed to be considerably distressed when they had lost their aprons, and crept about with their hands in the position of the Medicean Venus, in attitudes which presented a beautiful spectacle to the philosophic observer. Those who had not been deserted by their garments were particularly anxious to adjust them properly. . . .

We were not, however, allowed a long time to make philosophical observations upon our new Venuses; for one after another they vanished, hand-in-hand with the sailors, to the interior of the ship, while the goddess of night threw her dark veil over the mysteries that were celebrated. Thus ended, with a scene altogether new and extraordinary to us, the first day of our stay in the harbour of Nukahiwa [sic]. Early on the following morning, the beauties skipped one after another upon deck, and leaping into the water, swam away gaily, carrying with them presents of various kinds.

The sailors, who were not rich in treasures to bestow upon their nymphs, presented them with bottles, pieces of broken china and earthenware, coloured rags, and other things of a like kind, with which they seemed highly delighted. One sailor, who was at a loss in what way to testify sufficient gratitude for the favours he had received, tore out the lining from a pair of old breeches, and wrapped it round the neck of his beloved. This was so extraordinary a present, that the lady was no less delighted with her new ornament, and no less proud of it than a knight with the ribband of a new Order, and hastened home, probably thinking to herself, *Honi soit qui mal y pense*.[10]

Although Melville does not mention this work as one of the two "general narratives . . . that claim particular notice" touching the Marquesas, he does quote it as an authority in *Moby-Dick,* and there is good reason to suppose that he consulted it also for the composition of *Typee.* Here he gives a strikingly similar account of such a reception; but, of course, he may have seen only with his own eyes:

We had approached within a mile and a half perhaps of the foot of the bay, when some of the islanders, who by this time had managed to scramble aboard of us at the risk of swamping their canoes, directed our attention to a singular commotion in the water ahead of the vessel. At first I imagined it to be produced by a shoal of fish sporting on the surface, but our savage friends assured us that it was caused by a shoal of "whinhenies" (young girls), who in this manner were coming off from the shore to welcome us. As they drew nearer, and I watched the rising and sinking of their forms, and beheld the uplifted right arm bearing above the water the girdle of tappa, and their long dark hair trailing beside them as they swam, I almost fancied they could be nothing else than so many mermaids—and very like mermaids they behaved too.

We were still some distance from the beach and under slow headway, when we sailed right into the midst of these swimming nymphs, and they boarded us at every quarter; many seizing hold of the chain-plates and springing into the chains; others, at the peril of being run over by the vessel in her course, catching at the bob-stays, and wreathing their slender forms about the ropes, hung suspended in the air. All of them at length succeeded in getting up the ship's side, where they clung dripping with the brine and glowing from the bath, their jet-black tresses streaming over their shoulders, and half enveloping their otherwise naked forms. There they hung, sparkling with savage vivacity, laughing gaily at one another, and chattering away with infinite glee. Nor were they idle the while, for each one performed the simple offices of the toilet for the other. Their luxuriant locks, wound up and twisted into the smallest possible compass, were freed from the briny element; the whole person carefully dried, and from a little round shell that passed from hand to hand, anointed with a fragrant oil: their adornments were completed by passing a few loose folds of white tappa, in a modest cincture, around the waist. Thus arrayed they no longer hesitated, but flung themselves lightly over the bulwarks, and were quickly frolicking about the decks. Many of them went forward, perching upon the head-rails or running out upon the bowsprit, while others seated themselves upon the taffrail, or reclined at full length upon the boats.

What a sight for us bachelor sailors! how avoid so dire a temptation? For who could think of tumbling these artless creatures overboard, when they had swam miles to welcome us?

Their appearance perfectly amazed me; their extreme youth, the light clear brown of their complexions, their delicate features, and inexpressibly graceful figures, their softly moulded limbs, and free unstudied action, seemed as strange as beautiful.

The *Dolly* was fairly captured; and never I will say was vessel carried before by such a dashing and irresistible party of boarders! The ship taken, we could not do otherwise than yield ourselves prisoners, and for the whole period that she remained in the bay, the *Dolly*, as well as her crew, were completely in the hands of the mermaids. . . .

Our ship was now wholly given up to every species of riot and debauchery. Not the feeblest barrier was interposed between the unholy passions of the crew and their unlimited gratification. The grossest licentiousness and the most shameful inebriety prevailed, with occasional and but short-lived interruptions, through the whole period of her stay. Alas for the poor savages when exposed to the influence of these polluting examples! Unsophisticated and confiding, they are easily led into every vice, and humanity weeps over the ruin thus remorselessly inflicted upon them by their European civilisers. Thrice happy are they who, inhabiting some yet undiscovered island in the midst of the ocean, have never been brought into contaminating contact with the white man.[11]

It is interesting to note that this is one of the passages which suffered heavy expurgation in the revised American edition of *Typee*.[12]

The primitive grandeur of the Marquesan landscape, enlivened though it was by seductive human beauty, was tainted for Melville, however, even as it first opened to his sea-weary eyes. For something far different absorbed his attention and spoiled his initial impression. In the harbor, he says:

I saw nothing but the tri-coloured flag of France, trailing over the stern of six vessels, whose black hulls, and bristling broadsides, proclaimed their warlike character. . . . The whole group of islands had just been taken possession of by Rear-Admiral Du Petit Thouars, in the name of the invincible French nation. . . . It was in the summer of 1842 that we arrived at the islands; the French had then held possession of them for several weeks. During this time they had visited some of the principal places in the group. . . . At Nukuheva, there were about one hundred soldiers ashore. They were encamped in tents, constructed of the old sails and spare spars of the squadron, within the limits of a redoubt mounted with a few nine-pounders, and surrounded with a fosse.[13]

After some caustic remarks about this needless display of military power, Melville concludes that, though the natives looked on with savage admiration at the show, they indicated just as savage a hatred of the actors. What particularly impressed them was a horse, the first they had seen, brought over from Valparaiso by the "Achille," and ridden daily "by one of the officers at full speed over the hard sand beach," to the loud plaudits of the islanders.[14]

Max Radiguet, secretary to the *état-major général* on the frigate *La Reine Blanche,* has left some interesting particulars of this occupation—the beginning of an ambitious program of French colonial expansion in the Pacific. The squadron, consisting of *La Triomphante, La Boussole, L'Embuscade,* and *Le Bucéphale,* in addition to the flagship, sailed from Valparaiso at the end of March, 1842. Arriving at the Marquesas, they made a triumphant progress through the group, which culminated with the formal taking of possession at Anna Maria Bay, Nukahiva, on June 2, 1842. Here they landed about two hundred troops and set about building Fort Collet, the fortification which Melville referred to so scornfully. Even the horse brought over by the "Achille" and the equestrian display which Melville ridicules were likewise actualities. For about the middle of June *Le Jules-César,* a merchant ship from Valparaiso, arrived with supplies, and, in addition to some donkeys and two pregnant mares, she brought "un petit étalon du Chili." At first the natives were very much afraid of these animals; but soon Moana, the principal chief, learned to ride and enjoyed nothing more than racing up and down the beach at so reckless a speed as to astonish even the French officers themselves.[15]

This same Moana is the subject of a taunting aside in which Melville, with high mockery, sets forth the Frenchmen's justification of their seizure of the islands:

One example of the shameless subterfuges under which the French stand prepared to defend whatever cruelties they may hereafter commit in bringing the Marquesan natives into subjection is well worthy of being recorded. On some flimsy pretext or other Mowanna [*sic*], the king of Nukuheva, whom the invaders by extravagant presents have cajoled over to their interests, and move about like a mere puppet, has been set up as the rightful sovereign of the entire island—the alleged ruler by prescription of various clans who for ages perhaps have treated with each other as separate nations. To reinstate this much injured prince in the assumed dignities of his ancestors, the disinterested strangers have come all the way from France; they are determined that his title shall be acknowledged. If any tribe shall refuse to recognise the authority of the French, by bowing down to the laced chapeau of Mowanna, let them abide the consequences of their obstinacy.[16]

And yet, says Melville, notwithstanding such conduct in the far corners of the earth, the French have always "plumed themselves upon being the most humane and polished of nations."

Whatever the French pretensions to humane motives, they certainly left no stone unturned to build up the power of this local chief and then, by insinuating themselves into his good graces, to exert their authority through him, in accordance with their customary foreign policy. This Moana has an interesting history. His grandfather, Gattanewa (or Keatanui), had been previously set up as virtually and avowedly the king of the whole island of Nukahiva by the American captain, David Porter, after his conquest of the Typees in 1813; and at Gattanewa's death Moana I, the father of the present chief, succeeded to this honor. Stewart said that when he visited the island in the *Vincennes* in 1829 Moana I was dead, and that his son, the present Moana, a boy about eight years of age, was ruling under a regency: "All the tribes, including the Taipiis [Typees], partially at least acknowledge the boy—whose maternal grandmother is a chief woman of that tribe, still living at their principal valley—as the rightful prince of the whole." [17] Several years later, an attempt having been made on his life by the Taioas, a neighboring tribe, he left his native island in a merchant ship and visited England, where he took on a veneer of civilization. Sometime afterwards he was discovered in slavery at the Navigator Islands by a missionary named Thompson, who brought him back to Nukahiva on December 23, 1839. Here he was seen in 1840 by Captain Sir Edward Belcher, who has left a very unflattering picture of him:

In stature he is about five feet eight inches, not well built, sadly wanting in personal courage, is not a goodlooking person, and without any one feature to command respect or attachment; and, further, his best friends assert that he is not deficient in ingratitude, and every other bad feeling. Revenge, sulky, moody revenge, alone actuates him in the present war [against the Taioas].[18]

Such was the unprepossessing and corrupted ruler of the chief valley of Nukahiva when the French squadron arrived; and so Radiguet described him in 1842:

Te-Moana, principal chef de Taiohaë. C'était un jeune homme de vingt ans environ. . . . Vêtu d'un costume dont les pièces disparates semblaient sortir, celle-ci du sac d'un matelot baleinier, celle-là du vestiaire rebuté d'un officier anglais, les pieds nus, les cheveux incultes, le poil rare, on l'eût pris aux Antilles pour un mulâtre déserteur de l'armée de Soulouque.[19]

Rear-Admiral Dupetit-Thouars immediately began the work of creating his puppet, appealing to the naïve vanity of this half-spoiled native chief. In his report to the Minister of Marine, June 18, 1842, he set forth his procedure with such explicit candor as to deny any pretence that he was civilizing the Marquesans in the name of disinterested humanity:

Nous lui [Témoana] avons fait présent d'un uniforme rouge, d'une paire d'épaulettes de colonel, de chemises, d'un pantalon. Il porte tous ces vêtements avec aisance, et s'est montré très-reconnaissant de nos bons procédés. . . . Le roi se montrant fort enclin à la civilisation, il suffira de l'entretenir dans ces bonnes dispositions, chose facile en lui faisant de temps à autre des présents surtout de ceux qui peuvent favoriser son penchant pour nos goûts et nos mœurs, tels que des meubles pour orner une petite maison à l'européenne qu'il vient de faire bâtir, des vêtements pour lui et pour sa femme. Déjà le roi est vêtu en colonel et porte des souliers; étant resté à bord avec sa femme, après le coucher du soleil, pour assister à la représentation d'une petite pièce que l'on jouait, il a vu des matelots habillés en femmes, et aussitôt il nous a priés de faire faire des robes semblables pour sa femme, ce que nous nous sommes empressés de faire, convaincus que ces moyens sont les plus puissants sur eux pour nous les attacher: en leur créant des besoins, nous nous rendons nécessaires.[20]

More substantial aid than cast-off clothing and second-hand furniture, however, had to be rendered before Moana made himself the whole-hearted ally of Dupetit-Thouars. Early in June he came to the French admiral and complained that his enemies, the Taioas, refused to give up his wife, whom they were holding as a hostage. Accordingly, on the 9th of that month the admiral made an expedition to the bay of Acauï, where the Taioas lived, to undertake the diplomatic feat of rescuing a native queen. Radiguet was a member of this party, which, after some little difficulty, accomplished its mission.[21]

There was another visitor in the valley of the Taioas on that same day in early June. Herman Melville, several weeks before his desertion from the *Acushnet,* went there from Taiohaë with a party in one of the ship's boats, on a pleasure excursion, and entered the bay about noon, as he records in *Typee:*

It so happened that the very day I was in Tior [Taioa] the French admiral, attended by all the boats of his quadron, came down in state from Nukuheva to take formal possession of the place. He remained in the valley about two hours, during which time he had a ceremonious interview with the king. . . . The admiral came forward with head uncovered and extended hand, while the old king saluted him by a stately flourish of his weapon. The next moment they stood side by side, these two extremes of the social scale—the polished, splendid Frenchman, and the poor tattooed savage. They were both tall and noble-looking men; but in other respects how strikingly contrasted! Du Petit Thouars exhibited upon his person all the paraphernalia of his naval rank. He wore a richly decorated admiral's frock-coat, a laced chapeau-bras, and upon his breast were a variety of ribbons and orders; while the simple islander, with the exception of a slight cincture about his loins, appeared in all the nakedness of nature.[22]

Melville, intent upon his contrast between civilization and savagery and ignorant of the purpose of the expedition, missed the real import of this picturesque scene. For the French did not visit the valley of the Taioas to take formal possession—the chiefs of that tribe having taken part in the ceremonies at Taiohaë, June 2—but to persuade them to return Moana's wife; and, instead of coming in state with all his boats, Admiral Dupetit-Thouars brought only one *canot.*[23]

There is no doubt, however, that the two authors, Radiguet and Melville, were recounting the same incident. Melville's spelling of *Tior* for *Taioa* is merely typical of his usual phonetic inaccuracy;[24] for the two descriptions show that the same scene was under observation. Radiguet says that the Taioas lived in a narrow valley, four miles long and a quarter of a mile wide, shut in on one side by verdant slopes and on the other by "une muraille verticale de rochers noirs . . . haute de six à sept cents mètres;" he then spends himself lavishly in a description of this landscape of ravishing beauty, concluding: "Je n'en sais pas de plus charmante et de plus pittoresque aux Marquises." [25] Melville's picture tallies with this perfectly:

The glen of Tior . . . is not more than four miles in length, and varies in breadth from half a mile to less than a quarter. The rocky vineclad cliffs on one side tower almost perpendicularly from the base to the height of at least fifteen hundred feet; while across the vale—in striking contrast to the scenery opposite—grass-grown elevations rise one above another in blooming terraces. . . .

How shall I describe the scenery that met my eye, as I looked out from this verdant recess! The narrow valley, with its steep and close adjoining sides draperied with vines, and arched overhead with a fretwork of interlacing boughs, nearly hidden from view by masses of leafy verdure, seemed from where I stood like an immense arbour disclosing its vista to the eye, whilst as I advanced it insensibly widened into the loveliest vale eye ever beheld.[26]

This striking coincidence of Melville and Radiguet, strangers to one another in attitude as well as in person, observing the same obscure occurrence in a remote corner of the earth, and recording their impressions independently and without reference to each other, certainly gives validity to both accounts. Since Radiguet's book was not published until many years after *Typee*, there is no claim of literary influence; instead, here is an unexpected instance of how directly Melville wrote from actual experience when it suited his purposes to do so.[27]

By this intervention in native affairs which resulted in the reunion of the royal couple, the French hoped, for their own purposes, to cement the tie between the Taioas and the Teiis (the inhabitants of Taiohaë or Anna Maria Bay), and also between both of these and the Typees (Taipiis); for the wife of Moana was a Typee by birth and the heir to the supreme power in their valley.[28] Melville, in spite of a vaunted "four months residence" in Typee Valley, where he says he was in constant intimacy with their chief, Mehevi, seems to have remained strangely ignorant of any such family connections.

Apparently, however, he was more conversant with the supposed advantages that the French were bestowing on the natives by clothing them with the vesture of civilization. From a second visit to Nukahiva fifteen months later when, as an ordinary seaman on board the frigate *United States,* he touched again at this island before leaving the South Seas forever, Melville illustrates the thinness of this veneer by an incident which enables us to watch the author and artist at work, elaborating and embellishing his actual experiences:

Not . . . shy of exhibiting her charms was the Island Queen herself, the beauteous wife of Mowanna, the King of Nukuheva. Between two and three years after the adventures recorded in this volume [in reality, only a little more than one year], I chanced, while aboard of a man-of-war, to touch at these islands. The French had then held possession of the Marquesas some time, and already prided themselves upon the beneficial effects of their jurisdiction, as discernible in the deportment of the natives. To be sure, in one of their efforts at reform they had slaughtered about a hundred and fifty of them at Whitihoo—but let that pass. At the time I mention, the French squadron was rendezvousing in the bay of Nukuheva, and during an interview between one of their captains and our worthy Commodore, it was suggested by the former, that we, as the flagship of the American squadron, should receive, in state, a visit from the royal pair. The French officer likewise represented, with evident satisfaction, that under their tuition the king and queen had imbibed proper notions of their elevated station, and on all ceremonious occasions conducted themselves with suitable dignity. Accordingly, preparations were made to give their majesties a reception on board in a style corresponding with their rank.

One bright afternoon, a gig, gaily bedizened with streamers, was observed to shove off from the side of one of the French frigates, and pull directly for our gangway. In the stern sheets reclined Mowanna and his consort. As they approached, we paid them all the honours due to royalty; manning our yards, firing a salute, and making a prodigious hubbub.

They ascended the accommodation ladder, were greeted by the Commodore, hat in hand, and passing along the quarter-deck, the marine guard presented arms, while the band struck up "The King of the Cannibal Islands." So far all went well. The French officers grimaced and smiled in exceedingly high spirits, wonderfully pleased with the discreet manner in which these distinguished personages behaved themselves.

Their appearance was certainly calculated to produce an effect. His majesty was arrayed in a magnificent military uniform, stiff with gold lace and embroidery, while his shaven crown was concealed by a huge chapeau-bras, waving with ostrich plumes. There was one slight blemish, however, in his appearance. A broad patch of tattooing stretched completely across his face, in a line with his eyes, making him look as if he wore a huge pair of goggles; and royalty in goggles suggested some ludicrous ideas. But it was in the adornment of the fair person of his dark-complexioned spouse that the tailors of the fleet had evinced the gaiety of their national taste. She was habited in a gaudy tissue of scarlet cloth, trimmed with yellow silk, which descending a little below the knees, exposed to view her bare legs, embellished with spiral tattooing, and somewhat resembling two miniature Trajan's columns. Upon her head was a fanciful turban of purple velvet, figured with silver sprigs, and surmounted by a tuft of variegated feathers.[29]

That this royal visit actually took place is proved by the brief record of it preserved in an anonymous unofficial journal kept on board the frigate *United States* during this cruise. But this less poetic "Ship's Scribe" strips his account to the barest outline:

During our visit the King & Queen visited the Ship, he being dressed in a French uniform given him by the French Admiral, and she in a red skirt which reached a few inches below the knee, about 15 years of age, with handsome features, and tattooed on all visible parts.[30]

To this decorous memorandum, however, Melville contributes a sequel, in which he makes his most artistic flourish:

The ship's company crowding into the gangway to view the sight, soon arrested her majesty's attention. She singled out from their number an old *salt,* whose bare arms and feet and exposed breast were covered with as many inscriptions in India ink as the lid of an Egyptian sarcophagus. Notwithstanding all the sly hints and remonstrances of the French officers, she immediately approached the man, and pulling farther open the bosom of his duck frock, and rolling up the leg of his wide trousers, she gazed with admiration at the bright blue and vermilion pricking, thus disclosed to view. She hung over the fellow, caressing him, and expressing her delight in a variety of wild exclamations and gestures. The embarrassment of the polite Gauls at such an unlooked-for occurrence may be easily imagined; but picture their consternation, when all at once the royal lady, eager to display the hieroglyphics on her own sweet form, bent forward for a moment, and turning sharply round, threw up the skirts of her mantle, and revealed a sight from which the aghast Frenchmen retreated precipitately, and tumbling into their boat, fled the scene of so shocking a catastrophe.[31]

This "Characteristic Anecdote of the Queen of Nukuheva," as Melville entitles it, with its concluding flourish which is equally characteristic of the author of *Typee,* is undoubtedly more picturesque than it is veracious. The author of the "Abstract of a Cruise in the Frigate *United States*" would never have left unrecorded this piquant incident of a romantic queen who threw discretion and her own red skirt to the winds, if it had actually happened before his eyes; for he was neither an official journalist nor a prude, as is witnessed by his recording with evident relish a drunken dinner party on board the *United States* a year before, when the commodore had mounted the poop and danced the juba and the breakdown with the ship's Negroes.[32] Melville's embellishment was added for the sake of picturesqueness and for a good laugh at the French, which would be well received by his English audience (*Typee* being first published in London).[33] Although one example is not enough to impeach the veracity of a whole book, it strengthens one's suspicion that Melville was not altogether guided by the "anxious desire to speak the unvarnished truth" that he voices in the preface to *Typee.*[34]

Even if Moana's consort did behave with more propriety than Melville gave her credit for on this ceremonious occasion, he may, however, have heard gossip of her from some of the French garrison sufficient to give him at least a foundation for his anecdote. For, apparently, civilization lay on her as lightly as the garments which were, so far, its chief gift to savagery; whereas her primitive freedom from restraint remained beneath her skin as deeply and permanently dyed as the tattooing which symbolized her truer self. Radiguet, the French secretary, has left evidence of the more secret charms of this island queen, who, he says, was about sixteen years of age and one of the most beautiful Polynesians he had ever seen. In describing the artificial ornamentation by which she attempted to enhance her natural beauty, he remarks:

Quelques petites rayures verticales à ses lèvres, une sorte d'unsecte couvrant le lobe de l'oreille, des mitaines et des cothurnes du plus fin travail étaient les seuls tatouages apparents de son corps. Plus tard, elle ne se fit pas faute de nous montrer avec orgueil une splendide gerbe d'artifice, véritable chef-d'œuvre d'incrustation, qui lui couvrait les reins.[35]

This description tallies with the account Melville gives of the customary tattooing of Marquesan women—all but the finishing touch, which, itself, tallies with the unique additional decoration hinted at in the "Characteristic Anecdote of the Queen of Nukuheva." But, unfortunately, there are no documents extant to determine whether Melville himself attained the degree of intimacy enjoyed by Max Radiguet with Moana's beautiful consort.[36]

CHAPTER VI

MISSIONARIES AND CANNIBALS

THE natives of the Marquesas Islands, among the most primitive of the Polynesians, resisted the aggressions and allurements of European civilization with a persistence indicative of supreme contentment with their savage state—or rather, in the eyes of the first visitors, with a stubborn indifference to the bounty of Providence indicative of the total depravity in which they were sunk. As they met the aggrandizements of foreign governments with ferocity, so they defeated the propaganda of alien religions with the even more effective weapons of "indifference, levity, and licentiousness." The earliest apostles of Western culture, the missionaries, were far less successful here than at any of the other large Polynesian groups. "The Protestant Missions," observes Melville, "appear to have despaired of reclaiming these islands from heathenism. The usage they have in every case received from the natives has been such as to intimidate the boldest of their number." [1] Although efforts had been made to introduce Christianity at the Marquesas Islands coevally with the establishment of the missionary station at the Society Islands, in 1797, and twenty years before the first organized efforts at the Sandwich Islands, the Marquesans lagged far behind the natives of the other two groups in spiritual progress. Almost half a century of futile evangelizing followed before they accepted this blessing, and even then it was only a nominal acceptance, inspired by the bristling broadsides of the French squadron in the summer of 1842, on the eve of Melville's arrival.

For thirty-five years numerous abortive expeditions to convert the Marquesans had been sent out from the station of the London Missionary Society at Tahiti, but the teachers had all been placed on Santa Christina and La Magdalena in the southeastern group of the archipelago.[2] In 1833, the American Mission in the Sandwich Islands took a hand in the struggling enterprise and sent out three missionaries, Tinker, Withney, and Alexander, who landed with their wives at Nukahiva, the principal island of the northern cluster. They were greatly annoyed by the natives, who heaped upon them such unendurable insults—particularly in the form of the same indecorous curiosity that had frightened the Reverend Mr. Harris away from Santa Christina in 1797—that they left within a year.[3] In *Typee,* Melville gives a circumstantial account of the trials and tribulations of these first proselytizers to visit the island of Nukahiva:

. . . A short time before my visit to the Marquesas, a somewhat amusing incident took place in connection with these efforts, which I cannot avoid relating.

An intrepid missionary, undaunted by the ill-success that had attended all previous endeavours to conciliate the savages, and believing much in the efficacy of female influence, introduced among them his young and beautiful wife, the first white woman who had ever visited their shores. The islanders at first gazed in mute admiration at so unusual a prodigy, and seemed inclined to regard it as some new divinity. But after a short time, becoming familiar with its charming aspect, and jealous of the folds which encircled its form, they sought to pierce the sacred veil of calico in which it was enshrined, and in the gratification of their curiosity so far overstepped the limits of good breeding, as deeply to offend the lady's sense of decorum. Her sex once ascertained, their idolatry was changed into contempt; and there was no end to the contumely showered upon her by the savages, who were exasperated at the deception which they conceived had been practised upon them. To the horror of her affectionate spouse, she was stripped of her garments, and given to understand that she could no longer carry on her deceits with impunity. The gentle dame was not sufficiently evangelised to endure this, and, fearful of further improprieties, she forced her husband to relinquish his undertaking, and together they returned to Tahiti.[4]

None of the Protestant missionaries give the details of this fiasco, which apparently so outraged their sense of propriety that they merely observed that the Americans "relinquished the undertaking in the course of the following year" because of "the turbulent, licentious, and dishonest conduct of the natives."⁵ It is to the records of the Catholic priest, M. l'Abbé Mathias Gracia, who was stationed at Nukahiva in 1839–1840, that we must turn for a full authentication of Melville's anecdote:

... trois autres de ces messieurs [Protestant missionaries] ... se virent contraints à se retirer de la même île, en 1833, après mille vexations endurées durant un séjour prolongé de quinze mois. Nous tenons plusieurs détails du séjour et de l'expulsion de ces derniers, de la bouche des naturels euxmêmes. Ils avaient cru pouvoir amener leurs femmes pour les aider dans leur travaux de civilisation; et c'est justement ce qui les leur fit manquer. Les sauvages finirent par respecter assez peu ces dames, et leur firent même des outrages qu'il ne nous est pas permis de spécifier, et qui ne pouvaient entrer que dans le pensée de ces sauvages. Ces pauvres dames, après avoir usé en vain, pour mieux se faire respecter, elles et leur maison, de moyens qui parurent très-vexatoires à messieurs les cannibales, ne tardèrent pas à décider leurs maris à quitter une terre de déshonneur pour elles. Mais il leur fallut encore expier ce départ, en perdant tout leur avoir, sur lequel firent main basse les Nuku-Hiviens [*sic*], charmés de les voir partir à ce prix.⁶

The Frenchman's account seems to be reliable and unprompted by ulterior sectarian motives; but it is doubtful whether Melville was acquainted with this rare volume, or whether he read French fluently enough to have made any use of it had it come into his hands. What Melville's source of information was is not known, unless he learned the story from the natives themselves, just as Father Gracia had done.⁷ This futile attempt at introducing Christianity was the only sustained one that had been made by the Protestants at the island of Nukahiva before Melville's arrival.

The London Missionary Society, however, unwilling to abandon the Marquesans to their heathendom, continued its efforts in the lower group. In October, 1834, two missionaries, Messrs. Stallworthy and Rodgerson, arrived at Santa Christina to carry on the work which had been prosecuted so feebly by the Tahitian teachers. The official historian of the society records the prolonged but fruitless endeavor of these Englishmen to convert the fractious natives:

The chiefs received them kindly, . . . and the people treated them with respect, but regarded their message with the utmost aversion; and such was the ferocity of their character, and the profligacy of their habits, that Mr. Rodgerson, deeming it unsuitable to remain with his wife and children, returned to Tahiti in October, 1837.[8]

Mr. Rodgerson's wife, apparently, was subjected to insults similar to those which had driven the American missionaries from Nuka-hiva, and it is quite possible that Melville's anecdote refers to this occasion rather than to the former experience. Again Father Gracia gives the fullest account I have been able to discover:

À peu près à la même époque, sur un point différent, mais dans le même archipel, en l'île Sainte-Christine, un autre ministre protestant marié avait été obligé par les mêmes causes d'en venir à la même fin. La curiosité et l'impudence des naturels à l'égard de sa femme étant devenue chaque jour plus insultante pour lui et plus inquiétante pour son repos, il avait quitté ce poste, et était allé s'établir dans l'archipel de la Société. Son compagnon, M. Talworthy [*sic*], non marié, que nous avons vu là jusqu'en 1841 encore, après plus de dix ans de séjour, sans y avoir pu amener à sa croyance une seule personne, y était resté à jouir du moins d'une certaine aisance qu'il s'était acquise.[9]

So Mr. Stallworthy continued for four more years "amidst many privations, much suffering, and great discouragement to labour indefatigably for the benefit of the people," but the only progress he could make was through the desire of the native chief to get shipping to come to his port. Although he was reinforced in 1839 by Mr. Thompson—the missionary who had brought Moana, the chief of Nukahiva, back to his inheritance—by the close of 1841 "in concurrence with the opinion of the missionaries in Tahiti, they felt it their duty to retire from the islands." [10]

Thus the last of the Protestant missionaries withdrew from the Marquesas before Melville's arrival. There was another cause for their withdrawal, however, besides the stubbornness of the natives. In 1838, Dupetit-Thouars had landed two Catholic missionaries at Santa Christina, and the next year they were joined by ten more of their brethren, five of whom afterwards repaired to Nukahiva. One of these priests was Father Gracia, whose record of his residence at Nukahiva from February, 1839, to May, 1840, touches Melville's narrative closely at several points, as has been demonstrated; and another was Father Columban Murphy, whom Melville was later to know intimately at Tahiti.[11] But both of them had left the Marquesas before his arrival. In the meantime, however, the struggling little band of Catholics received the support requisite for success from the strong arm of the French squadron under Dupetit-Thouars in the spring of 1842. Where faith had failed, force of arms gave new hope.

If the Marquesans discouraged the traffic in souls by their indifference and even frightened the missionaries away by their licentiousness, they likewise discouraged the more material traffic with whalers and ships of commerce by their ferocity, and at times drove off by force those who sought to touch at their shores for refreshments. Much of their hostile conduct was probably the result of previous cruelty on the part of the Europeans, and their reputation for it was undoubtedly spread by the misrepresentations of impetuous captains and knavish crews; but there seems to be some evidence that the Marquesans were less friendly to overtures of all sorts than either the Society or the Sandwich Islanders. And of all the Marquesans, Melville attaches the most ferocious character to the Typees of Nukahiva:

Immediately adjacent to Nukuheva [Taiohaë], and only separated from it by the mountains seen from the harbour, lies the lovely valley of Happar [Hapa], whose inmates cherish the most friendly relations with the inhabitants of Nukuheva [the Teiis]. On the other side of Happar, and closely adjoining it, is the magnificent valley of the dreaded Typees, the unappeasable enemies of both these tribes. . . .

Deterred by the frightful stories related of its inhabitants, ships never enter this bay, while their hostile relations with the tribes in the adjoining valleys prevent the Typees from visiting that section of the island where vessels occasionally lie. At long intervals, however, some intrepid captain will touch on the skirts of the bay, with two or three armed boats' crews, and accompanied by an interpreter . . . , who . . . leaps ashore with the goods intended for barter, while the boats, with their oars shipped, and every man on his thwart, lie just outside the surf, heading off from the shore, in readiness at the first untoward event to escape to the open sea. As soon as the traffic is concluded, one of the boats pulls in under cover of the muskets of the others, the fruit

is quickly thrown into her, and the transient visitors precipitately retire from what they justly consider so dangerous a vicinity.[12]

On the other hand, when the frigate *United States* touched at
Anna Maria Bay (Taiohaë) in the fall of 1843, with Melville on
board, the Ship's Scribe observed: "Tipee [*sic*] Bay, about six miles
to leeward of where we lay, is equally safe as an anchorage, the
Inhabitants of which are at continual war with the neighboring
tribes." [13] Unfortunately, this isolated statement is somewhat ambiguous. It may mean safety in a nautical sense only, and not in
other respects because of the belligerent attitude of the Typee
natives. Again, it may mean that Typee Bay was equally safe in all
respects, the warlike nature of its inhabitants being merely a
descriptive and not a qualifying clause. Certainly if the Typees
enjoyed a "prodigious notoriety over all the islands" for their
peculiar ferocity, as Melville says, it is beyond belief that the observant journalist of the frigate would have failed to add this terrifying fact unambiguously to his otherwise casual observation
that "Tipee Bay . . . is equally safe as an anchorage." Most of the
shipping, however, went to Anna Maria Bay, whose inhabitants,
the Teiis, were the hereditary enemies of the Typees; consequently,
it was the former who gave them their bad reputation. Stewart
implies that this was the case:

It was soon ascertained from them, that their tribe and the Taipiis
were, as usual, at war. . . . Their grimaces of detestation and deadly
hatred to their enemies—as they pointed to their habitations and valley
—and pantomimic representations of the battle, the discharge of the
muskets, and effect of the shot, were quite amusing; while they used
all the eloquence of speech and gesture to induce us to espouse their
cause, and pour destruction on the poor Taipiis, whose very name
seemed to be a watchword of terror among them.[14]

Whatever the actual character of the Typees may have been, Melville plays up their reputation for ferocity and makes the dread of
falling victim to them the chief motive of suspense throughout his
volume.

The role that Melville assigns to the Typees, moreover, seems to
have some foundation in fact. For, by way of giving concreteness to

his specification of charges against them, he cites several instances of their ferocity that are testified to by other witnesses:

Even before visiting the Marquesas, I had heard from men who had touched at the group on former voyages some revolting stories in connection with these savages; and fresh in my remembrance was the adventure of the master of the *Katherine,* who only a few months previous, imprudently venturing into this bay in an armed boat for the purpose of barter, was seized by the natives, carried back a little distance into their valley, and was only saved from a cruel death by the intervention of a young girl, who facilitated his escape by night along the beach to Nukuheva.[15]

Francis Allyn Olmsted, who went out as a passenger on a whaler for the purpose of recruiting his health, reports the same story in a fuller form as it was told to him at Honolulu, May 25, 1840, by the captain of the *Catharine:*

Captain Brown, of the whale ship "Catharine," of Nantucket, arrived here the other day [direct from the Marquesas]. . . . In conversation with him, he gave me an account of a personal adventure among the Marquesas Islands, which I relate, as it illustrates the treacherous character of the natives of many of the Polynesian Islands. Leaving Nookaheva [*sic*] bay in the Island of Nookaheva, he sailed around to the opposite side of the Island, for the purpose of trafficking with the natives that assembled in great numbers upon the beach, as his boat lay on the water, a few yards from the shore. The Tipaiis [*sic*], the name of this tribe, are very ferocious, and to gratify their cannibal appetites, they are not very scrupulous in making choice of their victims. Capt. B., aware of their reputation for ferocity, disregarded all their solicitations to land, but made an agreement with them to supply his ship with a number of swine, which were to be brought down to the beach on the coming day. Accordingly, at the appointed time, these animals were exhibited upon the beach tied together, and every appearance of good faith was observed to induce the captain to come on shore. For a long time he hesitated about entrusting himself within their power, until after assurances from a Spanish boy (who had accompanied him from the opposite side of the island,) that there would be no danger, he landed upon the beach. He was instantly seized by a party of natives, and hurried off to some distance from shore, while the swine were cut loose that the savages had collected together to decoy the captain within their reach. They now thronged around him with horrid yells of

triumph, and clamorously demanded of him, as a ransom, forty mus-
quets and six kegs of gunpowder. As he was unable to comply with
their extravagant demands, a dreadful doom was prepared for him.
With awful anticipations of his horrid fate, he saw them collecting together piles of dry wood, and digging holes in the ground, to be used as
ovens for roasting him, upon the following morning; and it was with
the agony of despair that he found himself surrounded at night upon
every side by his merciless captors. About midnight, however, he stole
away from his sleeping guards, in company with the Spanish boy, and
after wandering about among the mountains, he made his escape to
the tribe to which the Spanish boy belonged, by whom he had been
adopted, after running away from some vessel which had stopped at
Nookaheva. Capt. B., soon regained his ship, when the crew were eager
to take vengeance upon the savages for their treachery, but he wisely
restrained them, believing that any thing of this kind would be retaliated upon the next ship that might visit them. The day after his
escape, the Tipiaiis challenged the friendly tribe [Teiis?] to mortal
conflict, upon their refusal to give up into their power the man who had
fled to them for protection. A battle ensued between the tribes, in which
two men were killed upon each side, and hostilities then ceased to allow
the contending parties the luxury of feeding upon their respective
prisoners.[16]

This account certainly has the virtue of directness, coming as it
does from the lips of the near-victim, and in one respect it verifies
Melville's anecdote—though it is possible that Olmsted's *Incidents
of a Whaling Voyage* was merely the source of his information.
But it is also possible that Captain Brown, in justifiable terror,
mistook a shrewd and mischievous prank (for which the Marquesans were famed) for a more murderous intent. In support of this
view Captain Sir Edward Belcher, who not only defends the Marquesans in general against the charge of licentiousness but also
defends the Typees themselves against the special charge of ferocity,
relates a story which he picked up during his visit to Nukahiva,
January 21–30, 1840, that sounds very much like a comic version
of the harrowing story related by Melville (and Olmsted) of the
captain of the *Catharine:*

In the case of the captain and mate of a whaler, not many years since
cut off by the natives in Comptroller's Bay [Typee], . . . said to be

the most ferocious on the island, seldom communicating with their neighbours, and never with foreigners,—how did they act? They amused themselves by exciting their fears. Having made a fire sufficiently large to bake them, a hog was substituted, which, when cooked, they were invited to partake of. They were afterwards ransomed. On no other island would their lives have been saved.[17]

And even this may have been in justifiably provoked retaliation for an act of cruelty perpetrated in this same valley by the captain of an American whaler, who, in March, 1829, had kidnaped three of the natives—one of them the only son of a high chief and a great favorite in his tribe—and forced them to fill the place of deserters on his ship. Even Captain Brown himself was aware that if he allowed his men to avenge his injury he would only invoke the law of an eye for an eye on some future visitor. In such a long running feud it is difficult to put one's finger on the initial guilt.

The second example cited by Melville in proof of his accusation is much more bloody:

I had heard, too, of an English vessel that many years ago, after a weary cruise, sought to enter the bay of Nukuheva, and arriving within two or three miles of the land, was met by a large canoe filled with natives, who offered to lead the way to the place of their destination. The captain, unacquainted with the localities of the island, joyfully acceded to the proposition—the canoe paddled on and the ship followed. She was soon conducted to a beautiful inlet, and dropped her anchor in its waters beneath the shadows of the lofty shore. That same night the perfidious Typees, who had thus inveigled her into their fatal bay, flocked aboard the doomed vessel by hundreds, and at a given signal murdered every soul on board.[18]

No confirmation of this specific instance of the peculiar ferocity of the Typees has been turned up. On the other hand Frederick Debell Bennett, the surgeon of a whaler that spent a week in the southern group, February 27–March 4, 1835, tells of a similar slaughter which occurred there:

A few years ago, two boats from the English South-Seaman Coquette, sent ashore to procure supplies from La Dominica [Hivaoa], were seized by the natives of that island, and their crews (with the exception of two individuals) massacred.[19]

It is quite possible, of course, that the Typees also were guilty at times of such apparent outrages (as Melville charges), but their reputation on the whole was no worse than that of the other inhabitants of this archipelago; moreover, it is equally possible that all of these demonstrations of barbarity were provoked by the unthinking cruelty of ships that had previously touched there. Those who came to know most intimately the Marquesans—even the Typees—invariably gave them the best character. And Melville himself, before his book was done, became their most ardent apologist.

Pursuing the dramatic preparation for his own visit to Typee Valley, Melville continues to build up a fear of this dreaded tribe by showing how even the conquering squadron of Admiral Dupetit-Thouars was reluctant to pay an official call at their bay:

The French, although they had gone through the ceremony of hoisting their colours for a few hours at all the principal places of the group, had not as yet visited the bay of Typee, anticipating a fierce resistance on the part of the savages there, which for the present at least they wished to avoid. Perhaps they were not a little influenced in the adoption of this unusual policy from a recollection of the warlike reception given by the Typees to the forces of Captain Porter, about the year 1814, when that brave and accomplished officer endeavoured to subjugate the clan merely to gratify the mortal hatred of his allies the Nukuhevas [Teiis] and Happars.

On that occasion I have been told that a considerable detachment of sailors and marines from the frigate *Essex,* accompanied by at least two thousand warriors of Happar and Nukuheva, landed in boats and canoes at the head of the bay, and after penetrating a little distance into the valley, met with the stoutest resistance from its inmates. Valiantly, although with much loss, the Typees disputed every inch of ground, and after some hard fighting obliged their assailants to retreat and abandon their design of conquest.

The invaders, on their march back to the sea, consoled themselves for their repulse by setting fire to every house and temple in their route; and a long line of smoking ruins defaced the once-smiling bosom of the valley, and proclaimed to its pagan inhabitants the spirit that reigned in the breasts of Christian soldiers. Who can wonder at the deadly hatred of the Typees to all foreigners after such unprovoked atrocities? [20]

Melville was apparently writing from first-hand information when he said that the French had not visited Typee Bay at the time of his arrival early in July, 1842, for the official report of Dupetit-Thouars on June 18, 1842, makes no mention of such a visit up until that time, and the account of Max Radiguet, his secretary, seems to indicate that they never went through any formal ceremony of taking possession there.[21] But the explanation that they were deterred by a recollection of Porter's trouble in subduing the Typees thirty years before is not necessarily true, for the general policy of the French was to perform this ceremony only once at each island, inviting the chiefs of the neighboring tribes to attend, as had been the case at Anna Maria Bay.

Perhaps it was Melville and not the French who called to mind Porter's invasion of Typee Valley. It will be remembered that he cites David Porter's *Journal* as one of the two general narratives of the Marquesas Islands that claim particular notice. Although he adds: "This is a work, however, which I have never happened to meet with," there is considerable evidence, as will appear throughout the ensuing chapters, not only that he was acquainted with Porter's volumes, but even that they formed—together with Stewart's two volumes—the chief source of his information for his own narrative of Marquesan life. It is true that Melville gives the title inaccurately as the *"Journal of the Cruise of the U. S. Frigate Essex, in the Pacific, during the late War,"* but this is not necessarily indicative of unfamiliarity with the work. For, even in his descriptive sketches, "The Encantadas," where he acknowledges Porter as one of his authorities, he again misquotes the title, giving it as Porter's *Voyage into the Pacific;* and, what is more to the point, he borrows from it there much more extensively than he admits—often *verbatim,* in fact.[22] Melville was never scrupulously exact in his bibliographical citations.

One proof of Melville's first-hand acquaintance with Porter's *Journal* is the very accuracy of his account of the invasion of Typee Valley just quoted. Since Captain Porter, according to his own record of this incident, feared that his conduct would be misrepresented as wanton and unnecessary (or, as Melville charges, "merely to gratify the mortal hatred of his allies the Nukuhevas and Happars"), he tried to justify his subjugation of this remote tribe, by declaring that their insubordination endangered the peace of the island during his occupation.[23]

Reluctantly, on November 27, 1813, he sent twenty war canoes and five of his own boats, protected by the *Essex Junior,* to Typee Bay. Here they were joined by other warriors of the Teii and Hapa tribes, the entire force amounting to almost five thousand natives in addition to two score of Porter's men. After his final offer of peace had been rejected, Porter advanced with his forces about two miles up the valley. But they met with such stout resistance that they were deserted by their native allies and, by nightfall, were forced to return to the beach "much fatigued and harassed with marching and fighting, and with no contemptible opinion of the enemy we had encountered or the difficulties we should have to surmount in conquering them." [24] The attack by sea was thus given up, and Porter's forces returned to Anna Maria Bay with the contemptuous threats of the Typees ringing in their ears, daring them to renew the battle. Three days later, crossing the intervening Hapa Valley and scaling the precipitous mountain ridges between, Porter launched a second attack, this time by land only. The Typees again offered a formidable resistance, disputing every inch of ground, and they were not subdued until many had been killed and ten of their beautiful villages burned. With two hundred seamen Porter marched the whole length of the valley, laying waste and conquering—his native allies, as he had anticipated, offering little assistance except to plunder in his wake. The conquest was complete, and the Typees sued for peace on any terms; yet, though Porter had accomplished his purpose and though he felt justified by the necessity that had forced him to it, he could not refrain from indulging in romantic regrets as he looked back over the once-smiling valley:

When I had reached the summit of the mountain, I stopped to contemplate that valley which, in the morning, we had viewed in all its beauty, the scene of abundance and happines[s]—a long line of smoaking [sic] ruins now marked our traces from one end to the other; the

[97]

opposite hills were covered with the unhappy fugitives, and the whole presented a scene of desolation and horror. Unhappy and heroic people! the victims of your own courage and mistaken pride, while the instruments of your own fate, shed the tears of pity over your misfortunes, thousands of your countrymen (nay, brethren of the same family) triumphed in your distresses! [25]

Although in Melville's version Porter's two invasions of Typee Valley are condensed into one, with some few minor inaccuracies, there can be little doubt that he had really read Porter's *Journal*. Otherwise, it is difficult to see where he could have got his information, for none of the other secondary accounts of Porter's activities in the Marquesas are so specific as his. One further proof of this indebtedness, all but convincing in itself, is the fact that they both frequently use the same rather crude orthography for Polynesian names; this is especially true of the unique spelling of the word *Typee*, all other writers using the French rendering of *Taipii*, or some variant thereof. Moreover, as will be seen, Porter's notes on the social, political, and religious customs of the Typees are more extensive and are based on more personal observations than those of anyone else except Stewart, Melville's other principal authority; for these were the only two travel writers who reported a genuine visit to the valley of the Typees prior to 1842.[26] And Porter's account certainly adds to their reputation for ferocity, which Melville was deliberately building up for the sake of suspense against the occasion of his own more friendly meeting with them later.

At this point, however, lapsing into his customary artistic error, Melville drops the role of dramatist for that of propagandist, defending the savages of Polynesia against their civilized aggressors. The impartial student of humanity must be left to balance Captain Porter's explanation of his conduct with Melville's accusation that he was guilty of "unprovoked atrocities." But there was undoubtedly much truth in Melville's more general complaints of European cruelty:

Thus it is that they whom we denominate "savages" are made to deserve the title. When the inhabitants of some sequestered island first descry the "big canoe" of the European rolling through the blue waters toward their shores, they rush down to the beach in crowds, and with open arms stand ready to embrace the strangers. Fatal embrace! They fold to their bosoms the vipers whose sting is destined to poison all their joys; and the instinctive feeling of love within their breasts is soon converted into the bitterest hate.

The enormities perpetrated in the South Seas upon some of the inoffensive islanders well-nigh pass belief. These things are seldom proclaimed at home; they happen at the very ends of the earth; they are done in a corner, and there are none to reveal them. But there is, nevertheless, many a petty trader that has navigated the Pacific whose course from island to island might be traced by a series of cold-blooded robberies, kidnappings, and murders, the iniquity of which might be considered almost sufficient to sink her guilty timbers to the bottom of the sea. . . .

How often is the term "savages" incorrectly applied! None really deserving of it were ever yet discovered by voyagers or by travellers. They have discovered heathens and barbarians, whom by horrible cruelties they have exasperated into savages. It may be asserted without fear of contradiction, that in all the cases of outrages committed by Polynesians, Europeans have at some time or other been the aggressors, and that the cruel and bloodthirsty disposition of some of the islanders is mainly to be ascribed to the influence of such examples.[27]

If Melville needed confirmation in taking his stand as an apologist for the South Sea islanders, he could have found it in Stewart's volumes. That humane gentleman, after recounting an instance of wanton cruelty and extortion on the part of a French commander at the Glen of Taioa in the 1820's, delivers a polemic on the atrocities committed by Europeans in Polynesia:

Every new observation of the character of this wild race, persuades me more and more fully, that the fierce and vindictive deportment, reported of them in some instances towards foreigners, is attributable, in a great degree at least, and in a majority of cases, to the ill treatment and wrong suffered by them from previous visitors; and often, is the direct consequence of the imprudent measures and violent usage of the very persons who publish their ferocity to the world. That the Nukuhivans [sic] and their neighbors of the Marquesas have, in some instances, shown themselves treacherous and sanguinary in their intercourse with visitors, there can be no doubt; but, in my mind, there is as little, that it has principally been in resentment for some real or supposed outrage on the part of civilized men. Few who come among them deport themselves in a manner to secure their good will and respect. Regarding them as beings scarce above the brute in their nature and habits—as those alike ignorant and reckless of all distinction between that which is right and that which is wrong—they treat them with utter contempt, except when views of immediate selfishness dictate the contrary; and themselves too often lay aside, in their intercourse with them, both the principles and practices of morality, and even a customary regard to common justice and honesty. They care not what the impression left by them among such a people may be, and seem to have no foresight of the evils that may result, from their ill conduct, to others who may come after them.[28]

This similarity of attitude furnishes one more indication of how deeply Melville was influenced by Stewart's *Visit to the South Seas*.

Having spent his anger against civilization for the present, Melville returns to the business of his dramatic preparation. Not content with presenting the Typees as the most ferocious of all the Marquesans, he brands them with the bloodiest of reputations for cannibalism—the theme of suspense which comes to dominate *Typee* and most of the subsequent South Sea romances modeled upon it. *Typee* discovered a new milieu for the romantic novelist, and with such passages as the following Melville furnished a new and exotic motive of terror for the sentimental reader:

These celebrated warriors appear to inspire the other islanders with unspeakable terrors. Their very name is a frightful one; for the word "Typee" in the Marquesan dialect signifies a lover of human flesh. It is rather singular that the title should have been bestowed upon them exclusively, inasmuch as the natives of all this group are irreclaimable cannibals. The name may, perhaps, have been given to denote the peculiar ferocity of this clan, and to convey a special stigma along with it.

These same Typees enjoy a prodigious notoriety all over the islands. The natives of Nukuheva [Anna Maria Bay] would frequently recount in pantomime to our ship's company their terrible feats, and would show the marks of wounds they had received in desperate encounters with them. When ashore they would try to frighten us by pointing to one of their own number, and calling him a Typee, manifesting no little surprise that we did not take to our heels at so terrible an announcement. It was quite amusing too, to see with what earnestness they disclaimed all cannibal propensities on their own part, while they denounced their enemies—the Typees—as inveterate gormandisers of human flesh. . . .

Although I was convinced that the inhabitants of our bay were as arrant cannibals as any of the other tribes on the island, still I could not but feel a particular and most unqualified repugnance to the aforesaid Typees.[29]

However much Melville himself may have been affected by such tidings of the dreaded Typees, there are certain demonstrable exaggerations and even errors in this account. In the first place, the word "Typee" in the Marquesan dialect did not signify "a lover of human flesh." The Abbé Boniface Mosblech in his Marquesan-French dictionary gives the word "Taipi" as meaning "ennemi" or "peuple ennemi." [30] This in itself is puzzling, for no people would take upon themselves voluntarily the name of enemy. Undoubtedly the Abbé got his information from the natives of Anna Maria Bay just as Melville did, for they were careful to translate their own name, "Teii," as meaning "jeune homme de condition noble"! In similar manner, the names of two other neighboring tribes, "Taioa" and "Hapa," were rendered to him as "fisherman" and "little fellow" or "boaster." [31] The transparency of such naïve vanity on the part of the Teiis needs no comment. Just what the word "Taipi" meant originally was perhaps unknown even to the Marquesans; but, if it really was interpreted as meaning "enemy," that designation could not have been applied to the tribe in question by themselves, but only by the Teiis and those who got their information from them. There is some indication that this was the case, for the name was applied in general to about a dozen different tribes, all hereditary enemies of the Teiis, known more specifically as Taipi-Vaii, Taipi-Avaange, Taipi-nui-a-Vaku, and so on. Whatever the meaning, there was nothing in the word "Typee," etymologically at least, to inspire anyone with unspeakable terrors.

Even in their reputation there seems to have been a similar kind of exaggeration. Melville himself, after recording that the Teiis "disclaimed all cannibal propensities on their own part, while they denounced their enemies—the Typees—as inveterate gormandisers of human flesh," says subsequently that, when he afterwards became the guest of the latter, "They likewise dwelt upon the cannibal propensities of the Happars [Hapas], a subject which they were perfectly aware could not fail to alarm us; while at the same time they earnestly disclaimed all participation in so horrid a custom." [32] Apparently the reputation and even the denomination of a people in the Marquesas Islands—as in more civilized parts of the world—was considerably affected by the source from which the information came; and, for the most part, this information came not from the Typees but from their avowed enemies, the Teiis of Anna Maria Bay, where most of the shipping touched.

It is extremely difficult to arrive at any satisfactory conclusions regarding the practice of such a custom as cannibalism in Polynesia, and far more so to discriminate between the degrees of cannibalism peculiar to various archipelagoes and the numerous tribes which inhabited them. By the time competent ethnologists came to visit them the custom, if it had ever existed, had died out under the rigorous inquisition of Christian civilization. The records of the travelers who touched at the Marquesas and other groups while cannibalism was still supposedly being practiced, on the other hand, are scanty, unscientific, and contradictory in the extreme, for their visits were brief and their sources of information unreliable. Their interpreters were usually ignorant runaway seamen who had gone native and would be tempted to distort the truth about cannibalism one way or another, either to frighten away European ships which might endanger their Crusoe paradise or to encourage the establishment of a regular trade which they could exploit. And the testimony of the natives themselves was equally untrustworthy, for they had the characteristic common to most primitive peoples when interrogated by their obvious superiors in power of being less concerned with telling the truth than with winning the favor of their questioners. Thus, when they denied cannibalism among themselves it was to win the whites as their friends; when they charged it upon their enemies it was to gain new allies for their wars. Nor is the information recorded by the early missionaries who took up their residence in the southern group any more dependable, because here again their informers, the natives, were more anxious to please by exaggeration than to serve as mediums for the preservation of scientific truth; and it must have been perfectly obvious to them that their Christian teachers were anxious to record the most revolting accounts of heathenism that could be collected, so as to heighten the contrast between savages before and after conversion, when they sent their reports to the London Missionary Society. Moreover, until the early nineteenth century there are none of even these unsatisfactory travel records and missionary reports worth consulting for the Marquesas, because the earlier voyagers merely touched there for a day or so and confined their remarks to the most superficial sort of observations.

Langsdorff, the naturalist, who remained at Nukahiva for ten days in 1804, was the first to make any real effort to secure information on the subject of cannibalism; but, unfortunately, his account is too pretentious and romantic to be given serious consideration. He was convinced that the Marquesans fed upon human flesh "on account of its delicacy and as the height of *gourmandise";* but just what evidence he found to establish the fact of cannibalism besides some mute skulls he does not record. His blood and thunder recitals made exciting reading—especially for a young man like Melville, who had a book of his own to endue with suspense—but they have little or no value as documents for the ethnologist.[33]

During his six weeks' residence at Nukahiva in 1813, Captain David Porter, who had the intellectual curiosity and skepticism together with some share of the perseverance requisite to scientific investigation, made a rather elaborate attempt to determine whether or not the Marquesans practiced cannibalism. The experiment that was conducted, he observed, "greatly staggered my belief of their being cannibals." [34] And, although the natives themselves confessed through an interpreter that they sometimes ate their enemies, Porter was doubtful that he had understood them correctly, owing to the difficulty of translating their language:

Kie-kie [kaikai] signifies *to eat,* it also signifies *a troublesome fellow;* may it not also have many other significations, with which we are unacquainted? it may signify *to cut up, to divide, to sacrifice, to keep as trophies;* whether it has these significations I am unable to say, and

Wilson [the interpreter] could not inform me; but many circumstances induce me to believe they meant no more, when they informed me they sometimes ate their enemies.[35]

Porter himself witnessed the offering of slain enemies as sacrifices to their gods and the preservation of their skulls and bones as trophies, but he was convinced that the bodies were not eaten. Perhaps when the Teiis told Melville that the Typees were *kaikais* they meant *troublesome fellows (peuple ennemi)* and not *canni bals*. In the European mind, at least, a considerably different degree of terror would have been inspired by the two several translations.

The third early visitor who gave some attention to social and religious customs at the Marquesas, C. S. Stewart of the *Vincennes*, preserved testimony that would have proved more acceptable to the author of *Typee*. On the occasion of a ceremonious visit to the chiefs of Typee Valley in 1829—Midshipman Thomas W. Melville being one of the party—he records the following conversation:

They admitted the practice of stealing from other tribes, victims to offer in sacrifice; and excused themselves by saying, that the Hapas and Teiis were guilty of the same outrage against them. In answer to the direct question, whether it was true, that they did eat the bodies of their enemies, and of prisoners taken in battle, they without a moment's hesitation declared positively and repeatedly that they did. On expressing our horror at such an abomination, they said they would do so no more.[36]

This evidence of cannibalism is specific enough, to be sure, but unfortunately it is based on nothing more reliable than native declarations, which, as we have seen, were usually untrustworthy because of purposeful distortion or because of mistranslation. Stewart was at Nukahiva for two weeks, but he seems to have made no investigations of his own to corroborate this confession. Although Melville cites him as the chief authority on the Marquesas that he consulted—and even though he probably drew on him for information about cannibalism and many other matters, as will be demonstrated—he discounts the reliability of Stewart's testimony concerning "human victims . . . daily cooked and served up upon the altars," saying that the *Vincennes* did not remain at the islands long enough to make any observations other than superficial ones.[37] Finally, if Stewart was right in saying that the Typees were confessedly arrant cannibals, we must also believe that they abandoned their horrid custom without a murmur at his request in 1829, more than twelve years before Melville's arrival.

The only direct eyewitness testimony to cannibalism in the Marquesas Islands that I have been able to discover—besides Melville's—is that of John M. Coulter, the surgeon of a whaling vessel, who in 1833 took up his residence for several weeks among the natives of Hivaoa (La Dominica) in the southern group. Coulter was an intelligent observer and his opportunities were unusual, for he submitted to being tatooed, put on the native dress, and became a chief. In his *Adventures in the Pacific,* he declares that cannibalism was an undisputed fact, and that it was practiced chiefly on the bodies of enemies killed in warfare. After a battle with a hostile tribe in which he had assisted his newly adopted brothers, he had the opportunity of witnessing a cannibal feast with his own eyes. He describes in detail the method of cooking the slain enemies, but politely skips over the eating of their bodies.[38] Whether the delicacy that restrained his palate and his pen also turned his eyes away from so uncivilized a sight, he does not say; but even with this point undetermined his story is the most convincing evidence yet found in proof of the cannibalism of the Marquesans, though it applies only to the natives of the lower group, who were notoriously more barbarous than the Nukahivans. From all indications, however, Melville was not acquainted with this highly interesting volume, which could have furnished him with much valuable information for his *Typee.*

The French visitors at Nukahiva have also left testimony of some value on the subject of cannibalism. One especially, Max Radiguet, whose presence at Nukahiva with Dupetit-Thouar's expedition coincided with Melville's visit, has left a brief but plausible note bearing on the subject. Although he seems to have acquired the usual prejudice against the Typees inculcated by the Teïis, calling them "la farouche tribu des Taïpis-Vaïs, vrais Lestrignons nukahiviens," he remarks:

> Les habitants de tout l'archipel sont anthropophages, après la guerre ou dans certaines cérémonies religieuses, mais ils n'avouent pas volontiers ce trait de leurs mœurs devant les Européens; chaque tribu s'en défend et accuse la tribu qui lui est ennemie. Les Taïpis-Vaïs sont braves et redoutés; aussi cherche-t-on, par cette accusation de cannibalisme, à exciter contre eux la haine et la défiance des étrangers.[39]

This concise statement of the case seems to be remarkably near the truth, both in generalization and in detail.

In default of more reliable information, the question of cannibalism in the Marquesas Islands will have to be left in this undetermined state. The testimony of the earliest visitors, we have seen, is meager, unreliable, and conflicting; and, unfortunately, there were no field ethnologists present on the scene while the natives were still in an unadulterated state of paganism. Moreover, the literary ethnologists of today are no more than compilers of the best accounts handed down by these same travel writers whose evidence has just been considered at first hand.[40] Making all allowances for contradiction, distortion, and mistranslation, it would seem that the Marquesans, along with most of the other Polynesian nations, had practiced cannibalism as a religious ceremony on the bodies of slain enemies—and possibly on those of their relatives and chief people at death—with the purpose of wreaking vengeance and of acquiring the virtues of the deceased. But the occasions of these ceremonies were certainly infrequent. (Eating the bodies of human beings when reduced to this dire necessity by starvation is beside the point, for this desperate means of preserving life has been resorted to by civilized people as well as by barbarous ones.) Finding that Europeans were horrified by such a custom, each tribe denied it among themselves and charged it upon their enemies, in the hope of winning the white man's favor and enlisting him as any ally against a hostile people—a diplomatic form of reputation mongering that put an unwarranted stigma on the character of the remote and rarely visited Typees, as has been demonstrated. In historic times, in fact, the ceremony may even have subsided into a mere "ritual cannibalism," such as has been observed authentically in recent times in more remote parts of the world. But the popular conception of grimacing savages dancing around a pot in which the bodies of kidnaped white men are cooking, after being fattened to the taste of these outlandish epicures, is one wholly to be ascribed to writers of highly wrought fiction and romantic adventure. There is no authenticated instance on record of human flesh being eaten as a delicacy, according to my discoveries, nor any reliable record of a white man being eaten by Polynesians for any reason whatever; finally, I have not been able to find a single unequivocal eyewitness account of a Marquesan eating the flesh of even a native enemy slain in battle, though in all likelihood this custom did exist at one time.

Melville, himself, in one of his digressions as an apologist for the South Sea islanders, limits the practice in somewhat the same way:

The reader will, ere long, have reason to suspect that the Typees are not free from the guilt of cannibalism; and he will then, perhaps, charge me with admiring a people against whom so odious a crime is chargeable. But this only enormity in their character is not half so horrible as it is usually described. According to the popular fictions, the crews of vessels, shipwrecked on some barbarous coast, are eaten alive like so many dainty joints by the uncivil inhabitants; and unfortunate voyagers are lured into smiling and treacherous bays; knocked on the head with outlandish warclubs; and served up without any preliminary dressing. In truth, so horrific and improbable are these accounts, that many sensible and well-informed people will not believe that any cannibals exist; and place every book of voyages which purports to give any account of them, on the same shelf with *Blue Beard* and *Jack the Giant-Killer*. While others, implicitly crediting the most extravagant fictions, firmly believe that there are people in the world with tastes so depraved, that they would infinitely prefer a single mouthful of material humanity to a good dinner of roast beef and plum pudding. But here, Truth, who loves to be centrally located, is again found between the two extremes; for cannibalism to a certain moderate extent is practised among several of the primitive tribes in the Pacific, but it is upon the bodies of slain enemies alone; and horrible and fearful as the custom is, immeasurably as it is to be abhorred and condemned, still I assert that those who indulge in it are in other respects humane and virtuous.[41]

But this apology is not introduced until Melville's tale is well done. Meanwhile, he has succeeded in building up such a reputation for the dreaded Typees that the first third of his book derives its suspense from his fear of falling into their hands, and the rest of the tale is still dominated by an unrelenting apprehension that his indulgent captors, in spite of their apparent hospitality, are merely fattening him for a delayed feast.

On the third night after his arrival in Typee Valley, Melville relates an incident calculated to keep this fear lurking in the back of his reader's mind for the remainder of the story:

I awoke from an uneasy nap, about midnight, as I supposed; and, raising myself partly from the mat, became sensible that we were enveloped in utter darkness. . . .

Apprehensive of some evil, I roused my comrade, and we were engaged in a whispered conference concerning the unexpected withdrawal of the natives, when all at once, from the depths of the grove, in full view of us where we lay, shoots of flame were seen to rise, and in a few moments illuminated the surrounding trees, casting, by contrast, into still deeper gloom the darkness around us.

While we continued gazing at this sight, dark figures appeared moving to and fro before the flames; while others, dancing and capering about, looked like so many demons.

". . . Depend upon it, we will be eaten this blessed night, and there is the fire we shall be roasted by. . . . There! I told you so! they are coming for us!" exclaimed my companion the next moment, as the forms of four of the islanders were seen in bold relief against the illuminated background, mounting the pi-pi, and approaching toward us.

They came on noiselessly, nay, stealthily, and glided along through the gloom that surrounded us, as if about to spring upon some object they were fearful of disturbing before they should make sure of it. Gracious heaven! the horrible reflections which crowded upon me that moment! A cold sweat stood upon my brow, and spell-bound with terror I awaited my fate.[42]

This hair-raising episode concludes as a fiasco, it is true, for the natives were merely preparing a midnight feast; and, when at this juncture they presented Melville and Toby with a trencher of steaming meat, the latter declared with comic relief:

"A baked baby, I dare say! but I will have none of it, never mind what it is. A pretty fool I should make of myself, indeed, waked up here in the middle of the night, stuffing and guzzling, and all to make a fat meal for a parcel of bloody-minded cannibals one of these mornings! No; I see what they are at very plainly, so I am resolved to starve myself into a bunch of bones and gristle, and then, if they serve me up, they are welcome! . . .

"A baked baby, by the soul of Captain Cook!" [43]

But the baked baby turned out to be a sucking pig, roasted to a gourmet's taste.

Neither comedy nor propaganda, however, destroys the effect that Melville has created by the fear of cannibalism. The suspense continues unabated to the very end of the book, where Melville relates at considerable length an "eyewitness" account of cannibalism as practiced by the Typees. From a war with the Hapas, he says, the bodies of three slain enemies had been brought home in triumph. Contrary to their usual indulgence of Melville's curiosity, the Typees on this occasion refused point blank to let him witness the ceremonies which afterwards took place at the Taboo Groves. Two days later, when he was allowed to go there, he confirmed the horrible suspicions that had been tormenting his mind:

After staying a short time, I took my leave. In passing along the piazza, previously to descending from the pi-pi, I observed a curiously carved vessel of wood, of considerable size, with a cover placed over it, of the same material, and which resembled in shape a small canoe. It was surrounded by a low railing of bamboos, the top of which was scarcely a foot from the ground. As the vessel had been placed in its present position since my last visit, I at once concluded that it must have some connection with the recent festival; and, prompted by a curiosity I could not repress, in passing it I raised one end of the cover; at the same moment the chiefs, perceiving my design, loudly ejaculated, "Taboo! taboo!" But the slight glimpse sufficed; my eyes fell upon the disordered members of a human skeleton, the bones still fresh with moisture, and with particles of flesh clinging to them here and there! [44]

The natives assured him that the skeleton was that of a pig, but this time Melville says he was convinced that he was being held captive by a tribe of irredeemable cannibals, and that, in spite of the hospitality he was enjoying, his ultimate fate was certain:

> All that night I lay awake, revolving in my mind the fearful situation in which I was placed. The last horrid revelation had now been made, and the full sense of my condition rushed upon my mind with a force I had never before experienced.[45]

Consequently, he says, he determined to escape; and by a combination of good fortune and desperate measures he managed to do so before a fortnight had passed.

This extended inquiry will be justified, it is hoped, by the dominant role which cannibalism plays throughout the whole of *Typee*. A thorough discussion of this important problem has made it necessary to abandon the chronological order temporarily; but, to return now to the early part of June, 1842, we find Melville sounding this note of alarm even as his ship first approaches the Marquesas:

> I shall never forget the observation of one of our crew as we were passing slowly by the entrance of this bay [Typee] in our way to Nuku-heva. As we stood gazing over the side at the verdant headlands, Ned, pointing with his hand in the direction of the treacherous valley, exclaimed, "There—there's Typee. Oh, the bloody cannibals, what a meal they'd make of us if we were to take it into our heads to land! but they say they don't like sailor's flesh, it's too salt. I say, matey, how should you like to be shoved ashore there, eh?" I little thought, as I shuddered at the question, that in the space of a few weeks I should actually be a captive in that self-same valley.[46]

The cannibal of *Typee*, however, was largely a straw man set up by Melville to be knocked down in a spirit of derring-do:

> Our ship had not been many days in the harbour of Nukuheva before I came to the determination of leaving her. That my reasons for resolving to take this step were numerous and weighty, may be inferred from the fact that I chose rather to risk my fortunes among the savages of the island than to endure another voyage on board the *Dolly* [*Acushnet*]. To use the concise, point-blank phrase of the sailors, I had made up my mind to "run away.". . .
>
> To be sure there was one rather unpleasant drawback to these agreea-

ble anticipations—the possibility of falling in with a foraging party of these same bloody-minded Typees, whose appetites, edged perhaps by the air of so elevated a region, might prompt them to devour one. This, I must confess, was a most disagreeable view of the matter.

Just to think of a party of these unnatural gourmands taking it into their heads to make a convivial meal of a poor devil, who would have no means of escape or defence: however, there was no help for it.[47]

Having established himself as a man of courage, willing to brave the dangers of a cannibal island in order to gain his freedom, Melville then feels it necessary, for the sake of his character, to free himself from the unflattering connotations usually attached to the word *deserter*. The first reason he gives for running away from the *Acushnet* was that the captain had broken his side of the contract by violating not only the implied but the specified conditions of the ship's articles:

The usage on board of her was tyrannical; the sick had been inhumanly neglected; the provisions had been doled out in scanty allowance; and her cruises were unreasonably protracted. The captain was the author of these abuses; it was in vain to think that he would either remedy them, or alter his conduct, which was arbitrary and violent in the extreme. His prompt reply to all complaints and remonstrances was— the butt-end of a handspike, so convincingly administered as effectually to silence the aggrieved party.

To whom could we apply for redress? We had left both law and equity on the other side of the Cape; and unfortunately with a very few exceptions, our crew was composed of a parcel of dastardly and mean-spirited wretches, divided among themselves, and only united in enduring without resistance the unmitigated tyranny of the captain.[48]

The affidavit of desertions from the *Acushnet*, registered by Captain Valentine Pease himself at the Sandwich Islands in June, 1843, shows that even by this date she had lost seven men out of a crew of twenty-six. This was rather a large number even for the lax discipline and abandoned characters of the whaling world of the 1840's; and it lends color to Melville's complaint of hard fare and harsh treatment. Before the four-and-a-half-year cruise was over, according to the memorandum left by Melville, five more seamen deserted, making a total of almost half the crew—and of these at least

three met with violent deaths, one by suicide and two with venereal diseases. Two more went ashore, by permission, to die; and the
first and third mates quit the ship at Payta, Peru—the former after
fighting with the tyrannical captain—so that of the original ship's
company only the captain, the second mate, the boatswain, the
cooper, the cook, and six of the mongrel crew returned with the
Acushnet from her maiden voyage.[49]

From such a record it is impossible after the lapse of a hundred
years to place the whole burden of the blame on either the "tyrannical captain" or the "dastardly and mean-spirited wretches" who
composed the crew. Wherever the fault lay, the highest pitch of the
fever of discontent seems to have been reached at the time of Melville's desertion, for four men left the ship at the Marquesas within
the space of two months. These were not the first seamen, moreover,
who had picked Nukahiva as their Utopian refuge from the tyranny
of life before the mast. Langsdorff had found two deserters on the
island when he touched there in 1804, and in spite of their low
character he made considerable use of them as interpreters since
they had been living for some years with the natives. All subsequent
visitors to these islands give similar reports; and the description of
these runaway seamen certainly does little to convince one that
they were any different from the knavish crew of the *Acushnet,* as
witness Father Gracia in 1840: "cette foule de déserteurs européens
et américains, rôdant de tous côtés dans ces îles, et corrompant le
reste des bonnes qualités physiques et morales de ces peuples." [50]
Melville, to be sure, was an exception to the generality of deserters,
and this gives some weight to his accusation that his captain was a
despot. But another motive impelled this young whaleman to take
leave of his ship—the desire for romantic adventure which, as we
have seen, had sent him to sea in the first place. He puts it indirectly,
saying that the length of the voyage ahead of him was unendurable; [51] but he had known what he had to expect in this particular
when he signed the ship's articles. At this restless period of his life,
any time and any place were alike bonds that chafed his spirit. In
all likelihood, Melville had entertained the prospect of going
ashore at Nukahiva before he ever sailed from New Bedford.

His mind once made up, says Melville, he lost little time in shaping his plan of escape. Desiring a companion for his adventures, he confided his scheme to one of his fellow seamen whom he calls Toby—"such was the name by which he went among us, for his real name he would never tell us":

He was a young fellow about my own age, for whom I had all along entertained a great regard. . . . He was active, ready, and obliging, of dauntless courage, and singularly open and fearless in the expression of his feelings. . . . Arrayed in his blue frock and duck trowsers, he was as smart a looking sailor as ever stepped upon a deck; he was singularly small and slightly made, with great flexibility of limb. His naturally dark complexion had been deepened by exposure to the tropical sun, and a mass of jetty locks clustered about his temples, and threw a darker shade into his large black eyes. He was a strange wayward being, moody, fitful, and melancholy—at times almost morose. He had a quick and fiery temper too, which, when thoroughly roused, transported him into a state bordering on delirium.[52]

As has long been known, this young man who shared the honors of *Typee* fame was Richard Tobias Greene of Rochester, New York. For his courage, his moodiness, his fiery temper, and the heroic qualities with which Melville endows him, there is no contemporary record to serve as a check. But the description of his personal appearance is confirmed by the daguerreotype of him found among Melville's possessions and by the brief memorandum noted on the crew list of the *Acushnet:* "Age 21, height 5 feet 5½ inches, complexion dark, hair black." [53] There is no doubt, then, that Toby was a real person and that he conformed to the description of him in *Typee,* at least in his extreme brunetteness, his small stature, and his age, which was exactly the same as Melville's.[54]

With such a companion Herman Melville deserted from the *Acushnet* at Nukahiva on July 9, 1842, to pursue on land the romantic adventure that he had wearied of at sea. The escape was effected during shore leave at Anna Maria Bay (Taiohaë) under cover of a tropical storm, according to Melville's version. A desperate flight, almost thwarted by a nearly impenetrable canebrake through which they had to cut their way, brought the runaway pair to safety on a mountain ridge by the middle of the afternoon. Melville then devotes some fifty pages to what has been aptly described as "Their five days of marvellous adventures that landed them finally in the valley of Typee [and that have] abidingly tried the credulity of Melville's readers—though never for an instant their patience." [55] There is no way to verify or disprove the thrilling conquests of seemingly insurmountable hardships that crowd on each other's heels and fill these days with excitement and suspense. We have no testimony but Melville's as to how they lost their way and were forced to live on half-a-dozen ship's biscuits for almost as many days, while scrambling up and down the ridges and ravines that honeycomb the interior of the island in bewildering confusion, or how they finally descended a sheer precipice hundreds of feet high by swinging themselves from creeper to creeper with horrid gaps between them.

There is one check, however, that can be brought to bear upon this part of Melville's narrative. The Reverend Titus Coan made a visit to Nukahiva in 1867, twenty-five years after Melville's visit, and his account dissipates to some extent the dramatic atmosphere of Melville's escape and even throws some doubt on the entire fabric of *Typee:*

From this bay [Anna Maria or Taiohaë] in 1842, the gifted Herman Melville, with his friend Toby, absconded to the hills, and made his devious and toilsome way to the Taipi valley, from which, in spite of its paradise-like beauty and its bewitching enchantments, he was but too glad to escape. I saw the valley he threaded, the cane-brake through which he struggled, the ridge he bestrode, the jungle where he concealed himself, and the towering summit over which he passed. Melville lost his reckoning of distances as well as his track. The enchanted valley of Taipi, Melville's "Typee," is only four hours' climb by the trail from Taiohai [sic]; and from ancient times there has been a well-known trail from the head of one valley to the other. This of course the young fugitive did not find. The distance is not over five miles, and the Marquesans walk it, or rather climb it, in three or four hours. The valley of Hapa, (Mr. Melville's Happar) lies between Taipi and Taiohae, and is only two or three hours' walk from the latter. These three valleys are all on the south side of the island, and adjoin each other. During all his four months' of romantic captivity, the gifted author of

"Typee" and "Omoo" was only four of five miles distant from the harbor whence he had fled.[56]

This certainly takes some of the thrill out of Melville's week of hair-raising adventures on the way to Typee Valley and even some of the terror out of his captivity in what seems to the reader to be the heart of barbarism—five miles from an outpost of civilization!

During this arduous journey Melville says he caught his first glimpse of Typee Valley, though at that time he still hoped it was the valley of the more friendly Hapas:

I chanced to push aside a branch, and by so doing suddenly disclosed to my view a scene which even now I can recall with all the vividness of the first impression. Had a glimpse of the gardens of Paradise been revealed to me, I could scarcely have been more ravished with the sight.

From the spot where I lay transfixed with surprise and delight, I looked straight down into the bosom of a valley, which swept away in long wavy undulations to the blue waters in the distance. Midway toward the sea, and peering here and there amidst the foliage, might be seen the palmetto-thatched houses of its inhabitants, glistening in the sun that had bleached them to a dazzling whiteness. The vale was more than three leagues in length, and about a mile across at its greatest width.

On either side it appeared hemmed in by steep and green acclivities, which, uniting near the spot where I lay, formed an abrupt and semicircular termination of grassy cliffs and precipices hundreds of feet in height, over which flowed numberless small cascades. But the crowning beauty of the prospect was its universal verdure; and in this indeed consists, I believe, the peculiar charm of every Polynesian landscape. Everywhere below me, from the base of the precipice upon whose very verge I had been unconsciously reposing, the surface of the vale presented a mass of foliage, spread with such rich profusion that it was impossible to determine of what description of trees it consisted.

But perhaps there was nothing about the scenery I beheld more impressive than those silent cascades, whose slender threads of water, after leaping down the steep cliffs, were lost amidst the rich herbage of the valley.

Over all the landscape there reigned the most hushed repose, which I almost feared to break, lest, like the enchanted gardens in the fairy tale, a single syllable might dissolve the spell.[57]

This description of Typee Valley proves to be remarkably accurate when compared with Captain David Porter's almost equally romantic sketch:

From the hill we had a distant view of every part, and all appeared equally delightful. The valley was about nine miles in length and three or four in breadth, surrounded on every part, except the beach, where we formerly landed, by lofty mountains: the upper part was bounded by a precipice of many hundred feet in height, from the top of which a handsome sheet of water was precipitated, and formed a beautiful river, which ran meandering through the valley and discharged itself at the beach. Villages were scattered here and there, the bread-fruit and cocoa-nut trees flourished luxuriantly and in abundance; plantations laid out in good order, inclosed with stone walls, were in a high state of cultivation, and everything bespoke industry, abundance, and happiness—never in my life did I witness a more delightful scene.[58]

Of course it is possible that here, as elsewhere, Melville may have drawn from Porter's experience rather than from any real experience of his own. In default of better proof to the contrary, however, we must assume that Melville finally made his way into this danger-beset paradise about the fifteenth of July, 1842. And even as he entered it, he says, there still remained the terrifying question: "Typee or Happar? A frightful death at the hands of the fiercest of cannibals, or a kindly reception from a gentler race of savages?"[59]

CHAPTER VII

THE NOBLE SAVAGES OF
TYPEE VALLEY

SAILORS are the only class of men who nowadays see anything like stirring adventure; and many things which to fireside people appear strange and romantic, to them seem as commonplace as a jacket out at elbows. . . .

There are some things related in the [following] narrative which will be sure to appear strange, or perhaps entirely incomprehensible, to the reader; but they cannot appear more so to him than they did to the author at the time. He has stated such matters just as they occurred, and leaves every one to form his own opinion concerning them; trusting that his anxious desire to speak the unvarnished truth will gain for him the confidence of his readers.[1]

THUS in the preface to *Typee: A Peep at Polynesian Life During a Four Months' Residence in a Valley of the Marquesas* Melville makes his *apologia* and signs his affidavit, anticipating the incredulity of his critics. It is impossible to follow him over the mountain ridges that inclose the valley of Typee (Taïpi-Vaï) and certify the events there recorded, for apparently no white man except Toby was present in this valley during his residence, even as he declares, nor did anyone leave a record of a visit to its confines for many years thereafter. Although his personal adventures among the Typees must remain, therefore, unverified, it is possible to test the general truth of his account of Marquesan life and to point to numerous sources from which he may have gathered his information. Not only will this furnish further material for a study of his technique of composition, but it will serve as a check upon his ethnological accuracy, and even upon the faithfulness of his "autobiographical" narrative. Since some contemporary reviewers were inclined to doubt the authenticity of *Typee,* and since modern readers probably set it down as outright fiction, it seems appropriate that an extended inquiry of this sort be made.

For one reason and another, the Marquesas Islands have been far less frequented by white men than other Pacific archipelagoes; prior to 1846 there were very few indeed who had established long residences there, and fewer still who had written of their experiences. Melville was not exaggerating, therefore, when he declared: "all that we know about them is from a few general narratives"—not more than a dozen, in fact, if one excludes the French accounts of the military occupation beginning in 1842, which were probably not accessible to Melville because of their language and were certainly not pertinent to his purposes because of their scope and interests. Among the general narratives, Melville says, there are two that claim particular notice: Captain David Porter's *Journal of A Cruise Made to the Pacific Ocean* and C. S. Stewart's *A Visit to the South Seas.* The first of these he says "is a work, however, which I have never happened to meet with"; and, although he tacitly acknowledges acquaintance with the second, he dismisses it as an authority by saying that its author was "a man who, according to his own statement, was only at one of the islands and remained there but two weeks, sleeping every night on board his ship, and taking little kidglove excursions ashore in the daytime, attended by an armed party." [2] In spite of such disavowals, conclusive internal evidence will be adduced to show that these are the two chief volumes to which *Typee* is indebted.

Less equivocally, Melville refers to William Ellis's *Polynesian Researches,* a work which he also cites in the preface to *Omoo,* and which he used, far more extensively than he intimates, in the composition of both volumes. Further, he quotes briefly from "a small volume entitled *Circumnavigation of the Globe*"—a volume, incidentally, which was included in the ship's library of the frigate *United States;* and he cites in the same connection "a volume by Fanning"—undoubtedly, Edmund Fanning's *Voyages Round the World.* [3] But his debt to these two volumes was necessarily small, for they have little to offer regarding the Marquesas. There are three other travel books dealing more largely with the Marquesas Islands which may have proved more useful to Melville, though he does not mention them: Langsdorff's *Voyages and Travels,* Bennett's *Narrative of a Whaling Voyage,* and Coulter's *Adventures in the Pacific.* Strong reasons have already been given to show that he was familiar with the first of these, and in the ensuing pages the possible extent of his indebtedness to it will be indicated; although the other two were written by surgeons of whalers, and thus held a double interest for Melville, it is doubtful whether he was acquainted with them at the time of writing *Typee.*

In view of the vast array of evidence which will be brought forward to show how largely Melville drew upon these authorities, his wholesale disparagement of travel books in general is misleading, for it deliberately intimates that he eschewed them altogether:

The fact is, that there is a vast deal of unintentional humbuggery in some of the accounts we have from scientific men concerning the religious institutions of Polynesia. These learned tourists generally obtain the greater part of their information from the retired old South Sea rovers, who have domesticated themselves among the barbarous tribes of the Pacific. Jack, who has long been accustomed to the longbow, and to spin tough yarns on a ship's forecastle, invariably officiates as showman of the island on which he has settled, and having mastered a few dozen words of the language, is supposed to know all about the people who speak it. A natural desire to make himself of consequence in the eyes of the strangers, prompts him to lay claim to a much greater knowledge of such matters than he actually possesses. In reply to incessant queries, he communicates not only all he knows but a good deal more, and if there be any information deficient still he is at no loss to supply it. The avidity with which his anecdotes are noted down tickles his vanity, and his powers of invention increase with the credulity of his auditors. He knows just the sort of information wanted, and furnishes it to any extent. . . .

Now, when the scientific voyager arrives at home with his collection of wonders, he attempts, perhaps, to give a description of some of the strange people he has been visiting. Instead of representing them as a community of lusty savages, who are leading a merry, idle, innocent life, he enters into a very circumstantial and learned narrative of certain unaccountable superstitions and practices, about which he knows as little as the islanders do themselves. Having had little time, and scarcely any opportunity, to become acquainted with the customs he pretends to describe, he writes them down one after another in an off-hand, haphazard style; and were the book thus produced to be translated into the tongue of the people of whom it purports to give the history, it would appear quite as wonderful to them as it does to the American public, and much more improbable.[4]

To the extent of its resemblance to such volumes, therefore, *Typee* itself could be similarly stigmatized for unreliableness.

Fortunately, the truth about Marquesan life in the period before its contact with civilization no longer needs to rest in such an undetermined state. Most of the ethnological treatises dealing with this subject, it is true, are merely literary compilations based upon no more conclusive evidence than that furnished by Melville and the other travel writers already alluded to. Hence, it is of little consequence that Melville is cited as an authority in such studies as those of Sir James George Frazer, Robert Wood Williamson, and Louis Rollin.

There is one series of modern studies, however, which gives far more authoritative information concerning the Marquesas. From September 21, 1920, to June 21, 1921, the Bayard Dominick Expedition—composed of competent ethnologists, anthropologists, and archeologists—remained on the islands of this group and made an elaborate study of its culture, ancient and modern; and the results of their investigations, including information derived from literary research as well as from field work, have been published in a series of bulletins issued by the Bernice Pauahi Bishop Museum of Honolulu (the most important being the studies by W. C. Handy, E. S. C. Handy, and Ralph Linton). These scientists knew the native language and consequently got their information direct. The informants, to be sure, had to rely on their memories of the genuine ancient culture, which is now dead save for a few lingering survivals; and frequently they were perforce giving second-hand information. But Marquesans have remarkably tenacious memories, according to these investigators, and they are by no means prone to invent or give false information when they recognize that their interlocutors are familiar with their culture in general. Moreover, errors were eliminated as far as possible by checking the various witnesses against each other, and, further, by comparisons with all

the standard literary sources and with the manuscript records of the
Catholic fathers preserved in the mission at Taiohaë.[5] Thus, although no study of a culture which has been obsolete for half a
century can be infallible, this series of bulletins offers the most complete and reliable information that the Western world will ever
have of pre-civilization life in the Marquesas Islands; and it serves
as an excellent authority for a thorough check on the accuracy of
Typee. On the other hand, the evidence of contemporary travel
writers—especially Langsdorff, Porter, and Stewart—will be cited as
possible source material upon which Melville levied in the composition of his book. During the course of this ethnological investigation the narrative order of *Typee* will be abandoned.

Following a long and ample tradition, both literary and philosophical, Melville consistently adopts a romantic attitude in his
account of the Noble Savages that he found in Typee Valley; and
nowhere is this more pronounced than in the extravagant praise
he lavishes upon their physical beauty. But, in this respect, he was
merely echoing the surprised eulogies of all the earlier visitors. Apprehensive that he might be suspected of overdrawing, he calls to
his defense the substantiations of Cook, Porter, Stewart, and Fanning, and quotes *verbatim* from a volume entitled the *Circumnavigation of the Globe* the vignette of Mendanna's historian in 1595,
the first European description of Marquesan beauty:

In complexion they were nearly white, of good stature, and finely
formed. . . . There came, among others, two lads paddling their canoe,
whose eyes were fixed on the ship; they had beautiful faces, and the most
promising animation of countenance, and were in all things so becoming, that the pilot-mayor Quiros affirmed, nothing in his life ever caused
him so much regret as the leaving such fine creatures to be lost in that
country.[6]

Melville declares that two and a half centuries have not altered the
truth of this picture, and he does not hesitate to assign to the Marquesans "great superiority over all other Polynesians," including
the "voluptuous Tahitians, . . . the dark-hued Hawaiians and the
woolly headed Feejees"; and in this opinion he is confirmed by all

of the previous commentators.[7] When he goes so far as to declare the
Typees similarly superior to all other Marquesans, however, one is
inclined to suspect him of playing favorites; yet, even here, there is
direct confirmation in the statement of Max Radiguet, secretary to
the French expedition in 1842:

Si l'on veut rencontrer le Nukahivien dans sa pureté, dans toute son
élégance native, ce n'est point chez les Teis, c'est chez les Taipis . . .
qu' il le faut chercher.[8]

It was during the large gathering of natives to celebrate a festival, which Melville calls the "Feast of the Calabashes," that he was
first struck by the physical strength and beauty of the Typees:

In beauty of form they surpassed anything I had ever seen. Not a
single instance of natural deformity was observable in all the throng
attending the revels. . . . But their physical excellence did not merely
consist in an exemption from these evils; nearly every individual of
their number might have been taken for a sculptor's model. . . .
The men, in almost every instance, are of lofty stature, scarcely ever
less than six feet in height, while the other sex are uncommonly di-
minutive. . . .
Nothing in the appearance of the islanders struck me more forcibly
than the whiteness of their teeth. The novelist always compares the
masticators of his heroine to ivory; but I boldly pronounce the teeth
of the Typees to be far more beautiful than ivory itself. . . . During
the festival, I had noticed several young females whose skins were almost
as white as any Saxon damsel's, a slight dash of the mantling brown
being all that marked the difference. . . . The distinguishing characteristic of the Marquesan islanders, [however], and that which at once
strikes you, is the European cast of their features—a peculiarity seldom
observable among other uncivilized people. Many of their faces present
a profile classically beautiful, and in the valley of Type, I saw several
who . . . were in every respect models of beauty.[9]

The descriptions by earlier travel writers are so strikingly similar,
even in phraseology, that it will be profitable to quote them at some
length. Langsdorff, after asserting the superiority of the Marquesans
over the Society Islanders, goes on to say:

The men are almost all tall, robust, and well made. . . . We did not
see a single crippled or deformed person, but such general beauty

and regularity of form, that it greatly excited our astonishment. Many of them might very well have been placed by the side of the most celebrated chef-d'œuvres of antiquity, and they would have lost nothing by the comparison. . . . The women are in general much smaller than the men, but are extremely well proportioned.[10]

On the whole, however, he found the men far more handsome than the women, and one in particular who attracted his attention by reason of his extraordinary height—above six feet eight inches—and his admirable proportions. His measurements were taken and found to correspond exactly with those of the Apollo Belvidere!

Porter, likewise, found the men striking:

The men of this island are remarkably handsome; of large stature and well proportioned: . . . they are far above the common stature of the human race, seldom less than five feet eleven inches, but most commonly six feet two or three inches, and every way proportioned: their faces are remarkably handsome, with keen, piercing eyes; teeth white, and more beautiful than ivory; countenances open and expressive, which bespeak every emotion of their souls; limbs which might serve as model for a statuary, and strength and activity proportioned to their appearance.

But, as Melville declares it was said of him, Porter was even more "vastly smitten by the beauty of the ladies":

The young girls, which we had an opportunity of seeing, were . . . handsome and well formed; their skins were remarkably soft and smooth, and their complexions no darker than many brunetts in America celebrated for their beauty. . . . I can say, without exaggeration, that I never have seen women more perfectly beautiful in form, features, and complexion, or that had playful innocence more strongly marked on their countenances or in their manners; all seemed perfectly easy and even graceful, and all strove by their winning attentions, who should render themselves most pleasing to us.[11]

Stewart, chaplain though he was, vied with the naval captain in gallantry, for, even as Melville says, he "expresses in more than one place, his amazement at the surpassing loveliness of the women; and says that many of the Nukuheva damsels reminded him forcibly of the most celebrated beauties in his own land":

Till now, I had begun to doubt, from all I had seen at the sea side, whether the natives of this group are so decidedly a finer race and handsomer looking people than the Society and Sandwich Islanders, as they are generally accredited to be. But, judging from those seen on this occasion, I am fully persuaded they are—particularly in the female sex. Many of these present were exceedingly beautiful—and two or three so strikingly like some of the most distinguished beauties in our own country I ever met, that the first glance brought them to my recollection. Their eyes have a rich brilliancy, softened by long glossy eyelashes, that can scarce be surpassed; which, with a regularity and whiteness of teeth unrivalled, add greatly to the impression of features of a more European mould than most uncivilized people I have seen. In complexion, many of them are very fair—scarce if any darker than a clear brunette—admitting even, in some cases, of a distinct mantling of color in the cheek and lips; while in figure, they are small, and delicately formed, with arms and hands that would bear comparison with any in the drawing rooms of the most polished noblesse.[12]

With such romantic models to draw from, it is not surprising to find Melville giving free range to his pen when he wishes to portray the most perfect specimens of Marquesan beauty that came under his notice. "Marnoo" he describes as the most handsome of the men, a true Polynesian Apollo. But it is upon the "beauteous nymph Fayaway," his peculiar favorite, that he expends his most lavish praise: her beauty of face and limb, "her strange blue eyes," her hands "as delicate as those of any countess," and "her easy unstudied grace" which marked her as a true child of nature.[13] In spite of some undeniable romancing in these descriptions, Marnoo and Fayaway were probably drawn in part from actual, living models, even as Melville declares. But it is equally certain that they owe something, if it is only the romantic overplus, to their literary antecedents; and the numerous passages quoted give an insight into how the author of *Typee* used these sources.

Perhaps the two elements in Melville's portraits that most tried the credulity of his readers were the "European cast of features" and the "strange blue eyes" that he ascribes to a pure-blooded Polynesian. Both of these apparent anomalies, indeed, have long been confirmed by ethnologists (though the latter is the exception rather than the rule); but they were also noted and commented upon by

Melville's contemporaries, as witness a member of the French expedition of 1842:

> A Taïti, on reconnaît réellement le type malais; c'est au contraire le profil européen qui distingue les sauvages de Nou-Hiva [*sic*]. . . . Leurs beaux yeux ne sont pas uniformement noirs comme chez les Taïtiennes, on en voit beaucoup de bleus, qui embellissent considérablement celles qui en sont gratifiées.[14]

To European explorers, accustomed to the more Mongoloid aborigines of America and the more Negroid primitives of Melanesia, the discovery of the Polynesians came as a pleasant and even exciting surprise, for here at the ends of the earth were Stone-Age savages who conformed closely to accepted European standards of beauty.

Not the least attractive of these resemblances was the unexpectedly light pigmentation of their skin, a characteristic that Caucasians had previously arrogated to themselves exclusively. The earliest visitors perhaps exaggerated the "whiteness" of the Marquesan's complexions, and they certainly erred in thinking it was entirely natural.[15] Melville was more conservative in his description, declaring that the "prevailing tint among the women of the valley was a light olive"; and he was undoubtedly nearer the truth in his explanation of how it was achieved:

This comparative fairness of complexion, though in a great degree perfectly natural, is partly the result of an artificial process, and of an entire exclusion from the sun. The juice of the "papa" root, found in great abundance at the head of the valley, is held in great esteem as a cosmetic, with which many of the females daily annoint their whole person. The habitual use of it whitens and beautifies the skin. Those of the young girls who resort to this method of heightening their charms, never expose themselves to the rays of the sun.[16]

But it was from Stewart's account that he drew this explanation, almost without change:

The uncommon fairness of many of the females is the result of an artificial process, followed by an almost entire seclusion from the sun. The juice of a small indigenous vine called *papa*, possesses the quality of whitening the skin; and such as are peculiarly desirous of fair complexions, wash their whole persons every morning in a preparation of this, and wrapping themselves closely in their garments, keep within doors most of the day.[17]

Sometimes, apparently, Melville worked with his authorities open before him. Just why he followed his sources so closely, even in phraseology it is hard to say. Perhaps, in *Typee* especially, he was conscious of his own inexperience as a writer; perhaps, also, his personal acquaintance with Marquesan life was not so full or so accurate as a "four months' residence" would have made possible.

Melville's further accounts of the attention which the Marquesans, both male and female, bestowed upon their personal appearance, such as plucking out unsightly hairs with a shark's tooth, dressing their hair with perfumed cocoanut oil, and ornamenting themselves with garlands, chaplets, and earrings of flowers—as well as his praise of their remarkable cleanliness—all find confirmation in contemporary travel books and in modern ethnologies. Perhaps the most lavish account, even surpassing Melville's in eulogy, is to be found in Ellis's *Polynesian Researches,* a work from which Melville confessedly borrowed much.[18] Similarly his accounts of native dress, both customary and ceremonial, accord with the best information available.[19]

No account of the Noble Savage is complete, however, without a description of the warrior in full costume. And from Melville's circumstantial portrait of the "noble Mehevi," chief of all the Typees, one can gain a good idea of the elaborate and detailed accuracy of his descriptions of costume:

At last, . . . a superb-looking warrior stooped the towering plumes of his head-dress beneath the low portal, and entered the house. . . . His aspect was imposing. The splendid long drooping tail-feathers of the tropical bird, thickly interspersed with the gaudy plumage of the cock, were disposed in an immense upright semicircle upon his head, their lower extremities being fixed in a crescent of guinea-beads which spanned the forehead. Around his neck were several enormous necklaces of boars' tusks, polished like ivory, and disposed in such a manner that the longest and largest were upon his capacious chest. Thrust forward through the large apertures in his ears were two small and finely-shaped sperm-whale teeth. . . .
The loins of the warrior were girt about with heavy folds of a dark-

coloured tappa, hanging before and behind in clusters of braided tas-
sels, while anklets and bracelets of curling human hair completed his
unique costume. In his right hand he grasped a beautifully carved
paddle-spear, nearly fifteen feet in length, made of the bright koa-
wood, one end sharply pointed, and the other flattened like an oar-
blade. . . . The warrior, from the excellence of his physical proportions, might certainly have been regarded as one of nature's noblemen.[20]

In this highly embellished description, moreover, Melville apparently was not drawing on a romantic imagination. More likely,
he was replenishing his own memory by drawing on the equally
elaborate account that Stewart gives of two Hapa warriors:

Both [were] men of the noblest stature—every limb, in its muscular
proportions, presenting a model for the skill of a statuary. Their dress
—in every respect alike—was singularly striking and imposing; especially
that of the head, which instantly attracted the admiration of the whole
party. It consisted of a crescent, three or four inches broad at its greatest breadth, fixed uprightly in front, . . . the middle [of which] was
entirely filled with the small scarlet berries of the *abrus precatorius*.
. . . The crescent formed the front of a cap fitting close to the head
behind, and the foundation in which the heavy plumage surmounting
it is fixed. This plumage consisted of the long, black, and burnished
tail-feathers of the cock—the finest I ever saw; those in the center being
more than two feet in length . . . , standing perpendicularly, and
becoming more and more vertical, till the lowest at the edges drooped
deeply over the shoulders. . . . Strings of whale's teeth hung around
their necks, and frizzled bunches of human hair were tied around
their wrists and ancles; their loins, also, being girt with thick tufts of
the same, over large maros of white tappa. Short mantles of white
cloth, tied in a knot on the chest, and floating gracefully in the wind
from their shoulders, with long spears, completed the costume.[21]

And this source Melville probably supplemented by turning to
Porter's somewhat briefer account:

I had seen several of their warriors since I had arrived, many of them
highly ornamented with plumes, formed of the feathers of cocks and
man-of-war birds, and with the long tail feathers of the tropic bird;
large tufts of hair were tied around their waists[?], their ancles, and
their loins: . . . with large round or oval ornaments in their ears,
formed of whales' teeth . . . ; from their necks suspended a whale's
tooth, or highly polished shell, and round their loins several turns of
the stronger kind of paper-cloth, the end of which hangs before in the

manner of an apron: this with a black and highly polished spear of about twelve feet in length, or a club richly carved, and borne on the shoulders, constitutes the dress and equipment of a native warrior.[22]

With such models to follow, Melville probably found little handicap in the fact that he kept no journal in the South Seas.

However imposing, even terrifying, the chief in ceremonial regalia may have seemed to outsiders, he was far from being a tyrannical despot among his own people. Indeed, he was very little elevated above them in power or authority, and on ordinary occasions he could scarcely be distinguished from them even in dress. "Previous to the Feast of the Calabashes," Melville says, "I had been puzzled what particular station to assign to Mehevi." And even from the evidence afforded by this large gathering of the natives of the valley, he was enabled to arrive at a conclusion only by supposition:

During the festival, I had not failed to remark the simplicity of manner, the freedom from all restraint, and, to a certain degree, the equality of condition manifested by the natives in general. No one appeared to assume any arrogant pretensions. There was little more than a slight difference in costume to distinguish the chiefs from the other natives. All appeared to mix together freely, and without any reserve; although I noticed that the wishes of a chief, even when delivered in the mildest tone, received the same immediate obedience which elsewhere would have been only accorded to a peremptory command. What may be the extent of the authority of the chiefs over the rest of the tribe, I will not venture to assert; but from all I saw during my stay in the valley, I was induced to believe that in matters concerning the general welfare it was very limited. The required degree of deference toward them, however, was willingly and cheerfully yielded; and as all authority is transmitted from father to son, I have no doubt that one of the effects here, as elsewhere, of high birth, is to induce respect and obedience . . . ; [but] the simplicity of the social institutions of the people could not have been more completely proved than by the fact, that after having been several weeks in the valley, and almost in daily intercourse with Mehevi, I should have remained until the time of the festival ignorant of his regal character.[23]

By reason of his important role on this occasion, Melville concluded that Mehevi was in some sort the "king" of Typee Valley, but that his government was certainly "of a most simple and patriarchal nature, . . . and wholly unattended by the ceremonious pomp which usually surrounds the purple." Melville then proceeds to heighten his praise of the simple and equitable Marquesan system by comparing it with the despotic monarchies found at Tahiti and Honolulu.

Langsdorff was similarly struck by the lack of any well-defined system of government. The chief of Taiohaë, Katanuah, was pointed out by the interpreters as being a "king," but he did not appear to exercise any political supremacy. There was nothing in his dress, either of clothing or of ornament, to distinguish him from the meanest of his subjects, who laughed at his commands and paid not the least respect to his dignity.[24] This was the same chief whom Porter tried to elevate to the rank of King of Nukahiva, with a hope of promoting peace among the various warring tribes. But he found his task a difficult one because of the lack of authority wielded by the chief in his own tribe. The situation was puzzling even to a democratic American:

The fact is that these people cannot be said to live under any form of government, except it be under a patriarchal one. The oldest man of the tribe, if he possess the most land, and is the owner of most breadfruit and cocoa-nut trees, is the most influential character among them. . . .

Although no external marks of respect were shown to Gattanewa [Katanuah], although he mixed unnoticed in the crowd, although he steered and sometimes paddled his own canoe, caught fish for his family, . . . and bore the reputation of being one of the most ingenious and industrious mechanics on the island, still Gattanewa had his rank, and that rank was known and respected.[25]

Moana, the puppet king established by the French in 1842 and ridiculed by Melville, it will be remembered, was the grandson of this patriarchal chief.

In 1829 Stewart found the young Moana nominally accepted as head of the whole island, but the same loose tribal system prevailed, with the chief practically powerless in all matters of influence and authority—more like "a highborn and wealthy citizen, respected and popular in the community in which he resides, than . . . a prince or lord"—and exacting from his followers only the ordinary marks of respect and good will:

> I am at a loss to determine under what form of government this should be classed. . . . I have been more than half tempted, with all deference to the dignity of our own happy government, to style it— will you forgive me?—a republic *en savage,* in which every man is the representative of his own rights, and the only law-giver, with liberty in all cases, promptly to wield the power of the executive, after having discharged, to his own satisfaction, the functions of the judge! [26]

This system, or lack of one, led to lawless retribution and revenge, according to Stewart, in whose eyes the Hawaiian missionary monarchy—so odious to Melville—was far preferable.

It was in just such matters of philosophical attitude that Melville forsook Stewart as an authority and followed the more congenial romantic reaction of Captain David Porter. A sample of the latter's praise of the law-abiding nature and innate goodness of the Marquesans, placed side by side with a similar passage from *Typee,* will furnish additional presumptive evidence of Melville's acquaintance with this fellow disciple of Rousseau. Porter remarks in this connection:

> Whether they have any mode of punishing offences or whether punishment is ever necessary among them, I cannot say. I am inclined to be, however, of the latter opinion. I saw no punishments inflicted, nor did I ever hear that there was any cause.
>
> Their fruit-trees, except those which are tabbooed, are without enclosure; their smaller and more delicate plants, as well as their roots, have only a wall to prevent the depredations of hogs. Their houses are open in front, and their furniture, many parts of which are of great value to them, is entirely exposed. Their hogs are wandering in every part of the valley; their fishing nets and their cloths [*sic*] are left exposed on the beach, and spread on the grass; no precautions are taken to guard against theft, and I therefore conclude, that thefts among themselves are unknown. . . .
>
> During our operations at the camp, . . . no article, of the most trifling nature, was ever missed by any person, . . . and I am inclined to believe that an honester or more friendly and better disposed people do not exist under the sun. They have been stigmatized by the name of savages; it is a term wrongly applied; they rank high in the scale of

human beings, whether we consider them morally or physically. We find them brave, generous, honest, and benevolent, acute, ingenious, and intelligent, and their beauty and [the] regular proportions of their bodies, correspond with the perfections of their minds.[27]

Such eulogy of the Noble Savage must certainly have caught the eye of the author of *Typee*. In fact, it is quite possible that Melville was actually paraphrasing Porter when he paid the following tribute to the innate goodness of the primitive Marquesans:

During the time I lived among the Typees, no one was ever put upon his trial for any offence against the public. To all appearances there were no courts of law or equity. There was no municipal police for the purpose of apprehending vagrants and disorderly characters. In short, there were no legal provisions whatever for the well-being and conservation of society, the enlightened end of civilised legislation. And yet everything went on in the valley with a harmony and smoothness unparalleled, I will venture to assert, in the most select, refined, and pious associations of mortals in Christendom. . . .

It may reasonably be inquired, how were these people governed? how were their passions controlled in their everyday transactions? It must have been by an inherent principle of honesty and charity toward each other. . . . It is to this indwelling, this universally diffused perception of what is *just* and *noble,* that the integrity of the Marquesans in their intercourse with each other is to be attributed. In the darkest nights they slept securely, with all their worldly wealth around them, in houses the doors of which were never fastened. The disquieting ideas of theft or assassination never disturbed them. Each islander reposed beneath his own palmetto thatching, or sat under his own bread-fruit tree, with none to molest or alarm him. There was not a padlock in the valley, nor anything that answered the purpose of one: still there was no community of goods. . . . Here is a spermwhale tooth, graven all over with cunning devices—it is the property of Karluna. It is the most precious of the damsel's ornaments. In her estimation its price is far above rubies; and yet there hangs the dental jewel, by its cord of braided bark, in the girl's house, which is far back in the valley; the door is left open, and all the inmates have gone off to bathe in the stream. . . . So pure and upright were they in all the relations of life, that entering their valley, as I did, under the most erroneous impressions of their character, I was soon led to exclaim in amazement: "Are these the ferocious savages, the bloodthirsty cannibals of whom I have heard such frightful tales! They deal more kindly with each other, and are more humane, than many . . . who repeat every night that beautiful prayer breathed first by the lips of the divine and gentle Jesus." [28]

As romantic as these accounts seem to be in their picture of an almost ideal social state existing among the primitive Marquesans —with government reduced to a minimum and economic justice extended to all—they seem to be surprisingly near the truth, at least in their statements of fundamental facts. According to E. S. C. Handy, the chiefs were democratic leaders in the original sense of the term, for they associated with their people without formality or etiquette, wore the same style of dress as other members of the tribe, and exercised only the mildest sort of paternal direction or control:

The actual relationship between the chief and his people was that of the head of a family to the other members of the family, and the relationship of the people among themselves was that of members of a large family. The political system may best be characterized as a patriarchal communism. . . . All evidence indicates that stealing within a tribe was very rare and that killing was more so.[29]

Objection must be taken, rather, to Melville's explanation that this apparent Utopia sprang from the innate goodness and nobility of primitive man unspoiled by civilization. He knew, as well as the other early visitors did, that the intercourse of the natives with each other was regulated in minute detail by an elaborate system of *tapu*, a code of prohibitions as rigid and as far reaching as any European legal system. He also knew that the isolation of tribes in secluded valleys made communal feeling and intra-tribal dependence inevitable, and that economic abundance within the valley made greed unprofitable and theft unnecessary. How quickly the virtuous Noble Savage was corrupted into dishonesty and covetousness at the first contact with civilization—upon the mere introduction of iron nails, cheap calico prints, and Dutch looking glasses—Melville himself is witness in his account of the state of morals at Tahiti.

In *Typee*, however, Melville was merely writing the preface to his brief against civilization, and his purpose was to show the idyllic relations that might subsist among men untainted by the complex of evils which invariably accompanied Western culture. So he attributed the felicity of the Marquesan character to amiability, benevolence of spirit, and brotherly love:

> There was one admirable trait in the general character of the Typees which, more than anything else, secured my admiration: it was the unanimity of feeling they displayed on every occasion. With them there hardly appeared to be any difference of opinion upon any subject whatever. They all thought and acted alike. . . . They showed this spirit of unanimity in every action of life: everything was done in concert and good fellowship. I will give an instance of this fraternal feeling.
>
> One day, in returning with Kory-Kory from my accustomed visit to the Ti, we passed by a little opening in the grove; on one side of which, my attendant informed me, was that afternoon to be built a dwelling of bamboo. At least a hundred of the natives were bringing materials to the ground, some carrying in their hands one or two of the canes which were to form the sides, others slender rods of the habiscus [*sic*], strung with palmetto leaves, for the roof. Everyone contributed something to the work; and by the united, but easy, and even indolent, labours of all, the entire work was completed before sunset. The islanders, while employed in erecting this tenement, reminded me of a colony of beavers at work. To be sure, they were hardly as silent and demure as those wonderful creatures, nor were they by any means as diligent. To tell the truth, they were somewhat inclined to be lazy, but a perfect tumult of hilarity prevailed; and they worked together so unitedly, and seemed actuated by such an instinct of friendliness, that it was truly beautiful to behold. . . .
>
> During my whole stay on the island I never witnessed a single quarrel, nor anything that in the slightest degree approached even to a dispute. The natives appeared to form one household, whose members were bound together by the ties of strong affection.[30]

In all the earlier travel books, moreover, Melville might have found ample warrant for such a characterization of the Marquesans; in particular, he seems here once again merely to be echoing the praise bestowed by Porter upon the natives of Taiohaë after they had built for him the village which he denominated "Madisonville":

> Nothing can exceed the regularity with which these people carried on their work, without any chief to guide them, without confusion,

and without much noise; they performed their labour with expedition and neatness; every man appeared to be master of his business, and every tribe appeared to strive which should complete their house with most expedition in the most perfect manner. . . .

It seems strange how a people living under no form of government that we could ever perceive, having no chiefs over them who appear to possess any authority, having neither rewards to stimulate them to exertion nor dread of punishment before them, should be capable of conceiving and executing, with the rapidity of lightning, works which astonished us; they appear to act with one mind, to have the same thought, and to be operated on by the same impulse; they can be compared only to the beaver, whose instinct teaches them to design and execute works [which] much claim our admiration.

And, commenting on the friendliness and generosity with which they divided the rewards for their labor among themselves, he adds:

So long as I remained on the island, I never saw or heard of the slightest difference between individuals, except in one instance, and they were of different valleys and tribes. The utmost harmony prevails among them, they live like affectionate brethren of one family, and the authority of their chiefs appears to be only that of fathers among their children.[31]

As for the incessant hostility and constant state of feud existing between the various tribes and flaring continually into open warfare, Melville offers a partial justification by declaring: "If our evil passions must find vent, it is far better to expend them on strangers and aliens, than in the bosom of the community in which we dwell." But he employs another more effective defense of the character of the Typees against the charges that they were fierce and belligerent in their relations with their neighbors: he represents their wars with the Hapas as being little more serious than the sham battles of American schoolboys. One of these conflicts he describes in mock heroics. Having been for a considerable time in the valley without witnessing any warlike encounters, Melville says, he had concluded that the Typees were a greatly traduced people, bearing an undeserved reputation for ferocity. But subsequent events, he adds, proved that he had been premature in reaching this conclusion. One day while enjoying a siesta at the "Ti" (the warriors' *tapu-*

house), he was awakened by a tremendous outcry. Starting up, he beheld the natives, armed with spears and the half-dozen muskets owned by the chiefs, striking across the valley toward the Hapa side:

Presently I heard the sharp report of a musket from the adjoining hills, and then a burst of voices in the same direction. At this the women, who had congregated in the groves, set up the most violent clamours, as they invariably do here as elsewhere on every occasion of excitement and alarm, with a view of tranquillising their own minds and disturbing other people.

When this female commotion had a little subsided, I listened eagerly for further information. At last bang went another shot, and then a second volley of yells from the hills. Again all was quiet, and continued so for such a length of time that I began to think the contending armies had agreed upon a suspension of hostilities; when pop went a third gun, followed as before with a yell. After this, for nearly two hours nothing occurred worthy of comment, save some straggling shouts from the hillside, sounding like the halloos of a parcel of truant boys who had lost themselves in the woods.

. . . At last, no sound whatever proceeding from the mountains, I concluded that the contest had been determined one way or the other. Such appeared, indeed, to be the case, for in a little while a courier arrived at the Ti, almost breathless with his exertions, and communicated the news of a great victory having been achieved by his countrymen: "Happar poo arva!—Happar poo arva!" (the cowards had fled!) Kory-Kory was in ecstasies, and commenced a vehement harangue, which, so far as I understood it, implied that the result exactly agreed with his expectations, and which, moreover, was intended to convince me that it would be a perfectly useless undertaking, even for an army of fire-eaters, to offer battle to the irresistible heroes of our valley. . . . The total loss of the victors in this obstinately contested affair was— in killed, wounded, and missing—one forefinger and part of a thumb-nail (which the late proprietor brought along with him in his hand), a severely contused arm, and a considerable effusion of blood flowing from the thigh of a chief who had received an ugly thrust from a Happar spear. What the enemy had suffered I could not discover, but I presume they had succeeded in taking off with them the bodies of their slain.

Such was the issue of the battle, as far as its results came under my observation; and as it appeared to be considered an event of prodigious importance, I reasonably concluded that the wars of the natives were marked by no very sanguinary traits.[32]

The effect of this burlesque account of savage warfare is to reconcile the reputation of the Typees for ferocity with the far more pacific and humane character which Melville says he found them to possess. How far Melville may have been forced to distort the truth in order to accomplish this end is another matter.

The evidence of contemporary travel writers is indeed conflicting on this point. Even E. S. C. Handy confesses that it is impossible to tell how sustained and how bloody the wars were in the ancient days. Informants on Hivaoa insisted that there had been one great war in which all the warriors on the eastern end of the island had been slain. But this he apparently considered a rare exception, for he concludes: "It seems very doubtful whether there were any engagements of a very serious nature, since to the native fighting was entirely a matter of individual personal combat, quick assault, and quick flight or pursuit." [33] Langsdorff's testimony even more nearly agrees with Melville's, for he says that they often quit the field as soon as they had slain one of their enemy, concluding: "it appeared as if their fights were very like the mock combats sometimes performed by our youths." [34] Porter, who not only witnessed their battles but took part in them, gives a circumstantial account of their method of warfare:

Their general mode of fighting consists in constant skirmishing. The adverse parties assemble on the brows of opposite hills, having a plain between them. One or two dressed out in all their finery, richly decorated with shells, tufts of hair, ear ornaments, &c. &c. advance, dancing up to the opposite party, amid a shower of spears and stones (which they avoid with great dexterity) and daring the other to single combat: they are soon pursued by a greater number, who are in turn driven back; and if in their retreat they should chance to be knocked over with a stone, they are instantly despatched with spears and warclubs and carried off in triumph.[35]

How little sanguinary such conflicts proved, however, may be seen from the consternation of the chief Katanuah, when, with the aid of

Porter's forces, the Teiis were enabled to rout the Hapas by killing the unprecedented number of five of their warriors:

We had gained a victory, which, to him, seemed incredible; and the number of dead which they had borne off as trophies had far exceeded that of any former battle within his recollection; as they fight for weeks, nay months sometimes, without killing any on either side, though many are, in all their engagements, severely wounded.[36]

Such evidence gives strong support to Melville's description of the war between the Typees and Hapas; indeed, it may have been the authority on which he based his account.

There is some evidence of destructive wars occurring on other Polynesian islands, but none for Nukahiva.[37] Stewart was apparently repeating beachcombers' gossip, therefore, when he remarked: "At times several tribes have combined in the utter extermination of a single weaker though independent body." [38] He was much nearer the truth when he reported what he had seen with his own eyes. At the time of his visit in 1829 the Typees were, as usual, at war with the Hapas. One day while in the valley of the Hapas, he was struck by a sight which was declared to be characteristic—a party of Typee warriors on the intervening mountain ridge, challenging the Hapas to combat:

Arrayed in battle dress, their lofty helmets of feathers, and light mantles sporting gayly in the wind, they stood in clearly defined outline, like giants against the sky—brandishing their spears over the valley, tossing their tufted war-clubs, by way of challenge, in the air; and, by every gesture, bidding defiance and showering contempt on their enemies below, while savage taunts and shouts of scorn echoed wildly over the surrounding cliffs. . . . This kind of insolent bravado, from the summit of a conspicuous hill, is very common among hostile neighbors: and here, on the borders of the neutral ground, the same precipice is not unfrequently occupied several times in one day, by alternate parties from the two sides—one ascending as soon as the other goes down to their own territory again—and this, generally, without leading to any direct engagement.[39]

So, from the Hapa side, might have appeared the conflict described by Melville.

[137]

Thus the more common form of warfare on Nukahiva seems to have consisted of gesticulations, threats, and oratorical combats, occasionally followed by sudden raids or brief skirmishes. And Melville is supported in his account of their mildness by his three chief sources of information: Langsdorff, Porter, and Stewart. More serious conflicts were apparently quite infrequent; and, if any such had occurred during Melville's brief stay in Typee Valley, it would have been a coincidence. It is certainly an exaggeration, however, to treat even their relatively bloodless encounters as comparable to the sham battles of a parcel of truant boys, for they were motivated by bitter, violent, and deep-seated hostility. Sometimes the purpose was to revenge a theft or other insult; sometimes, to destroy the hogs and breadfruit of a too-powerful enemy. But the most common cause was the seizure of victims for the purpose of religious sacrifice, upon the death of a priest or chief. This was apparently the occasion of the second war with the Hapas described by Melville, when the bodies of three slain enemies were brought home in triumph and afterwards disposed of at a "cannibal feast." But it was not until his story was nearly done that Melville definitely admitted the truth of this one unmitigable smirch on the character of the Typees. He had maintained until the end a nice balance between two conflicting purposes: the defense of the innate nobility of the unspoiled primitive and the maintenance of suspense for his narrative through a personal fear of cannibalism. In conclusion he could merely say, as we have seen: "But this only enormity in their character is not half so horrible as it is usually described, . . . [being practiced] upon the bodies of slain enemies alone; and horrible and fearful as the custom is, immeasurably as it is to be abhorred and condemned, still I assert that those who indulge in it are in other respects humane and virtuous." [40] The Noble Savages could not have asked for a more loyal apologist than Melville, who at times, for their sake, could thus fly in the face of his own art.

Sequestered in their own valley, however, the Typees apparently offered no such incongruities of character for Melville to reconcile. Within the tribe, according to his account, their relationships were without exception marked by spontaneous friendliness, selfless generosity, and perpetual good spirits. Particularly felicitous, he says, were their domestic life and the general relationship between the sexes:

If the degree of consideration in which the ever-adorable sex is held by the men be—as the philosophers affirm—a just criterion of the degree of refinement among a people, then I may truly pronounce the Typees to be as polished a community as ever the sun shone upon. . . . Far different from their condition among many rude nations, where the women are made to perform all the work, while their ungallant lords and masters lie buried in sloth, the gentle sex in the valley of Typee were exempt from toil—if toil it might be called—that, even in that tropical climate, never distilled one drop of perspiration. Their light household occupations, together with the manufacture of tappa, the platting of mats, and the polishing of drinking vessels, were the only employments pertaining to the women. And even these resembled those pleasant avocations which fill up the elegant morning leisure of our fashionable ladies at home. But in these occupations, slight and agreeable though they were, the giddy young girls very seldom engage. Indeed, these wilful, care-killing damsels were averse to all useful employment. Like so many spoiled beauties, they ranged through the groves—bathed in the stream—danced—flirted—played all manner of mischievous pranks, and passed their days in one merry round of thoughtless happiness.[41]

Again, as in all the aspects of Marquesan life that call forth praise, Melville's account is in circumstantial agreement with Porter's:

The women, different from those of almost every other Indian [*sic*] nation, are not subjected to any laborious work; their occupations are wholly domestic; to them belongs the manufacturing of cloth, the care of the house and children. . . . But the girls, from twelve to eighteen years of age rove at will; this period of their lives is a period of unbounded pleasure, unrestrained in all their actions, unconfined by domestic occupations, their time is spent in dancing, singing, and ornamenting their persons to render themselves more attractive in the eyes of man, on whom they indiscriminately bestow their favours, unrestrained by shame or fear of the consequences.[42]

This early period of unrivaled happiness and freedom from all cares, as described by Melville and Porter, has a very real historical substantiation in the social institution known as *ka'ioi,* a term used to designate all males and females from adolescence to the time of marriage. All natives during this period literally ran wild, and they were not only allowed to do so, but were expected to. Both sexes anointed their bodies with *eka* (Melville's "akar") to make them brilliant, soft, and sweet-scented; and they ornamented themselves with flowers and necklaces of pandanus seed. In fact, the prime motive of the *ka'ioi* was play, and they spent their time in beautifying themselves and in circulating about the valleys in pursuit of amusement in general, but of the satisfaction of their abundant sexual appetites in particular. They were not mere libertines, however, for as a group they performed very definite functions in society: for example, they supplied the singers and dancers for feasts and festivals; and the young men erected the special houses used in certain rites, such as tattooing.[43] Both Melville and Porter seem to have recognized the existence of this native convention which allowed complete freedom, sexual and otherwise, to its adolescents; but they were apparently not aware that it actually amounted to a social institution of considerable complexity and importance. They were chiefly impressed with the result produced: "a rabble rout of merry young idlers"—and the institution of *ka'ioi* certainly made for such a result.

The period of *ka'ioi* freedom terminated when a couple settled down to live together as more or less permanent mates, either upon the birth of a child or merely through the desire of the parties. But this union did not terminate their happiness nor completely restrict their freedom, for the marriage yoke was a loose one and could be terminated at will. Porter, for one, testifies to this flexibility of marriage as the explanation of their domestic felicity: "Before marriage they are at liberty to indulge themselves with whom they please, but after marriage the right of disposing of them remains with the husband. . . . [However,] the union is not binding, and the parties are at liberty to separate when they no longer like each other, provided they have had no children." Consequently, he was not surprised to find the wives "as firmly attached to their husbands as the women of any other country," and even more so.[44] This looseness of the marriage tie was probably one of the explanations of Melville's initial bewilderment over the matrimonial relations which he found in Typee. But there was another feature in their marriage scheme which Porter completely overlooked, and which perplexed Melville even more—a regular system of polyandry. Marheyo and Tinor, the old couple with whom he lived, "seemed to have a sort of nuptial understanding with one another," he says; "but for all that, I had sometimes observed a comical-looking old gentleman dressed in a suit of shabby tattooing, who had the audacity to take various liberties with the lady, and that too in the very presence of the old warrior her husband, who looked on as good-naturedly as if nothing was happening." And, again, he says that he happened upon the chief Mehevi several times when "he was romping—in a most undignified manner for a warrior king—with one of the prettiest little witches in the valley," although she herself was married and a mother.[45]

Finally the whole matter was explained to Melville by Kory-Kory:

A regular system of polygamy [*sic*] exists among the islanders, but of a most extraordinary nature—a plurality of husbands, instead of wives; and this solitary fact speaks volumes for the gentle disposition of the male population. Where else, indeed, could such a practice exist, even for a single day? . . . We [in America] are scarcely amiable and forbearing enough to submit to it.

I was not able to learn what particular ceremony was observed in forming the marriage contract, but am inclined to think that it must have been of a very simple nature. . . . The girls are first wooed and won, at a very tender age, by some stripling in the household in which they reside. This, however, is a mere frolic of the affections, and no formal engagement is contracted. By the time this first love has a little subsided, a second suitor presents himself, of graver years, and carries both boy and girl away to his own habitation. This disinterested and generous-hearted fellow now weds the young couple—marrying damsel and lover at the same time—and all three thenceforth live together as harmoniously as so many turtles. I have heard of some men who in civilised countries rashly marry large families with their wives, but had no idea that there was any place where people married supplementary husbands with them. Infidelity on either side is very rare. No man has more than one wife, and no wife of mature years has less than two husbands—sometimes she has three, but such instances are not frequent. The marriage tie, whatever it may be, does not appear to be indissoluble; for separations occasionally happen. . . . As nothing stands in the way of a separation, the matrimonial yoke sits easily and lightly, and a Typee wife lives on very pleasant and sociable terms with her husbands. On the whole, wedlock, as known among these Typees, seems to be of a more distinct and enduring nature than is usually the case with barbarous people.[46]

Even Stewart, who was usually slow to acknowledge any virtues in savagery, was forced to congratulate the Marquesans on their domestic felicity, while at the same time commenting in detail on their system of polyandry. Melville, as he wrote, apparently had Stewart's treatise open before him at the following passage:

The marriage tie, though existing almost exclusively in the baneful form of a singular polygamy—that of a plurality of husbands, instead of a plurality of wives—still seems more distinct, more binding, and more enduring here, than at the Society and Sandwich Islands. I have not been able to learn, that any particular ceremony attends the marriage engagement, except an interchange of presents . . . and the celebration of a feast.

We have yet met with no instance, in any rank of society, of a male with two wives, but are informed that for one woman to have two husbands is a universal habit. Some favorite in the father's household or retinue, at an early period becomes the husband of the daughter—who still remains under the paternal roof—till contracted in marriage to a second individual; on which, she removes with her first husband to his habitation, and both herself and original companion are supported by him. . . .

Instances of strong conjugal affection are reported of them. . . . All the domestic relations, indeed, appear to be under more propitious auspices here, than . . . [at the other Pacific] clusters.[47]

Wherever Melville got his information—from Stewart, from personal observation, or from a combination of the two—his account of the domestic relations of the Typees is quite accurate, as far as it goes. In fact, *The Popular Science Monthly* for October, 1891, printed an article on primitive marriage customs, based in general on scientific sources, which quoted approvingly the account of polyandry contained in *Typee*.[48] Thus, two weeks before his death, the

NOBLE SAVAGES OF TYPEE VALLEY

ghost of his first fame came back to harass the philosopher who had long been weary of being known as the "man who lived among cannibals." More recently, and more authoritatively, Edward Westermarck, in his *History of Human Marriage,* confirms Melville's account of a plurality of husbands among the Typees.[49] According to E. S. C. Handy, who discusses the marriage relationship in considerable detail, these secondary husbands were called *pekio;* and this term was likewise applied to secondary wives, though female *pekio* were rare even in chiefs' households. The practice of either polyandry or polygyny required the mutual consent of the original couple; and only temporary or occasional cohabitation was allowed to the *pekio*—that is, when the true husband (or wife) was absent. The marital relationship was further complicated by the extension of the right of temporary cohabitation to the father-in-law and brothers-in-law of the wife and to the mother-in-law and sisters-in-law of the husband.[50] To a foreign visitor, unacquainted with the intricacies of such a system, this wide range of sexual privilege might well have seemed like unbridled promiscuity, especially as the unmarried *ka'ioi* swelled the tide of seeming licentiousness.

The family life of the Marquesans, apparently, was just as stable and just as happy as Melville pictures it. One reason for this, in addition to the free and equitable relations between the sexes, was obviously the economy of abundance under which they could and did live. After describing the laborious process of primitive firemaking—the only form of hard work that came under his observation—Melville indulged in one of his many comparisons between savage and civilized life:

A gentleman of Typee can bring up a numerous family of children, and give them all a highly respectable cannibal education, with infinitely less toil and anxiety than he expends in the simple process of striking a light; whilst a poor European artisan, who through the instrumentality of a lucifer performs the same operation in one second, is put to his wit's end to provide for his starving offspring that food which the children of a Polynesian father, without troubling their parents, pluck from the branches of every tree around them.[51]

Providing food for the family was not quite so simple, however, even in a tropical paradise. The Marquesans were thrifty enough to take precautions against a future shortage by planting breadfruit and cocoanut trees with great care, especially upon the birth of a child. Every individual owned trees in the vicinity of his house, and the chiefs owned plantations of them, regularly laid out and cared for. Further, there were community pits for storing breadfruit against a time of famine. All of the early visitors commented on this cultivation and conservation of the food supply, but *Typee* is strangely silent on these matters.

On the other hand, Melville is much more circumstantial in his description of the various methods of preparing food than any of the travel books that, in so many other matters, seem to have served as sources for him. His information is apparently that of an eyewitness, and it is in these more prosaic passages that one finds the most convincing evidence that he actually lived the life of a native among the Marquesans for some weeks at least. Particularly full is his account of the various dishes made from breadfruit: "kokoo" (*ka'aku*), the roasted fruit pounded and mixed with cocoanut milk; "amar" (*ma*), a tart cake baked in earthen ovens from breadfruit paste which has been allowed to ferment for months, and even years, in pits dug in the ground; and the more famous "poee-poee" (*popoi*), a sort of pudding made by adding water to the latter. No other author that I have been able to find gives such detailed accounts of these dishes as Melville; and yet according to Handy, who checked them with information from manuscripts in the Catholic Mission and from native informants on Nukahiva, he was remarkably accurate except in a few minor points. Occasionally, he picked up a phrase from his sources, as when he says that *popoi* "resembles in its plastic nature our own book-binders' paste" (Stewart described it similarly, as having "the consistence and general appearance of bookbinders' paste"); but for the most part he seems to have been writing of the breadfruit from personal observation alone, contrary to his usual practice.[52]

Perhaps the second most important staple in the Marquesan diet was the cocoanut. In *Typee*, however, Melville has no extended account of the uses of this fruit. Besides incidental references, he merely describes the manner in which the nut is gathered, a description which seems to owe something to Porter. In *Omoo,* on the other hand, he supplements this with an elaborate account of its multifarious uses, which it seems best to include in the present discussion:

The blessings it confers are incalculable. Year after year, the islander reposes beneath its shade, both eating and drinking of its fruit; he thatches his hut with its boughs, and weaves them into baskets to carry his food; he cools himself with a fan plaited from the young leaflets, and shields his head from the sun by a bonnet of the leaves; sometimes he clothes himself with the cloth-like substance which wraps round the base of the stalks, whose elastic rods, strung with filberts, are used as a taper; the larger nuts, thinned and polished, furnish him with a beautiful goblet; the smaller ones, with bowls for his pipes; the dry husks kindle his fires; their fibres are twisted into fishing-lines and cords for his canoes; he heals his wounds with a balsam compounded from the juice of the nut; and with the oil extracted from its meat embalms the bodies of the dead.

The noble trunk itself is far from being valueless. Sawn into posts, it upholds the islander's dwelling; converted into charcoal, it cooks his food; and supported on blocks of stones, rails in his lands. He impels his canoe through the water with a paddle of the wood, and goes to battle with clubs and spears of the same hard material.

In pagan Tahiti, a cocoa-nut branch was the symbol of regal authority. Laid upon the sacrifice in the temple, it made the offering sacred; and with it the priests chastised and put to flight the evil spirits which assailed them. The supreme majesty of Oro, the great god of their mythology, was declared in the cocoa-nut log from which his image was rudely carved.[53]

Melville obviously culled this list of blessings from Ellis's *Polynesian Researches,* one of his admitted authorities for both *Typee* and *Omoo.* In this encyclopedic treatise there is a strikingly similar account:

The trunk of the tree is used for a variety of purposes; their best spears were made with cocoanut wood; wall-plates, rafters, and pillars for their larger houses were often of the same material; . . . their rollers for their canoes, and also their most durable fences, were made with its trunk. It is also a valuable kind of fuel, and makes excellent charcoal.

The timber is not the only valuable article the cocoanut-tree furnishes. . . . The leaflets are often plaited, when the whole leaf is called *paua,* and forms an excellent skreen [*sic*] for the sides of their houses, or covering for their floors. Several kinds of baskets are also made with the leaves. . . . They were also plaited for bonnets or shades for the foreheads and eyes, and were worn by both sexes. In many of their religious ceremonies they were used, and the *niau,* or leaf, was also an emblem of authority, and was sent by the chief to his dependents, when any requisition was made: through the cocoanut leaf tied to the sacrifice the god was supposed to enter; and by the same road the evil spirits, who, it was imagined, tormented those affected with diseases, were driven out. . . . On the tough and stiff stalks of the leaflets, the candlenuts, employed for lighting their houses, were strung when used. . . . A remarkably fine, strong, fibrous matting, attached to the bark under the bottom of the stalk, . . . is also occasionally employed in preparing articles of clothing. . . . All the cups and drinking vessels of the natives are made with cocoanut shells, . . . scraped very thin, and . . . often slightly transparent. . . . The fibres of the husk are separated from the pulp by soaking them in water, and are used in making various kinds of cinet and cordage, especially a valuable coiar rope; and, as the pious Herbert sung two hundred years ago,

> "The Indian's nut alone
> Is clothing, meat and trencher, drink and can,
> Boat, cable, sail and needle, all in one." [54]

These passages have been quoted at length because they offer a most instructive example of how Melville almost habitually leaned upon his authorities even in matters with which he certainly must have had a first-hand acquaintance. For some reason, he preferred to work from the descriptions of previous authors, which he found ready to hand, merely recasting this material to secure greater unity and artistic effect—a result which he usually achieved, as just illustrated. Even in his more poetic passages he often used this same method of composition, sometimes even retaining the exact phraseology of his original. An example of this is his description of the setting out of the young cocoanut plant:

The cocoa-nut is planted as follows: Selecting a suitable place, you drop into the ground a fully ripe nut, and leave it. In a few days, a thin, lance-like shoot forces itself through a minute hole in the shell, pierces the husk, and soon unfolds three pale-green leaves in the air; while, originating in the same soft white sponge which now completely fills the nut, a pair of fibrous roots, pushing away the stoppers which close two holes in an opposite direction, penetrate the shell, and strike vertically into the ground. A day or two more, and the shell and husk which, in the last and germinating stage of the nut, are so hard that a knife will scarcely make any impression, spontaneously burst by some force within; and, henceforth, the hardy young plant thrives apace; and needing no culture, pruning, or attention of any sort, rapidly arrives at maturity.[55]

This account also was lifted, with little change and with even less improvement, directly from the pages of Ellis's *Polynesian Researches;* yet Melville makes no mention of this book as a source, except to acknowledge in the preface that he consulted it on several points connected with "the history and ancient customs of Tahiti." Ellis's account follows:

If the cocoanut be kept long after it is fully ripe, a white, sweet, spongy substance is formed in the inside. . . . This fibrous sponge ultimately absorbs the water, and fills the concavity. . . . While this truly wonderful process is going on within the nut, a single bud or shoot, of a white colour but hard texture, forces its way through one of the holes in the shell, perforates the tough fibrous husk, and after rising some inches, begins to unfold its pale green leaves to the light and the air; at this time, also, two thick white fibres, originating in the same point, push away the stoppers or coverings from the other two holes in the shell, pierce the husk in an opposite direction, and finally penetrate the ground. If allowed to remain, the shell, which no knife would cut, . . . is burst by an expansive power, generated within itself; the husk and the shell gradually decay, and, forming a light manure, facilitate the growth of the young plant, which gradually strikes its roots deeper, elevates its stalk, and expands its leaves, until it becomes a lofty, fruitful, and graceful tree.[56]

Throughout his entire description of the cocoanut the author of *Omoo* obviously kept Ellis's volume open before him and borrowed from it without stint.

To return to *Typee*, we find that the native diet did not consist solely of fruit and vegetables, for the island abounded in hogs. Yet, as Melville says, pork was not a staple article of food: the hogs, which were permitted to run wild, were principally saved for feasts, when they were killed and eaten in large numbers. Melville describes such a slaughtering of hogs ("puarkee") in preparation for the "Feast of the Calabashes." His account of the method of cooking them on heated stones in earthen ovens apparently owes much to Porter's similar account; and both praise the results of this style of preparation.[57] The only other animal food eaten by the Marquesans was fish, which, as Melville states, was habitually eaten raw. A feast followed the fishing expeditions, a strict *tapu* being maintained until the distribution of the fish to all the inhabitants had been completed.[58]

The only other foods described by Melville are bananas, sugar cane, and seaweed. He makes no mention of taro, wild yams, apples, melons, and several other less important articles included by E. S. C. Handy in the Marquesan menu.[59] He does, however, give a full account of their national beverage *kava*, which is made from the juice of a root of the same name. Melville's description of the preparation of "arva," as he calls it, by masticating the root and mixing it with water, as well as his account of the narcotic effect produced by drinking it, is very similar to the one given by Porter. The latter also mentions a mineral water of strong taste, found in several springs on the island and held in high estimation by the natives for its medicinal qualities, which he calls *vie kava;* Melville says similarly that the Cheltenham of Typee was a spring called "Arva Wai," which he translates as "Strong Waters." [60] The only other drink of the Marquesans, besides water, was the milk of the young cocoanut.

In the equitable division of the simple labors necessary to life on the island, the men attended to the planting and gathering of food and shared the light burden of its preparation. The women, on the other hand, undertook the exclusive manufacture of the native cloth, *tapa*, made from the bark of the paper mulberry tree by beating it out to the desired thinness with a grooved mallet. Melville's detailed account of this remarkable industry, although prefaced with the statement that "no description of its manufacture has ever been given," follows very closely the one found in Ellis's *Polynesian Researches*, where he surely must have read it. Almost the only difference between the two accounts is in the concluding comments, which set apart the unsympathetic missionary from the romantic traveler. To Ellis the sound of the cloth-mallet, though not disagreeable at a great distance, was otherwise deafening and almost unendurable; to the ear of Melville, better attuned to savage delights, its "clear, ringing, musical sound [was] really charming." [61]

Most of the other industries and arts were left entirely to the men. The major occupations of fishing and canoe-building, which are treated at considerable length by most of the early visitors, are scarcely mentioned by Melville. Perhaps sufficient explanation for this omission may be found in his own declaration that he resided nine miles inland at the head of Typee Valley, and that his wanderings were rigidly circumscribed during his "indulgent captivity." [62] Further, the making and ornamenting of implements of war and domestic utensils, to which Porter gives so much space, are mentioned only incidentally, as are likewise stone and wood carving, and the weaving of mats.

Without a doubt the most striking and elaborate art practiced by the Marquesans was the adornment of their bodies with tattooing. Since this highly developed art amounted to a regular profession, with trained and paid artists, and since the entire population spent a considerable portion of its time under the hands of the tattooers, it can best be discussed here under the general head of industries, arts, and occupations, rather than as a characteristic of their personal appearance or as a feature of their social or religious systems. Certainly it was not a "religious observance" as Melville concluded, though it was abolished later by the missionaries because of a supposed connection with idolatry; nor was it "a sure indication of birth and riches" as he says elsewhere, though it was controlled somewhat by wealth, because of the attendant expense, and hence was proportioned in a measure to one's social rank.[63] In treating it as a widespread professional art, largely but not purely a matter of ornamentation, we are on surer ground. Melville's account can be checked for accuracy by comparison with Willowdean C.

Handy's authoritative study, *Tattooing in the Marquesas,* made during the Bayard Dominick Expedition in 1920; whereas numerous sources, especially for Melville's incorrect information, can be pointed out in contemporary travel books.

In his description of the designs used in tattooing Melville was apparently quite accurate when it suited his purposes to be. A complete suit of tattooing for a man, he says rightly, covered the entire body. In addition to every imaginable line and curve, he mentions birds, fishes, and an "artu" (?) tree among the various figures employed. W. C. Handy confirms this and says that throughout the historical record of tattooing in the Marquesas the two types of designs, geometric and naturalistic, have existed side by side even as they do today, citing numerous sources from Mendana's first description in 1595 on down through Langsdorff's drawings to the time of Melville's visit.[64] Not even the face, as a general rule, was spared. The most common designs used thereon, according to Melville, were as follows: three longitudinal or oblique lines crossing the eyes, nose, and mouth from ear to ear; three similar lines disposed in the form of a triangle; and squares over the eyes giving the grotesque effect of enormous glaring goggles. F. D. Bennett, here, seems to have come nearest to Melville's description, saying: "The three black bands across the face . . . give a strange harlequin-like appearance to the countenance . . . ; in one instance, . . . the tattooed bands were drawn obliquely. . . . When the face is profusely tattooed, a circle of unmarked skin is usually left around each eye, and produces a peculiarly glaring and almost terrific effect." [65] Whether Melville's descriptions of these designs are drawn from life or from some secondary source, they are correct in all particulars.

The women, on the other hand, were very much less embellished. Melville's descriptions of them, however, are slightly inconsistent and somewhat inaccurate. Fayaway and the younger girls, he says, had only three minute dots on either lip and a small design on the fall of the shoulder; all that was ever added to this was an elaborate design on the right hand and the left foot as the seal of marriage. Elsewhere, however, he says that the wife of Moana, king of Nukahiva, had her legs so "embellished with spiral tattooing" that they resembled "miniature Trajan's columns," and he concludes his description with a veiled reference to even more intimate "hieroglyphics on her . . . sweet form." Although this elaborate adornment of the queen is confirmed by two members of the French Expedition, who seemed to consider it unusual enough to call for especial comment, complete tattooing for all women, royal or plebeian, married or unmarried, included the lips, the lobes of the ears, the curve of the shoulder, both hands, both feet, and the entire expanse of the legs; and apparently there were no distinguishing marks to symbolize either marriage or rank.[66] Part of Melville's error may have come from misinformation derived from travel books; but he undoubtedly reduced and expanded the amount of tattooing on his Marquesan women to suit the romantic needs of his narrative.

Further, Melville's account of the operation of tattooing and of the instruments and the pigment used in its performance is accurate save in a few minor points; but here, again, there were numerous sources from which he could have drawn his information.[67] He touches off his discussion of the subject in *Typee* with an amusing personal anecdote which is not without confirmation, but which led him to a mistaken conclusion. The artist Karky, he says, became obsessed with the notion that Melville's white skin offered him an unusual opportunity for distinguishing himself in his profession. Melville, who is never as full in his praise of the beauty of tattooing as the other early visitors, declares that he was horrified at the mere thought of thus being rendered hideous for life. But, joined in his inexorable solicitations by all the other Typees, the artist became so insistent in his demands that Melville offered to have both arms tattooed if his face were spared—a compromise which was disdainfully rejected. A final discovery, he says, augmented his apprehensions to such an extent that escape from the valley now became imperative: "The whole system of tattooing was, I found, connected with their religion; and it was evident, therefore, that they were resolved to make a convert of me." [68]

Although Melville was mistaken in this conclusion, the Marquesans apparently did have some strong reason for wanting to tattoo

white men who came to live among them. One of the beachcombers
who served as an interpreter to Langsdorff was constrained against
his will to submit to this native custom; and Bennett tells of the
delight with which his own proposal to be tattooed was accepted.[69]
More to the point, and more suggestive of some social significance
connected with the custom, is John Coulter's account of his treatment on the island of La Dominica (Hivaoa). After he had lived
with the natives for several weeks as an adopted chief, he says, they
began to complain that various misfortunes were befalling them in
consequence of his not having been tattooed. Upon his denying
their request that he submit to the custom of the island, they became sullen and even threatened to take his life. Seeing that there
was no escape, he finally acceded to their demand, only stipulating
that his face and hands be not touched—a request which was readily
granted.[70] Melville may have modelled his anecdote on Coulter's,
though there is small evidence that he was acquainted with his volume; on the other hand, he may have undergone a similar personal
experience. In either case, the story is at least probable, though the
explanation of the natives' insistence remains obscure.

In *Omoo* Melville continues his remarks on the Marquesan system of tattooing. Before leaving the islands, he says, the whaling
captain who had rescued him from Typee Valley touched at La
Dominica to recapture some deserters. Here Melville talked with a
runaway sailor ("Lem Hardy, . . . a renegado from Christendom
and humanity—a white man in the South Sea girdle, and tattooed in
the face") who had lived as a chief among the natives for ten years.[71]
(Perhaps it was from this beachcomber that Melville picked up the
anecdote of Coulter's experience in being tattooed, on this very
island nine years before.) Along with other information that he says
he obtained from Hardy was much that dealt with tattooing as it
was practiced on this island:

Throughout the entire cluster the tattooers of Hivarhoo [Hivaoa]
enjoyed no small reputation. They had carried their art to the highest
perfection, and the profession was esteemed most honourable. No
wonder, then, that like genteel tailors, they rated their services very
high; so much so, that none but those belonging to the higher classes

could afford to employ them. So true was this, that the elegance of one's tattooing was in most cases a sure indication of birth and riches.

Professors in large practice lived in spacious houses, divided by screens of tappa into numerous little apartments, where subjects were waited upon in private. The arrangement chiefly grew out of a singular ordinance of the Taboo, which enjoined the strictest privacy upon all men, high and low, while under the hands of a tattooer. For the time, the slightest intercourse with others is prohibited, and the small portion of food allowed is pushed under the curtain by an unseen hand. The restriction with regard to food is intended to reduce the blood, so as to diminish the inflamation consequent upon puncturing the skin. As it is, this comes on very soon, and takes some time to heal; so that the period of seclusion generally embraces many days, sometimes several weeks. . . .

To begin the work, the period of adolescence is esteemed the most suitable. After casting about for some eminent tattooer, the friends of the youth take him to his house, to have the outlines of the general plan laid out. It behooves the professor to have a nice eye, for a suit to be worn for life should be well cut.

Some tattooers, yearning after perfection, employ, at large wages, one or two men of the commonest order—vile fellows, utterly regardless of appearances, upon whom they first try their patterns and practice generally. Their backs remorselessly scrawled over, and no more canvas remaining, they are dismissed, and ever after go about, the scorn of their countrymen.

Hapless wights! thus martyred in the cause of the Fine Arts.

Besides the regular practitioners, there are a parcel of shabby, itinerant tattooers, who, by virtue of their calling, stroll unmolested from one hostile bay to another, doing their work dog-cheap for the multitude. They always repair to the various religious festivals, which gather great crowds. When these are concluded, and the places where they are held vacated even by the tattooers, scores of little tents of coarse tappa are left standing, each with a solitary inmate, who, forbidden to talk to his unseen neighbours, is obliged to stay there till completely healed. The itinerants are a reproach to their profession, mere cobblers, dealing in nothing but jagged lines and clumsy patches, and utterly incapable of soaring to those heights of fancy attained by gentlemen of the faculty.[72]

Much of this account of tattooing, however, is inaccurate, according to W. C. Handy, who nevertheless confirms Lem Hardy's claim for the eminence of the artists of Hivaoa, saying that this island was the original and most famous center of the art.[73] But tattooing was not an indication of either birth or riches. Every father paid, in kind, for the work that was done on his eldest son (*opou*); but all the rest of the youths of the island (the *ka'ioi*) were tattooed free, being fed by the father of the *opou* during the process. It is perhaps these to whom Melville refers in speaking of the common fellows who were practiced on; but there is no evidence today that the work done on the *ka'ioi* was not of the same pattern and quality as that done on the *opou*. Moreover, Melville's statement that the tattooing was performed in large houses with numerous private apartments belonging to the artists (*tuhuna*), or in individual tents of *tapa* set up by itinerant tattooers at festival times, is equally without corroboration according to the information gathered by Handy in 1920. Instead, all were tattooed in special *tapu* houses erected for the occasion by the *ka'ioi* as their contribution to the work. Thus the patients being operated on were *tapu* during the process, just as Melville says, and all intercourse with others was forbidden to them. But there was no restriction put upon the kinds or quantity of food and water allowed to the patients. Finally, all present-day evidence denies Melville's suggestion that there were varying orders of *tuhuna*, though it is likely that there were itinerant members, who, however, were not at all "shabby reproaches to their profession, . . . doing their work dog-cheap for the multitude." [74]

Where did Melville get so much incorrect information? It is possible, of course, that he did meet such a person as Lem Hardy, for there were deserters from ships living on several of the islands who understood only imperfectly the customs of the natives, and yet who delighted in entertaining subsequent white visitors with their inaccurate and even extravagant tales. But it is hardly necessary to postulate such an actual meeting for Melville, since a very similar account of tattooing, particularly striking in the similarity of its misinformation, can be found in Langsdorff's pages as it was told to him by Jean Baptiste Cabri, a renegade on Nukahiva who may well have been the original of Melville's Hardy:

The operation of tattooing is performed by certain persons, who gain their livelihood by it entirely, and I presume that those who perform it with the greatest dexterity, and evince the greatest degree of taste in the disposition of the ornaments, are as much sought after as among us a particularly good tailor. Thus much, however, must be said, that the choice made is not a matter of equal indifference with them as with us; for if the punctured garment be spoiled in the making, the mischief is irreparable, it must be worn with all its faults the whole life through. . . . Although no real elevation of rank is designated by the superiority of these decorations, yet as only persons of rank can afford to be at the expence attendant upon any refinement in the ornaments, it does become in fact a badge of distinction. . . .

As soon as the inhabitant of Nukahiwa [*sic*] approaches towards the age of manhood, the operation of tattooing is begun, and this is one of the most important epochs of his life. The artist is sent for, and the agreement made with him. . . . While we were at the island, a son of the chief Katanuah [*sic*] was to be tattooed. For this purpose, as belonging to the principal person in the island, he was put into a separate house for several weeks which was *tabooed;* that is to say, it was forbidden to every body, except those who were exempted from the *taboo* by his father, to approach the house. . . . In the first year only the ground-work of the principal figures upon the breast, arms, back, and thighs, is laid; and in doing this, the first punctures must be entirely healed, and the crust must have come off before new ones are made. Every single mark takes three or four days to heal; and the first *sitting,* as it may be called, commonly lasts three or four weeks.

While the patient is going through the operation, he must drink very little, for fear of creating too much inflamation, and he is not allowed to eat early in the morning, only at noon and in the evening. . . .

The tattooing of persons in a middling station is performed in houses erected for the purpose by the tattooers, and *tabooed* by authority. A tattooer, who visited us several times on board the ship, had three of these houses, which could each receive eight or ten persons at a time. . . . The poorer islanders, who have not a superabundance of hogs to dispose of in luxuries, but live chiefly themselves upon breadfruit, are operated upon by novices in the art, who take them at a very low price as subjects for practice, but their works are easily distinguishable, even by a stranger, from those of an experienced artist.[75]

Thus Langsdorff parallels Melville not only in subject matter and even in specific phraseology, but also in half-a-dozen instances of identical misinformation. No better proof could be found of borrowing by one author from another than such a similarity of erroneous matter. It would certainly be a strange coincidence if two different interpreters, separated by the entire length of the archipelago, should have made exactly the same errors and exaggerations in giving their respective accounts of tattooing to Langsdorff and Melville, forty years apart. Even W. C. Handy, who was not concerned with literary influences, takes occasion to point out this resemblance while discussing a final instance of error made by both authors:

A special effort was made to find some trace of banqueting societies distinguished by marks tattooed on the chest, which Krusenstern, Langsdorff, and Melville describe; but no memory of anything in the nature of such fraternal orders supported by the chief and tattooed gratis is discovered today. . . . Indeed, Melville relates the "Hannamanoo" episode as an especial and unusual case; and it does not seem unlikely that the same story is at the basis of both his and the Russian's accounts.

In a footnote is added, more specifically, "It would not surprise me in the least if Melville made up his story of the 'Hannamanoo' episode after having read Langsdorff or Krusenstern." [76] Melville's entire account of the art of tattooing among the Marquesans is, indeed, an illuminating example of his method of composition.

The communal industry of house-building has already been discussed, as an example of the unanimity of spirit with which the Marquesans worked. (The erection by the *ka'ioi* of special houses for tattooing is a case in point.) Melville's description of the houses themselves, which is accurate enough, could have been drawn from any of half-a-dozen different sources, for all of the early visitors gave detailed information regarding their construction. [77] But it was in the stone platforms, or *pæ-pæ*, which formed the foundations for their houses and sacred places, that the natives left the most remarkable monuments to their industry and activity as group-builders. Those which served as burying grounds, *me'æ*, secluded in the depths of valleys or on mountain tops, were by far the most unusual in size and structure. Melville describes in detail one which he discovered at the head of Typee Valley, reminding him in its immense proportions and apparent antiquity of Stonehenge:

At the base of one of the mountains, and surrounded on all sides by dense groves, a series of vast terraces of stone rises, step by step, for a considerable distance up the hillside. These terraces cannot be less than one hundred yards in length and twenty in width. Their magnitude, however, is less striking than the immense size of the blocks composing them. Some of the stones, of an oblong shape, are from ten to fifteen feet in length, and five or six feet thick. Their sides are quite smooth, but though square, and of pretty regular formation, they bear no mark of the chisel. They are laid together without cement, and here and there show gaps between. The topmost terrace and the lower one are somewhat peculiar in their construction. They have both a quadrangular depression in the center, leaving the rest of the terrace elevated several feet above it.[78]

Melville was strangely unaware of the nature and uses of this remarkable monument of stone, remarking subsequently: "I never saw any of the ordinary signs of a place of sepulture in the valley." Moreover, he appears to have misunderstood the explanations of its origin that were given him by the natives, for he treated it as the work of an extinct and forgotten race:

These structures bear every indication of a very high antiquity, and Kory-Kory, who was my authority in all matters of scientific research, gave me to understand that they were coeval with the creation of the world; that the great gods themselves were the builders; and that they would endure until time shall be no more. Kory-Kory's prompt explanation, and his attributing the work to a divine origin, at once convinced me that neither he nor the rest of his countrymen knew anything about them.[79]

But Melville was of the opinion that all the stone-work in the valley was of such an ancient origin, even the smaller "pi-pis" (*pæ-pæ*) on which the houses were erected; especially did the "morais" (*me'æ*) or burying grounds, several of which were pointed out to him at Taiohaë, and the "hoolah-hoolah" (*tohua*) or festival grounds seem to him to bear incontestable marks of great age. Such structures, he says, were beyond the capabilities of the Marquesans that he knew:

Some of these piles are so extensive, and so great a degree of labour and skill must have been requisite in constructing them, that I can scarcely believe they were built by the ancestors of the present inhabitants. If indeed they were, the race has sadly deteriorated in their knowledge of the mechanic arts. To say nothing of their habitual indolence, by what contrivance within the reach of so simple a people could such enormous masses have been moved or fixed in their places? and how could they with their rude implements have chiselled and hammered them into shape? [80]

Melville was drawing unnecessarily on his imagination, however, in accounting for these massive stone platforms. Perhaps he actually misunderstood what the natives told him; perhaps it was simply more congenial to his romantic attitude to conjure up a race of Marquesan master builders coeval with those of ancient Egypt. However this may be, Ralph Linton, the archeologist of the Bayard Dominick Expedition in 1920, was thoroughly convinced that the ancestors of the present natives were the builders, and that the *pæ-pæ* were not of ancient date:

> The Marquesans possessed a surprising skill in stone construction. . . . The visitor is amazed by the extent of their ceremonial structures, the size of the stones used, and the skill with which they have been placed and fitted. . . .
> Many of the stones in ceremonial structures, and even in the dwelling platforms of chiefs and important persons, are of surprising size and weight [from three to ten tons]. To transport and place such masses of rock was an engineering feat of no mean order. . . . [But] I had many opportunities to observe the skill with which the natives use levers . . . , and I believe that any of the rough stone structures now in existence in the Marquesas could have been built by this method. The ancient builders had an abundance of labor, and time was no great object to them. It cannot be insisted too strongly that, in spite of the great extent of some of the sites and the huge size of the rocks used, there is no mystery as to the origin of the ruins found in the Marquesas. . . . Everything indicates that all the remains are the work of Polynesians who did not differ fundamentally from the present natives.[81]

The mortuary *me'æ*, he says, are almost all built on high ground and at some distance from the villages. On the island of Hivaoa they usually consisted of from two to eight terraces one behind another on a sloping hillside; and both at Taiohae and in Typee Valley he found several of considerable extent which followed this form. The early Catholic records listed thirty-two *me'æ* and fourteen *tohua* (festival places) in Typee Valley alone. Many of these Linton was unable to find, because the dozen natives left in the valley had forgotten about them; but his description of one of them, the *"me'æ* of Ahua,"* reads strikingly like the "prehistoric pi-pi" described by Melville.[82]

Of all the previous commentators that Melville may have consulted, Porter offers the most pertinent remarks on the communal industry of the Marquesans, and on their stone masonry in particular. His admiration of their coöperation in house-building has already been cited. In his account of their places of feasting, erected on platforms of large stones "neatly hewn and fitted together, with as much skill and exactness as could be done by our most expert masons," his astonishment is unfeigned:

Some of them are one hundred yards in length and forty yards in width, surrounded by a square of buildings executed in a style of elegance, which is calculated to inspire us with the most exalted opinion of the ingenuity, taste, and perseverance of a people, who have hitherto remained unnoticed and unknown to the rest of mankind. When we consider the vast labour requisite to bring from a distance the enormous rocks which form the foundation of these structures (for they are all brought from the sea side, and many of them are eight feet long and four feet thick and wide) and reflect on the means used in hewing them into such perfect forms, with tools perhaps little harder than the materials worked on, for the appearance of many of these places strongly mark[s] their antiquity, and their origin can no doubt be traced to a period antecedant [*sic*] to their knowledge of iron, and when we count the immense numbers of such places which are every where to be met with, our astonishment is raised to the highest, that a people in a state of nature, unassisted by any of those artificial means which so much assist and facilitate the. labour of the civilized man, could have conceived and executed a work which, to every beholder, must appear stupendous.[83]

Another circumstance which points out Porter as Melville's most likely source in the discussion of these monumental stone platforms is the fact that they are the only two who give the name of these structures as "morai," instead of the more correct form *me'æ*.[84] It never occurred to Porter, however, to attribute these enormous piles to another and superior race of people, for with his own eyes he had seen the Marquesans accomplish a prodigy of labor in raising one of his heavy guns, a six-pounder, to the top of a high and precipitous mountain.

Early writers made little if any distinction between the two types of tribal sacred places: the secluded ones such as Melville describes and the feasting places such as Porter describes. Indeed, there was little difference save in the uses to which they were put—the former being used chiefly as places of sepulture, although Melville was unaware of this, and the latter being used primarily for ceremonial rites performed at the festival places, of which they were a part. Both consisted of a central stone platform of quadrangular shape and usually of considerable size, surrounded by numerous more or less temporary structures; both were in the midst of a sacred grove; and both were rigidly *tapu,* especially to women. One of these festival places (*tohua*), of elaborate proportions, is the scene of much of *Typee,* and Melville describes it early in his narrative. Situated in the midst of the "Taboo groves" of the valley, he says, it was strictly *tapu* to women:

In the midst of the wood was the hallowed "hoolah-hoolah" ground— set apart for the celebration of the fantastical religious ritual of these people—comprising an extensive oblong pi-pi, terminating at either end in a lofty terraced altar, guarded by ranks of hideous wooden idols, and with the two remaining sides flanked by ranges of bamboo sheds, opening toward the interior of the quadrangle thus formed.[85]

Melville's description, elaborated at some length and verified by the best modern authority, is fuller than any single previous account, but it might easily have been compounded of Porter's and Stewart's accounts. Porter, in fact, saw the very *tohua* that Melville describes under the unique name of the "hoolah-hoolah" ground; during his war with the Typees he came upon what he says deserved to be called their "capital," almost at the head of their valley: "The beauty and regularity of this place was such, as to strike every spectator with astonishment, and their grand scite [*sic*], or public square, was far superior to any other we had met with." [86] It is unfortunate that he left no fuller account of this particular festival place, for he was apparently the only one of the early visitors besides Melville who saw it.

One of the most interesting adjuncts of the *tohua* was the warriors' *tapu* house, which was a part of the chief's establishment and as such was near his house and consequently near the festival place. It served as a gathering place for the men during peace times, but its main function was as an eating and sleeping place during the times of *tapu*, when all association with women was absolutely forbidden. Handy says that although he was never able to discover any generic name for this house, he found many that had particular names, such as the one in Typee Valley that Melville calls the "Ti." Melville, to be sure, was somewhat bewildered as to the nature of this building at which he spent so much of his time—he refers to it variously as the chief's "palace" and as a sort of "Bachelors' Hall," where the warriors gathered to eat, sleep, and talk over their affairs —but his description seems to be accurate and apparently drawn from his own observation:

In . . . [the vicinity of the hoolah-hoolah ground] was another remarkable edifice, built as usual upon the summit of a pi-pi, and at least two hundred feet in length, though not more than twenty in breadth. The whole front of this latter structure was completely open, and from one end to the other ran a narrow verandah fenced in on the edge of the pi-pi with a picket of canes. Its interior presented the appearance of an immense lounging-place, the entire floor being strewn with successive layers of mats, lying between parallel trunks of cocoanut trees, selected for the purpose from the straightest and most symmetrical the vale afforded.

To this building, denominated in the language of the natives the "Ti," . . . the merciless prohibitions of the taboo extended likewise, . . . and were enforced by the same dreadful penalty that secured the hoolah-hoolah ground from the imaginary pollution of a woman's presence.[87]

Langsdorff seems to have recognized the existence of these public *tapu* houses for men, but F. D. Bennett is the only visitor prior to Melville who left a description of them, two of which he saw on Santa Christina:

They are in the form of a shed, open on three sides, based upon a stone platform, and fenced, in front, either with poles or rails. . . . The largest is a lofty shed, fifty feet in length, and raised upon a stone platform about six feet high; its interior, and the posts which support the thatched roof, are decorated with red and black cinnet, and with long pennants of white cloth. . . . Women are forbidden to enter them under the severest penalties.[88]

Though these structures are of smaller dimensions, they tally in general with that of Melville. Moreover, in view of E. S. C. Handy's statement that the *tapu* houses had only local names, it is surprising to read the following account of one discovered by E. H. Lamont on the island of La Dominica (Hivaoa) in 1852:

[This] I subsequently learned was the "Tai," a kind of assembly-house, where a number of the warriors of the bay were now congregated. . . . The house, I learned, was set apart as a kind of gentleman's club, which by law, it was death for a woman's foot to desecrate.[89]

This furnishes an unexpected confirmation of Melville's "Ti," but of course he could not have seen it before the publication of *Typee;* yet Bennett's account he might have seen, though the evidence for this is slight.

The "hoolah-hoolah" ground, and the "Ti" in particular, is the scene of an elaborate festival, denominated by Melville "The Feast of the Calabashes," which occupies a central position in *Typee,* since it was the occasion that enabled him to gather his most important information relative to Marquesan life. From his observations during this three-day festival, Melville draws his most elaborate descriptions of the physical appearance of the Marquesans, their methods of preparing food, the nature of their civic and social relations, and, most important of all, their complex and incomprehensible religious system. The nature of the celebration itself remained somewhat of an enigma to him, but his full and detailed account of it is none the less interesting. The first day consisted principally of feasting:

The whole population of the valley seemed to be gathered within the precincts of the grove. In the distance could be seen the long front of

the Ti, its immense piazza swarming with men, arrayed in every variety
of fantastic costume, and all vociferating with animated gestures; while
the whole interval between it and the place where I stood was enlivened by groups of females fancifully decorated, dancing, capering, and
uttering wild exclamations. . . .

So soon as I mounted to the pi-pi I saw at a glance that the revels
were fairly under way. . . . All along the piazza of the Ti were arranged elaborately-carved canoe-shaped vessels, some twenty feet in
length, filled with newly-made poee-poee . . . ; hanging from the
branches of [trees], and screened from the sun by their foliage, were
innumerable little packages with leafy coverings, containing the meat
of the numerous hogs which had been slain, done up in this manner to
make it more accessible to the crowd. . . .

The banquet being thus spread, naught remained but for everyone
to help himself at his pleasure.[90]

The second and third days of the festival were given over to more
noisy celebration. In the Taboo groves were bands of young girls in
gala costumes of flowers, shouting and dancing. But what particularly attracted his attention there was "four or five old women, who
in a state of utter nudity, with their arms extended flatly down their
sides and holding themselves perfectly erect, were leaping stiffly
into the air . . . without a single moment's cessation." Kory-Kory
endeavored to explain this phenomenon to him: "But all I could
comprehend from what he said was, that the leaping figures before
me were bereaved widows, whose partners had been slain in battle
many moons previously; and who, at every festival, gave public evidence in this manner of their calamities." [91] It was in the spacious
quadrangle of the hoolah-hoolah ground, however, that the largest
concourse of people were assembled:

[Here] were arranged two parallel rows of cumbersome drums, standing at least fifteen feet in height, and formed from the hollow trunks
of large trees. Their heads were covered with shark skins, and their
barrels were elaborately carved with various quaint figures and devices.
. . . Behind these instruments were built slight platforms, upon which
stood a number of young men, who, beating violently with the palms
of their hands upon the drum-heads, produced those outrageous sounds
which had awakened me in the morning. . . .

Another most striking feature of the performance was exhibited by a score of old men, who . . . kept up an uninterrupted monotonous chant, which was nearly drowned in the roar of drums. . . .

But no attention whatever seemed to be paid to the drummers or to the old priests, the individuals who composed the vast crowd present being entirely taken up in chatting and laughing with one another, smoking, drinking arva, and eating. . . . All that day the drums resounded, the priests chanted, and the multitude feasted and roared till sunset, when the throng dispersed, and the Taboo groves were again abandoned to quiet and repose. The next day the same scene was repeated until night, when this singular festival terminated.[92]

None of the earlier visitors furnishes an account of a Marquesan festival that alone could have supplied Melville with the multitudinous details that embellish his description of the Feast of the Calabashes. Porter, one of the most circumstantial of the travel writers, unfortunately makes no mention whatsoever of such an occasion. Stewart, however, attended a dance in the Hapa Valley which may have furnished some suggestions. The assembly, he says, consisted of several hundred persons in their most gala and fanciful costumes; the *tohua,* or dance area, was a paved rectangle, about sixty feet by forty feet. But the performance was a much more orderly and elaborate one than Melville describes: a long and intricate dance by a young chief, accompanied by the music of "four drums on each side of the inner pavement, and the voices and loud clapping of hands of about one hundred and fifty singers." [93] Public exhibitions of this sort occurred on a great variety of occasions, he adds, but the most important was that celebrating the breadfruit harvests; unfortunately, however, he does not describe one of these. I am inclined to believe that Melville's Feast of the Calabashes was such a harvest festival (*ko'ina tapavau*). E. S. C. Handy—who, on the contrary, treats it as a memorial or funerary festival (*ko'ina tupapa'u*)—says that these feasts celebrating an abundant breadfruit harvest sometimes came in August, the very month of Melville's residence.[94] Bennett, whose description of the warriors' *tapu* house so closely resembles that of the "Ti," gives an account of them which more than suggests the Feast of the Calabashes:

About the time of the bread-fruit harvest, . . . the chiefs of this island give, each in his turn, entertainments to which the people of the adjacent valleys are invited. They are attended with much noisy festivity; feasting, dancing, and singing being continued, with but little inter- mission, for several successive days. The number of hogs killed on these occasions is immense; and troughs, eighteen feet long, and propor- tionately broad, filled with bread-fruit *poë*, are placed in the public banqueting-halls for the entertainment of the guests.[95]

Langsdorff supplements this with a much fuller account of the harvest festival:

In days of plenty, these gay people have a variety of amusements of different kinds. At the time of the year when the bread-fruit is ripe, so that there is great abundance of it, the chiefs and principal people of the valley make popular festivals: for this purpose they collect swine, cocoa-nuts, bananas, and many kinds of roots, so as to feast the people for some time. The principal of these assemblies are the dancing fes- tivals. . . .

At these balls, the company appear dressed in all their most costly ornaments. . . . Cabri [the interpreter] assured us. that only those girls, wives, and widows danced, whose husbands or lovers had been taken prisoners or conquered in combat, and that on these occasions they cut their skins with little stones, considering the dancing as a token of trouble and sorrow. When we consider that they are obliged to ap- pear naked, contrary to the usual custom, and that they are made ob- jects of sport and mockery to the people, it does indeed appear very probable that the dancing is imposed upon them as a sort of penance.

The place in which the company dance is in the most level part of the valley: it is paved with large broad flat stones, put together so close and even, that one could almost believe it to be done by an European workman: the place is seldom less than a hundred fathom long, and is tabooed. . . .

The music at these festivals consists of a wild sort of cry, and the beating of several drums, some of them very large. They have the form of an upright cylinder or cask, and are four feet, or four feet and a half high, with a diameter of a foot and a half or two feet; over the top is stretched the skin of a shark: the workmanship is extremely neat. The place where the music is ranged, I have already observed, is tabooed to the women.[96]

From such accounts Melville could have compounded at least the nucleus of his Feast of the Calabashes, though the unprecedented fullness of his description of this festival is one of the best pieces of evidence available to prove that he actually resided in the Marquesas Islands and sometimes wrote almost exclusively from his own observations.[97]

Just what prompted E. S. C. Handy to classify the Feast of the Calabashes as a funerary festival is not made clear; indeed, he similarly classifies the feast just quoted from Langsdorff, although the latter specifically calls it a harvest festival. Moreover, both Melville's and Langsdorff's descriptions more nearly fit Father Gracia's account of the ko'ina tapavau ("la fête de l'abondance ou de la grande récolte d'automne, au mois du juin pour eux"), cited by Handy as an accurate account of the harvest festival, than they do the typical funerary festival under which he describes them.[98] But all of their festivals had much in common, and without more specific information it is hard to say dogmatically just what was the nature of the feast described in *Typee*. Melville himself is the first to confess his bewilderment in this matter:

> Although I had been baffled in my attempts to learn the origin of the Feast of the Calabashes, yet it seemed very plain to me that it was principally, if not wholly, of a religious character. . . . In commemoration of what event, however, or in honour of what distinguished personage, the feast was . . . given, altogether passed my comprehension. Mehevi sought to enlighten my ignorance, but he failed as signally as when he had endeavoured to initiate me into the perplexing arcana of the taboo.[99]

In the preface to *Typee* Melville gives advance notice that in describing the unusual customs of the Marquesans he has refrained from entering into explanations concerning their origins and purposes, justifying such omissions by reason of the peculiar circumstances under which he lived among them. This apology applies particularly to his account of all matters that were connected, directly or indirectly, with their religious system. Indeed, considering the brevity of his residence, unacquainted as he was with the language and unaided by an interpreter, his reports seem incredibly full and accurate, until it is discovered that they were largely drawn from those of previous visitors. Such is the case with his account of the perplexing and complex system of *tapu*, which, enjoying the authority of a religious institution, apparently regulated the minutest as well as the most important transactions of their lives. For, although his list of the persons, things, and situations to which it applied is perhaps more complete than that of any single one of his predecessors, the shortcoming of his account of the system is precisely theirs: an inability to explain its origin or purposes.

A score of the specific operations of the *tapu* are described by Melville, all of which are confirmed by the most authoritative modern ethnologist of the Marquesas Islands; practically all of this information, however, he could have gleaned from the volumes of Langsdorff, Porter, and Stewart alone.[100] But he had the wisdom to pass by the pat and often facetious explanations suggested by these authors, remarking unpretentiously that he did not in the least comprehend the system.[101] Nor was Melville alone in his bewilderment. Not only were the other contemporary visitors equally bewildered, but the best modern scientific observers have had difficulty even in describing the mere facts of the system. As for the difficulty of arriving at the ultimate meaning of the institution of *tapu*, its origin and purposes, one need only imagine a complete stranger to Western civilization trying to explain its property system without any understanding of mortgages, land registry, money, and banking. For, contrary to popular notions, primitive cultures are anything but simple. The very perplexity just confessed by Melville—the apparently capricious operation of various *tapus*, the diversity of people affected by them, and the different authorities who imposed them—was occasioned by the actual complexity of the system and the variety of functions it performed. For example, any man could protect his private property by making it *tapu* himself; chiefs could lay temporary restrictions (*kahui*) on property belonging to others, especially on foods in preparation for great festivals; whereas most of the more widespread seasonal and ceremonial *tapus* had to be laid by the priests. Some of these last were also utilitarian, but others were based upon beliefs which, to the Western mind, can be described only as superstitious, such as the sacredness of the head and the contaminating power of blood.

In illustration of these more widespread and seemingly irrational *tapus*, Melville cites the law "which forbids a female to enter a canoe—a prohibition which prevails upon all the northern Marquesas Islands." [102] Stewart confirms this as being true at Nukahiva (remarking that he did not find any such restriction at other Pacific groups), whereas Coulter adds that the prohibition extended to the islands in the southern Marquesas also.[103] Moreover, E. S. C. Handy explains this as part of the general *tapu* of uncleanness which centered about woman as a reproducer, arising out of the polluting power of blood—the menstrual blood and blood at delivery.[104] So widespread, rigid, and tenacious was this prohibition that a mild attempt to preserve it survives even today, more than half a century after all other *tapus* have been discarded.[105] Hence, it is obvious that Melville was romancing with a high-handed disregard for truth when he wrote his piquant episode of canoeing with Fayaway, who had been granted a special dispensation by the priests as a result of Melville's eloquent persuasion.[106] It is such passages as this, indeed, which even for the general reader have thrown doubt on the truthfulness of the entire fabric of Melville's narrative.

Most of Melville's deviations from the truth in his discussions of the Marquesan religious system, however, come not from his deliberate inventions, but from his own mistaken observations or from his reliance upon the very authorities whom he disparages because of their small opportunity for becoming acquainted with the customs they describe. Sir James George Frazer recognized the untrustworthiness of Melville's narrative in this respect, remarking in his chapter on Marquesan religious beliefs: "His personal observations are valuable, but as he did not master the native language, he was not able to throw much light on the inner life of the people, and in particular on their religious ideas"; yet he quotes *Typee* with approval more than a score of times. Moreover, Robert Wood Williamson accepts Melville as an authority without even a nominal qualification. Fortunately, a reliable check on Melville's accuracy is furnished by E. S. Craighill Handy, whose study, confined to the Marquesas and based on information unknown to other ethnologists, deals more critically with all its source materials.[107] Melville was the first to confess his lack of any real understanding of the theology of the Typees; [108] but this handicap did not deter him from describing at length the outward manifestations of their religion. In his accounts of the native gods and the food sacrifices laid before them he was particularly accurate; [109] but these may be traced to their obvious sources in the similar accounts of Porter and Stewart, respectively.[110]

In discussing the priests of Typee, however, he was not so felicitous. For, on the very second day of his residence, Melville came in close personal contact with one of the highest priests of the valley without being in the least aware of his official rank. But Melville's description identifies him beyond question as an inspirational priest (*tau'a hiko etua*).[111] This powerful dignitary, whom Melville mistook for a mere leech, was called in to examine his injured leg; and the treatment which he administered is then described in an amusing scene, the meaning of which Melville failed to comprehend:

After diligently observing the ailing member, he commenced manipulating it; . . . he fastened on the unfortunate limb as if it were something for which he had been long seeking, and muttering some kind of incantation continued his discipline, pounding it after a fashion that set me well-nigh crazy. . . . My physician, having recovered from the fatigues of his exertions, as if anxious to make amends for the pain to which he had subjected me, now took some herbs out of a little wallet that was suspended from his waist, and moistening them in water, applied them to the inflamed part, stooping over it at the same time, and either whispering a spell, or having a little confidential chat with some imaginary demon located in the calf of my leg.[112]

This method of healing sickness by exorcism is rightly described by Stewart as being practised solely by the *tau'a*, or inspirational priest:

The Tauas alone act the part of physicians. Every internal disorder is believed to be inflicted by some god—who has taken possession of the person for that purpose . . . ; and the Tauas, being inspired, are applied to, as alone capable of contending with the evil. When sent for by a sick person, their practice principally consists in feeling for the mischievous deity, and in smothering him when found, by rubbing him between the palms of their hands! [113]

But apparently Melville overlooked this account of the Marquesan practice of the healing art, unless one assumes that he deliberately rejected Stewart's explanation of its religious character. Rather, such passages in *Typee*—blindly describing only half-understood customs when explanations were readily available in the travel books which he consulted—furnish strong evidence that Melville sometimes wrote solely from his own limited observations.

One of the next order, the ceremonial priests (*tuhuna o'ono*), Melville did recognize, partially by the prominent part he took in the Feast of the Calabashes, but "above all, [by] the mitre he frequently wore, in the shape of a towering head-dress, consisting of part of a cocoa-nut branch, the stalk planted uprightly on his brow, and the leaflets gathered together and passed round the temples and behind the ears." But this description he might well have taken from Stewart: "The Tahunas [*sic*] have a distinctive dress, consisting of a cap formed from a cocoanut leaf. A part of the stem, six or eight inches in length, is placed perpendicularly over the forehead, and the leaflets still attached to it are passed round the head on each side, and neatly fastened together behind." [114] This suspicion receives confirmation from the fact that Stewart apparently also furnished the cue for the strange religious rite which Melville then describes, with the ceremonial priest, "Kolory," as the chief actor:

His . . . grace very often carried about with him what seemed to me the half of a broken war-club. It was swathed round with ragged bits of white tappa, and the upper part, which was intended to represent a human head, was embellished with a strip of scarlet cloth of European manufacture. It required little observation to discover that this strange object was revered as a god. . . . In fact, this funny little image was the "crack" god of the island; lording it over all the wooden lubbers who looked so grim and dreadful; its name was Moa Artua. And it was in honour of Moa Artua, and for the entertainment of those who believe in him, that the curious ceremony I am about to describe was observed. . . . The priest comes along dangling his charge as if it were a lacrymose infant he was endeavouring to put in a good humour. Presently, entering the Ti, he seats himself on the mats as composedly as a juggler about to perform his sleight-of-hand tricks; and, with the chiefs disposed in a circle around him, commences his ceremony.

In the first place he gives Moa Artua an affectionate hug, then caressingly lays him to his breast, and, finally, whispers something in his ear, the rest of the company listening eagerly for a reply. But the baby-god is deaf or dumb—perhaps both, for never a word does he utter. At last Kolory speaks a little louder, and soon growing angry, comes boldly out with what he has to say, and bawls to him. He put me in mind of a choleric fellow, who, after trying in vain to communicate a secret to a deaf man, all at once flies into a passion and screams it out so that everyone may hear. Still Moa Artua remains as quiet as ever, and Kolory, seemingly losing his temper, fetches him a box over the head, strips him of his tappa and red cloth, and, laying him in a state of nudity in a little trough, covers him from sight. At this proceeding all present loudly applaud, and signify their approval by uttering the adjective "mortarkee" [good] with violent emphasis. Kolory, how-ever, is so desirous his conduct should meet with unqualified approba-tion, that he inquires of each individual separately whether, under existing circumstances, he has not done perfectly right in shutting up Moa Artua. The invariable response is "Aa, Aa" (yes, yes), repeated over again and again in a manner which ought to quiet the scruples of the most conscientious. After a few moments Kolory brings forth his doll again, and, while arraying it very carefully in the tappa and red cloth, alternately fondles and chides it. The toilet being completed, he once more speaks to it aloud. The whole company hereupon show the greatest interest; while the priest, holding Moa Artua to his ear, interprets to them what he pretends the god is confidentially com-municating to him. Some items of intelligence appear to tickle all pres-ent amazingly; for one claps his hands in a rapture; another shouts with merriment; and a third leaps to his feet and capers about like a madman.

What under the sun Moa Artua on these occasions had to say to Kolory I never could find out. . . . At any rate, whatever, as coming from the god, was imparted to those present, seemed to be generally of a complimentary nature—a fact which illustrates the sagacity of Kolory, or else the time-serving disposition of this hardly used deity.

Moa Artua having nothing more to say, his bearer goes to nursing him again, in which occupation, however, he is soon interrupted by a question put by one of the warriors to the god. Kolory hereupon snatches it up to his ear again, and after listening attentively, once more officiates as the organ of communication. A multitude of ques-tions and answers having passed between the parties, much to the satis-faction of those who propose them, the god is put tenderly to bed in the trough, and the whole company unite in a long chant, led off by Kolory. This ended, the ceremony is over; the chiefs rise to their feet in high good-humour, and my Lord Archbishop, after chatting a while, and regaling himself with a whiff or two from a pipe of tobacco, tucks the canoe under his arm and marches off with it.

The whole of these proceedings were like those of a parcel of children playing with dolls and baby-houses.[115]

Yet this abused and priest-ridden little baby god, says Melville, was the tutelary deity of Typee. And Kory-Kory once informed him that it would be the easiest thing in the world for Moa Artua "to take the whole island of Nukuheva in his mouth, and dive down to the bottom of the sea with it."

Stewart's account of such a ceremony is very brief, but sufficient to have suggested Melville's much longer and fuller description:

But to return to the Tahunas [*sic*], or priests, and their ceremonies. Sometimes a bundle, which is called the "clothed god"—consisting of a wooden log, wrapped in cloth, with four conch shells fastened upon it—is lifted up and carefully laid down again by the priests; all the people standing and making responses to an unintelligible jargon, during its elevation.[116]

It was undoubtedly from Captain David Porter, however, that Melville took most of the details for his elaborate and almost incredible account of this religious ritual—in spite of his flat denial of any acquaintance with the former's volume. Porter's account follows:

[They informed me] that I had not yet seen their greatest of all gods . . . ; and on my expressing a desire to see him, after a short consultation among themselves, they brought him out on the branch of the cocoa-nut tree, when I was surprised to find him only a parcel of paper cloth secured to a piece of a spear about four feet long; it in some measure resembled a child in swaddling cloths, and the part intended to represent the head had a number of strips of cloth hanging from it about a foot in length; I could not help laughing at the ridiculous appearance of the god they worshipped, in which they all joined me with a great deal of good humour, some of them dandling and nursing the god, as a child would her doll. They now asked me if I should like to see some of their religious ceremonies, and on my answering in the affirmative, they seated themselves in a ring, and placed the god, with the cocoa-nut branch under him, on the ground; one of them stood in the circle before the god, and as soon as the others began to sing and clap their hands, he fell to dancing with all his might, cutting a number of antic capers, then picking up the god, and whirling it over his shoulders several times, laid it down again, when a pause ensued: they now began another song, when the dancer, with no less violence than before, after whirling the god about, carried it out of the circle and laid it down on the ground: then shifted it from place to place, and afterwards returned it to the cocoa-nut branch within the circle. After a short pause the dancer asked the singers several questions with great earnestness, and on their all answering in the affirmative, he took up the god on the branch and deposited it in the house. I inquired of Wilson [the interpreter] the purport of the song, he told me they were singing the praises of their god; but this was all he could tell me. The inquiries of the dancer were whether this was not the greatest of all gods, whether they were not bound to sacrifice their lives to preserve him, and whether, if they should lose him, there would not be an end of their race. . . . Their religion, however, is like a plaything, an amusement to them, and I very much doubt whether they, at any moment, give it a serious thought; their priests and jugglers manage those matters for them; what they tell them they believe, and do not put themselves to the trouble of considering whether it is right or wrong. . . .

In religion these people are mere children; their morais are their babyhouses, and their gods are their dolls.[117]

E. S. C. Handy, however, found no evidence for such a ritual in the Marquesan religious system. He is extremely doubtful that portable images were ever used in public ceremonial. More specifically, he declares: "Melville's description of the priest of Tai-pi consulting a small roughly carved image wrapped in cloth is of questionable authenticity." [118] If this conclusion is accepted, the probability of Melville's literary indebtedness for this scene is almost beyond question, for it is far more likely that he and Stewart simply repeated Porter's error than that all three reported independently a custom which did not exist. Porter's original mistake resulted, perhaps, from his reliance on an ignorant interpreter. In any case, the resemblance of Melville to Porter in this, and in several other matters pertaining to religion, is too striking to be coincidental. But Melville always improved upon his original.

He is evidently again merely echoing Porter, for example, when he comments on the indifference and even the irreverence of the Marquesans to their religion. Walking through the "Taboo Groves" with his companion one day, Melville came upon a wooden image about six feet high, bruised and battered and partially rotted away:

I drew near to inspect more closely this strange object of idolatry, but halted reverently at the distance of two or three paces, out of regard to the religious prejudices of my valet. As soon, however, as Kory-Kory perceived that I was in one of my inquiring, scientific moods, to my astonishment he sprang to the side of the idol, and pushing it away from the stones against which it rested, endeavoured to make it stand upon its legs. But the divinity had lost the use of them altogether; and while Kory-Kory was trying to prop it up, by placing a stick between it and the pi-pi, the monster fell clumsily to the ground, and would infallibly have broken its neck had not Kory-Kory providentially broken its fall by receiving its whole weight on his own half-crushed back. I never saw the honest fellow in such a rage before. He leaped furiously to his feet, and, seizing the stick, began beating the poor image, every moment or two pausing and talking to it in the most violent manner, as if upbraiding it for the accident. When his indignation had subsided a little, he whirled the idol about most profanely, so as to give me an opportunity of examining it on all sides. I am quite sure I never should have presumed to have taken such liberties with the god myself, and I was not a little shocked at Kory-Kory's impiety.[119]

A cue for this all but incredible scene Melville evidently found in Porter's *Journal:*

Observing that they treated all their gods with little respect, frequently catching them by their large ears, drawing my attention to their wide mouths, their flat noses, and large eyes, and pointing out to me, by signs, all their other deformities, I told Wilson to inform them I thought they treated their gods very disrespectfully—they told me that those [the images] were like themselves, mere attendants on their divinity, as they were on the priest.[120]

It is Stewart, however, who furnished Melville with the most apt material for his anecdote illustrating this irreverence. On one of his strolls through the valley of Taiohaë, the chaplain stopped in front of a *tapu* house containing three large wooden images:

I commenced a sketch of them as they stood; which being perceived by one of the natives, he immediately without ceremony seized the two godships having their backs towards me, and whirled them over with as much carelessness and familiarity as I should myself, had I been disposed to make thus free with the objects of their superstition. I was somewhat surprised at the little veneration shown for the idols of their own worship, though not ignorant of the great inconsistency often discovered among the heathen in the grossness of the adulation of their gods at one time, and their disregard, and even abuse of them at another. I recollect to have heard, while living at the Sandwich Islands, of instances in which persons disappointed in their expectations and prayers, have not only scolded and upbraided, but actually beaten their images of wood and stone.[121]

Although Melville, just on the point of freeing himself from the religious tyranny of an overstrict Calvinism, indulges in none of the missionary's evangelical dreams of reclaiming a "back-slidden generation" of heathens—and even treats their "religious sloth" with levity, if not actual rejoicing—he certainly makes full use of Stewart's impressions that the Marquesan religion was in a state of decay.

Melville, indeed, never treats the pure paganism of the Marquesans forthrightly and in sober earnest. Sometimes his high-sounding but irreverent fooling gives place to a half-serious effort to embellish the superstitious practices of these primitives with the trappings of romance. Such is his description of the burial place of a chief—the ceremonies connected with death and with the ancestral cult being one of the central features of their religion:

On all sides, as you approached this silent spot, you caught sight of the dead chief's effigy, seated in the stern of a canoe, which was raised on a light frame a few inches above the level of the pi-pi. The canoe was about seven feet in length; of a rich, dark-coloured wood, handsomely carved, and adorned in many places with variegated bindings of stained sinnate, into which were ingeniously wrought a number of sparkling sea-shells, and a belt of the same shells ran all round it. The body of the figure—of whatever material it might have been made—was effectually concealed in a heavy robe of brown tappa, revealing only the hands and head; the latter skilfully carved in wood, and surmounted by a superb arch of plumes. These plumes, in the subdued and gentle gales which found access to this sequestered spot, were never for one moment at rest, but kept nodding and waving over the chief's brow. The long leaves of the palmetto dropped over the eaves, and through them you saw the warrior, holding his paddle with both hands in the act of rowing, leaning forward and inclining his head, as if eager to hurry on his voyage.

Glaring at him forever, and face to face, was a polished human skull, which crowned the prow of the canoe. The spectral figure-head, reversed in its position, glancing backward, seemed to mock the impatient attitude of the warrior.

When I first visited this singular place with Kory-Kory, he told me—or, at least, I so understood him—that the chief was paddling his way to the realms of bliss and bread-fruit—the Polynesian heaven—where every moment the bread-fruit trees dropped their ripened spheres to the ground, and where there was no end to the cocoa-nuts and bananas; there they reposed through the live-long eternity upon mats much finer than those of Typee; and every day bathed their glowing limbs in rivers of cocoa-nut oil. In that happy land there were plenty of plumes and feathers, and boars' tusks and sperm-whale teeth, far preferable to all the shining trinkets and gay tappa of the white men; and, best of all, women, far lovelier than the daughters of earth, were there in abundance. "A very pleasant place," Kory-Kory said it was; "but, after all, not much pleasanter, he thought, than Typee." [122]

It was to Porter rather than to Stewart that Melville turned for information in the composition of his more romantic passages, as here:

On the right of this grove, distant only a few paces, were four splendid war canoes, furnished with their outriggers and decorated with ornaments of human hair, coral shells, &c. with an abundance of white streamers; their heads were placed toward the mountain, and in the stern of each was a figure of a man with a paddle steering, in full dress, ornamented with plumes, earings made to represent those formed of whales' teeth, and every other ornament of the fashion of the country. One of the canoes was more splendid than the others, and was situated nearer the grove. I inquired who the dignified personage might be who was seated in her stern, and was informed that this was the priest who had been killed, not long since by the Happahs [Hapas]. The stench here was intolerable from the number of offerings which had been made, but; attracted by curiosity, I went to examine the canoes more minutely, and found the bodies of two of the Typees, whom we had killed, in a bloated state lying in the bottom of that of the priest, and many other human carcases, with the flesh still on them, lying about the canoe. The other canoes, they informed me, belonged to different warriors who had been killed, or died not long since. I asked them why they had placed their effigies in the canoes, and also why they put the bodies of the dead Typees in that of the priest; they told me (as Wilson interpreted) that they were going to heaven, and that it was impossible to get there without canoes. . . . I endeavoured to ascertain whether they had an idea of a future state, rewards and punishments, and the nature of their heaven. As respects the latter article, they believed it to be an island, somewhere in the sky, abounding with everything desirable; that those killed in war and carried off by their friends go there, provided they are furnished with a canoe and provisions, but that those who are carried off by the enemy, never reach it unless a sufficient number of the enemy can be obtained to paddle his canoe there, and for this reason they were so anxious to procure a crew for their priest, who was killed and carried off by the Happahs. They have neither rewards nor punishments in this world, and I could not learn that they expected any in the next.[123]

But even Porter, at times, was not romantic enough to suit the needs of the author of *Typee,* who preferred to cover up the stench of human sacrifices—the procuring of victims for which brought about their internecine feuds, upon the death of chiefs and priests—and, instead, to apostrophize the departed warrior with sentimental eloquence.[124]

Thus, according to the record of *Typee,* the Marquesan savage was no less noble in death than in life, and no less happy. Yet, though his heaven was a challenge to the paradise of the Mahometan, he was in no hurry to leave the bliss that he found more ready to hand in his earthly paradise. The canker in his flower was of another sort, and it was of recent and exotic origin. Even as Melville landed at Nukahiva, civilization was making its first raid on this unspoiled Happy Valley under the auspices of the French expedition. So it was that *Typee* came to be the first chapter in Melville's brief against civilization, the first book in a trilogy of which *Omoo* and *White-Jacket* are the logical and chronological sequels. The French had come at the behest of their missionaries—and their ambitious emperor—to save from eternal damnation these fine people whom the pious Mendana had so regretted leaving to be lost in their heathenism, two centuries before. To them Melville flings the challenge:

But the voluptuous Indian [sic], with every desire supplied, whom Providence has bountifully provided with all the sources of pure and natural enjoyment, and from whom are removed so many of the ills and pains of life—what has he to desire at the hands of civilisation? . . .

Ill-fated people! I shudder when I think of the change a few years will produce in their paradisiacal abode; and probably when the most destructive vices, and the worst attendances on civilisation, shall have driven all peace and happiness from the valley, the magnanimous French will proclaim to the world that the Marquesas Islands have been converted to Christianity! [125]

However, although *Typee* is liberally punctuated with disparagements of civilization, particularly the semicivilization of the Sandwich Islands, this affirmative side of Melville's attack is the especial thesis of *Omoo*.[126] *Typee*, on the other hand, is a wholehearted defense of the Noble Savage and a eulogy of his happy life, his external beauty, and his inward purity of heart. Virtually the whole book is written in the romantic literary tradition inaugurated by Rousseau a century before. But just how much Melville owed specifically to Rousseau in the composition of his first volume it is hard to say, for *Typee* contains only one explicit reference to him,[127] and there are no extant biographical facts which show an acquaintance with his writings prior to 1846. The only direct evidence of this sort throughout his entire life, so far discovered, is a single but pertinent reference in the journal that Melville kept during his trip to London in 1849, in which, under date of December 13, he records: "At last succeeded in getting the much desired copy of Rousseau's *Confessions*." [128] Although there is no external proof of any earlier acquaintance with the great apologist of the Noble Savage, the internal evidence of *Typee* suggests a long and ardent discipleship. It is this quality of romantic exaggeration, indeed, that has led many readers to suspect that in his first book Melville was not writing an altogether literal transcript of his travels.

CHAPTER VIII

TRUTH AND FICTION IN "TYPEE"

T HE controversy over the authenticity of *Typee,* and later of *Omoo,* has been a long and interesting one, marked by violent partisanship and still unsettled after almost a century. The problem is really a twofold one: How faithful was Melville to autobiographical fact? How reliable is his account of Marquesan life? Although the first of these questions cannot be answered even now as specifically as the biographer could wish, the question of ethnological accuracy can at last be determined with considerable definiteness. Before summing up the evidence of the preceding chapter, however, it seems pertinent to review briefly the history of this controversy.

As an appropriate prelude to the career of a persecuted genius, Melville's biographers have treated the immediate and undeniable success of his first two books as a mere *succès de scandale.* Taking the author's protestations too seriously, perhaps, they have pointed out that Melville himself threw down the glove to skeptical critics when he bowed himself out of the preface to the first edition of *Typee* "trusting that his anxious desire to speak the unvarnished truth will gain for him the confidence of his readers." [1] His first biographer then amplifies this author's affidavit: "When Melville's brother Gansevoort offered *Typee* for publication in England, it was accepted not as fiction but as ethnology, and was published as *Melville's Marquesas* only after Melville had vouched for its entire veracity." [2] But, he continues, both author's and publisher's guarantees were insufficient to establish it as fact: "Though Melville published *Typee* upright in the conviction that he had in its composition been loyal both to veracity and truth, his critics were not prone to take him at his word. . . . Both *Typee* and *Omoo* were

[179]

scouted as impertinent inventions, defying belief" and the reviewers were "scandalized by his boastful lechery." In proof of this assertion, a violent and even vituperative attack in the *American Review* is cited as typical, no other reviews being referred to.[3]

Carrying his thesis abroad, this same biographer declares: "Both
Typee and *Omoo* stirred up a whole regiment of critics, at home,
in England and in France. . . . In England, Melville was flattered . . . by vitriolic evangelistical damnation." [4] Documentary
evidence is then added in the form of a long quotation from a scandalized critic in the *Eclectic Review*. This hostile attack is cited as
typical of Melville's reception abroad: thus, laments his biographer, Melville "unloosed upon himself exhibitions of venom of the
whole-hearted sort that enamour a misanthrope to life." [5] This account of Melville's literary debut has been accepted without question by subsequent commentators.

Recent examination of the contemporary reviews, however, has
shown this to be quite the reverse of the truth, for Melville's critics
were not nearly so unanimous or so serious in their unbelief as this
widely accepted dictum would indicate. Such incredulity as manifested itself was largely prompted by the will to disbelieve on the
part of the sanctimonious few, who, scandalized by Melville's "voluptuousness" as well as by his uncomplimentary comments on the
missionaries in Polynesia, retaliated by accusing him of gross dishonesty in foisting off on the public a palpable fiction in the guise
of an authentic travel book. But such unbelievers formed a small,
if boisterous, minority.

Out of fifteen major American magazines that took cognizance
of Melville's debut, only two (besides the *American Review*) were
hostile to *Typee* and but one of these was hostile to *Omoo;* however,
these few did attack him roundly on all three scores: dishonesty, un-
founded abuse of the missionaries, and personal immorality. The
remaining twelve were all favorable to both works in general; and,
though a few of them were more or less noncommittal as to the truth
of one or the other as veracious travel books, seven were outspoken
in their opinion that *Typee* was authentic and ten were converted
upon the appearance of *Omoo*.[6] Examination of a similar number

of British magazines has shown an even smaller proportion of un-favorable reviews abroad. Indeed, the critic in the *Eclectic,* instead of being typical, was the only one who was hostile in his reaction to Melville's first two books. All the rest can be classed as favorable, for they unanimously testified in varying degrees of praise that *Typee* and *Omoo* were eminently readable, and they made no ob-jections to Melville's strictures on the missionaries or to his "im-morality." Even such doubts as they confessed were indirect com-pliments to the young author: first, his style is so cultivated and so free from provinciality that it could not possibly come from the pen of an ordinary seaman or from any American whatsoever; second, his books are so entertaining that they must be embel-lished autobiography if not an actual blending of fiction with fact.[7] Thus the only noticeable difference between Melville's reception in America and in England was just what one would expect, a differ-ence in tone: the former was heavy and patriotic in its praise; the latter, light and urbane. America was proud of Herman Melville; England enjoyed him. And her seasoned critics took his measure more accurately as a light-hearted raconteur of picaresque travel fiction, comparable to Defoe in *Robinson Crusoe.*

Similarly astute was the one contemporary French reviewer who followed with interest the controversy over the authenticity of Mel-ville's first two books. Though treating *Typee* as the record of an actual voyage, Philarète Chasles declared that the author was in-toxicated with the glamor of Polynesia and guilty of the same ro-mantic exaggeration that characterized all eulogists of the Noble Savage since Rousseau:

Malheureusement le style de M. Melville est si orné, ses teintes à la Rubens sont si vives et si chaudes, et il a tant de prédilection pour les effets dramatiques, que l'on ne sait pas exactement le degré de confiance que l'on doit lui accorder. Nous ne nous portons pas caution le moins du monde de ses descriptions efflorescentes; il est, comme tous les voyageurs, très enthousiaste de Noukahiva. Depuis les pages où le docteur Saaverde a décrit ces voluptueux parages, jusqu'aux récits aphrodisiaques de Bougainville et de Diderot, ces latitudes ont la propriété singulière d'échauffer la plume des voyageurs et de la tremper dans une encre composée par les fées. M. Melville a subi la même influence; il écrit comme tous ses prédécesseurs, à cette exception près que don Christoval Saaverde de Figueroa était plus mystique, c'est-à-dire plus homme de son temps; Cook plus simple, plus naïf et plus marin; Bougainville plus orné, plus dixhuitième siècle et plus raffiné dans ses peintures à la Vanloo; tandis que M. Melville, notre contemporain, hardi, violent et brusque, vise surtout à la terreur, à l'intérêt et à l'imprévu. C'est à lui, non à nous, de répondre de la fidélité complète des descriptions et des narrations que nous analyserons brièvement, et qui nous fourniront de curieux détails sur un recoin obscur de ces archipels à peine explorés.

Sans doute, il raconte des choses un peu romanesques et fait des peintures extraordinaires; mais la violence du coloris est bien naturelle chez un marin.[8]

Melville's attacks on the colonial policy of France, to which this reviewer called attention, would have been sufficient to provoke in return an attack on the absolute fidelity of *Typee* by any French critic. But the objection of Chasles seems to have been a purely literary one, directed against a school that was losing favor everywhere by the middle of the nineteenth century. Yet in spite of these reservations as to style, the reviewer was convinced of the authenticity of the details set forth in Melville's book.

In a second critique several years later, Chasles took up the controversy in earnest. Referring to his earlier voucher of the essential truth of *Typee,* he explained that an English journal had made sport of his credulity; and, believing himself to have been deceived, he did not reply.[9] Instead, having been advised that both *Typee* and *Omoo* were romances "qui attestent une vigoureuse puissance d'imagination et une grande hardiesse à mentir," he reread them both. But the result was that he was more convinced than ever of their authenticity: "Il y avait là un cachet de vérité, une saveur de nature inconnue et primitive, une vivacité d'impressions qui me frappaient. Les nuances me paraissaient réelles, bien qu'un peu chaudes et à l'effet; les aventures romanesques de l'auteur se déroulaient avec une vraisemblance suffisante." [10] But not caring to fly in the face of a critic who unhesitatingly treated the books as fiction, he contented himself with his own beliefs.

In the Pacific as well as in Europe *Typee* and *Omoo* attracted attention. Though at this early date there were no literary magazines published in the various island groups, there were two weekly newspapers at Honolulu, both of which noticed these new books on Polynesia. Since the only references made by Melville to the Sandwich Islands were disparaging in the extreme, it is only natural that his reception there would be unfavorable. Further, as is true of every hostile review of *Typee* and *Omoo*, special grounds for pique are readily discernible. The first of these weeklies, though bearing the ominous title of the *Temperance Advocate and Seamen's Friend*, dealt far less harshly with the castigator of Christendom than might have been expected. As early as October 15, 1846, the Reverend Samuel C. Damon, seamen's chaplain and editor of this missionary paper, commented rather pleasantly of *Typee:*

We hope that ere long, a copy of the work may find its way to our shores, for we have been led to entertain, by no means, an unfavorable opinion of the Sailor-Author's talents.

. . . That he possesses a talent for observation and description is very evident from such extracts as appear in the papers which have reached these Islands. We regret that the limits of our columns will not allow us to copy Melville's account of the Typee, a tribe of Marquesans. . . . The picture [however] is evidently overdrawn. It is too beautiful. . . . The whole population are in the full enjoyment, according to our author, of what Rousseau styles a "buoyant sense of healthful physical existence!" Which means, we suppose, that they more resemble animals than men, the brute than the human species.[11]

Some months later, when the book itself arrived, the Reverend Mr. Damon expressed his approval that it had been revised by omitting some of the "objectionable" passages, and even suggested a few more that might likewise be deleted. Yet in spite of this prudishness, his objections to the book and the author were certainly couched in restrained language:

On the islands of Polynesia, are scattered multitudes of young men from Europe and America, who are living in the same condition of Rosseau[sic]-society, and it only needs the pen of a Melville to make such a life worthy of praise!

It surely is not strange that such a man could find but little to praise and much to blame in the efforts of his missionary countrymen.[12]

Coming from the professional guardian of seamen's morals, this is certainly no more censure than one would expect; and even this is directed at the immorality of Melville's book rather than at its authenticity.

As for the second, since the despotism of the missionary monarchy at Honolulu had been a special target of Melville's criticism, it is not surprising to find that the *Polynesian,* the official organ of the Hawaiian government, was violently hostile to the young author. In an advance notice of *Typee,* the editor, the Reverend Charles E. Hitchcock, merely hinted his willingness to disbelieve: "A doubt has existed on the part of some reviewers, whether it is the genuine production of the reputed author." [13] And eighteen months later the same journal published a full and scathing criticism of both *Typee* and *Omoo:*

Blackwood in reviewing Mr. Melville's works, expresses doubts as to the author's identity with the common sailor, as well as misgivings respecting the truth of his entire adventures, but declares them "skilfully concocted Robinsonades, where fictitious incidents are ingeniously blended with genuine information." So far as *genuine information* is concerned, we think those acquainted with the incidents he pretends to narrate, differ entirely from the reviewer in Blackwood. That Mr. Melville did ship in a whale ship in 1838 [sic] there is no doubt; but that all the incidents which he relates as having befel him, are truthful narrations of facts, no one in this barbarous part of the world is inclined to believe. . . . We can state for the information of the reviewer in Blackwood, that we actually met the gentleman in New York a few evenings previous to our embarkation for this place in the spring of 1845. We have experienced pleasure in the perusal of Mr. Melville's writings, mingled we must confess with regret at his unblushing avowal of licentiousness and its kindred vices. Those who are at all familiar with the character of the South Sea islanders know what value to place upon his *truthful* description of the happy paradise in Typee Valley, his pure, lovely, and unsophisticated Fayaways and Kory-Korys. His kind greetings and affectionate *aloha's* [sic] are no more than are bestowed upon every run-away sailor who goes among them and pampers [panders?] to their depraved tastes.—The account of his intercourse with this degraded and licentious people, though in glowing terms, does not fail to convey to the mind the naked truth respecting his real principles and character. . . .

TRUTH AND FICTION IN "TYPEE"

Doubtless most of our readers have read Typee and Omoo. As works of fiction, written in a brilliant and captivating style, and abounding with graphic sketches of sea-faring life, Typee and Omoo are unequalled. The vividness of the forecastle revelations—the masterly picture of a whale ship fore and aft—the genial flow of humor and good nature, and the terse descriptions he gives of his wanderings through quiet valleys and leafy glens, are truly delightful. . . .

We are not disposed to detract from Mr. Melville's literary fame; but so far as he makes pretensions to accuracy as a historian, or claims for his writings credibility as truthful relations, we have something to say. . . . He would fain have his readers believe that the inhabitants of the valley of Typee are a race of pure and unsophisticated savages, knowing neither the galling fetters of law nor the odious distinctions of civilization. Those who have visited the islands in the Pacific know how to estimate his glowing descriptions of *innocent* social intercourse; and those who have not may glean some information from the records of Foreign Missions and the writings of more candid travelers. . . .

We have already extended our remarks upon Mr. Melville's works farther than we intended, and regarding his statements as we do, should never have alluded to them had it not been for the purpose of exposing the utter worthlessness of authority which some are disposed to quote in order to support their own declarations respecting Missionary operations in this part of the world. So far as authority in matters of history are [sic] concerned, Typee and Omoo are about as much to be relied upon as the writings of Baron Munchausen or the Adventures of Robinson Crusoe.[14]

Here, then, is another bit of venom that was unloosed upon Melville, fit to stand by the side of the calumnious attacks in the *American Review* and the English *Eclectic,* and prompted by the same partisan purpose—a defense of missionary activity in Polynesia. Yet the balance of unfavorable reviews still stands at no more than ten percent.

What then of the "whole regiment of critics" stirred up by the publication of *Typee* and *Omoo* which made their contemporary reception a mere *succès de scandale?* Even if one turns to the newspapers of the period, the number of responsible charges of dishonesty and immorality launched against Melville are found to be very few. Some of the religious sheets did make such accusations, but in general the reaction of the newspapers paralleled that of the

literary periodicals.[15] Apparently, a mere handful of adverse criticisms, as belligerent and vituperative as the one just quoted from
the *Polynesian,* were capable of raising a momentary sound and
fury almost equal to the general chorus of praise which in actuality
greeted Melville's debut as an author. And certainly they would
have been sufficient to persuade a timorous publisher to delete the
most "objectionable" passages at the first opportunity.[16] But the
publication of this revised edition of *Typee* in the summer of 1846
is not evidence that the book was considered immoral by the general public. Indeed, the reaction of publisher, critics, and reading
public to *Typee* and *Omoo* is an entirely different matter from the
authenticity of the books themselves.

Before proceeding to the solution of this problem, it will be interesting to inquire into the author's own attitude towards the controversy over his book. The evidence on this point is meager and
somewhat conflicting, but it is at least clear that Melville considered
his narrative of adventures among the Marquesans to be essentially
true. His prefatory avowal in *Typee* that he was speaking "the unvarnished truth" is positive evidence of this. And the ironical preface to *Mardi* is negative testimony to the veracity of both his earlier
books:

Not long ago, having published two narratives of voyages in the Pacific,
which, in many quarters, were received with incredulity, the thought
occurred to me, of indeed writing a romance of Polynesian adventure,
and publishing it as such; to see whether, the fiction might not, possibly, be received for a verity: in some degree the reverse of my previous experience.

But it is hard to say just how righteous his indignation was when
certain critics accused him of having written fiction rather than
fact. A recently discovered letter, written on May 23, 1846, seems to
indicate that Melville was seriously solicitous of maintaining the
credit of *Typee* as a genuine narrative, at least for practical reasons.
In this letter the particular object of his irritation was a review in
the New York *Courier and Enquirer,* which cast doubt on his truthfulness, and which, being copied into other newspapers, he feared
would seriously impair the success of his first book. Hence he was

vexed that whereas foreign editors, like those of *Chamber's Edinburgh Journal*, "endorse the genuineness of the narrative, . . . so ma[n]y numskulls [in America] should heroically avow their determination not to be 'gulled' by it." And he added with finality: "The fact is, those who do not beleive [*sic*] it are the greatest 'gulls'— full fledged ones too." [17]

In the midst of this controversy, as has long been known, the unexpected happened: Toby, the companion of Melville's strange adventures, turned up in Buffalo as Richard Tobias Greene and wrote to the *Commercial Advertiser* on July 1, 1846: "I am happy to testify to the entire accuracy of the work so long as I was with Melville." [18] The author of *Typee* took this occasion to convert the "politely incredulous Mr. Duyckinck," declaring that this strange resurrection "can not but settle the question of the book's genuineness" and projecting as a sequel the narrative of Toby's adventures after leaving the island.[19] In a subsequent meeting with Greene he learned this story, and, before the summer had passed, the sequel was added to the revised edition. Thus, one side of the contemporary picture shows Melville, annoyed by the incredulity of some of his readers, bringing Toby triumphantly into court as the unsought, unhoped-for, and sole possible eyewitness of his outlandish experiences.

On the other hand, a curious anecdote has been preserved, though at third hand, which shows Melville playing the other half of a dual role—unwilling to forego such a splendid opportunity of mystifying downright souls. According to Philarète Chasles, a purely chance meeting brought him in contact with a friend of Melville—a distinguished American citizen of literary bent, who kept abreast of the intellectual affairs of his country and who cleared up for Chasles the whole problem of the authenticity of *Typee* and *Omoo*, once and for all. This anonymous worthy assured him that Melville was a real person of distinguished family, who was at that moment married and living in Boston in the enjoyment of a deserved but singular celebrity, which he accepted rather equivocally. The anecdote of his American interlocutor follows:

Sa famille, qui sait que les aventures racontées par lui sont *genuine,* n'est point flattée de la part d éloges accordée à M. Hermann Melville en faveur de son imagination aux dépens de sa moralité. Son cousin, chez lequel j'ai passé l'été dernier, se récriait beaucoup contre cette obstination des lecteurs qui ne voulaient voir dans *Typee* et *Omoo* que des scènes fantastiques.—Mon cousin, disait-il, écrit fort bien, surtout quand il reproduit exactement se qu'il a senti; n'ayant pas fait d'études dans le sens ordinaire et accepté de ce mot, il a conservé la fraîcheur de ses impressions. C'est précisément à sa vie de jeune homme passée au milieu des sauvages qu'il a dû cette sincérité, cette vigeur, ce parfum de réalité bizarre qui lui donnent un coloris extraordinaire; jamais il n'aurait inventé les étranges scènes qu'il a décrites. Le plaisant de l'aventure, c'est que, charmé de sa reputation improvisée, il n'a pas contredit ceux qui attribuent à l'éclat et à la fécondité créatrice de son imagination le mérite qui n'appartient qu'à la fidélité de sa mémoire. Il serait fâché, je crois, que l'on reconnût la vérité essentielle de ce curieux épisode de la vie d'un jeune marin. La réapparition de son compagnon Toby ou Richard Green, personnage très réel et qui a partagé tous ses périls, l'a contrarié jusqu'à un certain point; elle le faisait descendre de son piédestal de romancier jusqu'au rôle ordinaire de narrateur.—Pour moi qui connais la mauvaise tête de M. Melville et l'emploi fait par lui de ses premières années, pour moi qui ai lu son journal, ses *Rough-Notes,* actuellement entre les mains de son beau-père, et causé avec Richard Green, son fidèle Achate, je ris de la préoccupation du public. Vous voyez le mensonge où est la vérité et la vérité où est le mensonge. Relisez *Typee,* je vous le demande; je ne parle pas d'*Omoo,* qui en est une pâle contre-épreuve; relisez ce livre, non plus comme un roman, mais comme portant l'empreinte la plus naïve des idées et des mœurs communes à ce grand archipel polynésien si mal connu.[20]

This authentic information, concluded the French critic, did not astonish him; on the contrary, it merely confirmed his former opinion as to the relative truthfulness of Melville's first two books.

This is indeed a dark anecdote, for, from the few scanty records that survive, all the evidence lies the other way, revealing an anxiety on Melville's part to defend the truth of *Typee*—though the preface and the contents of *Mardi* may be cited as proof of his enjoyment of the ambiguous role of romancer and autobiographer. Moreover, the reference to the diary or "Rough-Notes" of his voyage, which the American told Chasles he had seen with his own eyes, is in direct contradiction to Melville's explicit statement in the preface to *Omoo:* "No journal was kept by the author during his wanderings in the South Seas"—nor has any record of such a journal been discovered to date. In spite of all objections, however, this anecdote has a convincing ring; and it is quite possible that Melville found a curious pleasure in mystifying his critics by posing as a romancer when they refused to take his first books as straightforwardly as he had intended them to be taken, and further it is quite possible that Melville did keep a South Sea journal. Translating Chasles's essay into the New York *Literary World,* Melville's friend Evert Duyckinck commented upon the truthfulness of this story, correcting a few mistakes such as the statement that Melville was a resident of Boston; but, unfortunately, an overdelicate sense of propriety made him withhold the very information most pertinent to the biographer:

It is natural, of course, that there should be some slight errors in the chance anecdotes of an American author, picked up in conversation in Paris. . . . The information of Mr. Melville, derived through the medium of the "cousin," is as true as such authoritative narratives generally are; and the reference to his early years, with the phrenological indications of his head, as favorable as the appreciation in most families of the youthful book-writer and "genius"—at least until admiration is forced back upon them by the world at large. . . . Of his married life, and of the family inspection of his papers, we say nothing, for they are not subjects of public comment.[21]

And so, after the lapse of a century, the matter remains dark. At any rate, Chasles's American informant was very close to the truth when he said that *Typee* is more dependable and more credible than the Polynesian narratives of Bougainville, Diderot, and Ellis, in spite of an overwrought style and occasional romantic exaggerations.

Thus the popular notion that *Typee* and *Omoo* were scouted as impertinent inventions by Melville's contemporaries must be revised. In spite of some righteous objections in religious quarters and some amused speculation in literary circles, the books were on the whole accepted as authentic. On the other hand, whereas the modern reader is the one who is more inclined to treat *Typee* as an outlandish fiction, all of the most competent modern ethnologists have relied upon it as an authority in their compendious treatises upon Polynesia.[22] And thanks to the exhaustive researches of the Bayard Dominick Expedition to the Marquesas Islands in 1920, the truth about *Typee* can now be determined with scientific accuracy. From the published studies of E. S. Craighill Handy, Willowdean C. Handy, and Ralph Linton practically every detail of Melville's discussion of the natural habitat, the material culture, the social customs, and the religious and political institutions of the Marquesans can be checked. For the general student of Melville, the detailed analysis and verification of these matters in the preceding chapter probably reveals an accuracy of information in *Typee* scarcely to be expected. Without hesitation it can be said that in general this volume presents a faithful delineation of island life and scenery in precivilization Nukahiva, with the exception of numerous embellishments and some minor errors—very much as Lieutenant Henry A. Wise observed during a visit in 1848.[23] Some of these embellishments are dramatic exaggerations, such as the overemphasis on the dangers of cannibalism to the white man; others are purely romantic, such as the extravagant praise of their physical beauty and their moral perfection. Stripping *Typee* of its Rousseauistic overplus, the careful reader can find a central core of fact that will give him a fairly comprehensive understanding of ancient Marquesan native culture, for the amount of specific misinformation—exclusive of obvious fictions—is relatively inconsiderable.

The evidence of the preceding chapter, moreover, furnishes another and equally surprising conclusion; and it satisfactorily answers the question of how Melville, without a knowledge of the language and without the aid of an interpreter, could have gathered so much and such esoteric information in less than a month. This conclusion is that *Typee* itself is a compilation, similar to the literary ethnologies which quote it as an authority, and which cite in proof the very sources whence it was drawn. And the answer is that Melville gathered almost every shred of this information from contemporary travel books—especially those of Langsdorff, Porter, and Stewart—after leaving the scene of his story. Indeed, it can be said almost without exaggeration that, with these sources open before him and with a lively imagination to body them forth, Melville might have written *Typee* without ever having seen the Marquesas Islands. But Captain Pease's affidavit to his desertion at Nukahiva on July 9, 1842, precludes any such hypothesis. Since Melville did visit the Marquesas Islands in his own person, it may be asked, what then is the explanation of such wholesale dependence upon the information of previous visitors?

One ready answer to this question is that Melville, as an inexperienced writer, was not sure of himself; and this possibility is borne out by the fact that he frequently borrowed not only the subject matter and plan of arrangement, but also the specific phraseology and figures of speech of his source books. Consciously or unconsciously, most authors of first books probably contract similar literary debts, though not often such large ones as Melville's. A second explanation is that he may have used these repositories of information merely to supply the place of the journal which he says he neglected to keep while he was in the South Seas. If this were the precise explanation, one would expect to find him merely prompting his own memory by culling from the accounts of his predecessors all the information that was correct and suited to his purposes, leaving in them a fringe of material that he found erroneous or unsuitable. But such is not the case; for part of what he borrowed was inaccurate, and much of what he passed by was both accurate and appropriate. Consequently it is necessary to consider a third explanation: Melville's own acquaintance with Marquesan life may have been so brief, so limited, and so imperfect that he was forced to turn to printed authorities for the facts necessary to give substance to his narrative.[24]

Though there is no longer any problem as to the ethnological truth of *Typee,* there is very little new light that can be shed upon its autobiographical veracity, in addition to what the preceding chapters afford. Whereas it is impossible to say just what was the extent of Melville's actual experiences among the Marquesans, they were probably sufficient to exert a genuine influence on his life—though not such a thoroughgoing one as his previous biographers imply.²⁵ For his residence in Typee Valley was extremely brief, and almost all of his recorded experiences there were lived vicariously in the travel literature which he consulted upon his return. Hence they are not dependable facts in the life of Herman Melville. This is by far the most important kind of check that can be made upon the autobiographical truth of *Typee*. In the place of this tissue of vicarious adventures, very little of a positive sort can be substituted, beyond the simple statement that for several weeks Melville did live on the island of Nukahiva—in all probability in Typee Valley, just as he affirms—and that his experiences there in sober fact were probably neither more nor less glamorous than those of hundreds of other deserters scattered throughout Polynesia. What effect this relatively slight contact with primitive life may have had upon the spiritual biography of a sensitive young man is largely a matter of conjecture.

None of the specific individual experiences which Melville relates as personal were of any considerable significance. Indeed, the thread of "autobiographical" narrative upon which is strung the mass of ethnological information in *Typee* is remarkably slight. About ten days after his arrival in the valley (or about July 25), some boats came to Typee Bay, according to Melville, and Toby was permitted to go in one of them to Taiohaë, for the avowed purpose of securing medical aid from the French for his companion's injured leg. About three weeks after this, the story proceeds, there was a report that boats were again approaching the bay; but Melville was indignantly refused permission to go to the beach, and this frustrated opportunity to escape is thus used merely to·increase the reader's suspense.²⁶ In all likelihood, it may be ventured, this was the actual occasion of Melville's escape, for this incident must have occurred about August 15, 1842, the approximate date of his rescue from Typee Valley according to the chronology set forth in the ensuing chapter.

Since Melville's story was just begun, however, he allots himself three more months of residence to complete his observations. During this period, he says, he spent his time at first in tormenting himself about Toby's fate, and his own, but later in trying to forget his fears by plunging whole-heartedly into the life of the valley. Thus he drifts on through an imaginary three months of idyllic life among the Typees, explaining his chronological vagueness by saying, in his preface, that "the author lost all knowledge of the days of the week, during the occurrence of the scenes herein related"—scenes which he later drew from travel books! There was nothing to disturb the serenity of these days which followed one another, he says, like a perpetual "June just melting into July" (or July just melting into August, to be more literal); nor does he mention any contact with the outside world from which the biographer can arrive at a calendar date for reference.

All good things must end, however—even a fictitiously prolonged residence in a cannibal valley. After three pleasant months among the Typees, Melville's fear of being eaten alive returned with redoubled force upon his discovering what he says was indisputable evidence that a cannibal feast had taken place in the Taboo Groves. His resolution to escape revived with renewed emphasis, but a month of futile attempts followed before his real opportunity came. At last one day—"it must have been more than four months since I entered the valley"—news came that Toby had arrived at the beach in a boat. By ardent persuasions, Melville says, he finally wrung from the reluctant natives permission to go to the beach, where he found not Toby but a whale boat, in need of men, which had come to ransom him. Melville had never before been allowed to go into the lower part of the valley, and his description of it on this occasion is vague and sketchy in the extreme. For example, he makes no reference to the elaborate fort which blockaded the only path leading to the beach, nor any mention of the river which had to be forded numerous times during the last two miles of the journey—both of which are commented upon by Porter and Stewart.[27] Moreover, the whole scene of the rescue itself is romantic and unconvincing, apparently written in haste and more with a view to making himself a hero than with a proper regard to logic and dramatic finesse.

There is no doubt, however, that Melville did leave the Mar-

quesas Islands about the middle of August, 1842, on board a Sydney whaler—not the "Julia," as he calls her in *Omoo,* but the *Lucy
Ann.* And from the evidence now available, the presumption is
that this ship, in need of men, actually came round to Typee Bay
to accomplish his rescue. An anecdote to this effect, recorded by
Arthur Stedman, is casual and straightforward enough to be worthy
of record:

> Meeting with Mr. Charles Henry Webb ("John Paul") the day after
> Mr. Melville's death, I asked him if he were not familiar with that
> author's writings. He replied that "Moby-Dick" was responsible for his
> three years of life before the mast when a lad, and added that while
> "gamming" on board another vessel he had once fallen in with a mem-
> ber of the boat's crew which rescued Melville from his friendly impris-
> onment among the Typees.[28]

There is one piece of contrary evidence, on the other hand, in
the strange and unique version of Melville's escape recorded in the
critique of Philarète Chasles. After a detailed and accurate summary of the contents of *Typee,* this commentator departed widely
from the standard version of the escape by concluding the story on
the night after Melville's discovery of the remains of the cannibal
feast:

> Sa résolution fut prise; au milieu de la nuit, il profita du sommeil
> profond de Fayaway et de Kori-Kori, et pris sa course à travers les bois,
> pendant que ses hôtes fatigués dormaient autour des bûches enflam-
> mées et des débris de leur repas. Après trois jours et trois nuits sans
> sommeil et sans alimens, il parvint à s'orienter et vint tomber à demi
> mort au milieu de notre campement, où les soins généreux qui lui
> furent prodigués lui sauvèrent la vie et lui permirent de s'embarquer
> pour New-York, où il a écrit son livre, publié à Londres.[29]

Where could Chasles have picked up this story? It is unthinkable
that such a careful critic could have so garbled the conclusion to
a volume which he had analyzed painstakingly and minutely; and
it is equally unthinkable that he would have fabricated this conclusion through pique at Melville's attacks on the French. A satisfactory explanation is hard to come by.[30] It is possible that Chasles
got this story from some member of the French naval expedition

to the Marquesas who simply remembered some vagabond sailor coming into the French camp from Typee Valley, and who thus confused Toby's escape overland with Melville's. It is barely possible, of course, that Melville similarly escaped overland, was cared for by the French, and was then permitted to ship on a passing whaler—the *Lucy Ann*. The Frenchman's anecdote is frankly puzzling. But one thing is certain: Melville did not ship direct for New York. Instead, he spent the next year in a series of romantic adventures, roving through the South Seas.

BOOK THREE

"MR. OMOO," THE ROVER

CHAPTER IX

MUTINY ON THE "LUCY ANN"

NOWHERE, perhaps, are the proverbial characteristics of sailors shown under wilder aspects than in the South Seas. For the most part, the vessels navigating those remote waters are engaged in the Sperm Whale Fishery; a business which is not only peculiarly fitted to attract the most reckless seamen of all nations, but in various ways is calculated to foster in them a spirit of the utmost licence. These voyages, also, are unusually long and perilous; the only harbours accessible are among the barbarous or semi-civilised islands of Polynesia, or along the lawless western coast of South America. Hence, scenes the most novel, and not directly connected with the business of whaling, frequently occur among the crews of ships in the Pacific.

Without pretending to give any account of the whale-fishery (for the scope of the narrative does not embrace the subject), it is partly the object of this work to convey some idea of the kind of life to which allusion is made, by means of a circumstantial history of adventures befalling the author. . . .

The present narrative necessarily begins where Typee *concludes, but has no further connection with the latter work.*[1]

THUS, in an explanatory Preface, Melville foreshadows the nature of the events that are related in *Omoo: A Narrative of Adventures in the South Seas* (1847). And, as will be demonstrated, most of these adventures were drawn almost literally from actual experiences, in this perhaps the most strictly autobiographical of all Melville's works. A concise introductory note then summarizes for the new reader the contents of *Typee*, and without more ado the author takes up his narrative where he had broken off at the end of his first book.

Herman Melville escaped from Typee Valley on "a bright tropical afternoon" some time between the first and fifteenth of August, 1842, according to the best conjecture from evidence now available.[2] The ship that rescued him, he says, was a Sydney whaling barque, the "Julia,"[3] which had touched at the island of Nukahiva in distress for men, her crew having been depleted by desertion.

Melville gives a circumstantial account of his "Little Jule," as the sailors familiarly styled her, which has the ring of reality about it:

> She was a small barque of a beautiful model, something more than two hundred tons, Yankee-built, and very old. Fitted for a privateer out of a New England port during the war of 1812, she had been captured at sea by a British cruiser, and, after seeing all sorts of service, was at last employed as a government packet in the Australian seas. Being condemned, however, about two years previous, she was purchased at auction by a house in Sydney, who, after some slight repairs, dispatched her on the present voyage. . . .
> But all this had nothing to do with her sailing; at that, brave Little Jule, plump Little Jule, was a witch. Blow high, or blow low, she was always ready for the breeze; and when she dashed the waves from her prow, and pranced, and pawed the sea, you never thought of her patched sails and blistered hull. How the fleet creature would fly before the wind! rolling, now and then, to be sure, but in very playfulness. Sailing to windward, no gale could bow her over; with spars erect, she looked right up into the wind's eye, and so she went.[4]

Lieutenant Henry A. Wise, who made inquiries concerning Melville at Tahiti in 1848, identified this "Julia" as the *Lucy Ann,* Captain Vinton.[5] Fortunately, numerous references to an Australian whaler of this name survive to confirm the identification beyond any doubt. The *Australian,* a Sydney newspaper, records on June 27, 1827, that the *Lucy Ann* first arrived from London on that date, and on September 21, 1827, that she was bought by Governor Darling for £2,170, to be used by the government of Australia. On October 20, 1835, there is a notice in the same newspaper that the *"Lucy Ann,* a remarkably fast-sailing schooner," was dispatched up the coast in pursuit of a stolen sloop. And two months later she is reported to have sailed for the sperm whale fishery. In the Shipping Register, Customs Department, Sydney, there is an entry on December 10 of the same year which shows that she was then owned by Messrs. George and Edward Weller, merchants; and attached thereto, under date of August 17, 1841, is a deed of transfer to two other Sydney merchants in trust for the benefit of the creditors of the former owners. In this record the *Lucy Ann* is described as a barque of two hundred and thirteen tons burden, which had been built at Frederickton in the province of New Brunswick, Canada, in 1819.[6]

Thus, except that any service in the War of 1812 is precluded by the date of her launching, Melville's account of the "Julia" squares perfectly with these established facts pertaining to the *Lucy Ann*. Both ships are described as whaling barques from Sydney, old and Yankee-built (or just over the line in Canada), a little over two hundred tons burden, remarkably fleet in sailing, for some years employed as government packets in the Australian seas and afterwards as sperm whalers, and now recently disposed of by bankrupt owners. Moreover, confirmatory records of the present voyage survive. The departure from Sydney is listed as follows: "*Lucy Ann*, barque, left for sperm fishery February 14, [1842], Captain Ventom [*sic*]"; and the return: "Arrived May 20, [1843], *Lucy Ann*, whaler, Ventun [*sic*]. She has had a remarkably unfortunate cruise, having obtained only 250 barrels of sperm oil." [7] At the time of his shipping, Melville says, only two whales had been taken; during the period of his residence on board not a barrel was added to this meager catch; and before she left on her final brief cruise "a good part of what little oil there was aboard had to be sold for a song to a merchant of Papeetee," in order to engage a new crew.[8] The *Lucy Ann*, therefore, was Melville's "Julia," and this was the unlucky cruise of 1842–1843 to which Melville has given a modest immortality in his *Omoo*.[9]

Just how much truth there was in Melville's other references to the "Julia's" appearance, and to her lack of seaworthiness, it is impossible to say. Although he pays tribute to her sailing qualities, he adds that she was all the more to be distrusted on that very account:

Notwithstanding the repairs, she was still in a miserable plight. The lower masts were said to be unsound; the standing rigging was much worn; and, in some places, even the bulwarks were quite rotten. . . . Who knew but that, like some vivacious old mortal all at once sinking into a decline, she might, some dark night, spring a leak and carry us all to the bottom? . . .

All over, the ship was in a most dilapidated condition; but in the forecastle it looked like the hollow of an old tree going to decay. In every direction the wood was damp and discoloured, and here and there soft and porous. Moreover, it was hacked and hewed without mercy, the cook frequently helping himself to splinters for kindling wood from the bitts and beams.[10]

Everything, indeed, indicated an ill state of affairs on board, he says. The provisions were scanty and poor in quality; in fact, they had been purchased by the owners "at an auction sale of condemned navy stores in Sydney." Of the original ship's company of thirty-two, twelve had deserted, including three of the mates and three of the harpooneers. Of those who remained, "villains of all nations and dyes," more than half were sick and wholly unfit for duty. Worst of all, "Captain Guy," as Melville renames Captain Vinton, was essentially a landsman—a young Cockney recently emigrated to Australia—whom the seamen derisively called "The Cabin Boy" and "Paper Jack," but who was shrewd enough to leave the management of his ship to his mate, "Jermin," a bluff and efficient though habitually drunken seaman.[11]

A small amount of light can be thrown on these remarks. It is indeed true that on her very next whaling voyage, beginning June 25, 1843, the *Lucy Ann* sailed under a new commander, Captain Lee, and under the auspices of new owners, Messrs. Lyons and Jones—facts suggestive of an unsatisfactory previous voyage.[12] And, as will shortly be seen, her crew in 1842 probably deserved the reputation Melville has given them. But another decade passed before the *Lucy Ann* was finally condemned, after a venerable career of thirty-five years, twenty of which had been spent in the sperm whale fishery. Moreover, Edward Lucett, a merchant at Tahiti during these years, in identifying Melville's "Julia" offers an observation on this score: "It was the Sydney whaling barque Lucy Ann, Captain Ventom [*sic*], that had the honour of bringing Typee-Omoo Herman Melville to Tahiti; and in the month of June 1848, this said barque Lucy Ann was lying at Anatam, one of the New Hebrides, taking in sandal wood. So much for the way in which the cook used to pick her to pieces for firewood." [13]

However Melville may have dramatized the deplorable plight of the ship to which he had now entrusted his fortunes, his second whaling venture was certainly a futile one, terminating even more disastrously than his first one had, as subsequent events will show. According to the chronology shortly to be set forth, the *Lucy Ann* must have left Typee Bay about the end of the first week in August, 1842. But the cruise itself will have to be told in Melville's own words, for no other record of it has yet been discovered. Turning to the opening pages of *Omoo,* we read that the "Julia," after rescuing the author, sailed round to "Nukuheva Bay" (Taiohaë, the port at which Melville had deserted from the *Acushnet* exactly a month before), where a boat was sent ashore the next morning with the *tapu* natives who had rescued him. "Captain Guy" then shaped his course for Santa Christina (Tauata), an island in the lower Marquesas, to recapture eight seamen who had deserted there some weeks before. Two days later he reached his destination, the bay of "Hytyhoo" (Vaitahu), where he found a French corvette riding at anchor.[14] Counting on her for aid in case of any difficulty, he decided to spend the night in harbor. Early the next morning, as he had feared, it was discovered that several more of the crew had deserted, but with the assistance of the Frenchman all of these and five of the former deserters were brought back to the ship. On the following day the "Julia" stood over to the neighboring island of La Dominica, or "Hivarhoo" (Hivaoa), to ship some beachcombers reported to be there. It was at the bay of "Hannamanoo" (Hanamenu) on this island that Melville says he met the South Sea vagabond Lem Hardy, who gave him the spurious information on Marquesan tattooing mentioned in a previous chapter.[15] But the opportunity of being adopted as a native chief did not tempt Melville, at least, to leave his ship a second time for life in an island paradise. Instead, a Marquesan native shipped on board the little barque as she finally got under weigh on her whaling voyage to the westward, after six days consumed in cruising about the islands in an effort to replenish her crew.

Of this voyage absolutely nothing, beyond Melville's account, is now known. The half hundred pages devoted to it in *Omoo* are mostly consumed in introducing the ship and the ship's company more intimately to the reader. Even Melville has little to say of the voyage itself: "How far we sailed to the westward after leaving the Marquesas, or what might have been our latitude and longitude at any particular time, or how many leagues we voyaged on our passage to Tahiti, are matters about which, I am sorry to say, I cannot with any accuracy enlighten the reader. Jermin, as navigator, kept our reckoning; and, as hinted before, kept it all to himself." [16] Tahiti is less than a thousand miles from the Marquesas, and sailing ships never took more than a week or ten days to make the direct passage. But according to Melville's scattered references, the "Julia" sailed right into the setting sun for nearly a month before her course was altered for Tahiti, "with the South-East Trades strong on our bow"—so that she must have sailed far to the westward. Not a single whale had been sighted, and affairs on board had grown steadily worse. Since most of the crew remained unfit for duty—two had actually died, and the captain himself was reported to be sinking rapidly—the mate finally agreed to take the ship into port. Finally, they sailed past the westernmost of the Coral Islands (Paumotu Group) and on the next day came abreast of Tahiti.

When it was discovered that the captain's real plan was to have himself set ashore until he could recuperate and to have the "Julia" continue her course and merely touch at the island later to take him off, says Melville, the uneventful nature of the voyage suddenly changed. The crew threatened immediate and outright mutiny. Melville and his companion "Doctor Long Ghost" succeeded in quieting them by proposing that a round robin be sent to the consul on shore, stating their grievances and requesting that he come on board at once and investigate the situation. Melville himself by his own confession, was the author of this seditious letter, indited on the flyleaf of "a damp, musty volume entitled *A History of the most Atrocious and Bloody Piracies"*; and the following names were signed to it, in a circle: "Doctor Long Ghost, Typee, Van, Navy Bob, M'Gee, Jingling Joe, Antone, Pat, Wymontoo, Bungs, Long Jim, Salem, Black Dan, Flash Jack, Beauty, and Bill Blunt alias Liverpool"—sixteen in all.[17] When the English consul came off the next day, however, he ignored the petition and refused to listen to complaints. Instead, he declared that, the sick being taken care of on shore, there was no reason why the voyage should not be resumed at once. At first the men were submissive, but, mustering courage, "Salem" finally stepped forward and declared: "I'm nothing more nor a bloody *beach-comber* . . . ; we're all a parcel of mutineers and pirates!" [18] And for a moment mutiny seemed inevitable, some physical violence actually breaking out, but order was restored at last and the consul departed, promising to return the next day.

The next twenty-four hours aboard ship were marked by riotous drinking and general disorder, says Melville, mutiny constantly imminent and once again, at least, openly threatened. The consul not making his appearance as promised, on the fourth morning the mate took the "Julia" into the port of Papeete upon his own responsibility, not even waiting for the harbor pilot to come off to him. Shortly after, the English consul again came on board, where he proceeded to separate the crew into two classes, the "mutineers" and those who had remained loyal. He then withdrew and went aboard the French frigate *La Reine Blanche,* which lay at anchor nearby. The men now suspected what their fate was to be, and their suspicion was soon confirmed: "In an hour's time, the first cutter of the *Reine Blanche* came alongside, manned by eighteen or twenty sailors, armed with cutlasses and boarding-pistols—the officers, of course, wearing their side-arms, and the consul in an official cocked hat, borrowed for the occasion." [19] The roll of recalcitrants, including Melville, was called, and all who still refused to do duty were declared mutineers and ordered into the cutter. They were then taken on board the French frigate and put in the brig. Here they were kept in irons and given poor food and, worst of all, a watery wine instead of their usual grog—discomforts which were probably responsible, in part, for Melville's uncomplimentary remarks on the French navy, which fill the succeeding chapter.

Quite naturally, the casual reader of Melville might treat this entire episode as a pure fiction, and even the student looking for autobiographical passages might be inclined to suspect the author of romancing here, as in similar scenes elsewhere. Yet a mild mutiny did in fact take place on board the "Julia," that agrees in broad outline with the bloodless one recorded in *Omoo*, though the confirmatory records are meager in the extreme. "Le journal de bord de la REINE BLANCHE (1841–1845)," the flagship of Rear-Admiral Dupetit-Thouars, offers a rare bit of evidence in the following entry:

23 Septembre 1842 . . . a une heure et demie de l'après-midi, expédié le canot major, armé en guerre, avec un officier, à bord du baleinier le LUCY ANN, mouillé sur rade le matin, à l'effet d'y rétablir l'ordre dérangé par plusieurs matelots. Le canot revient à bord avec dix de ces hommes.[20]

Here, then, is the whole story of the first part of *Omoo* confirmed, though in barest outline!

In addition to a general substantiation of the mutiny and of the subsequent incarceration on board *La Reine Blanche,* this brief record offers other valuable information. Melville says that just as the "Julia" arrived off Papeete four days previously, the booming of the guns of *La Reine Blanche* came to his ears across the harbor: "She was firing a salute, which afterward turned out to be in honour of a treaty; or rather—as far as the natives were concerned—a forced cession of Tahiti to the French, that morning concluded." [21] But Melville's arrival was not in fact quite so spectacular. For it was on September 9, 1842, that Admiral Dupetit-Thouars, after threatening to bombard Queen Pomaré, had finally obtained her "request" for French protection and issued a proclamation to that effect, accompanied by a salute.[22] Melville always preferred the picturesque date to the exact one. At any rate, the island was still in a state of considerable excitement over the event when the *Lucy Ann* arrived off the harbor about ten days later; and it was perhaps because of this confusion that her little teapot tempest received no fuller notice in public records. Elsewhere, Melville says that when the "Julia" came to anchor at Papeete, "This must have been more than forty days after leaving the Marquesas." If, in lieu of better evidence, this statement be relied upon (and *Omoo* seems to offer the most veracious autobiography of all his South Sea volumes), Melville must have been rescued from Typee Valley at least as early as August 8; for we now find him arriving in the harbor at Tahiti on September 23, 1842, in the *Lucy Ann*—"mouillé sur rade le matin" —after six days cruising round the Marquesas Islands and forty days cruising for whale.[23]

Again, the Log Book of *La Reine Blanche* records that ten of the mutineers were brought on board the frigate. This checks approximately with the account in *Omoo*. It is true that there were sixteen names signed to the round robin, but several of the signers withdrew from the ranks of the mutineers and agreed to do duty before it was too late—two such being named scornfully by Melville as apostates. Reckoned from another approach, the tally is even closer. At the time Melville shipped on the "Julia," the whole ship's company, he says, numbered only twenty souls; but this figure was increased by six before the Marquesas were left behind and later reduced by two through deaths at sea. Of these twenty-four, two were taken ashore sick (probably Van and Long Jim), and ten more (the captain, the mate, the cooper, the cook, the steward, Bembo, Rope Yarn, Wymontoo, Sydney Ben, and the Dane) are specifically declared by Melville to have remained with the ship. Thus by actual count the list of mutineers is reduced to twelve, and, since nothing more is heard of Beauty or Antone, it is safe to list them as loyal and to accept as correct the estimate of ten recorded by *La Reine Blanche*.[24]

Moreover, the whole affair of the mutiny takes on the substance of reality when it is discovered that two of the chief participants from shore were actual characters, bearing the same names which Melville assigned to them. Melville was writing of historical facts when he said: "Pritchard, the missionary consul, was absent in England; but his place was temporarily filled by one Wilson, an educated white man, born on the island, and the son of an old missionary of that name still living." [25] George Pritchard, who had come out to Tahiti as a missionary in 1824, was appointed English consul in 1837; but, after serving four years in this capacity, he left on a visit to England in February, 1841.[26] For a while one Cunningham served in his stead, but at the time of the French occupation in 1842 Charles B. Wilson, the son of the missionary resident at Point Venus, was acting English consul.[27]

Not only was Melville accurate in his facts, but he was apparently justified in his low estimate of Wilson's character. "With natives and foreigners alike," he declares upon first introducing the consul, "Wilson the younger was exceedingly unpopular, being held an unprincipled and dissipated man, a character verified by his subsequent conduct." Throughout the succeeding hundred pages or more Melville pillories this official with merciless satire, so that Wilson becomes in effect the villain, or more precisely the buffoon, of the first half of *Omoo*.[28] Even if one sets down to vengeful prejudice many of the scenes in which he stands target for Melville's abuse, the two main charges—that he was "an unprincipled and dissipated man"—are substantiated by reliable sources.

Commodore Charles Wilkes, commanding the United States Exploring Expedition, 1838–1842, reported an anecdote that can hardly be said to reflect credit on a missionary's son. In April, 1840, Wilkes was called upon to settle a dispute between the natives of Tongatabu and Wilson, at that time captain of the English schooner *Currency Lass:*

On inquiry, it proved that two of the crew of the Currency Lass, with the knowledge of the commander and owner, (who was present,) had taken [some] Feejee women on board at Vavao, knowing it to be against the laws of that island; they thence sailed for Tonga. . . . I thought that the conduct of the Currency Lass had been improper, and the decision being left to me, I determined that the . . . women [should be] given up.[29]

Later, on one of the Fiji Islands, Wilkes picked up an anecdote showing up another aspect of Wilson's bad character—that of petty villainy. The *Currency Lass* had got on shore in attempting to go out of the harbor. The natives gathered round, threatening to plunder, and Wilson was helpless; but the native king proved friendly to him and restrained his subjects. In his extremity, Captain Wilson promised him a handsome present if they could get the ship clear. After much difficulty the king and his men accomplished this, but "The only thing the owner gave him was a whale's tooth and a small looking-glass!" [30] Finally, Lieutenant Wise left an after-picture of the missionary's son that tallies with Melville's second disparagement. Having recorded that another of Melville's former acquaintances at Tahiti had taken to hard drink, he remarks in conclusion: "H. M. *ci-devant* Consul, Mr. Wilson, was in the like vinous state, and occupied his leisure in the pursuit of shells at the Navigator Islands." [31] These corroborations certainly establish the truth, if not the propriety, of Melville's denunciation of the character of Consul Charles B. Wilson.

The second person living at Tahiti whom Melville holds up to ridicule, and does so without disguising his name, is "Doctor Johnson [*sic*], an Englishman, and a resident physician of Papeetee." There was actually such a Doctor Johnston then living at Tahiti, who is mentioned by W. T. Pritchard, the son of the missionary-consul, as being the family physician of the Pritchards at about this time.[32] He it was who in September, 1842, came aboard the *Lucy Ann* with Consul Wilson and passed judgment upon the condition of the seamen who had declared themselves unfit for duty. In a sense he may be said to share with Wilson the honors of Melville's abuse, though the disparagement of his character is limited to the charge that he was mercenary and incompetent in his professional capacity. Naturally, he resented Melville's caricature of him, for which there is little if any corroboration. Yet, ironically enough, it was the courtesy extended by this hardly-used man to Lieutenant Wise (to whom he expressed his resentment) that furnished the clue which has led to the discovery of much of the new light here first presented on Melville in Tahiti. But most of Doctor Johnston's connections with the mutineers came after they had been taken ashore, and it is there he will be found serving as the butt of Melville's naïve jests.[33]

A slight digression is perhaps warranted here for the purpose of identifying a third character mentioned at this point in *Omoo* and employed by Melville in a comic interlude. As the "Julia" was finding her way into Papeete harbor without waiting for the arrival of the regular pilot, an elderly native in an old naval frock coat was seen paddling out to them in a canoe. Flourishing his paddle and jabbering incomprehensibly, Melville says, he came alongside:

Presently we made out the following:—"Ah! you *pemi,* ah!—you come!—What for you come?—You be fine for come no pilot.—I say, you *hear?* I say, you *ita maitai* (no good).—You *hear?*—You no pilot. Yes, you d—— me, you no pilot 't all; I d—— you; you *hear?*" . . .

But Jermin was in no humour for nonsense; so, with a sailor's blessing, he ordered him off. The old fellow then flew into a regular frenzy, cursing and swearing worse than any civilised being I ever heard.

"You *sabbee* me?" he shouted. "You know me, ah? Well: me *Jim,* me *pilot*—been pilot now long time."

"Ay," cried Jermin, quite surprised, as indeed we all were, "you are the pilot, then, you old pagan. Why didn't you come off before this?"

"Ah! me *sabbee*—me know—you *piratee* (pirate)—see you long time, but no me come—I *sabbee* you—you *ita maitai nuee* (superlatively bad)."

"Paddle away with ye," roared Jermin in a rage; "be off! or I'll dart a harpoon at ye!"

But, instead of obeying the order, Jim, seizing his paddle, darted the canoe right up to the gangway, and, in two bounds, stood on deck. Pulling a greasy silk handkerchief still lower over his brow, and improving the sit of his frock-coat with a vigorous jerk, he then strode up to the mate; and, in a more flowery style than ever, gave him to understand that the redoubtable "Jim" himself was before him; and that the ship was *his* until the anchor was down; and he should like to hear what anyone had to say to it.

As there now seemed little doubt that he was all he claimed to be, the *Julia* was at last surrendered.

Our gentleman now proceeded to bring us to an anchor, jumping up between the knight-heads, and bawling out "Luff! luff! *keepy off! keepy off!*" and insisting upon each time being respectfully responded to by the man at the helm. At this time our steerage-way was almost gone; and yet, in giving his orders, the passionate old man made as much fuss as a white squall aboard the Flying Dutchman.

Jim turned out to be the regular pilot of the harbour; a post, be it known, of no small profit; and, in *his* eyes, at least, invested with immense importance. Our unceremonious entrance, therefore, was regarded as highly insulting, and tending to depreciate both the dignity and the lucrativeness of his office.

The old man is something of a wizard. Having an understanding with the elements, certain phenomena of theirs are exhibited for his particular benefit. Unusually clear weather, with a fine steady breeze, is a certain sign that a merchantman is at hand; whale-spouts seen from the harbour are tokens of a whaling vessel's approach; and thunder and lightning, happening so seldom as they do, are proof positive that a man-of-war is drawing near.

In short, Jim, the pilot, is quite a character in his way; and no one visits Tahiti without hearing some curious story about him.[34]

Jim, the native pilot, whose full English name was "James Mitchell," [35] was indeed a famous character in the history of the island, and, just as Melville declares, almost all the visitors to Papeete a century ago paid their respects to him. The earliest mention of him, probably before he had been appointed pilot, is recorded by Captain F. W. Beechey in 1826: "I used to laugh at Jim, our interpreter, a good-natured intelligent fellow, for his belief in these [superstitious] tales." [36] By 1834, however, he was definitely established in his new office, as F. D. Bennett found him:

The present occupant of the pilot's office is an eccentric native, named Jim; he is a travelled man, speaks English fluently, and has some little knowledge of seamanship; but the only duty for which he is responsible, or with which it would be safe to entrust him, is that of pointing out the reef entrances and the different anchorages.[37]

But it is Commodore Wilkes, in 1839, who gives the fullest account of him:

"English Jim" . . . is quite a respectable-looking man, dresses in the European fashion, and speaks English, which he has acquired on board of whale-ships, tolerably well. Although a good pilot, so far as a knowledge of the shoals goes, he does not understand what to do with a vessel, in case of difficulty. He told me that he had been looking out for vessels for some days, for it had thundered. . . .

A stormy evening having occurred previous to our leaving Matavai Bay [nine miles to leeward of Papeete], "Jim," the pilot, desired to see me; on his coming into the cabin, to my great amusement, he urged me to allow him to go to Papieti [sic], where he was sure he would be wanted; and when I asked for what purpose, he told me that the "thunder and lightning would bring in ships of war." He was displeased when I laughed and said, that he was engaged on board my ship, I would wait until I saw the ships before I could give him permission. He then reminded me of the night before we arrived, when there was plenty of thunder and lightning, and that he had told me as soon as he came on board that he expected us. He went on to repeat that he was sure that they would want him early in the morning at Papiete [*sic*], but I persisted in my refusal; and in the morning he appeared much disconcerted to find that there was nothing in sight out of which he could make a ship of war.[38]

The final touch is given by Admiral S. R. Franklin in reference to the voyage of the frigate *United States* in 1843, when he was a shipmate of Melville—to whom, incidentally, his account seems to owe at least a suggestion:

In a few days we reached Tahiti, where we took a pilot, which I mention only because he insisted on calling Point Venus Point "Wenus"; I can see him now on the poop, in the most emphatic manner telling the Captain from time to time that he must "weather Point Wenus before he could fetch the anchorage." [39]

Such are the fragments that compose a corroborative mosaic of Jim, the Pilot. Just how much Melville's account may have owed to these authors it is hard to say, for it is not at all improbable that he sketched him from life, having come in contact with this famous character as the *Lucy Ann* stood in to Papeete harbor, September 23, 1842.

To return to the frigate *La Reine Blanche,* in whose brig the ten mutineers were confined, we find Melville speculating on his fate:

In a day or two the Frenchman was to sail for Valparaiso, the usual place of rendezvous for the English squadron in the Pacific; and doubtless Wilson meant to send us thither to be delivered up.

This conjecture may have coincided with the consul's original intentions, but if so the plans were soon changed, for Melville adds:

Five days and nights, if I remember right, we were aboard the frigate. On the afternoon of the fifth, we were told that the next morning she sailed for Valparaiso. Rejoiced at this, we prayed for a speedy passage. But, as it turned out, the consul had no idea of letting us off so easily. To our no small surprise, an officer came along toward night, and ordered us out of irons. Being then mustered in the gangway, we were escorted into a cutter alongside, and pulled ashore.[40]

However, according to the Log Book of *La Reine Blanche,* she actually got under weigh for Valparaiso early on the morning of September 26, only three days after the mutineers had been brought on board; and, though this journal makes no further mention of the *Lucy Ann's* crew, it is certain that they were disposed of before she sailed.[41]

On the afternoon of September 25, it may be concluded, Melville and his fellow mutineers were taken on shore at Papeete. Under a native escort, says Melville, they were marched down the famous Broom Road about a mile from the village to the British jail—the "Calabooza Beretanee"—a native house that was so styled because it had been used by the consul for the past year or so as a house of confinement for refractory sailors: "The only piece of furniture was the 'stocks,' a clumsy machine for keeping people in one place, which, I believe, is pretty much out of date in most countries."[42] There was, in fact, just such a place of confinement near Papeete, and, even as Melville says, it had been established only a short while before the time of his incarceration. Even so late as September, 1839, Commodore Wilkes had complained in a letter to Queen Pomaré of "the absolute necessity of providing a jail or place for their [the deserters'] safe keeping until they can be sent on board."[43] At the time of the second visit of his expedition in January, 1841, accordingly, it was found that his suggestion had been acted upon in earnest, and that a virtual curfew law had been enacted: "We learned that the police regulations were such that any seaman would be taken up and put in the Caliboose [*sic*] if seen out after 8 P. M."[44] More specifically, Edward Lucett, upon his first arrival at Papeete in January, 1842, refers to a "calliboose [*sic*], or lock-up, supplied with stocks to fetter the limbs of the drunken or disorderly" which, he adds, was about three-quarters of a mile down the Broom Road from the village.[45] Here Melville spent the next six weeks, according to the record of *Omoo,* in indulgent confinement, but with the freedom of a prisoner on parole.

Before entering into an account of life at the Calabooza Beretanee, however, it seems best to pursue the affair of the mutiny to its conclusion. After about two weeks had passed, the prisoners were taken in to the consul's office at Papeete for trial, according to Melville. On this occasion Wilson read several documents specifying the charges against them: first, the affidavit of John Jermin, the mate, a long statement of matters from the time of leaving Sydney down to the arrival at Tahiti, which was fairly correct in details, though it bore rather hard on the seamen and was silent as to the mate's own derelictions; second, the affidavit of the seamen who had remained on board and who had turned ship's evidence, a grossly biased account; third, the captain's own deposition; and, finally, the ship's articles.[46] What a treasure to the biographer would be these documents which are said to tell the whole story of the mutiny on the *Lucy Ann!* But all search for them has proved unavailing. Neither the Log Book nor any of the ship's papers can be found at Sydney, and the spasmodically kept records of the English consular office at Tahiti one hundred years ago contain no trace of the whole affair.[47] Similarly, the records of the British Foreign Office have been searched without result. Indeed, such an inconsequential matter as a mutiny on a privately owned Sydney whaler was either passed by as a routine affair of no interest to the home office, or else omitted from official correspondence in the confusion created by the French seizure of Tahiti early in September, an event of international importance. For an official letter written at this time by the acting English consul, Charles B. Wilson, has been preserved: it is dated Papeete, September 26, 1842, while Wilson was in the midst of his difficulties with the crew of the *Lucy Ann,* but no mention is made of any mutiny on any vessel, though much space is given to the recent operations of the French.[48]

The apparent purpose of this trial, according to Melville, was to intimidate the mutineers into submission, the consul threatening that all preparations had been made to send them to Sydney for trial, and that transportation had been arranged for them on the "Rosa," an Australian schooner then lying in the harbor, which was to sail within ten days.[49] Meantime, they were told that they would be given one more opportunity to repent and do their duty before the "Julia" sailed, one week from that day. But the whole affair was gradually allowed to blow over, says Melville, and the mutineers

were never brought to further trial. At last Captain Guy managed
to ship a new crew and sailed from Tahiti to try his luck on another
whaling cruise. Melville remarks in farewell:

It was Sunday in Tahiti, and a glorious morning, when Captain Bob
[the jailor], waddling into the Calabooza, startled us by announcing,
"Ah—my boy—shippy you—harree—maky sail!" In other words, the
Julia was off. . . .
Thus disappeared Little Jule, about three weeks after entering the
harbour; and nothing more have I ever heard of her.⁵⁰

Again, a confirmatory account is furnished by a Sydney newspaper:

The *Lucy Ann,* whaler, belonging to Sydney, had touched at Tahiti,
and left again on the 15th of October. She had been out nine [eight]
months but had only 120 barrels of sperm oil on board. Her crew had
been in a state of mutiny, and fourteen of them were in irons at that
time.⁵¹

This entry, supported by the one in the Log Book of *La Reine
Blanche,* leaves no doubt as to the actual existence of a mutiny on
board Melville's ship, even as he describes. Brief as it is, this record
contains several points of interest. For one thing, October 15, the
date of sailing of the *Lucy Ann,* was exactly three weeks and a day
after she had arrived, on September 23; and, further, just as Melville says, this day fell on a Sunday, according to the Tahitian calen-
dar.⁵² When there was no dramatic effect to be sacrificed by accuracy, Melville's memory seems to have been accurate enough.
Again, the number of men in irons—fourteen—tallies reasonably
well with Melville's figure. The reckoning of ten given by *La Reine
Blanche,* however, seems to be the more reliable of the two, for
Melville calls only this number by name as his companions in the
British jail: "Typee" (himself), Long Ghost, Salem, Black Dan,
Flash Jack, Navy Bob, Jingling Joe, Bill Blunt (alias "Liverpool"),
Pat, and M'Gee.⁵³

Melville and his fellow mutineers at the Calabooza Beretanee, to
be sure, paid visits to Papeete other than those in the character of
prisoners brought to trial. Captain Bob, the Tahitian jailor, played
the role of a kind and indulgent father to his charges, allowing
them to roam pretty much at will after the first week of semicon-

finement had demonstrated that they had no intentions of running away; and the men took advantage of this parole to diversify the monotony of their enforced idleness. The route to the village lay along the famous "Broom Road," which Melville says was built by the natives who were assigned tasks of this sort as punishments for law-breaking—so many fathoms for murder, so many for adultery, and so on—but which he celebrates for its beauty with a felicitous pen:

As we proceeded, I was more and more struck by the picturesqueness of the wide, shaded road. In several places, durable bridges of wood were thrown over large water-courses, others were spanned by a single arch of stone. In any part of the road, three horsemen might have ridden abreast.

This beautiful avenue—by far the best thing which civilisation has done for the island—is called by foreigners the "Broom Road," though for what reason I do not know. Originally planned for the convenience of the missionaries journeying from one station to another, it almost completely encompasses the larger peninsula; skirting for a distance of at least sixty miles along the low, fertile lands bordering the sea. . . .

The uninhabited interior, being almost impenetrable from the densely wooded glens, frightful precipices, and sharp mountain ridges absolutely inaccessible, is but little known, even to the natives themselves; and so, instead of striking directly across from one village to another, they follow the Broom Road round and round. . . .

For miles and miles I have travelled the Broom Road, and never wearied of the continual change of scenery. But wherever it leads you—whether through level woods, across grassy glens, or over hills waving with palms—the bright blue sea on one side, and the green mountain pinnacles on the other, are always in sight. . . .

The finest orchard of cocoa-palms I know, and the only plantation of them I ever saw at the islands, is one that stands right upon the southern shore of Papeetee Bay. They were set out by the first Pomaree, almost half a century ago; and the soil being especially adapted to their growth, the noble trees now form a magnificent grove, nearly a mile in extent. . . . The Broom Road passes through its entire length.[54]

Many other travelers have described this Polynesian boulevard, at least two of whom may have served as models for Melville. C. S. Stewart, whose volume yielded valuable source material for *Typee*, says of the Broom Road:

This road is a fine and praiseworthy work for such a people—the labor principally of convicts, proved guilty of various breaches of the laws. It is a broad, gravel way, extending, for the most part, in a direct line from point to point along the coast, smoothly and well finished, and provided with narrow bridges of plank over the water courses and streamlets, running from the mountains to the sea. Thickly embowered with luxurious groves of various trees—skirted, here and there, with the humble but comfortable habitations of the islanders—opening occasionally upon a bright glade or extensive meadow land, with fine views of the mountains on one side, and the ocean on the other, it is, in many places, beautiful as a drive in the pleasure grounds of an American mansion, or the park of a gentleman in England.[55]

And Charles Wilkes, whose volumes are cited elsewhere in *Omoo*, added most of the other details which appear in Melville's description:

The Broom Road . . . extends completely around the island. It is in places almost arched over by trees, that grow on each side of it, and form a delightful shade. . . . At short intervals are groves of cocoanut trees, planted along the road; these are called the queen's, and travellers are at liberty to help themselves to the fruit. . . . The natives travel a great deal on this road, and some use it in going to visit places on the opposite side of the island, in preference to passing over the mountains.[56]

But, whatever his literary debt, Melville certainly must have passed along this road many a time during his sojourn at the Calabooza.

Nothing need be said of Melville's general accounts of Papeete itself, for Tahiti was a famous place even in those days, and many of the contemporary books of travel in the Pacific contain descriptions of the island and the village which might have served as models to refresh his memory. But some of his more detailed vignettes may be checked to show how closely he was sketching from life at times. Especially convincing is his description of a sight which could only have been seen at approximately the time of his visit:

What greatly added to the picturesqueness of the bay at this time was the condemned hull of a large ship, which at the farther end of the harbour lay bilged upon the beach, its stern settled low in the water, and the other end high and dry. From where we lay, the trees behind seemed to lock their leafy boughs over its bowsprit; which, from its position, looked nearly upright.

She was an American whaler, a very old craft. Having sprung a leak at sea, she had made all sail for the island, to heave down for repairs. Found utterly unseaworthy, however, her oil was taken out and sent home in another vessel; the hull was then stripped and sold for a trifle.

Before leaving Tahiti, I had the curiosity to go over this poor old ship, thus stranded on a strange shore. What were my emotions when I saw upon her stern the name of a small town on the river Hudson! She was from the noble stream on whose banks I was born; in whose waters I had a hundred times bathed. In an instant, palm-trees and elms—canoes and skiffs—church spires and bamboos—all mingled in one vision of the present and the past.[57]

There was indeed such a dismantled ship lying in the harbor of Papeete at this time. She was the *Alexander Mansfield,* a large ship of three hundred and twenty tons, which had sailed from Hudson, New York, in 1839, and had been condemned at Tahiti in 1840, her cargo of one thousand barrels of sperm oil being saved and shipped home. Another American, F. A. Olmsted, who visited Papeete at about this time, saw this same superannuated ship, though he did not conclude his description of her, as Melville does, with a nostalgic note:

There was an . . . American whale ship, the "Alexander Mansfield" of Hudson, lying dismantled near the shore. Not long ago, she had left Papeete bay, bound on a cruise, when, after being at sea for a few days, it was accidentally discovered that the stern timbers of the ship were falling to pieces. To have proceeded on the voyage in this dangerous condition would have been madness, and she returned to Papeete, where she was "condemned" as unseaworthy, and dismantled, a frequent occurrence whenever ships are found to be incompetent for service, either through age, or from injury. . . . The "Mansfield" was formerly a Liverpool packet, sailing from New York many years since, an exaltation that would hardly be surmised from the appearance of the dingy looking hulk lying condemned at Papeete.[58]

It is the accuracy of such casual digressions that convince one of the reality of Melville's experiences in *Omoo,* for Olmsted's account certainly reads like an independent corroboration rather than a source from which he drew.

On another one of his visits to the village of Papeete, Melville says, he paddled out in a canoe to a little island lying in this bay.

Although a sentry prevented his landing, he has left a description of it which readily shows how it could have struck his fancy as a spot worth exploring:

Right in the middle of Papeetee harbour is a bright, green island, one circular grove of waving palms, and scarcely a hundred yards across. It is of coral formation. . . .

The island is called Motoo-Otoo [sic]; and around Motoo-Otoo have I often paddled of a white moonlight night, pausing now and then to admire the marine gardens beneath.

The place is the private property of the queen, who has a residence there—a melancholy-looking range of bamboo houses—neglected and falling to decay among the trees.

Commanding the harbour as it does, her majesty has done all she could to make a fortress of the island. The margin has been raised and levelled, and built up with a low parapet of hewn blocks of coral. Behind the parapet are ranged, at wide intervals, a number of rusty old cannon, of all fashions and calibres. They are mounted upon lame, decrepit-looking carriages, ready to sink under the useless burden of bearing them up. Indeed, two or three have given up the ghost altogether, and the pieces they sustained lie half buried among their bleaching bones. Several of the cannon are spiked; probably with a view of making them more formidable; as they certainly must be to anyone undertaking to fire them off.

Presented to Pomaree at various times by captains of British armed ships, these poor old "dogs of war," thus toothless and turned out to die, formerly bayed in full pack, as the battle-hounds of Old England.[59]

This bright green spot attracted the attention of many visitors to Tahiti as they admired the scenery of the bay. Among those whose descriptions might have come under Melville's notice is F. D. Bennett, who has left an account of the island as it appeared at the time of his visit in 1834:

Near the entrance to Pápeéte [sic] harbour there is a low coral islet, covered with cocoa-nut and other litoral trees, and named by the natives *motu uta,* or the islet near the shore. It is surrounded by a platform built of coral blocks, on which are mounted eight cannon, commanding the village and harbour of Pápeéte. . . . Several native dwellings are erected upon it; including one belonging to the Queen of Tahiti, with whom this, her citadel, is a very favourite residence.[60]

It was the Reverend Daniel Wheeler, however, who in 1835 made the exploration of the island that Melville was so anxious to make seven years later, and at the time of writing *Omoo* the author may have satisfied his curiosity by turning to Wheeler's *Memoirs* (a volume which he cites, incidentally, in another connection) and reading the following description:

In the afternoon, we went on shore upon the Queen's Island. On this small spot of ground much is concentrated: a small chapel, with sides of upright bamboos (wicker-work), is standing, with seats and a pulpit, at one time probably in use: there were also several pieces of cannon in a useless state, one placed on a platform formed of loose stones and coral, and others lying about in a condition equally harmless. These have been left as presents by the ships of different nations which have visited these seas, and stand as memorials against them, by showing that their dependence is upon the arm of flesh for protection: England, France, and Russia seem to have been the donors of them. Part of one building is fitted up as an armory, with an inscription to this import over the arms, which consist of three worthless muskets without locks. We cannot wonder at young and barbarous nations being eager to possess weapons of a destructive nature, when they see in what high estimation they are held by those who are called Christians; but, alas! their conduct proclaims aloud that such are not the followers of the Prince of Peace, nor are living under the blessed influence of the gospel.[61]

But, although Melville later found space for pacifist propaganda of a similar sort in *White-Jacket,* another message was in his heart at the time of writing *Omoo*—an attack on the semi-civilization wrought in Polynesia by the missionaries themselves—and he passed by the good Quaker's denunciation of the decrepit war dogs turned out to die, old and toothless, on Motu-Uta.

Beyond Papeete, on the Broom Road leading to Matavai, is a place called Papaoa. Here at one time stood an immense native church which Melville describes in considerable detail, apropos of a remark that the early buildings, not being erected with a view to durability, went to pieces in a few years:

One, built many years ago in this style, was a most remarkable structure. It was erected by Pomaree II., who, on this occasion, showed all the zeal of a royal proselyte. The building was over seven hundred feet in length, and of a proportionate width; the vast ridgepole was, at intervals, supported by a row of thirty-six cylindrical trunks of the bread-fruit tree; and, all round, the wall-plates rested on shafts of the palm. The roof—steeply inclining to within a man's height of the ground—was thatched with leaves, and the sides of the edifice were open. Thus spacious was the Royal Mission Chapel of Papoar [sic].

At its dedication, three distinct sermons were, from different pulpits, preached to an immense concourse gathered from all parts of the island.

As the chapel was built by the king's command, nearly as great a multitude was employed in its construction as swarmed over the scaffolding of the great temple of the Jews. Much less time, however, was expended. In less than three weeks from planting the first post, the last tier of palmetto leaves drooped from the eaves, and the work was done.

Apportioned to the several chiefs and their dependents, the labour, though immense, was greatly facilitated by everyone's bringing his post, or his rafter, or his pole strung with thatching, ready for instant use. The materials thus prepared being afterward secured together by thongs, there was literally "neither hammer, nor axe, nor any tool of iron heard in the house while it was building."

But the most singular circumstance connected with this South Sea cathedral remains to be related. As well for the beauty as the advantages of such a site, the islanders love to dwell near the mountain streams; and so, a considerable brook, after descending from the hills and watering the valley, was bridged over in three places, and swept clean through the chapel.

Flowing waters! what an accompaniment to the songs of the sanctuary; mingling with them the praises and thanksgivings of the green solitudes inland.

But the chapel of the Polynesian Solomon has long since been deserted. Its thousand rafters of habiscus have decayed, and fallen to the ground; and now the stream murmurs over them in its bed.[62]

In all probability, this Tahitian cathedral had completely gone to destruction at the time of Melville's visit. And even if he did wander about its ruins in 1842, his description, at any rate, is obviously taken wholesale from William Ellis's *Polynesian Researches,* a work which Melville confesses in his preface that he had consulted "Upon several points connected with the history and ancient customs of Tahiti":

This building, which is called the Royal Mission Chapel, and might, not inappropriately, be termed the cathedral of Tahiti, is certainly, when we consider the imperfect skill of the artificers, their rude tools, the amazing quantity of materials used, and the manner in which its workmanship is completed, an astonishing structure. It is seven hundred and twelve feet in length, and fifty-four wide. Thirty-six massy cylindrical pillars of the bread-fruit tree sustain the centre of the roof, and two hundred and eighty smaller ones, of the same material, support the wall-plate along the sides, and around the circular ends, of the building. The sides or walls around are composed of planks of the bread-fruit tree, fixed perpendicularly in square sleepers. . . . The building was covered with the leaves of the pandanus. . . . The roof was too low, and the width and elevation of the building too disproportioned to its length, to allow of its appearing either stupendous or magnificent. . . .

The most singular circumstance, however, connected with the interior of the Royal Mission Chapel is the number of pulpits. There are no fewer than three. They are nearly two hundred and sixty feet apart, but without any partition between. . . .

This immense building was opened for divine service on the 11th of May, 1819, when the encampment of the multitudes assembled stretched along the sea-beach, on both sides of the chapel, to the extent of four miles. On this occasion, three distinct sermons, from different texts, were preached at the same time, to three distinct congregations. . . . The whole number of hearers, according to the nearest calculation, was about seven thousand. . . .

A long aisle or passage, between the forms, extends from one end to the other. In walking along this aisle on my first visit, I was surprised to see a watercourse five or six feet wide, crossing, in an oblique direction, the floor of the chapel. On inquiry of the people who accompanied our party, they said it was a natural watercourse from the mountains to the sea; and that, as they could not divert its channel so as to avoid the building without great additional labour and constant apprehension of its returning, they had judged it best to make a grating at each side under the wall, and allow it to pass in its accustomed course. As it was not during the rainy season that we were there, it was dry; the sides were walled, and the bottom neatly paved; but in the rainy season, when the water is constantly flowing through, its effect must be rather singular on the minds of those sitting near it during public worship. . . .

It has appeared matter of surprise to many that the natives should desire, or the missionaries recommend, the erection of such large places of worship; and I have often been asked, how we came to build such immense houses. The Royal Chapel at Papaoa, however, is the only one of the kind in the islands. It originated entirely with the king, and in its erection the missionaries took no part. The king, determined in his purpose, levied a requisition for materials and labour on the chiefs and people of Tahiti and Eimeo, by whose combined efforts it was ultimately finished. . . . It is probable, also, that, considering the Tahitians as a Christian people, he had some desire to emulate the conduct of Solomon in building a temple, as well as surpassing in knowledge the kings and chieftains of the islands.

. . . In 1822, when I last visited it, the roof had already begun to decay. The labour of keeping so large a place in repair would be very great; and the occasions for its use so seldom occur, that no repairs have been made since the king's death; and the exposure being constant, it will not probably last many years longer. The texture of the palm-leaves composing the thatch is not such as to resist for any protracted period the intense heat of the climate.[63]

Such were some of the sights that Melville saw in and around Papeete, either with his own eyes or through the eyes of others.

According to Melville's narrative, most of his six weeks in Tahiti, however, were spent at the Calabooza Beretanee. Little is known of the life enjoyed by him and his fellow mutineers there, but several checks can be made that will give color of reality to the experiences recorded at that place in *Omoo*. Shortly before the "Julia" sailed, says Melville, they were honored by a visit from three Catholic priests:

They had settled themselves down quite near our habitation. A pleasant little stroll down the Broom Road, and a rustic cross peeped through the trees; and soon you came to as charming a place as one would wish to see. . . .

On the summit of a knoll, was a rude chapel, of bamboos; quite small, and surmounted by the cross. Between the canes, at nightfall, the natives stole peeps at a small portable altar; a crucifix to correspond, and gilded candle-sticks and censers. Their curiosity carried them no farther; nothing could induce them to worship there. Such queer ideas they entertained of the hated strangers! Masses and chants were nothing more than evil spells. As for the priests themselves, they were no better than diabolical sorcerers; like those who, in old times, terrified their fathers.

Close by the chapel, was a range of native houses; rented from a chief, and handsomely furnished. Here lived the priests; and, very comfortably, too. They looked sanctimonious enough abroad; but that went for nothing: since, at home, in their retreat, they were a club of Friar Tucks; holding priestly wassail over many a good cup of red brandy, and rising late in the morning.

Pity it was they couldn't marry—pity for the ladies of the island, I mean, and the cause of morality; for what business had the ecclesiastical old bachelors, with such a set of trim little native handmaidens? These damsels were their first converts; and devoted ones they were.

The priests, as I said before, were accounted necromancers: the appearance of two of our three visitors might have justified the conceit.

They were little, dried-up Frenchmen, in long straight gowns of black cloth, and unsightly three-cornered hats—so preposterously big, that in putting them on, the reverend fathers seemed extinguishing themselves.

Their companion was dressed differently. He wore a sort of yellow, flannel morning gown, and a broad-brimmed Manilla hat. Large and portly, he was also hale and fifty; with a complexion like an autumnal leaf—handsome blue eyes—fine teeth, and a racy Milesian brogue. In short, he was an Irishman—Father Murphy, by name—and, as such, pretty well known and very thoroughly disliked throughout all the Protestant missionary settlements in Polynesia. In early youth he had been sent out to a religious seminary in France; and, taking orders there, had but once or twice afterward visited his native land. . . .

[Immediately] we all turned Catholics, and went to mass every morning . . . ; and so, every few days, we strolled down to the priest's residence, and had a mouthful to eat, and something generous to drink. In particular, Doctor Long Ghost and myself became huge favorites with [Father Murphy]; and many a time he regaled us from a quaint-looking travelling-case for spirits, stowed away in one corner of his dwelling. It held four square flasks, which, somehow or other, always contained just enough to need emptying. In truth, the fine old Irishman was a rosy fellow in canonicals. His countenance and his soul were always in a glow. It may be ungenerous to reveal his failings, but he often talked thick, and sometimes was perceptibly eccentric in his gait.

I never drink French brandy, but I pledge Father Murphy. His health again! And many jolly proselytes may he make in Polynesia! [64]

However much of scandalous invention there may be in Melville's picture of these three convivial Catholic priests, he was at least writing about real characters, for numerous records survive of Pères Armand Chausson, François d'Assise Caret, and Columban Murphy, who were in charge of the Mission de Notre Dame de Foi à Tahite in 1842. In his *History of the Catholic Mission in the Hawaiian Islands* Father Reginald Yzendoorn records that when the Pacific Islands were committed to the care of the Order of the Sacred Heart, as the Vicariate Apostolic of Oriental Oceanica, the first party of missionaries, which arrived at the Gambier Islands in 1834, included Columban Murphy, then a choir-brother. He was ordained a priest in 1837 and for the next two years was stationed at Honolulu.[65] The story of his subsequent life is told in a valuable collection of letters from missionary priests in the South Seas, entitled *Lettres Lithographiées,* which are in the possession of Father Yzendoorn at Honolulu. On April 16, 1840, Père Columban Murphy was sent to the Marquesas Islands; but he left there before Melville's arrival and went to Tahiti, for a traveling priest who stopped at the latter place on November 13, 1841, reported that he spent three days with Pères Armand and Murphy, remarking in conclusion: "Il paraît qu'ils ont beaucoup à souffrir dans cette mission, où ils n'ont d'autre appui que Dieu seul." [66] During the hardships of their first years at Tahiti the French missionaries did indeed need the support of God, as Melville also remarks, for they got none from Queen Pomaré, who was under the complete domination of the Protestant mission.

On February 21, 1842, Père Caret, the second of the two French priests whom Melville describes, wrote that he had joined Murphy and Armand at Tahiti, and that their work was being made difficult for them by the Protestants, in spite of Queen Pomaré's promise to receive them and give them land for their mission:

Nous attendons ici la fin des difficultés que les Protestans opposent à notre établissement; et nous sommes obligés de louer une petite maison, à douze piastres par mois, n'ayant pu encore entrer en possession du terrain promis par la Reine, ni de celui que nous a loué un Irlandais pour 99 ans. . . . Les depenses sont extraordinaires ici; et, si nous ne recevions pas plus de secours, nous ne pourrions pas longtemps tenir dans ce poste.[67]

But by June 2, 1842, a visit of the French corvette *L'Aube* straightened out most of the difficulties of the mission, and the priests were put in legal possession of the land they had rented as well as that which the queen had promised them for the erection of a church. Père Armand reported that wood had been bought for the church and for a house, the estimated costs of which would be fifteen thousand and three thousand piastres respectively.[68] Finally, with the arrival of Rear-Admiral Dupetit-Thouars in *La Reine Blanche* and the establishment of the French protectorate, the Catholic Mission began to show its first signs of prospering. On September 24, 1842, the day after Melville's arrival off Papeete, Père Caret joyfully reported this good news, concluding:

Quant à nous, mon Très Révérend Père, nous bâtissons une maison en briques séchées: nos murs commencent à sortir de terre. Mais nous depenserons bien des piastres. Ce qui nous encourage, c'est que nous avons l'espoir que cette île donnera beaucoup de vrais enfans à l'Église Catholique. Déja une famille toute entière s'était décidé à suivre nos instructions, lorsque la persécution durait encore; et voila que la liberté de conscience vient d'être stipulée dans le traité provisoire conclu par M. le Contre Amiral Du Petit Thouars avec la Reine de Tahiti.[69]

Pères Murphy, Armand, and Caret were beyond question the three kindly priests—Father Murphy, of Dundalk, Ireland, and his two French confrères—who visited Melville and his fellow mutineers at the Calabooza Beretanee. The difficulties which the Protestants put in the way of the propagation of their faith among the natives seem to have been quite as Melville recounted, and the church and houses they were building and renting were equally drawn from life by him. But whether any of the eighteen thousand piastres asked by them from the Society of Picpus for these purposes were applied to filling the never-empty brandy flasks, or whether the "famille toute entière" which first embraced the faith under their tutelage contained the "set of trim little native handmaidens" who Melville hints were something more than "their first and devoted converts"—these are matters that are securely sealed forever beyond investigation.[70]

There was another visitor to the British jail during Melville's incarceration who was not so welcome as the Catholic fathers, but who became the unsuspecting comedian in a little farce which can now be verified. Melville records the episode with evident relish:

We had not been many days ashore, when Doctor Johnson was espied coming along the Broom Road.

We had heard that he meditated a visit, and suspected what he was after. Being upon the consul's hands, all our expenses were of course payable by him in his official capacity; and, therefore, as a friend of Wilson, and sure of good pay, the shore doctor had some idea of allowing us to run up a bill with him. True, it was rather awkward to ask us to take medicines which, on board the ship, he told us were not needed. However, he resolved to put a bold face on the matter, and give us a call.[71]

With the prospect of some good sport, the mutineers feigned illness, hoping also that their prescriptions would be well seasoned with ardent spirits. Meeting with some success, they openly demanded a bottle of Pisco when the doctor paid his second visit. But the climax came on the third day, when Melville's hero "Long Ghost," by means of his familiarity with medical terms, persuaded Dr. Johnston to prescribe for him a laudanum compound, with which the whole band of mutineers pretended to indulge in an opiate sleep, much to the consternation of the doctor.[72] This sailor's joke, or at any rate the publication of it in *Omoo*, seems to have been resented by Doctor Johnston, who was the actual resident physician at Tahiti in 1842, as has been previously demonstrated. Lieutenant Henry A. Wise gave evidence of this resentment in his record of a meeting with the doctor six years later at Papeete:

Mr. Melville's friend, Dr. Johnstone whom he has immortalized in *Omoo,* was excessive wroth, and refused to be pacified, resolving shortly to prosecute the English publishers for libel. He politely permitted me to translate some items from his dose book, declaring, however, that the "embrocation" so relished by the Long Ghost, was a villainous preparation, having the least taste of gin in the world, and made up from laudanum, turpentine, and soap liniment! Here is the memorandum:—

  Ship, Lucy Ann, Captain Vinton.
  October 15, 1842. Melvil [*sic*], Herman. Stocks.
 Embrocation..,..75
 19th. Do..75
                    $1.50

I felt no inclination to task it, since I found the Doctor's other prescriptions unexceptionable. The Ghost must have been seriously in-
disposed; he had a large quantity.[73]

This, indeed, is a most unexpected confirmation of the escapade
described in *Omoo*—a passage which reads like anything but a sober
recital of actual fact.

In spite of his admission of the truth of Melville's anecdote, however, Doctor Johnston still had good moral justification for bringing a libel suit. For Melville was not content merely to ridicule the
good doctor by making him the butt of ingenuous pranks. He went
still further and branded him as incompetent and mercenary in his
professional capacity:

The day before the *Julia* sailed, Doctor Johnson paid his last call. He
was not quite so bland as usual. All he wanted was the men's names to
a paper, certifying to their having received from him sundry medica-
ments, therein mentioned. This voucher, endorsed by Captain Guy,
secured his pay. But he would not have obtained for it the sailors' signs
manual, had either the doctor or myself been present at the time.

Now, my long friend wasted no love upon Johnson; but, for reasons
of his own, hated him heartily. . . .

For my own part, I merely felt a cool—purely incidental—and passive
contempt for Johnson, as a selfish, mercenary apothecary; and hence
I often remonstrated with Long Ghost when he flew out against him, and
heaped upon him all manner of scurrilous epithets.[74]

It is next to impossible, of course, to verify or disprove such a defa-
mation of an obscure man's character a century afterwards. But
from the few records that survive, most of the evidence runs contrary to Melville's estimate, and it seems only fair to present the
other side, since it is quite possible that Melville was motivated by
personal pique. Even Lieutenant Wise—who was definitely favorable to Melville in his note—although he makes light of Johnston's
righteous indignation, represents the doctor as a gentleman who
treated him courteously and hospitably.

In another contemporary account, Edward Lucett—who, on the
other hand, was a man of violent prejudices, with a particularly
strong animus against Melville—takes the author of *Typee* and

Omoo to task, in general for want of truth and in particular for heaping calumny on an innocent and even meritorious man:

His sketches are amusing, and skilfully drawn, but bear as much relation to truth as a farthing does in value to a sovereign. It is as if the said Herman Melville had burnished and gilded the farthing, and then circulated it as the gold coin. With those unable to detect the difference, it would of course pass current. Herman Melville—I love to repeat his name—working upon detached images profusely scattered throughout Polynesia, has drawn largely upon a fertile imagination in grouping them, and thrown together an exceedingly spirited narrative; but regardless of all truth, gratitude, or manliness, has grossly scandalized by name some worthy men living at Tahiti, who very probably have done more good, gratuitously, to their fellows since their residence there, than Herman Melville has done during his whole existence. I allude more particularly to Dr. Johnstone, who has been most grievously misrepresented, and considerably to his injury. . . .

I had the curiosity to search Dr. Johnstone's medical diary: the names of all the mutineers were enrolled there, and amongst them stands Herman Melville's. The whole of the doctor's charges for medicine and medical attendance amounts to but a few dollars, and the only item charged against Herman Melville is a bottle of embrocation, as the man complained of pains in his limbs: but the doctor believing him to be an imposter, which by the way I think he has clearly shown himself to have been, paid no further heed to his complaints. His pains, I expect, might be traced to the same source as the valley which he describes in Moorea [Eimeo], and which has existence only in the regions of his imagination.

Herman Melville possesses a felicitous pen, with a humorous knack of hitting off little peculiarities of character; and if he had confined himself to these, without publishing names, or making gross aspersions upon worthy men, his works might have gone down the stream with other harmless and amusing productions; but he has passed base coin as sterling, and for so doing, deserves exposure and contempt.[75]

Thus another is added to the list of those who took offense at Melville's spirited volumes. Whether favorable or unfavorable, his critics almost invariably took sides with fervor. In spite of the outspoken malice which Lucett bore Melville—for which, indeed, he thought he had more than sufficient justification, as will be seen—his remarks throw considerable light on the ambiguous character under discussion. While resenting the injustice of giving publicity to names, he tacitly implies that Melville was not giving an altogether false picture when "hitting off little peculiarities of character" pertaining to Doctor Johnston—such as, one suspects, the pompous naïveté which made him such an easy dupe for the practical jokes of the mutineers. But the charge of being mercenary in his professional calling is specifically refuted; and, if the medical diary consulted by both Wise and Lucett was an honest account, this Melville's principal aspersion on the doctor's character was certainly without foundation. In retaliation, Lucett pours forth such a flood of calumny on the calumniator that Melville himself might have been prompted in turn to bring suit for libel against the author of *Rovings in the Pacific*, if that abusive volume ever came under his notice.

Finally, E. H. Lamont, a subsequent visitor to Tahiti who was apparently ignorant of the feud between Melville and Johnston, and therefore impartial in that respect at least, described the doctor in 1852 as "one of the oldest residents in the island, whose generous and amiable qualities have made him deservedly popular, both among natives and foreigners." [76] Thus ends this diverting battle of reputations waged across the wide Pacific a century ago, with the spoils more evenly distributed than the reader of *Omoo* alone would be aware.

These two glimpses of the life Melville led at the Calabooza Beretanee, when added to the authentication of the mutiny on the "Julia," give a basis in fact to *Omoo* that is really astonishing for a volume that has been commonly accepted as semifictitious. But the rest of Melville's adventures in the Society Islands cannot be subjected to quite so critical a check. After the "Julia" sailed, on October 16 (Tahitian calendar), Wilson seems to have dropped the prosecution of charges against the mutineers, perhaps because he considered the whole fiasco successfully concluded, or because, as Melville says, "For the part he had been acting, we learned that [he] was the laughing-stock of all the foreigners ashore, who frequently twitted him upon his hopeful protégés of the Calabooza Beretanee." [77] At any rate, unexpectedly and without more ado, the prisoners were given their liberty.

For the time being Melville and his companions remained where they were, however, since they had no where else to go, and since their reputation as mutineers made captains touching at Tahiti wary of shipping them. But Jermin had left them their seamen's chests, says Melville, and while their wealth lasted they fared well:

The islanders are much like the rest of the world; and the news of our good fortune brought us troops of "tayos," or friends, eager to form an alliance after the national custom, and do our slightest bidding.

The really curious way in which all the Polynesians are in the habit of making bosom friends at the shortest possible notice is deserving of remark. . . .

Among others, Kooloo was a candidate for my friendship; and being a comely youth, quite a buck in his way, I accepted his overtures. . . .

The way this "tayo" of mine expressed his regard was by assuring me over and over again that the love he bore me was "nuee, nuee, nuee," or infinitesimally [*sic*] extensive. . . . He was, alas! as sounding brass and a tinkling cymbal; one of those who make no music unless the clapper be silver.

In the course of a few days, the sailors, like the doctor and myself, were cajoled out of everything, and our "tayos," all round, began to cool off quite sensibly. So remiss did they become in their attentions that we could no longer rely upon their bringing us the daily supply of food, which all of them had faithfully promised.[78]

This ingenuous custom of forming instantaneous friendships was indeed widespread throughout Polynesia—being reported by all of the first visitors as one of the most striking characteristics of these newly discovered Noble Savages. But among the Tahitians, even as Melville says, "vitiated as they are by sophisticating influences, this custom . . . in most cases degenerated into a mere mercenary relation." As early as 1803, a voyager with whose volumes Melville was acquainted witnesses this sad taint of civilization:

It is indeed no easy matter to withstand the smooth insinuating manner of the natives. . . . They accordingly assaulted [us] with all the blandishment, and natural endearment, which to minds of benevolence is the most resistless kind of flattery. . . . Each man had his friend or Tayo, who paid his court so assiduously and insinuatingly, as to leave the poor fellows scarcely a rag to wear.[79]

Stripped of their few worldly goods, the mutineers now found themselves also without any dependable food supply. Moreover, Melville and Long Ghost began to tire of this indolent life and to long for activity, of any sort, once more. Finding themselves judged by the company they kept at Tahiti, they decided to take advantage of an offer to work on a plantation in "Imeeo" (Eimeo), the island immediately adjoining, as field laborers at fifteen silver dollars a month. Thus the two companions traded the career of prisoners at the Calabooza Beretanee for that of Polynesian farmers in the fertile valley of "Martair." This, says Melville, was a little more than three weeks after the "Julia" had sailed; and, since from internal evidence they left on a Wednesday night, the date of Melville's departure from Tahiti can be placed with reasonable accuracy (insofar as the testimony of *Omoo* can be relied upon) as Wednesday, November 9, 1842.[80]

Before following Melville's adventures on the island of Eimeo, it is necessary to consider at this point a curious anecdote which is related as having its setting in the Calabooza at about this time. For Edward Lucett, the author of the anonymous volume entitled *Rovings in the Pacific, from 1837 to 1849,* lays claim to the distinction of having paid a visit, though an unceremonious and an unwilling one, to the British jail while Herman Melville was still incarcerated there. And from his lively though incredible account of this experience, there can be no wonder that he bore a grudge against Melville, as has been previously demonstrated by his effort to turn the tide of abuse from the head of Doctor Johnston back upon the author of *Omoo* himself. Arriving at Tahiti in January, 1842, Lucett made this place the headquarters for his far-flung trading enterprises in the Pacific during the next ten or twelve years. His first venture was a business trip to Valparaiso, from which he returned to Papeete on November 9, 1842, in the midst of the confusion resulting from the French seizure. At this point his anecdote begins:

Two or three evenings subsequently to our return, in taking a stroll in the cool shady walk at the back of the settlement, I stopped at an open native house to light a cigar. Suddenly the house was surrounded by men, and two or three of them entered and commenced jostling me. Not dreaming that any violence was intended, I merely pushed the intruders good humouredly from me, and finished kindling my cigar. . . . In a moment I was prostrate: some of the younger of the party had precipitated themselves to the ground and jerked me by the ancles, which had caused me to stumble backwards across their bodies; and before I could recover myself, I was elevated on the shoulders of ten or a dozen of them, who clutched my body wherever they could find hand-room. . . . In this way I was conveyed for about three quarters of a mile, when, to my horror, I discovered that they were taking me to a calliboose [sic], where a party of mutineers were confined. Again I struggled to free myself, and once more we were rolling in the dust. But without troubling themselves to raise me a third time, they caught me by the heels, and dragged me along the ground until they had forced my ancles into a massive pair of wooden stocks, in which six or seven of the worst of the mutineers were also confined. My passion at this outrageous indignity was so great, that my tongue refused its office, and with my throat, became parched as if by fire. The mutineers appeared mightily tickled at my position, and indulged in exceedingly gross and insulting remarks,—one of them excepted, who, feeling for my situation, kindly doubled his mattress under my back, which brought my head to a level with my heels. But there was another of them who had contrived to liberate himself when the stocks were raised for the reception of my legs; and this fellow, apparently the ringleader and spokesman for the others, commenced an oration, addressing me in the most offensive style, instituting comparisons, rejoicing that one of the "swells" had got a taste of the stocks, and offering me a highly spiced dish of ironical sympathy: this loosened my tongue.

"You cowardly ruffian! Can't you confine your remarks to those of your own station, without taking advantage of the ignorant folly of these natives to insult a man who never offered you any injury, but whom a caprice of fortune has thrown into this degraded position—a position doubtless well merited by you? If I but had my limbs as free as you have got your tongue, I'd play such a peal about your ears as should teach you for the future to confine it to its proper sphere."

Uttering a volley of oaths, the dastardly dog hereupon drew his sheath knife, and threw himself upon me, helpless as I lay; and such was the maddened state of excitement I was in, that, regardless of all consequences, I turned to grasp him; and it was well that his companions interferred, for if I had caught him, I should have inflicted upon him summary justice. The natives outside, hearing the scuffle, made their appearance, and quickly disposed of this specimen of the bowie-knife

genus, by making his head take the place of his heels, and again reducing the latter to the loving embrace of the heavy timber; but whilst he
was undergoing the operation, four of them held me like a vice in my
position. Order restored, and the peace-makers having retired, the same
kind fellow who had given me up his mattress volunteered to liberate
me from my confinement; but this service I could not accept at his
hands, for infamous as the treatment was to which I was subjected, I
could not render myself the accomplice of a mutineer.[81]

Lucett was liberated that same night, however, with an apology
on the part of the constabulary for making the mistake of thinking
that he was subject to the curfew law, and thirteen of the natives
were fined twenty dollars each for the assault.[82] The facts of this
strange story, unconvincing enough in themselves, end here. But
Lucett supplies a sequel which borders on the proposterous. Three
pages later—but in reality after the lapse of six years—he adds what
purports to be a subsequent and wholly independent passage, attacking Herman Melville in the most abusive language ever applied
to him and identifying him as the "dastardly ruffian of the bowie-
knife genus":

Since the above entry was made in my journal, two works have appeared, "Typee" and "Omoo," purporting to have been written by
Herman Melville. By his own showing Herman Melville has been a
most reckless loafer, caring not a pin what enterprises were ruined so
long as he could indulge the gratification of his own propensities.
Gratitude for his escape, and horror at the reminiscences of the hardships to which he had been exposed, impel him to acknowledge the
kind manner in which he was received on board the Julia, where he
met with every attention. [Here follows the denunciation of Melville
for his unwarranted abuse of Doctor Johnston.] . . . But as Herman
Melville has been so free in giving publicity to certain names, it is a
pity he did not extend his candour,—perhaps his memory failed him,
as he "kept no notes." However, I will try and jog it for him. After the
first desertion with which he pleases to acquaint the public, and his
subsequent escape from the horrors of a residence in a narrow ravine,
shut in by boulders and inaccessible cliffs, his companions naked
savages, hideously tattooed, and ferocious as demons, unable to speak
their language, trembling for his life, and without food adapted to his
European origin,—I say, after his escape from this wretched state of
existence, in his first deep-felt emotion at the mercy that had been

vouchsafed to him, he acknowledges the debt and expresses his gratitude; but how does he ultimately repay it? Why, according to his own
account, he is incapable of all bodily exertion; and he knows no other
way of repaying the obligation he has incurred but by being the insti-
gator of a mutiny, that he, and others like him, may be sent ashore at
Tahiti, where they could loaf and sponge at will, till the chance offered
of their ruining some other voyage, if peradventure any one could be
found to receive such worthies on board his vessel.

. . . Herman Melville, undoubtedly the ringleader of the mutineers,
was lying in the calliboose when I was dragged there; and from the un-
English way in which the ruffian who assaulted me handled his knife, I
have the strongest suspicion that it was Herman Melville who threw
himself upon a bound defenceless man; and I only regret that, amongst
his other reminiscences, he omitted to take notice of this. That he was
in the calliboose at the time, there is not a question; and that the man
was a Yankee who threw himself upon me I will swear, not only from
the peculiar intonation of his voice, his pale unwhiskered face, and
the thatch-like way in which his hair fell on either side of it, but from
the glib-like nature of his tongue—a qualification by no means uncommon with ordinary American seamen, which may be accounted
for from the fact, that many of them are grown men before they think
of gratifying a roving fancy, and are much more devoted to loafing and
reading, than attending to their duties.[83]

It seems hardly necessary to give serious consideration to an incident so obviously manipulated for the purposes of vituperation.
Yet this aspersion upon Melville, if it were true, would necessitate
such a complete reëvaluation of his character and personality that
a brief refutation must be made in passing. Lucett states without
hesitation, but also without the slightest attempt at proof, that Melville was undoubtedly in the calaboose at the time the attack was
made on him. But the most accurate conjecture as to the date of
Melville's departure from Tahiti places it at least four days previous
to Lucett's arrest on the night of November 12 (Sunday, November
13, Tahitian calendar). Further, the latter's mention of only "six
or seven" mutineers seems to confirm this by the inference that the
original ten had been thus reduced in consequence of the departure
of Melville and Long Ghost. On the other hand, the only evidence
which Lucett adduces to prove that Melville was the proper object of
his contumely is of one piece with the inflated oratory which he puts

in his own mouth at the moment of crisis and with the egotistical texture of the whole anecdote. Of course, it never occurred to him to connect Melville with the "one kind fellow" among the mutineers. Certainly, before identifying an unknown man in order to villify him in print, one should have convincing proofs of identification. And this applies particularly· to Lucett since his chief accusation against Melville was that he himself had, in *Omoo,* "grossly scandalized by name some worthy men living in Tahiti" without warrant or justification.

Who, then, could Lucett's villain have been? Perhaps the most impetuous and ruffianly of the mutineers mentioned by Melville as one of the ten prisoners at the Calabooza was "a young American who went by the name of Salem"—the only other American among them. He it was who in *Omoo,* during the incipient mutiny aboard the "Julia," turned furiously on one of his fellow rebels merely because he would not stand his ground against Consul Wilson and "dashed out from among the rest, and fetching the cooper a blow that sent him humming over toward the consul, flourished a naked sheath-knife in the air, and burst forth with, 'I'm the little fellow that can answer your questions; just put them to me once, *counsellor.*' " [84] A fair guess would be that Salem was the "dastardly ruffian of the bowie-knife species" who threw himself upon Lucett, "a bound and defenceless man." For Melville was at this time undoubtedly on the neighboring island of Eimeo, if the record in *Omoo* can be trusted, engaged in the peaceful occupation of farming in the fertile valley of "Martair"; and on this very Sunday night, November 13, according to his own internal evidence, he was returning from a visit to the nearby bay of "Afrehitoo," where he had been attending service at a mission chapel—a family habit of church-going which followed him throughout his wanderings in Polynesia, but with a difference in attitude which will be examined in the next chapter.

CHAPTER X

TAHITI IN 1842

*ANOTHER object proposed is, to give a familiar account of the present con-
dition of the converted Polynesians, as affected by their promiscuous intercourse with foreigners, and the teachings of the missionaries, combined.*

*As a roving sailor, the author spent about three months in various parts of
the islands of Tahiti and Imeeo, and under circumstances most favourable for
correct observations on the social conditions of the natives.*

*In every statement connected with missionary operations, a strict adherence
to facts has, of course, been scrupulously observed; and in some instances, it
has been deemed advisable to quote previous voyagers, in corroboration of what
is offered as the fruit of the author's own observations. Nothing but an earnest
desire for truth and good has led him to touch upon this subject at all. And
if he refrains from offering hints as to the best mode of remedying the evils
which are pointed out, it is only because he thinks, that after being made acquainted with the facts, others are better qualified to do so.*

*Should a little jocoseness be shown upon some curious traits of the Tahitians,
it proceeds from no intention to ridicule: things are merely described as, from
their entire novelty, they first struck an unbiased observer.*

THUS in his Preface to *Omoo* Melville prepares the way for his
polemical central chapters, which contain the heart of the
message he brought back to civilization from his residence
in Tahiti. Glowing accounts of the felicity, purity, and nobleness
of primitive life—such as those that embellish the pages of *Typee*—
are palatable food for the polite tables of a world-weary society.
But it is quite another matter when, growing eloquent over these
exotic dishes, an erstwhile pleasant dinner companion begins to
elaborate philosophical comparisons which are derogatory to Western culture itself, and which disparage the efforts of its evangelists.
In his first book Melville had included a few passages which, he
warned, "may be thought to bear rather hard upon a reverend
order of men." And his prognostication was correct. For, in spite
of the immediate and widespread popularity of *Typee*, Melville's

[237]

publishers felt it necessary to issue a revised edition before the summer of 1846 had passed, purged of all offensive matter: its mockery of the missionaries' efforts to Christianize the Marquesans, its satire of the French attempts to civilize them, and its eulogies of the Polynesian way of life as superior to that of Europe.[1] As disheartening as this censorship must have been to Melville, he was evidently prepared for it, as a hitherto unpublished letter reveals. Writing in July, 1846, to Evert Duyckinck, his close friend and literary adviser, he points out his American publishers, Wiley and Putnam, as the authors of these expurgations, remarking without bitterness or surprise: "Typee has come out measurably unscathed from the fiery ordeal of Mr. Wiley's criticisms. I trust as it will stand the book will retain all the essential features which formerly commended it to the public favor." [2]

Melville's first attack on civilization and its emissaries had been largely a negative one, however, for in 1842 the Marquesas Islands were as yet little tainted by contact with Europe, and *Typee* is chiefly a defense of unspoiled primitivism. But in *Omoo* he planned a more positive attack, for Tahiti furnished an example of the semicivilization of half a century of missionary and commercial intercourse which, in his eyes at least, had wrought unspeakable havoc in this New Cytherea of the early explorers. His first tilt with the censors fresh in his memory, Melville had some misgivings about his new manuscript, completed in the late fall of 1846. On December 8, he sent the first chapter of *Omoo* to Duyckinck for an opinion, with the explanation: "I address you now not as being in any way connected with Messrs. W[iley] and P[utnam] but presume to do so confidentially as a friend." [3] Two days later he followed this up with the rest of the book, as is revealed in a significant letter to the same friend, now published for the first time:

My Dear Sir
   Herewith you have the remaining chapters. Those marked in the Table of Contents as *Nos.* V, VII, & XVII have been rejected altogether —but this does not break the continuity of the book. I have not as yet altered the numbers of the chapters as thus affected.

I beg you to pay particular attention to the following chapters—*33, 34*—& 45, 46, 47, 48, *49, 50*.—They all refer more or less to the missions & the conditions of the natives.

> Very Faithfully Yours
> Herman Melville

Thursday Afternoon.[4]

These brief lines contain much of interest to the student of Melville. What manner of "boastful lechery," of impious satire, of Rousseauistic castigation was contained in these lost chapters of *Omoo* will never be known, for there is no manuscript copy of the book extant, and Melville does not even indicate what their titles were to have been. Indeed, it is difficult to conjecture what offensive matter could have been contained in two of them—Nos. V and VII—for the first ten chapters of the published work are devoted to a very matter-of-fact narrative of the week spent by the "Julia" cruising about the Marquesas Islands in the hope of replenishing her depleted crew. The third rejected chapter—No. XVII—would have fallen in a more provocative context, for No. XVIII in the published version contains a general historical account of Tahiti that could easily have been preceded by an offensive contrasting chapter on its degenerate condition in 1842. Indeed, it is possible that this one alone was ultimately rejected and that the first two were restored, for a comparison of the rest of the chapter numeration in the letter with that in *Omoo* indicates a discrepancy of only one.

The second paragraph of Melville's letter is perfectly clear. He simply calls attention to eight central chapters which deal with the missionaries and the condition of the natives, requesting Duyckinck's judgment on their literary merit and propriety. The first two—"*33, 34*"— evidently refer to chapters XXXII and XXXIII of *Omoo,* dealing respectively with the French attack on Tahiti and the less demonstrative but equally insidious inroads of European diseases there. The others—"45, 46, 47, 48, *49, 50*"—refer similarly to the published sequence XLIV–XLIX, whose chapter titles alone indicate their controversial content: "The Church of the Cocoanuts," "A Missionary's Sermon; with Some Reflections," "Something About the Kannakippers [the moral police]," "How They Dress in Tahiti," "Tahiti As It Is," "Same Subject Continued." These six chapters contain the gist of Melville's discussion of the religious, moral, and social status of Tahiti in 1842, the result of a fifty-year experiment in civilizing and Christianizing the Noble Savages of Polynesia.

What Duyckinck's advice in the matter was can only be conjectured, for his reply to Melville's note is not extant. But he at least read the book and realized the small chance of persuading Wiley and Putnam to publish it, as is evidenced in a letter to his brother a few lays later:

Melville is in town with new MSS agitating the conscience of John Wiley and tempting the pockets of the Harpers. I have read it. His further adventures in the South Seas after leaving Typee. He owes a sailor's grudge to the Missionaries and pays it off at Tahiti.[5]

Whatever deletions may have been made were probably Melville's own; but they were not sufficient to pacify the American sponsors of *Typee*. So, in the end, Wiley and Putnam apparently set principle above profit, one experience with such an author being enough for them; for it was undoubtedly a disagreement over the propriety of publishing this provocative material that brought about the rift between Melville and his former publishers. At any rate, when *Omoo* appeared in America on May 5, 1847, it bore the imprint of Harper & Brothers—the publishers of Melville's next six volumes, until even their hardihood was dampened by the moral ambiguities of *Pierre*.

As with many other Victorians, the *Sturm und Drang* of Melville's adolescence centered about a reëvaluation of his religious faith. But Melville gave the problem its maximum complexity by shouldering on "Christian" the whole burden of the multitudinous ills attributable, in the eyes of an idealist, to Western civilization. With a philosopher's inclusiveness, he debated the relative merits of two entire cultures; for him it was heathendom versus Christendom. And this was just as true when he gave a metaphysical expression to his conflict later in *Clarel* (1876) as when he had con-

fined himself to a discussion of externals in *Omoo*. How deep the
roots of this conflict went back into his childhood, and how long
the noxious perfumes of the full flower of disillusion tormented
his restless head, we can only know by dark hints of a stern Cal-
vinistic upbringing and vague reports of withdrawal into a confused philosophical seclusion during his last years.[6] But, for the
adolescent Melville's reactions to the effects of Christian civilization in Polynesia, and for the accuracy of his observations, the
evidence is more explicit. Melville carried his interest in religion
with him through all his wanderings in the South Seas, attending
church whenever possible, observing, reflecting, and commenting;
and the biographer can now follow him in this strange pilgrimage.

"On Sundays," says Melville, "I always attended the principal
native church on the outskirts of the village of Papeetee, and not
far from the Calabooza Beretanee."[7] This chapel, considered the
best specimen of architecture on the island, Melville christened
the "Church of the Cocoa-nuts." His description of it follows:

> The present metropolitan church of Tahiti . . . [compared with the
> cathedral of Pomaré II] is of moderate dimensions, boarded over, and
> painted white. It is furnished also with blinds, but no sashes; indeed,
> were it not for the rustic thatch, it would remind one of a plain chapel
> at home. . . .
> Within, its aspect is unique, and cannot fail to interest a stranger.
> The rafters overhead are bound round with fine matting of variegated
> dyes; and all along the ridge-pole, these trappings hang pendant, in
> alternate bunches of tassels and deep fringes of stained grass. The floor
> is composed of rude planks. Regular aisles run between ranges of na-
> tive settees, bottomed with crossed braids of the cocoa-nut fibre, and
> furnished with backs. . . .
> Nor does the church lack a gallery, which runs round on three sides,
> and is supported by columns of the cocoa-nut tree.[8]

Commodore Charles Wilkes described this chapel during his visit
three years before as:

> [Pritchard's] church, a large frame building, much like a New England
> meeting-house. It has numerous windows, a large gallery, and pews
> capable of containing a great number of people.[9]

And Captain Fitzroy, commander of the famous expedition of which Darwin was the botanist, registered his disapproval of its mixed European and Tahitian architecture:

I was sorry to see the new church, a large wooden structure capable of holding six hundred people, covered by a partly Otaheitan [*sic*] roof, in lieu of one formed completely in their own style. Instead of the circular end, an ugly gable terminates a high box-shaped house, resembling a factory.[10]

These two corroborations serve to identify Melville's "Church of the Cocoa-nuts" as an actual chapel at Papeete in 1842, though the elaborate ornamentation inside, which he says made the natives set such a high estimate on its æsthetic worth, may have been drawn from imagination only.

The congregation attending this church, according to Melville, was composed of the better and wealthier natives, superior in healthfulness, personal beauty, and dress to the common people, who were more exposed to the debasing effects of foreign intercourse. The latter frequently had to be driven to their places of worship, but the communicants of the Church of the Cocoa-nuts went voluntarily, arrayed in all their finery:

It was the first place for Christian worship in Polynesia that I had seen; and the impression upon entering during service was all the stronger. . . .

The place is well filled. Everywhere meet the eye the gay calico draperies worn on great occasions by the higher classes, and forming a strange contrast of patterns and colours. In some instances, these are so fashioned as to resemble as much as possible European garments. This is in excessively· bad taste. Coats and pantaloons, too, are here and there seen; but they look awkwardly enough, and take away from the general effect.

But it is the array of countenances that most strikes you. Each is suffused with the peculiar animation of the Polynesians, when thus collected in large numbers. Every robe is rustling, every limb in motion, and an incessant buzzing going on throughout the assembly. The tumult is so great that the voice of the placid old missionary, who now rises, is almost inaudible. Some degree of silence is at length obtained through the exertions of half a dozen strapping fellows, in white shirts and no pantaloons. Running in among the settees, they are at great pains to inculcate the impropriety of making a noise by creating a most unnecessary racket themselves. This part of the service was quite comical. . . . [Then a hymn was announced.]

The first air fairly startled me; it was the brave tune of Old Hundred, adapted to a Tahitian psalm. After the graceless scenes I had recently passed through, this circumstance, with all its accessories, moved me forcibly.

Many voices around were of great sweetness and compass. The singers, also, seemed to enjoy themselves mightily; some of them pausing, now and then, and looking round, as if to realise the scene more fully. In truth, they sang right joyously, despite the solemnity of the tune. . . .

A chapter of the Tahitian Bible was now read; a text selected; and the sermon began. It was listened to with more attention than I had anticipated.[11]

This spirited sketch by Melville seems on the whole to be a fair picture of a native church service, though he was called to account for it by one or two pious reviewers of *Omoo*. To arrive at a fair judgment, therefore, it seems best to consider the reports of several visitors who attended native worship at Papeete during this period.

Otto von Kotzebue, the Russian navigator whose accounts of the state of Christianity at Tahiti had set the missionary world by the ears a decade before and had brought forth loud comments of malicious exaggeration, passed by the actual church services rather lightly, merely remarking:

Notwithstanding the seriousness and devotion apparent among the Tahaitians [*sic*], it is almost impossible for an European, seeing them for the first time in their Sunday attire, to refrain from laughter.[12]

In 1839 Commodore Wilkes, in general an impartial observer, was likewise impressed chiefly by the grotesque apearance of the half-civilized congregation, and he also added a note on the lack of religious seriousness among the natives:

I thought the attendance on worship small, compared with what I had been led to anticipate. There were less than two hundred persons present, and they did not appear to be as attentive as they had been represented. The women were more numerous than the other sex, and were dressed in a most unbecoming manner. They wore high flaring chip bonnets of their own manufacture, loose gay-coloured silk frocks, with showy kerchiefs tied around their necks. Nothing can appear more *outré* than they do in these habiliments.[13]

Strangely enough, one of the most unfavorable acounts is that of the good Quaker Wheeler, himself a missionary, but an independent one with no defensive justification to make of his own good works, such as might have colored his report:

The continual talking and light behavior of a large portion of the people were truly painful, although several attempts were made to restore order amongst them; and the sound of some sharp strokes of the long sticks by the agents employed to keep order, was distinctly heard amongst the younger people.[14]

On the other hand, there were favorable reports of Sunday services by visitors whose accounts seem to be equally impartial. Captain Fitzroy's is one of the fullest of these:

At Mr. Pritchard's church we found an orderly, attentive and decently dressed congregation. I saw nothing "grotesque," nothing "ludicrous," nor anything which had a tendency to "depress the spirits" or "disappoint one's expectations." [Note: "I had read Kotzebue's voyage a few days previously."]

The church was quite full and many were sitting outside; I suppose six hundred people were present besides children, who, like others of their happy age, required an occasional touch with the white wand of a most stern looking old beadle, to prevent their chattering to one another about the strangers, and their "money."

Mr. Pritchard's fluent delivery in the native language surprised and pleased us much. The greater part of the natives were very attentive. Two were making notes upon paper, of the subject of his discourse. A few were careless, but only a very few; and their eye-wanderings were caused chiefly by the strangers in uniform. Where is the English congregation of five or six hundred persons, in which a captious observer could not occasionally detect inattention to the clergyman? Hymns were sung with much propriety, and a very pleasing musical effect. The language is so soft and so full of vowels, that the good voices and very correct ears of the natives succeed admirably in hymns.[15]

Charles Darwin, who was present at the same service, was not quite so enthusiastic, however. He found Pritchard's service an "interesting spectacle," but he adds:

I was rather disappointed in the apparent degree of attention; but I believe my expectations were raised too high. At all events the appearance was quite equal to that in a country church in England.[16]

[244]

These oversanguine expectations were probably the result of having read the glowing reports of native worship sent home by the missionaries. Typical of the exaggeration caused by such excess zeal are the accounts written by the Reverend George Pritchard himself in his *Missionary's Reward*. And it may be added that Fitzroy was possibly an exceptionally enthusiastic lay visitor, for it is notable that his testimony is singled out by Pritchard to substantiate his own eulogiums.[17]

It was undoubtedly Melville's report of the sermon itself, however, which scandalized the pious. Having been informed that the discourses of the missionaries, calculated to engage the attention of their simple auditors, were to strangers an amusing combination of paternal advice and exhortations to economic ambition, Melville says, he provided himself with an interpreter. The resulting notes are farcical in the extreme. The native girls were warned not to have anything to do with the sailors from whale ships: "Where they come from no good people talk to 'em—just like dogs." Similarly the French usurpers were inveighed against as a set of robbers, with the added warning: "Wicked priests here, too; and wicked idols in woman's clothes." But the most insidious propaganda attributed by Melville to this missionary was an appeal to the lowest mercenary motivations for embracing Christianity, followed by a plea for contributions to the missionary's own well-being:

"Good friends, this very small island, but very wicked, and very poor; these two go together. Why Beretanee so great? Because that island good island, and send *mickonaree* to poor *kannaka*. In Beretanee, every man rich: plenty things to buy; and plenty things to sell. Houses bigger than Pomaree's, and more grand. Everybody, too, ride about in coaches, bigger than hers; and wear fine tappa every day. (Several luxurious appliances of civilisation were here enumerated, and described.)

"Good friends, little left to eat at my house. Schooner from Sydney no bring bag of flour; and kannaka no bring pig and fruit enough. Mickonaree do great deal for kannaka; kannaka do little for Mickonaree. So, good friends, weave plenty of cocoa-nut baskets, fill 'em, and bring 'em to-morrow." [18]

Unfortunately, there are no contemporary records of sermons preached at Tahiti by which this can be checked, for none of the visitors who attended native services undertook to make such stenographic reports of them, probably not understanding the native language well enough; and the missionaries, quite naturally, would not have reported such defamatory accounts of themselves even if they had been true. All that can be said is that Melville's version of the sermon, though not beyond the bounds of probability, was in all likelihood touched up in the retelling.

Yet this sermon Melville says, ironically, was admirably suited to the minds of the islanders:

> The Tahitians can hardly ever be said to reflect: they are all impulse; and so, instead of expounding dogmas, the missionaries give them the large type, pleasing cuts, and short and easy lessons of the primer. Hence anything like a permanent religious impression is seldom or never produced.
>
> In fact, there is, perhaps, no race upon earth less disposed by nature to the monitions of Christianity than the people of the South Seas.[19]

In amplification of this sweeping statement Melville analyzes the Tahitian character as naturally indolent, both physically and mentally, and constitutionally voluptuous—averse to any restraint—qualities which, however suited to the luxurious state of nature in the tropics, are the greatest possible hindrances to the strict moralities of Christianity. Added to these is the inherent childlike eagerness to please, induced by fear or by the desire to court the favor of their superiors in power, that leads them to assume a passionate interest in matters for which they really feel little or none whatever, and that can only be classified by the categorical Western mind as hypocrisy. Yet these very qualities, appearing to the early explorers as merely docility, ingenuousness, and amiability, misled the London Missionary Society into regarding them as the most promising subjects for conversion. In the half-century since the establishment of the Tahitian Mission, Melville admits, some changes have been effected. The entire system of idolatry has been done away with, for example; but this he ascribes not so much to the missionaries as to the general civilizing effects of a long and

constant intercourse with whites of all nations, citing the voluntary abolition of the institution of *tapu* in the Sandwich Islands
long before the arrival of the Christian teachers there. Again, the
"atrocities" formerly reported as committed by the natives on
visiting ships have now given place to peaceful trading; but this
is true only because the whites themselves no longer provoke such
retaliation by acts of wanton and unthinking cruelty practiced
upon "mere savages." Finally, there is one achievement which Melville ascribes solely to the missionaries: they have translated the
entire Bible into the language of the island. But the character of
the natives continues to present an almost insurmountable barrier
to any genuine improvement in morals or religion.

Nor is there any lack of substantiation for the first part of this
discouraging picture. The early missionaries themselves were the
most eloquent of all in their reports to the home office of Polynesian depravity. By way of explaining why, for a quarter of a
century, they had made so little progress, they did not fail to paint
the native character in its darkest aspects.[20] But once they began
to make headway, however nominal, they changed their minds
about the inherent nature of the Tahitians and strongly asserted
their innate qualifications for conversion, attributing to contamination with renegade frontier whites whatever of indolence, sensuality, and dishonesty they admitted still to remain after half a
century of Christianizing. Melville, likewise, was not entirely consistent in this respect. Having branded them as constitutionally
"depraved," from the Christian point of view, in order to prove
that they were unsuited to Christianity, he later takes the stand
that their depravity is attributable to the effects of civilization—
"their promiscuous intercourse with foreigners, and the teachings
of the missionaries, combined"—and that the natives in their original state had been pure and noble, even as he had painted the
Marquesans in *Typee*. But opinions as to the true nature of Tahitian character, both before and after contact with Christian civilization, are as diverse as they are numerous, as will be shortly
demonstrated.

Facts are more reliable than theories, however, and nowhere

more so than in regard to primitive man. It is undeniable that the first missionaries, who had come out in 1797, found it hard to make any progress whatever, and that a large part of their failure was attributable to the habitual indolence and sensuality of the natives (according to the white man's standard of conduct).[21] But they met with obstacles other than indifference. John Turnbull, a voyager who visited Tahiti in 1803, says that the London Society had made little headway in getting the natives to understand Christianity; and, by way of example he reports a conversation that he had after a Sunday service with King Otoo, the first Pomaré:

He asked me, upon the departure of the missionaries, whether it was all true, as they had preached. I replied in the affirmative, that it was strictly so according to my own belief, and that of all the wiser and better part of my countrymen. He demanded of me where Jehovah lived; I pointed to the heavens. He said he did not believe it. His brother was, if possible, still worse. Edeah [his mother] was looking on with a kind of haughty and disdainful indifference. It was all k[n]avery or falsehood, adding, they would not believe unless they could see; and observed, we could bring down the sun and moon by means of our quadrant, why could we not bring down our Saviour by similar means? [22]

But this same doubting Otoo, first brought to the attention of the Western world by Captain Cook, died before the close of this year, a stout pagan to the end.

At this point Melville takes up the history of the Christianization of Tahiti:

He was succeeded by his son, Pomaree II., the most famous prince in the annals of Tahiti. Though a sad debauchee and drunkard, and even charged with unnatural crimes, he was a great friend of the missionaries, and one of their very first proselytes. During the religious wars into which he was hurried by his zeal for the new faith, he was defeated, and expelled from the island. After a short exile he returned from Imeeo, with an army of eight hundred warriors; and, in the battle of Narii, routed the rebellious pagans with great slaughter, and re-established himself upon the throne. Thus, by force of arms, was Christianity finally triumphant in Tahiti.[23]

Even the Reverend Michael Russell in his *Polynesia,* a work compiled from many sources for the avowed purpose of defending the
missionary cause, admits that Pomaré II accepted Christianity from
economic rather than religious motives:

> There cannot be any doubt that it was with the view of improving his
> subjects in the mechanic arts, and more especially augmenting his
> military resources, rather than with any reference to spiritual advan-
> tages, that Pomaré finally resolved to abjure the absurdities of the
> superstition in which he had been educated.[24]

And bloody wars indeed followed this wholesale national acceptance of Christianity, just as Melville says. Otto von Kotzebue,
whose disparagements of the Christian civilization of Tahiti were
denied in so many other respects, left an account of this religious
warfare which none have dared to challenge, except to say that it
was exaggerated:

> This conversion was a spark thrown into a powder magazine, and was
> followed by a fearful explosion. The Marais [temples] were destroyed—
> every memorial of the former worship defaced—the new religion forcibly
> established, and whoever would not adopt it put to death. With the
> zeal for making proselytes, the rage of tigers took possession of a people
> once so gentle. Streams of blood flowed—whole races were exterminated;
> many resolutely met the death they preferred to the renunciation of
> their ancient faith. Some few escaped by flight to the recesses of the lofty
> mountains, where they still live in seclusion, faithful to the gods of
> their ancestors. . . . I really believe that these pious people were them-
> selves shocked at the consequences of their zeal; but they soon consoled
> themselves.[25]

It is true that Pomaré II died in 1821, two years after being
baptized into the church, and that the islands rocked along under
a regency for the next ten years—during the reign of the boy king,
Pomaré III, and the first few years of the reign of Aimata, Queen
Pomaré I—but the royal sanction had been given to Christianity,
and the work of conversion proceeded at a rapid pace. It is from
this time on, however, that the greatest diversity of opinion prevails as to the actual state of Christianized Tahiti. The missionaries, to be sure, sent home reports of wholesale conversions; but

[249]

to many visitors the result was a mere nominal Christianity, based upon anything but spiritual understanding and conviction. Melville himself has much to say on this head. Instead of estimating the result of missionary labors by the number of heathens who have actually been made to understand and practice the precepts of Christianity, he declares, reports have been broadcast of the thousands who, without any genuine change of heart or of religious philosophy, have been induced in any way to abandon idolatry and conform to certain outward observances. To Melville such "conversions" were misleading, since they were prompted merely by the hope of worldly benefit, and since they were dictated to the natives by their chiefs. In illustration of this superficiality, he cites a pseudo-Pentecostal visitation staged by the natives of Raiatea in order to curry favor with the missionaries, the "Great Revival" of 1836 in Hawaii which had been followed by an orgy of licentiousness, and the voluntary revival of heathen customs by an island professing Christianity as related by Williams the martyr of Erromanga.[26] And all of these examples are sober historical facts recorded by the missionaries themselves, but with a difference.

Melville then brings forward tacit evidence to prove in what low estimation even the missionaries held the state of Christianity and morals among the converted Polynesians in 1842:

> On the island of Imeeo (attached to the Tahitian mission) is a seminary under the charge of the Rev. Mr. Simpson and wife, for the education of the children of the missionaries, exclusively. Sent home—in many cases, at a very early age—to finish their education, the pupils here are taught nothing but the rudiments of knowledge; nothing more than may be learned in the native schools. Notwithstanding this, the two races are kept as far as possible from associating; the avowed reason being, to preserve the young whites from moral contamination. The better to ensure this end, every effort is made to prevent them from acquiring the native language.[27]

This illustration Melville probably found ready to hand in the *Narrative* of Commodore Wilkes, a work which he cites in other connections:

> Mr. and Mrs. Simpson have the care of a school for the children of missionaries and respectable white parents: these are kept entirely

separate from the children of the natives; the reason assigned for this exclusiveness is, that the danger of the former receiving improper ideas is such as to preclude their association with the latter. This may be a good policy as far as the white children are concerned, although I doubt its having a good effect on their minds if they are destined to spend their lives among the islands. The habit they will thus acquire of looking upon the natives as their inferiors, cannot fail to have an injurious influence on both. . . .

This, I must say, appeared to me the worst feature I had seen in the missionary establishment.[28]

Yet the missionaries, says Melville, kept up the pretense of the success of Christianity in Polynesia not only by their reports of wholesale conversions, which misled the Church at home, but also by the enforcement of at least a strict outward observance of the forms of piety, which might have misled the casual visitor, and possibly even some of the optimistic teachers themselves. One of these Connecticut Blue Laws pertained to keeping the Fourth Commandment. The Reverend Messrs. Daniel Tyerman and George Bennet, sent out as delegates from the London Missionary Society to visit the various stations in the South Seas, pointed with pride to the observance of the Sabbath by the Tahitians:

Not a fire is lighted, neither flesh nor fruit is baked, not a tree is climbed, nor a canoe seen on the water, nor a journey by land performed, on God's holy day; religion—religion alone—is the business and delight of these simple-minded people on the Sabbath.[29]

But many lay visitors objected to this "more than Presbyterian manner of keeping the Sabbath" which they found enjoined on the natives by the overzealous missionaries, even as Melville registers his own quiet disapproval:

The Sabbath is no ordinary day with the Tahitians. So far as doing any work is concerned, it is scrupulously observed. The canoes are hauled up on the beach; the nets are spread to dry. Passing by the hencoop huts, on the roadside, you find their occupants idle, as usual; but less disposed to gossip. After service, repose broods over the whole island; the valleys reaching inland look stiller than ever.

In short, it is Sunday—their "Taboo Day"; the very word formerly expressing the sacredness of their pagan observances, now proclaiming the sanctity of the Christian Sabbath.[30]

Similarly, Kotzebue, who helped to form many of Melville's judgments about Tahiti, made light of the importance of such evidences of Christianity:

The inhabitants of Tahaiti [*sic*] were celebrating the Sunday, on which account they did not leave their houses, where they lay on their bellies reading the Bible and howling aloud; laying aside every species of occupation, they devoted, as they said, the whole day to prayer. . . . [The missionaries] have ever since continued to watch with the most vigilant severity over the maintenance of every article of their faith. Hence, . . . their former admirable industry, and their joyous buoyancy of spirits, have been changed for continual praying, and meditating upon things which the teachers understand as little as the taught.[31]

These Blue Laws were administered by a set of officers whom Melville calls "Kannakippers," a native corruption of the word *constables.* One of their duties was to drive the natives to church:

On Sunday mornings, when the prospect is rather small for a full house in the minor churches, a parcel of fellows are actually sent out into the highways and byways as whippers-in of the congregation. This is a sober fact.[32]

Lest his readers be incredulous, as indeed they might have been, Melville substantiates his statement by a reference to the *Memoirs of the Life and Gospel Labors of the Late Daniel Wheeler,* saying that this recent benevolent visitor at the island alluded to the custom with abhorrence and disgust. This is indeed true, and it is by means of such frank and yet tempered criticism of missionary activity at Tahiti that the Quaker minister commends himself as an impartial observer. His condemnation follows:

There are so many aggravated circumstances which contribute to lessen the desire of the people for religion, that the present aspect of things here is truly discouraging; none of these seems to operate more powerfully to produce dislike and disgust than the arbitrary laws that have been made to compel the people to attend the places of worship and the schools; the neglect of which has no less a penalty attached to it than the forfeiture of their lands . . . ; but this coercion, of course, does no more than enforce a ceremony, if indeed, from its unchristian character, it does not operate as a hindrance to the progress of Christianity.[33]

This incredible Pharisaism was vividly described by Kotzebue, ten years before:

> To pray and to obey are the only commands laid upon an oppressed people, who submissively bow to the yoke, and even suffer themselves to be driven to prayers by the cudgel!
>
> A police-officer is especially appointed to enforce the prescribed attendance upon the church and prayer-meetings. I saw him in the exercise of his functions, armed with a bamboo canoe, driving his herd to the spiritual pasture. He seemed himself to be conscious of the burlesque attaching to his office,—at least he behaved very absurdly in it, and many a stroke fell rather in jest than in earnest. The drollery of the driver did not, however, enliven the dejected countenances of his flock.[34]

According to Melville, the Kannakippers did not confine their activities to the enforcement of attendance upon church services:

> On week days, they are quite as busy as on Sundays; to the great terror of the inhabitants, going all over the island, and spying out the wickedness thereof. . . . These gentry are indefatigable. At the dead of night prowling round the houses, and in the daytime hunting amorous couples in the groves.[35]

He then tells of an instance in which a pair of transgressors of the Seventh Commandment fled from the police and completely baffled pursuit for three months; but, while Melville was at the Calabooza, they were captured and sentenced to make one hundred fathoms of Broom Road. Consequently, he says, the natives not only feared the moral constables but hated them. He is borne out in this declaration by F. A. Olmsted, a visitor who had preceded him at Tahiti by only two years:

> Next to these [the judges] are the police officers, a numerous class, whose particular province is to make domiciliary visits to check the erratic propensities of the natives during the night. They are pronounced to be a band of great rascals.[36]

And, in the very year of Melville's residence there, his own severest critic, Edward Lucett, joined him in denouncing the whole system of moral police for its failure to lessen the prevalent licentiousness:

The missionaries, instead of trying to suppress this evil by examples of the strictest continence in their own persons, have endeavoured to check it by the institution of sumptuary laws, making the crime a marketable offence, to be atoned for by the payment of so many dollars. This system of punishment is eluded and laughed at; or, if the parties are detected, the paramour pays the fine, and the crime continues.[37]

And the only result, he adds, was to superinduce on their other bad qualities "hypocrisy of the deepest dye."

This is, indeed, the principal charge which Melville makes against the coercive superintendence of the spiritual well-being of the natives. Many of the women were professing Christians, he says: "Yet after eating bread-fruit at the Eucharist, I knew several of them, the same night, to be guilty of some sad derelictions." Puzzled by such inconsistencies, he determined to find out for himself what understanding, if any, they entertained of religion. Accordingly, he paid a visit to a household of communicants who lived near the Calabooza:

We dropped in one evening, and found the ladies at home. . . . I lounged on a mat with Ideea, the eldest, dallying with her grass fan, and improving my knowledge of Tahitian.

The occasion was well adapted to my purpose, and I began.

"Ah, Ideea, mickonaree oee?" the same as drawling out—"By the by, Miss Ideea, do you belong to the church?"

"Yes, me mickonaree," was the reply.

But the assertion was at once qualified by certain reservations; so curious that I cannot forbear their relation.

"Mickonaree *ena*" (church member *here*), exclaimed she, laying her hand upon her mouth, and a strong emphasis on the adverb. In the same way, and with similar exclamations, she touched her eyes and hands. This done, her whole air changed in an instant; and she gave me to understand, by unmistakable gestures, that in certain other respects she was not exactly a "mickonaree." In short, Ideea was

"A sad good Christian at the heart—
A very heathen in the carnal part."

The explanation terminated in a burst of laughter, in which all three sisters joined; and, for fear of looking silly, the doctor and myself. As soon as good-breeding would permit, we took leave.[38]

It was undoubtedly such anecdotes as this that scandalized the pious.[39]

In addition to the handful of readers who were shocked into disbelief by Melville's "boastful lechery," many others may have felt that he was guilty of some invention in such a piquant episode as this. Yet the damsels of Nukahiva, at any rate, seem to have practiced similar hypocrisy. E. H. Lamont, who visited the bay of Taiohaë ten years after Melville's desertion there, recorded an anecdote so surprisingly like the one in *Omoo* as to furnish full substantiation for it. On a ramble through the settlement one Sunday, he looked in upon the household of the royal Moana, where all were engaged in praying and reading the Bible. Later on in his walk up the valley, he surprised some native girls bathing in a stream. They fled to a native house, and he followed:

One of the lovely trio proved to be a backslider from the group of devotees I had a few minutes before seen so piously occupied at the king's house. I pointed significantly towards the place where I had previously seen her, uttering the word "missionary," which she repeated, indicating at the same time, by a sufficiently expressive sign, that she was "missionary" only from the lips—an avowal at which the other frail ones laughed immoderately. . . . The character of the natives was unchanged; they merely acted a lie in their semblance of devotion.[40]

At Tahiti, likewise, this species of mummery seems to have become almost a ritual with the natives when guilty of transgressing the Blue Laws laid upon them by the missionaries. In fact, the famous Charles Darwin was the witness of such a scene during an excursion which he made into the mountains back of Papeete with two native assistants. Indeed, he himself was the unwitting tempter on this occasion, being ignorant at the time of the law prohibiting the sale or use of intoxicating liquors on the island:

I took with me a flask of spirits, which they could not resolve to refuse; but as often as they drank a little, they put their fingers before their mouths, and uttered the word "Missionary."[41]

One need only call to mind the similar role constantly being enacted on every hand in America by another race of semi-Christianized primitives in order to be persuaded of the validity of Melville's anecdote.

The very existence of such numerous, severe, and perpetually violated laws against licentiousness of all kinds was in itself, according to Melville, an index of the continual increase of immorality. And the hypocrisy and discontent were aggravated by the fact that the missionaries, in the excess of their zeal to stamp out the last trace of heathenism, exercised no discretion in the application of their prohibitory laws:

Many pleasant and seemingly innocent sports and pastimes are likewise interdicted. . . . Among their everyday amusements were dancing, tossing the football, kite-flying, flute-playing, and singing traditional ballads—*now*, all punishable offences; though most of them have been so long in disuse that they are nearly forgotten.

In the same way, the "Opio," or festive harvest-home of the bread-fruit, has been suppressed; though, as described to me by Captain Bob, it seemed wholly free of any immoral tendency. Against tattooing, of any kind, there is a severe law. . . .

Doubtless, in thus denationalising the Tahitians, as it were, the missionaries were prompted by a sincere desire for good; but the effect has been lamentable. Supplied with no amusements in place of those forbidden, the Tahitians, who require more recreation than other people, have sunk into a listlessness, or indulge in sensualities, a hundred times more pernicious than all the games ever celebrated in the temple of Tanee.[42]

The testimony of many lay visitors corroborates this dark picture of the state of religion, conduct, and general morale in Tahiti as brought about by the misguided efforts of the missionaries. One sample, drawn from the *Narrative* of Captain F. W. Beechey, will suffice:

Ignorance of the language prevented my obtaining any correct information as to the progress that had been made generally towards a knowledge of the Scriptures by those who were converted; but my impression was . . . that it was very limited, and but few understood the simplest parts of them. . . . In general those who were *missi-narees* [as the converted term themselves] had a proper respect for the book, but associating it with the suppression of their amusements, their dances, singing, and music, they read it with much less good will than if a system had been introduced which would have tempered religion with cheerfulness, and have instilled happiness into society. . . . Without amusements, and excessively indolent, they now seek enjoyment in idleness and sensuality, and too much pains cannot be bestowed to

arouse them from their apathy, and to induce them to emerge from
their general state of indifference to those occupations which are most
essential to their welfare.[43]

This commentator, whom Melville cites in several specific connections, undoubtedly furnished him also with a suggestion for his
general attitude, as in the passage just quoted. And Beechey must
be given considerable weight as an authority, in spite of many
pious objections leveled at his book, for he remained at Tahiti
over six weeks in the constant company of the missionaries, who,
he said, treated him well; he simply felt called upon, in his own
words, to restore the balance of judgment which had been over-
turned by the too favorable accounts of the Christian teachers.

Having examined the religious and moral condition of the
natives, Melville next turns to their economic and social status as
it had been affected by their contact with Christian civilization:

It has been said that the only way to civilise a people is to form in
them habits of industry. Judged by this principle, the Tahitians are
less civilised now than formerly. True, their constitutional indolence
is excessive; but surely, if the spirit of Christianity is among them, so
unchristian a vice ought to be, at least, partially remedied. But the reverse is the fact. Instead of acquiring new occupations, old ones have
been discontinued. . . .

This, however, would be all very well, were the natives to apply
themselves to such occupations as would enable them to supply the few
articles they need. But they are far from doing so; and the majority being unable to obtain European substitutes for many things before made
by themselves, the inevitable consequence is seen in the present wretched
and destitute mode of life among the common people. . . .

In Tahiti the people have nothing to do; and idleness, every where,
is the parent of vice. "There is scarcely anything," says the good old
Quaker Wheeler, "so striking, or pitiable, as their aimless, nerveless
mode of spending life." [44]

Wheeler, or rather his son Charles, did report that he found the
habits of the natives deplorably indolent, and apparently he attributed this as much to their state of semicivilization as to any
constitutional defect, adding after the sentence quoted by Melville: "The community, with the exception of a few foreigners or

foreignized natives, might seem to exist to fish, pluck and eat fruit, bask in the sun, dabble in the water, or frolic on the sand . . . ; and it is difficult to imagine any very different state under their circumstances." [45]

The resident missionaries themselves testified to this indolence, but they all ascribed it to an inherent shortcoming of the Polynesians which defied all the efforts of their teachers to correct. William Ellis's *Polynesian Researches,* one of the ablest of the early accounts of Tahitian life and character, offers the fullest history available of these efforts on the part of the missionaries to engraft the industry of Western culture on the indolent and unresponsive native stock:

During the early periods of their residence in the islands, our predecessors often endeavoured to rouse them from their abject and wretched modes of life. . . . While the inhabitants continued heathens, their endeavours were altogether unavailing. The people frequently said, "We should like some of these things [European articles] very well, but we cannot have them without working; *that* we do not like, and therefore would rather do without them. The bananas and the plantains, &c. ripen on the trees, and the pigs fatten on the fruits that are strewed beneath them, even while we sleep; these are all we want, why therefore should we work?" . . .

They furnish a striking illustration of the sentiment, that to civilize a people they must first be Christianized. . . .

Industry, however, soon languishes, unless nurtured by more powerful motives than the effect of abstract principles upon partially enlightened and ill-regulated minds. To increase their wants, or to make some of the comforts and decencies of society as desirable as the bare necessities of life, appeared to us the most probable method of furnishing incitements to permanent industry. . . . We therefore recommended them to direct their attention to the culture of cotton. . . . They labored diligently and perseveringly. . . . [But the small price received for the crop] together with the length of time and the constant attention that a cotton plantation required, before any return could be received, greatly discouraged them, and prevented their continuing its culture.[46]

This tragi-comic experiment occurred in 1818, many years before Melville's arrival. Although he makes no acknowledgement of any indebtedness to Ellis save a general one in the Preface, Mel-

ville undoubtedly had this work open before him as he wrote of
this agricultural failure and of the industrial fiasco which followed:

> Attempts have repeatedly been made to rouse them from their slug-
> gishness; but in vain. Several years ago, the cultivation of cotton was
> introduced; and, with their usual love of novelty, they went to work
> with great alacrity; but the interest excited quickly subsided, and now
> not a pound of the article is raised.
>
> About the same time, machinery for weaving was sent out from Lon-
> don; and a factory was started at Afrehitoo, in Imeeo. The whiz of the
> wheels and spindles brought in volunteers from all quarters, who
> deemed it a privilege to be admitted to work; yet, in six months, not a
> boy could be hired; and the machinery was knocked down, and packed
> off to Sydney.[47]

And this disastrous sequel actually occurred very much as Melville
describes.

In spite of the fact that the small returns from the sale of the
raw cotton had discouraged the natives from raising it, the London
Missionary Society concluded that their great desire for cotton
cloth might persuade them to resume its culture if they were taught
to do their own manufacturing. Consequently, Mr. Armitage, an
artisan, was sent out with appropriate machinery to teach the natives to spin and weave the cotton grown in their own gardens. He
arrived in 1821, but because of the opposition of the native chiefs
there was considerable delay in getting started. Consequently, it
was not until May, 1824, that the factory was set up at Papetoai
on the island of Eimeo. According to Ellis:

> The work commenced with cotton belonging to the native missionary
> societies. Mr. Armitage taught them to card the cotton, and Mrs. Armi-
> tage instructed them in spinning. Their first attempts, as might be ex-
> pected, were exceedingly awkward, and the warp they furnished was
> exceedingly difficult to weave. One piece of cloth, however, fifty yards
> in length, was finished and presented to the king. Its appearance was
> coarse, and inferior to the calicoes of British manufacture; it was never-
> theless grateful to the chiefs, from the fact of its being the first ever
> manufactured in their own islands.
>
> Cotton for another piece was prepared, and the natives commenced
> spinning; but the confinement required being irksome and their ex-
> pectations rather lowered as to the quality of the cloth they were to

receive as wages for their labour,—before the warp was ready for the loom they simultaneously discontinued their work. When interrogated as to their reasons for this sudden change in their conduct, it was found that they had not indeed struck for higher wages, but had left off to think about it, and that until their minds were made up they could not return. The spinning-wheels and the loom now stood still. . . .

In every undertaking of this kind the greatest embarrassments attend its outset. . . . The indolent habits of these young persons, their impatience of control, and the fugitive mode of life to which many had been accustomed, were not to be at once removed.[48]

It was not until five years after the failure of this first experiment at Papetoai that Mr. Armitage moved his equipment to the other side of the island and set up a second factory in 1829 at Afareaitu (Melville's "Afrehitoo"); [49] but this proved even more unsuccessful, and the project was ultimately abandoned for good. Coulter, who in 1834 visited the remains of this old cotton mill, records the final tragedy of this last attempt to industrialize the Society Islanders:

When the mill was erected, from the novelty of the thing at first, the men, women, and children attended; but after some time, they all got tired, saying it was no use to work, when they could buy all the cloth they wanted for very little, out of a ship. Then they began stealing; one took away one piece of iron work; another, something else, until the chief part of the works disappeared, and rendered all further exertion, on the part of Mr. Armitage, futile.[50]

Thus the real sequel was even more disastrous than Melville states, for apparently there was little if any machinery left to be "knocked down, and packed off to Sydney." But Commodore Wilkes was undoubtedly right in his diagnosis of the situation when he declared that this failure was no argument against the probable success of less complex arts. The missionaries, in their zeal, simply attempted too much at the outset. These primitive people, just emerging from the Stone Age, were not prepared to pass at once from habits of desultory exertion to the regular and confining occupation of the mill.[51]

One other effort to rouse the natives from their indolence and to instill in them Western notions of industry is recorded by Melville, but the results were again negative:

It was the same way with the cultivation of the sugar-cane, a plant indigenous to the island; peculiarly fitted to the soil and climate, and of so excellent a quality that Bligh took slips of it to the West Indies. All the plantations went on famously for a while; the natives swarming in the fields like ants, and making a prodigious stir. What few plantations now remain are owned and worked by whites, who would rather pay a drunken sailor eighteen or twenty Spanish dollars a month, than hire a sober native for his "fish and Taro." [52]

This experiment had been started even before the one in the culture and manufacture of cotton, but it lingered on down to the time of Melville's arrival. Ellis again tells the story from which Melville may have drawn; but, in reality, it was not so much the indolence of the natives as the greed of their new European discoverers that brought about this failure.[53] For the machinery was taken over by white men, and the industry carried on. At the time of Melville's visit there were several such prosperous sugar plantations at Papetoai (Melville's "Partoowye") on the island of Eimeo, producing over one hundred tons annually, one of which came to be connected with Melville's own adventures there, as will be seen.[54]

Such are the facts that Melville sets forth to prove that the Polynesian is no more suited in disposition and talent for Western civilization than he is qualified in attitude and spiritual endowment for the morals and dogmas of the Christian religion. Faithful to his promise in the Preface of *Omoo,* Melville now brings forward the testimony of other visitors at Tahiti to corroborate his own judgments:

Upon a subject like this, however, it would be altogether too assuming for a single individual to decide; and so, in place of my own random observations, which may be found elsewhere, I will here present those of several authors, made under various circumstances, at different periods, and down to a comparatively late date. A few very brief extracts will enable the reader to mark for himself what progressive improvement, if any, has taken place. . . .

After alluding to the manifold evils entailed upon the natives by foreigners, and their singularly inert condition; and after somewhat too severely denouncing the undeniable errors of the mission, Kotzebue, the Russian navigator, says, "A religion like this, which forbids every innocent pleasure, and cramps or annihilates every mental power, is a libel on the divine founder of Christianity. It is true that the religion of the missionaries has, with a great deal of evil, effected some good. It has restrained the vices of theft and incontinence; but it has given birth to ignorance, hypocrisy, and a hatred of all other modes of faith, which was once foreign to the open and benevolent character of the Tahitian." [55]

Such was indeed the testimony of Otto von Kotzebue after his visit in 1824. And Melville might have quoted further:

True, genuine Christianity, and liberal government, might have soon given to this people, endowed by nature with the seeds of every social virtue, a rank among civilized nations. Under such a blessed influence, the arts and sciences would soon have taken root, the intellect of the people would have expanded, and a just estimation of all that is good, beautiful, and eternally true, would have refined their manners and enobled their hearts. Europe would soon have admired, perhaps even envied Tahaiti [*sic*]: but the religion taught by the missionaries is not true Christianity, though it may possibly comprehend some of its doctrines, but half understood even by the teachers themselves. [56]

From these passages, and others quoted elsewhere in the present chapter, there can be no doubt that Kotzebue's narrative substantiates Melville's observations, and even goes beyond.

Indeed, Melville could not have found an authority better suited to his purposes, unless it were his second witness (whose disparaging testimony has already been quoted at some length). According to *Omoo:*

Captain Beechey says, that while at Tahiti he saw scenes "which must have convinced the greatest sceptic of the thoroughly immoral condition of the people, and which would force him to conclude as Turnbull did many years previous, that their intercourse with the Europeans had tended to debase, rather than exalt their condition." [57]

Such was the actual recorded opinion of this English captain in regard to the royal household itself, after spending an evening in the company of the queen regent. And even more explicit—perhaps too much so for Melville's sense of decorum—was his observation on the common people, which follows:

Of the rest of the population, though their external deportment is certainly more guarded than formerly, in consequence of the severe penalties which their new laws attach to a breach of decorum, yet their morals have in reality undergone as little change as their costume. Notwithstanding all the restrictions imposed, I do not believe that I should exceed the bounds of truth in saying, that, if opportunity offered, there is no favour which might not be obtained from the females of Otaheite [*sic*] for the trifling consideration of a Jew's harp, a ring, or some other bauble.[58]

And Beechey himself was accurate in his reference to Turnbull's conclusions, for that visitor had found similarly deplorable conditions among the Tahitians twenty-three years before, after they had been exposed to only six years of continuous contact with civilization:

In the comparison of their present and former situation one inference is clear, that they have reaped no advantage from their intercourse with Europeans: The greater part of their characteristic simplicity has now vanished, and has given place to selfish cunning, and the artifice of low minds.[59]

Not content with such full substantiation, however, Melville attempts to pyramid his authorities, citing what purports to be a pious voucher for Kotzebue and Beechey:

Nor must it be overlooked that, of these authorities, the two first in order are largely quoted by the Right Reverend M. Russell, in a work composed for the express purpose of imparting information on the subject of Christian missions in Polynesia. And he frankly acknowledges, moreover, that they are such as "cannot fail to have great weight with the public."[60]

But here, for once, Melville is guilty of deliberate misrepresentation. For, although The Reverend Michael Russell did "advert to the less favorable opinions entertained by writers whose sentiments cannot fail to have much weight with the public," he did so "not without pain"; and his quotations from Kotzebue, Beechey, and Turnbull, which follow, were made for the express purpose of refuting them, or at least lessening their weight with the public.

Russell, on the other hand, made at least an attempt to be fair and temperate in his own conclusions:

> But a great question remains to be solved as to the result of missionary exertion on the character of the natives, and the permanence of the change which has been effected by the advent of a civilized people among them. In attempting to arrive at truth on these interesting points, we are impeded by the difficulty which arises from the marked disagreement prevailing among voyagers in regard to the actual condition of the inhabitants, both at the Society and Sandwich Islands. Such discrepancy, we are satisfied, does not arise so much from want of candour, as from the different aspect under which the same objects are contemplated by two classes of persons who have so little in common as seamen and ministers of the gospel.[61]

Of the two opinions, however, he expressly favored that of the missionaries, calling the works of William Ellis to the defense. It is at this point that the discussion becomes indeed complicated. For Ellis was the very authority pointed out by Beechey as being deficient on some essential matters concerning conditions at Tahiti, even as Melville quotes:

> It is hardly to be expected, that the missionaries would send home accounts of this state of things. Hence, Captain Beechey, in alluding to the *Polynesian Researches* of Ellis, says, that the author has impressed his readers with a far more elevated idea of the moral condition of the Tahitians, and the degree of civilization to which they have attained, than they deserve; or, at least, than the facts which came under his observation authorised.[62]

With such conflicting evidence, where is one to turn for the truth? All of the religious writers rebuke Melville's first authority, Kotzebue—especially William Ellis, the fairest and best informed of them, who calls his censure of the missionaries "absurd and petulant" and his accounts of the islanders "erroneous and ludicrous" in the extreme.[63] On the other hand, as has been demonstrated, Melville's second authority, Beechey, accuses the missionaries, and especially Ellis, of professional bias. At this critical impasse it will be illuminating to examine the reports of two visitors who arrived at Tahiti ten years later, in 1836, on the now famous surveying voyage of H. M. S. *Beagle,* and whose judgments, there should be every reason to believe, were both impartial and intelligent. Captain Robert Fitzroy, the commander, was content to conclude the whole matter with a rather noncommittal generalization:

The moral conduct and character of these islanders have undergone so much discussion; so various have been the decisions, and so varying are the opinions of voyagers and residents, that I, for one, am satisfied by the conclusion, that the good and the bad are mixed in Otaheite [*sic*], much as they are in other parts of the world exposed to the contamination of unprincipled people.[64]

Charles Darwin, the botanist of the expedition, was more deliberate and more critical in drawing his conclusions. His *Journal and Remarks* is filled with the acute and inquisitive observations of the scientific mind; yet his final judgment rests, likewise, in a somewhat inconclusive middle position:

From the varying accounts which I had read before reaching these islands, I was very anxious to form, from my own observation, a judgment of their moral state—although such judgment would necessarily be very imperfect. A first impression at all times very much depends on one's previously-acquired ideas. My notions were drawn from Ellis's "Polynesian Researches"—an admirable and most interesting work, but naturally looking at everything under a favourable point of view; from Beechey's Voyage; and from that of Kotzebue, which is strongly adverse to the whole missionary system. He who compares these three accounts, will, I think, form a tolerably accurate conception of the present state of Tahiti.[65]

In one sense of the word, Melville himself may be said to have taken such a middleground; for he certainly is not guilty of the extremes to which every one of these three authorities goes, though he quotes from all of them. But his "middle ground" was not a happy one, for his total picture is undeniably unfavorable to the Christian teachers in almost every detail; whereas both Darwin and Fitzroy, while deprecating the unnecessarily severe Blue Laws, declared that the popular representation of the licentiousness at Tahiti was exaggerated, that the natives had not become a gloomy race, and that they did not fear the missionaries. Their remarks were so favorable in many respects, indeed, that they were both quoted approvingly by two of the chief defenders of Polynesian Missions, George Pritchard and William Ellis. Upon the *Beagle's* return to England, moreover, Captain Fitzroy abandoned his impartial attitude and became a spokesman of the cause, testifying publicly before the London Missionary Society to the progress of Christianity in the Society Islands and castigating its censorious critics.[66] And, somewhat later, in a letter to the astronomer Sir John Herschel he declared:

On the whole, it is my opinion that the state of morality and religion in Tahiti is highly creditable. . . .

With respect to those who have severely censured the interference and effects of the missionary system, I subscribe entirely to the following remarks of Dr. Darwin:

"I do believe that, disappointed in not finding the field of licentiousness so open as formerly, and as was expected, they will not give credit to a morality which they do not wish to practise, nor to the effects of a religion which is undervalued, if not quite despised." [67]

In spite of the shortness of their stay at Tahiti—less than two weeks—and in spite of this shift in emphasis after their return from the South Seas, it must be confessed that the contrary evidence of these two eminent men goes hard against Melville's case; and there is undoubtedly some truth in the charge that such as he may have been prejudiced by personal pique at finding the Blue Laws so strictly enforced. Certainly, in Melville's own narrative there is no evidence that he, for one, exerted himself in any way to improve the moral or religious condition of the natives.

It will be interesting, therefore, to compare the testimony of other whalemen who visited the island. Arriving with less ceremony than more official visitors, they would be likely to come in contact with the normal everyday life of the natives rather than the dress parade which was undoubtedly staged by the missionaries for their distinguished guests; and if they were not biased for personal reasons such as Darwin suggests—but which can rarely be proved—their accounts should be reasonably reliable.

At about this time, during the decade preceding Melville's arrival, two surgeons of whaling vessels visited Tahiti, coming last from the Marquesas Islands, even as he, where their evidence has already been cited in connection with *Typee*. The first of these, John M. Coulter, praised the work of the missionaries in highest terms, concluding his rhapsody as follows:

Here all was peace—man and nature were in harmony with each other. The power of religion had completely altered the naturally uncontrolled character of the native, and effectually subdued barbarism.[68]

But F. D. Bennett, whose account is the fuller and more thoughtful of the two, was more chary of his praise. Although the Tahitians seemed to him at first to be good Christians, compared with the rest of the world, he found, on inquiry, a rather disconcerting explanation for these appearances:

The strictness, however, with which the island laws enforce the observance of religious forms leaves the native but little latitude to gratify his inclination in this respect; consequently, on the Sabbath the churches are filled with the entire population, clothed in decent attire, and presenting an orderly and contented appearance which makes a very favourable impression upon the foreign visitor. . . .

Notwithstanding these points of improvement, the resident missionaries speak of the native character in terms of severe reprobation, describing it as strongly marked by ingratitude and deceit. Nor had we at this visit any reason to admire the conduct of the people, as displayed on the coast: the abundance and indiscriminate sale of ardent spirits, as well as the laxity of the laws which permitted the sensuality of a seaport to be carried to a boundless extent, caused scenes of riot and debauchery to be nightly exhibited at Pápeéte [*sic*] that would have disgraced the most profligate purlieus of London. By partaking in these, the natives had degraded their physical no less than their moral state, and in the slovenly, haggard, and diseased inhabitants of the port, it was vain to attempt to recognize the prepossessing figure of the Tahitian, as pictured by Cook.[69]

A third visitor in a whale ship at this period, Thomas Beale, the foremost authority in his day on the natural history of the sperm whale, denounces the conduct of the missionaries as well as that of the natives in terms that would have seemed strong even to Melville, the deserter and beachcomber:

Although I am far, very far from an intention of casting any reflections on the general character of perhaps as ardent and devoted a body of

Christian missionaries as have ever assisted in spreading the voice of the gospel in distant lands, among dangers and privations of every kind; yet, from what I have myself witnessed and deplored, I fervently hope that the eyes of the public may be widely opened to the necessity of some more strict supervision into the character and conduct of many of the missionaries, who now disgrace their country and their creed in some of the islands of the South Sea. . . .

When these doings of the missionaries are taken into consideration, . . . can we wonder that farther progress has not been made among these people? . . . can we wonder at seeing the Society Islanders at the present time in a worse state than they ever were before? . . .

At the time of our visit to these islands [1832], the mass of the people were in the utmost state of demoralization, and had been in that condition for some time; everything had gone into disorder. . . . In fact, we found them the very worst people we had met with during our travels, although forty years' expense and trouble had been devoted to them.[70]

Omoo is more than corroborated by the testimony of fellow whalemen.

With judicious procedure, Melville reserved his strongest witness for the last. He ferreted out at least one religious observer, Daniel Wheeler, an independent Quaker missionary, who was doubtful of the progress of Christianity in Polynesia. Though many of his observations accorded with Melville's, only one remark of a general nature is quoted from his *Memoirs:*

About the year 1834, Daniel Wheeler, an honest-hearted Quaker, prompted by motives of the purest philanthropy, visited, in a vessel of his own, most of the missionary settlements in the South Seas. He remained some time at Tahiti; receiving the hospitalities of the missionaries there, and, from time to time, exhorting the natives.

After bewailing their social condition, he frankly says of their religious state, "Certainly, appearances are unpromising; and however unwilling to adopt such a conclusion, there is reason to apprehend that Christian principle is a great rarity." [71]

But Melville is guilty of some slight misrepresentation in this instance, for he took the sentence out of the following context in which Wheeler placed it:

It is nearly impossible for a visitor, who cannot even speak the language, to pronounce with much certainty on a subject of such moment as the religious state of the community. *Certainly appearances are unpromising; and however unwilling to adopt such a conclusion, there is reason to apprehend that Christian principle is a great rarity.* Far, however, be it from me to depreciate the labors of those who have been the instruments of the change produced in this island. So far from considering the beneficent results of their efforts as unimportant and insignificant, I regard them as of the highest moment, and as fully equal to what could in reason have been anticipated.[72]

Nevertheless, although the Quaker evangelist attributed most of the evil to the contamination of foreign residents and visiting ships rather than to the shortcomings of the missionaries, his opinion of the state of morals, religion, and social well-being at Tahiti was decidedly unfavorable on the whole; and Melville was justified in citing his testimony for corroboration. Wheeler, moreover, remained in the Society Islands for six full months in constant association with the missionaries, working with them among the better class of natives, so that his opinions should receive the fullest possible weight. All that can be said in mitigation of his doubts is that, being a Quaker, he probably exacted a more idealistic standard of spirituality than Polynesians—or Europeans— could be expected to live up to in the strictest sense.

It is possible, of course, that in such a recently established outpost of civilization every decade might produce a notable improvement, so that it is desirable to bring the evidence forward as near as possible to the actual time of Melville's visit, in order to arrive at a just conclusion. In September, 1839, the United States Exploring Expedition spent about three weeks at Tahiti, and it will be interesting to compare the comments of the official published volumes of the expedition with the private manuscript journals kept by the various officers. An example of the latter follows. It was written by an officer on board the flagship, with none of the reticence that an intent to publish might have imposed:

Notwithstanding the Missionary account of the chastity of these people, judging by our standards of virtue I should say there were few of this class among them. For my own part I was much astonished when seeing the contrast between the Missionary account and the actual state of morals among them. It is not uncommon for a man to prostitute his own daughter for a dollar and even his own wife has been disposed of in the same manner; neither is this confined to a few individuals, but the whole population without one single exception [is given] to this libidenous [*sic*] practise. And still you hear the missionaries preaching up the great change they have wrought in their morals! If there is any change it certainly must be for the worse, for they have learnt them the use of money and [the natives] will go to almost any length in libidenousness to obtain [it]. . . .

In walking among the Villages I was much reminded of our camp meetings. The natives attend church regular [*sic*] and [are] kept much in awe of the missionaries, so long as they suppose themselves in their sight.[73]

The author of *Omoo* could not ask for fuller corroboration; and this sample is in every respect representative of the many journals kept by the members of this expedition—by officers and seamen, by the surgeon and the botanist—over a score of which have been examined.

Yet in the five official volumes published by the expedition there is a slightly different story. Here, Commodore Wilkes himself admitted that licentiousness did still exist, that only the outward forms of religion were actually observed, and that the teachers themselves complained of the lack of much sincere piety. But he exonerated the missionaries from all responsibility for these conditions and laid the blame heavily on the other foreign residents, of whom there were about a hundred on the island: merchants, the descendants of the missionaries who "seem to have forgotten utterly the principles instilled into them in their infancy," and, chiefly, "a band of vagabonds, without trade or occupation," the "outcasts and refuse of every maritime nation." On these last, beachcombers such as the mutineers with whom Melville was associated at the Calabooza Beretanee, he was even more severe than Darwin and Fitzroy had been:

Many of those who bear testimony to the laxity of their morals, visit their shores for the very purpose of enticing them into guilt, and of rioting without fear or hindrance in debauchery. Coming with such intentions, and finding themselves checked by the influence of the missionaries, they rail against them because they have put an end to the obscene dances and games of the natives and procured the enactment of laws forbidding illicit intercourse.[74]

Such as these, he declared, opposed an almost insuperable barrier to the improvement of the natives in morals and religion. And even the more respectable residents, the merchants, tried to evade the Blue Laws for similar reasons, or because they were opposed to the missionaries sincerely and on fundamental principle:

[These latter] argue seriously, that this mild and amiable people had no need of instruction in divine revelation; that they would have been much happier had they been left to follow their own inclinations; and that they have been rendered miserable by being taught their responsibility as accountable human beings.[75]

Apparently there were other disciples of Rousseau in the South Seas besides Herman Melville! In fairness to Commodore Wilkes it must be said that he took no exception to such honest differences in philosophical attitude. He, for one, however, was convinced that what the natives needed was more and better civilization; or he felt, at least, that his position as commander of the United States Exploring Expedition to the South Seas necessitated such an avowal in his official *Narrative*.

F. A. Olmsted, a young Harvard graduate who went as a passenger on a whaling voyage for his health (much as Dana had done a year or two before), spent ten days at Tahiti in September, 1840. Although he joined the chorus of unfavorable commentators, he sided with Wilkes in placing the blame upon the foreign residents, of whom he said:

They are all united in representing the native character, as the worst that can be imagined; but many of them are not very solicitous about improving it, as far as my observation extended. There are doubtless, many natives of unexceptionable moral character, and many, it is to be hoped, that are truly pious people, but the tide of morality is at a very low ebb at Papeete.[76]

From the lowest class of foreigners one would naturally expect prejudiced and indeed wholly unreliable reports of conditions, though no written records have been left by mutineers, deserters,

or beachcombers—save Melville's record in *Omoo*. But what were
the opinions of the more permanent and more respectable residents?

Fortunately, representative of this class is the testimony of Edward Lucett, a merchant resident at Tahiti for many years. Even
at the time of Melville's visit his headquarters had been established at Papeete for almost a year. His observations recorded at
the very period covered by *Omoo*, therefore, are most apropos:

I will not sully the pages of my journal with recording the details that
have been given me, both by natives and Europeans; but if one tithe
of them be correct, and, unfortunately, I have seen corroborative testimony in certain instances, instead of improving the native character,
the missionaries have superinduced upon their other bad qualities
hypocrisy of the deepest dye. I speak dispassionately when I say, that I
conscientiously believe the moral character of the natives has not been
improved by missionary intercourse. It is true, that by long sojourning
with them the missionaries have instilled the conviction of the power
and grandeur of European nations; by this means taming their ferocity,
and rendering them more harmless to visitors, and less dangerous to
shipwrecked mariners; but fear, and not religious restraint, is the
governing principle.[77]

It is true that Lucett has been established previously in the present volume as a man of violent prejudices and extravagant language, but these characteristics were exhibited when he was defending his own respectability, and that of several prominent citizens
of Papeete, against the physical and verbal attacks of a set of
rascals whom he had known only as mutineers confined in the
Calabooza Beretanee. Of course, it is quite possible that some
similar personal grudge may have motivated this declaration
against the missionaries; but, if any such existed, there is no trace
of it in his two volumes of *Rovings in the Pacific*. Further, the
passage just quoted is, comparatively speaking, sufficiently restrained and temperate to carry considerable conviction.

In this survey of the testimony of almost two score authorities
on the state of religion, morals, and general well-being at Tahiti
during the period just prior to and contemporary with Melville's
residence, the bulk of the evidence certainly substantiates the un-

favorable opinions set forth in *Omoo*. Half a dozen of this number, to be sure, attempt to defend the state of Christian civilization there, yet all but one of these were missionaries and therefore chargeable, reasonably enough, with professional bias. The only layman who subscribes without reservation to the missionary version is John Coulter, the surgeon of a whaling vessel, who remained on the island but one week. It is also true that three others make a half-hearted attempt to exonerate the Christian teachers and to lay the whole blame on the other foreign residents and visitors, but all of them admit that the state of morals at Tahiti was deplorable and that the effects of religion were only skin deep. The first of these, Captain Fitzroy, only took this stand in public utterances made after his return to England; the second, Darwin, was merely lukewarm in his defense; and the third, Commodore Wilkes, was specifically refuted by every manuscript journal kept on board the ships of his expedition. All of the rest—more than three-fourths of the commentators—corroborate Melville to the fullest extent, some even going far beyond him in disparagement; and these witnesses include, besides one actual missionary, explorers, scientists, surgeons, passengers, and officers of merchantmen, whalers, and men-of-war—ranging chronologically from the first decade of missionary activity down to the very month of Melville's visit, at which time he is explicitly and fully vindicated in his pronouncements against the missionaries by a prominent citizen of Papeete, Edward Lucett, who had undertaken in the same volume to denounce him publicly for misrepresentation in other matters.

This chorus of agreement with Melville, moreover, was echoed at home in nine-tenths of the contemporary reviews of *Omoo*, contrary to the traditionally accepted version of its reception.[78] And ten years later, under the caption "Christian Missions: Their Principle and Practice," the *Westminster Review* (quoting *Omoo* throughout with approval) concluded from the evidence of fourteen books on Polynesia:

Alas! thus it is. Coal scuttle bonnets for the garland and palm-leaf! The Old Hundred for the national ballad! Levitical law for heroic tradition! A taboo-Sunday every week, and no harvest-home once a year! Idleness, breeding slander and dissoluteness, for the easy but willing occupation of former days! All distinctive character covered over with hypocrisy, and native prattle absorbed by cant! . . .

The natural question here arises— How we happen to have foreign missions still, if these are the results? [79]

Undoubtedly, the confusion attendant upon the French seizure of Tahiti on September 9, 1842, had served to magnify the havoc wrought by civilization upon the religious, moral, and social status of the natives which Melville so deplored; and it will be remembered that the author of *Omoo* had arrived in the midst of these events. In his account of the proceedings of the French he says: "My information was obtained at the time from the general reports then rife among the natives, as well as what I learned upon a subsequent visit, and reliable accounts which I have seen since reaching home." [80] Melville was, in fact, well qualified to speak on this subject, for he had lived at Papeete during the six weeks, more or less, which marked the peak of this excitement—September 26–November 9, 1842, or thereabout—in constant contact with the natives and within hearing of what the English consul and both the Protestant and the Catholic missionaries had to say. The "subsequent visit" was the week spent at anchor at Matavai, a neighboring harbor, on board the frigate *United States*, October 12–19, 1843, shortly before the French took formal possession. And there is good evidence that he consulted numerous accounts upon reaching home.

One cause of the French occupation of Tahiti Melville traces back to the attempts made to establish a Roman Catholic mission there that had met with such violent opposition from the English Protestants:

In one instance, two priests, Laval and Caset [Caret], after enduring a series of persecutions, were set upon by the natives, maltreated, and finally carried aboard a small trading schooner, which eventually put them ashore at Wallis Island—a savage place—some two thousand miles to the westward.

Now, that the resident English missionaries authorised the banishment of these priests, is a fact undenied by themselves. I was also repeatedly informed that by their inflammatory harangues they instigated the riots which preceded the sailing of the schooner. At all events, it is certain that their unbounded influence with the natives would easily have enabled them to prevent everything that took place on this occasion, had they felt so inclined.

Melancholy as such an example of intolerance on the part of Protestant missionaries must appear, it is not the only one, and by no means the most flagrant, which might be presented.[81]

The "reliable account" which he consulted for this incident was undoubtedly the *Narrative of the United States Exploring Expedition,* in which Commodore Wilkes, otherwise the defender of the English missionaries, declared that the priests would have been permitted by the chiefs to remain. And with undisguised censure he concluded:

The people, however, excited by the preaching of the English missionaries, broke into the building, and compelled the priests to embark on board a small vessel, which carried them to Uea, or Wallis Island, about two thousand miles to the west of Tahiti. . . . The resident missionaries may justly be held responsible, as they unquestionably had it in their power to prevent any positive ill treatment on the part of the natives.[82]

Although such conduct on the part of the English missionaries was wanting in civility, this was the only ground upon which Rear-Admiral Dupetit-Thouars had any cause for demanding satisfaction in the name of France, the rest of his charges being wholly without justification, according to Melville. "There now seems little doubt," he adds, "that the downfall of the Pomarees was decided upon at the Tuileries." [83] Melville's account of the resulting seizure of Tahiti—strongly pro-English on the whole and calculated to appeal to his London audience—is merely a continuation of the running attack against the French policy of South Sea colonization already noticed as one of the minor themes of *Typee.*[84] And his chronicle in *Omoo* of these proceedings, both during the time of his residence and subsequently, is substantially correct: the mock treaty under which the protectorate was established, the formal taking of possession a year later (November 7, 1843), the growing native resentment of French rule, and "the gallant, though useless warfare, so soon to follow my [second] departure." [85]

The facts for Melville's history of these events were probably garnered principally from the English periodical press, which was full of "reliable accounts" of the French outrage at the very period when Melville returned to America. In fact, the very month of his arrival, October, 1844, the *Foreign Quarterly Review* summarized the whole affair in a dramatic review of half-a-dozen books on the subject, declaring with uncompromising severity: "Now we maintain that the dominion of France in the Society Islands was ushered in by falsehood, established by violence, and followed by the foulest oppression." [86] Such accounts, however, Melville had the propriety to tone down for his American audience, where the strong pro-French sentiment might have demanded an expurgated edition (as in the case of *Typee*) from any publisher less hardy than Harper & Brothers. But, in spite of the misgivings of the author of *Omoo* as confided to Duyckinck before publication, the strictures against the French were allowed to stand, along with the disparagements of Christian civilization at Tahiti in 1842.[87]

Only a small part of the woes of Tahiti at the time of Melville's visit, however, could be attributed to the new invaders under Dupetit-Thouars. Indeed, his attack on the French, as well as his more extended one on the English missionaries, is but a fragmentary statement of a much larger thesis. For it will be remembered that *Omoo* was the second indictment in his brief against civilization, the obverse side of the bright gold coin of *Typee*. In his first book his attack was chiefly negative, a eulogy of the unspoiled primitive. In his sequel, taking Rousseau's famous 1750 *Discourse* as a text, he preaches an implicit sermon on the evil effects of civilizing the Noble Savage. This thesis underlies the whole of *Omoo*, though it is seldom explicitly stated. At least once, however, Melville lets slip the thought that must have been constantly in the back of his mind as he wrote these controversial central chapters on Tahiti: "To me, so recently from a primitive valley of the Marquesas, . . . a comparison [was unavoidable], immeasurably to the disadvantage of these partially civilised islanders." [88]

As is frequently true of primitives when suddenly brought in contact with a more advanced and more complex civilization, the Tahitians first acquired, in the eyes of the idealist, the vices rather than the virtues of the new culture—and, even in the eyes of the realist, its semblance rather than its substance. After almost fifty years of constant intercourse with white men, these islanders had not advanced far in their acquisitive desires beyond the Dutch looking glasses, scraps of iron, and gaudy beads dangled before their enchanted eyes by their earliest white visitors. According to Melville, at the time of his visit their economic ambitions reached no higher than the bright calicoes of the traders and the cast-off pantaloons of the visiting seamen. Most of his ridicule is directed at the incongruous mixture of European and native costumes worn by the men, and Melville undoubtedly saw many droll sights at Tahiti. But, in view of his penchant for working from literary sources in preference even to his own observations, it is not surprising to find convincing originals for his half-civilized manikins in the volumes of Ellis and Wilkes. Further, on the Tahitian women he showers good-humored raillery for their "coal scuttle" bonnets, which he declares, correctly, were introduced by the missionaries' wives.[89] Besides ridiculing the appearance of the natives in the half-dress of civilization, and hinting here and there at the price frequently paid by the women for their foreign finery, Melville makes a more serious charge in his chapter "How They Dress in Tahiti." The introduction of European clothing, he declares, has largely contributed to their present exasperating indolence, for it has caused them to abandon one of their principal employments of former days, the manufacture of *tapa*. And their passion for European fripperies has merely provided a new temptation to licentiousness.[90]

Undoubtedly, much of the beauty of the Polynesians reported by the first white visitors could be ascribed to the appropriate costumes of a healthy people living in a state of nature; at any rate, conversely, much of the decline in Tahitian beauty remarked half a century later was attributable to the unbecoming and even ludicrous half-dress of dirty and disease-ridden natives, imitating in a listless and bewildered fashion the externals of civilization in an outpost of the Western world. And Melville was not slow to make capital of this anomalous state of affairs.[91]

This complaint as to the superficial degeneracy of the Noble Savage, incongruously decked out in the gew-gaws of civilization, is merely a prelude to the far deeper romantic lament over the devastation wrought by its vices and diseases. As early as 1842, in Melville's eyes, theirs was an impending doom:

Their prospects are hopeless. . . . Years ago brought to a stand, where all that is corrupt in barbarism and civilisation unite, to the exclusion of the virtues of either state; like other uncivilised beings brought in contact with Europeans, they must here remain stationary until utterly extinct.[92]

Then with an account of the staggering decrease in their population since the first visits of the white man, he brings his polemical chapters on "Tahiti As It Is" to a dramatic conclusion:

About the year 1777 [1767], Captain Cook estimated the population of Tahiti at about two hundred thousand. By a regular census, taken some four or five years ago, it was found to be only nine thousand. This amazing decrease not only shows the malignancy of the evils necessary to produce it, but from the fact the inference unavoidably follows that all the wars, child murders, and other depopulating causes, alleged to have existed in former times, were nothing in comparison to them.

These evils, of course, are solely of foreign origin. To say nothing of the effects of drunkenness, the occasional inroads of the small-pox, and other things which might be mentioned, it is sufficient to allude to a virulent disease which now taints the blood of at least two-thirds of the common people of the island; and, in some form or other, is transmitted from father to son.

Their first horror and consternation at the earlier ravages of this scourge were pitiable in the extreme. The very name bestowed upon it is a combination of all that is horrid and unmentionable to a civilised being.

Distracted with their sufferings, they brought forth their sick before the missionaries, when they were preaching, and cried out, "Lies, lies! you tell us of salvation; and, behold, we are dying. We want no other salvation than to live in this world. Where are there any saved through your speech? Pomaree is dead; and we are all dying with your cursed diseases. When will you give over?" [93]

Captain James Cook did indeed estimate the population of Tahiti at two hundred thousand. And the Reverend M. Russell in his *Polynesia,* a volume with which Melville was familiar, quoted this figure as reliable. Comparing this with the pitiful handful of natives remaining in 1842, he concluded mournfully:

> But amidst . . . tokens of improvement, painful proofs are everywhere making themselves manifest, that the natives are doomed to extinction, from the operation of causes more or less connected with the arrival of the white men.[94]

But Cook's estimate of the population at the time of his visit was obviously a very hasty and unreliable generalization, based upon mere conjecture, as Melville must have known from his reading. Even Kotzebue, whom Melville acknowledged to be prejudiced, preferred the figure of one hundred and thirty thousand given by the elder Forster, the botanist of Cook's expedition.[95] But Ellis considered even this as grossly in error; while admitting that there had been considerable depopulation, he considered James Wilson's estimate of sixteen thousand in 1797 as more nearly correct.[96] Certainly, whatever decrease had occurred in the thirty years between Cook's visit and the arrival of the first missionaries could not be attributed to the introduction of Christian civilization! Finally, the very authority whom Melville cites for the pitiful remnant of the population at the time of his own visit, Commodore Wilkes, summarized the whole discussion convincingly as follows:

> A census recently taken, gives for the population of Tahiti nine thousand. . . . When this is compared with the estimates of the navigators who first visited these islands, an enormous decrease would appear to have taken place. The first estimates were, however, based on erroneous data, and were unquestionably far too high; yet there is no doubt that the population has fallen off considerably in the interval. The decrease may be ascribed in part to the remains of the old custom of infanticide, in part to new diseases introduced from abroad, and the evils entailed upon them by foreigners, and in part to the transition now going on from a savage to a civilized life.[97]

Melville simply chose the figures and the explanation which best suited his thesis.

The sudden exposure to European diseases, however, undoubtedly wrought unspeakable havoc in the peaceful valleys of Tahiti, even as Melville declares. Not only were the facilities of medical science practically nonexistent at this far-flung outpost of the Western world, but even the mildest of the diseases of civilization are known to have made unprecedented ravages among primitive peoples who have had no opportunity to build up a gradual constitutional immunity. The most dramatic example of this in Polynesia —a calamity that shocked all of Europe—was the sudden death of the Hawaiian King Kamehameha II and his queen from an attack of measles during their visit to London twenty years before.[98]

For his own purposes Melville chose to bewail the inroads of a "far more virulent disease at Tahiti" which, under the bungling treatment of missionaries and natives, had tainted the blood of "at least two-thirds of the common people," and which was transmitted from father to son in the form of horrible spinal distortions and other deformities. He quotes, for substantiation, the testimony of a missionary:

"How dreadful and appalling," breaks forth old Wheeler, "the consideration that the intercourse of distant nations should have entailed upon these poor, untutored islanders a curse unprecedented and unheard of in the annals of history." [99]

So far Melville quotes. The rest of the sentence was omitted, probably because he preferred his own figure of "two-thirds" to Wheeler's estimate:

It is said that one-fourth of the whole population is miserably affected with diseases brought amongst them and kept up by the licentious crews of the shipping. Will not, shall not, the Lord visit for these things? [100]

But even Wheeler's estimate was high according to the more explicit and unquestionably more accurate observation of the surgeon of the United States Exploring Expedition:

I was informed by some of the foreign residents in Tahiti that the people were very sickly, and that the Venereal disease in particular was destroying great numbers of them—I saw less evidence of the disease among them than can be seen among the lower orders of any American city or port and should consider them, so far at least as external appearances go, remarkably free from disease of any kind— The disease is treated by the Missionaries by mercury and this probably does much more injury than if the cases which occur were left to themselves as they cannot be expected to know the cases in which it might be useful or the proper manner of administering it. . . . There is no Physician in the Islands and the treatment of the sick is in the hands of the missionaries— It had much better be in the hands of the natives, as nature would cure most of their diseases which the Missionaries are far from doing.[101]

In his facts and figures dealing with depopulation, Melville was certainly guilty of romantic exaggeration, to say the least.

Melville has now built up his case against civilization with all the witnesses he could muster, but without overscrupulous consideration in every instance as to their reliability. With all the evidence in, he now brings his clients themselves to the stand to testify:

The islanders themselves are mournfully watching their doom. Several years since, Pomaree II. said to Tyreman [Tyerman] and Bennet, the deputies of the London Missionary Society, "You have come to see me at a very bad time. Your ancestors came in the time of men, when Tahiti was inhabited; you are come to behold just the remnant of my people." [102]

This pathetic declaration of the most famous of all the Pomarés is recorded in Ellis's *Polynesian Researches,* whence Melville probably drew it, with some slight change in phrasing:

When some visiters from England, I think the deputation from the Missionary Society, waited upon him at his residence . . . [Pomaré] addressed them to the following effect: "You have come to see us under circumstances very different from those under which your countrymen formerly visited our ancestors. They came in the era of men, when the islands were inhabited, but you are come to behold just the remnant of the people." [103]

Then, with a melancholy peroration of simple but eloquent poetry, in the best traditional courtroom manner, the case of Melville versus mankind is rested:

Of like import was the prediction of Teearmoar, the high-priest of Paree; who lived over a hundred years ago. I have frequently heard it chanted, in a low, sad tone, by aged Tahitians:—

> "A harree ta fow,
> A toro ta farraro,
> A now ta tararta."

> The palm-tree shall grow,
> The coral shall spread,
> But man shall cease.[104]

It made little difference to Melville that this prophecy of annihilation was an ancient one, dating from pagan days. Like other folk songs, however, it had been handed down from generation to generation, and William Ellis recorded a version of it that survived into the Christian era:

The present generations, deeply sensible of the depopulation that has taken place even within the recollection of those most advanced in years, have felt acutely in prospect of the annihilation that appeared inevitable. Their priests formerly denounced the destruction of the nation, as the greatest punishment the gods could inflict, and the following was one of the predictions: *E tupu te fau, e toro te farero, e mou te taata:* "The *fau* (hibiscus) shall grow, the *farero* (coral) shall spread or stretch out its branches, but man shall cease." [105]

Allowing for the difference occasioned by the French orthography of Ellis's version, this accords with Melville's rendering save for one word. But here is a unique example of the devil quoting scripture whichever way the matter is viewed. On the one hand, Melville reaches back a century into heathen Tahiti and, taking his jeremiad out of the mouth of a priest of Oro. finds its fulfillment in the depopulation brought by a Christian civilization of which this "Teearmoar" never dreamed. On the other hand. Ellis declares that infanticide, human sacrifice, and savage warfare—all of which were sponsored by the same priest who had announced the oncoming destruction of the nation—would have fulfilled this same prophecy had not Christianity stepped in and saved them from their self-annihilation! [106] To the tribulations of the prophet who is unhonored in his own country must be added the affront of being misinterpreted abroad.

Such prognostications of a righteous visitation of judgment on an erring people, of course, have always and everywhere been part of the stock in trade of priests who rule by divination. And even when Melville arrived in America in the fall of 1844, he found the Millerites making ready their ascension robes and clamorously announcing that the day of doom was at hand. But in *Omoo* this prophecy was introduced for its artistic rather than its ethical value. Melville here struck a keynote of wistfulness that had been hinted at in *Typee,* and that was to be echoed down through a century of South Sea romances: the Noble Savages of Polynesia, under the blight of a corrupt and unsought civilization, have assumed the tragic role of the passing race and are tending to extinction even while they chant their song of doom:

> The palm-tree shall grow,
> The coral shall spread,
> But man shall cease.

CHAPTER XI

BEACHCOMBER

P ART TWO of *Omoo* is chiefly a narrative of Melville's free-
footed adventuring at Tahiti and on the neighboring island
of Eimeo. In explaining the meaning of the title of his
second book, Melville christened himself with a romantic name
appropriate to this part of his Polynesian career:

Omoo . . . is borrowed from the dialect of the Marquesas Islands,
where, among other uses, the word signifies a rover, or rather, a person
wandering from one island to another, like some of the natives known
among their countrymen as "Taboo kannakers." [1]

And "Omoo" came to share honors with "Typee" as a popular
appellation for the young author, among critics and friends alike,
until Melville declared himself heartily sick of the euphonious
nicknames he had supplied by his own choice. Yet he had undoubtedly chosen "Omoo," deliberately, as the title for his recog-
nizably autobiographical book because it was more respectable
than the more accurate English designation of "Beachcomber"—
a word that was already in disrepute a hundred years ago. When
Melville undertook to define the latter, indeed, he applied it to
"Salem," the most disreputable of his fellow mutineers, rather
than to himself:

This is a term much in vogue among sailors in the Pacific. It is applied to certain roving characters, who, without attaching themselves
permanently to any vessel, ship now and then for a short cruise in a
whaler; but upon the condition only of being honourably discharged
the very next time the anchor takes hold of the bottom; no matter
where. They are, mostly, a reckless, rollicking set, wedded to the Pacific,
and never dreaming of ever doubling Cape Horn again on a homeward-
bound passage. Hence their reputation is a bad one. [2]

However unsavory the term, "beachcomber" fits Melville's career in the South Seas for the next nine months—though this role was of course merely temporary with him—far better than the romantic title of "Mr. Omoo," by which the youthful Julian Hawthorne, among others, afterwards called him.

Melville's experiences at Tahiti have already been rehearsed, as well as the controversial chapters which serve as an interlude between these and his further experiences upon the neighboring island of Eimeo. Leaving behind the Calabooza and its derelict party of mutineers, Melville set out for fresh Polynesian adventures in the company of his chosen companion, "Doctor Long Ghost." One would like to know more about this picaresque hero of *Omoo* to whom Melville played both Boswell and Sancho Panza. Early in the story he is set forth in all the trappings appropriate to his mock-epic proportions:

His early history, like that of many other heroes, was enveloped in the profoundest obscurity; though he threw out hints of a patrimonial estate, a nabob uncle, and an unfortunate affair which sent him a-roving. All that was known, however, was this. He had gone out to Sydney as assistant-surgeon of an emigrant ship. On his arrival there, he went back into the country, and after a few months' wanderings, returned to Sydney penniless, and entered as doctor aboard of the *Julia*.

His personal appearance was remarkable. He was over six feet high—a tower of bones, with a complexion absolutely colorless, fair hair, and a light, unscrupulous gray eye, twinkling occasionally with the very devil of mischief. Among the crew, he went by the name of the Long Doctor, or more frequently still, Doctor Long Ghost. And from whatever high estate Doctor Long Ghost might have fallen, he had certainly at some time or other spent money, drunk Burgundy, and associated with gentlemen.

As for his learning, he quoted Virgil, and talked of Hobbes of Malmsbury, besides repeating poetry by the canto, especially "Hudibras." He was, moreover, a man who had seen the world. In the easiest way imaginable, he could refer to an amour he had in Palermo, his lion-hunting before breakfast among the Caffres, and the quality of coffee to be drunk in Muscat; and about these places, and a hundred others, he had more anecdotes than I can tell of. Then such mellow old songs he sang, in a voice so round and racy, the real juice of sound. How such notes came forth from his lank body was a constant marvel.

Upon the whole, Long Ghost was as entertaining a companion as one could wish; and to me . . . an absolute godsend.[3]

As has already been mentioned, Lieutenant Henry Wise made inquiry about the Long Ghost at the time of his visit to Tahiti in 1848. From Doctor Johnston he got the corroboration of the laudanum anecdote previously quoted; but the only other information he could gather, according to his published memorandum, was purely conjectural: "The Ghost . . . was supposed at the period of our visit to be in Sydney, or after gold in California, but, with his ubiquitous propensities, may have been in both places."[4] An examination of the manuscript journal upon which Wise's volume was based has revealed no further secrets. But perseverance was rewarded when the jumbled mass of rough notes which furnished the material for this journal was consulted. There, within parentheses following the sobriquet "Long Ghost," was, apparently, the adventurous doctor's real name: JOHN TROY![5] This journal jotting, brief as it is, gives some color of reality to a figure whom Melville's previous biographers have never brought out of the land of fiction. But the search ended, unfortunately, at the very point where it began, because no trace of a "Doctor John Troy" survives in contemporary records at Sydney or Tahiti, the only known places of his residence.[6] Ghosts are frequently as hard to raise as they are to lay, especially when they masquerade under aliases. For one suspects, from Melville's account of his mysterious companion, that, even as he stalks through the pages of *Omoo* under a nickname, he must have sailed on the *Lucy Ann* under a purser's name.

However this may be, on or about November 9, 1842, disguising their mutinous past under the new aliases of "Peter and Paul," the two companions set sail in a small boat across the channel that separated Tahiti from Eimeo, five leagues to the westward.[7] Their destination, according to Melville, was a plantation in the valley of "Martair," directly opposite the village of Papeete, where they had been hired as field laborers. Since Edward Lucett declared that "the valley which he describes in Moorea [Eimeo] . . . has existence only in the regions of his imagination,"[8] however, it seems pertinent to establish first of all the existence of this supposedly fictitious valley. Since Matea—such is the more usual French spelling of the name—was indeed a small and obscure settlement, seldom visited at the period of Melville's story, it can best be identified by reference to the more populous village of Afareaitu, located in a beautiful neighboring bay.

On the first Sunday after his arrival, says Melville, he made a journey to this place, the seat of an important mission, for the purpose of attending the church services there:

In Afrehitoo [sic] is a large church and school-house, both quite dilapidated; and planted amid shrubbery on a fine knoll, stands a very tasteful cottage, commanding a view across the channel. In passing I caught sight of a graceful calico skirt disappearing from the piazza through a doorway. The place was the residence of the missionary.

A trim little sail boat was dancing out at her moorings, a few yards from the beach.

Straggling over the low lands in the vicinity were several native huts —untidy enough—but much better every way than most of those in Tahiti.[9]

This mission was the very first post assumed by William Ellis upon his arrival in the Society Islands in 1817. Tahiti being at this time in the throes of the religious wars that had driven Pomaré II and the missionaries from its shores, Ellis chose this lovely spot across the channel as the location for his church and printing press. He has left a description of it as it first appeared to him:

The next morning we examined the district, and were delighted with its fertility, extent, and resources. Afareaitu is on the eastern side of Eimeo, opposite the district of Atehuru in Tahiti, and is certainly one of the finest districts in the island. It comprises two valleys, or rather one large valley partially divided by a narrow hilly ridge, extending from the mountains in the interior towards the shore. The soil of the bottom of the valley is rich and fertile, well stocked with cocoanuts and bread-fruit trees.[10]

The dilapidated schoolhouse that Melville mentions was nothing less than the building formerly occupied by the South Sea Academy, founded there in 1824, but later moved to Papetoai on the other side of the island.[11] Afareaitu was likewise the scene of Mr.

Armitage's second effort to establish a native cotton factory, as Melville himself relates.[12] Stewart, who visited the village at about this time, 1829, found it flourishing and attractive:

Afareaitu is a lovely spot, surrounded by magnificent and beautiful objects. The South Sea Academy, chapel, and cottages of the natives—stretching in a long line of whiteness around the bay, at the water's edge, beneath mountains springing almost perpendicularly more than three thousand feet high—present a delightful scene as you row in from the sea.[13]

Moreover, Ellis had found not only the scenery enchanting, but the natives pure and unspoiled. In praise of them he declared:

We reposed the most entire confidence in the people . . . ; though sometimes the door was left open all night, yet we do not know that one single article was stolen from us by the natives during the eighteen months we resided among them.[14]

In the quarter-century that had elapsed since the period of his residence, however, the natives had been guilty of considerable backsliding in this very matter of thieving, if one credits Melville's account of the sermon that he listened to on this very subject at Afareaitu:

We attended service at the church, where we found but a small congregation; and after what I had seen in Papeetee, nothing very interesting took place. But the audience had a curious, fidgety look, which I knew not how to account for, until we ascertained that a sermon with the eighth commandment for a text was being preached.

It seemed that there lived an Englishman in the district, who, like our friends, the planters, was cultivating Tombez potatoes for the Papeetee market.

In spite of all his precautions, the natives were in the habit of making nocturnal forays into his enclosure, and carrying off the potatoes. One night he fired a fowling-piece, charged with pepper and salt, at several shadows which he discovered stealing across his premises. They fled. But it was like seasoning anything else: the natives stole again with a greater relish than ever; and the very next night, he caught a party in the very act of roasting a basketful of potatoes under his own cooking-shed. At last, he stated his grievances to the missionary; who, for the benefit of his congregation, preached the sermon we heard.

Now, there were no thieves in Martair; but then the people of the valley were bribed to be honest. It was a regular business transaction between them and the planters. In consideration of so many potatoes "to them in hand, duly paid," they were to abstain from all depredations upon the plantation. Another security against roguery was the permanent residence upon the premises of their chief, Tonoi.[15]

Ellis, indeed, had found the inhabitants of the valley where Melville was farming a similarly satisfactory and dutiful set of parishioners, declaring: "Once a week the people of Maatea [*sic*], a neighboring district, brought our family a present of bread-fruit and other articles of food." [16] But, again, the picture in *Omoo* is of a different sort and indicates the tendency of the Polynesians to fall from grace when the watchful eye of the Christian teachers was not upon them:

Tonoi's men, the fishermen of the grove, were a sad set. Secluded in a great measure, from the ministrations of the missionaries, they gave themselves up to all manner of lazy wickedness. Strolling among the trees of a morning, you came upon them napping on the shady side of a canoe hauled up among the bushes; lying under a tree smoking; or, more frequently still, gambling with pebbles; though, a little tobacco excepted, what they gambled for at their outlandish games, it would be hard to tell. Other idle diversions they had also, in which they seemed to take great delight. As for fishing, it employed but a small part of their time. Upon the whole, they were a merry, indigent, godless race.[17]

And so the Quaker Wheeler had found them in 1835. Extending his ministry to the island of Eimeo, he had conducted a meeting at Afareaitu. The inhabitants of Matea, a settlement about one league round the coast, he said, were invited but did not come. So, with Mahometan perseverance, the undaunted Wheeler sought out the slothful in their own habitations. But the chief—probably the same "Tonoi, the old sinner"—gave him a very poor welcome, and, in spite of his earnest preaching, he recorded mournfully, many slept during the meeting he held there.[18]

The mission station at "Afrehitoo" (Afareaitu) and the unredeemed neighboring valley of "Martair" (Matea), therefore, were not figments of Melville's imagination after all, but were geographical and spiritual realities very much as he has described them. Very little else of Melville's career as a Polynesian farmer, however, can be established with any certainty, though his employers at least were apparently drawn from living originals. In his thumbnail sketches of these two agricultural soldiers of fortune, Melville's felicitous pen earns the praise that even Lucett grudgingly bestowed upon him of "a humorous knack of hitting off little peculiarities of character":

The planters were both whole-souled fellows; but, in other respects, as unlike as possible.
One was a tall, robust Yankee, born in the backwoods of Maine, sallow, and with a long face; the other was a short little Cockney. . . .
The voice of Zeke, the Yankee, had a twang like a cracked viol; and Shorty (as his comrade called him) clipped the aspirate from every word beginning with one. The latter, though not the tallest man in the world, was a good-looking young fellow of twenty-five. His cheeks were dyed with the fine Saxon red, burned deeper from his roving life; his blue eyes opened well, and a profusion of fair hair curled over a well-shaped head.
But Zeke was no beauty. A strong, ugly man, he was well adapted for manual labor; and that was all. His eyes were made to see with, and not for ogling. Compared with the Cockney, he was grave, and rather taciturn; but there was a deal of good old humour bottled up in him, after all. For the rest, he was frank, good-hearted, shrewd, and resolute; and, like Shorty, quite illiterate.
Though a curious conjunction, the pair got along together famously.[19]

Six years later Lieutenant Wise made inquiries about these two former associates of Melville, and in his published account he established the actuality of the little Cockney at least. At Papeete he was informed, he said, that "Shorty was still devoting his talents to the culture of potatoes at Aimeo [*sic*], and strongly suspected of shooting his neighbor's cattle." [20] This libelous last clause, however, seems to have been a gratuitous comment contributed by Wise on his own authority, for the memorandum in his rough notes made on the spot reads simply: "Shorty still devotes himself to potatoes at Aimeo—this is all the information I could gather." [21] An equally unflattering after-picture of Zeke also survives, as will be seen shortly.[22]

The reality of the place and the people is certainly strong presumptive evidence of the reality of the experiences which Melville records during the brief period that he and Doctor "John Troy" spent in the valley of Matea. Although he devotes a dozen chapters to this part of his career as a roving sailor, however, the events are so strictly personal and the locale so obscure that it would be futile to look for any confirmation of them.[23] "Peter and Paul," according to Melville's own showing, spent most of their time in trying to evade the irksome labor of extracting Tombez potatoes from the stubborn soil of primitive Polynesia. Long Ghost, in particular, put on an elaborate and comical show of superiority calculated to convince his employers that his talents were above such menial duties. Zeke was duly impressed, and, hoping to induce these two learned adventurers to take up permanent residence in the valley as partners in a Utopian farming project which he vaguely outlined, he declared a holiday and took them on a bullock hunt in the mountains by way of diversion. This adventure Melville describes with spirit. Incidentally, all of the cattle on the island were wild, he says, and though they belonged technically to Queen Pomaré, the planters had obtained her permission to shoot as many of them as they needed—so much for the scandalous report of Wise in 1848 that Shorty was "suspected of shooting his neighbor's cattle." [24]

On the whole, Melville declares, the valley of Matea would have proved a very peaceful and habitable spot were it not for the mosquitoes which infested the place and made their nights miserable.[25] These pests and uncongenial labor combined to send the rovers once more on their way, to the great disappointment of Zeke and Shorty. Indeed, one suspects that almost any kind of work that restricted their freedom would have proved disagreeable to these young beachcombers. Hence, after less than two weeks of farming, they began to make new plans:

> The doctor was all eagerness to visit Tamai, a solitary inland village, standing upon the banks of a considerable lake of the same name, and embosomed among groves. From Afrehitoo [sic] you went to this place by a lonely pathway, leading through the wildest scenery in the world.

Much, too, we had heard concerning the lake itself, which abounded in such delicious fish that, in former times, angling parties occasionally came over to it from Papeetee.

Upon its banks, moreover, grew the finest fruit of the islands, and in their greatest perfection. . . .

Besides all this, in Tamai dwelt the most beautiful and unsophisticated women in the entire Society Group. In short, the village was so remote from the coast, and had been so much less affected by recent changes than other places, that, in most things, Tahitian life was here seen as formerly existing in the days of young Otoo, the boy-king, in Cook's time.[26]

After obtaining all necessary information and refurbishing their depleted wardrobes, they set out for this secluded village, some three or four leagues distant, on or about November 20, 1842, according to the chronology of *Omoo*.[27] William Ellis has left a description of this place that tallies with Melville's, as source or proof of the truth of his narrative:

On the north-eastern side of Eimeo, between the mountain and the sea, is an extensive and beautiful lake, called Tamai, on the border of which stands a sequestered village, bearing the same name. The lake is stocked with fish, and is a place of resort for wild ducks, which are sometimes taken in great numbers. . . . Occasionally we passed through the inland village of Tamai; and although whenever we took this route we had to wade three-quarters of a mile along the margin of the lake, up to our knees in water, yet we have always been amply repaid by beholding the neatness of the gardens and the sequestered peace of the village, by experiencing the generous hospitality, and receiving unequivocal proofs of the simple piety, of its inhabitants. Once or twice, when approaching Tamai, about sunrise, we have met the natives returning home from the bushes, whither by the break of day they had retired for meditation and secret prayer.[28]

The last part of Ellis's account of the natives of this inland village, however, does not find corroboration in *Omoo*. Melville was indeed struck by their health, beauty, and hospitality—all of which he attributed to the fact that their primitive purity was as yet little tainted by the deplorable evils of civilization which he had found so abundant at Tahiti. But, similarly, he found them as little touched by the teachings of the missionaries:

The people of Tamai were nominally Christians; but being so remote from ecclesiastical jurisdiction, their religion sat lightly upon them. We had been told, even, that many heathenish games and dances still secretly lingered in their valley.

Now the prospect of seeing an old-fashioned "hevar," or Tahitian reel, was one of the inducements which brought us here.[29]

Accordingly, after some persuasion, the chief was induced to arrange a dance for them that very night, though the preparations had to be somewhat secret for fear a few old gossips would report them to the church fathers.

What a treat this must have been for Melville, homesick for the "happy valley" of Typee, even if the surreptitious manner in which it had to be given somewhat diminished its full spontaneous freedom. But Melville describes it right joyously:

We waited impatiently; and at last they came forth. They were arrayed in short tunics of white tappa; with garlands of flowers on their heads. . . . [Then] the girls advanced a few paces; and, in an instant, two of them, taller than their companions, were standing, side by side, in the middle of a ring formed by the clasped hands of the rest. This movement was made in perfect silence.

Presently the two girls join hands overhead; and, crying out, "Ahloo! ahloo!" wave them to and fro. Upon which the ring begins to circle slowly; the dancers moving sideways, with their arms a little drooping. Soon they quicken their pace; and, at last, fly round and round; bosoms heaving, hair streaming, flowers drooping, and every sparkling eye circling in what seemed a line of light.

Meanwhile, the pair within are passing and repassing each other incessantly. Inclining sideways, so that their long hair falls far over, they glide this way and that; one foot continually in the air, and their fingers thrown forth, and twirling in the moonbeams.

"Ahloo! ahloo!" again cry the dance queens; and, coming together in the middle of the ring, they once more lift up the arch, and stand motionless.

"Ahloo! ahloo!" Every link of the circle is broken; and the girls, deeply breathing, stand perfectly still. They pant hard and fast, a moment or two; and then, just as the deep flush is dying away from their faces, slowly recede, all round; thus enlarging the ring.

Again the two leaders wave their hands, when the rest pause; and now, far apart, stand in the still moonlight, like a circle of fairies.

Presently, raising a strange chant, they softly sway themselves, gradually quickening the movement, until at length, for a few passionate moments, with throbbing bosoms, and glowing cheeks, they abandon themselves to all the spirit of the dance, apparently lost to everything around. But soon subsiding again into the same languid measure as before, they become motionless; and then, reeling forward on all sides, their eyes swimming in their heads, join in one wild chorus, and sink into each other's arms.

Such is the Lory-Lory, I think they call it; the dance of the backsliding girls of Tamai.

Only the pious could object to this description as being lascivious. Moreover, it has a more authentic ring to it than any of the accounts of dances recorded in *Typee,* though I have not been able to find a parallel for his "Lory-Lory," other than the suggestive outline in Captain Cook's *Voyages:*

Among other amusements, they have a dance called Timorodee, which is generally performed by ten or a dozen young females, who put themselves into the most wanton attitudes, keeping time during the performance with the greatest nicety and exactness.[30]

Melville was right, it may be added, in saying that all dances were prohibited by the missionaries, but that they were frequently performed in secret in spite of all that could be done. And Captain Beechey has left an account of a dance surreptitiously performed in 1824 for his benefit at Tahiti in the queen regent's house, right under the nose of the framers of the Blue Laws:

This was an indulgence we hardly expected, such performances being prohibited by law, under severe penalties, both against the performer, and upon those who should attend such exhibitions; and for the same reason it was necessary that it should be executed quietly, and that the *vivo,* or reed pipe, should be played in an undertone, that it might not reach the ears of an aava, or policeman, who was parading the beach, in a soldier's jacket, with a rusty sword; for even the use of this melodious little instrument, the delight of the natives, from whose nature the dance and the pipe are inseparable, is now strictly prohibited. None of us had witnessed the dances of these people before they were restrained by law; but in that which was exhibited on the present occasion, there was nothing at which any unprejudiced person could take offense; and it confirmed the opinion I had often heard expressed, that Pomarree [*sic*], or whoever framed the laws, would have more effectually attained his object had these amusements been restricted within proper limits, rather than entirely suppressed. To some of us, who had formed our opinion of the native dance of this island from the fascinating representation of it by Mr. Webber, who accompanied Captain Cook, that which we saw greatly disappointed our expectation.[31]

According to Melville's account, he and Long Ghost remained at Tamai for a week of uninterrupted pleasures. They were just beginning to entertain the prospect of an indefinite or even permanent stay at this idyllic spot when their plans were suddenly interrupted:

Several women came running into the house, and hurriedly besought us to "heree! heree!" (make our escape), crying out something about the "mickonarees."

Thinking that we were about to be taken up under the act for the suppression of vagrancy, we flew out of the house, sprang into a canoe before the door, and paddled with might and main over to the opposite side of the lake.[32]

Fearful of being apprehended as runaway seamen, they were thus forced to flee from their sequestered paradise. With blighted hopes, they returned to Matea, where they spent several days making plans for further adventures. Of course, the whole episode of Melville's visit to Tamai may have been manufactured. The very accuracy of his orthography—a rare occurrence with him—suggests the possibility that he may have taken the description of the inland lake and village from Ellis and merely added the account of the dance and their flight at the approach of visiting elders as a satire upon the missionaries, by suggesting that other things than prayers went on in secret during their absence. On the other hand, such a trip might easily have been included in the itinerary of an inveterate sight-seer, for it was certainly not far off the known route of Melville and Long Ghost.

"Taloo, the only frequented harbour of Imeeo," was picked as their next destination. There were several reasons, Melville says, for making this choice. In the first place, this offered their most likely chance of shipping, especially since a whaler had been reported to be lying at anchor there in want of men. Again, on one shore of the bay stood the prosperous settlement of "Partoowye" (Papetoai), where they might hope to find employment of some sort, since, among other openings, there was the prospect of hiring out as day laborers on a Sydney-owned sugar plantation in the vicinity. Finally, "there were hopes to be entertained of being promoted to some office of high trust and emolument about the person of her majesty, the queen." For this village, he declares, was one of the occasional residences of the court, which at the present time was permanently settled there, Pomaré having fled thither from Tahiti:

> We were told that, to resist the usurpation of the French, the queen was rallying about her person all the foreigners she could. . . . Should this prove true, a surgeon's commission for the doctor, and a lieutenancy for myself, were certainly counted upon in our sanguine expectations. . . .
> All things considered, I could not help looking upon Taloo as offering "a splendid opening" for us adventurers.[33]

Surprising as it may seem, all of these inducements were actually in prospect in the fall of 1842, including even the most romantic one of the three. The reality of the whaler and the sugar plantation will be established shortly. As for Pomaré, she had indeed fled to Taloo upon the arrival of Rear-Admiral Dupetit-Thouars, remaining there until the return of George Pritchard in a British man-of-war, in February, 1843, offered her protection. And in view of the aggressive warfare against the French which followed soon after, it is reasonable to assume that even at the time Melville mentions she was building up an army of English and American residents, as well as natives, against this eventuality.[34]

Although Melville says he kept no journal in the South Seas, he dates his rovings for the next two months with some show of accuracy, by reference to an event which must have happened about the end of November, 1842. He begins this calendar in mock-epic style by saying that he and Doctor Long Ghost set out for Taloo "on the fourth day of the first month of the Hegira, or flight from Tamai."[35] To these deserters this was indeed a significant date, for the circumstances of their inglorious departure from the fishing village had filled them with some misgivings, as *Omoo* records: "The truth is, that the rewards constantly offered for the apprehension of deserters from ships, induce some of the natives to eye all strangers suspiciously." This fear of being recaptured apparently followed Melville, the gentleman's son turned beachcomber, throughout all his Polynesian wanderings; and well it might, for the natives in their passionate desire for money were only too glad to serve in the capacity of police, as many ship captains testify.[36] Consequently, the two rovers carried with them a testimonial furnished by Zeke as to their character and previous employment. This was their only equipment for the journey, since they relied upon native hospitality en route to supply them with food and shelter.

Taloo, says Melville, lay on the opposite side of Eimeo from Matea, but, wishing to see as much of the island as possible, they decided to go round by the beach, some twenty to thirty miles, in preference to the overland route which was only one fourth of that distance. They set out on foot, hoping soon to fall in with a canoe, for the natives commonly used the smooth canal within the coral breakwater as the best means of communication between the various settlements. All this accords perfectly with the actual facts of travel at this period between the two settlements in question. William Ellis, for example, remarked that he frequently made the trip from Afareaitu to Taloo, sometimes along the beach and sometimes by canoe, usually covering the twenty miles in a day.[37] But Melville and Long Ghost made a more leisurely journey, consuming a whole week in sight-seeing and philandering. There is no confirmation for the events of this week, which fill half-a-dozen merry chapters, except their entire reasonableness and the convincing autobiographical veracity of *Omoo* throughout, wherever it can be checked. So with reasonable safety it may be assumed that the two travelers, even as Melville says, actually spent several pleasant days at the hamlet of "Loohooloo," where the manners of the natives remained unchanged from ancient days—enjoying the generous hospitality, fishing by torchlight, and sometimes canoeing with the beautiful young girls (who were not restricted by *tapu,* as at the Marquesas Islands)—that they continued their journey for some miles by water with a party from this settlement, and that they spent the last night of their week of travel in the disreputable hut of a comical old "dealer in contraband," who in defiance of the missionaries continued to make the vicious native drink *kava.*[38]

It must have been about the end of the first week in December —"the tenth day of the Hegira"—that Melville and Long Ghost covered the last two leagues of their journey and arrived at the village of Papetoai. They accepted the kindly invitation of the first house they came to, according to *Omoo,* and were apparently fortunate in their choice. For the proprietor, who introduced himself as "Eeremear (Jeremiah) Po-Po," was a wealthy native, related to the chief, and an elder in the church. This comical name, incidentally, had been forced upon him at his christening, says Melville. The missionaries, taking exception to his native patronymic —"Narmo-Nana Po-Po (something equivalent to The-Darer-of-Devils-by-Night)"—had insisted upon substituting a Christian name for at least part of it, with the resulting ludicrous hybrid of "Jeremiah-in-the-Dark." But there was nothing equivocal about the actual conversion of his new host, Melville declares emphatically: "Po-Po was, in truth, a Christian: the only one, Arfretee [his wife] excepted, whom I personally knew to be such, among all the natives of Polynesia." [39] All of this may be somewhat touched up in the telling, but to anyone familiar with Polynesian names and missionary ingenuousness it reads plausibly enough— though there were assuredly some reports more favorable than Melville's as to the amount of sincere piety to be found among the converted natives. However this may be, the two beachcombers found a pleasant home in this pious and hospitable household for the next several weeks, according to the record of *Omoo.*

The reality of the harbor and the village, on the other hand, do not have to depend upon conjecture. Melville's descriptions of them certainly establish the fact of his residence there beyond question. His sketch of the bay is as accurate as it is charming:

Going from Po-Po's house toward the anchorage of the harbour of Taloo, you catch no glimpse of the water, until coming out from deep groves, you all at once find yourself upon the beach. A bay, considered by many voyagers the most beautiful in the South Seas, then lies before you. You stand upon one side of what seems a deep green river, flowing through mountain passes to the sea. Right opposite, a majestic promontory divides the inlet from another, called after its discoverer, Captain Cook. The face of this promontory towards Taloo is one verdant wall; and at its base the waters lie still and fathomless. On the left hand, you just catch a peep of the widening mouth of the bay, the break in the reef by which ships enter, and, beyond, the sea. To the right, the inlet, sweeping boldly round the promontory, runs far away into the land; where, save in one direction, the hills close in on every side, knee-deep in verdure and shooting aloft in grotesque peaks. The open space lies at the head of the bay; in the distance it extends into a broad, hazy plain lying at the foot of an amphitheatre of hills. Here is the large sugar plantation previously alluded to. Beyond the first range of hills, you descry the sharp pinnacles of the interior; and among these, the same silent Marling-spike which we so often admired from the other side of the island.[40]

Upon this harbor, which Ellis declared was "one of the most secure and delightful anchoring-places to be met with in the Pacific," [41] the occasional travelers who chanced to visit this out-of-the-way place lavished their praise. Wheeler, for one, was highly enthusiastic:

This is a most romantic spot, surrounded by almost perpendicular hills, towering nearly four thousand feet, with a broken, fantastic outline. . . . Its scenery is wilder and more diversified, and the ridges are more angular and rugged than those of Tahiti; some of them, where huge black rocks and foliage blend in the obscurity of distance, resembling the broken fragments of a stupendous ruin.[42]

And Commodore Wilkes in 1839 completed the corroborative picture:

Taloo harbour is an inlet about three miles in depth, situated in a glen enclosed by precipitous sides rising in places to the height of two thousand feet; at its head is an extensive flat of rich alluvial soil, now employed in the culture of sugar, and studded with trees, shrubs, and other interesting objects. The ship lay at anchor close beneath a high mountain on the left, in contrast with which her dimensions seemed those of a cock-boat.[43]

For the time being, however, the land rather than the sea held Melville's interest. On the first morning after his arrival at Pape-toai he went for a ramble through the village, observing and recording his impressions:

The settlement of Partoowye [*sic*] is nothing more than some eighty houses, scattered here and there, in the midst of an immense grove. . . . The houses, constructed without the slightest regard to the road, peep into view from among the trees on either side; some looking you right in the face as you pass, and others, without any manners, turning their backs. Occasionally, you observe a rural retreat, enclosed by a picket of bamboos, or with a solitary pane of glass massively framed in the broad-side of the dwelling, or with a rude, strange-looking door, swinging upon dislocated hinges. Otherwise, the dwellings are built in the original style of the natives; and never mind how mean and filthy some of them may appear within, they all look picturesque enough without. . . .

Strolling on, we turned a sweep of the road, when the doctor gave a start; and no wonder. Right before us, in the grove, was a block of houses: regular square frames, boarded over, furnished with windows and doorways, and two stories high. We ran up and found them fast going to decay; very dingy, and here and there covered with moss; no sashes nor doors; and on one side, the entire block had settled down nearly a foot. On going into the basement, we looked clean up through the unboarded timbers to the roof; where rays of light, glimmering through many a chink, illuminated the cobwebs which swung all round. . . .

Curious to know who on earth could have been thus trying to improve the value of real estate on Partoowye, we made inquiries; and learned that some years previous the block had been thrown up by a veritable Yankee (one might have known that), a house-carpenter by trade, and a bold, enterprising fellow by nature. [The local chief was persuaded to underwrite this new subdivision to improve the appearance of his vil-lage, and the carpenter went to work.] . . .

Presto! the castle rose; but alas, the roof was hardly on, when the Yankee's patron, having speculated beyond his means, broke all to pieces, and was absolutely unable to pay one "plug" of tobacco on the pound. His failure involved the carpenter, who sailed away from his creditors in the very next ship that touched at the harbour.

The natives despised the rickety palace of boards; and often lounged by, wagging their heads and jeering.[44]

This real estate boom at Papetoai had evidently taken place before 1835, for the Quaker Wheeler had observed these Europeanized structures at that time. Although his comment was likewise unfavorable, his objection, diametrically opposed to Melville's, was that this progress in material civilization simply had not gone far enough:

Among the enclosures of the natives here, there is greater indication of industry than we remarked in Tahiti, and many of the houses are built in the civilized manner, with windows, plastered walls, etc. Nevertheless, the dwellings we have seen have by no means a comfortable aspect, and the general effect of the native settlements is not particularly pleasing. Unfurnished, dirty huts, surrounded with lumber, the remains of food, etc., naked children, and all but naked parents, working or rolling about, smoking or playing, sleeping or waking, as the case may be, with groups of half-starved hogs and dogs occupying every corner in the neighborhood, do not constitute the most delightful objects, though viewed in the far-famed South Sea Islands.[45]

The principal building in the village, the native church, however, receives due praise from Melville:

In Partoowye is to be seen one of the best constructed and handsomest chapels in the South Seas. Like the buildings of the palace, it stands upon an artificial pier, presenting a semicircular sweep to the bay. The chapel is built of hewn blocks of coral; a substance which, although extremely friable, is said to harden by exposure to the atmosphere. To a stranger, these blocks look extremely curious. Their surface is covered with strange fossil-like impressions, the seal of which must have been set before the Flood. Very nearly white when hewn from the reefs, the coral darkens with age; so that several churches in Polynesia now look almost as sooty and venerable as famed St. Paul's.

In shape, the chapel is an octagon, with galleries all round. It will seat, perhaps, four hundred people. Everything within is stained a tawny red; and there being but few windows, or rather embrasures, the dusky benches and galleries, and the tall spectre of a pulpit, look anything but cheerful.[46]

[301]

Stewart, the chaplain of the *Vincennes,* gave a corroborative picture of this same church, which had just been completed at the
time of his visit in 1829:

Papetoai does not differ materially from Matavai and Papeeté [*sic*],
in the evidences of civilization and piety it presents. The chapel is very
superior, and more substantial than any other building yet erected in
the South Seas, being of hewn coral, not dissimilar in its appearance to a
light free-stone or marble. It is an octagon, sixty or seventy feet in diameter, well plastered and whitewashed within and furnished with convenient seats constructed of the timber of the bread-fruit tree. The gallery, and a handsome pulpit, are of the same material.[47]

Here, Melville says, he and Long Ghost attended services every
Sunday. But he gives no satirical notes on the sermons he heard
at this place. Perhaps the two beachcombers were not anxious to
repeat the roles they had played at Tahiti. "Going in the family
suite of Po-Po," he remarks piously, "we, of course, maintained a
most decorous exterior; and hence, by all the elderly people of the
village, were doubtless regarded as pattern young men." [48] Papetoai offered a "splendid opening" to the two young adventurers,
which they did not choose to forfeit by ill-chosen word or deed.

It must not be thought, however, that Melville spent all of his
time at Papetoai in establishing a decorous reputation. Throughout his South Sea travels he remained, first of all, a sight-seer, with
a professional's eye for beauty as well as an amateur's love of adventure. But romance did not always follow where his observant
eye led him, as he records in an abortive anecdote:

One day, taking a pensive afternoon stroll along one of the many
bridle-paths which wind among the shady groves in the neighbourhood
of Taloo, I was startled by a sunny apparition. It was that of a beautiful
young Englishwoman, charmingly dressed, and mounted upon a spirited little white pony. Switching a green branch, she came cantering
toward me.

I looked round to see whether I could possibly be in Polynesia. There
were the palm-trees; but how to account for the lady?

Stepping to one side, as the apparition drew near, I made a polite
obeisance. It gave me a bold, rosy look; and then, with a gay air, patted
its palfrey, crying out, "Fly away, Willie!" and galloped among the
trees. . . .

The next day, our inquiries resulted in finding out, that the stranger had been in the island about two years; that she came from Sydney; and was the wife of Mr. Bell (happy dog), the proprietor of the sugar plantation to which I have previously referred.

To the sugar plantation we went the same day.

But Mrs. Bell proved to be a phantom: she had left that morning on a visit to Papeete! And although her husband, "a sun-burnt, romantic-looking European," did the honors of the plantation—even treating the two beachcombers to some spicy French sherry, served in goblets made of fresh citron melons—politeness could not compensate for her absence. Melville returned home, he declares, much chagrined:

> To be frank, my curiosity had been wonderfully piqued concerning the lady. In the first place, she was the most beautiful white woman I ever saw in Polynesia. But this is saying nothing. She had such eyes, such moss-roses in her cheeks, such a divine air in the saddle, that, to my dying day, I shall never forget Mrs. Bell.
>
> The sugar-planter himself was young, robust, and handsome. So, merrily may the little Bells increase and multiply, and make music in the land of Imeeo.[49]

It is the accuracy of such incidental episodes as this that convinces one of the essential autobiographical truth of *Omoo*. For, however embellished this little unfinished romance may be, the principal actors were real persons. Indeed, following his practice throughout this volume, Melville did not even undertake to disguise their names. Proof of this is found in the record of a visitor to Papetoai in 1847: "Mr. Bell, a young Englishman, has got a large sugar-manufactory here, but now all his works are suspended; the men whom he employed are either in the camp or else will not work until the question of their freedom is settled." [50] But all of Mr. Bell's worries were not caused by the decline of his plantation owing to the disorders growing out of the French occupation. Lieutenant Wise, who in 1848 tracked down so many of Melville's former associates, had a word to say about this tropical planter's wife, who had proved such a lovely apparition on horseback: "Charming Mrs. Bell had taken to hard drink, *before* Mr.

Melville's rencontre, and may have been slightly elevated on that occasion." [51] From these two side lights, one fears that the Bells did not prosper in domestic harmony to the extent that Melville had wished for them. The sequel, in fact, was tragic, but for an entirely different reason as will be seen later.

While killing time agreeably in Papetoai, says Melville, he and Doctor Long Ghost sallied forth as usual one day on a tour through the settlement:

Passing, on our route, a long, low shed, a voice hailed us—"White men, ahoy!" Turning round, who should we see but a rosy-cheeked Englishman (you could tell his country at a glance), up to his knees in shavings, and planing away at a bench. He turned out to be a runaway ship's carpenter, recently from Tahiti, and now doing a profitable business in Imeeo, by fitting up the dwelling of opulent chiefs with cupboards and other conveniences, and once in a while trying his hand at a lady's work-box. He had been in the settlement but a few months, and already possessed houses and lands.

But though blessed with prosperity and high health, there was one thing wanting—a wife. And when he came to speak of the matter, his countenance fell, and he leaned dejectedly upon his plane.

"It's too bad!" he sighed, "to wait three long years; and all the while, dear little Lullee living in the same house with that infernal chief from Tahar!"

Our curiosity was piqued; the poor carpenter, then, had been falling in love with some island coquette, who was going to jilt him.

But such was not the case. There was a law prohibiting, under a heavy penalty, the marriage of a native with a foreigner, unless the latter, after being three years a resident on the island, was willing to affirm his settled intention of remaining for life.

William was therefore in a sad way. He told us that he might have married the girl half a dozen times, had it not been for this odious law; but, latterly, she had become less loving and more giddy, particularly with the strangers from Tahar. Desperately smitten, and desirous of securing her at all hazards, he had proposed to the damsel's friends a nice little arrangement, introductory to marriage; but they would not hear of it; besides, if the pair were discovered living together upon such a footing, they would be liable to a degrading punishment—sent to work making stone walls and opening roads for the queen.

Doctor Long Ghost was all sympathy. "Bill, my good fellow," said he, tremulously, "let *me* go and talk to her." But Bill, declining the offer, would not even inform us where his charmer lived.

Leaving the disconsolate Willie planing a plank of New Zealand pine (an importation from the Bay of Islands), and thinking the while of Lullee, we went on our way. How his suit prospered in the end we never learned.[52]

There was in fact just such a law at this time in the islands prohibiting marriage between whites and natives, according to Commodore Wilkes.[53] And it had evidently been in force some time, for Wheeler declared approvingly:

This is a very useful restriction, as, previously to its adoption, the most worthless characters have caused much disorder and misery by settling among the natives and marrying, to remain only till caprice dictated the desirableness of a move, when their families have been deserted without scruple or redress.[54]

What is indeed surprising, moreover, is to find a complete confirmation of this trivial and purely incidental anecdote. Though Melville never learned how "Willie's" suit prospered, the reader can now satisfy whatever curiosity he may have on the subject by reference to one of the most detailed, most unexpected, and most convincing of all the corroborations of Melville's Polynesian experiences. Edward T. Perkins, who spent six months in the Society Islands, is the narrator. Just like Melville, he had gone out as an ordinary seaman on a whaler, and, again with striking similarity, he had spent several years according to his own descriptive phrase in "Reef-Rovings in the South Seas." Having read *Omoo*, he was just the person to follow successfully in the tracks of his fellow whaleman and beachcomber of a decade before. In Chapter XXI of his *Na Motu: . . . A Narrative of Adventures at the Hawaiian, Georgian, and Society Islands,* he gave the result of his discoveries under the conventional and noncommittal title: "In Which the Reader Will Probably Meet An Old Acquaintance." In the spring of 1853 he had visited Eimeo en route from Tahiti to Raiatea, being forced by adverse weather conditions to spend the night there. He does not name the harbor he entered, but merely says that he took a

ramble through a small settlement of fifteen or twenty native houses
—probably Papetoai or Matea, either of which would have offered a
convenient haven on such a trip. His remarkable anecdote follows:

Emerging from the grove to an open space, the principal objects were
a dilapidated house and a carpenter's shop. . . . Certain sounds from
the house indicated revelry of some description; as I passed, a head
with a very significant expression of countenance was protruded, and,
after stammering some kind of an apology for the interruption, begged
me to come in and make myself at home. A jug and bottle bore unequivocal testimony as to the cause of the merriment. The occupants
consisted of the before-mentioned individual, the carpenter, a middle-
aged man, and his partner, who was perfectly sober. Two young girls,
in high spirits, together with the carpenter's (native) wife (minus the
left visual organ), completed the company. . . .

"I hope you'll excuse my house," said the carpenter. "If those I hired
had done as they agreed to, I should have had a comfortable place by
this time. But there's no use talking; you can't get the natives to do
anything, unless they are amind to. They've got their orange rum agoin,
and are on a bust now; and the foreigners about here don't seem to behave much better."

"I say, carpenter," said our first acquaintance, "hold your temper,
and don't expose yourself before strangers, for you know your failings."
Then, to me—"There's no mistake about it; the carpenter *is* pretty well
to do, for a person on these islands; but, as he says, you can't do anything
with these lazy beggars—they will drink. For my part, I'm going home
as quick as I can settle my business and arrange some little family
matters." (Here he cast a knowing look towards one of the girls, whose
deshabillé bespoke an indifference to observation.) "I say, Matéa! *hére
mai!* and join your sweetheart in a glass—no, a bowl of Old Tom." She,
"nothing loth," complied; and, having drained it, twined her arms lovingly around the waist of her partner. "I'm a down-east Yankee, bound
home to the land of steady habits." These and a few similar expressions
terminated with his whistling "The girl I left behind me." . . .

While sitting upon the bedstead a thought suddenly occurred to me,
suggested by my host's occupation, the island, and his long residence
upon it; I casually inquired whether he had ever heard of Omoo.

At the sound of that word our down-east friend started, as if by magic,
from his *tête-à-tête* with the native girl. "What!—Omoo! Ha, ha! I say,
Chips, tell us all about the work-box and shavings, *old boy*. Well, now,
didn't he give it to us! Carpenter got his share. I dont know what the

devil *has* become of Shorty. Perhaps, though, you are Herman Melville, come to spy us out." [His precise words.]

I assured him to the contrary.

"Are you really the person mentioned in that book?" I inquired of the carpenter.

"I am that; and I don't thank Mr. Omoo for saying I was up to my—knees in New-Zealand pine shavings, making a work-box; nor insinuating that that scamp of a Long Ghost offered to do my courting for me."

"O, the girl! Did you get her at last?"

"Yes, indeed; and a good one she's proved to me."

I turned to have a view of the woman, who, by some intuitive perception, thinking herself the subject of our conversation, was looking up with inquiring glances. Whatever she might have been, her present appearance afforded no criterion for judging. Add ten years to the existence of a young Tahitian woman, and time will leave its indelible trace upon her features. At my request her husband inquired whether she recollected either of the persons mentioned. She could call to mind Long Ghost, who lived upon Mr. Bell's plantation, but all recollection of the other had escaped her. Poor Mrs. Bell's fate was tragical; the family having removed to the Navigator Islands, she was drowned in one of the streams of Upólu. Long Ghost led a free-and-easy life for some time, and afterwards took his departure. The carpenter was disposed to be vexed at the position he had been made to assume, but I soon convinced him that although Mr. Melville had handled his subject familiarly, he had said nothing to his disparagement, and he finally concluded it was "a good joke after all." [55]

This plain tale furnishes a rich reward for the student of Melville who has made his way through several hundred volumes of South Sea travels—all too frequently with negative results—constantly on the alert for any tidbit of information that might throw light on the Polynesian wanderings of an embryonic author, whether it be a confirmation of his actual adventures or merely a source for his published narratives. Yet this corroborative anecdote, like most of its fellows, while giving proof of reality to Melville's autobiographical records of his experiences, puts a pinprick in several of his miniature romances. "William," the English carpenter, had served out his probationary period and was rewarded with his cherished Polynesian bride, but in a brief ten years her beauty had been sadly blighted by premature aging and by the loss of one of her coquettish eyes. And charming Mrs. Bell had come to a tragic end by drowning, though one assumes not because of an "elevated" condition occasioned by strong drink.

Equally shocking is the discovery of what ten years had done to Zeke—Zeke of the homespun strength of will and redoubtable industry—for the "down-east Yankee," who was whistling "The girl I left behind me" even while in the embrace of his Tahitian sweetheart, could be none other than he. The lure of a tropical paradise had proved too much for even this paragon of honest toil and the homely virtues. He had given up his ambitions as a potato farmer and had turned to orange rum and philandering; but there is some show of his old New England ruggedness in his resolution to wind up his amorous affairs and return home to a new start in the land of steady habits. And Shorty, ever the silent partner, had already disappeared from the scene, probably to pursue the nomadic career of a typical beachcomber in the South Seas.

Probably the most interesting reference in this remarkable post-mortem of the characters in *Omoo* is the one to Long Ghost. One wonders if Melville ever ran across this passage in Perkin's *Na Motu,* for he had remarked at the close of his own book, upon his departure from the island: "I shook the doctor long and heartily by the hand. I have never seen or heard of him since." [56] Something of his future the reader now learns. As was his wont in *Omoo,* the doctor had come off with all the honors, especially in his chosen avocation of *chevalier d'amour.* Perhaps Melville's old envy of him in this respect was again aroused if he ever discovered that his former competitor at the court of love in Polynesia had lingered on for some time at Papetoai on the very plantation which the romantic Mrs. Bell had endowed with such attractions for the two young adventurers. Then at last, surfeited with this free-and-easy life, he had taken his departure—according to Wise's conjecture—for the more tangible rewards in prospect on the gold fields of California.

Most ironical of all, even the faded beauty "Lullee" remembered the Long Doctor, who, Tristram-like, had offered to woo her by proxy for the carpenter. But she had lost all recollection of Melville

—if she had ever really known him—the one who had celebrated her charms in print and had given her, and all the rest of this strangely assorted company, what small share of immortality they could claim. Finally, it is interesting to note that Melville had possibly gone by the name of "Omoo" during his actual residence on the island, long before the book had been conceived, even as he had been known on the *Lucy Ann* as "Typee," if his own record can be credited.

Thus, by and large, *Omoo* is a sort of traveler's portfolio of the genre of Irving's *Sketch-Book* and the *Tales of a Traveller*, though it differs from the former in that most of its episodes were personally experienced, and from the latter in that it is bound together by a continuous thread of autobiographical narrative. Rather than a novel it is a series of stereopticon scenes skilfully interlarded with a gallery of grotesque portraits, the slender line of continuity being furnished by the off-hand reminiscent chat of a graceful raconteur. Here, on a far-flung outpost of the Western world, where a pioneer civilization flourished incongruously in the midst of Bougainville's Nouvelle Cythère, missionaries hobnobbed with converted cannibals, rogues rubbed elbows with buffoons, romantic beachcombers dallied with island nymphs, and comic heroes performed their pygmy exploits. In spite of some embellishment here and there, always obviously motivated, the entire fabric seems to be remarkably veracious, as one astute reviewer perceived when he declared of this volume: "There is positively nothing which may not be literally true; the utmost that can be suspected, even by a jealous critic, is that the author made the most of his materials and opportunities." And whatever *Omoo* may have owed to the tradition of frame stories and travel books in general, Melville may be said to have created here, as elsewhere, his own medium.

Beneath all its high-spirited entertaining exterior, moreover, *Omoo* is also a propagandist document, as has been seen; for Melville was ever thesis-ridden. To give perspective to his indictment of civilization, he weaves in the historical background of Tahiti. Just as he had ushered in the narrative of his residence there with an account of the economic and moral chaos at the time of the French seizure in 1842, so he concludes with a sweeping survey of the house of Pomaré, from the days of its pristine glory through its decline and fall. To Melville, this royal tragedy was symbolic of the fate brought upon the entire Tahitian nation by the last "barbarian" invasion:

The truth is, that with the ascendency of the missionaries, the regal office in Tahiti lost much of its dignity and influence. In the days of Paganism, it was supported by all the power of a numerous priesthood, and was solemnly connected with the entire superstitious idolatry of the land. The monarch claimed to be a sort of by-blow of Tararroa, the Saturn of the Polynesian mythology, and cousin-german to inferior deities. His person was thrice holy; if he entered an ordinary dwelling, never mind for how short a time, it was demolished when he left; no common mortal being thought worthy to inhabit it afterward.

"I'm a greater man than King George," said the incorrigible young Otoo, to the first missionaries; "he rides on a horse, and I on a man!" Such was the case. He travelled post through his dominions on the shoulders of his subjects; and relays of immortal beings were provided in all the valleys.[57]

In his Preface Melville acknowledges William Ellis as his authority in historical matters, and it was undoubtedly from his *Polynesian Researches* that this information was drawn. After commenting on the sacred *tapu* placed upon everything connected with the pagan kings of Tahiti, so that whatever they touched—even the ground beneath their feet!—became theirs, Ellis went on to say specifically:

The sovereign and his consort always appeared in public on men's shoulders, and travelled in this manner wherever they journeyed by land. They were seated on the neck or shoulders of their bearers, who were generally stout. athletic men. . . . A number of attendants ran by the side of the bearers, or followed in their train; and when the men who carried the royal personages grew weary, they were relieved by others. . . . It is said that Pomare II once remarked that he thought himself a greater man than King George, who only rode a horse, while he rode on a man.[58]

Melville, by a slight anachronism, simply applied the saying to Pomaré I (Otoo).

This first king of the reigning dynasty, Melville reminds the reader, was the same "Otoo" whom Captain Cook had found ruling over the larger part of Tahiti in 1767, and whom the mutineers of the *Bounty* had aided with their muskets to extend his rule over the

entire island shortly thereafter.⁵⁹ How he came to change his name
to Pomaré is told elsewhere in *Omoo:*

The giving of nicknames is quite a passion with the people of Tahiti
and Imeeo. No one with any peculiarity, whether of person or temper,
is exempt; not even strangers.

A pompous captain of a man-of-war, visiting Tahiti for the second
time, discovered that, among the natives, he went by the dignified title
of "Atee Poee"—literally Poee Head, or Pudding Head. Nor is the highest rank among themselves any protection. The first husband of the
present queen was commonly known in the court circles as "Pot Belly."
He carried the greater part of his person before him, to be sure; and so
did the gentlemanly George IV.—but what a title for a king consort!

Even "Pomaree" itself, the royal patronymic, was, originally, a mere
nickname, and literally signifies, one talking through his nose. The first
monarch of that name [Otoo], being on a war party, and sleeping overnight among the mountains, awoke one morning with a cold in his head;
and some wag of a courtier had no more manners than to vulgarise him
thus.⁶⁰

Part of this information Melville probably found in Beechey's *Narrative,* where the custom is described:

It is very desirable to secure a favourable impression by liberality on
your first arrival at this island; it being a constant custom with the
natives to mark those who have any peculiarity of person or manner by
a nickname, by which alone the person will be known as long as any
recollection of his visit may remain.

As examples, Beechey cited an English Captain who came to be
known as "Tapane Matapo (Captain Blind-Eye)" and the first husband of Queen Pomaré, to whose royal name "in allusion to his
figure, and in conformity with their usual custom, they had added
the appropriate but not very elegant surname of 'Aboo-rai,' or big-
belly" ⁶¹—even as *Omoo* records. The rest of his information Melville evidently took from Ellis, though in a slightly garbled form:

The name of the king's father ["Otoo"] was originally *Vairaatoa,* but
travelling on one occasion among the mountains, and sleeping in an
exposed situation, he felt cold, and was affected with coughing. One of
his companions remarked in the morning, that it had been a night of
cough, *Po mare; po* night, and *mare,* cough; the chief was pleased with
the combination, and adopted it as his name.⁶²

Such was the actual origin of the royal patronymic of Tahiti.

Melville's account of the turbulent career of Pomaré II has already been given. From this point he brings his history rapidly down to the sovereign reigning at the time of his arrival:

Pomaree II., dying in 1821, was succeeded by his infant son, under the title of Pomaree III. This young prince survived his father but six years; and the government then descended to his elder sister, Aimata, the present queen, who is commonly called Pomaree Vahine I., or the first female Pomaree. Her majesty must be now upward of thirty years of age. She has been twice married. Her first husband was a son of the old King of Tahar, an island about one hundred miles from Tahiti. This proving an unhappy alliance, the pair were soon after divorced. The present husband of the queen is a chief of Imeeo.[63]

Melville is quite accurate, on the whole, in the facts he gives about Pomaré Vahine I. Her maiden name, Aimata, incidentally, was also royal in its own pagan way: it signified "eye-eater," the eye being the offering made to the sovereign at the time of human sacrifice.[64] The missionaries, in all likelihood, had a hand in persuading her to change this for the less objectional name of her father at the time of her succession to the throne in 1827. This famous queen was born on February 28, 1813, and hence was nearly thirty years old, just as Melville says, at the time of his visit.[65] In December, 1822, at the tender age of nine, she was indeed married to a son of the old chief of Taha'a, who later became Tapoa II of Borabora and Taha'a.[66] William Ellis, who was present at the wedding, has left a sentimental account of it:

During the ceremony I observed a tear moistening the eye of the youthful bride. Agitation of feeling perhaps produced it, as I have every reason to believe no cloud of anticipated evil overshadowed her prospects; and she is reported to have said, that had she not been betrothed, but free to choose her future partner, she should have selected the individual her friends had chosen for her.[67]

But, in spite of such good omens, the young royal couple proved to be ill-mated and soon separated. A subsequent visitor gave as the reasons for their divorce, which occurred in 1834, that Tapoa led a vicious life, was impotent, and would not give up living at Borabora

nor she at Tahiti.[68] Melville was not quite so accurate in the identification of Queen Pomaré's second husband, however, for he was a
chief of Huaheine and Raiatea, in the Georgian Islands, rather than
of Eimeo; in fact, the people of this last-named island objected
strenuously to the marriage, according to Ellis, and a mild civil war
ensued.[69]

In his account of the domestic warfare that continued to be
waged between the queen and her new husband, on the other hand,
Melville seems to be historically correct, even in his most apparently
theatrical passages:

The Tahitian princess leads her husband a hard life. Poor fellow!
he not only caught a queen, but a Tartar, when he married her. The
style by which he is addressed is rather significant—"Pomaree-Tanee"
(Pomaree's man). All things considered, as appropriate a title for a
king-consort as could be hit upon.

If ever there was a henpecked husband, that man is the prince. One
day, his "cara-sposa" giving audience to a deputation from the captains
of the vessels lying in Papeetee, he ventured to make a suggestion which
was very displeasing to her. She turned round, and boxing his ears, told
him to go over to his beggarly island of Imeeo if he wanted to give
himself airs.

Cuffed and contemned, poor Tanee flies to the bottle, or rather to the
calabash, for solace. Like his wife and mistress, he drinks more than he
ought.[70]

Daniel Wheeler has left a sketch of the king consort as he appeared
in 1835, one year after his marriage to Pomaré, which gives color to
Melville's declaration that "Tanee" was completely under the
queen's power:

[He] appears to be about twenty years of age [in reality about sixteen],
and is a mild, intelligent, unassuming youth. His countenance is not
strictly handsome, but it is truly Tahitian and pleasing, and his slender
form, dark expressive eye, and gentle manner, which are completely
Asiatic, give something feminine to his appearance.[71]

This mild submissiveness, it seems, was merely due to his extreme youth; Pomaré, being almost ten years his senior, naturally
took the upper hand in domestic as well as governmental affairs. But
when he reached his majority, he began to assert himself. A visitor

in 1840, F. A. Olmsted, has left a full description of him at this turning point in his career:

> The husband of the queen, *Pomare-tane* [*sic*], "Pomare's-man" as he is called, sustains the relation of a prince Albert to the government. He is a young man, of about twenty-one years of age, while her majesty is not far from thirty, a disparity on the side of the lady, highly averse to our notions of propriety. In the affairs of the government, he has no power, as he was an inferior chief before his marriage with Pomare, but in domestic matters is very tenacious of his rights. Pomare-tane is a good looking man, with very much of the *bon vivant* in his appearance, and an easy goodhumored way about him. Although so young, his hair is very grey, an indication of age, prematurely developed I doubt not, by the repeated floggings he received from her majesty many years since, when he was but a mere boy; occurrences entirely contrary to the order of nature. Pomare-tane, however, was very restive under her authority, and stimulated by the foreigners, had many desperate contests with his spouse, until she was compelled to succumb to his superior prowess. Since then, if reports speak true, he has not only administered wholesome chastisement for offences coming under his immediate supervision, but repays with compound interest, her maternal care over him in his boyish days. Invested in a brilliant crimson uniform, decked with gold epaulets, a sword at his side and his chapeau surrounded with white ostrich feathers, his majesty presented a highly imposing appearance. It would have been a matter of deep envy to all henpecked husbands, acquainted with the past history of his household, to have witnessed with what utter nonchalance his majesty attended his royal spouse, appearing entirely regardless of her presence.[72]

Indeed it was just about this time that Pomaré-Tani gave a public demonstration of his prowess which Melville records in all the boisterous details of low comedy:

> Six or seven years ago, when an American man-of-war was lying at Papeetee, the town was thrown into the greatest commotion by a conjugal assault and battery, made upon the sacred person of Pomaree by her intoxicated Tanee. . . .
>
> It seems, that on a Sunday morning, being dismissed contemptuously from the royal presence, Tanee was accosted by certain good fellows, friends and boon companions, who condoled with him on his misfortunes—railed against the queen, and finally dragged him away to an illicit vender of spirits, in whose house the party got gloriously mellow. In this state, Pomaree Vahine I. was the topic upon which all dilated—

"A vixen of a queen," probably suggested one. "It's infamous," said another; "and I'd have satisfaction," cried a third. "And so I will!" Tanee must have hiccoughed; for off he went; and ascertaining that his royal half was out riding, he mounted his horse and galloped after her.

Near the outskirts of the town, a cavalcade of women came cantering toward him, in the center of which was the object of his fury. Smiting his beast right and left, he dashed in among them, completely over-turning one of the party, leaving her on the field, and dispersing every-body else except Pomaree. Backing her horse dexterously, the incensed queen heaped upon him every scandalous epithet she could think of; until at last, the enraged Tanee leaped out of his saddle, caught Pomaree by her dress, and dragging her to the earth, struck her repeatedly in the face, holding on meanwhile by the hair of her head. He was pro-ceeding to strangle her on the spot, when the cries of the frightened attendants brought a crowd of natives to the rescue, who bore the nearly insensible queen away.

But his frantic rage was not yet sated. He ran to the palace; and before it could be prevented, demolished a valuable supply of crockery, a recent present from abroad. In the very act of perpetrating some other atrocity, he was seized from behind, and carried off with rolling eyes and foaming at the mouth.

This is a fair example of a Tahitian in a passion. Though the mildest of mortals in general, and hard to be roused, when once fairly up, he is possessed with a thousand devils.

The day following, Tanee was privately paddled over to Imeeo, in a canoe; where, after remaining in banishment for a couple of weeks, he was allowed to return, and once more give in his domestic adhesion.[73]

This story Melville says he got from Captain "Bob," the jailor of the Calabooza Beretanee, who acted out the scene with Melville standing proxy for the queen. But he could have found it likewise in several books of travel, the account in Wilkes's *Narrative* being his most probable source:

On the 7th of May [1840], one of the unhappy domestic feuds of the royal family threw the whole of Papieti [sic] into a ferment. The queen, followed by all her attendants, with great lamentations, rushed into a foreigner's house, to escape from her royal consort, who was pursuing her, uttering dreadful menaces. The facts of the quarrel, as derived from authentic sources, are as follows. As Pomare was on her way to Papieti from her residence at Papaoa, she was met by Pomare-tani riding furiously. Owing to the turn of the road, he did not perceive the queen's party in time to stop, and ran over one of the maids, knocking her down, and bruising her. Pomare, attributing the accident to his being intoxicated, began to abuse him in opprobrious terms. Enraged at it, he dismounted, and began not only to abuse, but also to strike her. Not content with this, he caught her by the hair, threw her down, and attempted to strangle her, which he was only prevented from doing by the attendants, who held him until Pomare fled for her life. Disappointed in overtaking her, he hurried to her new palace at Papieti, and vented his anger by demolishing the windows, breaking open her boxes and trunks, tearing her wardrobe and finery to pieces,—thus doing injury to the amount of some two thousand dollars.

On the perpetration of this outrage, the queen at first declared her intention of summoning the judges and suing for a divorce; but soon changed her mind, and forgave her husband on his promising future good behaviour.

Although this may appear extraordinary conduct on the part of the king-consort, yet when one learns that the queen has been in the habit of giving him a sound cudgelling, even on the highway, his conduct is not so surprising, particularly as it is said that she administered her punishments with such earnestness and force that he would not be likely soon to lose the remembrance of them.[74]

Melville's version is thus seen to be accurate even down to the date. But apparently he was not right in leaving the impression that, in spite of such an occasional flare-up, Pomaré-Tani remained on the whole a henpecked husband. Once the king consort came of age and began to assert his rights, the domestic tables seem to have been turned once and for all. Six years later, almost at the very moment when Melville was writing this scene in *Omoo,* Edward Lucett was recording Pomaré's continued woes in his journal:

It is reported that Ariifaite, her husband, treats her very cruelly, because she will not submit to the French and return to Tahiti. On more than one occasion, she has been compelled to fly to others for protection against his brutality. When taxed with his cowardly inhuman conduct, he at first denied it, but subsequently confessed, "that when he was first married to Pomare, he was only a boy, and she used to beat him; and why shouldn't he beat her now?" Ariifaite, like his father, is an awful fellow for ardent spirits, and when under their influence is capable of any excess.[75]

Melville continues his account of the downfall of the Pomarés by showing how the coming of the missionaries, and later of the French conquerors, had broken down the power of the throne:

Though Pomaree Vahine I. be something of a Jezebel in private life, in her public rule she is said to have been quite lenient and forbearing. This was her true policy; for an hereditary hostility to her family had always lurked in the hearts of many powerful chiefs, the descendants of the old Kings of Taiarboo, dethroned by her grandfather Otoo. Chief among these, and in fact the leader of his party, was Poofai; a bold, able man, who made no secret of his enmity to the missionaries, and the government which they controlled. But while events were occurring calculated to favour the hopes of the disaffected and turbulent, the arrival of the French gave a most unexpected turn to affairs.

During my sojourn in Tahiti, a report was rife—which I knew to originate with what is generally called the "missionary party"—that Poofai and some other chiefs of note [Kitoti, Tati, Utamai, and Paraita] had actually agreed, for a stipulated bribe, to acquiesce in the appropriation of their country. But subsequent events have rebutted the calumny. Several of these very men have recently died in battle against the French.

Under the Pomarees, the great chiefs of Tahiti became something like the barons of King John. Holding feudal sway over their patrimonial valleys, and, on account of their descent, warmly beloved by the people, they frequently cut off the royal revenues by refusing to pay the customary tribute due from them as vassals.[76]

The foreigners at Tahiti had indeed broken the natives into two opposing camps. Even Wheeler remarked on this condition, declaring: "The queen and two of the most influential chiefs entertain a very friendly feeling towards the missionaries, . . . but there is an opposite faction who would doubtless be glad if it were otherwise." [77] Commodore Wilkes gave a much fuller account of this political unrest that was probably the source from which Melville drew:

There are two distinct parties: the one led by the queen and the missionaries; the other, by some of the chiefs. The leaders of the latter are Paofai, Hitoti, and Taua, who are descended from the ancient kings dethroned by Pomare I. These chiefs have large domains, and many of the raatiras (landholders) take part with them. They are, besides, distinguished by qualities which give them consideration among the islanders. Paofai, who has more than once been spoken of, holds the office of chief judge, and is considered as the best statesman on the island. . . .

Of the three leaders, Hitoti alone is wholly free from reproach. Paofai is accused of covetousness, and a propensity to intrigue; and Taua, of a fondness for intoxicating drinks.

The queen, however, contrives to rule in all matters that rightfully belong to her; and, by the aid of the missionaries, maintains her ground against this strong opposition, although its leaders have generally the power to determine the course of policy to be pursued, and entire authority over the execution of the laws. They are much opposed to foreigners, and have made several attempts to have them banished from the island. They are supposed to entertain the design of setting aside the queen, on account of her irregular behaviour and vices; but this plan is not likely to succeed, because of the personal popularity she enjoys, and the number of adherents she possesses among the people. In conformity with such a design, these chiefs are said to be continually watching for opportunities to increase their own power and diminish the royal authority.[78]

And the French seizure, three years later, did much to complete the breakdown of the royal authority, as has been previously demonstrated, agreeably to Melville's account. To epitomize this pathetic illustration of the transiency of human greatness, Melville has one word to say in conclusion:

Some years since, Pomaree Vahine I., the granddaughter of the proud Otoo, went into the laundry business; publicly soliciting, by her agents, the washing of the linen belonging to the officers of ships touching in her harbours.

And, distressing as this may seem, he was writing of actual facts.[79]

Turning to Queen Pomaré's private character, Melville finds no relief from this disheartening picture:

The reputation of Pomaree is not what it ought to be. She, and also her mother, were, for a long time, excommunicated members of the Church; and the former, I believe, still is. Among other things, her conjugal fidelity is far from being unquestioned. Indeed, it was upon this ground chiefly that she was excluded from the communion of the Church.

Previous to her misfortunes, she spent the greater portion of her time sailing about from one island to another, attended by a licentious court;

and wherever she went, all manner of games and festivities celebrated her arrival.[80]

However libelous Melville's picture, it has at least the defense of truth. The Reverend C. S. Stewart, who in general reported so favorably on the status of Christianity at Tahiti, declared that at the time of his visit in 1829 Pomaré and her suite of followers were said to be the most lawless company in that part of the Pacific:

> The reputation of the Tahitian chieftains is far from being unspotted. The regent and dowager [Pomaré's mother] are both excommunicated members of the church; and the young queen's character, according to common report, is not *sans reprôche*. . . . The appearance of the rabble, constituting a principal part of her train, in contrast to that of most of the islanders we have seen, either at the Georgian group or at this place, goes far to prove the reputed licentiousness of her household.[81]

And Wheeler, another witness who represented the missionary's point of view, confirmed this with a specimen of her conduct that occurred during the very period of his residence in 1835:

> Although Pomare appears to favor the cause of the missionaries, . . . she is by no means a woman on whose principles full dependence can be placed. At a national assembly held annually, when nearly the whole population of the island come together to see, hear, and enjoy themselves, which took place a week or two back at Papáoa, she is said to have sanctioned great disorders, and allowed some of the ancient heathen customs„ of a shameful nature, to be indulged in.[82]

All of this discussion of Queen Pomaré and her royal house is merely preparatory to Melville's personal introduction to Tahitian majesty—and here the denouement is swift and decisive. The ostensible purpose of Melville's visit to the palace was to seek employment in the queen's household, as before intimated; but, from the use to which he put this audience in *Omoo,* he was merely resorting to the device of eyewitness testimony to clinch his thesis that the civilization at Tahiti was a travesty, at once ludicrous and pathetic. There is, unfortunately, no way to determine how authentic Melville's relation of his audience is. None of the travel books contain an account of the royal residence at Papetoai, which Melville describes in some detail, but contemporary descriptions of the palace at Papeete are similar enough to serve as a corroboration, unless, indeed, Melville simply used them as source material for an otherwise fanciful sketch.[83] However this may be, after some difficulty he and Doctor Long Ghost obtained permission to enter the queen's immense hall, he says. Here, amidst an incongruous assemblage of the gew-gaws of civilization cheek by jowl with the rudest native articles, all in hopeless disarray, they witnessed the arrival of the famous Pomaré:

> She wore a loose gown of blue silk, with two rich shawls, one red and the other yellow, tied about her neck. Her royal majesty was barefooted.
>
> She was about the ordinary size, rather matronly; her features not very handsome; her mouth, voluptuous; but there was a care-worn expression in her face, probably attributable to her late misfortunes. From her appearance, one would judge her about forty; but she is not so old.
>
> As the queen approached one of the recesses, her attendants hurried up, escorted her in, and smoothed the mats on which she at last reclined. Two girls soon appeared, carrying their mistress's repast; and then, surrounded by cut-glass and porcelain, and jars of sweetmeats and confections, Pomaree Vahine I., the titular Queen of Tahiti, ate fish and "poee" out of her native calabashes, disdaining either knife or spoon.[84]

All that can be said is that this sketch sounds so convincingly authentic that it could have been drawn from life. Almost every voyager to Tahiti during the reign of Queen Pomaré described her majesty, and, though there is some difference of opinion, most of this is attributable to the early maturing and aging of women in the tropics, for the descriptions range over a period of twenty years. In general, these accounts are agreed on the fundamental points of Melville's picture in *Omoo:* she dressed in a mixture of native and civilized attire, she was of middle stature and inclined to corpulence, she was not handsome but had a rather composed and intelligent countenance, and she looked considerably older than her actual years warranted.[85] Even the final gesture of disdain for the ways of civilized life expressed by the royal Pomaré, through the lips of Melville, finds confirmation in the account of another visiting whaleman, F. D. Bennett, at about this period:

In her domestic habits the queen differs but little from native women in a very inferior grade of life. . . . Hence, it is usual to see the queen Aimata, clad in a loose cotton gown, bare-headed, and bare-footed, mingling familiarly with natives of every class. Her meals, also, are equally unostentatious; the bread-fruit, *poe,* cocoa nuts, and baked pig, intended for her food, being placed on a layer of fresh leaves, spread on the ground, while the partaking party display, by the use of their fingers, a thorough contempt for the modern innovation of knives and forks, in the use of which, however, they are perfectly well versed.[86]

Regardless of interrupting the evening meal of royalty, says Melville, the impetuous Long Ghost insisted upon an immediate audience. It was then that Queen Pomaré first became aware of the presence of the two intruding beachcombers:

She seemed surprised and offended, and issuing an order in a commanding tone to several of her women, waved us out of the house. Summary as the dismissal was, court etiquette, no doubt, required our compliance. We withdrew; making a profound inclination as we disappeared behind the tappa arras. . . .

The next day Po-Po informed us that strict orders had been issued to admit no strangers within the palace precincts.[87]

Thus ended their royal audience and their hopes of preferment at court. But Melville does not omit this last opportunity for a comparison to drive home his thesis. The courtier who had admitted them into the royal palace was none other than a Marquesan in the train of Pomaré, by the name of "Marbonna"—"large and muscular, well made as a statue, and with an arm like a degenerate Tahitian's thigh." This contrast Melville elaborates with romantic enthusiasm:

The first time my eyes lighted upon the Marquesan, I knew his country in a moment; and hailing him in his own language, he turned round, surprised that a person so speaking should be a stranger. He proved to be a native of Tior, a glen of Nukuheva. I had visited the place more than once; and so, on the island of Imeeo, we met like old friends.

In my frequent conversations with him over the bamboo picket, I found this islander a philosopher of nature—a wild heathen, moralising upon the vices and follies of the Christian court of Tahiti—a savage, scorning the degeneracy of the people among whom fortune had thrown him.

I was amazed at the national feelings of the man. No European, when abroad, could speak of his country with more pride than Marbonna. He assured me, again and again, that so soon as he had obtained suffici- ent money to purchase twenty muskets, and as many bags of powder, he was going to return to a place, with which Imeeo was not worthy to be compared.[88]

After some two months in Papetoai, Melville himself,—because of homesickness for his own native land and people, combined with "a naturally roving disposition"—was being urged on to new scenes. His abortive audience with Queen Pomaré had taken place "about the middle of the second month of the Hegira," or about January 10, 1843, if the reckoning of time in *Omoo* can be credited. Failing in one of their projected schemes, and unwilling to under- take any employment that involved actual work such as that of field laborers on the sugar plantation of Mr. Bell, the two rovers turned to their one remaining possibility—shipping on the American whaler that was still lying in the harbor of Taloo. This ship, says Melville, was the "Leviathan," and her captain was a native of Martha's Vineyard.

.These names must have sounded sonorously sweet in the ears of the far-wandering whaleman who had sailed from the nearby port of Fairhaven on the *Acushnet* two years before. The account of Mel- ville's shipping on this his second Yankee whaler occupies the con- cluding chapter of *Omoo*. Several days passed before he succeeded in making the acquaintance of this captain, he says. But when he did, he set him down at once as "a sailor and no tyrant" and applied for a berth for himself and his companion, carefully concealing their former mutinous connections with the *Lucy Ann*. The Vine- yarder, mellow with wine at the time, pronounced Melville a Yan- kee in every beat of his pulse and heartily agreed to ship him; but he insisted that the Long Ghost was a "bird" from Sydney and swore he would have nothing to do with him—a grotesque but not entirely inappropriate resolution of the career of *Omoo's* pica- resque hero.

Melville was loth to desert his companion, but the Long Doctor insisted that he ship, declaring that for his own part he had already made up his mind to tarry a while longer in Eimeo. The lure of the sea and the prospect of eventually reaching home, says Melville were too much to be resisted, especially since the "Leviathan" would be doubling Cape Horn in little more than a year. But Melville merely bound himself for the coming cruise, leaving his subsequent movements unrestrained. After long and hearty leave-takings of Doctor Long Ghost and the hospitable family of Jeremiah Po-Po— none of whom he was ever to see again—Melville signed the ship's articles. The next day at dawn, he says, the "Leviathan" sailed. By noon the island of Eimeo had gone down in the horizon, and before him was the wide Pacific: "So, hurrah for the coast of Japan! Thither the ship was bound." [89]

CHAPTER XII

HONOLULU

ELVILLE'S career for the first half of 1843 remains some-what obscure. What ship was disguised under the sobriquet of the "Leviathan," and what waters Melville cruised on board her before arriving at Honolulu, are yet to be discovered. But there are two theoretical routes, never before presented, which may be outlined now for what they are worth. The first of these fits the already established facts of his itinerary with surprising exactness, except that it leaves no place for the "cruising for whale off the coast of Japan," which in all likelihood was merely a rhetorical flourish. In the Archives of Hawaii there is fortunately preserved a manuscript notebook kept by William Paty, the first harbor master of Honolulu. It contains about two hundred ledger pages, half of which are a spasmodically kept journal devoted to business matters, missionary gossip, and odds and ends about ships (the entries ranging from January 1, 1842, to January 28, 1845), and the other half devoted to a tabulated list of ships entering Honolulu harbor between January 1, 1843, and December 31, 1849. The entry which strikes the eye of the student of Melville is this:

Arrived, Feb. 2, [1843], Brig *Julia,* Commander Milne, owned at Sidney [*sic*], 110 Tons, from Tahiti, bound for Sidney, sailed Mar. 11.[1]

Certainly no other entry in this list—which was presumably complete—fits the circumstances of Melville's arrival in Honolulu with such precision. In the first place, the actual existence in these waters and at this time of a whaler from Sydney named the *Julia* is striking; and, what is even more to the point, this ship had been lying in the harbor at Papeete during most of the six weeks that Melville spent at the Calabooza and was very likely one of those vessels which he mentions visiting on nocturnal foraging parties, when provisions were running low.[2] In the second place, the sailing dates of this *Julia* and Melville's "Leviathan" coincide with almost incredible exactness. For Melville's departure from the Society Islands has been established with reasonable certainty, although from internal evidence only, as the middle of January, 1843; now his arrival at Honolulu by this ship would seem fixed with almost equal certainty as February 2—the normal time required for the passage of 2,500 miles from Tahiti to Honolulu by sailing ships being eighteen days.[3] If this theory be accepted, one point only remains to be explained—the apparent contradiction of Melville's arriving at Honolulu on the very ship, the *Julia*, from which he says, in *Omoo*, he had mutinied at Tahiti. But a satisfactory solution to this would be easy: he wanted to disguise the identity of the unfortunate *Lucy Ann*, on which the actual mutiny took place; and, casting about for a suitable name, he chose, naturally enough, the Sydney trader *Julia* on which he had actually shipped a few months later at Eimeo. The *Julia*, in turn, was then rechristened the "Leviathan" for his real voyage in her from Papetoai to Honolulu. But, of course, fortuitous coincidence could explain even such a neatly synchronized chronology and such a pat juggling of names.

The second theory is based almost altogether on conjecture, derived from apparently autobiographical passages in Melville's books. The only explicit statement that Melville makes as to the time of his residence in the Sandwich Islands is that he spent "four months at Honolulu, the metropolis of the group." [4] Thus, reckoning from the date of his subsequent departure, shortly to be established as August 17, 1843, he must have arrived in this flourishing little village at least as early as the middle of April, 1843—three months after his departure from Eimeo. But there is no reason why Honolulu should necessarily have been the port of his arrival from the Society Islands on board the "Leviathan"—hence, the harbor master's list of ships arriving at Honolulu, given in support of the first theory, is not conclusive. There were watering places on other islands in the group that were frequented by whalers, particularly Lahaina on the island of Maui and Hilo Bay on Hawaii, the largest island of the group. And in scattered references throughout *Typee*

[325]

and *Omoo,* there are indications that Melville personally visited one or both of these islands, as will be seen.

Another possible route, therefore, will now be outlined for Melville's cruise on the "Leviathan" from the Society to the Sandwich Islands—other than the direct passage taken by the brig *Julia.* In *Omoo* Melville speaks familiarly of "Roorootoo, a lone island, some two days' sail from Tahiti, . . . where the vessel touched to which I then happened to belong." [5] Now, Rurutu is an island in the Austral group, some several hundred miles to the southwest of Tahiti, and if Melville had sailed on the *Julia* how could he have touched at this out-of-the-way place?

The next clue comes from the anomalous *Mardi,* that volume whose opening pages—in poor prophecy of the fanciful allegory that follows—seem to mark it as the third in the trilogy which Melville later referred to lightly, in echo of Blackwood's banter, as "Peedee, Hullabaloo, and Pog-dog." [6] On the very first page of this book Melville says, with apparent literalness:

We sail from Ravaivai, an isle in the sea, not very far northward from the tropic of Capricorn, nor very far westward from Pitcairn's island, where the mutineers of the *Bounty* settled. At Ravaivai I had stepped ashore some few months previous; and now was embarked on a cruise for the whale, whose brain enlightens the world.

And from Ravaivai we sail for the Gallipagos [*sic*], otherwise called the Enchanted Islands, by reason of the many wild currents and eddies there. [7]

This completes the conjectured route: the "Leviathan" sailed from Papetoai to Rurutu, touched at Ravaivai in the same group—a few hundred miles due south of Tahiti—then cruised along the tropic of Capricorn past Pitcairn Island, and finally turned northward to the Encantadas. What gives support to such a theory is the fact that this was a favorite cruising ground for whalers: along the thirtieth parallel south—below Tahiti and the Marquesas—from Australia to the western coast of South America, thence to meet the Season-on-the-Line at the Galapagos Islands, and finally to the Sandwich Islands to recruit. [8]

It may be objected that *Mardi* is obviously a romance and therefore altogether untrustworthy as autobiography. But from one point of view, *Mardi* is two books in one; and, for the student seeking clues for Melville's itinerary in the South Seas, it may be characterized as a good whaling story gone wrong. For the first fifty pages of this otherwise fanciful romance have the ring of actuality. Indeed, Edward Lucett, one of Melville's most persistent critics, noted this dual personality of the book and even doubted that "Typee-Omoo Herman Melville," the reputed author, actually composed the two seemingly disparate parts:

It has not been my chance to peruse the whole; but, from what I have seen, it would appear the opening part *might* have come from the "ready pen" to which common rumour has ascribed it, but that the fustian rant of the great bulk would indicate other paternity.[9]

But, though one and the same man was assuredly the author of these ill-assorted twins, it was a different Melville who penned the second part—the "transcendental pseudo-philosophical rifacciamento of Carlyle and Emerson," in the words of the outraged *Knickerbocker*.

Indeed, it is just at the point where *Mardi* plunges headlong into those depths which Hawthorne himself declared "compel a man to swim for his life" that Melville gives the final data that seem to complete the circuit of his cruise to the Sandwich Islands. Passing Massafuero off the coast of Chili two weeks out, he says, his ship then consumed an indefinite period cruising for whale on the Off-Shore Ground. But the catch proved small, and Melville continues:

At the time I now write of, we must have been something more than sixty degrees to the westward of the Gallipagos. And having attained a desirable longitude, we were standing northward for our arctic destination: around us one wide sea.[10]

It so happens that the Galapagos Islands are located on the Equator near the ninetieth parallel west longitude, and it seems to be more than mere coincidence that the Sandwich Islands are clustered about the one hundred and fiftieth parallel—sixty degrees to the westward. Melville's ship, therefore, was headed due north towards Hawaii at the time when he says he made his escape in an open boat, determined once more to give up whaling for an island paradise, this time one of the Kingsmill group lying far to the west. But, from this point on, *Mardi* rapidly leaves the world of reality; and what is more reasonable than that Melville here abandoned the actual route of his cruise for allegory instead of following the "Leviathan" on to her real destination in the Sandwich Islands, several hundred miles to the north, and so completing his trilogy of island travel books with an account of his residence in Honolulu and on the neighboring Sandwich Islands.

Thus, though the evidence is somewhat divided, the most reasonable hypothesis seems to be that Melville arrived at some Hawaiian port other than Honolulu, and that he spent some time rambling about the group before proceeding to the metropolis about the middle of April, 1843; and the cruise just outlined could have been accomplished considerably under three months, so as to leave sufficient time for such adventures as he may have had. But this part of Melville's career can only be conjectured from random allusions in *Typee* and *Omoo*.

Melville's references to the island of Hawaii do not carry the conviction of an eyewitness's testimony. In *Typee* he mentions, in an aside, the monument on this island marking the spot where Captain Cook met his death: "At Karakikova [Kealakekua], the scene of that tragedy, a strip of ship's copper nailed against an upright post in the ground used to inform the traveller that beneath reposed the 'remains' of the great circumnavigator." [11] But Melville does not say that he himself visited this famous spot; and, besides, the monument he refers to had been replaced by a new one twenty years before his visit.[12] Again, in *Omoo* he refers to the famous "Mouna Roa [Mauna Loa] and Mouna Kea," on the island of Hawaii, as "perhaps the most remarkable volcanoes in the world," but here also the reference does not seem to be based on personal observation. In fact, the tenor of his note is quite the opposite, for he merely cites the volumes of William Ellis, Commodore Wilkes, and George Anson, Lord Byron, as containing interesting accounts of three expeditions to their summits, which he certainly would have described more personally had he made such an expedition himself. And from one of these volumes, incidentally, he could have drawn the information for the reference in *Typee* to Cook's monument.[13] There is no evidence extant, therefore, to prove that Melville visited Hawaii, the largest island in the Sandwich group.

The chances are stronger that the "Leviathan's" port of arrival was Lahaina on the island of Maui, for Melville's allusions to this important town are more convincing. In *Typee,* describing the dowager queen of the Sandwich Islands as a "gigantic . . . woman of nearly four-hundred pounds weight," who was known in a fit of anger sometimes "to snatch up an ordinary-sized man who had offended her, and snap his spine across her knee," he declares:

While at Lahainaluna—the residence of this monstrous Jezebel—a hump-backed wretch was pointed out to me, who, some twenty-five years previously, had had the vertebræ of his backbone very seriously discomposed by his gentle mistress.[14]

Commodore Wilkes left a confirmatory report of this Polynesian strong woman, though he did not cite any instance of such a brutal display of her strength; he merely said:

This lady is upwards of six-feet in height; her frame is exceedingly large and well covered with fat. . . . She was altogether one of the most remarkable-looking personages I have ever seen.[15]

A second and more commonplace allusion occurs also in *Typee,* in illustration of the intricacies of the Polynesian language: "In the Missionary College at Lahainaluna, on Mowee [Maui], . . . I saw a tabular exhibition of a Hawaiian verb, conjugated through all its moods and tenses. It covered the side of a considerable apartment, and I doubt whether Sir William Jones himself would not have despaired of mastering it." [16] This certainly has the ring of authenticity. Again, Wilkes furnishes corroboration. He had visited the seminary at Lahaina just a year or two before, and though he made no reference to the complexity of Hawaiian grammar as taught there, he did complain that the college was badly conducted and perhaps doomed to failure, since manual training and vocational education had been abandoned for the pursuit of higher abstract studies—a comment that certainly must have proved agreeable to Melville, if he read it.[17]

Lahaina, indeed, was a favorite resort for whalers and just the place at which Melville's "Leviathan" might have touched to reprovision. Since Melville, according to his own account, had shipped for the cruise only, he would have been at liberty to step ashore immediately and resume the carefree life of a beachcomber in the Pacific. Without better evidence to draw upon, therefore, it is reasonable to conjecture that Melville did begin his residence in the Sandwich Islands at this port, probably sometime in February or March, 1843, though how he occupied himself and how long he stayed there it is impossible to say. It is with something of a shock that one recalls at this point his unceremonious leave-taking of another whaler, at Nukahiva, less than a year before. For this same ship, the *Acushnet,* now came to anchor in this very port, Lahaina, and on June 2, 1843, filed with the United States Commercial Agency there an affidavit of Melville's desertion.[18] But the runaway seaman thus advertised for recapture was already at this date, as will be seen shortly, at a safe distance in Honolulu, whither he had probably removed as early as the middle of April. Otherwise, there might have been a different conclusion to his South Sea travels.

The known facts of Melville's life at Honolulu, during his residence there of "four months" or more, are scanty in the extreme. On March 7, 1843, William Hooper, Acting United States Commercial Agent at Honolulu, wrote to Secretary of State Daniel Webster: "A census of American citizens resident at these islands taken under my direction gives the number of 404, a large proportion of which are more or less interested in landed property." [19] This list would probably yield pertinent information about Melville, but it is not to be found in the State Department or Census Bureau at Washington or in the government archives of Hawaii. Further, Melville's name is not mentioned in any local newspaper or periodical during the year 1843. Over a year after his departure, however, there is an entry in the *Temperance Advocate and Sea-*

men's Friend, a weekly newspaper published at Honolulu, that piques one's curiosity:

To whom it may concern. . . . If Mr. Herman Melville, formerly officer on board Am[erican] W[hale] S[hip] Acushnet, is in this part of the world, and will call upon the seamen's chaplain, he may find several letters to his address.[20]

How one would like to see those letters, unopened for a century! Romantic conjecture would suspect the unknown correspondent to be Richard Tobias Greene, the Toby of *Typee,* or Doctor John Troy, alias Long Ghost, the companion of his adventures in *Omoo,* unless his friends and relatives in America had been informed of his whereabouts. But dead-letter offices tell no tales, and all search for these priceless documents has proved futile. A reappearance of the same notice, long after Melville had left the Pacific, is evidence that he never received these letters which might have altered the course of his subsequent wanderings.[21] The reference to him as formerly an "officer" on the *Acushnet* is not clear; unless the statement was a careless error, the title must have been assumed by Melville in his sea-gossip or in his letters home—if he wrote any—for he had shipped at Fairhaven as an ordinary seaman and apparently had not been promoted during the cruise.

Whatever his former rank on board this whaler, he now occupied the uncomfortable position of one who had unceremoniously renounced that rank by taking French leave of his ship at Nukahiva. He must have experienced an unpleasant shock, therefore, when this same Flying Dutchman of a whaler, the *Acushnet* herself—standing over from Lahaina as if in unconscious pursuit— dropped anchor in Honolulu Bay, June 7, 1843, with only nine hundred barrels of oil for all her two and a half years of cruising.[22] Whatever Melville's fears of being apprehended—for, whether he knew it or not, he was listed with responsible authorities in the islands as a deserter—they must have been short-lived. For, true to the character that Melville has given her in *Moby-Dick,* the

Acushnet rested from her zealous pursuit of the whale, white or otherwise, only long enough to take on provisions and weighed anchor the next day,[23] leaving her "former officer" free to return to America and immortalize her as the "Pequod" at his leisure, without undergoing the humiliation of being recaptured. There is one further ray of light that can be shed on Melville's fictionized account of his connection with the *Acushnet* before she slips back into the ghost ship that he has made of her. On August 5 there arrived in Honolulu the American barque *Elizabeth,* in mourning for the loss of her captain and a boat's crew who had been taken down by a whale.[24] From her Melville may have learned the story that he later told in *Moby-Dick* of the ship "Rachel" which, after a similar catastrophe, pleaded in vain for assistance from the fanatical Captain Ahab, though such disasters were perhaps not uncommon in the cruel world of whaling.[25]

From supposition, it is heartening to be able to turn at this point to one documented fact concerning Melville's life at Honolulu. Arthur Stedman, one of the few close friends of his last years, asserts that Melville was "employed as a clerk" during his residence there, but he throws no further light on his business duties or on his social standing.[26] By good fortune the actual contract establishing this clerkship was rescued from oblivion some fifty years ago, though it remained unknown to all modern students of Melville until 1935. The Reverend Samuel C. Damon, seamen's chaplain at Honolulu—the very man who had occupied this station at the time of Melville's residence—was apparently the discoverer of this unique document, which he published in the Bethel's weekly journal in 1873 as "A Curiosity Relating to a Literary Author." [27] It was found, he said, among the papers of Isaac Montgomery, Esq., a wealthy merchant who had recently died at Honolulu. This Montgomery, a storekeeper who advertised himself in the *Polynesian* (Honolulu) in 1843 as a "Dealer in General Merchandise," was the man who hired Melville as a clerk on June 1 of that year. The stipulations of the contract are simple but interesting. By its covenants Melville was employed as a bookkeeper and general clerk in Montgomery's business at an annual salary of one hundred and fifty dollars in addition to board, lodging, and washing. The term of employment ran for one year, beginning July 1, 1843; and during the intervening month of June, Melville was further to receive the domestic perquisites mentioned above without additional charges. Thus Melville was apparently making plans for a long stay at Honolulu, in pursuit of a more respectable kind of life than that of a beachcomber. But some unknown event—possibly the arrival of the *Acushnet* a week later and his consequent fear of recapture—caused him to bring to an end this business career before it had run seven weeks and to ship for home on the frigate *United States.* The contract shows no legal cancellation, but on the other hand there is no evidence of any disagreement between Melville and Montgomery; the assumption, therefore, must be that it was terminated by mutual consent, employer and employee parting as friends.

Although the record of Melville's residence in Honolulu is rather bare of personal matter, it is full of events of international importance that were taking place there at the time. For several years both England and France had trained covetous eyes on the various South Sea islands. The French occupation of the Marquesas and Society Islands during Melville's residence at those places in the summer of 1842 has already been noticed. Now, the English seizure of the Sandwich Islands and the ensuing five months of unauthorized occupation, full of diplomatic turmoil and moral confusion, took place under his very eyes. His reactions to these somewhat similar episodes were widely different.

Late in 1842 the British Consul, Charlton, who had long been at odds with the native government, left Honolulu to present, en route to London, certain personal claims and official complaints against the native king to the British naval force on the South Pacific station. He did not return, but the result of his errand was the arrival at Honolulu on February 11, 1843, of Lord George Paulet, commanding H. B. M. *Carysfort.* After three unsuccessful efforts to obtain a personal interview with King Kamehameha III, Captain Paulet presented written demands, with a threat of immediate hostilities upon noncompliance, as follows: (1) the adjustment of Charlton's personal claims; (2) the recognition of Mr. Alexander Simpson, the delegated successor of Mr. Charlton, as acting consul; (3) a guarantee that no British subject in the future be imprisoned unless accused of a felony under the laws of England; (4) a guarantee to British subjects in civil disputes of trial by jury, one-half of whom should be Englishmen, approved by the consul; (5) direct communication between King Kamehameha (instead of through the medium of his interpreter, Dr. G. P. Judd) and the British acting-consul for the immediate settlement of all cases of grievance on the part of British subjects against the government of the Sandwich Islands. Unwilling to submit to these demands and unable to offer successful resistance to the hostilities threatened as an alternative, the king made a provisional cession of the islands to Lord George Paulet in the name of Queen Victoria on February 25—just about the time of Melville's arrival—sending out a plea to President Tyler for the United States to intercede with Great Britain and secure justice to the native government.

By a proclamation of Captain Paulet, the government was immediately placed in the hands of a commission composed of King Kamehameha, acting through his deputy, G. P. Judd, and Lord George Paulet, Duncan Forbes Mackay, Esq., and Lieutenant John Frere, R. N. Dr. Judd resigned on May 11, after a protest against some of the acts of the commission, and thus withdrew the king from all further participation. But the remaining members continued to administer the government and perform various sovereign functions. Commodore Lawrence Kearney, United States frigate *Constellation,* arrived on July 11 and promptly protested the king's deed of cession and also the acts of the commission wherein the rights of American citizens had suffered. Finally, on July 26 Rear-Admiral Richard Thomas, H. B. M. *Dublin,* arrived at Honolulu from Valparaiso, having just heard of Captain Paulet's movements. After friendly conferences between the king and the admiral, an agreement was signed disavowing Lord Paulet's act of seizure and restoring the Hawaiian flag, July 31, 1843.[28]

A large part of this stirring episode Melville must have witnessed with his own eyes, and he has recorded the events and his reactions in an appendix to *Typee*.[29] His account squares so perfectly with the official records as far as facts go, and evinces such insight into the intricacies of British policy and such sympathy with it, that one is inclined to credit his statement that he "was in the confidence of an Englishman who was much employed by his lordship [Lord George Paulet]." [30] This Englishman was quite probably his employer, Isaac Montgomery, a native of Cumberlandshire, who in the normal line of his business might very well have furnished supplies to the British man-of-war and local information to its commander. Moreover, the fact that Montgomery was only three years Melville's senior should have made for some natural intimacy and confidence between the two.[31] Otherwise, it is difficult to explain his intimate knowledge of facts that would naturally have been confined to official papers.[32]

Melville's reactions to the British seizure, however, are a more personal matter. His predilections were as strongly pro-English as they were anti-French.[33] Comparing the operations of the two nations in the South Seas, he exclaims:

And yet this piratical seizure of Tahiti [by the French], with all the woe and desolation which resulted from it, created not half so great a sensation, at least in America, as was caused by the proceedings of the English at the Sandwich Islands. No transaction has ever been more grossly misrepresented than the events which occurred upon the arrival of Lord George Paulet at Oahu. . . . Great was the author's astonishment on his arrival at Boston, in the autumn of 1844, to read the distorted accounts and fabrications which had produced in the United States so violent an outbreak of indignation against the English. He deems it, therefore, a mere act of justice toward a gallant officer briefly to state the leading circumstances connected with the event in question.
. . . High in the favour of the imbecile king at this time was one Dr. Judd, a sanctimonious apothecary-adventurer, who, with other kindred and influential spirits, was animated by an inveterate dislike to England. The ascendancy of a junta of ignorant and designing Methodist elders in the council of a half-civilised king, ruling with absolute sway over a nation just poised between barbarism and civilisation, and exposed by the peculiarities of its relations with foreign states to unusual difficulties, was not precisely calculated to impart a healthy tone to the policy of the government.[34]

[335]

This spirited defense of the British policy was perhaps calculated partly to promote the sale of *Typee* in England as well as partly to set American opinion right. That America repudiated Melville's Anglomania is evidenced by the deletion of this appendix from the second American edition, which followed close upon the heels of the first.[35]

Undoubtedly Melville's animosity towards the "piratical seizure" of the French and his justification of the "proceedings" of the English were also colored by his attitudes towards the natives whose freedom and happiness were affected by these European interventions. Here again is a manifestation of the brief he directed against civilization. For him, virtue flourished as one fled from the institutions erected by man's inhumanity to man, and vice showed its head in the islands of the Pacific paradise only when brought there by the evangelists of Western culture. Especially distasteful to him was the brand of civilization forced down the throat of the Noble Savage by overzealous missionaries. The Tahitians, who had been only slightly tainted, he found congenial and amusing; to the Marquesans, if one is to believe his record in *Typee*, he gave his heart. The fear that these unspoiled primitives might be polluted by the French, or anyone else, roused him to eloquence. But the Sandwich Islanders he evidently considered already polluted beyond redemption; it was of little moment, then, that the English or any nation should usurp control of their mock civilization which was already in the hands of a foreign rabble.

The conclusion to his defense of the English occupation of Hawaii was in reality an attack on the degeneracy of the Hawaiians themselves. When Admiral Thomas restored the native flag, Melville says:

The event was made an occasion of riotous rejoicing by the king and the principal chiefs, who easily secured a display of enthusiasm from the inferior orders, by remitting for a time the accustomed severity of the laws. Royal proclamations in English and Hawaiian were placarded in the streets of Honolulu, and posted up in the more populous villages of the group, in which his majesty announced to his loving subjects the re-establishment of his throne, and called upon them to celebrate it by breaking through all moral, legal, and religious restraint for ten consecutive days, during which time all the laws of the land were solemnly declared to be suspended.

Who that happened to be at Honolulu during those ten memorable days will ever forget them! The spectacle of universal broad-day debauchery, which was then exhibited, beggars description. The natives of the surrounding islands flocked to Honolulu by hundreds, and the crews of two frigates, opportunely let loose like so many demons to swell the heathenish uproar, gave the crowning flourish to the scene. It was a sort of Polynesian saturnalia. Deeds too atrocious to be mentioned were done at noon-day in the open street, and some of the islanders, caught in the very act of stealing from the foreigners, were, on being taken to the fort by the aggrieved party, suffered immediately to go at large and to retain the stolen property—Kekuanoa [the governor of Oahu] informing the white men, with a sardonic grin, that the laws were "hannapa" (tied up).

The history of these ten days reveals in their true colours the character of the Sandwich Islanders, and furnishes an eloquent commentary on the results which have flowed from the labours of the missionaries. Freed from the restraints of severe penal laws, the natives almost to a man had plunged voluntarily into every species of wickedness and excess, and by their utter disregard of all decency plainly showed that, although they had been schooled into a seeming submission to the new order of things, they were in reality as depraved and vicious as ever.

Such were the events which produced in America so general an outbreak of indignation against the spirited and high-minded Paulet.[36]

In almost every reference that Melville makes to the Sandwich Islands he drives home his thesis against civilization. Out of a score of allusions in *Typee* and *Omoo,* more than two-thirds contain some attack of this sort, usually directed at the missionaries or at the absolute monarchy they had set up there. In making his appeal that the unspoiled primitives of Typee Valley be saved from the curse of civilization, he cites a warning example:

Let the once smiling and populous Hawaiian Islands, with their now diseased, starving, and dying natives, answer the question. The missionaries may seek to disguise the matter as they will, but the facts are incontrovertible; and the devoutest Christian who visits that group with an unbiased mind, must go away mournfully asking—"Are these,

[337]

alas! the fruits of twenty-five years of enlightening?" . . . Better will it be for [the Marquesans] to remain the happy and innocent heathens and barbarians that they now are, than, like the wretched inhabitants of the Sandwich Islands, to enjoy the mere name of Christians without experiencing any of the vital operations of true religion, whilst, at the same time, they are made the victims of the worst vices and evils of civilised life.[37]

Even the Reverend Michael Russell, in commenting on Kotzebue's disparagements of the effects of civilization in these islands, admitted that "there is too much ground for the dark colouring applied by this author to the picture which he draws of the inhabitants, who have unquestionably lost much of the simplicity and innocence which formerly distinguished them." [38]

Sometimes Melville is much more specific, and much more devastating, in the denunciations that he calls down upon the heads of the missionaries:

Not until I visited Honolulu was I aware of the fact that the small remnant of the natives had been civilised into draught horses, and evangelised into beasts of burden. But so it is. They have been literally broken into the traces, and are harnessed to the vehicles of their spiritual instructors like so many dumb brutes!

Among a multitude of similar exhibitions that I saw, I shall never forget a robust, red-faced, and very ladylike personage, a missionary's spouse, who day after day for months together took her regular airings in a little go-cart drawn by two of the islanders, one an old gray-headed man, and the other a roguish stripling, both being, with the exception of the fig-leaf, as naked as when they were born. Over a level piece of ground, this pair of *draught* bipeds would go with a shambling, unsightly trot, the youngster hanging back all the time like a knowing horse, while the old hack plodded on and did all the work.

Rattling along through the streets of the town in this stylish equipage, the lady looks about her as magnificently as any queen driven in state to her coronation. A sudden elevation, and a sandy road, however, soon disturb her serenity. The small wheels become imbedded in the loose soil—the old stager stands tugging and sweating, while the young one frisks about and does nothing; not an inch does the chariot budge. Will the tender-hearted lady, who has left friends and home for the good of the souls of the poor heathen, will she think a little about their bodies and get out, and ease the wretched old man until the ascent is mounted?

Not she; she could not dream of it. To be sure, she used to think nothing of driving the cows to pasture on the old farm in New England; but times have changed since then. So she retains the seat and bawls out, "Hookee! Hookee!" (pull, pull). The old gentleman, frightened at the sound, labours away harder than ever; and the younger one makes a great show of straining himself, but takes care to keep one eye on his mistress, in order to know when to dodge out of harm's way. At last the good lady loses all patience: "Hookee! hookee!" and rap goes the heavy handle of her huge fan over the naked skull of the old savage; while the young one shies to one side and keeps beyond its range. "Hookee! hookee!" again she cries—"Hookee tata kannaka!" (pull strong, men)— but all in vain, and she is obliged in the end to dismount and, sad necessity! actually to walk to the top of the hill.[39]

Such degradation of the lower class natives by their Christian teachers, incredible as it may seem, was actually one of the results of the caste system fostered by the missionary monarchy at Honolulu. And Melville may have witnessed just such a scene as he describes—though one suspects some embellishment—either with his own eyes or through the eyes of Thomas Beale, an author whose acquaintance he acknowledges in *Moby-Dick*. In his *Natural History of the Sperm Whale,* apropos of the menial condition to which the bulk of the natives had been reduced, Beale declared:

But not only is this the case, but they are obliged also, in many instances, to act as slaves to the missionaries. If the Christian white man moves from one district to another, he or his family and baggage must be carried about in a sort of "palanquin," or "settee," of course greatly to the delight of the poor native, who frequently gets nothing for his trouble; for when his shoulder aches from the weight he has sustained in a hot climate, or perhaps over uneven or broken ground, or through an entangled forest, he is repaid with a prayer or godly blessing for his pains, and which is considered as a full equivalent for his labour.[40]

What few actual evidences of civilization were at this period scattered throughout the South Seas, according to Melville, pertained exclusively to the foreign residents, though they were frequently cited by the missionaries as proofs of the elevated condition of the natives. This he found to be strikingly true in the Sandwich Islands, where the greatest progress in all Polynesia was claimed: "Thus, at Honolulu, . . . there are fine dwelling-houses, several hotels, and barber-shops, ay, even billiard-rooms; but these are all owned and used, be it observed, by whites." [41] The observation of W. S. Ruschenberger, a visitor just five years before, largely confirms this remark: "There . . . is a seaman's chapel and a reading room, as yet almost without readers; to which may be added, as additional evidence of the march of civilization, billiard tables, bowling allies, grog shops, livery stables, and *restaurans*, both foreign and native, and they all meet with a sufficient patronage, because the vices are more aptly acquired than the virtues of civilized life." [42] In this connection, however, it must be remarked that the figures which Melville quotes from this same author to show the almost incredible depopulation of the Sandwich Islands since the introduction of civilization are quite misleading; Melville merely chose those figures which showed by far the greatest decrease and gave them as representative.[43]

Perhaps the most insistent charge that Melville brings against the Christian mission at this place, which incidentally was manned exclusively by Americans, was that they had bolstered up the power of a pompous and tyrannical monarchy:

The chiefs swagger about in gold lace and broadcloth, while the great mass of the common people are nearly as primitive in their appearance as in the days of Cook . . . ; so that the measure of gewgaw refinement attained by the chiefs is only an index to the actual state of degradation in which the greater portion of the population lie grovelling.[44]

And pyramided precariously on this feudal pile was the absurd and even despicable king:

The republican missionaries of Oahu cause to be gazetted in the Court Journal, published at Honolulu, the most trivial movements of "his gracious majesty" King Tammahammaha III. [*sic*], and "their highnesses the princes of the blood royal."—And who is his "gracious majesty" . . . ?—His "gracious majesty"—is a fat, lazy, negro-looking blockhead, with as little character as power. He has lost the noble traits of the barbarian, without acquiring the redeeming graces of a civilised being; and although a member of the Hawaiian Temperance Society, is a most inveterate dram-drinker.[45]

Partial confirmation of this may be found in the observation of the Quaker Daniel Wheeler, who always reported frankly and without bias whatever came under his honest eyes:

The government is inefficient, partly from the character of the king, who is very much influenced by the whites and half-castes, whose interest leads them to encourage his dissipated, thoughtless course of life, and partly because his native simplicity and inexperience are ill adapted to cope with designing adventurers, who are ready to take every advantage.[46]

These same designing adventurers are the subject of Melville's last thrust at the missionary monarchy:

Even upon the Sandwich Islands, a low rabble of foreigners is kept about the person of Tammahammaha, for the purpose of ministering to his ease or enjoyment.

Billy Loon, a jolly little negro, tricked out in a soiled blue jacket, studded all over with rusty bell-buttons, and garnished with shabby gold lace, is the royal drummer and pounder of the tambourine. Joe, a wooden-legged Portuguese, who lost his leg by a whale, is violinist; and Mordecai, as he is called, a villainous-looking scamp, going about with his cups and balls in a side pocket, diverts the court with his jugglery. These idle rascals receive no fixed salary, being altogether dependent upon the casual bounty of their master. Now and then they run up a score at the dance houses in Honolulu, where the illustrious Tammahammaha III. afterward calls and settles the bill.[47]

Whether Melville was always reporting facts in his disaparagements of the king and court at Honolulu it is hard to say. But the editor of the *Polynesian,* the official organ of the native government to which Melville alluded above, undertook to discredit *Typee* and *Omoo* on this score as well as in all their attacks on the missionaries, though he made no attempt to produce contrary evidence:

The whole of his *genuine* information is about on a par with his assertion that "the Monarch of the Sandwich Islands has three foreigners about his Court—a negro to beat the drum—a wooden-legged portuguese to play the fiddle, and Mordecau, a juggler, to amuse his Majesty with cups and balls and slight [*sic*] of hand." Mr. Melville does very well as a romancer, but tarnishes all by his attempts to ape the historian.[48]

It is interesting to note that this critic of Melville's books, Charles E. Hitchcock, though residing in a remote part of the world, lays claim to acquaintance with Melville, having met him, he says, in New York previous to his own embarkation for the Pacific islands in the spring of 1845. Thus, though he arrived too late to be a fellow citizen of Melville in Honolulu, he found traces of his residence there of two years before, declaring: "There are those residing here who have had the honor of being shipmates with Mr. Melville, as well as those who were acquainted with him during his residence here." [49] But whoever these former associates were, they have left no written reminiscences of his life in the Hawaiian capital.

Indeed, what Melville's personal experiences in Honolulu were like can only be conjectured, though his respectable position as a merchant's clerk is evidence that he turned aside from the free ranging life of a beachcomber. Perhaps his life there was so circumspect and tawdry that he decided it would fall short of the high pitch of his first two volumes. The biographer can only wish that he had written a sequel to *Omoo,* completing the account of his Pacific island rovings. He seems, in fact, to have had some such plan temporarily in mind when he wrote the opening chapters of *Mardi;* but, apparently on second thought, he altered his course and shifted from travel writing to allegorical romance. Beyond the conjectured route of Melville's passage from the Society to the Sandwich Islands, outlined at the opening of this chapter, it would be useless to look; for *Mardi* furnishes no further foothold, even for speculation, as a memoir of the author.

Yet it would be as big a mistake to accept *Mardi* as all imaginative fiction as to be gulled by the prefatory challenge and "receive the fiction for a verity." For although in this volume Melville abandoned the use of autobiographical experiences such as had formed the backbone of *Typee* and *Omoo,* he clung to his old habit of borrowing material from earlier travelers. The four chief sources upon which he levied were already familiar to him: the volumes of Daniel Tyerman, William Ellis, F. D. Bennett, and Charles Wilkes. Almost all of the legends, customs, and beliefs which make up the Polynesian background of *Mardi* (comprising roughly the central third of the book) came from these authorities. In some instances Melville drew upon his sources for factual information only; but in the main he selected the most bizarre materials he could lay his hands on, and these he embellished for purposes of satire.[50]

What, then, of the other two-thirds of *Mardi?* To any one acquainted with Polynesian life, it is obvious that the major part of this book has only the most superficial connection with the islands of the Pacific. And at least two contemporary reviewers pointed out that, though it began as a sea story, *Mardi* was chiefly an allegory that mirrored the world [51]—the intellectual world, it should be added, that Melville was becoming acquainted with in the salons of New York. Returning from his wedding trip in the summer of 1847, he settled down to a promising life of authorship in the rising literary metropolis. From previous visits connected with the publication of his first two books, he was already widely acquainted with the *literati* of the city—especially the groups centering around Anne C. Lynch, N. P. Willis, and E. A. Duyckinck.[52] His most intimate relations with them now began just as he was writing the opening chapters of his new book. That *Mardi* was originally planned as a continuation of *Typee* and *Omoo* is evidenced in a letter written by Evert Duyckinck to his brother on September 22, 1847, in which he remarked: "Herman Melville is preparing a third book which will exhaust the South Sea marvels." [53] But that this plan had been changed in the process of composition was apparent to Duyckinck as the book neared completion; in a letter of March 9, 1848, he declared: "Melville the other night brought me a few chapters of his new book, which in the poetry and wildness of the thing will be far ahead of Typee & Omoo." [54]

Students of Melville have long been aware that in *Mardi* Melville turned to satire of the contemporary world in Europe and America, but not until recently has a convincing explanation been suggested for this change.[55] The first of his books to be written entirely in New York City under the full influence of his new associations, *Mardi* was at least in part a reflection of the new world of ideas in which the young author was now moving. The Duyckinck circle, with whom Melville spent many evenings during 1847–1848, consisted of artists, actors, publishers, editors, doctors, lawyers, politicians, and military men, as well as authors. Five important events of this period—the Oregon boundary dispute, the Mexican War, the discovery of gold in California, the presidential election, and the French Revolution of 1848—inevitably stirred up interesting conversations in such a diversified group. It is only natural that such spirited talk on a wide variety of subjects of current interest should have found a place in a literary omnibus like *Mardi*. So it was that under the thin guise of a Polynesian allegory, Melville satirized the gold rush, the jury system, the exploitation of the Indian, the blatant spirit of nationalism, the controversy over slavery, the Mexican War, and national figures like Clay, Webster, and General Zachary Taylor.[56]

Nor was it only through the salon that new worlds were opening up for Melville to make use of in *Mardi*. Evert Duyckinck's extraordinary private library of rare books consisting of nearly twenty thousand volumes—half as large as that of the New York Library Society—was at the disposal of his friends; and his regularly kept list of "Books Lent" shows that Melville took full advantage of this generosity. The very first volumes that he borrowed—between October, 1847, and March, 1848—show the author of *Mardi* at work gathering new materials for his new book: the works of Sir Thomas Browne, the works of Rabelais, and Esaias Tegner's *Frithjof's Saga*.[57] Browne, as many readers have suspected, was probably responsible for the pedantry and the highly involved, sometimes cumbersome, sentences that replaced the straightforward narrative of *Typee* and *Omoo*. And Rabelais, in addition to a general influence on the type of humor now first essayed by Melville, was undoubtedly the inspiration of certain new stylistic devices.[58] Finally, the general framework and story of *Mardi* certainly owe something to the symbolic voyage of Panurge and Pantagruel and the constant journeyings of Frithjof seeking the realization of his love with Ingeborg—echoed by Melville in Taji's symbolic visits to Europe and North America, and in his futile pursuit of Yillah and ideal love.

All of this, however, is a long way from the South Seas, so that most of *Mardi* lies outside the strict limits of the present study. Such was the book that Melville offered an audience of readers eager for a continuation of the pleasant travels with which he had entertained them in his first two books. Romance, allegory, and satire were substituted for the more prosaic adventures of his residence of several months in the Sandwich Islands. And the biographer, without clues in Melville's writings to prompt investigation, can throw no additional light on that portion of his South Sea experiences which he rejected as literary copy—his life at Honolulu.

At any rate, it was now nearing an end, and no further record of it survives than has been here presented. Melville had been busy in his new employment of clerking little more than a month when, in the midst of the bedlam that he has described as ensuing on the restoration of the Hawaiian flag, the American frigate *United States* arrived in the harbor, on August 4. The next day the American sloop *Cyane* came to anchor at her side. It was the crews of these two ships, unquestionably, that Melville referred to as "opportunely let loose like so many demons to swell the heathenish uproar." Apparently he struck up an acquaintance with some of them on shore leave during the ten days that followed before order was finally restored. For, weary of his adventures in the borderlands of civilization, Herman Melville shipped on board the frigate *United States* shortly after noon on August 17, 1843,[59] as an ordinary seaman, for three years or the length of the cruise. With eyes set on home, he traded the easy freedom of the roving life he had enjoyed during the past year for the stern discipline of a man-of-war.[60]

FAREWELL TO THE PACIFIC

FROM this point on, for the last fourteen months of Melville's career in the South Seas, hypothesis gives way to the more trustworthy chart and compass of the frigate *United States*. On the very first morning after his enlistment Melville was called, along with all hands, to witness the punishment of several of his fellow seamen: "John Hall, twelve lashes for striking sentry on post; George Clark, twelve lashes for smuggling liquor; Joseph Stanly, apprentice, twelve lashes with the kittens for fighting; William Ewing, six for provoking language." Even the petty officers seem to have grown restless during the idleness in port, for the boatswain himself, who was something of a police officer, was suspended from duty "for disrespectful conduct to the Officer of the Deck, by replying when ordered to call all hands stand by their washed clothes, that he would receive no more orders in this ship, or words to that effect." Despite the vigilance of the officers, some of the liquor smugglers seem to have succeeded, for on the following day three of the bandsmen, George Davis, William Stewart, and Antonio Guavella, were given twelve lashes each for drunkenness.[1] Although Melville was accustomed to the merciless brutality of the merchant marine, these first scenes of punishment on an American man-of-war must have made a lasting impression on him, for his first and fullest tirade against the institution of corporal punishment is launched by a scene in which "Antone, the Portuguese," is one of the victims.[2]

On Sunday, August 20, 1843, the *United States* weighed anchor and made all sail out of the harbor of Honolulu Bay. Rounding the southwestern side of Oahu, the frigate headed for the Marquesas Islands, running into tropical squalls of wind and rain for the first few days and then enjoying fine weather for the rest of the trip.[3] On August 26 Melville had his first exercise at the great guns during General Quarters; on Sunday, September 3, he was first mustered at the capstan to hear the monthly reading of the Articles of War, the code of prohibitions and punishments which so rigorously circumscribed the conduct of a man-of-war's men—with the constant refrain, "Shall suffer death"—and which Melville complained of so bitterly in *White-Jacket*. On the 23d of the same month a fellow seaman died of heart disease, and shortly after morning quarters "all hands were called to '*bury the Dead.*' The body of 'Conly Daugherty' was then brought to the Gangway by his Messmates, and, after the funeral Service being read by the Revd. Mr. Bartow, his remains were committed to the deep." [4] This was undoubtedly the "Shenly," White Jacket's messmate, whose death from a "pulmonary complaint" during a calm at the Equator Melville uses as a point of departure for a detailed description of a burial at sea.[5] Just before the Marquesas were sighted, another seaman lost his life, by falling overboard, but this incident will receive fuller treatment in a subsequent chapter.[6]

Without further mishap the frigate *United States* cast anchor in Anna Maria Bay (Taiohaë), Nukahiva, on the afternoon of October 6, after a passage of over seven thousand miles, accomplished in forty-seven days—an average sailing of one hundred and fifty miles a day. The "Ship's Scribe" (the anonymous author of a journal kept on board the *United States*, 1842–1844) was captured by the grandeur and novelty of the scene spread before him in the harbor. When Melville had entered this same bay fifteen months before, one of the mistreated crew of the *Acushnet*, he had been similarly impressed with the natural scenery, spending himself lavishly in a description of its wild beauty. Then, as now, the French frigate *La Reine Blanche* had been lying in the harbor, for Rear-Admiral Dupetit-Thouars had just taken possession of the Marquesas in the name of France. And ten weeks later Melville had made a more intimate acquaintance with this French flagship, imprisoned on board her for several days at Tahiti as one of a mutinous crew.[7] It was with more equanimity that he now looked out on her black hull and bristling broadsides from his own safe berth on board a similarly warlike American frigate and watched the operations of the French on shore. They were establishing a colony of settlers on their new possession—four hundred convicts planted in the Happy Valley! Melville's heart must have sunk within him. But six miles to the eastward lay Typee, still unblessed by such benefits of civilization, though Melville had no opportunity to visit his old paradise on this occasion, nor even to set foot ashore at Taiohaë.

The next day King Moana and his consort paid the visit of state to the American flagship which Melville turned to such good account in *Typee*.[8] Then, after lying at anchor only thirty-three hours, the frigate *United States* stood out of Anna Maria Bay, skirted the neighboring islands of Fetu-Hugo and Roa-Pua, and made all sail for Tahiti. Melville, after far too brief a second peep at this part of Polynesia, said goodbye forever to the Marquesas; but before turning for home he was given a last look at the Society Islands, the scene of his adventures in *Omoo*. The passage was made in less than a week.

On October 12 the frigate arrived at Matavai Bay, Tahiti, but the native pilot would not take the ship in after dark because of the Dolphin Shoal. It was in maneuvering past this same dangerous reef, it will be remembered, that Melville had become acquainted with the picturesque pilot "Jim," probably the same native, a year before.[9] Matavai Bay was selected for anchorage because it was easy of access and the stay was to be short. Melville does not record any previous visit to this particular bay, but only eight or nine miles to the eastward lay the harbor and village of Papeete, the capital of the island, where so much of the action of *Omoo* takes place.[10] Connecting the two ports was the famous Broom Road, and, granted the opportunity, Melville would certainly have revisited this sylvan thoroughfare, so crowded with memories for him, and the village of Papeete and the Calabooza beyond, where he had spent six weeks in semi-confinement. But none of the ship's company were given shore liberty, and the chances are that Melville was not allowed to leave the decks of his man-of-war home during the week of this second visit.

With typical confusion, Rear-Admiral S. R. Franklin remembered the Society Islands as the place where Melville shipped on board the *United States:*

At Tahiti we picked up some seamen who were there on the Consul's hands. They were entered on the books of the ship, and became a portion of the crew. One of the number was Herman Melville, who became famous afterwards as a writer and an admiralty lawyer. He had gone to sea for his health, and found himself stranded in the South Pacific. I do not remember what the trouble was, but he and his comrades had left the ship of which they were a portion of the crew.[11]

The patent inaccuracies of this reminiscence have already been pointed out by another biographer—Melville, of course, shipped at Honolulu, he did not go to sea for his health, and he was never an admiralty lawyer—but it is well to notice again how Franklin's memory of Melville is trustworthy only on such points as could have been strengthened by his reading of Melville's volumes. But he himself, in his easygoing way, was the first to confess:

I do not think that I remember Melville at all; occasionally will flash across my memory a maintop-man flitting about the starboard gangway with a white jacket on, but there is not much reality in the picture which it presents to my mind.[12]

Six men were shipped at Tahiti, however—William H. Carter, James McDonnel, Albert Brissie, Benjamin Thornton, Rufus F. Hill, and Alban Patterson.[13] And one cannot help wondering if any of these "seamen who were on the Consul's hands" were Melville's fellow mutineers of a year before—"Sydney Ben," for example, or "Long Jim."

Aside from these disreputable beachcombers, most of Melville's former associates in the Society Islands were undoubtedly still here in the fall of 1843, as the bits of gossip already cited as having been picked up by visitors five and even ten years later definitely prove. Though Melville would not have cared to renew his acquaintance with such dignitaries as Consul Wilson and Doctor

Johnston, a mutually warm reunion would have ensued had he struck up again with Captain Bob, the native jailor who had been such an indulgent guardian, or the worldly Father Murphy, who had ministered to his comfort while he was in the Calabooza. It is just possible, also, that Shorty and Zeke may have come over from Eimeo with an order of potatoes for the Papeete market during this week. Most desirable of all would have been the opportunity to relive, in table talk, his picaresque adventuring with that gangling and ghostly Falstaff, Doctor "John Troy." But Melville says specifically at the end of *Omoo* that he never again saw or heard of the Long Ghost, his roving apothecary companion, who, more than anyone else gives verve and color to the bright pages of this book. Though he may have seen or at least heard of some of the others, he chose not to risk anticlimax by bringing them back to life in any of his books. And so, hypothesis, however provocative, must give way again to the slender records of his second visit that actually are available.[14]

During the stay of a week at the Society Islands the ship was watered and repaired, half-a-dozen new men were shipped and half-a-dozen old ones were flogged, the boatswain was restored to duty, and the French and English consuls were saluted. Finally, on October 19, the barge and fourth cutter were dispatched to Papeete to convey Queen Pomaré and the royal family to the ship. But only the royal consort honored them with a visit: "He is about 45 years of age, very stout, and speaks english [*sic*] remarkable [*sic*] well, and very polite in his manners. He was dressed in a military undress. On his departure saluted him with 13 guns." [15] Thus Melville did get a glimpse of at least one familiar face on his second visit to Tahiti. But Pomaré-Tani's dissipations had evidently aged him, for the Ship's Scribe set him down by conjecture at twice his actual years! The queen herself did not come, but she was described, probably from ship's gossip, as being "about 32 years of age, of good personal appearance, and is represented as superior in morals and intellect to any of her contemporarys [*sic*] of the adjoining Islands"; and, what is more doubtful, she was praised as being "At present . . . an exemplary member of the Christian Church." [16] Whether Melville ever saw the famous Pomaré must be left in uncertainty; but his description of her in *Omoo*, though considerably less flattering, is undoubtedly more veracious.

On this same afternoon, October 19, the frigate hove up the anchor and stood out from "this Fairey Island which lies reposing on the bosom of the wide Pacific, like some glittering gem on the brow of the beautiful," to quote the ambitious phrase of the Ship's Scribe. Coasting to the westward round the island of Eimeo, the scene of the second half of *Omoo*, and passing the beautiful bay of Taloo, from which Melville had sailed in the "Leviathan" for Honolulu less than a year before, the *United States* after a brief calm got underweigh for the coast of South America.[17] And life in the South Seas became for Melville a thing of the past, but a past that was to prove inexorable.

The passage from Tahiti to Valparaiso, a distance of over five thousand miles, was accomplished in thirty-two days. Ten days out a seaman, James Craddock, fell from a yard to the quarter-deck, fracturing an arm and a leg.[18] Since this was the only accident of the kind that happened on the entire cruise, it must have been the basis for the indignant chapter in *White-Jacket* entitled "The Commodore on the Poop, and One of 'The People' Under the Hands of the Surgeon." [19] "Baldy," Melville's little Scotch captain of the mizzentop and a messmate, took his fall to the quarter-deck more dramatically, however, during a competitive sail-furling staged by the American squadron in the harbor of Rio, while the commodore satisfied his vanity by showing off the excellent discipline of his flagship. Such was the use Melville made of his actual experiences for the rest of the homeward-bound cruise, namely, to attack what he considered abuses in the United States Navy, not scrupling to transform and embellish the facts to suit his purposes.[20] Meanwhile, beyond Craddock's misadventure, the voyage back to civilization was uneventful, the fast-sailing frigate bowling along the thirty-third parallel south before steady winds at an average speed of one hundred and seventy miles a day. Two days out of Valparaiso the ship ran close in under the island of Juan Fernandez,

described by Melville in "The Encantadas," [21] where the Ship's
Scribe delivered himself of some poetic comments on the scenery
and some philosophic reflections on Alexander Selkirk's residence
there.[22] On November 21 anchor was cast in Valparaiso "after the
most agreeable passage we have had since leaving home sweet
home." [23]

During the brief stay at this port the colors were kept at half
mast for three successive days, in memory of the late Honorable
Hugh S. Legaré, Secretary of State, and the late Commodores Isaac
Hull and David Porter.[24] But of course none of this dampened the
pent-up spirits of the crew; the temptations of a civilized port after
so long an absence took their toll, four men deserting and a dozen
going under the lash for sundry misdemeanors.[25] An uneventful
passage of ten days brought the ship on December 15, 1843, to the
Pacific Squadron Station, Callao, Peru, "that land of fogs, Cheri-
moyas, and snakes," where she lay at anchor for seventy days during the winter season, the longest period of idleness during the
entire cruise.

Christmas day was passed on board ship by the crew, without
other observance than the customary doubling of the grog allowance for holidays. However, between December 28, 1843, and
January 3, 1844, the two sections of the starboard watch, to one of
which Melville belonged, enjoyed a forty-eight-hour shore liberty.[26]
It is quite possible, therefore, that Melville spent New Year's Day
at the historic city of Lima, eight miles distant from its seaport
at Callao, making the journey inland over the robber-infested highway. In *Omoo* he speaks familiarly of the "herds of panniered
mules, driven . . . by mounted Indians, along the great road
from Callao to Lima." [27] And in *Moby-Dick* he makes several references to visiting the Peruvian capital, once describing it in a
memorable thumbnail sketch.[28] That he visited Lima at some time
during his Pacific wanderings there can hardly be any doubt, for
he explicitly states that he did, and such a description as he has
recorded strongly argues the literalness of an eyewitness.[29]

One of the seamen in the Pacific squadron at this time—William
H. Meyers, the gunner of the *Cyane*—has left a ribald description

of the drunken debauches with which sailors refreshed themselves
on shore leaves such as the present one.[30] Of course, one is not
warranted in assuming that Melville himself indulged in such
riotous conduct ashore in Peru; but, if he did not, he was an
exception to the generality of sailors, according to all contemporary
accounts, for the seaports of Spanish-America offered little else in
the way of diversion for them.[31] Melville's only reference to the
institution of shore liberty, in *White-Jacket*, is similar to Meyers's
in tone though not so detailed. The setting for this he places at
Rio de Janeiro; and for his own part, he says: "With Jack Chase
and a few other discreet and gentlemanly top-men, I went ashore
on the first day, with the first quarter-watch. Our own little party
had a charming time; we saw many fine sights; fell in—as all sailors
must—with dashing adventures." [32] One reason for the noncommittal character of this account is that in reality Melville did not
go ashore at Rio, for the Log Book of the frigate *United States*
shows that no liberty was given to the crew during the week spent
there.[33] Apparently, during the entire fourteen months of Melville's
life in the United States Navy, from Honolulu to Boston, the only
places that he visited were the port Callao and the Peruvian capital
eight miles inland. The Ship's Scribe, in the account of his own
visit, furnishes a decorous guidebook to Lima, detailing the many
sights to be seen in this city of fifty-five thousand inhabitants,
which, even a century ago, had already weathered over three hundred years of turbulent history.[34]

The monotony of this protracted stay in port was further broken
by a man-of-war race out of the harbor:

On the 21st of January the Constellation sailed for *home,* having on
board Commodore Jones, he having been recalled. H. B. M. Frigate
Vindictive and this Frigate accompanied her out for the sake of trying
the speed of the Vessels. It is unnecessary to say that the *"Old Waggon"*
did her duty, distancing her competitors.[35]

Midshipman A. C. Jackson adds enthusiastically: "The Constellation could not hold a candle to us in working ship," though he
admits that the *Vindictive* passed them during the night.[36] The
circumstantial account of this race in the Log Book gives a clear

victory to the British ship, though the *United States* did outstrip her rival American frigate.[37] Thus, with an exchange of courtesies and salutes, with the rigging manned, and with a farewell speech to his men and an answering three cheers, Commodore Thomas ap Catesby Jones left Melville's ship and hoisted his broad blue pennant on the *Constellation,* bound for home—though, for dramatic reasons Melville kept him on board in *White-Jacket* until the frigate reached America. "The next day stood back to Callao with light hearts, knowing it to be our turn next," was the hopeful conclusion of the Ship's Scribe.[38]

It was almost six months, however, before the *United States* started for home; and the high spirits of her crew were probably somewhat dampened when the new commodore, Alexander J. Dallas, arrived on the station a month later and gave orders to Captain Armstrong on February 23, 1844, to proceed to Mazatlán, Mexico, to procure money for the squadron.[39] More than three months were consumed in the accomplishment of this mission. "Nothing could have been more uninteresting than this long and tedious voyage, which occupied more than a hundred days," is Rear-Admiral Franklin's painful memory, half a century afterwards.[40] All that Melville saw of Mexico, in spite of a three weeks' stay in the harbor of Mazatlán, was probably from the decks of his frigate. At last this tedious trip was over, however, and the *United States,* bearing in her money bags some fifty thousand Mexican dollars, stood back into the harbor of Callao on June 6, 1844. The Ship's Scribe records the sad news that was made known to them as they worked up to the anchorage:

We heard minute guns, and perceived the coach whip at the mast head of the Savannah. Upon coming to an anchor, we received the meloncholly [sic] intelligence that Commo. Alexander J. Dallas had departed this Life on the 3d. of June.[41]

By the commodore's demise, Captain James Armstrong, Melville's commander for the past ten months, fell in command of the entire Pacific Squadron, until he should be relieved by the Navy Department. On June 7 he transferred his commodore's pennant to the new flagship *Savannah,* sent out to relieve the *United States.* Captain Cornelius K. Stribling, being next in seniority, took command of Melville's ship.

The next thirty days were spent preparing for the homeward-bound cruise. A number of men and officers whose terms of service had not expired were transferred to ships that were to remain on the station. Among these were Midshipmen Samuel R. Franklin, sent to the *Relief,* and Alonzo C. Jackson, to the *Savannah.*[42] Henceforward we are deprived of their confirmatory records of the cruise. The *United States* was stripped of its charts and maps and all excess equipment. The most interesting part of this was the ship's library, consisting of the following: "Prescott's *Ferdinand and Isabella,* 3 volumes; Bancroft's *History of the United States;* Darwin's *Voyages of H. B. M. 'Adventure' and 'Beagle,'* 4 volumes; Livingstone's *Atlas;* Hough's *Military Law Authorities* and *Courts Martial;* and *Harper's Family Library.*"[43]

This forms Melville's earliest known reading list, and it has proved of considerable value for literary source-hunting in his South Sea volumes. In *White-Jacket* he speaks of reading voraciously while on board the *United States,* especially as his principal antidote against ennui while lying in port, and mentions specifically a dozen or more volumes that he read.[44] Since none of the ones he mentions are in the list of those transferred from his ship at Callao, the implication is that this was only part, and perhaps a small part, of the ship's library. During the one hundred and fifty days that Melville spent in port on this cruise—and only three of them were spent on shore leave—he must have had ample time to exhaust what the ship had to offer in the way of readable literature. Consisting chiefly of biographies, histories, travel books, and handbooks of general knowledge, "Harper's Family Library" should have been particularly well suited to his interests after his experiences of the past three years.[45] Melville declares, and rightly so, that reading was a common pastime among sailors;[46] but there were none of them on the frigate *United States* who later put their reading to such profitable literary use as he did.

There was little time for reading during the month of June, 1844, however, for there were busy days ahead repairing and provisioning the ship for her homeward voyage. The official records for this period offer little of interest to the student of Melville, and a few notes will suffice to sketch in this month of activity. On June 17 the colors were at half-mast for the death of the Honorable William Gilmer, late Secretary of the Navy, and on the next day for the death of Commodore Kennon. They and several other dignitaries had been killed by an accidental explosion on board the *Princeton,* when the "Peacemaker"—a new wrought-iron twelve-inch gun—had burst during its trial firing.[47] In *White-Jacket* Melville comments on this satirically:

While lying in harbour, intelligence reached us of the lamentable casualty that befell certain high officers of state, including the acting Secretary of the Navy himself, some other member of the President's cabinet, a commodore, and others, all engaged in experimenting upon a new-fangled engine of war. At the same time with the receipt of this sad news, orders arrived to fire minute-guns for the deceased head of the naval department. . . . I thought it a strange mode of honouring a man's memory who had himself been slaughtered by a cannon.[48]

On June 20 the entire squadron hoisted the English ensign in honor of the anniversary of Queen Victoria's accession. During the next ten days the ship's company were given a twenty-four-hour shore liberty, the second and last that Melville was to enjoy while on the *United States.* On July 1 Josiah Faxon, the ship's sailmaker, died, and on the following day he was buried on the island of San Lorenzo. It was probably in reference to this sad occasion that Melville remarked in *White-Jacket:*

Protestant sailors dying in Callao . . . are shoved under the sands of St. Lorenzo, a solitary, volcanic island in the harbour, overrun with reptiles, their heretical bodies not being permitted to repose in the more genial loam of Lima.[49]

On July 4 all the men-of-war in the harbor fired a national salute in honor of Independence Day. Finally, on July 6 Acting-Commodore Armstrong dispatched the frigate *United States* for home. Before she sailed, the following passengers were taken on board: the Honorable Manuel C. Lima—Brazilian Minister to Peru—with his lady, five children, and servants; and the Brazilian Minister to the United States, the Honorable William W. Caldwell.[50] Excluded from notice in the records of the Log Book by the presence of all these dignitaries was an undistinguished member of the after-guard who later made this voyage known to the public in the entertaining but scandalous pages of *White-Jacket*.

CHAPTER XIV

THE FRIGATE "UNITED STATES"

"All hands up anchor! Man the capstan!
High die! my lads, we're homeward bound!" [1]

THESE hearty words open Melville's *White-Jacket*, which is a narrative of the last leg of his homeward-bound voyage from Callao, Peru, by Cape Horn to Rio, and thence to Boston, Massachusetts. Although the passage occupied only three months, July 6 to October 4, 1844, into this short space Melville telescopes most of the interesting experiences of his entire residence of fourteen months on board the frigate *United States*. Because of the nature of the source materials now available, the chief present concern with this part of the voyage is to study the artist at work, so that it seems best to abandon the chronological order for an analysis of his technique of composition. Approximately half of *White-Jacket* is a straight-forward account of daily life on board a man-of-war, with detailed descriptions of the ship and the ship's company. Doubtless this factual part is accurate enough, though the manuscripts at hand are naturally silent about matters that must have been commonplace knowledge to every seaman on board.[2] For the narrative part of *White-Jacket* Melville made use of the following methods of dealing with his materials: expedient alterations of fact to suit the exigencies of his tale; dramatic elaboration of actual events; and deliberate invention of his most powerful scenes. This study will furnish a significant commentary upon Melville's declaration that he was writing "an impartial account . . . inventing nothing." [3]

Melville felt, however, that a certain anonymity would be desirable in such a controversial book. In the Preface to the first

[361]

English edition, which, incidentally, was not reprinted in the American, he says:

As the object of this work is not to portray the particular man-of-war in which the author sailed, and its officers and crew, but, by illustrative scenes, to paint general life in the Navy, the true name of the frigate is not given. Nor is it here asserted that any of the persons introduced in the following chapters are real individuals.⁴

This statement, apparently, was not intended to disavow the essential truth of *White-Jacket,* which he elsewhere stoutly defends, but to save the uninformed English reader from being misled by the fictitious names under cover of which he was writing. So it was that he rechristened the frigate *United States* as the "Neversink," a name that its long and admirable history bore out.⁵ Similarly, the members of the American squadron in the harbor at Rio when the *United States* arrived there—the frigates *Constitution, Congress,* and *Raritan,* and the sloop *Cyane*—were disguised as the "Mohawk," the "Malay," the "Buccaneer," and the "Algerine."

Each of the officers was likewise given a descriptive sobriquet. "Captain Claret," who earned his from a fondness for wines and brandy, may have been either Captain James Armstrong, who left the frigate in Callao to take temporary command of the Pacific Squadron, or Captain Cornelius K. Stribling, who actually commanded the *United States* during the period covered by *White-Jacket;* but the following anecdote is presumptive evidence in favor of Captain Armstrong:

On the 22ᵈ of Feb. [1843, at Mazatlán, Mexico] the Commodore gave a splendid dinner to the Officers of H. B. M. Ship Champion, Sloops of War Cyane & Yorktown, with a number of invited guests from shore. . . . Captain A[rmstrong] was in high glee but was lifted to his Cabin, being too fatigued to walk without support.⁶

This gentleman, Melville says, was a "Harry the Eighth afloat, bluff and hearty"; and, not content with one pun, he continues his satirical portrait:

Captain Claret was a portly gentleman, with a crimson face, whose father had fought at the battle of the Brandywine, and whose brother had commanded the well-known frigate named in honour of that engagement. And his whole appearance evinced that Captain Claret himself had fought many Brandywine battles ashore in honour of his sire's memory, and commanded in many bloodless Brandywine actions at sea.

And, to dispel any final doubt, it may be mentioned that one of Melville's shipmates wrote opposite this description in his copy of *White-Jacket,* the year after its publication, the following note: "Capt. James Armstrong is described as 'Capt. Claret'— He did not however command the 'U. S.' on her voyage home round Cape Horn in 1844— He was relieved in that command by Capt. Stribling." [7] Elsewhere Melville puts this amusing sketch of Armstrong to use in a dissertation upon naval incompetence.[8]

He has little to say of the lieutenants except one whom he calls "Mad Jack," [9] apparently a composite of several characters well-known in naval history. The immediate original was Latham B. Avery, a lieutenant on the present cruise. Two of Melville's shipmates so identify him; and one of them, later Rear-Admiral Samuel Franklin, adds a description of him as the best sea officer he had ever known:

His style was the best, his manner the most seaman-like, his voice was like music, and all the qualities that go to make up the best type of deck-officer were embodied in him. The men jumped at his call, and although he did not spare them, they adored him. No officer on board ship could get the work out of them that he could. The Captain had the most implicit confidence in him, and when we were buffeting about off Cape Horn, when he was Officer of the watch "all hands" were never called for getting the ship under short canvas, for he, with the watch on deck, was sufficient of himself. Herman Melville, in *White-Jacket,* calls him "mad Jack," and when he was making the ship snug in a heavy gale of wind he well deserved the sobriquet, although at other times he was as quiet as a lamb. To sum him up, he was a gentleman seaman of the first order.[10]

Agreeing in most respects with this is Melville's eloquent description of "this man who was born in a gale":

In some time of tempest—off Cape Horn or Hatteras—*Mad Jack* must have entered the world—such things have been—not with a silver spoon, but with a speaking trumpet in his mouth; wrapped up in a caul, as in a mainsail—for a charmed life against shipwrecks he bears—and crying, *Luff! luff, you may!—steady!—port! World ho!—here I am!*

Mad Jack is in his saddle on the sea. *That* is his home. . . . His loud, lusty lungs are two belfries, full of all manner of chimes; but you only hear his deepest bray in the height of some tempest—like the great bell of St. Paul's, which only sounds when the King or the Devil is dead. . . .

Mad Jack was a bit of a tyrant—they say all good officers are—but the sailors loved him all round; and would much rather stand fifty watches with him than one with a rose-water sailor.[11]

To this, however, Melville adds a final touch which seems to indicate that, though following a good tradition of the "gentleman seaman," he was anything but "quiet as a lamb":

Mad Jack, alas, has one fearful failing. He drinks. . . . The vice was inveterate; surely, like Ferdinand, Count Fathom, he must have been suckled at a puncheon. Very often this bad habit got him into very serious scrapes. Twice he was put off duty by the commodore; and once he came near being broken for his frolics.[12]

And Melville was not inventing here—he rarely invented except for definite propagandist purposes. The ship's records bear him out:

August 15 [1842]. Courtmartial for Lieut. Avery for leaving the deck whilst officer of the deck (he was drunk, etc.). Pleaded guilty and read his defense.

September 6 [1842]. All officers on board the flag ship to hear the sentence of Lieut. Avery the drunkard. He received his sword from the Commodore; was requested to go to [his] duty which he could so well perform; in fact, a complimentary address. He ought to have been broke. A perfect humbug. So it goes.[13]

Once this hard-drinking lieutenant came into collision with his even harder drinking captain, according to Melville, and countermanded his superior's orders during a gale; this anecdote seems to have been picked up from a similar breach of discipline recorded of Lieutenant David Farragut, and attached to the magnetic character of Mad Jack.[14] A third element in Melville's composite sea cavalier seems to have been Captain John Percival, who, according to a competent naval historian, was the original of Mad Jack and was so called because of an ungovernable temper rather than for any lack of sailing abilities or recklessness in handling ship.[15] It is quite possible that Percival did add something to the picture, for he had been a lieutenant on the *United States* in 1826–1827, and a famous character might well have been kept alive for fifteen years by ship's gossip.[16] In some such manner there came into being Lieutenant Mad Jack, no spotless hero, to be sure, but none the less Melville's beau ideal of a sea officer.

A number of petty officers who are mentioned in *White-Jacket* are identified by Franklin: "He [Melville] gives no names, but to any one who served in the Frigate *United States* it was easy to recognise the men by their sobriquets." [17] The gunner, Asa G. Curtis, Melville calls "Old Combustibles," and makes him the type of all bad-tempered men who acquire their disposition from their ill-chosen vocation, while admitting that he was the most efficient of all the forward officers. Franklin also remembers him as a rare character, who guarded his battery jealously, even putting spikes in his match tubs to keep the men from using them for seats.[18] William Hoff, the boatswain, of whom Melville has little to say, was an Englishman who had risen from the ranks and was a good seaman, but he drank heavily and frequently got into trouble. Franklin recalls one occasion when he had delirium tremens; perhaps this was the occasion, already pointed out, when he peremptorily announced his intention of "receiving no more orders in this ship" and was accordingly suspended from office.[19] Of course, all of the names of the ship's company, both officers and men, can be had from the Muster Rolls, but a careful check shows that Melville consistently used fictitious names—except in two instances, noted below—whether they were obvious sobriquets like those already discussed or names that have more of a sound of reality, like "Lieutenant Bridewell" and "John Ushant," the captain of the forecastle. Sometimes his titular inventions reached the height of the fantastic, as in the transformation of William Johnson, Surgeon of the Fleet, into "Cadwallader Cuticle, M. D." Only in one instance does he place a character on board who we know was not there. This was the commodore, Thomas ap Catesby Jones, who had already sailed for home in the *Constellation* on

January 22, 1844. But in *White-Jacket* Melville postpones his re-call for six months and allows the "Neversink" to sail back into the home port still flying his broad blue pennant. His dramatic sense told him that a flagship would make a more impressive set-ting, and, even if the fiction made him keep his commodore dis-creetly in the background, he could use his presence on board ship to give point to some of his attacks on naval abuses.[20]

After this array of highly-colored *dramatis personæ*, it is a little surprising to find that Melville did, for two characters, use actual names. "Williams," his Yankee friend from Maine, was obviously the Griffith Williams who had shipped with him at Honolulu[21]—probably a beachcomber whom he had made friends with in his rovings among the Pacific islands. The other is far more impor-tant. "Jack Chase, our noble first captain of the top," who is the real hero of *White-Jacket,* was the veritable John J. Chase listed on the Muster Roll as No. 513. Much more will be said of him later.

One further identification will be made which, barring that of Jack Chase, is the most significant of all. There are several indi-cations which lead to the conclusion that the Ship's Scribe, the anonymous author of the very journal which has furnished the information for these concluding chapters, was the "gentlemanly young member of the after-guard" whom Melville so obviously admired, and whom he called "Lemsford the poet." It is chiefly in this role that he appears in *White-Jacket,* as the author of a sheaf of poems called the *Songs of the Sirens,* which were accident-ally "published" in the bay of Rio de Janeiro by being fired through the muzzle of one of the main-deck guns, their hiding-place, during a national salute.[22] Jack Chase, according to Mel-ville, was Lemsford's patron, frequently inviting him up into the maintop to recite some of his verses.[23]

The ornate style of the *Journal of a Cruise in the Frigate United States* itself suggests the hand of an ambitious young poet, espe-cially since it contains several fragments of poetry that were evi-dently the author's own handiwork.[24] But this alone would not be enough to identify the Ship's Scribe as Lemsford. Good luck has saved for posterity what would seem to be the only one of the

Songs of the Sirens that escaped destruction. Tucked in between the leaves of the Log Book of the *United States,* as though hastily concealed from uncongenial and prying eyes, has been found a poem of twelve lines, written in the identical autograph of the *Journal* and headed: "Respectfully inscribed to J. J. C. by his sincere Friend G. W. W." [25] Here seems to be the dedication written by the sailor-Virgil to his Mæcenas. According to the Muster Rolls, "J. J. C." can be no one but John J. Chase; and the poet and author of the *Journal* must be, with equal certainty, one and the same person—in all likelihood George W. Wallace, listed as an ordinary seaman during this cruise. Finally, in the closing pages of *White-Jacket,* as the ship nears home, Melville has Lemsford exclaim: "I venerate the sea, and venerate it so highly, shipmates, that evermore I shall abstain from crossing it"; with striking similarity, in an appendix to his journal, "G. W. W." has written opposite Boston, under the column headed Days in Port: "Forever for me!" [26] Since only one of the *Songs of the Sirens* chanced to survive, how fortunate that it was the very one which so fittingly and convincingly links together this little literary trio of Melville, Chase, and Wallace—thus vividly re-creating the reality of life on board the *United States* in 1844 as it is described in *White-Jacket.* For, unless there were two poet-protégés of Jack Chase among this frigate's crew, "G. W. W." must have been Melville's good friend "Lemsford the poet." [27]

It was not only by the use of pseudonyms that Melville sought to disguise his narrative in *White-Jacket.* The chronology of the homeward cruise also he altered to his purposes. He lets the frigate rightly sail from "Callao, on the coast of Peru—her last harbour in the Pacific," but he helps to shield himself from recognition by selecting Norfolk rather than Boston for her destination.[28] Sometimes he sacrifices accuracy to felicity of phrase: "The *Neversink* had summered out her last Christmas on the Equator; now she was destined to winter out the Fourth of July not very far from the frigid latitudes of Cape Horn." [29] Both holidays, as a matter of fact, were spent idly in port at Callao. Once, he reaches back into the earlier part of the cruise to get a dramatic setting for an abuse of naval authority: "while making a long, tedious run from Mazatlán to Callao on the Main, baffled by light head-winds and frequent intermitting calms," he says, an unwarranted flogging was administered by Captain Claret solely because the monotonous and threatening calm had put him out of sorts. This was undoubtedly a reference to the portentous calm of a month's duration between Mazatlán and Valparaiso in the spring of 1843, so grimly recorded by the Ship's Scribe. Although it occurred before Melville became a member of the crew of the *United States* and the Log Book records no punishments administered at that time, he declares that the disgraceful episode happened right before his own eyes; during the cruise that Melville made from Mazatlán to Callao, April 16–June 6, 1844, neither calms nor floggings are recorded.[30] A final alteration of chronology was in the length of the stop-over at Rio. In actual fact the ship only touched at this last harbor for a week; but Melville, when he finds his fast-sailing frigate rapidly outrunning his narrative, expands this one week into such endless weeks "that a saying went abroad among the impatient sailors that our frigate would at last ground on the beef-bones daily thrown overboard by the cooks." More than one-fourth of the entire book is then given over to the imaginary events of this fictitiously prolonged stay in the "Bay of all Beauties." [31]

These minor alterations of fact for the sake of anonymity and expediency are but the prelude to Melville's more elaborate embellishments of actual events for dramatic effect. It has already been pointed out how, by transferring a death at sea from the pleasant latitude off Nukahiva to the sweltering heat of a calm on-the Equator, he opens the way for a denunciation of the wretched conditions in the sick bay of a man-of-war.[32] And it has also been shown how, by shifting the setting of a fall from the main yard to the quarter-deck—which happened in the normal performance of necessary duty—to the harbor of Rio during a show-off of disciplinary excellence in competitive sail-furling, he brutalizes a mere accident into the needless and deliberate sacrifice of one of "the people" in order to glorify the commodore on the poop.[33]

This method is used throughout the narrative for some of his most effective scenes.

Only once do the manuscripts at hand offer a purely pictorial scene of everyday life on a man-of-war for comparison with Melville's exuberant descriptions. Early in the cruise the Ship's Scribe confesses himself an apprentice by checking his narrative long enough to sketch admiringly a typical divine worship at sea:

Sunday Morning came, calm as a sunday [*sic*] morning should come, with a light air skipping o'er a sea rolling in long swells, as though it were sleeping never to be disturbed. . . . The sails are hanging lazily against the masts. The starbd. watch are buisaly [*sic*] engaged holystoning the decks, cleaning their bright work, and getting the Ship ready for inspection, while the larbd. watch are still in their hammocks paying their respects to Morpheus. At 10 O'Clock the Ship in all her parts is as clean as the most fastiduous [*sic*] Northern housewife keeps her cottage. At 10.30 the shrill notes of the Boatswains Pipe, assisted by his mates, is heard, "All hands to Muster." The crew were then mustered around the Capstan. After muster the Capstan Bars were arrainged [*sic*] on the Shot Boxes, both sides of the Quarter Deck, for the accomodation of the crew during Divine Service. As the Men passed aft, I was struck with the beauty of the scene, the men and boys all drest in their snowy frocks and Blue Jackets and Trowsers.[34] Commo. Jones, . . . Capt. A[rmstrong], and Ward Room Officers then took their seats. Our Chaplain, *"the Revd. Theo. Bartow of New York,"* then stept forward to the Desk, which was covered with the American Flag. The Service of the Episcopal Church was then read. All was quiet save the soft toned voice of the Chaplain, who gave us a most eloquent and impressive Sermon. And who were his hearers? Who were gazing anxiously in his face as he explained the word of God? Some "450 Children of the Storm" whose daily life cause[s] them frequently to be amidst danger on the high and giddy mast, furling or reefing the canvass [*sic*] when the vessel staggers under more than she [can] bear, or aloft wrestling with the fury of the gale. It was a solemn [occasion], one that would have gladdened the heart of a pious philanthropist—" 'twas truly divine worship at sea." [35]

How different from this naïve and unexceptionable picture is the same scene viewed through Melville's disillusioned eyes, in the chapter entitled: "The Chaplain and Chapel in a Man-of-War":

The next day was Sunday; a fact set down in the almanac, spite of merchant seamen's maxim, that *there are no Sundays off soundings.*

No Sundays off soundings, indeed! No Sundays on shipboard! You may as well say there are no Sundays in churches; for is not a ship modelled after a church? has it not three spires—three steeples? yea, and on the gun-deck, a bell and a belfry? And does not that bell merrily peal every Sunday morning, to summon the crew to devotions?

At any rate, there were Sundays on board this particular frigate of ours, and a clergyman also. He was a slender, middle-aged man, of an amiable deportment and irreproachable conversation; but I must say that his sermons were but ill-calculated to benefit the crew. He had drunk at the mystic fountain of Plato; his head had been turned by the Germans. . . . He enlarged upon the follies of the ancient philosophers. . . .

Fancy, now, this transcendental divine standing behind a gun-carriage on the main-deck, and addressing five hundred salt-sea sinners upon the psychological phenomena of the soul, and the ontological necessity of every sailor's saving it at all hazards. . . . He was particularly hard upon the Gnostics and Marcionites of the second century of the Christian era; but he never, in the remotest manner, attacked the everyday vices of the nineteenth century, as eminently illustrated in our man-of-war world. Concerning drunkenness, fighting, flogging, and oppression—things expressly or impliedly prohibited by Christianity—he never said aught. But the most mighty commodore and captain sat before him; and in general, if, in a monarchy, the state form the audience of the church, little evangelical piety will be preached. . . .

During these Sunday discourses, the officers always sat in a circle round the chaplain, and, with a business-like air, steadily preserved the utmost propriety. In particular, our old commodore himself made a point of looking intensely edified; and not a sailor on board but believed that the commodore, being the greatest man present, must alone comprehend the mystic sentences that fell from our parson's lips. . . .

The accomodations of our chapel were very poor. We had nothing to sit on but the great gun-rammers and capstan-bars, placed horizontally upon shot-boxes. These seats were exceedingly uncomfortable, wearing out our trowsers and our tempers, and, no doubt, impeded the conversion of many valuable souls.

To say the truth, man-of-war's men, in general, make but poor auditors upon these occasions, and adopt every possible means to elude them. Often the boatswain's mates were obliged to drive the men to service, violently swearing upon these occasions, as upon every other.

"Go to prayers, d——n you! To prayers, you rascals—to prayers!" In this clerical invitation Captain Claret would frequently unite.

At this Jack Chase would sometimes make merry. "Come, boys, don't hang back," he would say; "come, let us go hear the parson talk about his Lord High Admiral Plato, and Commodore Socrates."

But, in one instance, grave exception was taken to this summons. A remarkably serious, but bigoted seaman, a sheet-anchor man . . . once touched his hat to the captain, and respectfully said, "Sir, I am a Baptist; the chaplain is an Episcopalian; his form of worship is not mine; I do not believe with him, and it is against my conscience to be under his ministry. May I be allowed, sir, *not* to attend service on the half-deck?"

"You will be allowed, sir!" said the captain haughtily, "to obey the laws of the ship. If you absent yourself from prayers on Sunday mornings, you know the penalty."

According to the Articles of War, the captain was perfectly right; but if any law requiring an American to attend divine service against his will be a law respecting the establishment of religion, then the Articles of War are, in this one particular, opposed to the American Constitution, which expressly says, "Congress shall make no law respecting the establishment of religion, or the free exercise thereof." But this is only one of several things in which the Articles of War are repugnant to that instrument.

How can it be expected that the religion of peace should flourish in an oaken castle of war? How can it be expected that the clergyman, whose pulpit is a forty-two-pounder, should convert sinners to a faith that enjoins them to turn the right cheek when the left is smitten? [36]

Four years previously, en route to the South Seas, Melville would probably have seen with the more reverent eyes of the Ship's Scribe; but his vagabondage had cost him dear, and not the least of the price he paid was the unquestioning faith of his childhood. The United States Navy had to bear part of the burden of his quarrel at being cheated.

If Melville looked at commonplace scenes through darkened glasses, the coloring that he added to more dramatic moments amounts to propagandism. Into the narrative of rounding Cape Horn goes a complex blending of fact and fiction that shows the shaping hand of the reformer. In the actual records of this cruise, beginning a week out of Callao, a rather normal passage is indicated:

July 13, [1844], we are making rapid headway for Cape Horn, having a stiff breeze & a heavy sea, the old ship half burying herself at every plunge. On the morning of the 15th it fell calm and continued so untill the afternoon, when the wind came out from the Sd. & Ed., which continued with moderate breezes untill the 25th when the weather became very squally. On the same Sail ho! was proclaimed from the Mast head, which proved to be the American Ship Natchez [64 days from New York, bound to Valparaiso] under Courses, topsails, topgallant sails, Royals, Skysails, Lower, topmast, topgallant & Royal Studdingsails, on both sides Jib a Jib, flying jib, Jib and Foretopmast staysail, Maintopmast, topgallant and Royal staysails, Fore & Main Spencers, Spanker and Gaff Topsail, Ringtail, and water sails—we being at the time under topgallant sails and single reefed topsails. [Spoke her at 6:30 P.M.] On the 28 blowing a gale, we lay *too*, under Main & Mizen staysails & Fore Storm Staysail, for 6 hours, not being able to carry sail. The wind abated and then shifted in our favour, and we were on our way once more towards Rio, under all sail.[37]

The calm occurred north of the latitude of Valparaiso, some two thousand five hundred miles from Cape Horn; the ship *Natchez* was passed ten days later, still some seven hundred miles from it; and only the gale itself occurred as the *United States* turned east to round the Cape, which was not actually passed until two days later, but then under another stiff gale which sped the ship along at more than two hundred and fifty miles in one day.[38]

The actual passage was thrilling enough, but Melville heightens the effect of his account, first by bringing all three events together off the very point of the Cape. He further dramatizes the situation by making the calm longer, two days of bitter cold instead of a few hours in the temperate zone; the gale more violent and dangerous; and the incident of passing the ship more picturesque. On the second day of the calm, according to *White-Jacket*, a sail was discerned from the masthead at a great distance:

What was she, and whence? There is no object which so excites interest and conjecture, and, at the same time, baffles both, as a sail, seen as a mere speck on these remote seas off Cape Horn.

A breeze! a breeze! for lo! the stranger is now perceptibly nearing the frigate; the officer's spyglass pronounces her a full-rigged ship, with all sail set, and coming right down to us, though in our vicinity the calm still reigns.

She is bringing the wind with her. Hurrah! Ay, there it is! Behold how mincingly it creeps over the sea, just ruffling and crisping it.

Our topmen were at once sent aloft to loose the sails, and presently they faintly began to distend. As yet we hardly had steerage-way. Toward sunset the stranger bore down before the wind, a complete pyramid of canvas. Never before, I venture to say, was Cape Horn so audaciously insulted. Stun'-sails alow and aloft; royals, moonsails, and everything else. She glided under our stern, within hailing distance, and the signal-quarter-master ran up our ensign to the gaff.

"Ship ahoy!" cried the lieutenant of the watch, through his trumpet. . . .

"The *Sultan*, Indiaman, from New York, and bound to Callao and Canton, sixty days out, all well. What frigate's that?"

"The United States ship *Neversink*, homeward bound." . . .

By this time the *Sultan* had swept past, but the lieutenant of the watch could not withhold a parting admonition.

"D'ye hear? You'd better take in some of your flying-kites there. Look out for Cape Horn!"

But the friendly advice was lost in the now increasing wind. With a suddenness by no means unusual in these latitudes, the light breeze soon became a succession of sharp squalls, and our sail-proud braggadocio of an Indiaman was observed to let everything go by the run, his t'gallant stun'-sails and flying-jib taking quick leave of the spars; the flying-jib was swept into the air, rolled together for a few minutes, and tossed about in the squalls like a football. But the wind played no such pranks with the more prudently managed canvas of the *Neversink*, though before many hours it was stirring times with us.[39]

This elaborate setting merely paves the way for one of Melville's most striking inventions—a dramatic climax from which Mad Jack emerges covered with glory and Captain Claret stands target for Melville's unsparing denunciation of naval incompetence:

About midnight, when the starboard watch, to which I belonged, was below, the boatswain's whistle was heard, followed by the shrill cry for "*All hands take in sail! jump, men, and save ship!*"

Springing from our hammocks, we found the frigate leaning over to it so steeply, that it was with difficulty we could climb the ladders leading to the upper deck.

Here the scene was awful. The vessel seemed to be sailing on her side . . . the quarter-deck and forecastle were plunging through the sea, which undulated over them in milk-white billows of foam. . . . By this time the deck was alive with the whole strength of the ship's company, five hundred men, officers and all, mostly clinging to the weather bulwarks. . . .

In a sudden gale, or when a large quantity of sail is suddenly to be furled, it is the custom for the first lieutenant to take the trumpet from whoever happens then to be officer of the deck. But Mad Jack had the trumpet that watch; nor did the first lieutenant seek to wrest it from his hands. Every eye was upon him, as if we had chosen him from among us all, to decide this battle with the elements, by single combat with the spirit of the Cape; for Mad Jack was the saving genius of the ship, and so proved himself that night. I owe this right hand, that is this moment flying over my sheet, and all my present being to Mad Jack. The ship's bows were now butting, battering, ramming, and thundering over and upon the head seas, and with a horrible wallowing sound our whole hull was rolling in the trough of the foam. The gale came athwart the deck, and every sail seemed bursting with its wild breath. . . .

"Hard *up* the helm!" shouted Captain Claret, bursting from his cabin like a ghost, in his nightdress.

"Damn you!" raged Mad Jack to the quarter-masters; "hard *down—* hard *down,* I say, and be damned to you!"

Contrary orders! but Mad Jack's were obeyed.[40]

Then, in one of the most exciting passages that Melville ever wrote, Mad Jack pilots the ship through the tempest to safety, without even a reprimand for having countermanded his superior's orders. This leads Melville to a chapter of scathing commentary on Captain Claret's weakness for brandy and poor seamanship, Paper Jack captains, and incompetent officers in the American Navy in general.[41] Though just such an extraordinary anecdote of unpunished insubordination is recorded of another officer, David Farragut, on another ship, and at an earlier time,[42] the records of the *United States* do not admit of any such scene as the one Melville describes. Though such a breach of discipline might naturally have been expunged from official documents, one suspects that the unofficial Scribe of the frigate would never have let it pass without comment.

In the minor details of this harrowing passage of Cape Horn Melville is more literal and accurate. For all his eager searching on this occasion, he says, he caught no sight of the gleaming snow-white barrenness and solitude of Staten Land, with its unnumbered white albatross, though he describes it vividly from his recollections of its appearance outward bound.[43] The reason for this was that a strong breeze from the southwest swept the ship several hundred miles out to sea just as it was rounding the Horn. So, also, the pleasant weather that Melville records as coming with such a welcome relief about a week northward is recorded officially as well. Finally, the gradual increase of the ship's sick list, from the usual dozen on July 15 to thirty-two on August 2, seems to corroborate Melville's epidemic of "Cape Horn Fever," which filled the sick bay, off the pitch of the Cape, with men who chose "to submit to this dismal hospital . . . in order to escape hard work and wet jackets." [44]

So it appears that White Jacket's thrilling passage of Cape Horn owes much to actual experience but still more to a dramatic imagination, heightened in its most extraordinary scene by an anecdote which he had garnered, perhaps, from the tall talk of the maintop. In conclusion, it may be added that something more than a hint was derived from that famous volume which Melville refers to so enthusiastically in *White-Jacket* as his "friend Dana's unmatchable *Two Years Before the Mast*," whose "chapters describing Cape Horn must have been written with an icicle." We know that a copy of this book was included in the ship's library of the frigate *United States*.[45]

The man-of-war race of the American squadron out of Rio de Janeiro furnished Melville with another opportunity for dramatic elaboration. In addition to the fact that his hero, Jack Chase, takes color from the embellishment, Melville's artistic flourishes are chiefly spent upon heightening the excitement of the race itself and drawing from it a sermon against naval abuses. The actual event must have been not without its stirring moments, for even the usually placid Ship's Scribe caught something of the spirit of this "man-of-war Derby":

We remained at anchor [in Rio] untill the 24th, when on signal from the Commo. [Daniel Turner of the Raritan] we weighed and stood out in company with Congress, Raritan, Bainbridge, and French Sloop Coquette for a race. On starting the odds was 3 to 1 on the Raritan, she having been represented as a crack Ship on her keel. Got underweigh Saturday at 5.45 [A.M.]. [Until meridian standing out of the harbor of Rio.] At 12 the Bainbridge abeam, the others astern. [At 2 P.M. still working out of the harbor of Rio.] At 4 the Bainbridge 1 mile ahead, others astern, wind very light. [At 6 P.M. passing Raza Island and Sugar Loaf Mountain, at the entrance to the harbor. At 8 the Raritan tacked close aboard to avoid running into us. At 8.40 the Coquette ahead, the others alongside, all hull down. At 10 the Coquette on the lee bow, the Bainbridge on the weather beam, others astern. At 11 P.M. set the Royals and Flying Jib, a strong breeze springing up.] At Midnight Raritan ½ mile astern & to leeward, Congress off the lee quarter hull down, Coquette out of sight astern, and Bainbridge just visible on weather Quarter. At 4 in the morning [August 25] Raritan on wr. Quarter dist. 4 miles, Bainbridge 1 mile on weather beam, Congress not in sight. At 8 Raritan astern 2 miles, Congress on lee beam, dist. 3 miles, Bainbridge on weather quarter 5 miles. At 11 Bainbridge stood back to Port, Congress & Raritan on lee bow & beam [in company] dist. 6 miles. On signal from the Commo. stood down for them, run within hail, and hove to at 3[P.M.]. At 3.30, having received the letter bags from the two Frigates, filled away and stood to the Nd. & Wd. with a Royal breeze, which continued for several days.[46]

To translate this nautical language into simple terms: the five ships weighed anchor at daybreak on August 24 and spent the morning and afternoon working out of the harbor of Rio. During this time the *United States* held the lead; but, when the entrance of the harbor was passed, the *Bainbridge,* a light brig, forged a mile ahead and kept this lead for four hours, the wind being too light to give the heavier frigates much headway. At eight o'clock in the evening the French corvette *Coquette* took first place for a few hours, but by ten o'clock the *United States* and the *Bainbridge* were alongside contending for the lead. At eleven P. M. a strong breeze sprang up, and the *United States,* setting her Royals

and Flying Jib, forged into the van and kept an undisputed lead
throughout the rest of the race. The *Coquette* had dropped out of
sight astern by midnight, and the *Bainbridge,* the only other real
rival, stood back to Rio the next morning. (The *Raritan,* in spite
of her reputation, remained astern throughout.) By this time the
race was virtually over, and the *United States* was left without
a challenger.

In *White-Jacket* the racing frigates are not only at the beck and
call of the winds, but further they are puppets for Melville to
manipulate. Bright and early one morning, as the sun rose in the
east, says the author, the "Neversink" weighed anchor and
dropped down the bay. In her wake came two frigates, one French
and one English, the latter being the "President," a prize ship
that had been captured from America by the English during the
War of 1812: [47]

Both Englishman and Frenchman were resolved on a race; and we
Yankees swore by our topsails and royals to sink their blazing banners
that night among the southern constellations we should daily be extinguishing behind us in our run to the north.

"Ay," said Mad Jack, "St. George's banner shall be as the *Southern
Cross,* out of sight, leagues down the horizon, while our gallant stars, my
brave boys, shall burn all alone in the north, like the Great Bear at
the Pole! Come on Rainbow and Cross!"

But the wind was long languid and faint, not yet recovered from
its night's dissipation ashore, and noon advanced, with Sugar Loaf
pinnacle in sight.

Now it is not with ships as with horses; for though, if a horse walk
well and fast, it generally furnishes good token that he is not bad at
a gallop, yet the ship that in a light breeze is outstripped, may sweep
the stakes, so soon as a t'-gallant breeze enables her to strike into a canter.
Thus fared it with us. First, the Englishman glided ahead, and bluffly
passed on; then the Frenchman politely bade us adieu, while the old
Neversink lingered behind, railing at the effeminate breeze. At one
time, all three frigates were irregularly abreast, forming a diagonal
line; and so near were all three that the stately officers on the poops
stiffly saluted by touching their caps, though refraining from any further civilities. At this juncture, it was a noble sight to behold those fine
frigates, with dripping breast-hooks, all rearing and nodding in con-
cert, and to look through their tall spars and wilderness of rigging, that

seemed like inextricably entangled, gigantic cobwebs against the sky.

Toward sundown the ocean pawed its white hoofs to the spur of its helter-skelter rider, a strong blast from the eastward, and, giving three cheers from decks, yards, and tops, we crowded all sail on St. George and St. Denis.

But it is harder to overtake than outstrip; night fell upon us, still in the rear. . . . It was a misty, cloudy night; and though at first our look-outs kept the chase in dim sight, yet at last so thick became the atmosphere, that no sign of a strange spar was to be seen. But the worst of it was that, when last discerned, the Frenchman was broad on our weatherbow, and the Englishman gallantly leading his van.

The breeze blew fresher and fresher; but, with even our main-royal set, we dashed along through a cream-coloured ocean of illuminated foam. White Jacket was then in the top, and it was glorious to look down and see our black hull butting the white sea with its broad bows like a ram.

"We must beat them with such a breeze, dear Jack," said I to our noble captain of the top.

"But the same breeze blows for John Bull, remember," replied Jack, who, being a Briton, perhaps favoured the Englishman more than the *Neversink*.

"But how we boom through the billows!" cried Jack, gazing over the top-rail.[48]

Then, flinging forth his arm, the self-tutored Briton recited some glowing lines from Camoens's *Lusiad*. This launched him on a grandiose eulogy of sea captains and sea poets—ranging from Noah, St. Paul, Columbus, and Shakespeare, down through Shelley and Byron—concluding with a lament that "We Homers who happen to be captains of tops must write our odes in our hearts, and publish them in our heads." But this lyric interlude was rudely interrupted. Midnight came, and still all the officers were on deck; neither of the rival ships, however, was in sight:

"Call all hands!" roared the captain. "This keel shan't be beat while I stride it."

All hands were called, and the hammocks stowed in the nettings for the rest of the night, so that no one could lie between blankets.

Now, in order to explain the means adopted by the captain to en-sure us the race, it needs to be said of the *Neversink* that, for some years after being launched, she was accounted one of the slowest vessels in the American Navy. But it chanced upon a time that, being on a cruise in the Mediterranean, she happened to sail out of Port Mahon in what was then supposed to be very bad trim for sea. Her bows were rooting in the water, and her stern kicking up its heels in the air. But, wonderful to tell, it was soon discovered that in this comical posture she sailed like a shooting-star; she outstripped every vessel on the station. Thenceforward all her captains, on all cruises, *trimmed her by the head;* and the *Neversink* gained the name of a clipper.[49]

To return. All hands being called, they were now made use of by Captain Claret as make-weights, to trim the ship, scientifically, to her most approved bearings. Some were sent forward on the spar-deck, with twenty-four-pound shot in their hands, and were judiciously scattered about here and there, with strict orders not to budge an inch from their stations, for fear of marring the captain's plans. Others were distributed along the gun and berth decks, with similar orders; and, to crown all, several carronade guns were unshipped from their carriages, and swung in their breechings from the beams of the main-deck, so as to impart a sort of vibratory briskness and oscillating buoyancy to the frigate.

And thus we five hundred make-weights stood out that whole night, some of us exposed to a drenching rain, in order that the *Neversink* might not be beaten. But the comfort and consolation of all make-weights is as dust in the balance in the estimation of the rulers of our man-of-war world.

The long anxious night at last came to an end, and, with the first peep of day, the look-out on the jib-boom was hailed; but nothing was in sight. At last it was broad day; yet still not a bow was to be seen in our rear, nor a stern in our van.

"Where are they?" cried the captain.

"Out of sight astern, to be sure, sir," said the officer of the deck.

"Out of sight *ahead,* to be sure, sir," muttered Jack Chase in the top.

Precisely thus stood the question: whether we beat them, or whether they beat us, no mortal can tell to this hour, since we never saw them again; but for one, White Jacket will lay his two hands on the bow-chasers of the *Neversink,* and take his ship's oath that we Yankees carried the day.[50]

It will be seen that Melville makes three separate transformations of his material, each with a distinctive dramatic appeal. First of all, he endows the race with an international character, reducing the original five contestants—the American squadron plus a

French corvette which early dropped out of the race—to three, each representing a different nation. Melville himself sponsors the *United States;* Jack Chase, the true Briton, is divided in his loyalty but leans towards the English frigate; and the French corvette remains unsponsored by anyone, unless by the sympathetic reader. This new alignment of the contestants was obviously designed as a setting for the dialogue in the maintop between Melville and Jack Chase, to show that the latter was a true-blue Briton, and also to show the London reading public that Melville was something of an Anglophile though he wasted no love on the French. The next change was for the sake of the excitement of the race itself. In reality, the *United States* sprang into a lead early in the race and maintained it throughout; but Melville heightens the suspense by having darkness and fog close in on the scene just as the "Neversink," though still in the rear, is getting into true form and crowding all sail on her rivals. He seems to be guilty of a breach of dramatic technique when on the next day he sacrifices this gain in suspense by leaving the outcome of the race in disappointing uncertainty. But this was undoubtedly deliberate, for Melville's interest, and the reader's, has now shifted from the race itself to anti-naval propaganda.

This third change is pure invention; for the seamen are made to stand out on deck through a drenching night with twenty-four-pound shot in their hands, as ballast to trim the ship scientifically to her most approved bearings, whereas the ship's records show that fair weather prevailed all night and that no call was made for all hands. (Such an important maneuver on board ship would have been noted in the Log Book as a matter of routine, had it actually taken place.) There is no denying that the inhumanity of this is rendered doubly effective and ironical by making it extremely doubtful whether the sacrifice brought any real glory to the captain on the poop. This serio-comic trick of "trimming by the head" for speed, however, was sometimes practiced on board the *United States* in emergencies.[51] During the race out of Callao the previous January—in which, incidentally, the English frigate *Vindictive* won a clear victory—the Log Book records: "shifted Shot forward to trim Ship" and "shifted the two after guns in the Cabin abreast of the Galley."[52] Twenty years before, a former sailor on the *United States* records another example of this in a race to overtake the Spanish privateer *Moriendra,* which reads like a source for Melville's anecdote:

> The chase which was right before the wind lasted all day. For some time we did not gain upon her, owing to the ship being somewhat out of trim, a defect which we remedied in a manner something similar to that practised by Captain Staunch in "Sailors and Saints," not exactly by piping down the hammocks, and sending the watch to bed "with a thirty-two pound shot for a bedfellow;" but every man took a thirty-two pound shot in his hands and went on the forecastle, as we had found by experience that the ship sailed best with her nose in the water, like a pig rooting in a gutter.[53]

It made little difference to Melville that no such method was resorted to on the night of August 24, 1844, out of Rio. He knew of the trick, and he was less interested in recording an actual event than in adorning his tale and pointing his moral.

Sometimes Melville's elaborations were not vehicles for propagandist attacks on naval abuses, directly or indirectly, but were purely for heightening the dramatic effect of characters and scenes. Such is his treatment of an incident concerning the past history of Jack Chase. The noble proportions of this ideal sailor are so suggestive of a picaresque hero that one is inclined to attribute to pure invention all of the anecdotes which fill in his generous outlines. Yet one of them, one of the least credible, has at least a foundation in fact, however embroidered by the worshipful pen of Melville. Records in the Navy Department show that John J. Chase, boatswain's mate, deserted from the United States vessel of war *St. Louis* on November 18, 1840, at Callao, Peru: "All the men returned who went on liberty yesterday, except John Bates, James Egan, G. Barrett, F. Gold, George Nixon, John Chase."[54] Though several of these men came back to the ship the next day, there is no entry of Chase's return subsequently on the Log Book of this ship. A year and a half later the frigate *United States* came to anchor at Callao, and her Log Book records:

Callao, Peru. May 18, 1842. Commodore Jones visited the Peruvian Admiral's ship [Tungay]. . . . May 19, Peruvian Minister of Marine visits ship. . . . May 22. Peruvian Admiral visits ship. . . . May 29, Received on board John J. Chase, a deserter from the U. S. S. St. Louis, with a particular request to Como. Jones, from the Peruvian Admiral (in whose service he had shipped) that he might be pardoned, which was complied with by Com. Jones.[55]

It is noteworthy that although the *St. Louis* was at this time lying in Callao also, Chase was reinstated in the service on board the *United States*, probably to cover up the remission of the usual corporal punishment meted out to deserters.

Though attributable to international courtesy, this procedure was extraordinary enough in itself; but it was not highly colored enough to content Melville when he was sketching in the heroic background of his favorite:

On this present cruise of the frigate *Neversink*, Jack had deserted; and after a certain interval had been captured.

But with what purpose had he deserted? To avoid naval discipline? to riot in some abandoned seaport? for love of some worthless signorita? Not at all. He abandoned the frigate from far higher and nobler, nay, glorious motives. Though bowing to naval discipline afloat, yet ashore he was a stickler for the Rights of Man and the liberties of the world. He went to draw a partisan blade in the civil commotions of Peru, and befriend, heart and soul, what he deemed the cause of the Right.'

At the time, his disappearance excited the utmost astonishment among the officers, who had little suspected him of any such conduct as deserting.

"What? Jack, my great man of the main-top, gone!" cried the captain: "I'll not believe it."

"Jack Chase cut and run!" cried a sentimental middy. "It must have been all for love, then; the signoritas have turned his head." . . .

Months passed away, and nothing was heard of Jack; till at last the frigate came to anchor on the coast, alongside of a Peruvian sloop of war.

Bravely clad in the Peruvian uniform, and with a fine mixed martial and naval step, a tall, striking figure of a long-bearded officer was descried, promenading the quarter-deck of the stranger, and superintending the salutes which are exchanged between national vessels on these occasions.

This fine officer touched his laced hat most courteously to our captain, who, after returning the compliment, stared at him, rather impolitely, through his spyglass.

"By heaven!" he cried at last; "it is he—he can't disguise his walk—that's his beard; I'd know him in Cochin China. Man the first cutter there! Lieutenant Blink, go on board that sloop of war, and fetch me yon officer."

All hands were aghast. What? when a piping-hot peace was between the United States and Peru, to send an armed body on board a Peruvian sloop of war, and seize one of its officers, in broad daylight?—Monstrous infraction of the Law of Nations! What would Vattel say?

But Captain Claret must be obeyed. So off went the cutter, every man armed to the teeth, the lieutenant commanding having secret instructions, and the midshipmen attending looking ominously wise, though, in truth, they could not tell what was coming.

Gaining the sloop of war, the lieutenant was received with the customary honours; but by this time the tall, bearded officer had disappeared from the quarter-deck. The lieutenant now inquired for the Peruvian captain; and being showed into the cabin, made known to him that on board his vessel was a person belonging to the United States ship *Neversink;* and his orders were to have that person delivered up instanter.

The foreign captain curled his moustache in astonishment and indignation; he hinted something about beating to quarters, and chastising this piece of Yankee insolence.

But resting one gloved hand upon the table, and playing with his sword-knot, the lieutenant, with a bland firmness, repeated his demand. At last, the whole case being so plainly made out, and the person in question being so accurately described, even to a mole on his cheek, there remained nothing but immediate compliance.

So the fine-looking, bearded officer, who had so courteously doffed his chapeau to our captain, but disappeared upon the arrival of the lieutenant, was summoned into the cabin, before his superior, who addressed him thus:—

"Don John, this gentleman declares, that of right you belong to the frigate *Neversink.* Is it so?"

"It is even so, Don Sereno," said Jack Chase, proudly folding his gold-laced coat-sleeves across his chest; "and as there is no resisting the frigate, I comply.—Lieutenant Blink, I am ready. Adieu! Don Sereno, and Madre de Dios protect you! You have been a most gentlemanly friend and captain to me. I hope you will yet thrash your beggarly foes."

With that he turned; and entering the cutter, was pulled back to the frigate, and stepped up to Captain Claret, where that gentleman stood on the quarter-deck.

"Your servant, my fine Don," said the Captain, ironically lifting his chapeau, but regarding Jack at the same time with a look of intense displeasure.

"Your most devoted and penitent captain of the main-top, sir; and one, who, in his very humility of contrition, is yet proud to call Captain Claret his commander," said Jack, making a glorious bow, and then tragically flinging overboard his Peruvian sword.

"Reinstate him at once," shouted Captain Claret; "and now, sir, to your duty; and discharge that well to the end of the cruise, and you will hear no more of your having run away."

So Jack went forward among crowds of admiring tars, who swore by his nut-brown beard, which had amazingly lengthened and spread during his absence. They divided his laced hat and coat among them, and on their shoulders carried him in triumph along the gun-deck.[56]

Perhaps some of these flourishes were picked up from the lips of the hero himself, for these events happened long before Melville came on board the *United States*. Besides the eloquent phrasing, the striking difference between the real and the embroidered accounts is that Jack Chase emerges from Melville's version covered with personal glory. He is reinstated in his *old* position as captain of the maintop on board his *old* frigate (he had really deserted as boatswain's mate from the *St. Louis* and had been reinstated as an ordinary seaman on the *United States*), and all punishment is foregone by reason of his own personal worth in the eyes of his captain. Though this change of motive is apparently slight, it is a far cry from the impersonal diplomatic reasons, the request of the Peruvian Admiral, that in actuality spared him from disgrace at the gangway. Naturally, Jack Chase was a man of far larger mold in the admiring eyes of Melville than in those of the officers of the frigate *United States;* and perhaps it was such anecdotes as the one just given that prompted Rear-Admiral Franklin's memory:

He [Melville] speaks of a certain seaman, Jack Chase, who was Captain of the maintop, of whom I have a very distinct recollection. He was about as fine a specimen of a seaman as I have ever seen in all my cruising. He was not only that, but he was a man of intelligence and a born leader. His topmates adored him, although he kept them up to the mark, and made every man do his share of work. Melville has given him considerable space in his book, and seems to have had intense admiration for him.[57]

But there is at least one official testimony to Chase's worth, for the Log Book of the *United States* records that he was promoted from a seaman to the important petty office of captain of the maintop within six weeks after he had been captured as a deserter.[58] Perhaps even this was something of an anticlimax to his temporary glory as a full-fledged officer on board the Peruvian man-of-war, although nothing is actually known of his eighteen-months' career as a soldier of fortune. However, some account of the guerilla warfare between Peru and Bolivia, in which he took part, may be found in the contemporary journal of William Meyers.[59]

It may be felt that a man-of-war cruise in the South Seas a century ago should have furnished some experiences sufficiently thrilling to serve the dramatist unadorned. There is at least one considerable incident in *White-Jacket* that was an almost literal transcription from life, although the wary reader would be inclined to suspect Melville, at first blush, of romancing here as elsewhere:

It was the morning succeeding one of these *general quarters* that we picked up a lifebuoy, descried floating by.

It was a circular mass of cork, about eight inches thick and four feet in diameter, covered with tarred canvas. . . . The whole buoy was embossed with barnacles, and its sides festooned with seaweed. . . . Long ago, this thing must have been thrown overboard to save some poor wretch, who must have been drowned; while even the lifebuoy itself had drifted away out of sight.

The forecastle men fished it up from the bows, and the seamen thronged round it.

"Bad luck! bad luck!" cried the captain of the head; "we'll number one less before long."

The ship's cooper strolled by: he, to whose department it belongs to see that the ship's lifebuoys are kept in good order.

In men-of-war, night and day, week in and week out, two lifebuoys are kept depending from the stern; and two men, with hatchets in their hands, pace up and down, ready at the first cry to cut the cord and drop the buoys overboard. Every two hours they are regularly relieved, like sentinels on guard. No similar precautions are adopted in the merchant or whaling service. Thus deeply solicitous to preserve human life are the regulations of men-of-war. . . .

"There, Bungs!" cried Scrimmage, a sheet-anchor man, "there's a good pattern for you; make us a brace of lifebuoys like that; something that will save a man, and not fill and sink under him, as those leaky quarter-casks of yours will the first time there's occasion to drop 'em. I came near pitching off the bowsprit the other day; and, when I scrambled inboard again, I went aft to get a squint at 'em. Why, Bungs, they are all open between the staves. Shame on you! Suppose you yourself should fall overboard, and find yourself going down with buoys under you of your own making—what then?"

"I never go aloft, and don't intend to fall overboard," replied Bungs.

"Don't believe it!" cried the sheet-anchor man; "you lopers that live about the decks here are nearer the bottom of the sea than the light hand that looses the main-royal. Mind your eye, Bungs—mind your eye!"

"I will," retorted Bungs; "and you mind yours!"

Next day, just at dawn, I was startled from my hammock by the cry of *"All hands about ship and shorten sail!"* Springing up the ladders, I found that an unknown man had fallen overboard from the chains; and darting a glance toward the poop, perceived, from their gestures, that the life-sentries there had cut away the buoys.

It was blowing a fresh breeze; the frigate was going fast through the water. But the one thousand arms of the five hundred men soon tossed her about on the other tack, and checked her further headway.

"Do you see him?" shouted the officer of the watch through his trumpet, hailing the mainmast-head. "Man or *buoy,* do you see either?"

"See nothing, sir," was the reply.

"Clear away the cutters!" was the next order. "Bugler! call away the second, third, and fourth cutters' crews. Hands by the tackles!"

In less than three minutes the three boats were down. More hands were wanted in one of them, and, among others, I jumped in to make up the deficiency.

"Now, men, give way! and each man look out along his oar, and look sharp!" cried the officer of our boat. For a time, in perfect silence, we slid up and down the great seething swells of the sea, but saw nothing.

"There, it's no use," cried the officer; "he's gone, whoever he is. Pull away, men—pull away! they'll be recalling us soon."

"Let him drown!" cried the strokesman; "he's spoiled my watch below for me."

"Who the devil is he?" cried another.

"He's one who'll never have a coffin!" replied a third.

"No, no! they'll never sing out, '*All hands bury the dead!*' for him, my hearties!" cried a fourth.

"Silence," said the officer, "and look along your oars." But the sixteen oarsmen continued their talk; and, after pulling about for two or three hours, we spied the recall signal at the frigate's fore-t'-gallant mast-head, and returned on board, having seen no sign even of the lifebuoys.

The boats were hoisted up, the yards braced forward, and away we bowled—one man less.

"Muster all hands!" was now the order; when, upon calling the roll, the cooper was the only man missing.

"I told you so, men," cried the captain of the head; "I said we would lose a man before long."

"Bungs, is it?" cried Scrimmage, the sheet-anchor man; "I told him his buoys wouldn't save a drowning man; and now he has proved it!" [60]

When the almost equally dramatic record of this episode in the *Journal of a Cruise on the Frigate United States* is set in juxtaposition with Melville's account, the resemblance is so striking, down to the minutest detail of "not even the lifebuoys" being found, that one would be tempted to credit Melville with being the author of both, were this not, in fact, impossible: [61]

October 4th. [1843] at 5.22 A. M. the appalling cry of Man overboard was sung out from the cat head. The life Bouys [sic] were instantly cut away. The Ship hove to, the Barge & 4th. Cutters lashing out, a strong breeze from S. S. E. at the time and a heavy sea running. In an instant all was commotion. The boats being manned, "Lower!" exclaimed the Officer. The Barge fell to the water and drifted rapidly astern. I thought it impossible for her to live in such a sea, but the man who held the helm was a skillfull seaman and brought the head of the gallant boat on to each high sea that would otherwise have sunk her. The 4th. Cutter followed her with equal success. They continued the search untill 8 O'Clock [A. M.], when the Cornet was hoisted for their recall to the ship. Fresh crews were then put in and sent in search but of no avail, not finding the life bouys [sic], as he must have sunk or been devoured by the sharks, as a number were seen playing round the ship. Tacked repeatedly to keep our position with the boats. At 10:45 [A. M.], all search proving ineffectual, picked up the boats and made all sail on our course. From the report of the Man on the Look at the cat head it appears that David Black, "Cooper," was in the head towing his hammock and, having tied the 4 corners of it singly with lanyards, threw it over the water.

[Water?] instantly caught in the Bag, which jerked him into the sea. When making the life Bouys [*sic*] a few weeks before, he was told that they leaked. His answer was, "If a man cannot save himself with these, he ought to drown." Poor fellow, he little thought he would have the first chance at them.[62]

In this remarkable piece of literal transcription from experience Melville found it necessary to invent little. The episode itself, stark and unclothed, was sufficient to make reality thrilling enough to pass as fiction. Beyond the necessary transposition of the scene from off Nukahiva to the vicinity of Cape Horn, his only embellishment is to give the anecdote a setting in sailor superstition. A derelict lifebuoy presages the cooper's death; and, on the night following his loss, Melville in his White Jacket up aloft is taken for the cooper's ghost by the frightened seamen, who give him a spill from the main-royal-yard to test his corporeality.[63] It is interesting to note, in conclusion, that in this one autobiographically veracious scene Melville has only good words to say of the humanity and efficiency of the Navy; when he wants to launch a propagandist attack, he invents, or at least elaborates, with a free hand.

As far as the ship's records offer verification, this is the only incident of any size or consequence which Melville reproduced in *White-Jacket* as it actually occurred. There are numerous minor references, however, mostly to time and place, which check with known facts. Accuracy in detail may be claimed for half-a-dozen trivialities during Melville's residence on board, some of which have already been mentioned in passing. A few other examples will recall their inconsequential nature. Melville says that no land was sighted all the way from Callao round Cape Horn to Rio de Janeiro, and this was, in fact, the case; although it was customary to get at least a glimpse of gleaming Staten Land while rounding the Horn, there was nothing to relieve the monotony of shoreless seas on this trip.[64] Further, "The whole of our run from Rio to the Line was one delightful yachting," says Melville, "so far as fine weather and the ship's sailing were concerned." The official records bear this out, by and large, though they are naturally silent about the pleasant quarter watches when Melville and Chase "lounged in the main-top, diverting ourselves in many agreeable ways." [65] But this fine weather did not hold out: "After running with a fine steady breeze up to the Line, it fell calm, and there we lay, three days enchanted on the sea," says Melville. Ten degrees north of the Equator the Log Book records this calm that lasted through parts of three days; but it was the artist, and not the journalist, who took this occasion to invite the reader to an inspection of the ship's hospital, where a fellow seaman lay dying of heart trouble, suffocating in the stuffy air of the hold.[66] A few brief allusions to events occurring earlier in the present voyage of the *United States,* before Melville joined it, are equally accurate. The frigate had really touched at Madeira, outward bound, and there, even as *White-Jacket* records, the "commodore and captain had laid in a goodly stock of wines for their own private tables, and the benefit of their foreign visitors"; [67] and further out, in the summer of 1842, she had lain at anchor for a month at Coquimbo, where, according to Melville, Jack Chase had first started his famous nut-brown beard.[68]

Melville's allusions to events in American naval history are, as he declares in the Preface to the first English edition, "supported by the best authorities." A pertinent example is his reference to Commodore Jones's gallant conduct at New Orleans during the war of 1812.[69] Because of wounds received in this engagement, he had a body-servant's pay allowed to him in addition to his regular salary, and, according to Melville, this valet was a Polynesian, picked up in the Society Islands. But of the dozen men listed on the Muster Rolls as shipped in Polynesia, none seems to fit this role unless "Aben Patterson, 1st. Cabin Boy, Tahiti, October 17, 1843," was a native with a Christian surname.[70]

A more extended and equally accurate use of history is Melville's account of the capture of H. B. M. frigate *Macedonian* by the "Neversink," during the same war. This checks with known facts not only in the external details recorded by official historians,[71] but also in the personal details (naturally unmentioned in official records) which Melville puts in the mouth of an old sheet-anchor man, a Negro whom he calls "Tawney," who was serving on the *Macedonian* during the battle and who was later a member of the crew of the *United States* with Melville. Samuel Leech, a seaman whose career was parallel to that of Tawney, has left his reminiscences of the battle as seen from the decks of the *Macedonian*, and it will prove interesting to compare his account with that in *White-Jacket.* Melville begins with a sidelight on impressment:

As the Briton bore down on the American . . . Tawney and his countrymen, who happened to be stationed at the quarter-deck battery, respectfully accosted the captain. . . . They assured him that they were not Englishmen, and that it was a most bitter thing to lift their hands against the flag of that country which harboured the mothers that bore them. They conjured him to release them from their guns, and allow them to remain neutral during the conflict. But when a ship of any nation is running into action, it is no time for argument, small time for justice, and not much time for humanity. Snatching a pistol from the belt of a boarder standing by, the captain levelled it at the heads of the three sailors, and commanded them instantly to their quarters, under penalty of being shot on the spot. So, side by side with his country's foes, Tawney and his companions toiled at the guns, and fought out the fight to the last; with the exception of one of them, who was killed at his post by one of his own country's balls.[72]

Compare Leech's version in *Thirty Years from Home, or a Voice from the Main Deck:*

The Americans among our number felt quite disconcerted, at the necessity which compelled them to fight against their own countrymen. One of them, named John Card, as brave a seaman as ever trod a plank, ventured to present himself to the Captain, as a prisoner, frankly declaring his objections to fight. That officer, very ungenerously, ordered him to his quarters, threatening to shoot him if he made the request again. Poor fellow! He obeyed the unjust command, and was killed by a shot from his own countrymen. This fact is more disgraceful to the captain of the Macedonian, than even the loss of his ship. It was a gross and a palpable violation of the rights of man.[73]

Another barbarity of war provoked a bitter comment from Melville:

Nor seems it a practice warranted by the Sermon on the Mount, for the officer of a battery, in time of battle, to stand over his men with his drawn sword (as was done in the *Macedonian*), and run through on the spot the first seaman who showed a semblance of fear. Tawney told me that he distinctly heard this order given by the English captain to his officers of divisions.[74]

Compare Leech:

A few of the junior midshipmen were stationed below, on the berth deck, with orders, given in our hearing, to shoot any man who attempted to run from his quarters.[75]

Tawney, in pointing out to Melville the place where he was stationed, said:

"This part of the ship . . . we called the *slaughter-house* on board the *Macedonian*. Here the men fell, five and six at a time. . . . About the hatchways it looked like a butcher's stall; bits of human flesh sticking in the ring-bolts. A pig that ran about the decks escaped unharmed, but his hide was so clotted with blood, from rooting among the pools of gore, that when the ship struck the sailors hove the animal overboard, swearing it would be rank cannibalism to eat him."

Another quadruped, a goat, lost its forelegs in this fight.[76]

Compare Leech:

Certainly there was nothing very inspiriting in the aspects of things where I was stationed. So terrible had been the work of destruction round us, it was termed the slaughter-house. Not only had we had several boys and men killed or wounded, but several of the guns were disabled. [Six deaths described.] . . . Even a poor goat, kept by the officers for her milk, did not escape the general carnage; her hind legs were shot off, and poor Nan was thrown overboard.[77]

Leech recounts one moving scene where a sailor heaved a dead comrade overboard, talking to the corpse all the while, with tears streaming down his face. Melville makes much of a similar scene:

The captain of the next gun . . . turned over the heap of bodies to see who they were; when, perceiving an old messmate who had sailed with him in many cruises, he burst into tears, and, taking the corpse up in his arms, and going with it to the side, held it over the water a moment, and eyeing it, cried, "Oh God! Tom!"—"D——n your prayers over that thing! overboard with it, and down to your gun!" roared a wounded lieutenant. The order was obeyed, and the heart-stricken sailor returned to his post.[78]

Melville describes the dismantled condition of the *Macedonian* at the close of the battle:

At length, having lost her fore and main topmasts, and her mizen-mast [*sic*] having been shot away to the deck, and her fore-yard lying in two pieces on her shattered forecastle, and in a hundred places having been *hulled* with round shot, the English frigate was reduced to the last extremity.[79]

Compare Leech:

Our head braces were shot away; the fore and main topmasts were gone; the mizzen mast hung over the stern, having carried several men over in its fall: we were in the state of a complete wreck.[80]

The foolhardy stubbornness of a lieutenant at the time of surrender gets anything but praise from Melville:

According to the negro, Tawney, when the captain of the *Macedonian* —seeing that the *Neversink* had his vessel completely in her power— gave the word to strike the flag, one of his officers, a man hated by the seamen for his tyranny, howled out the most terrific remonstrances, swearing that, for his part, he would not give up, but was for sinking the *Macedonian* alongside the enemy. Had he been captain, doubtless he would have done so; thereby gaining the name of a hero in this world;—but what would they have called him in the next.[81]

And so Leech:

Any further resistance was therefore folly. So, in spite of the hot-brained lieutenant, Mr. Hope, who advised them [the council of officers] not to strike, but to sink alongside, it was determined to strike our bunting.[82]

In the confusion after the surrender, Melville depicts a harrowing anticlimax:

It is generally the case in a man-of-war when she strikes her flag that all discipline is at an end, and the men for a time are ungovernable. This was so on board of the English frigate. The spirit-room was broken open, and buckets of grog were passed along the decks, where many of the wounded were lying between the guns. These mariners seized the buckets, and, spite of all remonstrances, gulped down the burning spirits, till, as Tawney said, the blood suddenly spirted out of their wounds, and they fell dead to the deck.[83]

Leech's version is not quite so gory:

Most of the men who remained [on board the *Macedonian* after the battle] were unfit for any service, having broken into the spirit room and made themselves drunk. . . . What was worse than all, however, was the folly of the sailors in giving spirits to their wounded messmates, since it only served to aggravate their distress. . . . [One brave fellow had lost an arm.] Cheerful and gay as he was, he soon died. His companions gave him rum; he was attacked by fever and died. Thus his messmates actually killed him with kindness.[84]

Both accounts say that Commodore Decatur refused to take Captain Carden's sword. In explaining this on the basis of their previous friendship, Melville says:

Perhaps the victor remembered the dinner-parties that he and the Englishman had enjoyed together in Norfolk, just previous to the breaking out of hostilities—and while both were in command of the very frigates now crippled on the sea. The *Macedonian,* it seems, had gone into Norfolk with dispatches. *Then* they had laughed and joked over their wine, and a wager of a beaver hat was said to have been made between them upon the event of the hostile meeting of their ships.[85]

Commenting on the same visit to Norfolk before the war, Leech says:

Our officers . . . exchanged visits with Commodore Decatur and his officers, of the United States frigate, then lying at Norfolk. These visits were seasons of much wassail and feasting. I remember overhearing Commodore Decatur and the Captain of the Macedonian joking about taking each other's ship, in case of a war; and some of the crew said that a bet of a beaver hat passed between them on the issue of such a conflict. They probably little thought that this joking over a wine-cup, would afterwards be cracked in earnest, in a scene of blood and carnage.[86]

There is no external evidence that Melville read Leech's *Thirty Years from Home, or a Voice from the Main Deck,* but it is a reasonably safe guess that he did. Not only do the two accounts square with surprising consistency, but the sum and substance of everything that Melville puts in Tawney's mouth can be found in Leech's version. Of course, it is perfectly possible that such a person as Tawney was actually a shipmate of Melville and that the apparent borrowing is in fact only the natural agreement between two eyewitness accounts. If the former be true, here is a most unusual revelation of how Melville gathered the materials of his art; if the latter, here is an equally unhoped-for check on the accuracy of Tawney's intimate version of the human side of the battle between the frigates *United States* and *Macedonian,* during the War of 1812.

These trivialities, together with one major incident and the historical episode just cited, exhaust the list of possible material in *White-Jacket* that is specifically accurate. Although they prove that Melville could cleave to literalness when it suited him, yet their very existence, and their paucity, is conclusive proof that little of what went into the making of *White-Jacket* can be accepted as straightforward autobiography. His alterations and embellishments have already been noticed. Now, in strong contrast with his few literal transcriptions from life will be set his most powerful romantic episodes, which, it will be seen, were wholesale inventions. Nothing will be labeled as such, however, unless the ship's records flatly contradict it, or unless their failure to record it is strong presumptive evidence that it did not happen.

CHAPTER XV

"WHITE-JACKET" AS ROMANCE

C HANCE has preserved a copy of the first American edition
of *White-Jacket* that was owned by a shipmate of Melville
on the homeward-bound voyage. On one of the preliminary leaves of his copy, the owner, "Ha[rrison] Robertson," has left
a penciled comment of considerable interest and of unique value
because his note could not have been motivated by any of the ulterior purposes that attend more public utterances. His analysis of
White-Jacket, within the year after its publication, was brief but
to the point:

Some of the incidents & characters described in this book, occurred on
board the Frigate "United States"—in which I returned home, via Cape
Horn, in 1844. Other incidents described are either purely imaginary,
or happened at some other time & place— The author probably has
made his book, not from personal experience wholly, but has patched
together scraps picked up from some other person's journal, or conversation— Most of the characters & incidents described are grossly
caricatured, or exaggerated.[1]

This commentator was indeed well qualified, by reason of his official position, to pass judgment on the amount of fact and fiction
that went into the composition of Melville's narrative, for he was
"Harrison Robertson, Captain's Clerk," listed as No. 76 on the
Muster Rolls of the frigate *United States* during the voyage from
Callao, Peru, to Boston.[2] The correctness of his remarks on the
factual matter which Melville drew from his actual experiences on
this man-of-war has been evaluated in the preceding chapter. Ex-
emplification of the "purely imaginary" portions to which he refers will now be given. For it will be seen that, following closely
the route of the homeward-bound cruise, Melville's inventions
multiply in a soaring crescendo, from light comic preludes to the

stirring and eloquent climaxes by which *White-Jacket* is remembered.

"We were not many days out of port," says Melville, "when a rumor was set afloat that dreadfully alarmed many tars. It was this: that owing to some unprecedented oversight in the purser, or some equally unprecedented remissness in the naval storekeeper at Callao, the frigate's supply of that delectable beverage called 'grog' was well-nigh expended." After dilating on the extravagant love of the average seaman for his drink—to many of whom "the thought of their daily tots forms a perpetual perspective of ravishing landscapes, indefinitely receding in the distance"— and after deprecating the tendency of the Navy to become an asylum for all drunkards, Melville records some of the comments upon the receipt of this tragic news:

"The grog gone!" roared an old sheet-anchor man.
"Oh Lord! what a pain in my stomach!" cried a main-top man.
"It's worse than the cholera!" cried a man of the after-guard.
"I'd sooner the water-casks would give out!" said a captain of the hold.
"Are we ganders and geese, that we can live without grog?" asked a corporal of marines.
"Ay, we must now drink with the ducks!" cried a quarter-master.
"Not a tot left?" groaned a waister.
"Not a toothful!" sighed a holder, from the bottom of his boots.
Yes, the fatal intelligence proved true. The drum was no longer heard rolling the men to the tub, and deep gloom and dejection fell like a cloud. The ship was like a great city when some terrible calamity has overtaken it. The men stood apart, in groups, discussing their woes, and mutually condoling. No longer, of still moonlight nights, was the song heard from the giddy tops; and few and far between were the stories that were told.[3]

This mock tragedy finds no entry on any of the ship's records. Further, the Log Book furnishes contradictory evidence. At the time of Melville's enlistment at Honolulu, the ship's supply of whiskey on hand was 4,840 gallons. Weekly entries of the amount expended occur throughout the entire cruise with unvarying regularity. The last entry, on September 21, 1844, shows 1,559 gallons

on hand. This indicates an average of about ten gallons a day consumed, certainly a sufficient quantity to give the five hundred
members of the crew their "tot," or half-gill, twice a day. Not only
did the grog supply not give out, but there was an excess of over
a thousand gallons to be discharged to the storekeeper at Boston.[4]

Having once invented this melancholy mishap, Melville uses
it as a vehicle for several amusing scenes. For example, during
their "prohibition" days, he says, ten men were reported to be in-
toxicated, though everyone was at a loss to tell where they had obtained their liquor. Soon the secret leaked out that the purser's
steward had been selling them Eau de Cologne from a supply he
had brought out clandestinely to sell to South Sea natives. For
several days thereafter:

> The whole frigate smelled like a lady's toilet; the very tar-buckets were
> fragrant; and from the mouth of many a grim, grizzled old quarter-
> gunner came the most fragrant of breaths. The amazed lieutenants went
> about snuffing up the gale. . . . It was as if we were sailing by some
> odoriferous shore, in the vernal season of violets. Sabæan odours!
> > "For many a league,
> > Cheered with the grateful smell, old ocean smiled."
> But, alas! all this perfume could not be wasted for nothing; and the
> master-at-arms and ship's corporals, putting this and that together, very
> soon burrowed into the secret. The purser's steward was called to ac-
> count, and no more lavender punches and cologne toddies were drunk
> on board the *Neversink*.[5]

One feels certain that such wholesale drunkenness, as well as such
flagrant misconduct on the part of a petty officer, would have been
recorded in the Log Book as a matter of routine, had they been
real.

After chafing for some weeks over the stoppage of the grog—
particularly while rounding Cape Horn, where it was customary
to double the daily allowance as an offset to the cold weather—
Melville temporarily breaks the grog fast with a pleasant chapter
entitled: "Some Superior old 'London Dock' from the Wine-
Coolers of Neptune." Booming along towards Rio, he says, the
"Neversink" discovered some dark objects floating in the sea. The

ship's headway was stopped, a cutter was lowered, and soon "five goodly puncheons . . . covered with minute barnacles and shell-fish, and streaming with seaweed" were hoisted out of the water:

How long they had been tossing about, and making voyages for the benefit of the flavour of their contents, no one could tell. . . . They were *struck* into the gun-deck, where the eager crowd being kept off by sentries, the cooper was called with his tools.

"Bung up, and bilge free!" he cried in an ecstasy, flourishing his driver and hammer.

Upon clearing away the barnacles and moss, a flat sort of shellfish was found, closely adhering, like a California shell, right over one of the bungs. Doubtless this shell-fish had there taken up his quarters, and thrown his own body into the breach, in order the better to preserve the precious contents of the cask. The bystanders were breathless, when at last this puncheon was canted over and a tin-pot held to the orifice. What was to come forth? salt water or wine? But a rich purple tide soon settled the question, and the lieutenant assigned to taste it, with a loud and satisfactory smack of his lips, pronounced it Port! [A night of anticipation and uncertainty passed for the seamen.]

But next day all hands were electrified by the old familiar sound—so long hushed—of the drum rolling to grog.

After that the port was served out twice a day, till all was expended.[6]

Certainly the chatty Ship's Scribe would not have overlooked so ripe an opportunity for comment; and a Log Book so circumstantial as to record, "Lowered Whale Boat and picked up Hammock accidentally knocked overboard," [7] would not have missed this far richer haul. But they contain no mention of such an incident.

To compensate for the lack of grog for celebration purposes, says Melville, Captain Claret gave permission to the sailors, as the ship neared the latitude of Cape Horn, to get up any sort of amateur theatricals they desired with which to honor the approaching Fourth of July. Accordingly the stage-struck portion of the crew began rehearsals, and against the mainmast was tacked a placard, drawn up by Lemsford the poet, announcing that:

The managers of the Cape Horn Theatre beg leave to inform the inhabitants of the Pacific and Southern Oceans that, on the afternoon of

the Fourth of July 184—, they will have the honour to present the admired drama of

THE OLD WAGON PAID OFF!

Jack Chase . . . . Percy Royal-Mast.
Stars of the first magnitude.[8]

Captain Claret read and censored the manuscript, and, at the discharge of a marine's musket, the curtain rose at the appointed
hour. Then, frequently interrupted by uncontrollable bursts of
applause, Jack Chase starred to his own, and Melville's, heart's
content. As the romantic farce reached its climax, however, the
rowdy scene was brought to an unexpected end by the sudden appearance of a black squall on the horizon and the beating of the
drum calling all hands to quarters. The officers all "shipped their
quarter-deck faces," and holiday frolic gave way to the serious business of saving the ship. This pleasant episode, obviously designed
to heighten the stature of Melville's hero, was just as imaginary as
its setting; for the Fourth of July was celebrated in port at Callao,
just before sailing for home, merely by the firing of a national
salute. And if any amateur theatricals were staged on board the
United States during this cruise, no record of them, official or
otherwise, has survived. To dispel any lingering doubt, it may be
pointed out that Melville's censorious shipmate, Harrison Robertson, in his copy of *White-Jacket* opposite this chapter wrote with
finality the single word: "Fiction." [9]

By far the largest number of Melville's inventions are given a
setting in the Bay of Rio de Janeiro. It has already been pointed
out how he fictitiously prolongs the stay at this port from the actual one week to many weeks, and how most of the events put in
this setting—aggregating more than a fourth of the entire book—
are likewise manufactured. Some of these are mere details, such as
Melville's appointment as gigman to the captain, an honor which
he evaded, and the commodore's visit to a Portuguese marquis at
Praya Grande.[10] But several of them are significant contributions
to the picturesqueness and the dramatic appeal of *White-Jacket.*

Perhaps the most eloquent of all is Jack Chase's supplication
for a day's liberty on shore for "the people." With submissive at-

titude and a gallant flourish of his tarpaulin hat he presented the
petition of the commoners, breaking through the captain's reserve with quotations from Shakespeare, Waller, and Pope, and
beguiling the commodore's vanity with compliments to his "honourable wound, received in glorious battle." Two days later a
twenty-four-hour shore leave was granted, and Melville, with the
noble Chase "and a few other discreet and gentlemanly topmen,
. . . went ashore on the first day." The ensuing dissipations in Rio
of both officers and men, together with a few amusing incidents, are
then recounted, not without an occasional moral reflection.[11] The
Log Book, however, shows that no shore leave was given to any of
the ship's crew during the week's stay at Rio; it would have taken
longer than a week to get all four quarter watches on shore and
bring them back. Although it is recorded on one day that some
liberty men were sent on board the various ships of the American
squadron lying in port, these were probably a few unfortunate ones
who had missed their liberty on the Pacific coast for one reason or
another. [12] It will be remembered that the ship's company did have
a forty-eight-hour leave at Callao during Christmas week, 1843, and
another of twenty-four hours at the same port just before sailing
on July 6, 1844. But if Melville ever set foot on shore at Rio, it must
have been on his outward-bound voyage; and so the self-imposed
restriction of his narrative to "the world in a man-of-war," passing
over even Rio, "the bay of all beauties," was a practical as well as
an artistic limitation.[13] This invention, then, besides adding another laurel to Jack Chase's heroic brow, was undoubtedly for the
purpose of describing the institution of shore leave; it is incredible
that Melville would have passed up so lightly the picturesque sights
of Rio if he had really seen them on this trip.

Although the author of *White-Jacket* denies his readers the
privilege of vicarious sight-seeing on shore, he brings the color and
pomp of Brazil to the crew of the "Neversink" in a visit of state
made by the young Emperor, Dom Pedro II, and suite. This brilliant scene was likewise a pure fiction, though the lavish and detailed descriptions certainly give it a convincing verisimilitude.
Perhaps the recollections of some of Melville's fellow seamen, who

had caught a glimpse of his imperial majesty during the outward-bound cruise, helped him; [14] perhaps he drew something from his own recollections of the equally imposing regality of the King of the Sandwich Islands.[15] Besides atmosphere, this gorgeous spectacle furnishes subject matter for some democratic and even anarchic comments by Melville through the mouths of his Yankee seamen in the tops.[16] But no such royal visit was actually paid to the frigate *United States* during her brief stay in Rio on this cruise, and, so far as the records show, Melville never laid eyes on the Emperor of all the Brazils.[17]

Beyond doubt the most dramatic invention set in the splendors of Rio Bay, and one of the most memorable passages in the entire pageant of *White-Jacket,* is the brutal scene depicting the amputation of a seaman's leg by the Surgeon of the Fleet, "Cadwallader Cuticle, M. D.," and the subsequent, and perhaps unnecessary, death of the patient. Since to official eyes such an episode would have implied no especial brutality, there is no reason why it should have passed unrecorded on the ship's books. Moreover, both the sentry's shot which caused the fatal wound and the death of the seaman consequent upon the operation must necessarily have been recorded as a matter of official routine. But of the six men who died on board the *United States* during Melville's residence, one died of "Inflamation of the Bowells," two of "Consumption of the Lungs," one of "Disease of the Heart," one "Apoletic [apoplectic?]," and one "Fell Overboard." [18] And none of these deaths occurred in Rio. The conclusion is unavoidable that Melville fabricated out of whole cloth.

Naval surgery was undoubtedly crude enough a hundred years ago. Nathaniel Ames recorded that fifty-two men died during a three-and-a-half-year cruise on board the *United States* twenty years before, and most of these deaths he lays to the incompetence of the medical department.[19] But conditions on land were not much better in the days before ether and aseptic surgery. And whereas it is one thing to launch a virulent propagandist attack from authentically observed grievances, it is quite another to base such an attack on a purely hypothetical case. If Dr. William Johnson, the surgeon of the Pacific squadron, ever recognized himself in the grotesque caricature of "Cadwallader Cuticle, M. D.," he must have been dismayed at finding this barbaric role hung upon him.[20] There is no discounting the power of this scene as propaganda, however, just as there was no inconsiderable effect in the melodramatic death of Uncle Tom at the hands of Simon Legree two years later.

From beginning to end Melville gives himself without stint to the unfolding of this drama. Swift could not have made the details more revolting or the comments more sardonic. At a mock consultation of surgeons Cuticle forces the operation over the better judgment of his assistants, merely because his professional hand itches for employment. The amputation itself is a libel on unimpassioned science. With incredible inhumanity Surgeon Cuticle interrupts his butchery at the most painful climax and "turning to the assistant surgeons, he said, 'Would any of you young gentlemen like to apply the saw? A splendid subject!' " After a bungling novice has used the helpless seaman's leg for a few minutes of experimentation, Cuticle snatches the saw from his hands and dispatches the operation with professional zeal—if not skill. He has just announced that the limb will be on the table for further examination on the morrow, when it is discovered that he has dispatched his patient as well as the operation. "The body, also, gentlemen, at ten precisely," is his only comment as he takes his leave from the scene. Melville devotes over twenty pages to the elaboration of this tragedy. His biographers have also made much of it; and though one has recognized it as satire rather than fact, another treats it as one of the most lurid experiences of his life.[21] Certainly an imaginary nightmare could have had no effect on even Melville's spiritual biography!

For this scene Melville certainly owes an inspirational debt, at least, to Smollett's account of his experiences as a surgeon's mate in the British navy, as recorded in *Roderick Random* (Chapters XXIV–XXXVIII). In the first place, one is struck by the fact that the surgeon's first mate in Smollett's story was named "Cadwallader Morgan." Barring unlikely coincidence, Melville undoubtedly found a suggestion here for the stage name of his chief surgeon, "Cadwallader Cuticle." Moreover, the general tone and content of Smollett's complaints against the incompetence, brutality, and negligence of the medical service in the British Navy are congenial with Melville's animadversions. An instance of this is found in the former's description of the "hospital" on board ship:

Here I saw about fifty miserable distempered wretches, suspended in rows, so huddled one upon another, that no more than fourteen inches space was allotted for each with his bed and bedding; and deprived of the light of day, as well as of fresh air; breathing nothing but a noisome atmosphere of morbid steams exhaling from their own excrements and diseased bodies, devoured with vermin hatched in the filth that surrounded them, and destitute of every convenience necessary for people in that helpless condition.[22]

Even this deplorable treatment of the sick was mild, however, as compared with what followed when "Captain Oakum" came on board and took command. He declared that there should be no sick on board the "Thunder" while he was her captain, and straightway ordered all the patients to be brought on deck—many at the cost of their lives—for inspection. The chief surgeon then proceeded to decide upon the soundness of their complaints: one was ordered to receive a dozen lashes at the gangway for feigning sickness, but died before the discipline could be executed; another was declared fit for duty, "but being resolved to disgrace the doctor, died upon the forecastle next day"; a third, suffering from pleurisy, had exercise at the pump prescribed for him to promote expectoration, but "in less than half an hour he was suffocated with a deluge of blood that issued from his lungs"; a fourth was pronounced fit for duty and ordered into the rigging, from which he fell into the sea by reason of his weakness and was drowned. At this point, even Smollett felt called upon to halt a scene of such incredible brutality, concluding:

It would be tedious and disagreeable to describe the fate of every miserable object that suffered by the inhumanity and ignorance of the captain and surgeon, who so wantonly sacrificed the lives of their fellow-creatures. Many were brought up in the height of fevers, and rendered delirious by the injuries they received in this way. Some gave up the ghost in the presence of their inspectors; and others, who were ordered to their duty, languished a few days at work among their fellows, and then departed without any ceremony. On the whole, the number of the sick was reduced to less than a dozen.²³

But even though Melville may have taken the cue for his complaints against medical abuses in the Navy from Smollett, he had the good sense to tone down his descriptions; for, deplorable as the conditions were in Melville's time, they showed a vast improvement in humaneness of attitude if not in actual skill over the conditions of a century before.

Roderick Random provides another scene, however, that may have been of more direct use to the author of *White-Jacket*. "Jack Rattlin," an ordinary seaman on board the "Thunder," fell from a yardarm to the deck during a hurricane and fractured his leg. The chief surgeon was immediately called into consultation:

He examined the fracture and the wound, and concluding, from a livid colour extending itself upon the limb, that a mortification would ensue, resolved to amputate the leg immediately. This was a dreadful sentence to the patient, who, recruiting himself with a quid of tobacco, pronounced with a woeful countenance, "What! is there no remedy, doctor? —must I be dock'd?—can't you splice it?" "Assuredly Doctor Mackshane," said the first mate, "with submission, and deference, and veneration, to your superior abilities, and opportunities, and stations, look you, I do apprehend, and conjecture, and aver, that there is no occasion nor necessity to smite off this poor man's leg." . . . Mackshane, very much incensed at his mate's differing in opinion from him so openly, answered, that he was not bound to give an account of his practice to him; and, in a peremptory tone, ordered him to apply the tourniquet, at the sight of which, Jack, starting up, cried, "Avast, avast! d——n my heart, if you clap your nippers on me, till I know wherefore! Mr. Random, won't you lend a hand towards saving my precious limb? . . ." This pathetic address to me, joined to my inclination to serve my honest friend, and the reasons I had to believe there was no danger in delaying the amputation, induced me to declare myself of the first mate's opinion, and affirm, that the preternatural colour of the skin was owing to an inflamation occasioned by a contusion, and common in all such cases, without any indication of an approaching gangrene. Morgan [the first mate] . . . asked Thomson's sentiments in the matter, in hopes of strengthening our association with him too; but he, being of a meek disposition, and either dreading the enmity of the surgeon, or speaking the dictates of his own judgment, in a modest manner, espoused the opinion of Mackshane, who, by this time, having consulted with himself, determined to act in such a manner as to screen himself from censure, and at the same time revenge himself on us for our arrogance in contradicting him. With this view he asked if we would undertake to cure the leg at out peril—that is, be answerable for the consequence. [We agreed] . . . , and we had the satisfaction of not only preserving the poor fellow's leg, but likewise of rendering the doctor contemptible among the ship's company, who had all their eyes on us during the course of this cure, which was completed in six weeks.

Although Smollett's scene takes a different turn from Melville's, and no actual amputation follows, there is certainly a strong resemblance in the main purport of the two episodes; in both, the arrogance, brutality, and ignorance of the ship's surgeon is held up to ridicule—especially his effort to brow-beat his assistants into submission; in both, there is recognizable the hand of the propagandist, satirizing naval abuses in the hope of bringing about reforms. And Melville's amputation scene, throughout, has a distinct flavor of Smollett's style, with which we know he was acquainted, for he tells us in *Omoo* that he read his novels with great relish.[24]

On the heels of this tragedy comes one of the most rollicking scenes that Melville ever invented, a comic interlude which is typical of the dominant mood in which *White-Jacket* was written —the good humor of high animal spirits. This is the episode of the "Massacre of the Beards" and the bloodless "mutiny" which accompanied it. It is undoubtedly true that seamen in the United States Navy resented even the spasmodic efforts that were made at this period to standardize their uniforms and beards. A. T. Mahan calls attention to the periodically annoying regulations that were passed in the old Navy of sails concerning the size and style of beards, one of which, he remarks, furnished Melville with a striking chapter.[25] In the *Regulations for the Uniform and Dress of the Navy of the United States* approved on February 19, 1841—before the *United States* sailed from Norfolk—it was specified that

The hair of all persons belonging to the Navy, when in actual service, is to be kept short. No part of the beard is to be worn long excepting whiskers, which shall not descend more than an inch below the tip of the ear and thence in a line toward the corners of the mouth.[26]

Since this restriction of the personal masculine adornment of seamen was passed while George E. Badger was Secretary of the Navy, the hated standarized beards received the epithet of "Badger Whiskers." This was, of course, the regulation that Melville had in mind when he said:

According to a then recent ordinance at Washington, the beards of both officers and seamen were to be accurately laid out and surveyed, and on no account must come lower than the mouth, so as to correspond with the Army standard—a regulation directly opposed to the theocratical law laid down in the nineteenth chapter and twenty-seventh verse of Leviticus, where it is expressly ordained, *"Thou shalt not mar the corners of thy beard."* . . .

At last, when we had crossed the Northern Tropic, and were standing up to our guns at evening quarters, and when the setting sun, streaming in at the port-holes, lit up every hair, till, to an observer on the quarter-deck, the two long even lines of beards seemed one dense grove; in that evil hour it must have been, that a cruel thought entered into the heart of our captain.

A pretty set of savages, thought he, am I taking home to America; people will think them all catamounts and Turks. Besides, now that I think of it, it's against the law. It will never do. They must be shaven and shorn—that's flat.[27]

Melville merely postponed the enforcement of an actual law of 1841 long enough to bring the ensuing mock tragedy within the chronological scope of *White-Jacket*. For, according to Rear-Admiral Benjamin F. Sands, it had already reached the far-off Mediterranean squadron by the spring of 1843.[28] Moreover, William H. Meyers, on board the *Cyane* just two months out of Norfolk on the present cruise to the Pacific, remarks: "January 2, 1842. Started the badger whiskers on my jowls." And again, at Honolulu, he notes: "September 15, 1843. Shattuck 3rd. Luff ordered to cut his whiskers off or suffer an arrest." [29] The orders, then, were known to the Pacific squadron before sailing from the United States; and even this last recalcitrant offender on board the *Cyane* was brought to the mark a full year before anyone on board the *United States* was even apprized of the existence of the law, according to Melville! He explains this by reference to the indulgent nature of Captain Claret:

Throughout the cruise, many of the officers had expressed their abhorrence of the impunity with which the most extensive plantations of hair were cultivated under their very noses; and they frowned upon every beard with even greater dislike. They said it was unseamanlike; not *shipshape;* in short, it was disgraceful to the Navy. But as Captain Claret said nothing, and as the officers, of themselves, had no authority to preach a crusade against whiskerandoes, the Old Guard on the forecastle still complacently stroked their beards, and the sweet youths of the after-guard still lovingly threaded their fingers through their curls.[30]

But whatever the disposition of the captain, it will be remembered that the *United States* was the flagship; and one feels sure that Commodore Jones, always a stickler for naval discipline and even punctilio, would not have tolerated unlawful whiskers on board his model ship for a single month after sailing from Norfolk.

There was a purpose behind Melville's invention, however, for he makes it a vehicle for his second long attack on the institution of flogging. A number of rebels, chiefly old sailors, who refused to comply with the ordinance were brought to the mast and unhatted:

Such an array of beards! spade-shaped, hammer-shaped, dagger-shaped, triangular, square, peaked, round, hemispherical, and forked. But chief among them all was old Ushant's, the ancient captain of the forecastle. Of a Gothic venerableness, it fell upon his breast like a continual iron-gray storm.

Ah! old Ushant, Nestor of the crew! it promoted my longevity to behold you.

All of them finally gave in except this one staunch old hero, who refused to have his streaming beard trimmed. The next day he was flogged for his stubbornness:

"Lay on! I'll see his backbone!" roared the captain in a sudden fury. . . .

One, two, three, four, five, six, seven, eight, nine, ten, eleven, twelve lashes were laid on the back of that heroic old man. He only bowed over his head . . . [and muttered under his breath,] " 'tis no dishonour when he who would dishonour you only dishonours himself."

"What says he?" cried the captain; "what says that tarry old philosopher with the smoking back? Tell it to me, sir, if you dare! Sentry, take that man back to the brig. Stop! John Ushant, you have been captain of the forecastle; I break you. And now you go into the brig, there to remain till you consent to have that beard taken off." [And there he stayed until the end of the cruise, in confinement.] But he . . . spent many hours in braiding his beard, and interweaving with it strips of red bunting, as if he desired to draw out and adorn the thing which had triumphed over all opposition.[31]

But no such bloodless mutiny occurred on this particular cruise, for the names of the offenders must certainly have turned up on the ship's punishment lists.[32]

A second reason why this episode of the "Massacre of the Beards" was invented was for comic relief and for the sake of sheer merriment. A matchless specimen of Melville's bright foolery is Jack Chase's eloquent funeral oration over his own nut-brown beard when he surrendered it up to the executioner:

"My friend, I trust your scissors are consecrated. Let them not touch this beard if they have yet to be dipped in holy water; beards are sacred things, barber. Have you no feeling for beards, my friend? think of it;" and mournfully he laid his deep-dyed, russet cheek upon his hand. "Two summers have gone by since my chin has been reaped. I was in Coquimbo then, on the Spanish Main; and when the husbandman was sowing his autumnal grain on the Vega, I started this blessed beard; and when the vinedressers were trimming their vines in the vineyards, I first trimmed it to the sound of a flute. Ah! barber, have you no heart? This beard has been caressed by the snow-white hand of the lovely Tomasita of Tombez—the Castillian belle of all Lower Peru. Think of *that*, barber! I have worn it as an officer on the quarterdeck of a Peruvian man-of-war. I have sported it at brilliant fandangoes in Lima. I have been alow and aloft with it at sea. Yea, barber! it has streamed like an admiral's pennant at the mast-head of this same gallant frigate, the *Neversink!* Oh! barber, barber! it stabs me to the heart! Talk not of hauling down your ensigns and standards when vanquished—what is *that*, barber! to striking the flag that Nature herself has nailed to the mast!" [33]

One cannot forego a regret, in passing, that this native gift for high comedy was abandoned, two years later, for the disastrous attempt at psychological fiction in *Pierre*.

None of the inventions listed so far concern Melville himself, except incidentally. But the two remaining, the two most magnificent of all, are recorded as lurid personal experiences and are so treated by all his biographers, who then belabor themselves to show the far-reaching effects of these experiences on Melville's spiritual development.[34] The first of these was Melville's near-flogging, as recorded in *White-Jacket,* one day during that otherwise "delightful yachting" from Rio to the Equator, and the remission of his punishment just in time to keep him from becoming a murderer and a suicide. The order was given for all hands to tack ship. For such occasions every seaman in a man-of-war is supposed to have a particular station assigned to him. "But among the various *numbers* and *stations* given to me by the senior lieutenant, when I first came on board the frigate," says Melville, "he had altogether omitted informing me of my particular place [for this maneuver]." [35] Consequently, when no one let go the weather-lift of the main yard at the proper time, Captain Claret investigated the cause of the ensuing confusion. On the station-bill Melville's name was found opposite the post in question, and, a moment after, this unlucky name was bawled out by the boatswain's mates at all the hatchways.

All hands were called to witness punishment. Charged by the captain with having been absent from his proper station, Melville replied that he had never been assigned to any such place. But his solemn disclaimer was thrown in his teeth, and the captain ordered him to the gratings to be flogged. Melville tells his own emotional reactions incomparably:

There are times when wild thoughts enter a man's heart, when he seems almost irresponsible for his act and his deed. . . . My blood seemed clotting in my veins; I felt icy cold at the tips of my fingers, and a dimness was before my eyes. But through that dimness the boatswain's mate, scourge in hand, loomed like a giant, and Captain Claret, and the blue sea seen through the opening at the gangway, showed with an awful vividness. I cannot analyze my heart, though it then stood still within me. But the thing that swayed me to my purpose was not altogether the thought that Captain Claret was about to degrade me, and that I had taken an oath with my soul that he should not. No, I felt my man's manhood so bottomless within me, that no word, no blow, no scourge of Captain Claret could cut me deep enough for that. I but swung to an instinct in me—the instinct diffused through all animated nature, the same that prompts even a worm to turn under the heel. Locking souls with him, I meant to drag Captain Claret from this earthly tribunal of his to that of Jehovah, and let him decide between us. . . . The privilege, inborn and inalienable, that every man has, of dying himself, and inflicting death upon another, was not given to us without a purpose. These are the last resources of an insulted and unendurable existence.[36]

At this critical juncture a most unprecedented thing happened. "Corporal Colbrook," the foremost man among the marines, stepped forward and defended the culprit, saying that he was a most dutiful sailor and would not have been found absent from his station if he had known where it was. Jack Chase, foremost among the seamen, seconded this defense, deferentially but firmly. Captain Claret accepted this most unusual breach of naval procedure with apparent unconcern, dismissed Melville, and sauntered aft to his cabin—"while I, who, in the desperation of my soul, had but just escaped being a murderer and a suicide, almost burst into tears of thanksgiving where I stood." [37]

Of course such an occurence, however significant to Melville himself, would have been of no especial concern to the officers of a man-of-war, but it would have been officially recorded as a matter of routine. The Log Book, on the other hand, reveals that Melville consistently kept himself off the ship's punishment lists, not even receiving a reprimand throughout the entire cruise. To the objection that such an extraordinary matter as the remission of punishment would naturally be omitted as a confession of weak discipline, the Log Book has sufficient answer in the pardon of Jack Chase's deserved punishment for desertion, and, further in the remission of the last eleven lashes of a courtmartial sentence of fifty, imposed upon one Benjamin Furness earlier in the cruise, without assigning any reasons.[38] There is one bit of evidence that may be considered contradictory. In his personal journal kept on board the *Cyane,* William H. Meyers notes: "January 3, 1842. All hands witness punishment. Francis and Smith brought to the mast and cleared"; yet the official Log Book of the *Cyane* contains no record of this incident. But, although half-a-dozen journals, official and otherwise, have been searched, this is the only entry to be found which tells of a seaman brought to the mast and cleared; apparently it was a rare exception to normal procedure. Moreover, there is every reason to feel that even if Melville did narrowly escape both a flogging and the official recording of it, yet the author of the unofficial *Journal of a Cruise in the Frigate United States*—who was quite possibly his intimate friend "Lemsford the poet"—would certainly have found a place in his personal journal to comment on an event which so closely concerned his friends Melville and Chase.

Finally, no one acquainted with naval routine can accept Melville's account of the situation which he says brought him within range of punishment at the gangway. It is undoubtedly true that the complexity of the various assignments of a seaman on the old sailing frigate might readily have got a novice into a scrape on the first occasion when he was required to take a given station. But it is inconceivable that on every prior order to "tack ship" some other member of the crew should have filled Melville's place so that his failure to appear at his proper post could have come as a surprise to anyone after he had completed more than twelve-months' service on board. The evidence seems to indicate overwhelmingly that Melville invented this dramatic moment in his life. Yet all his biographers accept it as straightforward autobiography. One of them, after commenting on the headlong violence of Melville's passion throughout life, says that on this occasion "he seems to have been as murderously roused as at any other known moment in his life. . . . But for the timely intercessions, it is very likely that Melville would have ended that day as a suicide and a murderer." [39] Another, more interested in his writings than in his life, declares:

"It was with this moment of fury in his past that Melville, now safe, struck out [in *White-Jacket*], arguing that the lash was neither lawful nor necessary, and that it was an outrage which no man was good enough to have the right to inflict on any other, however bad." [40] An imaginary episode, however, could certainly have had no influence on Melville's life or on his writings. What occurred, apparently, was quite the reverse of this: wishing to give his propaganda against flogging the added effectiveness of personal resentment and revulsion, he simply invented a scene in which he himself was the near-victim.

The second fiction in which Melville is the chief actor is the thrilling account of his fall overboard—which, he says, occurred off the Capes of Virginia just a few days out from the home port— and his subsequent rescue. One pleasant midnight the talk of home in the maintop was interrupted by an order to set the main-topgallant stun'-sail, and one of the most difficult duties connected with this, reeving the halyards, was assigned to Melville by Jack Chase, his noble captain of the top. Melville's own account of this incident is one of the high spots in all his writing:

Having reeved the line through all the inferior blocks, I went out with it to the end of the weather-top-gallant yard-arm, and was in the act of leaning over and passing it through the suspended jewel-block there, when the ship gave a plunge in the sudden swells of the calm sea, and pitching me still further over the yard, threw the heavy skirts of my jacket right over my head, completely muffling me. Somehow I thought it was the sail that had flapped, and, under that impression, threw up my hands to drag it from my head, relying upon the sail itself to support me meanwhile. Just then the ship gave another sudden jerk, and, head foremost, I pitched from the yard. I knew where I was, from the rush of the air by my ears, but all else was a nightmare. A bloody film was before my eyes, through which, ghost-like, passed and repassed my father, mother, and sisters. An unutterable nausea oppressed me; I was conscious of gasping; there seemed no breath in my body. It was over one hundred feet that I fell—down, down, with lungs collapsed as in death. Ten thousand pounds of shot seemed tied to my head, as the irresistible law of gravitation dragged me, headforemost and straight as a die, toward the infallible centre of this terraqueous globe. All I had seen, and read, and heard, and all I had thought and felt in my life, seemed intensified in one fixed idea in my soul. But dense as this idea was, it was made up of atoms. Having fallen from the projecting yard-arm end, I was conscious of a collected satisfaction in feeling, that I should not be dashed on the deck, but would sink into the speechless profound of the sea.

With the bloody, blind film before my eyes, there was a still stranger hum in my head, as if a hornet were there; and I thought to myself, Great God! this is Death! Yet these thoughts were unmixed with alarm. Like frost-work that flashes and shifts its scared hues in the sun, all my braided, blended emotions were in themselves icy cold and calm.

So protracted did my fall seem, that I can even now recall the feeling of wondering how much longer it would be, ere all was over and I struck. Time seemed to stand still, and all the worlds seemed poised on their poles, as I fell, soul-becalmed, through the eddying whirl and swirl of the maelstrom air.

At first, as I have said, I must have been precipitated head foremost; but I was conscious, at length, of a swift, flinging motion of my limbs, which involuntarily threw themselves out, so that at last I must have fallen in a heap. This is more likely, from the circumstance, that when I struck the sea, I felt as if some one had smote me slantingly across the shoulder and along part of my right side.

As I gushed into the sea, a thunder-boom sounded in my ear; my soul seemed flying from my mouth. The feeling of death flooded over me with the billows. The blow from the sea must have turned me, so that I sank almost feet foremost through a soft, seething, foamy lull. Some current seemed hurrying me away; in a trance I yielded, and sank deeper down with a glide. Purple and pathless was the deep calm now around me, flecked by summer lightnings in an azure afar. The horrible nausea was gone; the bloody, blind film turned a pale green; I wondered whether I was yet dead, or still dying. But of a sudden some fashionless form brushed my side—some inert, soiled fish of the sea; the thrill of being alive again tingled in my nerves, and the strong shunning of death shocked me through.

For one instant an agonising revulsion came over me as I found myself utterly sinking. Next moment the force of my fall was expended; and there I hung, vibrating in the mid-deep. What wild sounds then rang in my ear! One was a soft moaning, as of low waves on the beach; the other wild and heartlessly jubilant, as of the sea in the height of a tempest. Oh soul! thou then heardest life and death: as he who stands upon the Corinthian shore hears both the Ionian and Ægean waves. The life-and-death poise soon passed; and then I found myself slowly ascending, and caught a dim glimmering of light.

Quicker and quicker I mounted; till at last I bounded up like a buoy, and my whole head was bathed in the blessed air.

I had fallen in a line with the main-mast; I now found myself nearly abreast of the mizen-mast [*sic*], the frigate slowly gliding by like a black world in the water. Her vast hull loomed out of the night, showing hundreds of seamen in the hammock nettings, some tossing over ropes, others madly flinging overboard the hammocks; but I was too far out from them immediately to reach what they threw. I essayed to swim toward the ship; but instantly I was conscious of a feeling like being pinioned in a feather bed, and, moving my hands, felt my jacket puffed out above my tight girdle with water. I strove to tear it off; but it was looped together here and there, and the strings were not then to be sundered by hand. I whipped out my knife, that was tucked at my belt, and ripped my jacket straight up and down, as if I were ripping open myself. With a violent struggle I then burst out of it, and was free. Heavily soaked, it slowly sank before my eyes.

Sink! sink! oh shroud! thought I; sink forever! accursed jacket that thou art! . . .

Being now astern of the frigate, I struck out boldly toward the elevated pole of one of the lifebuoys which had been cut away. Soon after, one of the cutters picked me up. As they dragged me out of the water into the air, the sudden transition of elements made my every limb feel like lead, and I helplessly sunk into the bottom of the boat.

Ten minutes after, I was safe on board, and springing aloft, was ordered to reeve anew the stun'-sail halyards.[41]

Thus Melville a second time narrowly escaped a fictitious death. He may have actually come face to face with death during his four years of adventure in the South Seas, but it was not by falling overboard from the yard of the frigate *United States*. Such an event would certainly have been recorded in the ship's books had it happened. Attention has already been called to the elaborate account of a fall overboard which resulted in the loss of the ship's cooper (Melville's "Bungs") and to the fall in which James Craddock (Melville's "Baldy") fractured an arm and a leg. The Log also tells of two men who fell overboard and were retrieved without injury, as in Melville's account of himself, and is even circumstantial enough to record that "Lieutenant Dulany lost a bag of clothes overboard but it couldn't be found." [42] Certainly Melville, though an obscure ordinary seaman, would have been equally worth searching for. And, though the official records might be silent on many matters that would throw interesting light on an unknown seaman whom few if any suspected of future authorship, they were businesslike and thorough in taking notice of everything and everybody that came on board or went overboard. Finally, Melville's shipmate, Harrison Robertson, scored the episode in his copy of *White-Jacket* with the definitive annotation: "Imaginary." [43]

For the skeptical, chance has turned up the unmistakable source of Melville's dramatic account of his close grappling with a watery death. Nathaniel Ames, who went on a South Sea cruise in the frigate *United States,* 1824–1827, has left a vivid description of an experience he had in Callao Bay in January, 1826, which is more than strikingly similar:

I have often read different descriptions of one's sensations when drowning, hanging, starving, being buried alive, etc. . . .

Having had, while in the Pacific, the pleasure of performing an aerial excursion, which commenced at the main cat-harpins of the frigate United States and terminated near the bottom of Callao Bay, I will take the liberty to give a history of my own voyage, and my reflections during it, for the benefit of future tumblers.

I was going aloft and had got as far as the futtock shrouds, when a ratlin broke under my feet, and I fell backwards. My first sensation was surprise; I could not imagine where I was, but soon ascertained from the rushing of the air by my ears that I was falling and that head-foremost.

Dr. Johnson says that the near approach of death wonderfully concentrates a man's ideas. I am sure it did mine for I never thought so *fast* before or since, as I did during the few seconds that I was tumbling.

In an instant the recollection came into my head that one of the quarterdeck guns (No. 20) was directly under me, and I should in all human probability, be dashed to pieces upon it. I would have given the world to vent my feelings in cries, I tried to gather my limbs together, to contract my muscles, to shrink my body into as small a compass as possible, and with unspeakable terror awaited the "death shock."

All this while there was a blood red light before my eyes, through which a thousand horrible forms were constantly gliding. Then I thought of home, and the forms of all I hold dear on earth, and many others, "strangers of distinction," beside, floated before me. Then the recollection of the infernal gun and the consequent smash across the breech of it, put all these phantoms to flight, and I felt that peculiar sickness and distress at the stomach, which it is said one experiences when on the point of undergoing a sudden and violent and painful death, and I thought to myself "surely it *must* be almost time for the shock."

A shock I certainly did receive, and that no very gentle one across the back of the head, neck and left shoulder, and in an instant all was dark and still. "It is all over," thought I, "this is the state between death and resurrection." I really thought I had passed the first and awaited with increased terror for the second, when to my utter dismay, I felt myself falling a second time, but the sensation was different; the blow that I had received had turned me, and I was descending feet foremost.

But no words can express my delight, my extacy, at finding myself *overboard,* instead of on the gun. I kept going down, down, till it appeared to me that the seven fathoms and a half, (the depth of water at our anchorage,) had more than doubled since we let go our anchor.

After a while I became stationary and soon began slowly to ascend. When I looked up, I saw high, very high above me, a dim, greenish light, which became brighter and brighter till at last I bounced on the surface like a cork.

I immediately swam to the accommodation ladder and went on board. My shoulder and neck were much bruised by striking against a spare maintop-sail yard, that was stowed over the starboard quarter, and my head felt "sort o' queer," from the sundry thumps and knocks and thumps it had received in the fall, which however were mere "cakes and gingerbread."

It may seem incredible, impossible, that I should be able to recollect my feelings after so long a time has elapsed, but my sensations are as fresh in my memory now as they were at the very moment when I was satisfactorily demonstrating, in my own unlucky person, the principles of gravitation.[44]

The surprising similarity of phraseology is certainly too close to be accidental. But the likeness is more than a mere verbal one. All of the fundamental facts tally, and the emotional content is convincingly alike in the two accounts. The differences are the natural changes that an artist would have made to heighten the dramatic effect. Melville's fall was more thrilling since it began about twice as high up on the mast; his courage in the face of death was more heroic; and his rescue was theatrically delayed while he cut his way out of his White Jacket, which nearly proved to be his shroud.

Otherwise the only difference between the two versions is Melville's elaboration of the descriptive passages. It is not only possible but quite natural and to be expected that he should have read Ames's book and every other account of cruises in the South Seas, especially when they had been made on board his own frigate. And yet, when Ames wrote down his reflections during his fall overboard "for the benefit of future tumblers," he little thought that they would chiefly be of service to a genuine *jongleur,* through whose hands they would pass—by a legerdemain known only to the profession— into a piece of dramatic prose which is one of the small master-pieces of American literature. For Melville has put his touch upon this raw material, and it is his by right of artistic conquest. However, his biographers, when they unwarily accepted his fiction for fact, did not realize that they were writing of Ames's life rather than Melville's when they remarked: "[He had now] faced life and death, not as abstractions, but as concrete events, when a sinew less of resolution would have meant his extinction . . . enveloped in the white jacket at sea"; [45] and "Melville always, even in the lowest abyss of despair, clung passionately to life." [46]

Finally, it is perhaps unnecessary as well as unkind to point out that Melville was resorting to fiction when he clothed himself with a White Jacket—instead of the official Blue Jacket required by naval regulations. On the opening page of *White-Jacket* he says:

> When our frigate lay in Callao, on the coast of Peru—her last harbour in the Pacific—I found myself without a *grego,* or sailor's surtout; and as, towards the end of a three years' cruise, no pea-jackets could be had from the purser's steward, and being bound for Cape Horn, some sort of a substitute was indispensable; I employed myself, for several days, in manufacturing an outlandish garment of my own devising, to shelter me from the boisterous weather we were so soon to encounter.[47]

But according to the clothing records of the *United States* and the storeship which accompanied the squadron, it would have been possible at any time for Melville to have drawn a pea jacket, if he had been willing to have it charged against his pay.[48] He might also have equipped himself with a similar coat at any of the South American ports touched at before rounding the Horn. But the artist preferred to invent the fitting symbol of the White Jacket to unify an otherwise disjointed narrative; throughout its ill-fated history it is the recurrent subject of comment, tragic and comic, superstitious and philosophical. Further, it served autobiographically as a coat-of-arms for the Gansevoort–Melville sense of family pride; though ostensibly mixing with the seamen as a common tar, Melville sets himself apart as a sheep from among goats, securely cloaked in the aristocratic tatters of his White Jacket.

This detailed study of *White-Jacket* should throw considerable light on Melville's methods of composition and his technique as an artist. An analysis of the evidence will enable certain conclusions to be drawn. In a dozen trivial details, and in one important incident, he transcribed from actuality as the ship's records show it. For the rest, the actual cruise of the *United States* in 1843–1844 supplied him only with the staple of his romance, and this he manipulated and embellished to suit his own purposes. He altered numerous facts, mostly names and chronology, for the purposes of anonymity, picturesqueness, and the exigencies of his narrative. A half-dozen major episodes were based upon real occurrences but were dramatically elaborated to heighten the effect of characters and scenes, or were given an invented twist at the end to point an attack on some naval abuse. Finally, more than a dozen of the most important scenes, making up almost half of the volume, were manufactured out of whole cloth. Several of them, at least, found their source in contemporary travel books; many more, perhaps, were revampings of sailor-lore, garnered from the tall tales he had heard in the maintop on pleasant nights. Some of these concoctions are the most delightful bits of foolery in this best-humored of all Melville's volumes; some are given as lurid personal experiences, traps for the unwary biographer; some are vehicles for Melville's most incisive attacks on the navy. A list of the pure inventions in *White-Jacket* is a roll call of its most powerful and memorable passages. If, then, *White-Jacket* emerges from this analysis shorn of most of its autobiographical value, it is enhanced as a piece of readable fiction; and, if Melville loses as a veracious travel writer, he gains as a propagan-

dist of high order and as an artist who could portray even his own
narrow escape from death so realistically that official records, and
the accidental discovery of a literary source, are necessary to prove
that it was imaginary.

CHAPTER XVI

"WHITE-JACKET" AS PROPAGANDA

IN CONCLUSION, it may be ventured that *White-Jacket* is something more than a plain narrative of a cruise in a man-of-war, overlaid with the romance of the sea. It is a novel of purpose, in which the plot has been supplanted by a sustained attack upon naval abuses, running beneath its comedy and tragedy, its story and picture, its fact and fiction. And at least one modern critic has recognized the true nature of the book and of Melville's propagandist purposes, declaring:

He was no longer able, or disposed, to tell as plain and consecutive a tale as he had told earlier about his Pacific paradise. . . . Nor is it [*White-Jacket*] so much a personal chronicle as a document intended for some use in the world.[1]

However slight its influence may have been as propaganda, most of the reforms advocated in its eloquent pages were subsequently effected. And however small an audience its message may have reached—a second edition was not called for until five years later, and a third not until 1892 [2]—it was sufficiently provocative to elicit comments from three rear-admirals of the United States Navy. The earliest, fullest, and bitterest of these—twenty-one foolscap pages of detailed criticism—is dated July, 1850, just four months after the publication of the book. This attempted refutation of *White-Jacket,* written by Rear-Admiral Thomas O. Selfridge, Sr., in the crucial summer that saw the passage of the Act of Congress abolishing corporal punishment in the Navy, must have been intended for immediate publication, but until 1935, apparently, it remained in manuscript.[3]

It was while Selfridge, with the rank of commander, was stationed at Boston as the Recruiting Officer of the United States Naval

Rendezvous that a copy of *White-Jacket,* just off the press, fell into his hands, with the result that his high sense of the dignity of the service prompted him to draft forthwith his reply to Melville's attack on abuses in the United States Navy. Commander Selfridge, at this time a veteran of thirty-two years on the sea (including one brief cruise on the frigate *United States*), was just the type of officer to be provoked to action by such propaganda. Naval tradition remembers him as a pious and temperate man, a seamanlike officer, and a strict disciplinarian. This last characteristic is borne out by a letter he wrote to a fellow officer a year later, at a time when many of the laced chapeaux felt that the recent abolition of corporal punishment had completely broken down the service and brought on a period of "anarchy and listlessness":

> Unless a reorganization takes place before long I am at a loss to know what we are to become. Efficiency & discipline are now mere words, & mean nothing when applied to the Navy. If a commander now goes afloat, & does his duty & makes others do theirs, he is immediately put down as a tyrant, . . . & the whole official force under him are continually striving to disregard or evade his orders.[4]

This cry of despair is the logical sequel to his vain essay to stem the tide of reform a year before—his official castigation of Melville the unofficial castigator:

> We have before us a book entitled White Jacket, or "the world in a man of war," by Herman Melville, which is presented to the reader as a correct and authentic account of the manners & customs of that world, & of the sayings & doings therein, but which is evidently intended to ridicule the etiquette & ceremonies of a ship of war, & to condemn the system of corporal punishment. . . .
> We have never known a work, professing as this does to give a true picture of men & things, in which was to be found so many misnomers, misstatements & inconsistencies—so many improbabilities, false premises & false conclusions—so much of the marvellous & absurd.—
> The author endeavours to make us believe that there is nothing but wrong & injustice within the wooden walls of a ship of war. He puts complaints into men's mouths that we never heard uttered. He denounces ceremony & etiquette, & all discipline that does not square with his own peculiar notions— He strives to convince his readers that all corporal punishment, for whatever offence, is no more nor less than

tyranny; & that men would be justified in resisting this mode of correction even so far as to bring their conduct under the title of mutiny.— This is the sum & substance of his doctrine.[5]

After this petulant prelude, Commander Selfridge undertook to discount the authority of *White-Jacket* by attacking the accuracy of Melville's knowledge of seamanship, but in this endeavor he was reduced in almost every case to hair-splitting and casuistry. In pointing out scenes where romance embellishes reality, however, he was more successful. But his chief concern was in refuting, collectively and severally, Melville's attacks on naval abuses:

White Jacket appears quite to have lost his temper when he opens his budget of complaints— His hammock, whether he is in it, or out of it, is a constant source of annoyance— He rails most bitterly against every thing that requires the least muscular exertion, or exposes him to a minimum of personal discomfort. General exercise—cleaning ship— washing clothes—scrubbing hammocks—sleeping—eating—drinking—in short, all that tends to keep a man of war healthy & efficient comes under his sledge hammer of denunciation.[6]

But of Melville's list of grievances Selfridge discussed less than half; and, aside from corporal punishment, he chose in general the most petty and the most personal for refutation.[7] Whether he considered some of Melville's major complaints as unanswerable or as too erroneous to deserve comment, it is hard to say. But it is apparent that he was just the type of man to be gulled by Melville's mock-serious thrusts as well as outraged by his more earnest satire. Over against Melville's list he outlined with approval the reforms which he declared were more generally advocated by sailors, such as higher pay and longer shore leaves. It is perhaps worthy of comment that these complaints of "Jack" (which Selfridge admitted were just) were based almost exclusively on self-interest; whereas the reforms advocated by Melville (which he set down as ill-tempered denunciations) were in almost every instance directed at general improvement in the discipline, efficiency, health, and humanity of the naval service. But Melville's proposed reforms were root-and-branch in their scope, and this naturally put every conservative naval officer on the defense.

The gravest subject of the book, corporal punishment, called forth Selfridge's most extended denunciations. Although he accused Melville of exaggerating the evils of this institution and endeavored, without much success, to undermine the authorities cited by *White-Jacket* as opposed to it, his chief argument, in the last analysis, was merely a statement of his fundamental disagreement with Melville's attitude. To the credit of this rigid disciplinarian, it must be recorded that he cherished the hope that some day the severity of this form of correction might be gradually lightened as the personnel of the Navy improved. But for the present he declared, with uncompromising redundancy: "We advocate the power of corporal punishment as essential & necessary to preserve order & insure discipline." [8] Moreover, Selfridge was not the only naval officer who took this stand. In reply to a circular issued by the Secretary of the Navy six months before, only four out of eighty-four officers had recommended the abolition of flogging.[9] Selfridge's conclusion, therefore may be considered as a representative response of the contemporary naval oligarchy to Melville's *White-Jacket:*

As a whole this book can give one but a very imperfect idea of what transpires within a ship of war; only, about as much as can be known of a rule from its exceptions— And this should not be thought strange, for the author's mind and feelings were so warped by prejudice--so elated by any advantage the sailor might obtain over the officer—that he could not, if he would, give a plain unvarnished tale of what actually occurred.[10]

Only the voice of justice and truth, he regretted, could have moved him "to treat with such severity the production of an author whose previous works have been so well received."

The second rear-admiral to comment in writing upon *White-Jacket* was Samuel R. Franklin, who had been a midshipman on the frigate *United States* in 1843–1844, and a shipmate of Melville. Writing in 1898 his *Memoirs of a Rear-Admiral,* long after the issue raised by *White-Jacket* had been resolved, he indulged in nothing but favorable comments upon this book and pleasant reminiscences of its author. His identifications of some of its characters and his confirmation of its essential accuracy are valuable, though memories recorded half a century after the fact are not entirely trustworthy, especially when many of them have obviously been prompted by the work in question. Although Rear-Admiral Franklin was inclined to remember the old Navy of sails more pleasantly than Melville, apparently he was not provoked by the scoffing at etiquette and ceremony or by the program of advocated reforms which had proved so distasteful to Selfridge. On the contrary, he admitted the justice of several of Melville's complaints, even including one that concerned midshipmen. Yet, in general, he preferred the less critical picture of life on board a wooden man-of-war contained in Captain Marryat's *Mishipman Easy*.[11]

Finally, the third and most recent criticism of *White-Jacket* by an officer in the United States Navy strikes happily between the opinions of Selfridge and Franklin. Writing in 1930 on "Herman Melville as a Naval Historian," Rear-Admiral Livingston Hunt objects to his satirical and disrespectful pictures of officers, saying: "There is not much of naval history in these sallies of humor and irony." "But," he adds, "his descriptions of life at sea on a man-of war are more to be noticed." He admits the charge of incompetence and excessive drinking among the officers, but says it was confined to a small group; he also admits the theoretical cruelty of the Articles of War and the actual cruelty of flogging. Although writing with a slightly professional bias, Hunt comes near putting his finger on the true Melville, charging him with adopting a florid and verbose style as if writing a romance:

Those who wish a picture of life in the old American navy of sails—about the time of the year 1843—will find no more detailed description of the manners and customs that prevailed before the mast, as well as abaft it, on a man-of-war of that day, than that in the pages of Herman Melville's *White-Jacket; or, the World in a Man-of-War*. But it should be remembered that it is a writer of exuberant and brilliant imagination, a devotee of poetic exaggeration, a propagandist for world peace, a scoffer at gold braid and salutes and ceremonials, an anti-militarist, an apostle of leveling and democracy, who writes the story of White Jacket. Melville in this book is both an historian and an autobiographer, and in the latter [former?] capacity he does not always show the judgment

and the power of interpreting naval facts that an historian should possess. . . . His railings at rank and the naval polity provoke a smile.[12]

The chief cause of this smile, however, is merely a fundamental
difference in attitude; and the impartial critic of Melville must remember that he was not so much lacking in historical judgment as
he was lacking in a desire to interpret naval facts as a national-
minded historian should. Moreover, Melville was not alone in railing at rank and the naval polity. William H. Meyers, who was a seasoned tar and in general free from evangelical purpose, found
frequent occasion in his Journal for bitter criticism:

February 22, 1842. A row in the ward room. . . . Puffing about the
duello. This afternoon a Peruvian Schooner flogged a man with 36
lashes. . . . Humbug upon humbug. Cruelty and ungentlemanly conduct characterizes a man of war. . . .
March 16, 1842. Mr. Barton [midshipman] making a gony of himself,
wrenching a crazy man's ears off. Poor Jimmy Ducks! Think that the
navy as it is is a pattern for cruelty and oppression.[13]

And Meyers was not writing for publication. Melville, however, was
an avowed reformer, and he had the zeal as well as the intention of
one. He ransacked every nook and corner of his man-of-war world,
its organization and its discipline, to expose the vices and abuses
that he could find. The list of his complaints against the Navy, from
the barbarism of "flogging through the fleet" down to the baldness
caused by hard tarpaulin hats, makes a formidable thesis.[14] Beyond
the references already made to naval abuses, the manuscripts at
hand offer no further check, except in the matter of flogging. This,
however, was the principal target of Melville's attack; he devotes
more than fifty pages to a sweeping and detailed condemnation of
this institution, which seemed to him a relic of the Middle Ages.

His attack, moreover, seems justified from the records of his
experience on board the frigate *United States*. The punishment lists
for this cruise show that Melville witnessed the degradation at the
gangway of one hundred and sixty-three of his fellow seamen during
his residence of fourteen months on board. The usual punishment
was twelve lashes with the cat-o'-nine-tails (only one-fifth being less
than this), although this was the maximum that could be inflicted

by law. And this was true in spite of the fact that the offenses ranged
all the way from "Obscene Language"—which Melville says the
officers used with impunity—to "Desertion," both of which were
punished with the same unrelenting maximum of twelve lashes!
Further, almost half of all the punishments were for drunkenness
or smuggling liquor on board. This preponderance is a commentary
on the discrepancy between the proportion of punishments inflicted while in port and while at sea: ninety and ten percent, respectively. Obviously the temptations during idleness in port, and
the consequent restrictions placed on the liberty of the sailor to
keep him out of temptation's way, were largely responsible for the
supposed indispensableness of the cat-o-nine-tails for maintaining
discipline.[15] What few punishments did occur at sea were usually
the result of fights and quarrels among the seamen themselves; and
one is inclined to agree with Melville that such minor insubordination was not enough to warrant the inhuman and primitive discipline of flogging. In this connection, it may be remarked that Melville must have drawn most of the venom for his attack from the
earlier part of his residence on the *United States,* for during the
period covered by *White-Jacket* only seventeen men went under
the lash, largely because from Callao to Boston the ship was mostly
at sea.

The most extreme form of flogging, which Melville uses to clinch
his polemic, was the punishment called "flogging through the fleet."
This could be inflicted only by a court-martial for some flagrant
offense, and the maximum penalty was set at one hundred lashes.
In *White-Jacket* this barbarous custom is described in all its revolting details:

All hands being called "to witness punishment" in the ship to which
the culprit belongs, the sentence of the court-martial condemning him
is read, when, with the usual solemnities, a portion of the punishment is
inflicted. In order that it shall not lose in severity by the slightest ex-
haustion in the arm of the executioner, a fresh boatswain's mate is
called out at every dozen.
As the leading idea is to strike terror into the beholders, the greatest
number of lashes is inflicted on board the culprit's own ship, in order

to render him the more shocking spectacle to the crews of the other vessels.

The first infliction being concluded, the culprit's shirt is thrown over him; he is put into a boat—the Rogue's March being played meanwhile —and rowed to the next ship of the squadron. All hands of that ship are then called to man the rigging, and another portion of the punishment is inflicted by the boatswain's mates of that ship. The bloody shirt is again thrown over the seaman; and thus he is carried through the fleet or squadron till the whole sentence is inflicted. . . .

In some cases the attending surgeon has professionally interfered before the last lash has been given, alleging that immediate death must ensue if the remainder should be administered without a respite. But instead of humanely remitting the remaining lashes, in a case like this, the man is generally consigned to his cot for ten or twelve days; and when the surgeon officially reports him capable of undergoing the rest of his sentence, it is forthwith inflicted. Shylock must have his pound of flesh.[16]

Melville does not pretend that he was ever an eyewitness to such an affront to civilization. But Samuel Leech—whose volume has already been pointed out as the source of Melville's description of the battle between the *United States* and the *Macedonian* during the War of 1812—gives an account of flogging through the fleet in the British Navy a quarter of a century before, which not only corroborates Melville's account but undoubtedly supplied the information for it:

Fifty [lashes] were laid on alongside of the Macedonian, in conformity with a common practise of inflicting the most strokes at the first ship, in order that the gory back of the criminal may strike the more terror into the crews of the other ships. . . . The drummer beats a mournful melody, called the rogue's march, and the melancholy procession moves on. . . . This poor tortured man bore two hundred and twenty, and was pronounced by the attending surgeon unfit to receive the rest. . . . He was brought on board, and when his wounds were healed, the captain, Shylock-like, determined to have the whole pound of flesh, ordered him to receive the remainder.[17]

Melville drives home his point unsparingly:

To say, that after being flogged through the fleet the prisoner's back is sometimes puffed up like a pillow; or to say that in other cases it looks as if burned black before a roasting fire; or to say that you may track him through the squadron by the blood on the bulwarks of every ship, would only be saying what many seamen have seen.

Several weeks, sometimes whole months, elapse before the sailor is sufficiently recovered to resume his duties. During the greater part of that interval he lies in the sick-bay, groaning out his days and nights; and unless he has the hide and constitution of a rhinoceros, he never is the man he was before, but, broken and shattered to the marrow of his bones, sinks into death before his time. Instances have occurred where he has expired the day after the punishment. . . .

While the *Neversink* was in the Pacific, an American sailor, who had deposited a vote for General Harrison for President of the United States, was flogged through the fleet.[18]

This final point, however, seems to lack entire corroboration, though the Log Book of the *United States* does contain the following entry:

[At Sea. June 3, 1842.] By sentence of a general Courtmartial held on board the Yorktown [at Callao, May 29] Benj. Furness was to receive 50 lashes. Punished him with 39, Commo[dore] remitting remainder of sentence.

William H. Meyers leaves no doubt that the custom of "flogging through the fleet" was still in vogue in the United States navy as well as the British. Six months before Melville joined the Pacific Squadron Meyers recorded a wholesale case:

Mazatlán. February 12, 1843. Sentence of prisoners [for mutinous conduct] to be flogged through the fleet: John Ryneman, 100 lashes; John Ressick, 50; John Walker, 50; William Moore, 50; Yorktown's Balzen, 100; Maguire, 50. Fair sum for the merciful disposition of our Naval Officers.

February 13. Orders to flog prisoners on board the Yorktown and frigate [*United States*]. At 10 Gun fired; hoisted the Yellow flag at the fore of each Ship. At 7 bells [11.30], punishment over. John Ryneman recd 75, John Ressick 50, Wm. Moore 50, John Walker 50, Boy Maguire 36. Balzen received his 75 with perfect nonchalance. When the Commodore cried, "Stop!" at 75, he exclaimed, "Domino! that squares yards on both ships!" "Seise him up again!" said the Commodore. It was done. 25 more he got. "That's domino anyhow!" he cried. "Put him in irons!" said the Great Chieftain. It was done.[19]

It would be a bitter and hard-hearted smile indeed that would be provoked by railings, however fanatical, at such a naval polity.

The British press took no interest in Melville's propaganda,[20] but the contemporary American reviews devoted over half their space to expressing their approval of his attack on naval abuses. Even the conservative *Knickerbocker Magazine* joïned the chorus demanding reform:

> We would call especial attention, as a matter of present public interest, to the chapters descriptive of an instance of almost indiscriminate flogging on board a man-of-war, and the consequences of such inconsistent punishment, in the case of each offender. The force of public opinion, and the example of certain humane officers in the highest rank of the American navy, would seem to indicate that the time is not distant when corporeal [*sic*] punishment, if not mainly abolished, will at least be hereafter less frequently resorted to than formerly, and greatly lessened in its severity. The signs of the times would seem to point unerringly to this result.[21]

Only one American review took exception to Melville's strictures, and strangely enough this same magazine, the *Democratic Review*, just six months before had published a series of articles advocating the abolition of corporal punishment in the Navy.[22] Beyond this there was no adverse American comment on *White-Jacket*, nor was there any doubt expressed as to the actuality of the author's experiences. Undoubtedly the orthodox Christian tone of the volume helped to make it acceptable to the public, but the current agitation against flogging in the Navy probably did more. Yet, although Melville was again growing in fame after the popular failure of *Mardi*, his account of his experiences in the United States navy was far from being as successful as *Typee* and *Omoo* had been.[23]

Further, the influence of his new book as propaganda has been greatly overemphasized. A traditional error was started by Rear-Admiral Franklin when he declared:

> *White-Jacket* had more influence in abolishing corporal punishment in the Navy than anything else. This book was placed on the desk of every member of Congress, and was a most eloquent appeal to the humane sentiment of the country. As an evidence of the good it did, a law was passed soon after the book appeared abolishing flogging in the

Navy absolutely, without substituting any other mode of punishment in its stead; and this was exactly in accord with Melville's appeal.[24]

This extravagant dictum has been accepted by Melville's biographers without question,[25] but it needs considerable qualification, as do most of Franklin's recollections. A brief history of the abolition of flogging will throw light on the extent of *White-Jacket's* influence. Corporal punishment had first been established in the Navy by the Continental Congress in 1775. By an Act for the Better Government of the Navy, April 25, 1800, it was limited to twelve lashes by the captain's order and one hundred by a court-martial. As the century of reform wore on, however, the institution came under the notice of the humane, and by 1845 a strong feeling had developed in favor of abolishing both flogging and the grog allowance.[26]

The Naval Appropriations Bill, passed on August 3, 1848, contained a proviso which directed the Secretary of the Navy to report to Congress annually (and retroactive to 1846), the number of persons flogged, giving the name of the ship, the offense, and the number of the lashes inflicted.[27] During the congressional session of 1848–1849 a long debate took place in the House of Representatives on a resolution to abolish flogging in the Navy, but the proposal was defeated on the grounds that it was inadvisable to attach such an important change in naval discipline to a general appropriations bill.[28] In January, 1850, the Secretary of the Navy addressed a circular letter to the leading naval officers asking for their views; the answers were almost unanimous in favor of retaining the cat-o'-nine-tails, a few of the seamen, even, petitioning for the retention of this form of punishment as "manly."[29] Meanwhile, memorials and petitions had begun to flood Congress, mostly from the states which were also in favor of the abolition of Negro slavery.[30] And a resolution again came up in the session of 1849–1850, again attached to the Naval Appropriations Bill. It was passed in the House by a large majority, but in the Senate it met with strong opposition.[31] The Southern states chiefly were against it. Although they gave as their reasons that it was not advisable to attach such a revolutionary change as a proviso to an appropriations bill, and that no

substitute punishment was provided, their position was more probably dictated by their general policy of resistance to the aggressions
of Northern sentimental philanthropy. After a long debate the
proviso finally passed the Senate by the narrow margin of 26 to 24;
and from and after September 28, 1850, flogging became illegal in
the American Navy.[32]

In all the speeches delivered on this subject in Congress, pro and
con, Melville's name is not mentioned, nor is any allusion made
to *White-Jacket*, although it would have been quite in keeping with
congressional usage to bring in such a document as evidence. As
propaganda, Melville's volume did not have any extraordinary
vogue. The truth of the matter is that the fight to abolish flogging
was already substantially won when *White-Jacket* appeared in the
spring of 1850;[33] and, although it may have swelled the growing
tide of agitation, it was at most merely another coal carried to
Newcastle. Rear-Admiral Franklin's sweeping generalization, then,
may be judiciously modified by reversing it: so far from Melville's
White-Jacket bringing about the movement that resulted in the
abolition of flogging in the Navy, it was the very currency of this
agitation that brought forth his attack. Melville simply got on the
bandwagon of reform; he had an eye for the public taste, in his
earlier years, as keen as that of Defoe and Cotton Mather. And it
is interesting to remember that a similar technique guided another
partisan pen, two years later, in the cause of a more far-reaching
abolition—with greater power and more popular success, if with
less artistic skill.

White-Jacket draws to an end with the "Neversink" still at sea,
off the Virginia Capes. "I love an indefinite, infinite background,"
says Melville; "a vast, heaving, rolling, mysterious rear."[34] As a
matter of biography, it may be added that the *United States* proceeded to Boston for its home port, arriving on October 3, 1844.
Melville's three-year enlistment was only a little more than one-
third spent; but, since the frigate was to go into dry dock, and since
the term of service of the majority of the men had already expired,
Captain Stribling's request that the entire crew be discharged was
granted by the Secretary of the Navy.[35] The previous winter at

Callao Melville had more narrowly missed a prolongation of his seafaring years when Commodore A. J. Dallas had contemplated the transfer of two hundred men with unexpired enlistments from the *United States* to the *Cyane,* to return home by way of the East Indies. Only the untimely death of the commodore saved him then from two more years of service and a trip round the world.[36] After ten days spent in port helping to strip the ship for repairs, he received his discharge on October 14, 1844,[37] and began his years of freedom two years before he had bargained for them.

Melville was not the only one, however, to secure his freedom unexpectedly. Several days before, Robert Lucas, a landsman on the *United States,* had been delivered up to the civil authorities on a writ of *Habeas Corpus.* He was a slave owned by Edward Fitzgerald, purser of the ship and a Virginia gentleman, and had been received on board before sailing from Norfolk by special permission of the Secretary of the Navy; he had been a component part of the crew, however, and not in any way subject to his master except in the claim of the latter for his wages. At the suit of some Abolitionists, without the knowledge or authority of Lucas, he was granted his freedom on October 11, 1844, on the ground that he had been brought into a free state by his master "voluntarily," although the original sailing orders of the *United States* gave Norfolk as the port of return. The decision, which restricted the application of the Fugitive Slave Law, was rendered by Chief Justice Lemuel Shaw, who shortly afterwards became Melville's father-in-law and the dedicatee of *Typee.* In giving his opinion, the Chief Justice said that Fitzgerald had acted honorably in the transaction, disclosing all the facts in the case with entire frankness, and had even agreed that, whatever the decision of the court might be, Lucas should be left free to act according to his own wishes, either to return to Virginia or to remain in a free state, as he might elect.[38]

Melville tells a similar story in *White-Jacket:*

On board of the United States ship *Neversink,* during the present cruise, there was a Virginian slave regularly shipped as a seaman, his owner receiving his wages. Guinea—such was his name among the crew—belonged to the purser, who was a southern gentleman; he was employed as his body servant. Never did I feel my condition as a man-of-war's man so keenly as when seeing this Guinea freely circulating about the decks in citizen's clothes, . . . exempted from the disciplinary degradation of the Caucasian crew. Faring sumptuously in the ward-room; sleek and round, his ebon face fairly polished with content; ever gay and hilarious; ever ready to laugh and joke, that African slave was actually envied by many of the seamen. There were times when I almost envied him myself. Lemsford once envied him outright. "Ah, Guinea!" he sighed, "you have peaceful times; you never opened the book I read in." . . . Accustomed to light and easy duties from his birth, and so fortunate as to meet with none but gentle masters, Guinea, though a bondman, liable to be saddled with a mortgage, like a horse—Guinea, in india-rubber manacles, enjoyed the liberties of the world. . . . [To his master], from his pleasant, kind, indulgent manner towards his slave, I have always imputed . . . a generous heart, and cherished an involuntary friendliness toward him. Upon our arrival home, his treatment of Guinea, under circumstances peculiarly calculated to stir up the resentment of a slave-owner, still more augmented my estimation of the purser's good heart.[39]

Here was an instance of a kind master deprived of a contented slave by the intermeddling of Abolitionists; and Melville, himself a reformer, was the one to throw this denial of the good effects of their philanthropy in their face. But, bondslave and wage slave, they were all free now; and perhaps Lemsford and Melville, who had envied Guinea on board, were more pleased than even he at putting foot once more on dry land. At any rate, as already mentioned, the former made a last joyful note in his journal when he arrived in port: "Forever for me!"

As for Melville, though a nostalgia for the robust life of the sea grew upon him with the years, he regained his freedom now with eagerness and with a head full of literary plans. He arrived in Boston just in time, had he been so minded, to purchase a white muslin ascension robe and go to the Millerite Tabernacle to usher in the end of the world, which was predicted, for the third and last time, to come on October 23, 1844.[40] And for Melville it was, in some sort, the end of one world; but it was also the beginning of another. When doomsday passed without disturbing Boston's complacent routine, he made his way back to his native state and settled down to the mundane task of bridging the gap between his two worlds. He lost little time in setting up shop, where he passed the raw materials of his recent experiences through the magic crucible of his imagination. The distillate had its charms; but the ever-tempting route from alchemy to metaphysics was too alluring to resist. Within a decade the high priest of the South Seas had become, in his own eyes at least, the heretic of an inquisitional civilization. In spite of the consequences, he undoubtedly continued to think of himself always as the philosopher in his tower, castigating an unresponsive world. But posterity, no less than his contemporary world, prefers him rather as the *jongleur* of *Omoo* and *White-Jacket*, or, best of all, as the enchanter,

> the sea-compelling man,
> Before whose wand Leviathan
> Rose hoary-white upon the deep,
> With awful sounds that stirred its sleep;
> Melville, whose magic drew Typee,
> Radiant as Venus, from the sea.[41]

NOTES

I. Why Ishmael Went to Sea

1. *Moby-Dick*, I, 1.
2. Stedman, "Melville of Marquesas."
3. Stedman, *Typee*, p. xviii.
4. Mumford, p. 40.
5. Weaver, *Melville*, p. 131.
6. Records of the Copyright Office (Library of Congress), Southern District of New York, XIII, 171: title-page deposited, September 1, 1840; work deposited, October 6, 1840.

That Melville did read *Two Years Before the Mast* shortly thereafter we can be reasonably sure, for a copy of it was included in the ship's library on board the frigate *United States*, homeward bound, 1842–1844. (See p. 358, and Chap. XIII, note 45.) And there can be no doubt that he made use of it in his *White-Jacket* (1850), in which volume he refers to the author as "my friend Dana." Apparently, however, they were never intimate, the friendship being confined to several meetings, 1847–1850, and to several favors performed for Melville by Dana (Hart, "Dana").

7. Damon (pp. 281–283) places the school teaching in Pittsfield in 1836, following J. E. A. Smith, who got his information from Melville himself, rather than Arthur Stedman, who places it between 1837 and 1840 from information derived from Mrs. Melville.

A letter from Melville to his Uncle Peter Gansevoort, however, seems to clear this matter up once and for all. Melville's voyage of four months to Liverpool must have lasted from June to October, 1837 (a letter from his mother to his brother Gansevoort, June 1, 1837, says he had just left home— MS. in the Gansevoort-Lansing Collection, New York Public Library) ; and, after a brief visit in Albany, he returned to Pittsfield, where he had spent the previous year of 1836, to take charge of the school in the Sykes District, near Washington Mountain. From the tone of his letter to his uncle this was undoubtedly his first teaching experience, the winter of 1837–1838. (Paltsits, pp. 5–6.)

Major Thomas Melville, the uncle with whom he lived in 1836, had left Broadhall and moved to Illinois in 1837; hence Melville was "boarding round" with his pupils during this visit. (See pp. 17–19.)

8. *Redburn*, p. 1.
9. Weaver, *Melville*, p. 131. In his latest pronouncement on Melville, Weaver reaffirms his acceptance of this dramatic explanation, quoting the "Pistol and Ball" passage again, and adding: "Five times in his life, Melville

took to the ship. And the first four of these, at least, were instigated in desperation" (*Journal,* pp. iii, iv) .

10. *Moby-Dick,* I, 6–7.

11. Garnett, pp. 841–858.

12. *Redburn,* Chap. XXXI. (An article relative to this guide-book will soon appear in the *Publications of the Modern Language Association.*)

13. *Ibid.,* p. 44. These experiences were published by Captain DeWolf in 1861, as *A Voyage to the North Pacific and a Journey Through Siberia More Than Half a Century Ago.*

14. *Moby-Dick,* I, 260–261.

15. *Ibid.* See Munro, pp. 97–201; and Perry, pp. 48–50, 132.

16. Langsdorff, I, 77–178. A briefer account is given in Krusenstern, I, 110–185.

Weaver (*Melville,* p. 44) mentions this uncle and quotes the references to him in *Redburn* and *Moby-Dick.* But he failed to push his investigation far enough, for he concludes, ill-advisedly: "Just what, if anything besides two contradictory statements—Melville owed to this uncle it would be worthless to surmise."

17. "Genealogical Tree of the Gansevoort Family" (MS. in Gansevoort-Lansing Collection, New York Public Library). See also Smith, "Melville," p. 5.

18. Weaver, *Melville,* pp. 35, 69.

19. Reynolds, I, 62–68. Hamersly (p. 272) traces his naval career as follows: Midshipman, 1823; Lieutenant, 1837; Commander, 1855; Captain, 1862; Commodore, 1866.

20. Letter to the author, May 2, 1934, from Captain Dudley W. Knox, Officer-in-Charge, Naval Records and Library, containing a transcript of the naval service of Guert Gansevoort, 1823–1842, from Log Books and other records. The dates for the various leaves-of-absence were as follows: December 12, 1831–July 1, 1833; August 15–October 12, 1833; July 26, 1834–May 26, 1836; May 6–September 21, 1837. On September 21, 1838, he was ordered to the Mediterranean—an earlier order to accompany the United States Exploring Expedition round the world had been revoked—and did not return until after Herman Melville had sailed for the South Seas. All official communications were addressed to him at Albany.

In the Gansevoort-Lansing Collection, New York Public Library, there is preserved a letter from Guert Gansevoort, then a midshipman, to his uncle Peter Gansevoort, dated "U. S. Ship St. Louis, Callao, [Peru], March 13, 1831."

21. "Paternal Line of the Melville Family of Boston" (MS. in the Gansevoort-Lansing Collection, New York Public Library).

22. Smith, *Pittsfield,* p. 7.

23. *Ibid.,* pp. 399–400.

24. Hamersly, p. 489.

25. Herman Melville's sketch of his uncle is printed in Smith, *Pittsfield,* pp. 399–400.

NOTES FOR PAGES 19–26

26. "Captain Finch's Cruise in the U. S. S. Vincennes, 1826–1830" (MS. in the Naval Records and Library, Navy Department, Washington). Midshipman Melville's name is mentioned only incidentally and in the line of duty.

27. *Ibid.:* "No. 1. Narrative of Proceedings, On a Visit to Noohevah [*sic*], July and August, 1829, in the U. S. Ship Vincennes."

28. *Ibid.:* "No. 4. Observations upon Noohevah [*sic*]."

29. *Ibid.:* "No. 2. Visit to Otaheite, (or Tahiti) . . . August and September, 1829." The "Private Journal of Thomas A. Dornin [Lieutenant on the *Vincennes*, 1829–1830]" corroborates the above information (MS. in the Naval Records and Library).

30. *Typee,* pp. 3–4.

31. See especially Book Two, "The Man Who Lived Among Cannibals." Stewart, I, 207–357, "The Marquesas Islands"; II, 7–57, "The Society Islands"; II, 61–280, "The Sandwich Islands."

Raymond Weaver discovered the existence of this interesting and far-wandering cousin, Pierre François Henry Thomas Wilson Melville, who, he says, died in the Sandwich Islands in 1842. But, again, he failed to push his investigation far enough, merely remarking (*Melville,* p. 46) : "That Pierre's adventures to the far corners of the earth may have had some influence upon Melville's taking to a ship is a tempting surmise; but a surmise whose only cogency is its possibility." Emboldened by the influence already pointed out, one is now even tempted to make the further cogent surmise that this Pierre may have given the name to Melville's disastrous novel, *Pierre; or, The Ambiguities,* so desperately filled with attempts to probe into family influences.

II. New Bedford

1. *Moby-Dick,* I, 42.

2. See Pease.

3. *Moby-Dick,* I, 42–43.

4. See Pease.

5. *Ibid.* (The italics are mine.) The New York *Times,* December 31, 1916, expresses approval that a memorial is to be erected to Herman Melville in the New Bedford chapel in the form of a "Crow's Nest Pulpit" like the one described in *Moby-Dick;* but the reality does not bear out this prediction. though the pulpit does have the general form of a ship's bows.

6. *Moby-Dick,* I, 47–48.

7. Hart, *Coffin,* p. xvii.

8. *Moby-Dick,* I, 47–48.

9. See Pease.

10. *Ibid.* Mumford (p. 44) has called attention to this duality, merely saying that Melville "transformed [Father Mudge], through later acquaintance with Father Taylor of Boston, into Father Mapple in *Moby-Dick.*" The earliest notice of this likeness to Father Taylor appeared in the anonymous letter under "The Listener," the Boston *Transcript,* May 22, 1897: "Now that the authenticity of the story of Jonah is so vigorously questioned in clerical cir-

cles, it would be well to turn to a chapter in 'Moby Dick' (by Herman Melville) and read how the reverend sailor preacher there portrayed handles the subject. The author has evidently taken Father Taylor for his prototype, and the fidelity of the impersonation will commend itself to many of your older readers who can well recall his earnest labors among the seamen of all climes congregated in your city."

11. The New Bedford *Mercury*, May 3, 1832.

12. *Moby-Dick*, I, 46.

13. Dickens, pp. 25–26.

14. *Moby-Dick*, I, 49–50.

15. *Ibid.*, I, 57–59. (For further information about Father Taylor see Haven, and MacDonald.)

16. Macy, p. 31.

17. *Moby-Dick*, I, 193. (For a similar account see Crèvecœur, p. 115.)

18. Macy, p. 219.

19. *Moby-Dick*, I, 78–79.

20. Starbuck, p. 376.

21. Quoted in Weaver, *Melville*, pp. 160–161. The names in square brackets are from the official crew list of the *Acushnet*, by courtesy of W. H. Tripp, Curator of the Old Dartmouth Historical Society and Whaling Museum, New Bedford, Mass., where the original document is preserved. (Weaver says erroneously that it can be found in Starbuck.) Two of the identifications on Melville's list have been made by reference to another document, which gives a list of deserters from the *Acushnet*—one of whom, Jim Rosman, shipped during the cruise (see Chap. IV, notes 3 and 4).

22. *Moby-Dick*, I, 149, 233.

23. *Ibid.*, I, 214–221.

24. *Billy Budd and Other Prose Pieces*, "Daniel Orme," p. 117.

25. Crew list of the *Acushnet* (MS. in the Old Dartmouth Historical Society and Whaling Museum, New Bedford, Mass.).

III. A Whale Laboratory

1. See pp. 13–14.

2. Anon., "New Bedford Whalers."

3. *Moby-Dick*, II, 208. The volumes listed by Melville as having been consulted in the preparation of his masterpiece comprise the best authorities on the subject of whaling that were available in 1850. Further, a modern whaling expert pays convincing tribute to his knowledge and accuracy: "There is one writer of whaling fiction whose book may be taken seriously and unquestioningly. There could be no truer picture of whaling or finer story of the sea than Herman Melville's 'Moby Dick.' Melville knew his subject." (See Ashley, p. 106.)

4. Browne, pp. 262–263. That Melville was acquainted with this volume is evidenced by the numerous references that he made to it. And the chances

are strong that he was the author of the anonymous review of it in the New York *Literary World*, I, 105–106 (March 6, 1847). The reviewer called attention to the realism, the "unvarnished facts" in this "truthfully and graphically sketched . . . voice from the forecastle," saying that it does for the whale fishery what Dana's book did for the merchant marine. The brutal tyranny of the captain of Browne's *Styx* is specifically pointed out. (See Melville's letter to E. A. Duyckinck on February 3, 1847—MS. in the New York Public Library—promising to review a book just published by Harpers; Browne's volume was the first Harpers' book to be reviewed in the *Literary World* after that date.)

5. Browne, p. 560, quoting from Wilkes's narrative of a voyage on the *Vincennes*.

6. *Ibid.*, pp. 302–327.

7. *Ibid.*, pp. 496, 504, and *passim*.

8. *Ibid.*, pp. 76–96. Compare *Moby-Dick*, I, 310–330.

9. Browne, pp. 105–106, 249–250, 492. Compare *Moby-Dick*, I, 203–205; II, 242–244, 290–293.

10. Browne, pp. 51–61, 127–135. Compare *Moby-Dick*, II, 25–38, 47–52, 177–180.

11. Browne, pp. 62–63.

12. *Moby-Dick*, II, 20–24.

13. Browne, pp. 60–64.

14. *Moby-Dick*, II, 178–182.

15. Weaver, for example, in his latest critical remarks on Melville, again quotes this declaration as the true explanation of "Why Ishmael Went to Sea," describing Melville's South Sea jaunt as "a retreat from life, from reality and outward experience, from the world which has [*sic*] so early disappointed and blighted his soul" (Weaver, *Journal*, p. iv).

16. Browne, pp. 22–23. Compare *Moby-Dick*, I, 152–155. Weaver (*Melville*, p. 137) says: "Though in *Moby-Dick* Melville makes several references to J. Ross Browne's *Etchings of a Whaling Cruise* . . . he owes no debt to J. Ross Browne. Melville and Browne wrote with purposes diametrically opposed."

17. Browne, pp. 35–37. Compare *Moby-Dick*, I, 200–210. It was probably just such high-flown rhetoric as adorns this speech that an English reviewer was analyzing when he remarked, with some fitness, that Melville's Ahab "raves by the hour in a lingo borrowed from Rabelais, Carlyle, Emerson, newspapers transcendental and trans-Atlantic, and the magnificent proems of our Christmas pantomimes" (see "Sir Nathaniel").

18. Beale, pp. 131–135.

19. *Moby-Dick*, II, 161–162.

IV. Facts and Symbols in "Moby-Dick"

1. *Moby-Dick*, I, 293, 295–296, 346, 350; II, 124–125, 242, 252–253, 273–275.
2. *Omoo*, p. 6; *Typee*, p. 300.

3. MS. in the Old Dartmouth Historical Society and Whaling Museum, New Bedford, Mass. Photostat by courtesy of W. H. Tripp, Curator. This valuable document has been discovered and reprinted by another investigator, independently (see Forsythe, "Honolulu").

4. This affidavit, certified to by Captain Valentine Pease before John Stetson, the United States Commercial Agent at Lahaina (Maui, Sandwich Islands), on June 2, 1843, records the following information: David Smith deserted at Santa, Peru, on June 30, 1841; Richard T. Greene and Herman Melville deserted at Nukahiva on July 9, 1842; John Wright at the same place on September 14, 1842; Martin Brown at Roa-Pua, Marquesas Is., September 22, 1842; Jim Rosman at Salango, Ecuador, February 3, 1843; and Henry Harmer at Maui, on May 28, 1843 (see note 3, above). Subsequent points on the cruise of the *Acushnet* are: at Maui, September and October 15, 30, 1843; off Prince of Wales Is., January 18, 1844; at Maui, March 11, 1844; at Talcahuano, Chili, February 1, 1845; at New Bedford, Mass., May 13, 1845 (see the *Whalemen's Shipping List and Merchants' Transcript*, 1844–1845, *passim*).

5. The frigate *United States,* the fastest ship in the navy in 1844, took three months to a day for an uninterrupted voyage from Callao, Peru, to Boston, by the more direct route of Cape Horn; and her outward-bound voyage required several weeks more because of the difficulty of the westward passage round Cape Horn (see Anderson, *Journal,* pp. 71–72).

6. Browne, pp. 556–557.

7. *Ibid.*

8. *Mardi,* I, 120.

9. Log Book of the *Rousseau,* 1841–1845, New Bedford Free Public Library. Photostat through the courtesy of W. H. Tripp.

10. *The Piazza Tales,* "The Encantadas," p. 189.

11. Reference deleted in the present edition.

12. Darwin, III, 456.

13. Fitzroy, II, 486–487, 494.

14. Over fifty pages in this work are devoted to the Galapagos Islands (*ibid.,* II, 485–505; III, 453–478). In addition to the descriptions of flora and fauna and the general landscape, Melville may have picked up details such as his description of Rock Rodondo: "Some two hundred and fifty feet high, rising straight from the sea, . . . [Rock Rodondo] when first seen afar invariably is mistaken for a sail. Four leagues away, on a golden, hazy noon, it seems some Spanish Admiral's ship, stacked up with glittering canvas. Sail ho! Sail ho! Sail ho! from all three masts. But coming nigh, the enchanted frigate is transformed apace into a craggy keep." (*The Piazza Tales,* "The Encantadas," p. 193.) A suggestion for this may have been found in Fitzroy's description of a similar rock at the other end of the archipelago: "The Kicker Rock is a curious mass of stone, rising almost perpendicularly from the bottom of the sea, where it is thirty fathoms deep; and in the offing is another (called the Dalrymple, by Colnett), which looks exactly like a ship becalmed, with all sail set." (Fitzroy, II, 487.)

15. *The Piazza Tales,* "The Encantadas," pp. 182–183.

16. *Typee,* p. 1.

17. Browne, p. 557.

18. *Moby-Dick,* I, 257, 258.

19. *Ibid.,* I, 259–261. (See Langsdorff, II, 328–329.)

20. *Ibid.,* I, 259.

21. Macy, pp. 237–242.

22. *Moby-Dick,* I, 258–259.

23. *Ibid.* Compare Chase, pp. 23–35, 37–39, 52. The perilous voyages in open boats performed by the crews of both the *Union* and the *Essex* may have furnished suggestions for the escape of Melville and Jarl from the "Arcturion" in *Mardi.*

24. The New York *Times,* February 10, 1932, p. 21, announces that this valuable Melville copy was sold by the American Art Association Anderson Galleries, Inc., to an anonymous purchaser, under the buying name of J. B. Courtney, for $1,675. Unfortunately, it is not available for scholarly purposes.

25. Hart, *Coffin,* pp. 292–293. Melville, as we have seen, was also indebted to this volume for the inspiration of his nautically-built pulpit. Further details that he may have picked up are as follows: (1) "Peleg Folger," a Quaker, was the owner of the "Grampus," whereas one of the eccentric whaling-Quakers who owned the "Pequod" was likewise named "Peleg." (2) The last Nantucket Indian chief, according to Hart, was named "Tashima"; it is not improbable that this name furnished the root for Melville's "Tashtego," the full-blooded Indian from Gay Head. (Macy, p. 47, says that the Nantucket Indians served constantly on whaleships in the early days, and until the last one died in 1822.) (3) The "Leviathan" was the name of one of the principal whaleships owned by Miriam Coffin's husband; and "Leviathan" is the name that Melville gives at the end of *Omoo* to the Yankee whaler on which he left the Society Islands, bound for "the coast of Japan."

26. Howard (pp. 310–311) has called attention to most of these resemblances, which he discovered independently.

27. *Moby-Dick,* II, 359–367. (See Weaver, *Melville,* p. 137.)

28. Quoted in Weaver, *Melville,* pp. 319–320, 322.

29. Quoted in the *Whalemen's Shipping List and Merchants' Transcript* (New Bedford), November 4, 1851, p. 142.
Jenkins gives the most modern account of such a catastrophe that I have been able to find. This list of corroborative authorities certainly confirms the possibility of what has been scouted as fabulous by many of the readers of *Moby-Dick.*

30. No earlier report has been found than that in the *Whalemen's Shipping List* (see note 29, above). The records of the Copyright Office show that the title-page of *Moby-Dick* was deposited on October 15 and a copy of the work on November 19, 1851.

31. Sadleir, p. 229. It was reviewed in the *London Spectator,* the *Athenæum,* and *John Bull* as early as October 25. (See also Ament, p. 41.)

32. Minnegerode, p: 74. Melville's parenthetical remark in the eighty-fifth chapter of *Moby-Dick*—"down to this blessed minute (fifteen and a quarter minutes past one o'clock P. M. of this sixteenth day of December, A. D. 1851)"—is certainly chronologically erroneous. If it has any accurate application, it probably stands for the publication date as he prognosticated it and is thus another proof of the fact that he was still working on his manuscript up to the last minute.

33. *Literary World*, IX, 381–383, 403–404 (November 15, 22, 1851). After a condensed summary of the account in the *Panama Herald*, Duyckinck adds: "By a singular coincidence this extreme adventure is, even to very many of the details, the catastrophe of Mr. Melville's new book. . . .

"Such an infuriated, resolute sperm whale as pursued and destroyed the Ann Alexander is the hero, Moby Dick, of Mr. Melville's book. The vengeance with which he is hunted, which with Capt. Deblois was the incident of a single, though most memorable day, is the leading passion and idea of Captain Ahab of the Pequod for years, and throughout the seas of the world."

This confirmation he also preserved in his excellent account of Melville in his *Cyclopædia of American Literature*, New York, 1856, II, 673.

34. Final confirmation of the reality of this disaster, if any be needed, can be found in the Honolulu *Seamen's Friend* for May 6, 1854, which reported that, about five months after the *Ann Alexander* was sunk, this pugnacious whale was captured by the *Rebecca Simms* of New Bedford, and that two of the *Ann Alexander's* harpoons were found in him as well as pieces of the ship's timbers embedded in his head, which had sustained serious injuries.

35. *Whalemen's Shipping List,* December 23, 1851, p. 170.

36. *Moby-Dick,* I, 257. Most of the contemporary reviewers took this warning seriously. But a few ventured an interpretation of its allegory.

37. Van Doren, *Moby-Dick*, and "Lucifer"; and Canby, pp. 251–252.

38. Mumford, p. 184. Compare Weaver, *Melville,* pp. 26, 131.

39. Gleim, *Moby-Dick,* pp. 402–419.

40. Homans, pp. 699–730, and Wainger, pp. 35–62.

41. Brooks, p. 205.

42. Lawrence, pp. 214–240. (Curl finds, among other likenesses, that Melville as well as Hawthorne attacked transcendentalism under a thin veil of symbolism; see also White.)

43. Hawthorne, p. 307. (See Weaver, *Melville,* pp. 326–329.)

44. *Catalogue of the American Art Association,* New York, 1931, Sale No. 3911. The entire letter, bought by J. W. Bentley (buying name for an anonymous purchaser) for $3,100, is, unfortunately, not available for scholarly use.

45. A quarter of a century later, the shadowy bulk of Moby-Dick again breached, in late Victorian waters, under the new name of *Pehe Nu-e, The Tiger Whale of the Pacific,* by Captain Bill Barnacle (pseudonym for Charles Martin Newell), Boston, 1877. This purports to be the story of a fierce battle-scarred whale known to some sailors as Mocha-Dick. The author acknowledges that he has read *Moby-Dick,* and certainly his fictitious captain bears

resemblance to Melville's Ahab, having been crippled by the tiger-whale and having vowed vengeance on him. What Melville's attitude was towards this pale shade of Moby-Dick is not known, but he was at least safe in knowing that the shadow would never be mistaken for the reality. (See Birss, *Moby-Dick*.)

V. The French at Nukahiva

1. *Typee*, pp. 1–3, 9.
2. *Ibid.*, p. 28.
3. *Ibid.*, p. 19.
4. Vincendon-Dumoulin, *Marquises*, pp. 119–137: "Rapport adressé par le contre-amiral du Petit-Thouars à M. le ministre de la marine et des colonies . . . sur la prise de possession de l'archipel des îles Marquises . . . Baie de Taiohaë, frégate *La Reine-Blanche,* le 18 juin, 1842."
5. See pp. 47–48 and Chap. IV, notes 3 and 4.
6. *Omoo*, p. viii.
7. *Typee*, p. 13.
8. Stewart, I, 224–226. (See pp. 16–20, above.)
9. *Typee*, pp. 28–29. See also Porter, II, 18–19.
10. Langsdorff, I, 92–95. (See pp. 15–16, above.)
11. *Typee*, pp. 16–18.
12. For the expurgation of Melville's episode see Minnegerode, p. 12. (See also Wilson, pp. 130–140; Stewart, I, 226–227, 229–230; Porter, II, 15–16, 24–25; and Handy, *Culture*, p. 40.)
13. *Typee*, pp. 13–14.
14. *Ibid.*, pp. 19–21.
15. Radiguet, pp. 1–59, 71–73.
16. *Typee*, p. 21. Throughout this volume Melville keeps up a running fire against the French (*ibid.*, pp. 131, 184, 254, 263, 343); and, leading off with a bitter reproach: "Under cover of a similar pretence, have the outrages and massacres at Tahiti the beautiful, the queen of the South Seas, been perpetrated" (*ibid.*, pp. 21–22), he renews the attack at the Society Islands (*Omoo*, pp. 80, 123–129, 142–147).
17. Stewart, I, 227, 303; Porter, II, 107–111. Contrary to my usual policy of using the standard spellings of Polynesian names, as explained in the Preface, I have thought it best in the case of *Taipii* to retain Melville's spelling, *Typee*, to avoid the confusion that would otherwise result since numerous quotations from his work containing this word are necessary, and since the work itself bears the title of *Typee*.
18. Belcher, I, 356. M. l'Abbé Mathias Gracia, a French Catholic priest resident at Nukahiva at this time, says that Moana had been brought up from infancy by the Protestants and educated in their schools, with the ultimate project of uniting by force all the neighboring tribes under his authority. Whether this charge was valid or merely made in sectarian jealousy, the

French were actually the ones who finally perfected this scheme. (See Gracia, pp. 21, 28.)

19. Radiguet, p. 56. This author confirmed the charge that the Protestants were to blame for Moana's present state, saying that Moana had been converted to the Methodist church at the age of ten, that his subjects had objected, and that he had fled to Rarotonga and thence to Europe (*ibid.*, pp. 56–57).

20. Vincendon-Dumoulin, *Marquises,* pp. 130, 136–137.

21. Radiguet, pp. 72, 73–77. Caillot (p. 352) says that the manuscripts left by Dupetit-Thouars show that this expedition was made on June 9, 1842. This would mean that the *Acushnet* was at the Marquesas for a full month before Melville's desertion—a possibility that gains additional weight from Melville's own remark (*Typee,* p. 32) as his ship passed Typee Bay on the way to its anchorage: "I little thought . . . that in the space of a few weeks I should actually be a captive in that self-same valley."

22. *Typee,* pp. 36–37.

23. Radiguet, pp. 72–77. The symbol of French authority already adorned the bamboo hut of the chief: "A notre arrivée, nous aperçûmes le pavillon français qui flottait sur la maison du vieux chef Maheatete" (Gracia, p. 301).

24. Radiguet (p. vi) refers to Melville's volume as "un récit curieux et bien mené sous le titre, bizarrement ortographié: 'Typee.'" Stevenson, among others, has commented on this same shortcoming: "Our admirable friend Herman Melville, of whom, since I could judge, I have thought more than ever, had no ear for languages whatever: his Happar tribe should be Hapaa, etc." (Stevenson, *Letters,* II, 182.) In the transcription of a hitherto unwritten language, there is naturally considerable diversity of opinion; Melville, however, usually differs from most other writers, and often from all of them.

25. Radiguet, pp. 74–77.

26. *Typee,* pp. 35–36.

27. Stewart also visited this valley, and in his description (I, 280–281) Melville may have found a model, if he needed one:

"On the left side of the glen a stupendous range of cliffs rises more than two thousand feet perpendicularly from the beach, in such wild and singular formation, as to seem more like a highly wrought fancy sketch for a romance of the stage, than a scene in nature. . . .

"Directly opposite, on the right—across the thickly embowered glen, at the distance of half a mile only—imagery of a totally different character was presented: gently swelling hills of grass smiled beneath the morning sun with all the brightness and verdure of a lawn in June, as they rose one above another to the height of five or six hundred feet. . . .

"I have gazed on much beautiful and much noble scenery, in various parts of the world, and in a great variety of aspects; but must unhesitatingly proclaim triumph to the glen of Taioa over everything of the kind I ever beheld."

The similarity of tone, and even of phraseology, is indeed striking.

28. Gracia (p. 302) says that she had adopted the son of the chief of the

Typees, and upon this predicated her claim.

29. *Typee,* pp. 6-8.

30. Anderson, *Journal,* p. 58.

31. *Typee,* p. 8. Samuel R. Franklin, who was a midshipman on the frigate *United States* in 1842-1843, seems to substantiate Melville's spectacular sequel: "There was a Queen who came on board, but I do not remember whether it was Pomare, well known in the history of the [Society] Islands, or some other Queen. Ladies of that rank were not uncommon in those days in the South Seas. At all events, she was a Queen to be saluted, and we gave her five guns, which made her very happy. She was very much tattooed, and I remember she drew up her cotton skirt and exhibited her leg, covered with India-ink. She was treated with every consideration by the Commodore, and returned to her Island feeling more like a Queen than ever." (See Franklin, p. 63.)

Recollections half a century after the fact, however, are likely to be distorted and unreliable; and Franklin shows his confusion by placing the event at Tahiti instead of at Nukahiva. Moreover, instead of his account being an independent corroboration of Melville, it is very likely a garbled memory of the anecdote as he had read it later in *Typee,* for he was familiar with Melville's volumes and frequently prompted his own *Memories of a Rear-Admiral* by drawing from them.

32. Anderson, *Journal,* pp. 45-46.

33. It will be remembered that both *Typee* and *Omoo* contain a running attack against the French policy in the South Seas. It is interesting to note that this whole episode was expurgated from the revised (American) edition, 1846, and not restored in any American reprinting until Arthur Stedman's edition in 1892. (See Minnegerode, pp. 109-124, *passim.)*

34. *Typee,* p. ix.

35. Radiguet, p. 75. Ginoux (III, 366-367) confirms this description of the native queen. After remarking that in general the Marquesan women are only slightly tattooed—on the lips, the fore-arm, the legs, and the hands and feet—he says that women of high rank were allowed to tattoo certain other parts of their bodies. In illustration of this he pays tribute to the more intimate designs which adorned the queen of Nukahiva: "Le tatouage de la reine Tahiahoko, femme de Demoana [Te-Moana], roi de Nou-Hiva [*sic*], est un travail admirable. Quand on lui demande à la considérer, elle relève sans cérémonie sa *tapa* et découvre toute la richesse des formes de son corps. La jambe de cette femme est ravissante, sa main et son bras seraient copiés par nos statuaires."

36. The subsequent history of King Moana and his consort is recorded by Vergnes, p. 18.

VI. Missionaries and Cannibals

1. *Typee,* p. 5.

2. Wilson, pp. 139-140; Fanning, pp. 125 ff., 156 ff.; Porter, II, 134-135;

Ellis, *Researches*, III, 237, 238. In *Typee*, p. 5, Melville cites Ellis in this connection: "Ellis, in his *Polynesian Researches*, gives some interesting accounts of the abortive attempts made by the Tahiti Mission to establish a branch mission upon certain islands in the group."

3. Ellis, *History*, I, 271–272. See also Bennett, I, 324; Coulter, p. 241; and Alexander, p. 237.

4. *Typee*, pp. 5–6.

5. See note 3, above.

6. Gracia, pp. 19–20.

7. *Ibid.* Gracia says that these American missionaries fled to Tahiti, where they were interviewed by J. N. Reynolds, author of the *Voyage of the U. S. Frigate Potomac . . . in the years 1831–1834,* and he cites page 247 of that work as the source of his information. Melville was undoubtedly acquainted with Reynolds as the author of "Mocha-Dick; or, The White Whale of the Pacific," and so was probably acquainted with this work also. But the first edition (1835) of it makes no mention of the incident, and I have not been able to discover any subsequent editions.

8. Ellis, *History*, I, 272.

9. Gracia, p. 20.

10. Ellis, *History*, pp. 272–273.

11. Gracia, pp. 19–31.

12. *Typee*, pp. 30, 98–99.

13. Anderson, *Journal*, p. 57.

14. Stewart, I, 223. Coulter (p. 243), who touched at Anna Maria Bay in 1833, apparently took the word of the Teiis without questioning it: "We went round the point in one of our boats, to have a look at the bay of Oomii [Typee]. It was not large, nor so well adapted for anchorage as the one we lay in. We contented ourselves with an examination of it without landing, as the Tiapiis [*sic*] are very treacherous." Other travellers who got their information from such a prejudiced source were probably persuaded to the same belief.

15. *Typee*, p. 31.

16. Olmsted, pp. 197–199. Gracia (pp. 29–30) gives a similar version of the same story, saying that it occurred just before his departure from Nukahiva in May, 1840, slightly more than two years before Melville's arrival.

17. Belcher, II, 316, 317.

18. *Typee*, p. 31.

19. Bennett, I, 341.

20. *Typee*, pp. 32–33.

21. Vincendon-Dumoulin, *Marquises*, pp. 119–137. See also Radiguet, *passim.*

22. *Typee*, p. 5; *The Piazza Tales*, p. 246n. (See also Introduction, note 12.)

23. Porter, II, 59–60, 73; see also II, 102–103.

24. *Ibid.*, II, 74, 90–95.

25. *Ibid.*, II, 108; 97–109.

26. Porter's two expeditions through Typee Valley took place in the latter

part of November, 1813; Stewart's ship remained at Typee Bay August 5–12, 1829, using this anchorage as a point of departure for various excursions inland.

27. *Typee,* pp. 33–34. In later years, as a lecturer, he continued in this same vein to an audience in Boston, the breeding-ground of reformers: "The white race have a very bad reputation among the Polynesians. With few exceptions they were considered the most bloodthirsty, atrocious and diabolical race in the world." (Quoted in Weaver, *Melville,* p. 374, from the Boston *Journal* of January 31, 1859.) Apparently, this was always a favorite theme with Melville as a lecturer (Birss, "Lectures").

28. Stewart, I, 296–299, 317–318.

29. *Typee,* pp. 30–31. (Compare Stewart's similar remarks quoted on p. 91, above.)

30. Mosblech. The Marquesan for "cannibale" is given as "kaikai"; for "anthropophage" it is "kaikai a enata" (eater of men).

Hale (in a work compiled from the volumes of Langsdorff, Krusenstern, Stewart, Porter, and Melville) discusses the two translations of *Taipii* as given by Melville and Krusenstern in a note (p. 10) as remarkable for its avowed prejudice as for its curious etymology: "These two explanations of the literal meaning of 'Typee' widely differ. In Langsdorff, *tai* is given as meaning 'sea,' and *pehipehi* 'to strike'; this word (spelt *pippee*) in *Typee,* means 'to kill'; from this might be derived *pih,* meaning a striker, killer, or warrior; these two words would give Krusenstern's meaning ['warriors of the ocean']. On the other hand, *akai* or *kaikai* means 'to eat.' *Kaipih* might mean 'eater-of-warriors,' and *kaipih* would easily be corrupted into *Taipih.* But as I do not believe that any of the inhabitants of Nukahiwa are cannibals, I prefer the former explanation."

Buschmann contents himself with Krusenstern's definition. Dordillon makes no effort to translate proper names. His dictionary, based on numerous manuscripts kept by the Catholic fathers at Nukahiva from Melville's time down to the present, is by far the best of the available authorities.

31. See Mosblech. The latter is somewhat obscure, "Hapa" being translated "un peu; fraction indéfinie" and the corresponding verb "hapai" as "se vanter." On the other hand, *Teii,* as a shortened form of *te haka-iki,* seems actually to have been the term used in addressing a young male chief (Handy, *Culture,* p. 49).

32. *Typee,* pp. 31, 137. Other writers, particularly Stewart, record evidence of the same sort.

33. Langsdorff, I, 141–150. It will be remembered that Melville's uncle, Captain John DeWolf, was a friend of this scientist who accompanied the Russian expedition, and that in all likelihood Melville was acquainted with Langsdorff's volumes even before sailing for the South Seas. (See pp. 15–16, above.)

34. Porter, II, 44–45, 48–49, 58.

35. *Ibid.,* II, 50.

36. Stewart, I, 319.

37. *Typee*, p. 228.

38. Coulter, pp. 178–228, *passim;* 228–232. What purports to be a second eyewitness account of cannibalism is found in a volume by Torrey, pp. 125–130. But the most cursory glance at this progenitor of the ten-cent thrillers will suffice to condemn it as an obvious fabrication—a sailor's yarn which even the most credulous will balk at.

39. Radiguet, p. 52.

40. E. S. C. Handy is by far the best of the modern ethnological authorities on the Marquesas Islands, for his work is based upon actual field investigation as well as on literary research (see Chap. VII, note 5). His summary of the evidence on cannibalism (*Culture*, pp. 218–220) is in general agreement with the conclusions reached in the present study. Among the best of the other modern ethnologists on the Marquesas Islands are Andree, Rollin, Frazer, and Williamson; but their studies, unfortunately, are mere literary compilations.

41. *Typee*, pp. 276–277. Elsewhere (*ibid.*, p. 166) Melville remarks that a native has even less fear of being eaten in barbarous Polynesia than a civilized man of being drawn and quartered in enlightened England.

42. *Ibid.*, pp. 125–127.

43. *Ibid.*

44. *Ibid.*, pp. 310–321, *passim.*

45. *Ibid.*, p. 320.

46. *Ibid.*, p. 32. The pleasantry about European flesh being too salt seems to have been a commonplace. Gracia (p. 242) remarks similarly: "les étrangers étaient *tapus*, c'est-à-dire que leur chair étaient interdite à la dent cannibale, parce que, disaient les plaisants parmi eux, la chair des blancs leur paraissait trop salée."

47. *Typee*, pp. 24, 39.

48. *Ibid.*, p. 25. Levi Hunt (pp. 12, 22–23, 65–66) gives a similar list of grievances and hardships endured by the common seaman: flogging, brutal and tyrannical treatment, poor food and filthy cooking, and a despotic captain.

49. See pp. 33–34. This memorandum and the notation in Mrs. Melville's journal (which adds nothing to the information contained in *Typee*) that "he [Melville] left the ship, being oppressed with hard fare and hard usage, in the summer of 1842, with a companion, Richard T. Greene (Toby), at the bay of Nukuheva in the Marquesas Islands" are the only two documents used by Weaver for all the one hundred and fifty pages which he devotes to Melville's career in the South Seas (see Chap. V, note 4).

Records such as that of the *Acushnet*, though infrequent, were not unheard of. The desertions and near mutiny aboard the *Styx* in 1843, as related by J. R. Browne, have already been mentioned (see pp. 37–38, above). And to this T. W. Smith adds an account of the desertion of the entire crew of his ship in a body at Payta, Peru, in 1821, because of the tyranny of the second mate and the refusal of the captain to remedy the situation (*Narrative*, pp. 171–174).

50. Gracia, pp 245, 253. A number of such sailors, he says, were residing at Taiohaë in 1840, Peruvians, Chileans, and especially two Englishmen.

51. In emphasizing the longevity of South Sea whaling voyages, as one of his reasons for desertion, Melville falls into a slight exaggeration, saying that the *Acushnet* was still in the Pacific at the time of writing *Typee*, in the fall of 1845. In reality, she had returned to America on May 13, 1845, with 850 barrels of sperm oil, 1350 barrels of whale oil, and 13,500 pounds of whale bone—a normal cruise both as to time and cargo. (*Typee*, p. 28; see Chap. IV, note 4, above.)

52. *Typee*, pp. 40, 41.

53. MS. in the Old Dartmouth Historical Society and Whaling Museum, New Bedford, Mass. (The picture is reproduced in Weaver, *Melville,* opposite p. 164.)

54. According to Weaver (*Melville* pp. 163–166) Toby was only 16 at the time of sailing from New Bedford.

55. Weaver, *Melville,* pp. 200–201.

56. Coan, *Life,* pp. 199–200. Gracia (p. 267) confirms the declaration that there were well-known paths connecting the valleys. See also Porter, II, 98, 99, 107.

57. *Typee,* pp. 64–65.

58. Porter, II, 102.

59. *Typee,* p. 87.

VII. The Noble Savages of Typee Valley

1. *Typee,* pp. vii, ix.

2. *Ibid.,* pp. 5, 228.

3. *Ibid.,* p. 247 and note. Melville probably made no further use of these volumes than in the instance here cited (see note 6, below).

4. *Ibid.,* pp. 228–229.

5. Handy, *Culture,* pp. 3–5. The chief MSS. consulted were those of Pierre Geroud Chaulet, I. R. Dordillon, Jean Lecornu, and Siméon Delmars. The first three are old, dating even from the time of Melville's residence; the last, more modern, has recently been published as *La Religion ou la paganism des Îles Marquises.*

6. *Typee,* pp. 246–247. The quoted passage may be found in the anonymous *Circumnavigation of the Globe,* pp. 68–69. This volume, it will be remembered, was included in the ship's library of the frigate *United States* during Melville's residence on board (see p. 358, above, and Chap. XIII, note 45).

7. *Typee,* pp. 247–248. Compare Langsdorff, I, 108: "I am inclined to think that the people of the Marquesas . . . Islands excel in beauty and grandeur of form, in regularity of features, and in colour, all the other South-Sea islanders"; Porter, II, 136: "The natives of Nooaheevah [*sic*] are more beautiful in their proportions than [the Sandwich Islander, the Otaheitan, and the New Zealander]. . . . I have had those of the three other places on board

my ship, and in point of beauty and intelligence of countenance they bear no comparison." See also Stewart, I, 255; Ellis, *Researches*, III, 233; and Bennett, I, 316.

8. Radiguet, p. 121; compare *Typee*, p. 242. Stewart, I, 255–256, makes a similar comparison in favor of the Hapas.

9. *Typee*, pp. 242–243, 245, 248.

10. Langsdorff, I, 108, 110–111.

11. Porter, II, 14, 62; 15, 86. See *Typee*, p. 247.

12. Stewart, I, 255; 294, 330; see *Typee*, p. 247. Such testimonials could be multiplied: Coulter, p. 189; and Ellis, *Researches* III, 233. The last strikes the highest note of praise, declaring: "Physically considered, the Marquesans are described as among the most perfect of the human species."

The scientists of the Bayard Dominick Expedition, as would be expected, take little part in this contest of eulogiums. But an even more recent observer still awards the Marquesans a high degree of praise for their beauty and substantiates his own (and Melville's) claims with numerous photographs taken during his residence of almost a year among them (see Menard).

13. *Typee*, pp. 114–115, 181. Porter, II, 62.

14. Ginoux, III, 365.

15. Russell, pp. 76–77, 78; Ellis, *Researches*, I, 76.

16. *Typee*, p. 245.

17. Stewart, I, 256. For similar accounts see Langsdorff, I, 113–115; and Porter, II, 66, 86. Handy, *Culture*, p. 292, gives a confirmation of them.

18. *Typee*, pp. 117, 162–163, 216, 308–309, and *passim*. Compare Ellis, *Researches*, I, 110–114; and see also Handy, *Culture*, pp. 291–294.

19. *Typee*, pp. 110–111, 114–117, 216, 234–235, etc. Compare Handy, *Culture*, pp. 279–296.

20. *Typee*, pp. 103–104.

21. Stewart, I, 247–249.

22. Porter, II, 27. Compare Handy, *Culture*, pp. 128, 294–295.

23. *Typee*, pp. 250, 251, 252.

24. Langsdorff, I, 130–131.

25. Porter, II, 34, 68. It is interesting to note that for Typee Valley Porter lists three tribes, one of which, the "Attayiyas" [*sic*], was "a democracy without a chief."

26. Stewart, I, 264, 265–266.

27. Porter, II, 60–61, 62.

28. *Typee*, pp. 269–270, 272–273. As for the real estate on the island, Melville was inclined to think it was held communistically (*ibid.*, p. 271); but Stewart (I, 277) thought the system was feudal. The actual system, it seems, lay somewhere between these two extremes, but Melville was undoubtedly nearer the truth than Stewart. According to Handy, at the time of European contact most of the land on which the various tribes lived was regarded as the private property of the chief, but there was a definite, lingering conception of its belonging to the whole tribe which severely limited his rights in it (Handy, *Culture*, p. 57).

Although Melville evidently considered the Marquesan system as an un-expected realization of the hypothetical state of Rousseau, he was not will-ing to admit its kinship with the transcendental Utopias of his own day. As a lecturer in Boston, January 31, 1859, Melville is reported to have described "an interview he had with a poetical young man who called upon him to get his opinion upon what would be the prospects of a number, say four score, of disciples of Fourier to settle in the valley of Typee. He had not encour-aged the scheme, having too much regard for his old friends, the Polynesians" (quoted in Weaver, *Melville,* p. 374). Apparently this was a favorite quip with Melville as a lecturer (see Birss, "Lectures").

29. Handy, *Culture,* pp. 45, 49, 54, 56.

30. *Typee,* pp. 273–274, 275.

31. Porter, II, 60, 66–67.

32. *Typee,* pp. 172, 173–174.

33. Handy, *Culture,* p. 133; see also pp. 132, 139, 140.

34. Langsdorff, I, 151.

35. Porter, II, 36; 41. See also Gracia, pp. 80–81, 84–86.

36. Porter, II, 41.

37. See Ellis, *Researches,* I, 214–228, and Coulter, pp. 220–228. See also p. 105, above.

38. Stewart, I, 301–302.

39. *Ibid.,* I, 347.

40. *Typee,* pp. 276–277; 315–321. See pp. 100–111, above, for a full dis-cussion of Melville's treatment of the subject of cannibalism.

41. *Ibid.,* pp. 274–275.

42. Porter, II, 64, 121.

43. Handy, *Culture,* pp. 39–42. (See pp. 72–76, above, and Chap. V, note 12.)

44. Porter, II, 64, 121.

45. *Typee,* pp. 254, 255.

46. *Ibid.,* pp. 256–258.

47. Stewart, I, 339–340.

48. Ellis, "Polyandry." Stedman says this article appeared on September 28, 1891, about two weeks before Melville's death.

49. Westermarck, III, 146–148.

50. Handy, *Culture,* pp. 98–102. Gracia (p. 111) says he knew of only one example of polygyny in the Marquesas Islands.

51. *Typee,* p. 150.

52. *Ibid.,* pp. 151–156. Compare Ellis, *Researches,* I, 45–47; Langsdorff, I, 124–125; Porter, II, 56–58; Handy, *Culture,* pp. 187–196. For the metaphor applied to *popoi,* see *Typee,* p. 96, and Stewart, I, 289. It is possible, on the other hand, that Melville gathered such information from sources which have not yet come to light.

53. *Omoo,* pp. 310–311. For the description of gathering the nuts, see *Typee,* pp. 289–290; compare Porter, II, 53. Melville's account of the normal method of climbing the tree is prefaced by an anecdote illustrating a brand

of pantomimic, child-like humor which he and Porter alone attributed to the Marquesans (compare *Typee*, pp. 288–289, and Porter, II, 141).

54. Ellis, *Researches*, I, 53–59 *passim*.

55. *Omoo*, p. 311.

56. Ellis, *Researches*, I, 56–57. Compare *Omoo*, p. 312, and Ellis, *Researches*, I, 53, 57.

57. *Typee*, pp. 155–156, 213, 222–223; compare Porter, II, 86–87, 120. Porter, who gives the name as "pouarka," suggests the likeness to the Spanish *porca* and the possibility that the god who the natives said brought hogs to the island was Mendana (II, 53).

It is in connection with the preparation of pork that Porter complains of the lack of salt on the island (II, 56, 109). Melville comments on a similar scarcity, declaring: "I verily believe, that with a bushel of common Liverpool salt, all the real estate in Typee might have been purchased" (*Typee*, p. 152). See also Langsdorff, I, 125–126.

Besides hogs, Melville found very little other animal life on the islands. The following citations will afford sources and confirmations for his descriptions: (1) Birds: *Typee*, pp. 285, 290–291; compare Porter, II, 132–133. (2) Dogs and Cats: *Typee*, pp. 283–284; compare Porter, II, 130. (3) Lizards: *Typee*, pp. 284–285; compare Porter, II, 132. (4) Insects: *Typee*, pp. 285–286; compare Porter, II, 132; Bennett, I, 343–344.

58. *Typee*, pp. 278–282. Compare Gracia, pp. 70–73, and Handy, *Culture*, pp. 167–168, 196–197. Melville says that the fishing parties were always at full moon, but this is contradicted by Handy.

59. The first two, bananas and sugar-cane, are mentioned by all the early writers, but the only mention of seaweed I have been able to find besides Melville's is in Jardin, pp. 55–57. For a full discussion of foods see Handy, *Culture*, pp. 181–202 *passim*.

60. *Typee*, pp. 206, 221–222; compare Porter, II, 56. See also Handy, *Culture*, pp. 202–203.

61. *Typee*, pp. 197–199; compare Ellis, *Researches*, I, 145–149. See also Porter, II, 125–126; Bennett, I, 337–338; and Handy, *Culture*, p. 162.

62. The natives themselves, Melville says, conducted only four fishing expeditions during his stay, although they appeared to be extravagantly fond of fish (*Typee*, p. 278). A possible explanation for this seems to lie in Handy's report: "It is commonly said in Taiohae that the people of Tai-pi living up-valley were not allowed by the hostile lower valley tribe to go down to the sea to fish" (*Culture*, pp. 198–199). Just who is meant by this "hostile lower valley tribe" I have not been able to ascertain. Porter says that the valley was inhabited by three separate tribes (II, 35); and the existence of such a tribe may account for the confusion and quarreling among the natives at the beach which, according to Melville, facilitated his escape (*Typee*, pp. 329–339).

63. *Typee*, pp. 296–297; *Omoo*, p. 36. Compare Handy, *Tattooing*, pp. 1–3. The information in this excellent study was obtained from the few remaining natives who are tattooed and from the one surviving *tuhuna* or artist, c

well as from literary sources. The custom of tattooing has long been prohibited by French law. (See also Berchon.)

64. *Typee,* pp. 104, 111, 181–182; compare Handy, *Tattooing,* pp. 15–16.
See also Langsdorff, I, 122 (and illustrations); Porter, II, 14–15; Ellis, *Researches,* I, 207.

65. *Typee,* pp. 7–8, 104, 111, 296, 297; compare Bennett, I, 306–307. Handy
(Tattooing, p. 18) also confirms Melville's description. Berchon gives the specific confirmation that triangles, of which Handy found no evidence, were used only by the Typees as a facial design.

66. *Typee,* pp. 8, 115–116, 256; compare Handy, *Tattooing,* pp. 5, 14; and see, above, pp. 81–85, and note. Langsdorff (I, 120–121) and Porter (II, 124) add designs on the arms; Bennett (I, 309) mentions seeing them on the bust.

67. *Typee,* pp. 292–293; compare Handy, *Tattooing,* pp. 10–11. See also Langsdorff, I, 118; Porter, II, 124; Coulter, pp. 210–212. Melville's account of coming upon his artist at work in the midst of a thicket seems to be totally without foundation: the operation was always performed indoors, in a special *tapu* house.

68. *Typee,* pp. 294–296.

69. Langsdorff, I, 122; Bennett, I, 307.

70. Coulter, pp. 204–214.

71. *Omoo,* p. 32.

72. *Ibid.,* pp. 36–38.

73. Handy, *Tattooing,* p. 17.

74. *Ibid.,* pp. 3, 4, 5, 8, 9.

75. Langsdorff, I, 117–120 *passim.*

76. Handy, *Tattooing,* pp. 5–6. For the two accounts, which are quite similar, see *Omoo,* pp. 38–39, and Langsdorff, I, 121.

77. *Typee,* pp. 108–110. Compare: Langsdorff, I, 126–127; Porter, II, 43–44; Stewart, I, 233–236; Bennett, I, 302–303; Coulter, pp. 165–166; and Handy, *Culture,* pp. 62–63.

78. *Typee,* p. 207.

79. *Ibid.,* p. 208.

80. *Ibid.,* p. 209.

81. Linton, pp. 5, 7, 8.

82. *Ibid.,* pp. 33, 36, 114. The sacred places were deserted except during times of ceremonies: hence the unkempt appearance described by Melville, which he took as an indication that this was an ancient forgotten ruin.

83. Porter, II, 42–43.

84. *Ibid.,* II, 118; *Typee,* p. 209. Ellis (*Researches,* I, 261) gives the name of "maræ" to the pyramidical temples he found in the Society Islands; but the other travel writers, when they give any name at all to the Marquesan platforms, use the more correct form of *me'æ* (see Stewart, I, 239).

85. *Typee,* p. 122.

86. Porter, II, 105. See also *ibid.,* II, 42–43, 113–114; Stewart, I, 238–239, 257–258; and Handy, *Culture,* pp. 118–120, 205–206, 231–234.

87. *Typee,* p. 123; see Handy, *Culture,* pp. 126–127.

88. Bennett, I, 317; Langsdorff, I, 128.

89. Lamont, p. 26. He was at first under the impression, as Melville had been, that this was the chief's dwelling, a misconception that arose quite naturally since, like all the other "public" buildings, it was actually one of the chief's possessions.

90. *Typee*, pp. 219–220.

91..*Ibid.*, p. 224.

92. *Ibid.*, pp. 225–226.

93. Stewart, I, 254–260.

94. Handy, *Culture*, pp. 212–216, 218. See also Williamson, *Social and Political Systems*, I, 302.

95. Bennett, I, 318.

96. Langsdorff, I, 158–160. An account of their chants follows.

97. A fuller comparison of Melville's accounts of Marquesan music with those of contemporary observers may be made from the following citations: (1) Drums: *Typee,* pp. 225–226; compare Ellis, *Researches*, I, 156–157; Langsdorff, I, 160, 164; Stewart, I, 258, 275–276; Bennett, I, 333; Handy, *Culture*, pp. 310–311. (2) Chants: *Typee*, pp. 225–226, 305–306; compare Langsdorff, I, 160–168; Stewart, I, 261, 272–273; Bennett, I, 334; Handy, *Culture*, pp. 314–341. (3) Nasal Flute: *Typee*, pp. 306–307; compare Ellis, *Researches*, I, 159; Handy, *Culture*, pp. 311–312. In all such matters Melville would have had little difficulty in finding source material, and his descriptions, according to Handy, were accurate enough.

In his descriptions of their dances, however, he seems to have been guilty of some romancing. At the very opening of *Typee* (p. 18) he says: "The varied dances of the Marquesan girls are beautiful in the extreme, but there is an abandoned voluptuousness in their character which I dare not attempt to describe." Later (p. 204), he adds: "There are a great variety of these dances, in which, however, I never saw the men take part. They all consist of active, romping, mischievous evolutions, in which every limb is brought into requisition. Indeed, the Marquesan girls dance all over, as it were; not only do their feet dance, but their arms, hands, fingers, ay, their very eyes seem to dance in their heads. In good sooth, they so sway their floating forms, arch their necks, toss aloft their naked arms, and glide, and swim, and whirl, that it was almost too much for a quiet, sober-minded, modest young man like myself." But Melville was merely writing what his readers would demand of a book on the South Seas. None of the other visitors, with one exception (Coulter, pp. 167–171), found their dances lascivious; even Stewart, a former missionary, declares: "There was less of licentiousness in the dance than I had expected" (I, 262). And Handy confirms this repudiation of Melville's testimony still further. In spite of the fragmentary present state of knowledge of the ancient dances, he was able to establish three points which contradict Melville: (1) dances were done in solo rather than in groups; (2) they were performed principally by men; and (3) there was no hip and abdominal dance corresponding to the *hula* of Hawaii and the *upaupa* of Tahiti (*Culture*, pp. 304–307).

98. Handy, *Culture,* pp. 212–216, 218. (See also Gracia, pp. 72–74.)

99. *Typee,* pp. 215, 227.

100. *Typee,* pp. 16, 122–123, 175–178, 187, 274, 279, 297–302. Compare Langsdorff, I, 133–138; Porter, II, 22, 42, 68, 115, 119–120; Stewart, I, 240–243; Handy, *Culture,* pp. 46, 59–61, 89–90, 97–98, 257–263. It is interesting to note that Porter and Melville are the only ones who report that the men and women were permitted to eat together, all the other authorities, including Handy, declaring that this was prohibited by *tapu.* Porter also tells how he was taken under the especial protection of the chief and his person made *tapu,* just as Melville was; and, in confirmation, Handy quotes the Marquesan proverb: *"Mea tapu te manahi'i; ua tapapa te haka-iki* (The stranger is sacred, the chief entertains him)." Finally, Porter explains the *tapu kanaka* who, like Melville's "Marnoo," could go with impunity into a hostile valley —as one who had intermarried with the enemy tribe; Handy adds that a mere friendship with a member of the hostile tribe ratified by the ceremony of exchanging names was sufficient to invoke such a *tapu.*

101. *Typee,* pp. 297, 302. See Porter, II, 42, for a similar remark.

102. *Typee,* pp. 16, 302.

103. Stewart, I, 240, 242–243; Coulter, pp. 153–154. Vergnes (p. 33), records that it was still in force thirty years after the French occupation.

104. Handy, *Culture,* pp. 261–262. The curse that resulted from such defilement, he adds, was leprosy. According to Melville and Menard the penalty was death.

105. Menard, p. 462.

106. *Typee,* pp. 176–178.

107. Frazer, II, 373; 328–374. (See Williamson, *Religions and Cosmic Beliefs,* and Handy, *Culture, passim.*)

108. *Typee,* p. 239; see also pp. 229–230, 233, 238–239. Porter likewise testifies to his perplexity and remarks, just as Melville does, that he doubts if the natives themselves could explain the nature of their religion (II, 118).

109. *Typee,* pp. 233–234. Compare Handy, *Culture,* pp. 236–239.

110. See Stewart, I, 272; Porter, II, 114.

111. *Typee,* p. 106. Compare Stewart, I, 244, 328; Gracia, pp. 63–65; Handy, *Culture,* p. 227.

112. *Typee,* pp. 106–107.

113. Stewart, I, 270; compare Handy, *Culture,* pp. 269–270.

114. *Typee,* p. 234; Stewart, I, 271.

115. *Typee,* pp. 235, 236–238. The name "Moa Artua" is suggestive: *artua (etua)* means "god," as Melville rightly says; *moa,* on the other hand, means "temple assistant." The possible etymology of Melville's god is thus indicated.

116. Stewart, I, 274.

117. Porter, II, 116–117, 119.

118. Handy, *Culture,* pp. 238–239. This is said in spite of the supporting testimony of Stewart, which Handy quotes.

119. *Typee,* pp. 234, 239, 240–241.

120. Porter, II, 116.

121. Stewart, I, 239, 286, 292. This state of affairs led the chaplain to hope that the Marquesans would readily embrace Christianity. In the Hapa Valley, however, his heart sank, for he found paganism in a more flourishing condition there (*ibid.*, I, 331).

122. *Typee*, pp. 230–232.

123. Porter, II, 114–115, 117. (See also Stewart, I, 282, 284; and Bennett, I, 329.) Handy (*Culture,* pp. 121–122) quotes the accounts of Porter and Melville as indicative of a conception in the native mind that the soul of the dead went to heaven in a canoe. *Havai'i* (heaven), incidentally, seems formerly to have meant an ancient and distant region to the westward, vaguely identified with the land of their ancestors. The name occurs repeatedly in islands to the westward—notably in "Hawaii."

124. *Typee*, p. 233. The few remaining religious matters that Melville discusses are all connected with the cult of the dead. (1) A funeral ceremony which he says he witnessed at Taiohaë: *Typee*, pp. 260–261; compare Langsdorff, I, 154–155; Porter, II, 125; Stewart, I, 287–290; Gracia, pp. 116–118; Handy, *Culture,* pp. 106, 110, 117. (2) Mummified bodies suspended on the walls of dwelling houses in the glen of Taioa: *Typee*, p. 261; compare Wise, p. 390; Handy, *Culture,* p. 243. (3) The heads of enemies preserved as trophies: *Typee*, pp. 261–262, 311–312; compare Porter, II, 118; Handy, *Culture,* pp. 113–114, 258. On this last point Melville was apparently in error, and probably deliberately so. The anecdote in which he tells of discovering the mummified head of a white man, which he feared might be that of his lost companion Toby, is unconvincing, to say the least. For the Marquesans were not head-hunters in any sense of the word: the skulls and bones which they kept as relics were merely part of their ancestral cult.

125. *Typee*, pp. 165, 262. Melville's prophecy was not long in being fulfilled, though the Typees held out against French domination longer than any other Marquesan tribe. It was not until 1857, fifteen years after Melville's departure, that they were finally brought to terms after a devastating campaign had been conducted against them, their villages ravaged, and the inhabitants all but driven from the valley (Caillot, pp. 350, 370).

Ten years later a smallpox epidemic swept the whole island, taking in its toll the old puppet king Moana. But the tragic story of the Marquesas Islands is a somewhat different one from that of the other principal Pacific groups, such as the Sandwich Islands. For the French did not find commercial exploitation profitable here, as a visitor in 1869 recorded. The main body of settlers had evacuated Nukahiva in 1860, and there was no longer any trade to the islands, even the whalers having given them up as a watering place ("Cruise of the U. S. S. Jamestown to the Marquesas and other Islands in the Pacific, 1869–1870," MS. in the Naval Records and Library, Navy Department, Washington, D. C.).

A last unsuccessful commercial venture was begun about this time. An English planter from Tahiti bought about five hundred acres of land "situated in Tipi [*sic*] bay" and established a colony of thirty Chinese farmers there. The plantation flourished for a while, producing magnificent fields of sea-island cotton in the very valley which Melville had celebrated twenty-five years before as a primitive paradise. By 1873, however, it was bankrupt because of bad management (Vergnes, p. 16).

Thenceforth, the natives have been left pretty much to themselves, a desultory trade in *copra* being the only considerable pursuit of the white man in this archipelago. Not competition with a superior economic power, therefore, but ennui and the ravages of disease have wrought havoc with the Noble Savages whom Melville celebrated. Sentimental pilgrims have recorded the progressive stages of this decline. (See Gohdes; Stoddard, p. 279; Stevenson, *South Seas, passim;* O'Brien, pp. 306–309; Menard, p. 459.)

126. See Chap. X.

127. *Typee,* p. 170: "But the continual happiness which, so far as I was able to judge, appeared to prevail in the valley, sprung principally from that all-pervading sensation which Rousseau has told us he at one time experienced, the mere buoyant sense of a healthful existence." (For other passages in a strikingly similar vein see *ibid.,* pp. 166–168, 193–194, 202, 262, 273.)

128. Quoted in Weaver, *Melville,* p. 299. Some part of Melville's Rousseauistic attitude, moreover, may have been derived indirectly from authors who wrote of primitive life in a similarly romantic manner, such as Captain David Porter.

VIII. Truth and Fiction in "Typee"

1. *Typee,* p. ix.

2. Weaver, *Melville,* pp. 206–207. No source is cited for this information. But it is confirmed by a statement in the Boston *Literary World,* XXIII, 352–353 (October 8, 1892). In a review of Arthur Stedman's edition of *Typee: A Real Romance of the South Seas,* the anonymous critic declared: "When *Typee* was first published, in 1846, by Mr. John Murray of London, he—his plans not including fiction—accepted the manuscript on the assurance of the author's brother that it contained nothing which had not been really experienced by Herman Melville."

3. Weaver, *Melville,* pp. 207–208. Compare Mumford, p. 75.

4. Weaver, *Melville,* pp. 255–256.

5. *Ibid.,* pp. 224–225. It is true that in another connection Weaver did quote a sentence from each of two favorable magazine reviews, only to add that "such pronouncements were no earnest of fame," though "they may have contributed somewhat to augment Melville's royalties." This does little, if anything, to relieve the impression that the English reaction to *Typee* and *Omoo* was highly unfavorable. And in his most recent critical comments on Melville, Weaver repeats this misleading citation of the *Eclectic Review* as typical of Melville's contemporary reception (*Journal,* p. v).

6. Anderson, "American Debut."

7. Anderson, "English Debut."

8. Chasles, "Séjour."

9. Chasles, "Voyages," p. 547*n*. In this note Chasles acknowledges the authorship of the earlier review.

10. *Ibid.*, p. 542.

11. The *Seamen's Friend,* Honolulu, IV, 157 (October 15, 1846). The editor announced also that there was a letter in his possession addressed to Melville in care of the *Acushnet.*

12. *Ibid.*, V, 86 (June 1, 1847).

13. The *Polynesian,* III, No. 22 (October 17, 1846). An extract from the New Bedford *Mercury* follows. In the issue of November 18, 1846, a generous specimen from *Typee* is quoted, without any comment, however.

14. *Ibid.*, IV, 174 (March 18, 1848).

15. I am indebted for this information to Robert S. Forsythe of the Newberry Library, Chicago, who is at present compiling a definitive bibliography of Melville.

16. See Minnegerode, pp. 20–28, for a list of the passages deleted. See also pp. 238–239, above.

17. Forsythe, "Marquesas." The review in the New York *Courier and Enquirer* appeared in the issue of April 17, 1846.

18. Conveniently reprinted in Minnegerode, pp. 17–19.

19. *Ibid.*, pp. 14–15, 19.

20. Chasles, "Voyages," pp. 545–546.

21. The New York *Literary World,* V, 103 (August 11, 1849).

22. See pp. 119–121.

23. Wise, p. 399*n*: "In all the lighter sketches upon Polynesia, I cannot resist paying the faint tribute of my own individual admiration to Mr. Melville. Apart from the innate beauty and charming tone of his narratives, the delineations of Island life and scenery, from my own personal observations, are most correctly and faithfully drawn." This note has been reprinted by John H. Birss in the *Saturday Review of Literature,* VIII, 429 (January 2, 1932). Duyckinck quoted it in the New York *Literary World,* V, 355–356 (October 27, 1849), as proof of the truth of *Typee* and *Omoo.* Melville, in London at the time, secured a copy of Wise's book from his English publisher Bentley, as recorded in his "Journal," December 15, 1849, MS. in the Widener Library, Harvard; this volume, however, is not included in the list of books purchased as recorded by Weaver, *Melville,* pp. 299, 304. But Wise was not quite so sweeping in his corroboration of Melville when he took his notes at Nukahiva; for in the manuscript journal from which his published volume was drafted he observed that Melville's Marquesan scenes were "prettily" rather than "faithfully" drawn, and he qualified this even further by adding "with exception of some few embellishments." ("Journal of Lieutenant Henry A. Wise, U. S. N., Cruise of the U. S. S. Independence from Boston to the Pacific Ocean. September, 1846–May 1849," MS. in the Naval Records and Library, Navy Dept., Washington.)

Arthur Stedman, the companion of Melville's last years, reopened the question of the authenticity of *Typee* in an obituary notice. After discussing the abuse showered on his friend's early books by the missionaries, he remarked:

"It is a curious fact that both works [*Typee* and *Omoo*] proved of the greatest value to outgoing missionaries on account of the exact information contained in them with respect to the islanders" (Stedman, " 'Marquesan' Melville"). And the next year he added more specifically: "I have been told by Dr. Coan that his father, the Rev. Titus Coan, of the Hawaiian Islands, personally visited and verified in all respects the statements made in 'Typee' " (Stedman, *Typee*, p. xiv). But the Reverend Titus Coan's report, though entirely free of the abusive disparagement heaped upon Melville by the average missionary, is not quite so sweeping a verification; it seems to emphasize the romance rather than the reality of *Typee* (see pp. 114–115, above).

24. Strong evidence of this is found in the fact that his personal knowledge seems to have been insufficient to warn him that he was appropriating incorrect information when he borrowed his account of tattooing from Langsdorff and his description of naïve religious ceremonies from Porter and Stewart (see pp. 152–156, 169–175, above). Possible negative evidence may be found in a number of matters which Melville failed to mention, but which longer residents like Porter called attention to. Some of these omissions may be explained on the basis that they were not suitable to the thesis of *Typee:* for example, Melville says nothing about the elaborate stone fortifications, villages with regularly laid out streets, and cultivated plantations of breadfruit and cocoanut trees, but this was apparently because they indicated a higher degree of civilization than he cared to assign to his Noble Savages. But his omission of many other prominent features of Marquesan life mentioned by other travelers—stilt-walking, string-games, and the like—admits of no explanation save that because of the brevity of his visit he was entirely ignorant of them.

25. For passages indicating how completely previous biographers have leaned upon Melville's books as autobiography, see Introduction, note 11.

26. *Typee*, pp. 135–136, 141–144, 158–160.

27. Porter, II, 91, 94–95, 104–106; Stewart, I, 345–346. Compare *Typee*, pp. 323–328.

28. Stedman, " 'Marquesan' Melville."

29. Chasles, "Séjour."

30. A reasonable hypothesis would be that Chasles was reviewing a pirated French edition that contained this spurious version, but I have not been able to discover the existence of any French edition in 1846, pirated or otherwise (see *Bibliographie de la France, ou Journal général de l'imprimerie et de la librairie*, XXXVe, XXXVIe, Paris, 1846, 1847). Nor is there any record of a pirated edition of *Typee* having been brought out in any other country. From all indications he was reviewing a copy of the first English edition, which is identical with the text of the standard Constable edition.

IX. Mutiny on the "Lucy Ann"

1. *Omoo*, pp. vii, viii.

2. See p. 206, and Chap. IX, note 23. According to internal evidence Mel-

ville was rescued on a Monday afternoon. (*Omoo*, pp. 5, 9, 23–26, 28, 31, 34, 41, indicates that five days were spent in cruising about the Marquesas Islands, and that on the sixth, which was Sunday, the "Julia" stood out to sea westward from Hivaoa.) Thus, according to my conjectural chronology, the date of Melville's escape from Typee Valley can be placed tentatively as August 8 or 15, 1842—both of which fell on Monday.

An independent investigator of Melville's South Sea itinerary arrives at August 8, 1842, as the date of escape (see Forsythe, "Marquesas").

3. Information kindly furnished by Miss Ida Leeson, Mitchell Library, Sydney, Australia, from contemporary newspapers and documents, shows the existence of a small Sydney trader named the *Julia*, but her history and description as well as her arrival at Tahiti near the end of October, 1842, direct from Australia, preclude her identification as the "Julia" of *Omoo*.

4. *Omoo*, pp. 10–11.

5. Wise, p. 399*n*. (See Chap. VIII, note 23.) The manuscript journal from which this volume was drawn gives the spelling *Venton*. Various other spellings of this captain's name complicate the problem; for the sake of uniformity, therefore, I have adopted the form *Vinton*.

6. Other details included in the Shipping Register's description are as follows: "One & a half *Decks*, Three *Masts*, *Length* 87 *Feet* 7 *Inches*, *Breadth taken* above *the Main Wales* 23 *Feet* 10 *Inches*, *Height between Decks* five *Feet* three *Inches*, . . . *Rigged with a* standing *Bowsprit*, Square *sterned*, Carvel *built*, No *Galleries*, a Woman's Bust *[Figure-]Head.*" (The matter in italics was contained in the printed form.)

The author is indebted to W. H. Ifould, Principal Librarian, The Public Library of New South Wales, for a copy of The Shipping Register, No. 20 of 1835, and for various items, cited here and elsewhere, from Sydney newspapers referring to the *Lucy Ann*.

7. *Tegg's Almanac*, Sydney, 1843; the *Australian*, May 22, 1843.

8. *Omoo*, pp. 11, 176, and *passim*. See p. 215, above, and Chap. IX, note 51.

9. An American whale ship named the *Lucy Ann* from Wilmington, Delaware, Captain King, was also in the southern Pacific at this time. But from July to November, 1842, she was continuously at sea, cruising in the neighborhood of south latitude 34°–37° and east longitude 122°–125°, south of Australia. ("Journal" of John F. Martin, MS. in the Delaware Historical Society. Information by courtesy of A. T. Lincoln, custodian.)

10. *Omoo*, pp. 10, 11, 47.

11. *Ibid.*, pp. 11–12, 16–17, 18.

12. *Shipping Gazette and General Trade List*, Sydney, 1844.

13. Lucett, I, 294–295. This volume, published anonymously, is ascribed to Edward *Lucatt* in the catalogue of the Library of Congress; but the best evidence shows his name to have been *Lucett*.

14. This corvette was either *La Triomphante* or *L'Embuscade*, both of which had been dispatched thither from Taiohaë towards the end of June, 1842. *La Reine Blanche* was still at Taiohaë, though Melville does not mention seeing her when the "Julia" touched there. She herself sailed on August

19 and spent a few days at the bay of Vaitahu, Tauata, before proceeding to Tahiti for the purpose of further conquests. (See Radiguet, pp. 71, 78, and Vincendon-Dumoulin, *Marquises*, p. 135. The Ministère de la Marine, Paris, in a letter to the author on December 19, 1935, reports that there is no mention of any such incident in the Log Book of *La Triomphante*, and that the Log Book of *L'Embuscade* for this cruise is lost.)

15. See pp. 152–156. The conjecture that Melville got his information from Langsdorff and that he met no such adopted chief as Lem Hardy is strengthened by the fact that Radiguet (pp. 44–46) in his full account of a visit to Hanamenu only two months before makes no mention of any white man living there with the natives.

16. *Omoo*, p. 71.

17. *Ibid.*, pp. 86–90. An interesting variant of these signatures, in a page from the original manuscript of *Omoo*, is described by Forsythe ("Tahiti," p. 347).

18. *Omoo*, p. 95; see also pp. 88–90.

19. *Ibid.*, p. 121; see also pp. 99–100, 113–116, 119–120.

20. This manuscript is preserved in the Archives Nationales, Paris, Marine 4/J.222. The information was furnished through the courtesy of the Ministère de la Marine by le Contre-Amiral M. Geuson, Sous-Chef d'État-Major Général. There is no further reference to the *Lucy Ann* or her crew, nor is there any mention of the affair in the "Correspondance de l'Amiral Dupetit-Thouars (1842)," Archives Nationales, Marine BB4–615. Neither source, it may be remarked, contains any reference to a ship named the *Julia*.

This piece of documentary evidence was discovered independently by Forsythe, though his transcript differs in a few minor details of wording. This and several other matters in the present chapter are contained in his two articles on Melville in Tahiti.

21. *Omoo*, p. 80.

22. Vincendon-Dumoulin, *Taïti*, II, 956ff. The "treaty" by which the French took possession was not signed until March, 1843, six months later.

23. *Omoo*, p. 119. A round forty days, plus the six spent in cruising about the Marquesas, when subtracted from September 23 gives this approximate date of August 8, if *Omoo* can be thus relied upon. If the six days are counted as part of the "forty days cruising" the date is August 15. (See note 2, above.)

24. *Omoo*, pp. 11, 26, 34, 53–59, 97, 100–122. (See pp. 215–216, above, and Chap. IX, note 53. The estimate of ten is borne out by the fact that only this number are mentioned by name throughout the rest of the story.)

25. *Omoo*, pp. 87–88.

26. G. Pritchard, *passim;* Ellis, *History*, I, 352; W. T. Pritchard, pp. 3, 22.

27. Letter from Charles B. Wilson, Acting-Consul, September 26, 1842 (MS. in the Foreign Office, London, 58/16, Pacific Islands, 1840–1842); "Private Journal No. 515, U. S. Brig *Porpoise*, U. S. Exploring Expedition," entry dated January 21, 1841 (MS. in the Hydrographic Office, Navy Department, Washington, D. C.); Vincendon-Dumoulin, *Taïti*, II, 958, quoting a letter from "Th[Ch?] Wilson, consul de S. M. B.," on September 12, 1842, accepting

the French protectorate; and W. T. Pritchard, p. 29.

28. *Omoo*, pp. 88–98, 119–121, 130–132, 162–165, 172–174, 177.

29. Wilkes, III, 18–19.

30. *Ibid.*, III, 129. Compare Lucett, I, 298–300, contra.

31. Wise, p. 399n. Compare, especially, the anecdote in *Omoo*, pp. 172–174, which concludes with a most vilifying scene. "Mother Tot," an old hag who kept a sailor's grog shop, one night accosted Wilson being borne home in a drunken condition by two natives: " 'Ha, ha! my fine *counsellor*,' she shrieked; 'ye persecute a lone old body like me for selling rum—do ye? And here ye are, carried home drunk— Hoot! ye villain, I scorn ye!' And she spat upon him."

32. W. T. Pritchard, pp. 44–45. But in 1842 he was apparently a newcomer, for the surgeon of the U. S. Exploring Expedition in 1839 deplores the fact that "There is no Physician in the Islands" ("Surgeon's Journal, No. 505, Wilkes's Exploring Expedition," *Vincennes*. MS. in the Hydrographic Office, Navy Department); and Commodore Wilkes adds, "I was surprised to hear that the London Society did not employ any medical men" (Wilkes, II, 49).

33. See pp. 226–229.

34. *Omoo*, pp. 115–117.

35. See Fitzroy (II, 509), who says that this pilot was valuable in getting the ship past Point Venus and in avoiding the Dolphin Shoal.

36. Beechey, p. 187. Belcher (II, 4) adds under date of April 5, 1840: "we were taken through [the reefs] in good style by our pilot 'Jim,' of notoriety in Beechey's work. As a native pilot, he deserves great credit, and acquits himself with far more coolness and decision than many Europeans."

37. Bennett, I, 66–67. Coulter (p. 264) mentions him in the same year as " 'Jem' [*sic*], the native pilot."

38. Wilkes, II, 4, 39. In the manuscript journal on which Wilkes's volumes are based Jim is said to hold his pilot's commission officially from Queen Pomaré (MS. Volume II, 1838–1839, Hydrographic Office).

39. Franklin, p. 62.

40. *Omoo*, pp. 121, 130.

41. See Chap. IX, note 20.

42. *Omoo*, p. 135.

43. Manuscript letter from Charles Wilkes to Queen Pomaré, September 18, 1839, Wilkes: Exploring Expedition, Volume I, 1838–1839 (MS. in the Hydrographic Office).

44. "Private Journal of U. S. Brig *Porpoise*, No. 515, Wilkes's Exploring Expedition" (MS. in the Hydrographic Office). Wilkes (IV, 276) refers to this jail as "the stocks."

45. Lucett, I, 225, 288.

46. *Omoo*, pp. 162–165.

47. Letters to the author from W. H. Ifould, Principal Librarian of the Public Library of New South Wales, and from Miss Ida Leeson, Mitchell Library, Sydney. Another letter, dated Papeete, April 23, 1934, from M. le Secrétaire de la Société d'Études Océaniennes, Tahiti, says concerning the affair of the *Lucy Ann*: "J'ai le regret de vous informer que malgré toutes mes

recherches, je n'ai pu trouver ici aucun document concernant ce batiment";
and he adds, what seems to render further research futile: "Les archives du
Consulat anglais de Papeete ne datent que de 1845."

48. Foreign Office, London, 58/16 (Pacific Islands, 1840–1842). Other docu-
ments searched were: F. O. 58/20, 21, 22, 23, 24, 25 (1843–1844); F. O. 83/130
(Sailing Letters, 1832–1853); and Admiralty 1/5581 (Captain's Letters, Captain
J. T. Nichols, Tahiti, 1843).

49. This was probably the schooner *Sarah Ann,* which sailed from Tahiti
on October 23, 1842 (*Morning Herald,* Sydney, December 1, 1842).

50. *Omoo,* p. 176.

51. The Sydney *Morning Herald,* December 2, 1842. These 120 barrels were
probably the "little oil there was aboard [that] had to be sold for a song to a
merchant of Papeetee," according to Melville (see p. 201 and Chap. IX,
note 8).

52. Saturday, October 15, according to ship's reckoning, would have been
Sunday, October 16, in Tahiti. Melville explains this anomalous situation
in *Omoo,* p. 194:

"It must be known that the missionaries of the good ship *Duff* [the first to
come to Tahiti, 1797], who more than half a century ago established the
Tahitian reckoning, came hither by the way of the Cape of Good Hope. . . .
For this reason, vessels coming round Cape Horn—as they most all do nowadays
—find it Sunday in Tahiti, when, according to their own view of the matter, it
ought to be Saturday. But as it won't do to alter the log, the sailors keep
their Sabbath, and the islanders theirs.

"This confusion perplexes the poor natives mightily; and it is to no purpose
that you endeavor to explain so incomprehensible a matter."

This information Melville probably got from Tyerman (I, 51), who gives
the whole story of the *Duff's* mistake, adding that the missionaries have not
dared to correct the error, for fear of "occasioning worse confusion in the
minds of a people to whom it would probably be difficult to make the change
intelligible."

53. *Omoo,* pp. 122, 151, 154, 157, 158, 167, 168. See p. 207, above, and
Chap. IX, note 24.

54. *Omoo,* pp. 132–134, 312–313.

55. Stewart, II, 19.

56. Wilkes, II, 33–34. The account by Franklin (p. 62), on the other hand,
seems to be indebted to Melville. Another visitor, in 1846–1847, concluded
his description of this road with a brief mention of Melville: "On the other
side is . . . the *carabouse* [*sic*], or State-prison of former times, where Omo
[*sic*] passed, according to his own account, a most disagreeable captivity" (Walpole, II, 82ff., 111).

57. *Omoo,* pp. 118–119.

58. Olmsted, p. 275; Starbuck, pp. 242–243. If Melville borrowed anything
from Olmsted, this anecdote and the one referred to on pp. 92–93, above,
exhaust the list of possibilities, leaving a wealth of material untouched. The
indications are that he was unacquainted with this volume.

59. *Omoo*, pp. 192–193.

60. Bennett, I, 67. Coulter, another whaling surgeon who visited Tahiti· the same year, mentions "a pleasure house for the queen" on this little island, which he calls simply "Mothu" (Coulter, pp. 264–265). Bennett's spelling *motu uta*, and his translation "the isle near the shore," is adopted as correct, because of its linguistic soundness.

61. Wheeler, pp. 250–251. See Fitzroy, II, 515; Wilkes, II, 41.

62. *Omoo*, pp. 198–199.

63. Ellis, *Researches*, II, 278–281. Even by 1829 all of the building had fallen to pieces except one section which was kept in repair for use as a schoolhouse (Stewart, II, 21). The contemporary account of the baptism of Pomaré II at this chapel one week later, as it was printed at the mission press, Tahiti, May 18, 1819, is reproduced by Lovett (I, 219–223).

64. *Omoo*, pp. 166–167, 169–170.

65. Yzendoorn, pp. 86, 113, 115, 146.

66. *Lettres lithographiées* ("Lithographed Letters Written Before 1865"), being two volumes of about 1,500 pages of copied, facsimile, and lithographed letters of missionary priests of the Society of Picpus in the South Seas, compiled about 1870 for distribution to various institutions of the Order of Sacred Hearts (copy in the possession of Father Reginald Yzendoorn, Honolulu, Hawaii, pp. 677–678, 679). The author is indebted to Carl Stroven, University of Hawaii, Honolulu, for searching this large collection of letters for references to Father Murphy.

Murphy, a native of Dundalk, Ireland, had had many hostile encounters with Protestant missionaries in Polynesia. (For a detailed account of his early career see Forsythe, "Father Murphy.")

67. *Lettres lithographiées*, pp. 776–782.

68. *Ibid.*, pp. 785–786.

69. *Ibid.*, p. 787.

70. When Lieutenant Wise (p. 399*n*) inquired about this jovial priest in 1848, however, it was discovered that he, as well as Captain Bob, the elderly native jailor, was dead.

71. *Omoo*, p. 156.

72. *Ibid.*, pp. 159–161.

73. Wise, p. 399*n*.

74. *Omoo*, p. 230. Then ("a few days after Johnson *presented his bill*") there follows a final tilt between Long Ghost and Dr. Johnston, in which the latter was again duped (*ibid.*, pp. 231–234). Incidentally, it is notable that the dates given by Wise—October 15 and 19—tally reasonably well with Melville's datings of Dr. Johnston's last two visits as "the day before the *Julia* sailed" and "a few days after."

75. Lucett, I, 293–294, 295–296. Lucett's reference here to the pains that Melville complained of in his limbs brings to mind the strange malady that Melville complained of all through *Typee* and the first part of *Omoo*, declaring at the time of his escape from the cannibal valley that "three months elapsed before I recovered my health"—August, September, and October. It

is interesting to note that in this the only confirmatory reference to Melville's unaccountably injured leg, the doctor who examined it was suspicious of the reality of the malady—even as the reader has been all along.

76. Lamont, p. 61. He adds: "Besides a good and well-regulated public hospital, there is also a private one kept by Dr. Johnston"—probably the one referred to by Melville as "the sailor hospital at Townor [Taonoa], a small place on the beach between Papeetee and Matavai" (*Omoo*, p. 175).

Perkins (p. 295) speaks of visiting Dr. Johnston in 1853 in his house on the bay, surrounded by an exquisite garden, but he likewise makes no mention of Melville. (Several further facts about Dr. Johnston's character are given by Forsythe, "More Tahiti," pp. 9–12.)

77. *Omoo*, p. 177.

78. *Ibid.*, pp. 179, 185–186.

79. Turnbull, pp. 84–85.

80. *Omoo*, pp. 237–238, 239, 244, 254, 267. The fourth day on Eimeo, by this reckoning, was Sunday; hence the departure was on a Wednesday midnight.

81. Lucett, I, 287–290. Since this study was completed, Lucett's volume has been independently discovered by another investigator (see Aaron, "An English Enemy").

82. Lucett, I, 290–293. Previously, Lucett had described this curfew regulation under which he was falsely arrested (*ibid.*, I, 225–226).

83. *Ibid.*, I, 293–295.

84. *Omoo*, p. 94. See also pp. 95, 105, 106, 122. Perhaps the best proof that Melville was not present in the calaboose at the time of Lucett's arrest is the fact that there is not the slightest hint of such a scene to be found in the pages of *Omoo*. Had he known of this event, Melville would certainly have made copy of it.

X. *Tahiti in 1842*

1. Minnegerode, pp. 109–123, and the letter on p. 19.

2. MS. in the New York Public Library. This letter, which is not in the regular Duyckinck Collection, was kindly brought to my attention by Mr. John H. Birss. It is not dated, but a reference to Melville's immediate departure from New York City to visit Toby and get the information for his sequel to *Typee* places it as some time shortly after July 1, 1846. Mumford (pp. 75–77), inexplicably, attributes the expurgation to Duyckinck.

3. Minnegerode, pp. 28–29.

4. MS. in the Duyckinck Collection, New York Public Library, dated in pencil in Duyckinck's handwriting "December 10, 1846"—not included by Minnegerode.

5. E. A. Duyckinck to G. L. Duyckinck, December 15, 1846. MS. in the Duyckinck Collection, New York Public Library.

6. Weaver (*Melville*) gives the fullest discussion of these problems, though the facts recorded are few. Dr. John Murray of Harvard is said to have dis-

covered important new information shedding light on Melville's religion, which will be embodied in his forthcoming psychological study of Herman Melville. See also Braswell, "Christianity"; Braswell has collected all the available published material on the subject.

7. *Omoo*, p. 198. Melville also speaks of the "European chapel" in the village of Papeete, where "there were about forty people present, including the officers of several ships in the harbour" and ten mutineers. "It was an energetic discourse," he adds, "and the pulpit-cushion was well pounded." (*Ibid.*, pp. 186–187.)

Fitzroy (II, 523, 527) speaks of this same English chapel as a small wooden structure where he had attended service in 1835: "Mr. Pritchard . . . performed divine service in the manner of the Independents. Occasional visitors from ships at the island, and the few European residents who are within reach, frequent this chapel." Since Pritchard was absent in England at the time of Melville's visit, it is impossible to say who was preaching in his stead. Lovett (I, 793–794) lists fourteen missionaries as resident in the Society Islands during 1842.

But Melville was far more interested in the native churches, where he could observe the effect of Christianity on the Polynesians themselves.

8. *Omoo*, pp. 199–200.

9. Wilkes, II, 9.

10. Fitzroy, II, 515.

11. *Omoo*, pp. 201–204.

12. Kotzebue, I, 154–158.

13. Wilkes, II, 7. The congregation here described was that of the aged missionary Wilson at Matavai, near Point Venus.

14. Wheeler, p. 268.

15. Fitzroy, II, 523.

16. Darwin, III, 494. It will be remembered that these volumes formed part of the library of the frigate *United States* during Melville's residence on board.

17. G. Pritchard, p. 57; see also, for example, p. 80, where Pritchard declares: "But few congregations in England surpass them in serious attention and decent behavior in the house of God."

18. *Omoo*, pp. 204–205.

19. *Ibid.*, pp. 205–206.

20. See, for example, Wilson, and Ellis, *History*. (See also pp. 86–90, above, for similar impressions recorded by missionaries at the Marquesas Islands.)

21. See, for example, Russell, who admits that "the indolence of the Otaheitans [*sic*] is beyond the cure of any common remedy." (A copy of this volume, it will be remembered, was published in the Harpers' Family Library Series in time to be included in the ship's library of the frigate *United States* during Melville's residence.)

22. Turnbull, pp. 256–257.

23. *Omoo*, p. 358.

24. Russell, p. 104.

25. Kotzebue, I, 159, 169–170.

26. *Omoo*, pp. 206, 207, 222.

27. *Ibid.*, p. 223.

28. Wilkes, II, 57. But Melville may have visited this school himself, and seen with his own eyes, while he was on the island of Eimeo. Established at Afareaitu in 1824 as the South Sea Academy, it was moved to Papetoai—where Melville spent several weeks—under the mastership of Alexander Simpson, who was still presiding over it in 1842 (Lovett, I, 296, 297).

29. Tyerman, I, 50.

30. *Omoo*, p. 208. See also Darwin, III, 493.

31. Kotzebue, I, 150, 169–170.

32. *Omoo*, p. 211 and note 2.

33. Wheeler, pp. 285, 568. Melville's reference to p. 763 is to the London edition of 1842, where Wheeler adds: "The fact that the poor native is subjected to a penalty if he absents himself from the chapel, and the sight of a man with a stick ransacking the villages for worshippers, before the hour of service,—a spectacle we have witnessed,—are so utterly abhorrent to our notions, that I cannot revert to the subject without feelings of regret and disgust."

34. Kotzebue, I, 203–204.

35. *Omoo*, pp. 211, 212.

36. Olmsted, p. 291.

37. Lucett, I, 223.

38. *Omoo*, pp. 210–211.

39. See, for example, *American Review*, VI, 42 (July, 1847).

40. Lamont, pp. 18–19. It is possible, of course, that Lamont had read *Omoo* and based his anecdote thereon, but he makes no mention of any acquaintance with Melville's works.

41. Darwin, III, 490.

42. *Omoo*, pp. 216–217.

43. Beechey, pp. 195–196. (See especially Kotzebue, I, 170–175, and Wilkes, II, 14–15, for reference to the suppression of games and amusements, and the resulting listlessness.)

44. *Omoo*, pp. 225–226.

45. Wheeler, p. 566, quoting an extract from a letter of his son, Charles Wheeler, to the family at home. The sentence quoted by Melville is inaccurate in phrasing, but not sufficiently so to be chargeable with any misrepresentation of Wheeler's sentiments.

46. Ellis, *Researches*, II, 208–210, 215.

47. *Omoo*, p. 226.

48. Ellis, *Researches*, II, 223–224. (See also Tyerman, I, 78, and Beechey, p. 186.)

49. Stewart, II, 29.

50. Coulter, p. 286.

51. Wilkes, II, 15.

52. *Omoo*, p. 226.

53. Ellis, *Researches*, II, 211–212.

54. Tyerman, I, 79; Stewart, II, 18; Wilkes, II, 59. See also pp. 302–304, 308, above.

55. *Omoo*, pp. 220–221.

56. Kotzebue, I, 167–168. Melville's quotation follows, even as his footnote cites, on p. 168; as usual, it is slightly garbled, but this is the result of carelessness rather than of any purpose to misrepresent.

57. *Omoo*, p. 221.

58. Beechey, p. 185. Melville's quotation is found immediately preceding, on pp. 183–184; his reference (I, 287) is to the London edition (1831) of Beechey's *Narrative*.

59. Turnbull, pp. 263–264.

60. *Omoo*, pp. 220–221.

61. Russell, p. 394. The discussion of authorities will be found on pp. 111–117; Melville's reference to p. 96 must be an error, for he expressly refers to the "Harpers' Family Library Edition."

62. *Omoo*, p. 224. See Beechey, p. 173. Melville's quotation is in reality a close paraphrase; his reference (I, 269) is to the London edition of 1831.

63. Ellis, *History*, I, 269–270. See also Tyerman, I, xiv, and II, 217n; and Stewart, II, 26, 53–56. It is interesting to note that in *Omoo* Melville made no further use of Stewart's volumes, which had proved so fertile in the composition of *Typee*.

64. Fitzroy, II, 549.

65. Darwin, III, 492–493.

66. Quoted by G. Pritchard, p. 57.

67. Quoted by Ellis, *History* I, 331.

68. Coulter, pp. 268–269; see further pp. 270–278.

69. Bennett, I, 80–81.

70. Beale, pp. 379, 382, 383.

71. *Omoo*, pp. 221–222.

72. Wheeler, p. 570 (the italics are mine). Melville's reference (p. 757) is to the London edition of 1842, from which this, the American edition, was reprinted. (See pp. 252, 257–258, above.)

73. "Private Journal of a Cruise in the U. S. Flagship Vincennes . . . to the South Seas and Around the World, No. 512," entry under date of September 23, 1839 (MS. in the Hydrographic Office, Navy Department).

74. Wilkes, II, 12, 13, 14.

75. *Ibid.*, II, 14.

76. Olmsted, p. 298.

77. Lucett, I, 223–224.

78. See Anderson, "American Debut," and "English Debut." (See also pp. 179–181, above.)

79. "Christian Missions," *Westminster Review*, X [n.s.], 35; 1–51 *passim* (July 1, 1856).

80. *Omoo*, pp. 142–143.

81. *Ibid.*

82. Wilkes, II, 19–20.

83. *Omoo*, p. 143.

84. See Chap. V.

85. See *Omoo*, pp. 142–147. For the English version see Ellis, *History*, I, 403–422, and G. Pritchard, pp. xvii–xx (substantiated later by his son W. T. Pritchard, pp. 4–49), though none of these volumes mention the account of Mrs. Pritchard's heroism cited by Melville in *Typee*, pp. 22–23. For the French version see Vincendon-Dumoulin, *Taïti*, II, 940ff.

86. "French Aggressions in the Pacific," *Foreign Quarterly Review*, XXXIV, 90; 88–104 *passim* (October, 1844).

87. For a substantiation of his charges against the French by a visitor ten years later, see Warren, pp. 328–329.

88. *Omoo*, p. 215. Compare Ellis, *Researches*, II, 290–291; Wilkes, II, 42.

89. *Omoo*, pp. 214–215; see Ellis, *Researches*, II, 294, and Lamont, p. 58.

90. *Omoo*, pp. 214–215; .see Ellis, *Researches*, II, 297–299, and Wilkes, II, 15, 42.

91. *Omoo*, p. 216.

92. *Ibid.*, pp. 228–229.

93. *Ibid.*, pp. 227–228; see also pp. 148–150.

94. Russell, p. 410. The figure he gives for the population in 1842 is 8,000.

95. Kotzebue, I, 169.

96. Ellis, *Researches*, I, 89.

97. Wilkes, II, 48–49. (Compare *Omoo*, p. 227, note 2.) Kotzebue's ascription of the depopulation entirely to the wars ensuing upon the conversion of Pomaré II to Christianity is obviously an absurd exaggeration of only one factor involved (I, 159, 169–170, quoted above, p. 249).

98. See the account of Byron (pp. 65–70), who brought the bodies back to their native land.

99. *Omoo*, p. 228.

100. Wheeler, p. 250. Melville's quotation immediately precedes.

101. "Surgeon's Journal, Wilkes's Exploring Expedition, Vincennes, No. 505" (MS. in the Hydrographic Office, Navy Department).

102. *Omoo*, p. 229.

103. Ellis, *Researches*, I, 91–92. It is likewise quoted by Russell (p. 411), another authority with whom Melville was acquainted. There is no mention of this incident in Montgomery's official edition of the *Journal of Tyerman and Bennet*, however.

104. *Omoo*, p. 229.

105. Ellis, *Researches*, I, 91–92.

106. *Ibid.* This prophecy is also quoted by Tyerman (II, 223–224) to the same import.

XI. Beachcomber

1. *Omoo*, p. ix.

2. *Ibid.*, p. 95n.

3. *Ibid.*, pp. 14–15.

4. Wise, p. 399n.

5. "Journal of Lieutenant Henry A. Wise" (MS. in the Naval Records and Library, Navy Department, Washington, D. C.).

6. A letter to the present writer from W. H. Ifould, Principal Librarian of the Public Library of New South Wales, dated Sydney, May 18, 1934, says in part: "There is no record in Sydney directories of any Dr. John Troy, nor has a close search of newspapers disclosed him or any evidence whatever that a man of such name reviewed any of Melville's books." A letter from the secretary of the Société d'Études Océaniennes at Tahiti, dated Papeete, April 23, 1934, bears similar tidings.

Another conjecture as to the identity of Long Ghost has been put forward by an investigator in Sydney, Australia, who quotes Trood (p. 32) to the effect that a companion of the missionary martyr John Williams, who escaped the massacre at Erromango in 1839, claimed to be the original of Melville's hero. Upon somewhat slender evidence this "companion" has been identified as M. W. C. Cunningham, the acting English Consul at Tahiti for a short time in 1841. (See Simon, pp. 118–123.)

7. *Omoo*, p. 238. Stewart (II, 27) says, corroboratively, that the channel was twelve to fifteen miles across.

8. Lucett, I, 296.

9. *Omoo*, p. 267.

10. Ellis, *Researches*, II, 160.

11. Lovett, I, 296–297.

12. *Omoo*, p. 226. (See pp. 258–260, above.)

13. Stewart, II, 28–29.

14. Ellis, *Researches*, II, 185.

15. *Omoo*, pp. 267–268. The missionary who preached at this time was undoubtedly the Reverend William Howe, who was stationed at Afareaitu from 1839 until 1844 (Lovett, I, 312, 794).

16. Ellis, *Researches*, II, 185.

17. *Omoo*, pp. 241–242.

18. Wheeler, p. 304.

19. *Omoo*, p. 243.

20. Wise, p. 399n.

21. See "Journal of Lieutenant Henry A. Wise" (MS. in the Naval Records and Library).

22. See pp. 304–309.

23. *Omoo*, Chaps. LII–LXII.

24. *Ibid.*, pp. 249; 247–265. (See Wise, p. 399n.)

25. *Ibid.*, pp. 257–259. Compare Ellis, *Researches*, II, 162.

26. *Omoo*, p. 278.

27. *Ibid.*, pp. 239–280 *passim*. From internal evidence ten days to two weeks were spent at Martair, where they had arrived about November 9.

28. Ellis, *Researches*, I, 30; II, 183.

29. *Omoo*, p. 283.

30. *Ibid.*, pp. 285–286; Cook, I, 96.

31. Beechey, p. 183. Even today, travelers report that the *upa-upa*, a far more bacchanalian revelry, is secretly performed in the hills from time to time.

32. *Omoo*, p. 290.

33. *Ibid.*, pp. 291–294 *passim*.

34. See pp. 274–276, and especially Chap. X, note 85.

35. *Omoo*, p. 298. The week spent at Tamai, according to my chronology, must have been November 20–27.

36. *Ibid.*, p. 295. See, for example, Wilkes (II, 58), who tells of three deserters from his ship at Taloo in 1839 that were captured by the natives for a reward.

37. Ellis, *Researches*, II, 159. Compare *Omoo*, p. 291, 296.

38. *Omoo*, Chaps. LXVII–LXXII.

39. *Ibid.*, pp. 330, 332.

40. *Ibid.*, pp. 342–343.

41. Ellis, *Researches*, I, 30. He added, however, that the proper name of the harbor is "Opunohu"; "Taloo," or "Tareu," is the name of the rock on the right-hand entrance, which the natives probably thought Cook was pointing to when he asked them the name of the bay. Hence the traditional error.

42. Wheeler, p. 571.

43. Wilkes, II, 56.

44. *Omoo*, pp. 336–338.

45. Wheeler, p. 572.

46. *Omoo*, p. 352.

47. Stewart, II, 28; see also Lovett, I, 224.

48. *Omoo*, p. 352. The missionary who preached at this church was probably the same Alexander Simpson already mentioned as being in charge of the South Sea Academy at this place (see p. 250, above). But in this part of the narrative, strangely enough, Melville makes no reference to the famous academy or to its master.

49. *Omoo*, pp. 349–351.

50. Walpole, II, 156–157. This sugar plantation was the formerly prosperous one referred to a decade before by Wilkes (II, 59) as producing one hundred tons annually.

51. Wise, p. 399n.

52. *Omoo*, pp. 341–342.

53. Wilkes, II, 57.

54. Wheeler, p. 567.

55. Perkins, pp. 321–323.

56. *Omoo*, p. 375.

57. *Ibid.*, pp. 362–363.

58. Ellis, *Researches*, III, 81–82.

59. *Omoo*, p. 358.

60. *Ibid.*, p. 308.

61. Beechey, pp. 175–176.

62. Ellis, *History*, I, 169n. This version is likewise quoted by Russell (pp. 150–151, note) from Ellis (*Researches*, II, 70)—both familiar works to Melville.

This etymology is corroborated by Buschmann (p. 109).

63. *Omoo*, pp. 358–359.

64. Fitzroy, II, 526–527.

65. Henry, p. 249.

66. *Ibid.*

67. Ellis, *Researches*, III, 218; 214–218. Tyerman and Bennet, the delegates from the London Missionary Society, were also there and were similarly optimistic: "[Tapoa] was Aimata's own choice, and there was every prospect (according to human views) of their union being a happy one" (Tyerman, II, 136–137). Many other visitors have left brief accounts of this first marriage, and of the second one likewise.

68. Walpole, II, 128.

69. Ellis, *History*, I, 316; see also Henry, pp. 249ff.

70. *Omoo*, p. 360.

71. Wheeler, p. 567. See also Fitzroy, II, 227; Wilkes, II, 18.

72. Olmsted, pp. 282–283.

73. *Omoo*, pp. 360–362.

74. Wilkes, IV, 272. This story was picked up by the *Porpoise*, a member of the United States Exploring Expedition, upon a return visit to Tahiti in January, 1841. Perhaps the most authentic version is the one recorded by Belcher (II, 9–10), for he was present at Papeete at the time of the assault and took part in the negotiations which restored matrimonial peace in the royal household. But there is little evidence that Melville was acquainted with Belcher's work, though, it is true, this same version is recounted in the anonymous *Voyages*, pp. 384–385, which was probably in the library of the frigate *United States* during Melville's residence on board.

75. Lucett, II, 167–168.

76. *Omoo*, p. 362.

77. Wheeler, p. 569.

78. Wilkes, II, 18–19.

79. *Omoo*, p. 363. Compare, for example, Belcher, II, 4.

80. *Omoo*, p. 359.

81. Stewart, II, 42, 48.

82. Wheeler, p. 569. Of course, there is some testimony on the other side. Bennett (I, 76–77), for example, declares that although during the early part of her reign she had cast aside all restraints and had "shared unblushingly in the licentiousness for which this island is so notorious," a threatened revolt of her chiefs in 1831 had recalled her to a sense of duty, since when she has preserved "under the surveillance of chiefs and missionaries, a staidness of deportment which almost defies slander." (It is hard, however, to reconcile this with Wheeler's anecdote recorded the next year.) See also G. Pritchard, pp. 66–67.

83. *Omoo*, pp. 339, 365–368. Compare Fitzroy, II, 525, 526–527; and G. Pritchard, p. 169.

84. *Omoo*, pp. 368–369.

85. See, for example, Ellis, *Researches*, III, 216; Stewart, II, 43, 47; Bennett,

I, 75; Wheeler, p. 567; Fitzroy, II, 524–525, 528; Darwin, III, 496; Belcher, II, 11; Olmsted, p. 282.

86. Bennett, I, 77–78.

87. *Omoo*, p. 369.

88. *Ibid.*, pp. 364–365.

89. *Ibid.*, pp. 371; 370–375.

XII. Honolulu

1. This information was kindly furnished to me by Professor Carl Stroven, University of Hawaii, Honolulu. The only other ships listed as arriving between January 1, and August 17, 1843, which could possibly have had any connection with Melville are: "February 13, 1843, U. S. Ship *Boston*, Commander J. C. Long, from China via Tahiti, bound to U. S. via Valparaiso, sailed March 11; February 18, Barque *Jules*, Commander Simonet, from Valparaiso & Marquesas, bound to Marquesas & Society Islands, sailed April 15; June 7, Ship *Acushnet*, Commander Pease, 29 months out, 900 barrels of oil, sailed June 11; July 2, Ship *Hazard*, Commander Bell, from Tahiti, bound for San Blas, sailed August 7; July 25, Ship *B. Gosnold*, Commander Russell, 42 months out, 1650 barrels oil, sailed August 7, bound home after a short cruise in Japan; August 3, U. S. Ship *United States*, Commander Jones, from Callao, bound to Tahiti, sailed August 19 [with Melville on board]."

2. *Omoo*, pp. 188–191. Entries in the *Australian* (Sydney) show that this *Julia* arived at Tahiti in October, 1842, and remained there throughout the fall of that year.

3. Stewart, II, 61.

4. *Typee*, p. 343.

5. *Omoo*, pp. 149; 180.

6. Weaver, *Melville*, p. 290. At the time Melville spoke of himself as the author of *Peedee, Hullabaloo* and *Pog-Dog*, November 4, 1849, *Typee, Omoo*, and *Mardi* were the only three books of his that had been published, for according to the records of the Copyright Office the American edition of *Redburn* did not appear until November 23, though the English edition may have been somewhat earlier.

7. *Mardi*, p. 1. Melville's ship is called the "Arcturion" in this book.

8. See pp. 52–53, and Chap. IV, note 17.

9. Lucett, I, 296n.

10. *Mardi*, p. 12.

11. *Typee*, p. 314.

12. Byron (p. 202) tells of erecting this new monument to Cook in 1822.

13. *Omoo*, p. 250n. See Byron, pp. 175–190; Ellis, *Researches*, IV, 170–198, 285–309; Wilkes, IV, 109–231.

14. *Typee*, pp. 250–251.

15. Wilkes, IV, 4.

16. *Typee*, p. 303.

17. Wilkes, IV, 245–250.

18. See Chap. IV, note 4.

19. *U. S. Public Documents,* Serial No. 3062, p. 852.

20. The *Temperance Advocate and Seamen's Friend,* II, 84 (September 4, 1844). This news sheet was started in February, 1843, just about the time of Melville's arrival; but his name is not included in the long list, printed in I, 18 (April, 1843), of seamen for whom there were letters in the care of the seamen's chaplain.

21. *Ibid.,* III, 51 (April 1, 1845); and IV, 157 (October 15, 1846), in a review of *Typee.*

22. "Harbourmaster's Journal" (MS. in Archives of Hawaii), see "List of Vessels . . . arriving at and departing from Honolulu [January 1, 1843–December 31, 1849]."

23. The *Seamen's Friend,* I, 30 (June 27, 1843).

24. A. C. Jackson, "Journal of a Cruise in the Frigate *United States,*" August 5, 1843 (see Anderson, *Journal,* p. v).

25. *Moby-Dick,* II, 311–315. Elsewhere, however, Melville says that on one voyage to the Pacific his ship spoke no less than thirty whalers each of which had lost at least one man, and three of which had lost a whole boat's crew (*ibid.,* I, 257).

26. Stedman, *Typee,* p. xix.

27. This important article was kindly brought to my attention by Robert S. Forsythe of the Newberry Library, Chicago, to whom must go the credit of being the first modern student of Melville to turn it up in the files of the *Friend,* XXII [n.s.], 71 (August 1, 1873). This document he has published, along with some of the other material included in the present chapter, which he came by independently. (See Forsythe, "Honolulu.")

Damon arrived at Honolulu, as chaplain, on October 19, 1847.

28. The official records from which this summary has been made can be found in *U. S. Public Documents,* Serial No. 3062, pp. 817, 853–868.

29. *Typee,* pp. 343–348.

30. *Ibid.,* p. 343.

31. Forsythe, "Honolulu."

32. A thorough search of British government documents relating to the seizure has revealed no mention of Melville's name. The following records were searched: *Foreign Office,* 58/12, 13, 17, 18, 19, 30 (1840–1844); *Admiralty,* 50/128, 129 (1843), "Journal of Rear-Admiral Thomas."

33. Both *Typee* and *Omoo* contain a running attack against the French colonial policy in the Southern Pacific, as has been demonstrated above.

34. *Typee,* pp. 343–344.

35. Minnegerode, pp. 109–124.

36. *Typee,* p. 347. Compare Melville's account of a similar relapse into licentiousness consequent upon the morbid conditions engendered by fanatical preaching during the "Great Revival" in the Sandwich Islands in 1836 (*Omoo,* p. 206).

37. *Typee,* pp. 166, 244.

38. Russell, p. 318.

39. *Typee,* pp. 264–266. See also *Omoo,* pp. 203, 219, 223.

40. Beale, p. 381.

41. *Omoo,* p. 227.

42. Ruschenberger, p. 457.

43. *Omoo,* p. 227, note 2. Compare Ruschenberger, pp. 478–479. The population of Honolulu at this time he estimated at about seven thousand, less than two hundred of whom were whites (*ibid.,* p. 454). Ruschenberger's book, in general, gives one of the most intelligent and impartial accounts of the Sandwich Islands for this period that is available.

44. *Typee,* p. 253n; see also *Omoo,* p. 363.

45. *Typee,* pp. 253–254.

46. Wheeler, p. 582.

47. *Omoo,* p. 293.

48. "Typee and Omoo," the *Polynesian,* IV, 174 (March 18, 1848).

49. *Ibid.* See also Aaron, "Missionaries." Bingham, p. 446, says: "I have not altered my views of heathenism and Christianity since the uncivilized 'Tipee' has sought, through the presses of civilization in England and America, to apologize for cannibalism."

50. A full account of this borrowing can be found in David Jaffé's "Melville's Use of Some Sources in *Mardi*" (an unpublished master's thesis prepared under my direction at Duke University, 1936). Since none of this material relates to Melville's actual South Sea experiences, and since the similar use of source materials has been elaborately outlined in Chaps. V–XII of the present study, it seems unnecessary to reproduce it here. (See Jaffé, *Mardi,* for a published abstract of this thesis.)

51. *United States Magazine and Democratic Review,* XXV, 44–50 (July, 1849); *Dublin University Magazine,* XLVII, 47–54 (January, 1856).

52. See Mansfield, "Herman Melville."

53. MS. in the Duyckinck Collection, New York Public Library.

54. MS. in the Duyckinck Collection. (The book was finished two months later, though not published for another year, according to Weaver, *Melville,* pp. 271, 273.)

55. For the explanation given in this paragraph I am indebted to the able study of L. S. Mansfield, as yet unpublished, with whose permission I here sketch in broad outline what he has set forth in considerable detail (see Mansfield, "Herman Melville").

56. For a specific proof of this thesis see Mansfield, "Zachary Taylor."

57. MS. in the Duyckinck Collection, New York Public Library. These facts were first called to my attention by L. S. Mansfield.

58. See also Wells, p. 123.

59. Muster Roll, *United States,* 1842–1844. The Log Book gives the date of Melville's enlistment as August 18; but this discrepancy is accounted for by the fact that the ship's day ran from meridian to meridian, and Melville's enlistment was in the afternoon.

60. For an account of the naval manuscripts used in the following Chapters, see Introduction, note 10.

XIII. Farewell to the Pacific

1. Log Book, *United States*, August 17–19, 1843 (MS. in the Naval Records and Library, Navy Department, Washington, D. C.).

2. *White-Jacket*, pp. 166–189.

3. For the rest of the homeward-bound cruise details such as these will be used from the Log Book without citation.

4. Anderson, *Journal*, p. 56.

5. *White-Jacket*, pp. 421–432.

6. See pp. 385–388.

7. See pp. 205–207, 212–213, above. (For the descriptions of Anna Maria Bay by the Ship's Scribe and by Melville, see Anderson, *Journal*, pp. 57–58, and *Typee*, pp. 28–29.)

8. See pp. 81–85, above. Anderson, *Journal*, pp. 57–58.

9. Anderson, *Journal*, p. 60. Compare *Omoo*, pp. 115–117. For a full account of this interesting character see pp. 210–212, above.

10. Melville mentions Matavai twice in *Omoo* (pp. 77–78, 114–115), but the references are historical rather than personal.

11. Franklin, p. 64. Franklin's reminiscences of the cruise of the *United States*, 1842–1844, contained in this volume, are untrustworthy as to specific facts and dates, for they were written from memory fifty years later. With this caution, they will be cited hereinafter for what they are worth. (See Weaver, *Melville*, pp. 234–235.)

12. Franklin, pp. 64–65.

13. Log Book, October 12–19, 1843.

14. The reactions of the Ship's Scribe to the deplorable state of semi-civilization at Tahiti confirm the thesis of *Omoo* (see Anderson, *Journal*, pp. 59–62).

15. Log Book, October 19–20, 1843; Anderson, *Journal*, p. 61.

16. Anderson, *Journal*, p. 61.

17. *Ibid.*, p. 62.

18. Log Book, October 28, 1843.

19. *White-Jacket*, pp. 240–245.

20. See Chap. XVI. Gleim ("Journal") quotes Melville's manuscript record of his concern over a similar accident that occurred during his pleasure trip round Cape Horn in his brother's ship *Meteor* in 1860. This passage shows that Melville's compassion, like Whitman's, was just as deeply touched when he was confiding it to his intimate journal as when he was wearing it on his sleeve.

21. *The Piazza Tales*, pp. 200–202.

22. Anderson, *Journal*, pp. 62–63.

23. *Ibid.*, p. 63.

24. Log Book, November 21–December 5. Porter, it will be remembered, had been the first white man to report a visit to the valley of Typee in the Marquesas Islands, thirty years before. Melville's use of Porter's account as published in his *Journal* has been discussed previously (see Chaps. V–VIII).

25. Log Book, November 21–December 5, 1843.

26. *White-Jacket*, p. 7; Log Book, December 28, 1843–January 3, 1844.

27. *Omoo*, p. 272.

28. *Moby-Dick*, I, 241. Melville also makes Lima the setting of his "Town-Ho's Story" (*Moby-Dick*, I, 307–330): "For my humour's sake, I shall preserve the style in which I once narrated it at Lima, to a lounging circle of my Spanish friends, one saint's eve, smoking upon the thick-gilt tiled piazza of the Golden Inn."

29. Compare the picture painted at the time by W. H. Meyers (Anderson, *Journal*, opp. p. 32; see also p. 126, note 28, where Melville's description of Lima is conveniently reproduced).

30. Anderson, *Journal*, pp. 109–114.

31. *Ibid.*, p. 127, note 30.

32. *White Jacket*, pp. 223, 225 ff.

33. Log Book, August 16–24, 1844.

34. Anderson, *Journal*, pp. 32–37.

35. *Ibid.*, pp. 63–64; see p. 130, note 50, for an account of Commodore Jones's recall; and p. 119, note 3, for an account of the origin of the nickname "Old Wagon."

36. Jackson, "Journal," January 21, 1844 (see Anderson, *Journal*, p. v).

37. Log Book, January 21–22, 1844.

38. Anderson, *Journal*, p. 64.

39. *Ibid.*, p. 64; see also p. 130, note 50.

40. Franklin, p. 69.

41. Anderson, *Journal*, p. 64.

42. Had it not been for Dallas's death, Melville's career in the United States Navy would have been considerably prolonged, for Dallas's first plans had been to transfer the two hundred men on the *United States* who still had two years to serve to the *Cyane*, which he intended to keep on the station. When he had to give up this scheme because of the bad repair of the *Cyane*, he was still intending to dispatch the *United States* for home by way of the East Indies, thus completing her trip round the world. His sudden death prevented the execution of this latter plan, and the new commodore dispatched her for home by way of Cape Horn. (Pacific Squadron Letters: Dallas to Secretary of the Navy, February 24, 1844; April 24, 1844; and May 8, 1844; Armstrong to Secretary of the Navy, June 8, 1844. MSS. in Naval Records and Library.)

When the *United States* arrived at Boston, October 4, 1844, Melville was again fortunate in escaping the full service of his three year enlistment (see Anderson, *Journal*, p. 139, note 92).

43. Sharp, "Journal," July 6, 1844 (see Anderson, *Journal*, p. v).

44. *White-Jacket*, pp. 207–209.

45. The Log Book says that seventy-two volumes in the "Harpers' Family Library Series" were transferred. Melville's use of a number of these volumes, and of Darwin's *Voyages*, has been pointed out in previous chapters.

46. See Anderson, *Journal*, p. 17, for Meyers's account of his reading. Ames

(pp. 242, 255) throws some light on how sailors got their books: "We were generally well supplied with books by the kindness of the officers, whose friends sent out Scott's novels, and other new and interesting works, as fast as they were published in America."

47. Log Book, June 17–18, 1844. See Maclay, III, 18–19.

48. *White-Jacket*, p. 162.

49. *Ibid.*, pp. 210–211.

50. All these details are taken from the Log Book, June 6–July 6, 1844. For Melville's unflattering portrait of the Honorable Manuel C. Lima, see *White Jacket*, pp. 364–365.

XIV. The Frigate "United States"

1. *White-Jacket*, p. 4.

2. One exception to this is found in the circumstantial description of a typical scene of "Divine Worship" on Sunday. See pp. 369–371, where this is compared with Melville's far different picture.

3. *White-Jacket*, p. 59.

4. *Ibid.*, p. v.

5. This pseudonym was immediately recognized in America (see Anderson, *White-Jacket*, p. 126). And even in England Melville's ship was soon identified: "We need hardly say that the name Neversink is fictitious; but from various incidental statements we can easily learn that the real name of the frigate is the United States" (Anon., "A Trio," p. 52).

See also Hill, pp. 199–207. The *United States* was launched in 1797, the second frigate built under the Act of 1796 (the *Constitution*, "Old Ironsides," being built the same year). It served the Navy well during its long life of sixty-four years, and was finally destroyed with the other Federal ships in the Norfolk Navy Yard, April 20, 1861, to prevent them from falling into the hands of the Confederates.

6. Anderson, *Journal*, pp. 45–46. Commander Selfridge, moreover, indicated that Stribling was not Melville's original, saying that the *United States* was commanded from Callao to Boston by "a Captain other than the one designated in the book under the appellation of Capt. Claret" (Anderson, *White-Jacket*, p. 126).

7. *White-Jacket*, pp. 27, 192. See the "Harrison Robertson" copy of *White-Jacket*, p. 31 (for an account of this copy see Chap. XV, note 1).

8. *White-Jacket*, p. 139. See pp. 371–375, above.

9. *White-Jacket*, p. 38.

10. Franklin, p. 22. The "Harrison Robertson" copy of *White-Jacket* (see Chap. XV, note 1), p. 44, identifies "Mad Jack" as Lieutenant Avery, and on p. 41 annotates Melville's caricature of another lieutenant, "Selvagee," as follows: "Lt. Murray is probably here referred to—but the description is grossly exaggerated."

11. *White-Jacket*, pp. 41–42.

12. *Ibid.*

13. Meyers, "Journal," August 15, and September 6, 1842 (MS. in possession of Nelson B. Gaskill, Washington, D. C.).

14. Sands, pp. 20–21. See also pp. 371–375, above.

15. Hill, pp. 178, 206.

16. Pay Roll, *United States*, 1823–1827.

17. Franklin, p. 65.

18. *Ibid.*, pp. 32–33. Compare *White-Jacket*, pp. 51–52, 55–56, 160–162.

19. Franklin, pp. 31–32. See p. 349, above.

20. *White-Jacket*, pp. 23, 24 ff., 358–359.

21. *White-Jacket*, p. 65; Log Book, August 18, 1843.

22. *White-Jacket*, pp. 238–239. On p. 53 Melville describes an illustrated journal of the cruise, kept on board by another literary man, which reads strikingly like that of William H. Meyers kept on board the *Cyane*, a ship in the same squadron during the same cruise (Anderson, *Journal*, pp. 16–18).

23. *White-Jacket*, pp. 49–50.

24. Anderson, *Journal*, pp. 24–25, and note 13.

25. The MS. of this poem was kindly presented to the present writer by Nelson B. Gaskill, Washington, D. C., who discovered it.

26. See Anderson, *Journal*, pp. 14–16, for an explanation of this identification, and compare *White-Jacket*, p. 491. (See also Franklin, pp. 66–67.)

27. The validity of this identification of the fictitious with the real poetaster is not vitiated by the fact that "G. W. W.'s" untitled verses, though obviously presented to Jack Chase as an original composition, are nothing less than an almost literal transcription of Mrs. Hemans's "Lights and Shades," a juvenile poem published ten years before (*Poetical Works of Felicia Hemans*, Philadelphia, 1841, p. 428, and note).

28. *White-Jacket*, pp. 1, 500.

29. *Ibid.*, p. 112.

30. *Ibid.*, pp. 278–279. See Anderson, *Journal*, pp. 47–48; and Log Book, March 10–April 27, 1843, and April 16–June 6, 1844.

31. *White-Jacket*, pp. 198–337.

32. *Ibid.*, pp. 421–432. See Anderson, *Journal*, p. 56; also p. 350, above.

33. *White-Jacket*, pp. 240–245. See the Log Book, October 28, 1843. See p. 354, above.

34. See Anderson, *Journal*, p. 120, note 5, for new material now first brought to light dealing with the early history of uniforms in the American Navy, and Melville's description of the same.

35. *Ibid.*, pp. 22–23.

36. *White-Jacket*, pp. 193–197. Colton gives a picture of religious life on a man-of-war from the chaplain's point of view. But, although he condemns grog and recommends simple sermons, in many respects he resembles Melville's chaplain. For example, he condones flogging (p. 23) and upholds the honor and glory of war (pp. 136, 384). In the review of this volume in the N. Y. *Literary World*, VI, 347–348 (April 6, 1850), Duyckinck made frequent references to Melville's *White-Jacket*, as a truer picture than Colton's.

37. Anderson, *Journal*, p. 65. The information in square brackets is taken from the Log Book.

38. Log Book, and Sharp, "Journal," July 15–30, 1844.

39. *White-Jacket*, pp. 130–131.

40. *White-Jacket*, pp. 131–133.

41. *Ibid.*, pp. 138–143.

42. Sands, pp. 20–21.

43. *White-Jacket*, p. 145. Gleim ("Journal") quotes a similar description of Staten Land from the journal that Melville kept on his voyage round Cape Horn fifteen years later in his brother's clipper ship, the *Meteor*.

44. *White-Jacket*, p. 416. See Log Book, and Sharp, "Journal," July 15–August 15, 1844.

45. *White-Jacket*, p. 124. See Dana, pp. 32–42, 368–413.

46. Anderson, *Journal*, p. 66. (The details added in square brackets are from the Log Book, and Sharp, "Journal," August 24–26, 1844.)

47. *White-Jacket*, pp. 334–335. H. B. M. ship *America*, just such a war trophy, was actually anchored in Rio Bay at this time, but she did not participate in the race. (Sharp, "Journal," August 17, 1844.)

48. *White Jacket*, pp. 337–339.

49. For corroboration of the reputation of the *United States* as a fast sailer, see Anderson, *Journal*, p. 118, note 1; p. 119, note 3.

50. *White-Jacket*, pp. 339–343.

51. See Anderson, *Journal*, p. 118, note 1.

52. Log Book, January 21, 1844.

53. Ames, p. 205. For definite proof that Melville was acquainted with this volume and borrowed material for *White-Jacket* from it, see pp. 412–417, above.

54. Log Book, *St. Louis*, November 18, 1840. The history of Chase's previous career in the United States Navy is incomplete. He is listed as a seaman on the U. S. S. *Consort*, March 1–April 3, 1839. On April 4, he was promoted to a boatswain's mate, a position which he retained when he was transferred to the *St. Louis* on May 26, 1839. He still had fifteen months to serve at the time of his desertion from the *St. Louis*.

55. Log Book, *United States*, May 15–30, 1842. See Meyers, "Journal," May 10–31, 1842 (MS. in possession of Nelson B. Gaskill, Washington, D. C.).

56. *White-Jacket*, pp. 19–22. Commander Selfridge felt that Melville's "Jack Chase" was too overdrawn for a reality, and he was clearly doubtful of the authenticity of the anecdote just quoted, remarking: "The clemency shown towards Jack Chase, after his recapture as a deserter, is not in accordance with experience & usage— But if the circumstances were as has been stated, does it not imply that both the Commodore & Captain were more disposed to forgive offenders than to punish them—more inclined to be merciful than just" (Anderson, *White-Jacket*, p. 128).

57. Franklin, p. 65.

58. Log Book, *United States*, July 19, 1842.

59. Anderson, *Journal*, pp. 105–108.

60. *White-Jacket,* pp. 90–93.

61. The *Journal,* which covers the entire three years' cruise, was undoubtedly all the work of one man; Melville was on board only fourteen out of the thirty-four months. Moreover, the manuscript is not written in Melville's autograph.

62. Anderson, *Journal,* pp. 56–57.

63. *White-Jacket,* pp. 98–99.

64. *Ibid.,* p. 145. See Log Book, July 29–31, 1844.

65. *White-Jacket,* pp. 344, 389. See Log Book, August 24–September 6, 1844.

66. *White-Jacket,* p. 409. See Log Book, September 10–12, 1844. (See also p. 350, above.

67. *White-Jacket,* p. 192. See Anderson, *Journal,* p. 26. The Log Book, February 10, 1842, says that this wine was procured for the United States Minister at Rio de Janeiro; but Franklin (p. 27) corroborates Melville, declaring that it was for Commodore Jones.

68. *White-Jacket,* p. 454. See Anderson, *Journal,* pp. 38–40; and Log Book, July 2–30, 1842.

69. *White-Jacket,* p. 24; Franklin, p. 20. Compare Maclay, II, 40; Clowes, VI, 148–150.

70. *White-Jacket,* pp. 24, 147–148; Franklin, p. 20. See Log Book, October 12–19, 1843. Perhaps Melville's "Wooloo," the Commodore's Polynesian valet —who was the subject of some comments of a serio-comic nature arising from the incongruity of a simple-hearted savage trying to adapt himself to the civilized world in an American man-of-war—was merely a metamorphosis of "Bento Joachim," a Portuguese servant the commodore had picked up at Madeira (Log Book, February 8–11, 1842).

71. *White-Jacket,* pp. 391–398; Franklin, p. 25; and Hill, pp. 199 ff. Compare Maclay, I, 364–394; and Clowes, VI, 41–47, 62. See also Anderson, *Journal,* p. 119, note 3.

72. *White-Jacket,* pp. 391–392.

73. Leech, pp. 127–128. Both accounts give as one of the reasons for the British defeat the number of impressed American seamen on board the *Macedonian;* Melville adds that some of the guns found spiked after the battle were attributable to this fact. (*White-Jacket,* pp. 393–394; Leech, p. 150.)

74. *White-Jacket,* p. 394.

75. Leech, p. 127.

76. *White-Jacket,* p. 397.

77. Leech, pp. 132, 133.

78. *White-Jacket,* p. 398. Compare Leech, p. 145.

79. *White-Jacket,* p. 392.

80. Leech, pp. 135–136.

81. *White-Jacket,* p. 396.

82. Leech, p. 136.

83. *White-Jacket,* pp. 396–397.

84. Leech, p. 144.
85. *White-Jacket*, p. 392.
86. Leech, p. 103.

XV. *"White-Jacket" as Romance*

1. The "Harrison Robertson" copy of *White-Jacket*, New York, 1850, p. iii. This valuable first edition is now in the possession of Carroll A. Wilson of New York City, who very generously permitted me to see it and make full use of its annotations. (Curle reproduces a photograph of this memorandum opposite p. 104.)

2. Robertson was transferred to the *United States* on June 7, 1844, from the *Cyane*, following his commander, Captain C. K. Stribling.

3. *White-Jacket*, pp. 66–68.

4. Log Book, August 17, 1843–October 14, 1844 *passim*.

5. *White-Jacket*, pp. 68–70.

6. *Ibid.*, pp. 190–192.

7. Log Book, April 21, 1844.

8. *White-Jacket*, pp. 112–119. (For the origin of "Old Wagon" as a nickname for the *United States*, see Anderson, *Journal*, p. 119, note 3.)

9. "Harrison Robertson" copy of *White-Jacket*, p. 110 (see note 1, above). Similarly, on p. 402, at the beginning of the chapter in which Melville burlesques the midshipman's school on board ship, Robertson wrote: "All that follows is sheer fiction."

10. *White-Jacket*, pp. 201–204, 223. The first finds no confirmation in the ship's records; the second was impossible since Commodore Jones was not on board during the voyage from Callao to Boston.

11. *Ibid.*, pp. 265–268, 281–287. (For contemporary accounts of drunken rioting during shore leaves, see Anderson, *Journal*, pp. 109–114, 127 note 30.)

12. Log Book, August 19, 1844.

13. *White-Jacket*, pp. 199, 261.

14. Log Book, March 21, 1842.

15. Compare the description of Kamehameha III (Anderson, *Journal* p. 54) with that of Dom Pedro II (*White-Jacket*, p. 293).

16. *White-Jacket*, pp. 291–299.

17. Log Book, August 17–24, 1844.

18. See Anderson, *Journal*, p. 77. Of the seven casualties during the earlier part of the cruise, five died of consumption, one of paralysis, and one of inflammation of the bowels. An amputation did occur on board the *Cyane* during this cruise, and perhaps Melville based his incident on details he had picked up from ship's gossip; Meyers records in his "Journal": "MONTEREY. January 8, 1843. A subscription raised for Ambrose Tomlinson, who had his leg amputated. . '. . He made some money by having his leg amputated" (MS. in the possession of Nelson B. Gaskill, Washington, D. C.).

19. Ames, p. 224.

20. Commander Selfridge in a contemporary critique of *White-Jacket* rejected this scene of amputation as incredible and the caricature of Dr. William Johnson as preposterous, saying: "The description of the Surgeon & his coadjutors, & of the operation performed on one of the crew is full of improbability & absurdity, & doubtless originated in the fertile imagination of the author—Cuticle is no more like the real Surgeon of the ship, than 'hyperion [*sic*] to a satyr' " (Anderson, *White-Jacket*, pp. 128–129).

21. *White-Jacket*, pp. 310–333. See Mumford, p. 115, and Weaver, *Melville*, p. 243.

22. Smollett, II, 45. Compare *White-Jacket*, pp. 421–432.

23. Smollett, II, 55–58.

24. *Ibid.*, II, 63–66. Elsewhere Smollett complains of the inefficiency of his commanding officers, tyranny, bad provisions, and the neglect of the wounded in battle (II, 84, 85, 93–94, 95). It is interesting to note that a recent study has been made in which *Roderick Random* has been checked with manuscript naval records, with results similar to those set forth in the present chapters on *White-Jacket* (see Knapp).

In *Omoo*, p. 347, Melville speaks of reading *Peregrine Pickle* and *Ferdinand Count Fathom* during his idle days as a rover in the Society Islands. And in Duyckinck's list of "Books Lent" it is recorded that Melville borrowed a copy of *Roderick Random* in 1851 (MS. in the New York Public Library).

25. Mahan, p. 66.

26. Anon., *Regulations*, p. 14.

27. *White-Jacket*, p. 447.

28. Sands, p. 160.

29. Meyers, "Journal" (MS. in the possession of Nelson B. Gaskill, Washington, D. C.).

30. *White-Jacket*, pp. 446–447.

31. *Ibid.*, pp. 456–469.

32. The only entry in the Log Book that suggests any such wholesale punishment occurs on September 16, 1844: "Punished O. F. Dean, 'Sea,' with twelve lashes with the cats for disobedience of orders, Jos. L. Holland with 8 do. for disobedience of orders, H. O'Donnell 8 for abuse to B'mate, and David Foster 8 do for insubordinate conduct." But this noncommittal entry was far from the "Northern Tropic."

33. *White-Jacket*, p. 454.

34. Weaver, *Melville*, pp. 243–247; Mumford, pp. 58–60; Freeman, pp. 34–37; Van Doren, *White-Jacket*, pp. vii, xiii–xiv. Mumford is perhaps the worst offender. Several critics have already drawn attention to the fact that he used his material with the freedom of a dramatist rather than with the exactness of a biographer. (See, for example, Starke, Brown, and Forsythe, *Pierre*.)

35. *White-Jacket*, p. 348.

36. *Ibid.*, pp. 352–353.

37. *Ibid.*, p. 354.

38. Log Book, May 29, 1842; and June 2, 1842.

39. Weaver, *Melville*, p. 245.

40. Van Doren, *White-Jacket,* pp. vii–viii.

41. *White-Jacket,* pp. 494–498.

42. Log Book, November 23, 1842; December 19, 1842; and April 30, 1842.

43. The "Harrison Robertson" copy of *White-Jacket,* New York, 1850, pp. 456–457. (See Chap. XV, note 1.)

According to Commander Selfridge, this last adventure of the White Jacket was preposterous in the extreme: "In the first place the haliards [sic] in question, are always rove in a man of war, unless the yard is prepared to be sent down; secondly, how is it possible that a jacket, looped together, with short skirts, could, either by a light breese [sic], or by the motion of the ship, be thrown over one's head?; thirdly, an object falling from the position indicated, could hardly escape coming in contact with the topsail yard, the channels, or the spare yard projecting from the latter; & lastly, is it credible that a man, so exhausted & prostrated, could have the power to resume his duties in ten minutes— To any one who has the least knowledge of the sea, this adventure must carry on its very face its own refutation." Besides, as he had already pointed out, Melville was not assigned to the main royal yard in the first place: "We learn [that] he was stationed in the After-guard, & not in the Main top." (Anderson, *White-Jacket,* pp. 126, 130–131.)

44. Ames, pp. 227–230. Although Weaver was apparently familiar with Ames's volume (citing it in his *Melville,* pp. 79 and 87), he seems to have overlooked this striking and significant parallel.

This habit of literary borrowing, so frequently indulged in for the composition of *Typee* and *Omoo,* was resorted to only occasionally in *White-Jacket.* Yet even in this volume Melville's indebtedness was sufficient to call for a reprimand by one of the keenest of his contemporary critics. After praising *White-Jacket* as his masterpiece, "the best picture of life before the mast in a ship of war yet given to the world," this reviewer declared: "We could point out a good many instances, however, where the author has borrowed remarkable verbal expressions, and even incidents, from nautical books unknown to the general reading public (and this he does without a syllable of acknowledgement)." (Anon., "A Trio," p. 52.)

45. Mumford, p. 60.

46. Weaver, *Melville,* p. 249.

47. *White-Jacket,* p. 1.

48. The Log Book, December 2, 1843, for example, records that 200 Blue Jackets were received in the Purser's department at Valparaiso, just six months before leaving for home.

XVI. *"White-Jacket" as Propaganda*

1. See Van Doren, *White-Jacket,* p. vi.

2. Minnegerode, p. 156.

3. Published in Anderson, *White-Jacket.* (The manuscript of this critique is in the Naval Historical Foundation Archives, Navy Department, Washington, D. C., where it was recently deposited along with other papers of

Selfridge. I am indebted to Captain Dudley W. Knox, Officer-in-Charge, Naval Records and Library, for permission to publish.)

4. *Ibid.,* pp. 124–125. (The letter was to Commander Louis M. Goldsborough, June 26, 1851.)

5. *Ibid.,* pp. 125, 126.

6. *Ibid.,* p. 131.

7. See note 14, below, for Melville's list of grievances.

8. Anderson, *White-Jacket,* p. 140.

9. Paullin, XXXIII, 1463.

10. Anderson, *White-Jacket,* p. 140.

11. Franklin, pp. 29–30. Nathaniel Ames, himself an ordinary seaman, also found life on a man-of-war in the 1820's less objectionable than Melville, and far preferable to that on a merchantman; next to his three years at Harvard College, he declared, his three and a half years on the frigate *United States* were the happiest of his life (Ames, pp. 251–252, 259).

12. Livingston Hunt, pp. 22–30. Melville's railing at the naval polity may have provoked another and more costly smile; for it is said that when Commodore Perry returned from his expedition in Japan (1852–1854), by way of England, he stopped at Liverpool to see Hawthorne and asked him to suggest a collaborator for a projected narrative of his expedition. Melville was among those mentioned by Hawthorne, but Perry chose another. Perhaps he had read *White-Jacket,* and with distaste. (See Mordell, p. 946.)

13. Meyers, "Journal." See entries under dates cited. (MS. in the possession of Nelson B. Gaskill, Washington, D. C.)

14. *White-Jacket:* p. 23, need for officers above the rank of commodore; pp. 30 ff., too many midshipmen; pp. 34–37, three meals crowded into eight hours; pp. 103–106, hammocks not available in the daytime for the night watch to sleep; pp. 108–109, seamen's quarters damp from daily deck-washing; pp. 140–143, incompetent officers; pp. 205 ff., ceremonies unnecessary and injurious; p. 240, hard tarpaulin hats, which make the seamen bald-headed; pp. 240–245, life sacrificed for the sake of showing off the discipline of the ship; pp. 258–260, war, which brings hardship to seamen and glory to officers; pp. 269 ff., hierarchy of power, which makes even a midshipman's word law; pp. 367–371, the Articles of War, a barbarous code; p. 440, graft among petty officers at the expense of the seamen; pp. 471 ff., marines unnecessary; p. 473, immoralities of seamen unpunished, including the "sin of Gomorrah"; p. 478, lack of patriotism of crews filled with foreigners; p. 480, small pay, long cruises, and few "liberty days"; p. 482, idleness because crews are too large; pp. 485–486, the type of "happy jack" preferred by sea officers, a low order of person; and pp. 166–190, 346–355, 456–470, flogging.

In working himself up into the proper state of righteous indignation for the sake of his antinaval propaganda, Melville went far beyond his mild words about flogging recorded in *Omoo* three years before (pp. 126–127 and note): "I do not wish to be understood as applauding the flogging system practised in men-of-war. As long, however, as navies are needed, there is no substitute for it. War being the greatest of evils, all its accessories necessarily partake of the same character; and this is about all that can be said in defence of flogging." This comment, in a footnote, is apropos of the French policy of not administering regulation floggings to the boys on board their frigates. Melville adds, with apparent pride, that on American and English ships the younger men are brought right up to the gratings just as the seasoned sailors are, and that they stand up to their punishment like heroes. To this tough training he attributes the superior bravery of the American and English seamen to the French.

15. For accounts of drunkenness during shore leave on this cruise, see Anderson, *Journal*, pp. 109–114, 127–128.

16. *White-Jacket*, pp. 467–468.

17. Leech, pp. 61–62, 88.

18. *White-Jacket*, pp. 468–469.

19. Meyers, "Journal," February 12–13, 1843 (MS. in possession of Nelson B. Gaskill, Washington, D. C.).

20. One British reviewer, however, declared that *White-Jacket* was as realistic as Dana's *Two Years Before the Mast,* and that Cooper's *Pilot* was theatrical by comparison (*Athenæum,* XXIII, 123, February 2, 1850).

21. *Knickerbocker Magazine,* XXXV, 448 (May, 1850). Hetherington cites seven other favorable reviews: *Literary World* (New York), *Albion, Southern Literary Messenger, American Review, Littell's Living Age, Sartain's Union Magazine, Southern Quarterly Review.* It is interesting to note that of these the *Knickerbocker Magazine* and the *American Review* had been two of the severest critics of *Typee* and *Omoo* (see Anderson, "American Debut," pp. 3–9).

22. *Democratic Review,* XXVI, 384 (April, 1850). See "Flogging in the Navy," *ibid.,* XXV, 97–115 (August, 1849); 225–242 (September, 1849); 318–338 (October, 1849); 417–432 (November, 1849); and 538–543 (December, 1849). Moreover, this journal had printed one of the most favorable reviews of *Typee* and *Omoo* that appeared in America (Anderson, "American Debut," pp. 17–18).

23. Hetherington, pp. 150–175 *passim.*

24. Franklin, p. 64.

25. Weaver, *Melville,* p. 234; Mumford, pp. 117–118; Freeman, p. 36; Van Doren, *White-Jacket,* p. vii; and note 12, above.

26. Paullin, XXXIII, 1461–1463. (See also note 32, below.)

27. *U. S. Statutes at Large,* IX, 271.

28. The *Congressional Globe,* 30th Congress, 2nd Session (1848–1849), pp. 505–512. It may have been the newspaper reports of this prolonged debate which put the idea of *White-Jacket* in Melville's mind, for the book was begun during the early part of 1849 and was completed by September 12, 1849, six months before it was published (letter from E. A. Duyckinck to G. L. Duyckinck, September 12, 1849, MS. in the New York Public Library).

29. Paullin, XXXIII, 1464.

30. *U. S. Public Documents,* Serial No. 548, pp. 37, 38, 44, 57, 72, 94, 104, 140, 142, 147, 153, 157, 160, 204, 218, 228, 340, 401. The petitions came from

the citizens of Massachusetts, Pennsylvania, Maine, New Hampshire, Maryland, and New York; from public meetings at Troy, New York, and Hartford, Connecticut; and from the legislatures of Rhode Island and Indiana. The petition from New York City, February 15, 1850, may have been signed or even sponsored by Melville.

31. *U. S. Public Documents*, Serial No. 566, pp. 206–208, 464.

32. The *Congressional Globe*, 31st Congress, 1st Session (1849–1850), XXI, 2057–2061; *U. S. Statutes at Large*, IX, 515.

The first mention found regarding the abolition of flogging in the navy is in the report of the committee composed of Congressmen Edwards of Pennsylvania, Patterson of New Jersey, and White of Vermont on December 6, 1821. On September 26, 1832, Secretary of the Navy Woodbury issued an order which read: "Flogging is recommended to be discontinued when practicable, by courts as well as officers; and some badge of disgrace, fine, etc., substituted when discretion exists." Another circular, previously mentioned, was issued on January 29, 1850, requesting the views of the officers on this subject. Of the eighty-four replies, the answer was almost unanimous in favor of retaining this form of punishment, though a few requested modifications of its use. Only four recommended its abolition: Commodore F. Stockton, who later made the same advocacy from the floor of the Senate as the representative from New Jersey; Commander S. F. Dupont, a close friend of Commander Selfridge; Captain D. Conner; and Lieutenant J. J. Almy, whose answer took the form of a pamphlet entitled "Naval Discipline and Corporal Punishment." Another, Commodore U. P. Levy, was likewise a strong advocate of abolition, and his untiring efforts had great influence in securing passage of the Congressional Act on September 28, 1850.

However, corporal punishment, a legacy from older days, was still in 1850 generally considered by the officers as essential to the maintenance of discipline in the Navy. The assumption that cruelty was their prime motive would, of course, entirely overlook the difficulty in maintaining discipline among men of the character then common in the service and entirely ignore the crucial need of such strict discipline in any ship at sea. (Information by courtesy of Captain Dudley W. Knox, Officer-in-Charge, Naval Records and Library, Navy Department, Washington, D. C.)

33. Minnegerode (p. 155) says that the English edition was scheduled for publication at the end of March, 1850; Sadleir (p. 228) says, on the other hand, that it actually appeared on January 23, 1850. The title page of the American edition was deposited with the clerk of the United States Court, Southern District of New York, as early as January 9, 1850; but the work itself was not deposited until March 26, 1850. The Congressional debates which resulted in the abolition of corporal punishment in the Navy were virtually concluded by this date, though the bill was not actually passed by the Senate until the end of this long session, September 28, 1850, at which time the Southern senators made a final effort to block its passage in this form. If Melville had any influence as a propagandist it must have been on these last-minute speeches; but even in them, though numerous other docu-

ments were brought into the discussion, there is no reference to Melville or to *White-Jacket*.

34. *White-Jacket*, p. 500.

35. See Anderson, *Journal*, p. 139, note 92.

36. See Chap. XIII, note 42.

37. Log Book, October 4–14, 1844; Pay Roll, *United States*, 1844.

38. The *Liberator* (William Lloyd Garrison, ed.), October 18, 1844. See Commanders's Letters, 1844, No. 25, Boston, October 15, 1844 (Captain Stribling to Mason, Secretary of the Navy).

39. *White-Jacket*, pp. 477–478.

40. *Boston Recorder*, October 17, 1844. The dates previously set had been April 23 and September 23, 1843.

41. Buchanan, "Socrates," pp. 102–103. (The version of this poem printed in Buchanan's *Works*, II, 395–398, however, omits the lines on Melville, whether as a retraction or otherwise I have not been able to discover.) Melville saw this eulogy, written thirty years after his career as an author had come to an end, and expressed his appreciation of it in a letter to another English admirer (anon., "Some Melville Letters").

KEY TO THE NOTES

MANUSCRIPTS AND ANONYMOUS MISCELLANEA FROM
PERIODICALS ARE NOT INCLUDED

Anonymous. An Historical Account of the Circumnavigation of the Globe, . . . from the Voyage of Magellan to the Death of Cook. New York: 1839 (Harpers' Family Library Series).

—— "New Bedford Whalers: the Bark 'Platina,' " *Series of Reynolds Printing Sketches (No. 6).* New Bedford, Mass.: [n. d.].

—— Regulations for the Uniform and Dress of the Navy of the United States. Washington, D. C.: 1841.

—— "Some Melville Letters," *Nation and Athenæum,* XXIX, 712–713 (August 13, 1921).

—— "A Trio of American Sailor-Authors," *Dublin University Magazine,* XLVII, 47–54 (January, 1856).

—— Voyages round the World from the Death of Captain Cook to the Present Time. New York: 1839 (Harpers' Family Library Series).

Aaron, Daniel. "An English Enemy of Melville," *New England Quarterly,* VIII, 561–567 (December, 1935).

—— "Melville and the Missionaries," *New England Quarterly,* VIII, 404–408 (September, 1935).

Adkins, Nelson F. "A Note on Herman Melville's *Typee,*" *New England Quarterly,* V, 348–351 (April, 1932).

Alexander, James M. The Islands of the Pacific. New York: 1895.

Ament, W. S. "Bowdler and the Whale," *American Literature,* IV, 39–46 (March, 1932).

Ames, Nathaniel. A Mariner's Sketches. Providence, Rhode Island: 1830.

Anderson, Charles, ed. Journal of a Cruise in the Frigate United States, 1842–1844, with Notes on Herman Melville. Durham, North Carolina: 1937.

—— "Contemporary American Opinions of *Typee* and *Omoo,*" *American Literature,* IX, 1–25 (March, 1937).

—— "Me*ville's English Debut," *American Literature,* X (November, 1938).

—— "A Reply to Herman Melville's *White-Jacket,* by Rear-Admiral Thomas O. Selfridge, Sr.," *American Literature,* VII, 123–144 (May, 1935).

Andree, Richard. Die Anthropophagie: eine Ethnographische Studie. Leipzig: 1887.

Ashley, Clifford W. The Yankee Whaler. Boston: 1926.

Beale, Thomas. The Natural History of the Sperm Whale. London: 1839.

Beechey, Captain Frederick W. Narrative of a Voyage to the Pacific and Bering Straits. Philadelphia: 1832.

Belcher, Sir Edward. Narrative of a Voyage round the World, . . . 1836–1842. 2 vols. London: 1843.

Bennett, Frederick D. Narrative of a Whaling Voyage round the Globe, . . . 1833 to 1836. 2 vols. London: 1840.

Berchon, M. "Le Tatouage aux Îles Marquises," *Bulletins de la Société d'Anthropologie de Paris*, I, 99–117 (Paris, 1860).

Bingham, Hiram. A Residence of Twenty Years in the Sandwich Islands. New York: 1847.

Birss, J. H. "Herman Melville Lectures in Yonkers," *American Book Collector*, V, 50–52 (February, 1934).

—— "Melville's Marquesas," *Saturday Review of Literature*, VIII, 429 (January 2, 1932).

—— " 'Moby-Dick' under Another Name," *Notes and Queries*, CLXIV, 206 (March 25, 1933).

Braswell, William. "Herman Melville and Christianity." (An unpublished doctoral dissertation. University of Chicago: 1934.)

—— "Melville as a Critic of Emerson," *American Literature*, IX, 317–335 (November, 1937).

Brooks, Van Wyck. Emerson and Others. New York: 1927.

Brown, E. K. "Herman Melville and 'Ethan Brand,' " *American Literature*, III, 72–75 (March, 1931).

Browne, J. Ross. Etchings of a Whaling Cruise, to Which Is Appended a History of the Whale Fishery. New York: 1846.

Buchanan, Robert. Complete Poetical Works. 2 vols. London: 1901.

—— "Socrates in Camden," *Academy*, XXVIII, 102–103 (August 15, 1885).

Buschmann, Johann C. E. Aperçu de la langue des Îles Marquises. Berlin: 1843.

Byron, George Anson, Lord. Voyage of H. M. S. Blonde to the Sandwich Islands, in the Years 1824–1825. London: 1826.

Caillot, A. C. Eugène. Les Polynésiens au contact de la civilisation. Paris: 1909.

Canby, Henry S. Classic Americans. New York: 1931.

Chase, Owen. Narrative of the Most Extraordinary and Distressing Shipwreck of the Whale-Ship Essex, of Nantucket. New York: 1821.

Chasles, Philarète. "Séjour des deux Américains chez les Taïpies, dans l'Île Noukahiva," *Journal des débats* (Feuilleton), 22, 25 juin 1846.

—— "Voyages réels et fantastiques d'Hermann Melville," *Revue des deux mondes*, II, 545–577 (May 15, 1849). (Reprinted as Section III in Études sur la littérature et les mœurs des Anglo-Américains aux XIXᵉ siècle. Paris: 1851.)

Clowes, William Laird, *et al.* The Royal Navy, a History. 7 vols. London: 1897–1903.

Coan, Titus. Life in Hawaii, an Autobiographical Sketch of Mission Life and Labors (1835–1881). New York: 1882.

Coan, Titus M. "Herman Melville," Boston *Literary World*, XXII, 492–493 (December 19, 1891).

Colton, Walter. Deck and Port; or, Incidents of a Cruise in the U. S. Frigate Congress to California. New York: 1850.

[Cook, James]. A Collection of Voyages round the World, . . . Containing a Complete Historical Account of Captain Cook's Voyages. 2 vols. London: 1790.

Coulter, John. Adventures in the Pacific. Dublin: 1845.

Crèvecœur, J. H. St. John de. Letters from an American Farmer. London: 1782.

Curl, Vega. Pasteboard Masks: Fact as Spiritual Symbol in the Novels of Hawthorne and Melville. Cambridge, Mass.: 1931.

Curle, Richard. Collecting American First Editions. Indianapolis, Indiana: 1930.

Damon, S. F. "Why Ishmael Went to Sea," *American Literature*, II, 281–283 (November, 1930).

Dana, Richard Henry. Two Years before the Mast. New York: 1842 (Harpers' Family Library Series).

Darwin, Charles. Journal and Remarks (Vol. III of Fitzroy's Narrative, *q. v.*).

Dickens, Charles. American Notes for General Circulation. New York: 1842.

Dordillon, René. Grammaire et dictionnaire de la langue des Îles Marquises. Paris: 1931–1932.

Ellis, Lieutenant A. B. "On Polyandry," *Popular Science Monthly*, XXXIX, 802 (October, 1891).

Ellis, William. The History of the London Missionary Society. 1 vol. printed. London: 1844.

—— Polynesian Researches. 4 vols. London: 1833.

Fanning, Edward. Voyages round the World. New York: 1833.

Fitzroy, Captain Robert. Narrative of the Surveying Voyages of H. M. S. Adventure and Beagle . . . 1826–1836. 4 vols. London: 1839. (Vol. III, Journal and Remarks, by Charles Darwin.)

Forsythe, R. S. "Herman Melville's Father Murphy," *Notes and Queries*, CLXXII, 254–258 (April 10, 1937); 272–276 (April 17, 1937).

—— "Herman Melville in Honolulu," *New England Quarterly*, VIII, 99–105 (March, 1935).

—— "Herman Melville in the Marquesas," *Philological Quarterly*, XV, 1–15 (January, 1936).

—— "Herman Melville in Tahiti," *Philological Quarterly*, XVI, 344–357 (October, 1937).

Forsythe, R. S. "More on Herman Melville in Tahiti," *Philological Quarterly*, XVII, 1–17 (January, 1938).

—— "Mr. Lewis Mumford and Melville's *Pierre*," *American Literature*, II, 286–289 (November, 1930).

Franklin, Samuel R. Memories of a Rear-Admiral Who Has Served for More than Half a Century in the Navy of the U. S. New York and London: [1898].

Frazer, Sir James G. The Belief in Immortality and the Worship of the Dead. 3 vols. London: 1922.

Freeman, John. Herman Melville. New York: 1926.

Garnett, R. S. "Moby-Dick and Mocha Dick: A Literary Find," *Blackwood's Magazine*, CCXXVI, 841–858 (December, 1929).

Ginoux, Edmond de. "La Reine Pomaré: femmes de Taïti et des Marquises," *Nouvelles annales des voyages*, III, 365 (Paris, 1844).

Gleim, W. S. "Journal of Melville's Voyage in a Clipper Ship," *New England Quarterly*, II, 120–125 (June, 1929).

—— "A Theory of *Moby-Dick*," *New England Quarterly*, II, 402–419 (July, 1929).

Gohdes, Clarence. "Gossip about Melville in the South Seas," *New England Quarterly*, X, 526–531 (September, 1937).

Gracia, Mathias. Lettres sur les Îles Marquises. Paris: 1843.

Hale, Charles. A Vocabulary of the Nukahiwa Language: including a Nukahiwa-English Vocabulary and an English-Nukahiwa Vocabulary. Boston: 1848.

Hamersly, Thomas H. S. General Register of the United States Navy and Marine Corps. Washington, D. C.: 1882.

Handy, E. S. Craighill. Native Culture in the Marquesas. Honolulu: 1923.

Handy, Willowdean C. Tattooing in the Marquesas. Honolulu: 1922.

Hart, James D. "Melville and Dana," *American Literature*, IX, 49–55 (March, 1937).

Hart, Joseph C. Miriam Coffin, or The Whale-Fisherman: a Tale. San Francisco: 1873 (reprinted from the edition of 1834).

Haven, Gilbert, and Thomas Russell. Father Taylor, the Sailor Preacher. Boston: 1872.

[Hawthorne, Nathaniel]. The American Notebooks by Nathaniel Hawthorne, ed. Randall Stewart. New Haven: 1932.

Henry, Teuira. Ancient Tahiti: Based on Material Recorded by J. M. Orsmond. Honolulu: 1928.

Hetherington, Hugh. "The Reputation of Herman Melville in America." (An unpublished doctoral dissertation. University of Michigan: 1933.)

Hill, Frederic S. Twenty-Six Historic Ships. New York and London: 1903.

Holden, W. S. "Some Sources for Herman Melville's *Israel Potter*." (An unpublished master's thesis. Columbia University: 1932.)

Homans, G. C. "Dark Angel: the Tragedy of Herman Melville," *New England Quarterly*, V, 699–730 (October, 1932).

Howard, Leon. "A Predecessor of *Moby-Dick*," *Modern Language Notes*, XLIX, 310–311 (May, 1934).

Hunt, Levi. A Voice from the Forecastle of a Whale Ship. Buffalo: 1848.

Hunt, Livingston. "Herman Melville as a Naval Historian," *Harvard Graduates's Magazine*, XXXIX, 22–30 (September, 1930).

Jaffé, David. "Some Sources of Melville's *Mardi*," *American Literature*, IX, 56–69 (March, 1937).

Jardin, Édelestan. Essai sur l'histoire naturelle de l'archipel des Marquises. Paris: 1862.

Jenkins, Thomas H. Bark Kathleen Sunk by a Whale, as Related by the Captain. New Bedford, Mass.: 1902.

Knapp, L. M. "The Naval Scenes in *Roderick Random*," *Publications of the Modern Language Association*, XLIX, 593–598 (June, 1934).

Kotzebue, Otto von. A New Voyage round the World, . . . 1823–1826. 2 vols. London: 1830.

Krusenstern, A. Johann von. Voyage round the World, in the Years 1803–1806. 2 vols. London: 1813.

Lamont, E. H. Wild Life among the Pacific Islanders. London: 1867.

Langsdorff, Georg H. von. Voyages and Travels in Various Parts of the World, . . . 1803–1807. 2 vols. London: 1813.

Lawrence, D. H. Studies in Classic American Literature. New York: 1923.

Leech, Samuel. Thirty Years from Home, or a Voice from the Main Deck. Boston: 1847 (15th edition).

Linton, Ralph. Archæology in the Marquesas Islands. Honolulu: 1925.

Lovett, Richard. The History of the London Missionary Society. 2 vols. London: 1899.

[Lucett, Edward]. Rovings in the Pacific, from 1837 to 1849 . . . by a Merchant Long Resident at Tahiti. 2 vols. London: 1851.

McCutcheon, Roger B. "The Technique of Melville's *Israel Potter*," *South Atlantic Quarterly*, XXVIII, 161–174 (April, 1928).

MacDonald, Allan. "A Sailor among the Transcendentalists," *New England Quarterly*, VIII, 307–319 (September, 1935).

Maclay, Edgar S. A History of the United States Navy. 3 vols. New York: 1902.

Macy, Obed. The History of Nantucket . . . Together with the Rise and Progress of the Whale Fishery. Boston: 1835.

Mahan, Alfred T. From Sail to Steam. New York: 1907.

Mansfield, Luther S. "Glimpses of Herman Melville's Life in Pittsfield, 1850–1851," *American Literature*, IX, 26–48 (March, 1937).

—— "Herman Melville: Author and New Yorker, 1844–1851." (An unpublished doctoral dissertation. University of Chicago: 1936.)

—— "Melville's Comic Articles on Zachary Taylor," *American Literature*, IX, 411–418 (January, 1938).

Menard, Wilmon. "A Forgotten South Sea Paradise," *Asia*, XXXIII, 457–463, 510 (September–October, 1933).

Minnegerode, Meade. Some Personal Letters of Herman Melville and a Bibliography. New York: 1922.

Mordell, Albert. "Melville and 'White-Jacket,'" *Saturday Review of Literature*, VII, 946 (July 4, 1931).

Mosblech, L'Abbé Boniface. Vocabulaire Océanien-Français et Français-Océanien des dialectes parlés aux Îles Marquises, Sandwich, Gambier, etc. Paris: 1843.

Mumford, Lewis. Herman Melville. New York: 1929.

Munro, Wilfred H. Tales of an Old Seaport. Princeton, New Jersey: 1917.

Nathaniel, Sir [pseudonym]. "American Authorship. No. IV—Herman Melville," *New Monthly Magazine*, XCVIII, 300–308 (July, 1853).

Nichols, Thomas L. Forty Years of American Life. 2 vols. London: 1864.

O'Brien, Frederick. White Shadows in the South Seas. New York: 1919.

Olmsted, Francis A. Incidents of a Whaling Voyage. New York: 1841.

Paltsits, Victor H., ed. The Family Correspondence of Herman Melville, 1830–1904, in the Gansevoort-Lansing Collection. New York: 1929.

Paullin, Charles O. Naval Administration, 1775–1911. Annapolis: [n. d.].

Pease, Zephaniah W. "Historical Address," *One Hundredth Anniversary of the New Bedford Port Society*. New Bedford, Mass.: 1930.

Perkins, Edward T. Na Motu: or, Reef-Rovings in the South Seas. New York: 1854.

Perry, Calbraith B. Charles D'Wolf of Guadaloupe . . . Being a Complete Genealogy of the "Rhode Island D'Wolfs." New York: 1902.

Porter, Captain David. Journal of a Cruise Made to the Pacific Ocean, in the U. S. Frigate Essex, in the Years 1812, 1813, and 1814. 2 vols. Philadelphia: 1815.

Pritchard, George. The Missionary's Reward; or, The Success of the Gospel in the Pacific. London: 1844.

Pritchard, William T. Polynesian Reminiscences; or, Life in the Southern Pacific Islands. London: 1866.

Radiguet, Max. Les Derniers Sauvages: la vie et les mœurs aux Îles Marquises (1842–1859). Paris: 1929. (First published, in part, as

"La Reine-Blanche aux Îles Marquises: souvenirs et paysages de l'Océanie," *Revue des deux mondes*, XXII, 431–479; XXIII, 607–644, 1859.)

Reynolds, Cuyler, ed. Hudson-Mohawk Genealogical and Family Memoirs. 4 vols. New York: 1911.

Rollin, Louis. Les Îles Marquises. Paris: 1929.

Ruschenberger, William S. W. A Voyage round the World. Philadelphia: 1838.

Russell, Michael. Polynesia: or, an Historical Account of the Principal Islands in the South Sea. Edinburgh: 1845 (Harpers' Family Library Series).

Sadleir, Michael. Excursions in Victorian Bibliography. London: 1922.

Sands, Benjamin F. From Reefer to Rear-Admiral, Reminiscences and Journal Jottings of Nearly Half a Century of Naval Life. New York: [1899].

Scudder, H. H. "Melville's *Benito Cereno* and Captain Delano's Voyages," *Publications of the Modern Language Association*, XLIII, 502–532 (June, 1928).

Simon, Jean. "Recherches Australiennes sur Hermann Melville," *Revue Anglo-Américaine*, XIII, 114–129 (December, 1935).

Smith, Joseph E. A. Herman Melville. Written for the Evening Journal. Pittsfield, Mass.: 1891.

—— The History of Pittsfield (Berkshire County), Mass., from the Year 1800 to the Year 1876. Springfield, Mass.: 1876.

[Smith, Thomas W.]. A Narrative of the Life, Travels and Sufferings of Thomas W. Smith. Boston: 1844.

Smollett, Tobias. The Adventures of Roderick Random. London: [n. d.] (The Navarre Edition, ed. George Saintsbury).

Starbuck, Alexander. History of the American Whale Fishery from Its Earliest Inception to the Year 1876. Waltham, Mass.: 1876.

Starke, A. H. "A Note on Lewis Mumford's Life of Herman Melville," *American Literature*, I, 304–305 (November, 1929).

Stedman, Arthur. " 'Marquesan' Melville," New York *World*, XXXII, 26 (October 11, 1891).

—— "Melville of Marquesas," *Review of Reviews*, IV, 428 (November, 1891).

—— ed. Typee: a Real Romance of the South Sea. Boston: 1892.

Stevenson, Robert Louis. In the South Seas. London: 1888.

—— The Letters of Robert Louis Stevenson, ed. Sir Sidney Colvin. London: 1900.

Stewart, Charles S. A Visit to the South Seas, in the U. S. Ship Vincennes, . . . 1829–1830. 2 vols. New York: 1831.

Stoddard, Charles W. Summer Cruising in the South Seas. London: 1874.

Sundermann, Karl H. Herman Melvilles Gedankengut. Berlin: 1937.

Thomas, Russell. "Melville's Use of Some Sources in *The Encantadas*," *American Literature*, III, 432–456 (January, 1932).

—— "Yarn for Melville's *Typee*," *Philological Quarterly*, XV, 16–29 (January, 1936).

[Torrey, William]. Torrey's Narrative: or, the Life and Adventures of William Torrey, Who for the Space of 25 Months within the Years 1835–1837, Was Held a Captive by the Cannibals of the Marquesas. Boston: 1848.

Trood, Thomas. Island Reminiscences. Sydney, Australia: 1912.

Turnbull, John. A Voyage round the World, . . . 1800–1804. Philadelphia: 1810.

[Tyerman, Daniel, and George Bennet]. Journal of Voyages and Travels (Deputed by the London Missionary Society to Visit the South Seas, 1821–1829), ed. James Montgomery. 2 vols. Boston: 1832.

Van Doren, Carl. "Lucifer from Nantucket," *Century Magazine*, CX, 494–501 (August, 1925).

—— "Mr. Melville's *Moby-Dick*," *Bookman*, LIX, 154–157 (April, 1924).

—— ed. White-Jacket. London: 1924 (Oxford Worlds Classics).

Vergnes, P. E. Eyriaud des. L'Archipel des Îles Marquises. Paris: 1877.

Vincendon-Dumoulin, Clément A., et C. Desgraz. Îles Marquises, ou Nouka-Hiva, histoire, géographie, mœurs et considérations générales. Paris: 1843.

—— Îles Taïti, esquisse historique et géographique sur la colonisation française dans l'Océanie. Paris: 1844.

Wainger, B. M. "Herman Melville: a Study in Disillusion," *Union College Bulletin*, XXV, 35–62 (January, 1932).

Walpole, Lieutenant Fred. Four Years in the Pacific, . . . 1844 to 1848. 2 vols. London: 1849.

Warren, T. Robinson. Dust and Foam; or, Three Oceans and Two Continents. New York: 1859.

Weaver, Raymond. Herman Melville, Mariner and Mystic. New York: 1921.

—— ed. Journal Up the Straits, October 11, 1856–May 5, 1857. New York: 1935.

Wells, W. H. "*Moby-Dick* and Rabelais," *Modern Language Notes*, XXXVIII, 123 (February, 1923).

Westermarck, Edward. The History of Human Marriage. 3 vols. New York: 1922.

[Wheeler, Daniel]. Memoirs of the Life and Gospel Labors of the Late Daniel Wheeler. Philadelphia: [1842].

White, Viola C. "Symbolism in Herman Melville's Writings." (An unpublished doctoral dissertation. University of North Carolina: 1934.)

Wilkes, Commodore Charles. Narrative of the U. S. Exploring Expedition, . . . 1838–1842. 5 vols. Philadelphia: 1845.

Williamson, Robert W. The Religious and Cosmic Beliefs of Central Polynesia. 2 vols. Cambridge: 1934.

—— The Social and Political Systems of Central Polynesia. 3 vols. Cambridge: 1924.

Wilson, James. A Missionary Voyage to the Southern Pacific Ocean, . . . 1796, 1797, 1798. London: 1799.

Wise, Lieutenant [Henry A.]. Los Gringos: or an Inside View of . . . Polynesia. New York: 1849.

Yzendoorn, Father Reginald. History of the Catholic Mission in the Hawaiian Islands. Honolulu: 1927.

INDEX

Act abolishing corporal punishment, 420, 431

Act for the Better Government of the Navy, 430

Acushnet (ship), whaling voyage, 33 ff., 47, 48; crew, 33, 35; wrecked, 62; desertions, 111, 113; arrives in Lahaina, files affidavit of desertion, 330; in Honolulu Bay, 331; ray of light on fictionized account, 332

Adams, John, 34

Afareaitu, cotton factory set up at, 260; village and missions, 287 ff.

Ahab, Captain, 33, 47, 332; feud with Starbuck, 39; prototype of, 43; feud with Moby-Dick, 53, 63

Aimata, 312; *see also* Pomaré Vahine I

Albermarle Island, 49, 51

Alexander Mansfield (ship), 218

"Algerine," the, 362

Ambergris, Beale quoted on, 44; Melville's borrowed account of, 45

American Mission in the Sandwich Islands, 87

American Review, attack upon *Typee* and *Omoo*, excerpt, 180; defense of missionaries, 185

Ames, Nathaniel, 401; description of a fall overboard, 415

Amputation of leg, 401-5

Ann Alexander (ship) sunk by whale, 59 ff.

Anna Maria Bay (Taiohaë), 70, 91, 113, 350; Stewart's and Melville's descriptions of, quoted, 71; French take possession of, 77

Anonymity desirable in *White-Jacket*, 361

Anson, George, *see* Byron

Armand Chausson, 224, 225, 226

Armitage, Mr. and Mrs., efforts to teach cotton spinning and weaving to Tahitians, 259; second effort to establish factory, 288

Armstrong, James, 357, 359, 362; in command of Pacific Squadron, 357; original

of Captain Claret, 362; characteristics, 362

Articles of War, 350, 424

Arva (*kava*), 148

Aube, L' (corvette), 225

Autobiographical material, 3; semi-fictitious, semi-autobiographical travel books, 4; partly borrowed, partly fictionized, 5, 36; faithfulness of narratives, 52, 117, 179; books accepted as, 181; in *Omoo*, 191, 192, 199, 284, 297, 303, 342; *Typee*, 191, 192, 342; *White-Jacket*, 394, 409; *see also under titles of books*

Avery, Latham B., original of Mad Jack, 363

Badger, George E., 406

Bainbridge (frigate), 376

Barnard, Wilson, 34

Bartow, Theo., 350, 369

Bayard Dominick Expedition, 150, 158, 190; study of Marquesan culture, 120

"Bay of all Beauties," 400

Beachcomber, laxity of morals, 270; Melville's South Seas adventuring as, 284-323; term defined, 284

Beagle (ship), 50, 264, 266

Beale, Thomas, *Natural History of the Sperm Whale*, used by Melville, 44; excerpts, on ambergris, 44; on missionaries, 267; on condition of natives, 339

Beards, Navy regulations concerning, 405 ff.

Beechey, Captain F. W., 264; quoted, 211, 256, 262, 263, 294, 311

Belcher, Sir Edward, quoted, 78, 93

Bell, Mrs., 303, 307, 308

Bennet, George, 251

Bennett, Frederick Debell, 342; quoted, 94, 211, 219, 320 f.; *Narrative of a Whaling Voyage*, 119, 150; description of *tapu* house, 161 f.; of breadfruit harvest festival, 164; on character and conduct of Tahitians, 267

INDEX

Bernice Pauahi Bishop Museum of Honolulu, bulletins, 120

Beverages of Typees, 148

Bible translated by missionaries, 247

Blue Laws, 251, 265, 266; administered with a cúdgel, 252; respectable residents try to evade, 271

Bob, Captain, 215, 353

Bounty (ship), mutineers aid rule of Otoo, 310

Boussole, La (ship), 77

Bradford, Melvin O., 33

Brazil, glimpses of, in *White-Jacket*, 400

Breadfruit, cultivation, dishes made from, 144; harvest festival, 164, 256

Brissie, Albert, 352

Broom Road, Papeete, 216-17, 220, 351

Brown, Captain, adventure among the Marquesas, 92 ff.

Brown, Martin, 33

Browne, J. Ross, *Etchings of a Whaling Cruise*, compared with *Moby-Dick*, 37 ff.; theme of reform, 37; excerpts, 37, 38, 39, 41, 43; "Bob Grimsley's Ghost," 39; routes for whalers outlined, 48

Browne, Sir Thomas, 344; quoted, 45

"Buccaneer," the, 362

Bucéphale, Le (ship), 77

Burying grounds, *see* Me'œ

Byron, George Anson, Lord, 328

Cabri, Jean Baptiste, 154

Calabashes, *see* Feast of the Calabashes

Calabooza Beretanee, 213, 215

Caldwell, William W., 360

Callao, Peru, winter spent at, 355-58

Calm at sea, 372, 389

Cannibalism, of Polynesians, 93, 106; Marquesans branded with reputation for, 100 ff.; propensities denied, 100, 101; efforts to secure information regarding practice, 102 ff.; practiced only on bodies of enemies, 103-6 passim; Porter convinced that bodies are not eaten, 104; only direct testimony to, 105; question of, in Marquesas, undetermined, 106; "ritual cannibalism," 107; effect Melville created by fear of, 109; slain enemies disposed of at feast, 138; overemphasis on dangers of, 190; Melville's fear of being eaten, 193

Cannibals, man who lived among, 67-195; and missionaries, 86-116

Cape Horn, *see* Horn, Cape

Cape Horn Fever, 375

Carden, Captain, friendship with Decatur, 393

Caret, François d'Assise, 224; quoted, 225, 226; maltreated, 274

Carter, William H., 352

Carysfort (man-of-war), 333

Catharine (ship), 92

Catholic, *see* Roman Catholic

Chamber's Edinburgh Journal, 187

Chaplain and Sunday service, 369-71

Chase, John J., original of "Jack Chase," 366, 367; desertion from *St. Louis*, 381; reinstated on *United States*, 382; Rear-Admiral Franklin on, 384; promotion, 385

Chase, Owen, *Narrative*, 54

Chasles, Philarète, 188, 189; quoted, 181; belief in authenticity of *Typee* and *Omoo*, 187; version of Melville's escape from Marquesas, 194

Christianity, futile attempt to introduce, at Nukahiva, 88; treatment of pagans by Christians, 95, 97, 98, 99; triumphant by force of arms, 248; Great Revival of 1836, 250; converts, 249 ff., 298; coercion a hindrance to, 252; progress in Society Islands, 266; *see also* Civilization

Christmas on the *United States*, 355

Church, natives driven to, in Tahiti, 252; chapel at Papaoa, 220 ff.; at Papetoai, 301

Church of the Cocoa-nuts, 241

Church service, celebrated in *Moby Dick*, 22; in Tahiti, 242 ff.

Circumnavigation of the Globe, 118

Civilization, treatment of pagans by civilized man, 95, 97, 98, 99; Melville's brief against, 133, 178, 238; savage and civilized life compared, 143; first raid of, 177; Melville's attack on the semicivilization wrought by missionaries, 220; demoralizing influence of, 247, 262, 263, 269, 273, 277; effect on economic and social status of Tahitians, 257; *Omoo* the second indictment in Melville's brief against, 276, 309; effect upon Sandwich Islanders, 336 ff.; *see also* Christianity

Clarel, expression of author's religious conflict, 240

Claret, Captain, 373, 374, 407, 409; original of, 362

Coan, Titus, quoted, 114

Cocoanut, cultivation of trees, 144, 146; multifarious uses, 145

Collet, Fort, 77

INDEX

kidnaped by American captain, 94; **Melville** apologist for, 95 (*see also* South Sea islanders); reputation for cannibalism, 100 ff. (*see also* Cannibalism); no eyewitness account of practice, 107; general truth of account of Marquesan life, and sources of information, 117-78; ethnological treatises dealing with, unreliable, 120; tenacious memories, 120; superior to other Polynesians, 121, 122; described, 121 ff., 130 ff.; attention bestowed upon personal appearance, 126; communal industry, 133, 156, 159; hostility between tribes, mode of warfare, 134 ff.; domestic relations, 142; food, 144, 147; beverages, 148; occupations, 148, 149; tattooing, 148 ff.; insistence upon tattooing white men, 151; skill in stone construction, 156 ff.; Melville's information gathered at Feast of the Calabashes, 162 (*see also* Feast of the Calabashes); complex system of *tapu*, 166 ff. (*see also Tapu*); religious system, 168 ff.; *see also,* Gods; Nukahivans; Religion; Savages; Typees

Marquesas Islands, 16, 18 ff.; Stewart's narrative of, 21; *Acushnet's* voyage to, desertions, 52; taken possession of for France, 69, 76, 350; Melville's arrival, 69; Porter's activities in, 95 ff.; little frequented by white men, 118; books dealing with, 118; bulletins of the Bayard Dominick Expedition to, 120; government, 128 ff.; ideal social state, 132; Melville's departure from, 194; courtier of, in Tahitian court, 321; colony of convicts, 351; *see also* Hivaoa; Nukahiva; Typee Valley

Marriage, flexibility of, 140 ff.; between whites and natives, 304

Marryat, Frederick, *Midshipman Easy,* 424

"Massacre of the Beards," 405-8

Matavai Bay, Tahiti, 351

Matea, Society Islands, 286-95, 306

Mauna Loa volcano, 328

Mazatlán, Mexico, 357

Me'œ (term), 156, 158; great age of, 157; of Ahua, 159

Medical service in navy, 368, 401-5

Mehevi, described, 126; king of Typee Valley, 128; flirtations, 141

Melville, Allan, guidebook to Liverpool, 15

Melville, Gansevoort, 179

Melville, Herman, romantic genre;

"man who lived among cannibals," 143; literary discoverer of the South Seas, 5; yearning for philosopher's mantle, 5; career in Navy, 5 (*see also United States,* frigate); indebtedness to sources, 6, 126,146, 166, 190, 342, 358; why he went to sea, 11-21; spiritual turmoil, 14; seafaring kinsmen, 15 ff.; desertion at the Marquesas, 16, 52, 70, 111, 113, 191; whaling voyage on *Acushnet,* 33 ff.; described on crew list of the *Acushnet,* 35; letter to Mrs. Hawthorne, quoted, 64; at Nukahiva, 69-85; indebtedness to Stewart, 71; phonetic inaccuracy, 80; apologist for South Sea islanders, 95, 98, 99, 107, 138, 178; not exact in bibliographical citations, 96; acquaintance with Porter's *Journal,* 96; general truth of account of Marquesan life and sources of information, 117-78; kept no journal in South Seas, 128, 189; evidences that he actually lived among Marquesans, 144, 145; William Ellis one of his acknowledged authorities, 145, 310; tattooed, 151; deviations from truth, 168; always improved upon his original, 173; controversy over *Typee* and *Omoo,* 179 ff.; charges of dishonesty and immorality launched against, 180, 181, 185; reception of books in England and America, 180; in France, 181; attitude towards controversy, 186; considered his narrative of adventures essentially true, 186; diary or "Rough Notes," 188; books on the whole accepted as authentic, 190; escape from the Marquesas, 193, 199; among mutineers of the *Lucy Ann,* 212; in Calabooza Beretanee, at Papeete, 213; feud with Johnston, 227 ff.; departure from Tahiti, 232; Lucett's criticism of, 229, 232 ff.; habit of churchgoing, 236, 241; letter to Evert Duyckinck, 238; effect of adolescent reevaluation of religious faith, 240; guilty of deliberate misrepresentation, 263; his authorities disagree, 264 ff.; no evidence that he tried to improve moral or religious condition of natives, 266; corroborated in pronouncements against missionaries, 273; exaggeration in his figures dealing with depopulation, 281; "beachcomber" adventuring at Tahiti and on Eimeo, 284-323; nicknamed Omoo and Typee, 284; autobiographical veracity of *Omoo,* 284,

Melville, Herman (*Continued*)
297, 303, 342; knack of hitting off peculiarities of character, 290; date of
rovings, search for employment, 296;
fear of being recaptured, 297; propagandism in *Omoo*, 309; interview with
Queen Pomaré, 319-21; parts with Long
Ghost, 322; ships on "Leviathan," 322;
movements of, during first half of 1843,
324-28; possible routes taken, 325, 326;
date of departure from Society Islands,
325; date of arrival in Honolulu, 325,
328; contract establishing clerkship in
Honolulu, 332; differing reactions to
English and French seizures, 333, 335;
defense of British policy in Sandwich
Islands, 335 ff.; drives home thesis
against civilization in references to
Sandwich Islands, 337; use of satire in
Mardi, 343; connection with intellectual world, 343; return from wedding
trip, 343; influence of Rabelais, Sir
Thomas Browne and Esaias Tegner,
344; ships on the *United States*, leaves
Honolulu, 345; return trip on the
United States, 349-60; imprisoned on
La Reine Blanche, 350; use of actual
experiences to attack naval abuses, 354,
363, 366, 373, 374, 375; visit to Lima,
355; earliest known reading list, 358;
technique of *White-Jacket's* composition analyzed, 361-419; asserts essential
truth of *White-Jacket*, 361, 362; invents
or elaborates for propagandist attacks,
364, 388, 412; consistent use of fictitious names, 365; fantastic titular inventions, 365; use of actual names, 366;
propagandism in *White-Jacket*, 371,
402, 405, 412, 420-34; dramatic climaxes,
373, 396; good words for humanity of
navy, 388; allusions to events in naval
history, 389; reading of Smollett, 405;
lurid fictitious experiences and emotional reactions accepted as autobiography of, 409-17; native gift for high
comedy abandoned, 409; never on punishment list of *United States*, 410; fall
overboard episode one of high spots in
his writing, *text*, 412, 414; influence of
his efforts at naval reform, 420, 429,
431; reforms root-and-branch in their
scope, 422; faults in style, 424; in attitude, 425; an avowed reformer, list of
complaints against navy, 425; attitude
of press toward attack on naval abuses,

429; keen eye for the public taste, 431;
discharge from navy, 432; arrival in
Boston, use of his freedom, 433; posterity's preferences, 434; reactions to effects of Christian civilization in Polynesia, *see* Civilization
"Melville, Herman, as a Naval Historian"
(Hunt), 424
Melville, Pierre François Henry Thomas Wilson, *see* Melville, Thomas Wilson
Melville, Thomas Wilson, 17, 70; quoted
on cannibalism, 104
Melville's Marquesas, Typee published in
England as, 179
Men, Marquesan, described, 123; warrior
in full costume, 126; secondary husbands, 143; occupations, 148, 149; tattooing of, 149 ff.; *tapu* houses for, 161;
see also Warriors
Mexico, trip to, 357
Meyers, William H., 355, 385, 406, 411;
bitter criticism of naval polity, 425;
description of a flogging through the
fleet, 428
Millerites, 283, 433
Miriam Coffin or the Whale-Fisherman
(Hart), 24 ff.
Missionaries, and cannibals, 86-116; lack
of success in the Marquesas, 86; withdrawal of Protestant, landing of Catholic, 89; supported by French squadron,
90; accounts of heathenism, 103; hostility aroused by strictures on, 180;
Melville's attack on, 184, 220, 245; defense of activities, 185; French missionaries in Tahiti, 223 ff.; abolish idolatry, 246; translate Bible into native
language, 247; influence upon house
of Pomaré, 248, 317; reports of conversions, 249; children of, kept from
association with natives, 250; Blue
Laws imposed by, 251, 252, 265, 266,
271; hypocrisy induced by coercive
methods of, 254, 272; interdict sports
and pastimes of natives, 256; religion
taught by, not true Christianity, 262;
disagreement regarding results of exertions, 264 ff.; Melville corroborated
in his pronouncements against, 273;
Catholic priests banished by Protestants, 274; dancing prohibited by, 294;
influence over Sandwich Islanders,
335, 337 ff.; natives as slaves to, 338,
339

INDEX

Omoo (Continued)
South Seas, 3, 5, 405, 429; theme of reform, 37; excerpt on uses and cultivation of cocoanut, 145, 146, 147; on tattooing, 152; a sequel to *Typee*, 177, 199; controversy over authenticity, 179; success treated as a *succès de scandale*, 179; reviews, 180 ff., 273; most strictly autobiographical of Melville's works, 199; unlucky cruise of the "Julia," 201 ff.; veracity of, 206, 230, 309; Dr. Johnston's threat to bring libel suit against publishers, 227; Melville's attack on civilization, 238; chapter titles, 239; published by Harper & Brothers, 240, 276; only written record left by mutineer, deserter, or beachcomber, 272; bulk of evidence supports opinions set forth in, 273; chronicle of French policy of colonization substantially correct, 275; evil effects of civilizing the Noble Savage, 276; publishers allow strictures against France and Christian civilization to stand, 276; exaggeration in figures dealing with depopulation, 281; Melville's "Beachcomber" adventuring in Tahiti and Eimeo, 284-323; characters in, 285, 290, 303; principal actors real persons, names not disguised, 303; analyzed, 309; compared with Irving's *Sketch-Book* and *Tales of a Traveller*, 309; allusions to Melville's Sandwich Islands cruise, 326 ff., 337, 341; autobiographical material the background of, 342; scenes of action, revisited, 351, 354; description of Queen Pomaré, 354; references to Lima, 355
Opio (term), 256
Opou (term), 154
Otoo, King, *see* Pomaré I
Outward bound, 9-65

Pacific Ocean, routes for whalers, 48
Pacific Squadron, Armstrong in command of, 357
Pæ-pæ, 157, 158
Panama Herald, excerpt, 59 ff.
Paofai, chief, 317
Papaoa, Royal Mission Chapel, 220 ff.
Papa root, juice used as skin bleach, 125
Papeete, 351; "Julia" in port of, 205, 206; mutineers taken to Calabooza Beretanee at, 213; bay, 217; native worship, 243; riot and debauchery, 267
Papetoai, 296, 298, 300 ff.; cotton factory

set up at, 259, 288; sugar plantations, 261; South Sea Academy moved to, 287; real estate boom, 301; native church, 301
Patterson, Alban, 352
Paty, William, manuscript notebook, 324
Paulet, Lord George, seizure of the Sandwich Islands, 333 ff.; Melville's defense of, 335, 337
Peacock (ship), 54
Pease, Valentine, 33, 52, 111, 191
Pedro II, of Brazil, 400
"Pequod," the, 30, 33, 53, 55; crew, 34, 35; "trying out" scene, 42; voyage, 47; route ascribed to, 48
Percival, John, 364
Periodical reviews, *see* Reviews
Perkins, Edward T., 305; *Na Motu: . . . A Narrative of Adventures at the Hawaiian, Georgian, and Society Islands*, 305, 308; excerpt, 306
Pierre; or, The Ambiguities, 65; philosophico-nonsensical ambiguities of, 4; attempt at psychological fiction in, 409
Plantations of breadfruit and cocoanut trees, 144
Platforms, stone, 156, 158, 159
Police in Tahiti, *see* Kannakippers
Pollard, Captain, of *Essex*, 54
Polyandry, 141 ff.
Polygyny, 143
Polynesia, atrocities committed by Americans and Europeans in, 95, 97, 98, 99; Porter and Melville use crude orthography for names, 98; ethnologists rely upon *Typee* as an authority on, 190; Melville's attack on semi-civilization wrought by missionaries, 220; background of *Mardi*, 343, 344; *see also* Hawaii; Hivaoa; Marquesas Islands; Moorea; Nukahiva; Papeete; Society Islands; Tahiti; Typee Valley
Polynesian, the, 186; excerpt, 184, 341
Polynesian language, intricacies, 329
Polynesians, treacherous character, 92; cannibalism, 93, 106; defended by Melville, 98; custom of forming instantaneous friendships, 231; character of, a barrier to improvement in morals or religion, 247; indolence, 256 ff.; unsuited for Western civilization, 261; much of beauty ascribed to appropriate costumes, 277; contrast between Ellis's opinion of, and Melville's (*Omoo*), 288, 289, 292; giving of nicknames, 311; *see*

INDEX

also Marquesans; Tahitians

Pomaré I (Otoo), King, quoted, 310; change of name, 311; Kings of Taiarboo dethroned by, 317

Pomaré II, King, 220, 287; Christianization of, 248; quoted, 281, 310; death, heir, 312

Pomaré III, King, 249, 312

Pomaré, house of: survey of, 310-21; power broken by missionaries and French conquerors, 317

Pomaré (term), origin as nickname, 311

Pomaré-Tani, King consort, descriptions of, 313 ff., 353; domestic life, 313, 314 ff.; attack upon queen, 315; visit to *United States*, 353

Pomaré Vahine I, Queen, 19, 249, 312-21, 353; forced to cede Tahiti to French, 206; under domination of Protestant mission, 225; wild cattle belong to, 291; refuge at Papetoai, building army for warfare against French, 296; birth, 312; marriages, 312, 313; domestic life, 313, 315 ff.; fight with husband, 315; rule of, 317; political affiliates and enemies, 317; private character, 318; goes into laundry business on breakdown of authority, 318; Melville's interview with, 319-21; appearance, costume, residence, 320

Po-Po, Eereemear (Jeremiah), 298, 302, 323

Popular Science Monthly, the, 142

Porter, David, 50, 78, 355; invasions of Typee Valley, 95, 97, 98; *Journal*, 96, 98; efforts to secure information on cannibalism, 103; description of Typee Valley, 116; *Journal of a Cruise Made to the Pacific Ocean*, 118; as source material upon which Melville levied, 121; description of Marquesans, 123; of warriors, 127; king of Nukahiva, 129; styles government a republic *en savage*, 130; law-abiding nature and innate goodness of Marquesans, 130; praise of natives of Taiohaë, 133; on method of warfare, 136, 137; communal industry of Marquesans, 159; saw Melville's hoolah-hoolah ground, 160; account of religious ritual, 172; of irreverent treatment of gods, 174; human sacrifice to dead priest, 176

Press, *see* Reviews

Priests, inspirational, 169; ceremonial, 170; Christian, *see* Missionaries

Primitivism, *Typee* a defense of, 238

Princeton, explosion on, 359

Pritchard, George, 207, 266, 296; church at Papeete, 244; *Missionary's Reward*, 245

Pritchard, W. T., 209

Propaganda, *Omoo* an indictment of civilization, 309; *White-Jacket* as, 371, 402, 405, 412, 420-34; dramatic coloring equivalent to, 371; invention, or elaboration, for purposes of, 388, 412

Protestant missions, *see* Missionaries; Missions

Pseudonyms in *White-Jacket*, 362-67

Punishment, unnecessary among Typees, 130; Articles of War, code of prohibitions and punishments, 350; history of corporal punishment, 423, 430 (*see also* Flogging)

Queequeg, 30, 34

Rabelais, François, 344

Race, man-of-war, 357, 375-81

"Rachel," the, 332

Radiguet, Max, 77, 78, 96, 105; quoted, 79, 84, 106, 122

Raiatea, natives curry favor with missionaries, 250

Raritan (frigate), 362, 376, 377

Ravaivai, Austral Islands, 326

Raymond, Frederic R., 33

Read, Enoch, 34

Redburn: His First Voyage, excerpt, 13

Reform, *see* Propaganda

Regulations for the Uniform and Dress of the Navy . . ., 405

Reine Blanche, La (frigate), 69, 77, 350; mutineers incarcerated on, 205 ff.; Log Book cited, 206, 207, 215; Melville among mutineers, 212

Religious ceremony, slain enemies offered as sacrifices to gods, 104; cannibalism practiced as, 106; *see also* Cannibalism; Sacrifice

Religious ritual described, 170 ff.

Religious sacrifice, *see* Sacrifice

Religious system of Marquesans, Melville's apology for account of, 166; his deviations from truth, 168; priests, 169

Reviews, of *Typee* and *Omoo*, 180, 183, 185; of attack on naval abuses, 429

Reynolds, John M., "Mocha-Dick," 14, 36

Rio de Janeiro, scenes given setting at, 356, 399

Ritual cannibalism, 107

[509]

INDEX

170 ff.; civilization's first raid, 177; date of escape from, 199, 207

Uniforms, standardization, 405
United States, aids restoration of Sandwich Islands to natives, 334
United States (frigate), source material for Melville's trip on, 4; reception to king and queen of Nukahiva, 82; drunken dinner party, 84; "Abstract of a cruise in the frigate United States," 84; at Anna Maria Bay, 91; library, 118, 358, 375; Pilot Jim on, 212; Melville ships on, at Honolulu, 345; passage from Honolulu to the Marquesas, 349; flogging of sailors, 349, 355, 425, 426; sailing speeds, 350, 354, 357; record of "Ship's Scribe," 350, 353, 354, 355, 356, 357, 376; passage to Tahiti, 351; stay at Society Islands, king's visit to ship, 353; competitive sail-furling and sailor's fall to quarter-deck, 354, 368; passage from Tahiti to Valparaiso, 354; at Callao, Peru, 355; at Rio de Janeiro, 356; trip to Mexico, 357; race, 357, 375-81; preparation for homeward voyage, 358, 359; White-Jacket a narrative of homeward-bound voyage, 361; rechristened the "Neversink," 362; chronology of cruise altered in White-Jacket, 367, 368; Sunday service, 369-71; "trimming by the head" for speed, 380; race to overtake Moriendra, 381; battle with Macedonian, 389-94; crew discharged, 431
United States Exploring Expedition, 1838-1842, 208; comments of official published volumes, excerpts, 269 ff.; observation of surgeon on treatment of disease by missionaries, 281
Ushant, John, 365

Vicariate Apostolic of Oriental Oceanica, 225
Vincennes (ship), 18 ff., 70, 78
Vindictive (frigate), man-of-war race, 356, 380
Visit to the South Seas, in the U.S. Ship Vincennes (Stewart), 21, 70, 118

Wallace, George W., Lemsford the poet, 367; Songs of the Sirens, 367
Warfare, Typee method of, 134 ff.; man-of-war barbarities, 390-93
Warriors, costume of Typee, 126; of Hapa, 127; challenging enemy to combat, 137; tapu house, 161; see also Men
Webb, Charles Henry, 194
Wedding trip, Melville's return from, 343
Weller, George and Edward, 200
West, Andrew W., 37
Westermarck, Edward, History of Human Marriage, 143
Western culture, see Civilization
Westminster Review, excerpt, 273
Whale, curiosity about, 13; as a dish, 40; ships sunk by, 54-61
Whale, white, 14, 53; treated as symbolical, 36; sailors' superstitious dread of, 36; killed by West, 37; catastrophe in Moby-Dick, 53 ff.
Whale laboratory, 36-46
Whaleman's chapel, New Bedford, 22 ff.
Whalemen's Shipping List, 62
Whaling, 31; Browne's and Melville's description of technique of, 39; Beale quoted on nature and use of ambergris, 44; Melville's account of ambergris, 45
Whaling marine, despotism fostered in, 38; Pacific routes for, 48, 52; favorite cruising ground, 326; disasters, 332
Whaling voyage, motives for joining, 13 ff.; see also Acushnet
Wheeler, Charles, quoted, 257
Wheeler, Daniel, Memoirs of the Life and Gospel Labors of . . . , 220, 252; quoted, 220, 244, 252, 268, 280, 289, 299, 301, 305, 313, 317, 319, 341
Whiskers, see Beards
Whiskey allowances, 355, 396, 430
White Jacket, use of, a fiction, 417
White-Jacket; or the World In a Man-Of-War, 5, 37; a sequel to Typee, 177; complaint against code of prohibitions and punishments, 350; chapter on sailor's fall and resulting surgical operation, 354, 368; reference to shore liberty, 356; to man-of-war race, 357, 375-81; to reading, 358; to burial in Callao, 359; comment on gun explosion, 359; a narrative of homeward-bound voyage on United States, 361; Melville asserts essential truth of, 361, 362; his expedient alterations of fact, 361-68, 418; dramatic elaboration of actual events, 361, 368-85, 418; deliberate inventions, 361, 395-419; anonymity, 361; preface to English edition, 361 f., excerpt, 362; identification of characters in, 362-67; Harrison Robertson's analysis of, 363, 395, 399, 415; propagandism, 371, 402, 405, 412, 420-34;

CATALOGUE OF DOVER BOOKS

Books Explaining Science and Mathematics

WHAT IS SCIENCE?, N. Campbell. The role of experiment and measurement, the function of mathematics, the nature of scientific laws, the difference between laws and theories, the limitations of science, and many similarly provocative topics are treated clearly and without technicalities by an eminent scientist. "Still an excellent introduction to scientific philosophy," H. Margenau in PHYSICS TODAY. "A first-rate primer . . . deserves a wide audience," SCIENTIFIC AMERICAN. 192pp. 5⅜ x 8. S43 Paperbound **$1.25**

THE NATURE OF PHYSICAL THEORY, P. W. Bridgman. A Nobel Laureate's clear, non-technical lectures on difficulties and paradoxes connected with frontier research on the physical sciences. Concerned with such central concepts as thought, logic, mathematics, relativity, probability, wave mechanics, etc. he analyzes the contributions of such men as Newton, Einstein, Bohr, Heisenberg, and many others. "Lucid and entertaining . . . recommended to anyone who wants to get some insight into current philosophies of science," THE NEW PHILOSOPHY. Index. xi + 138pp. 5⅜ x 8. S33 Paperbound **$1.25**

EXPERIMENT AND THEORY IN PHYSICS, Max Born. A Nobel Laureate examines the nature of experiment and theory in theoretical physics and analyzes the advances made by the great physicists of our day: Heisenberg, Einstein, Bohr, Planck, Dirac, and others. The actual process of creation is detailed step-by-step by one who participated. A fine examination of the scientific method at work. 44pp. 5⅜ x 8. S308 Paperbound **75¢**

THE PSYCHOLOGY OF INVENTION IN THE MATHEMATICAL FIELD, J. Hadamard. The reports of such men as Descartes, Pascal, Einstein, Poincaré, and others are considered in this investigation of the method of idea-creation in mathematics and other sciences and the thinking process in general. How do ideas originate? What is the role of the unconscious? What is Poincaré's forgetting hypothesis? are some of the fascinating questions treated. A penetrating analysis of Einstein's thought processes concludes the book. xiii + 145pp. 5⅜ x 8. T107 Paperbound **$1.25**

THE NATURE OF LIGHT AND COLOUR IN THE OPEN AIR, M. Minnaert. Why are shadows sometimes blue, sometimes green, or other colors depending on the light and surroundings? What causes mirages? Why do multiple suns and moons appear in the sky? Professor Minnaert explains these unusual phenomena and hundreds of others in simple, easy-to-understand terms based on optical laws and the properties of light and color. No mathematics is required but artists, scientists, students, and everyone fascinated by these "tricks" of nature will find thousands of useful and amazing pieces of information. Hundreds of observational experiments are suggested which require no special equipment. 200 illustrations; 42 photos. xvi + 362pp. 5⅜ x 8. T196 Paperbound **$2.00**

THE UNIVERSE OF LIGHT, W. Bragg. Sir William Bragg, Nobel Laureate and great modern physicist, is also well known for his powers of clear exposition. Here he analyzes all aspects of light for the layman: lenses, reflection, refraction, the optics of vision, x-rays, the photoelectric effect, etc. He tells you what causes the color of spectra, rainbows, and soap bubbles, how magic mirrors work, and much more. Dozens of simple experiments are described. Preface. Index. 199 line drawings and photographs, including 2 full-page color plates. x + 283pp. 5⅜ x 8. T538 Paperbound **$1.85**

SOAP-BUBBLES: THEIR COLOURS AND THE FORCES THAT MOULD THEM, C. V. Boys. For continuing popularity and validity as scientific primer, few books can match this volume of easily-followed experiments, explanations. Lucid exposition of complexities of liquid films, surface tension and related phenomena, bubbles' reaction to heat, motion, music, magnetic fields. Experiments with capillary attraction, soap bubbles on frames, composite bubbles, liquid cylinders and jets, bubbles other than soap, etc. Wonderful introduction to scientific method, natural laws that have many ramifications in areas of modern physics. Only complete edition in print. New Introduction by S. Z. Lewin, New York University. 83 illustrations; 1 full-page color plate. xii + 190pp. 5⅜ x 8½. T542 Paperbound **95¢**

CATALOGUE OF DOVER BOOKS

THE STORY OF X-RAYS FROM RÖNTGEN TO ISOTOPES, A. R. Bleich, M.D. This book, by a member of the American College of Radiology, gives the scientific explanation of x-rays, their applications in medicine, industry and art, and their danger (and that of atmospheric radiation) to the individual and the species. You learn how radiation therapy is applied against cancer, how x-rays diagnose heart disease and other ailments, how they are used to examine mummies for information on diseases of early societies, and industrial materials for hidden weaknesses. 54 illustrations show x-rays of flowers, bones, stomach, gears with flaws, etc. 1st publication. Index. xix + 186pp. 5⅜ x 8.   T622 Paperbound **$1.35**

SPINNING TOPS AND GYROSCOPIC MOTION, John Perry. A classic elementary text of the dynamics of rotation — the behavior and use of rotating bodies such as gyroscopes and tops. In simple, everyday English you are shown how quasi-rigidity is induced in discs of paper, smoke rings, chains, etc., by rapid motions; why a gyrostat falls and why a top rises; precession; how the earth's motion affects climate; and many other phenomena. Appendix on practical use of gyroscopes. 62 figures. 128pp. 5⅜ x 8.   T416 Paperbound **$1.00**

SNOW CRYSTALS, W. A. Bentley, M. J. Humphreys. For almost 50 years W. A. Bentley photographed snow flakes in his laboratory in Jericho, Vermont; in 1931 the American Meteorological Society gathered together the best of his work, some 2400 photographs of snow flakes, plus a few ice flowers, windowpane frosts, dew, frozen rain, and other ice formations. Pictures were selected for beauty and scientific value. A very valuable work to anyone in meteorology, cryology; most interesting to layman; extremely useful for artist who wants beautiful, crystalline designs. All copyright free. Unabridged reprint of 1931 edition. 2453 illustrations. 227pp. 8 x 10½.   T287 Paperbound **$3.00**

A DOVER SCIENCE SAMPLER, edited by George Barkin. A collection of brief, non-technical passages from 44 Dover Books Explaining Science for the enjoyment of the science-minded browser. Includes work of Bertrand Russell, Poincaré, Laplace, Max Born, Galileo, Newton; material on physics, mathematics, metallurgy, anatomy, astronomy, chemistry, etc. You will be fascinated by Martin Gardner's analysis of the sincere pseudo-scientist, Moritz's account of Newton's absentmindedness, Bernard's examples of human vivisection, etc. Illustrations from the Diderot Pictorial Encyclopedia and De Re Metallica. 64 pages.   **FREE**

THE STORY OF ATOMIC THEORY AND ATOMIC ENERGY, J. G. Feinberg. A broader approach to subject of nuclear energy and its cultural implications than any other similar source. Very readable, informal, completely non-technical text. Begins with first atomic theory, 600 B.C. and carries you through the work of Mendelejeff, Röntgen, Madame Curie, to Einstein's equation and the A-bomb. New chapter goes through thermonuclear fission, binding energy, other events up to 1959. Radioactive decay and radiation hazards, future benefits, work of Bohr, moderns, hundreds more topics. "Deserves special mention . . . not only authoritative but thoroughly popular in the best sense of the word," Saturday Review. Formerly, "The Atom Story." Expanded with new chapter. Three appendixes. Index. 34 illustrations. vii + 243pp. 5⅜ x 8.   T625 Paperbound **$1.60**

THE STRANGE STORY OF THE QUANTUM, AN ACCOUNT FOR THE GENERAL READER OF THE GROWTH OF IDEAS UNDERLYING OUR PRESENT ATOMIC KNOWLEDGE, B. Hoffmann. Presents lucidly and expertly, with barest amount of mathematics, the problems and theories which led to modern quantum physics. Dr. Hoffmann begins with the closing years of the 19th century, when certain trifling discrepancies were noticed, and with illuminating analogies and examples takes you through the brilliant concepts of Planck, Einstein, Pauli, Broglie, Bohr, Schroedinger, Heisenberg, Dirac, Sommerfeld, Feynman, etc. This edition includes a new, long postscript carrying the story through 1958. "Of the books attempting an account of the history and contents of our modern atomic physics which have come to my attention, this is the best," H. Margenau, Yale University, in "American Journal of Physics." 32 tables and line illustrations. Index. 275pp. 5⅜ x 8.   T518 Paperbound **$1.50**

SPACE AND TIME, E. Borel. Written by a versatile mathematician of world renown with his customary lucidity and precision, this introduction to relativity for the layman presents scores of examples, analogies, and illustrations that open up new ways of thinking about space and time. It covers abstract geometry and geographical maps, continuity and topology, the propagation of light, the special theory of relativity, the general theory of relativity, theoretical researches, and much more. Mathematical notes. 2 Indexes. 4 Appendices. 15 figures. xvi + 243pp. 5⅜ x 8.   T592 Paperbound **$1.45**

FROM EUCLID TO EDDINGTON: A STUDY OF THE CONCEPTIONS OF THE EXTERNAL WORLD, Sir Edmund Whittaker. A foremost British scientist traces the development of theories of natural philosophy from the western rediscovery of Euclid to Eddington, Einstein, Dirac, etc. The inadequacy of classical physics is contrasted with present day attempts to understand the physical world through relativity, non-Euclidean geometry, space curvature, wave mechanics, etc. 5 major divisions of examination: Space; Time and Movement; the Concepts of Classical Physics; the Concepts of Quantum Mechanics; the Eddington Universe. 212pp. 5⅜ x 8.   T491 Paperbound **$1.35**

Nature, Biology

NATURE RECREATION: Group Guidance for the Out-of-doors, William Gould Vinal. Intended for both the uninitiated nature instructor and the education student on the college level, this complete "how-to" program surveys the entire area of nature education for the young. Philosophy of nature recreation; requirements, responsibilities, important information for group leaders; nature games; suggested group projects; conducting meetings and getting discussions started; etc. Scores of immediately applicable teaching aids, plus completely updated sources of information, pamphlets, field guides, recordings, etc. Bibliography. 74 photographs. + 310pp. 5⅜ x 8½.   T1015 Paperbound **$1.75**

HOW TO KNOW THE WILD FLOWERS, Mrs. William Starr Dana. Classic nature book that has introduced thousands to wonders of American wild flowers. Color-season principle of organization is easy to use, even by those with no botanical training, and the genial, refreshing discussions of history, folklore, uses of over 1,000 native and escape flowers, foliage plants are informative as well as fun to read. Over 170 full-page plates, collected from several editions, may be colored in to make permanent records of finds. Revised to conform with 1950 edition of Gray's Manual of Botany. xlii + 438pp. 5⅜ x 8½.   T332 Paperbound **$2.00**

HOW TO KNOW THE FERNS, F. T. Parsons. Ferns, among our most lovely native plants, are all too little known. This classic of nature lore will enable the layman to identify almost any American fern he may come across. After an introduction on the structure and life of ferns, the 57 most important ferns are fully pictured and described (arranged upon a simple identification key). Index of Latin and English names. 61 illustrations and 42 full-page plates. xiv + 215pp. 5⅜ x 8.   T740 Paperbound **$1.35**

MANUAL OF THE TREES OF NORTH AMERICA, Charles Sprague Sargent. Still unsurpassed as most comprehensive, reliable study of North American tree characteristics, precise locations and distribution. By dean of American dendrologists. Every tree native to U.S., Canada, Alaska, 185 genera, 717 species, described in detail—leaves, flowers, fruit, winterbuds, bark, wood, growth habits etc. plus discussion of varieties and local variants, immaturity variations. Over 100 keys, including unusual 11-page analytical key to genera, aid in identification. 783 clear illustrations of flowers, fruit, leaves. An unmatched permanent reference work for all nature lovers. Second enlarged (1926) edition. Synopsis of families. Analytical key to genera. Glossary of technical terms. Index. 783 illustrations, 1 map. Two volumes. Total of 982pp. 5⅜ x 8.   T277 Vol. I Paperbound **$2.25**
                                                              T278 Vol. II Paperbound **$2.25**
                                                                       The set **$4.50**

TREES OF THE EASTERN AND CENTRAL UNITED STATES AND CANADA, W. M. Harlow. A revised edition of a standard middle-level guide to native trees and important escapes. More than 140 trees are described in detail, and illustrated with more than 600 drawings and photographs. Supplementary keys will enable the careful reader to identify almost any tree he might encounter. xiii + 288pp. 5⅜ x 8.   T395 Paperbound **$1.35**

GUIDE TO SOUTHERN TREES, Ellwood S. Harrar and J. George Harrar. All the essential information about trees indigenous to the South, in an extremely handy format. Introductory essay on methods of tree classification and study, nomenclature, chief divisions of Southern trees, etc. Approximately 100 keys and synopses allow for swift, accurate identification of trees. Numerous excellent illustrations, non-technical text make this a useful book for teachers of biology or natural science, nature lovers, amateur naturalists. Revised 1962 edition. Index. Bibliography. Glossary of technical terms. 920 illustrations; 201 full-page plates. ix + 709pp. 4⅝ x 6⅜.   T945 Paperbound **$2.35**

FRUIT KEY AND TWIG KEY TO TREES AND SHRUBS, W. M. Harlow. Bound together in one volume for the first time, these handy and accurate keys to fruit and twig identification are the only guides of their sort with photographs (up to 3 times natural size). "Fruit Key": Key to over 120 different deciduous and evergreen fruits. 139 photographs and 11 line drawings. Synoptic summary of fruit types. Bibliography. 2 Indexes (common and scientific names). "Twig Key": Key to over 160 different twigs and buds. 173 photographs. Glossary of technical terms. Bibliography. 2 Indexes (common and scientific names). Two volumes bound as one. Total of xvii + 126pp. 5⅝ x 8⅜.   T511 Paperbound **$1.25**

INSECT LIFE AND INSECT NATURAL HISTORY, S. W. Frost. A work emphasizing habits, social life, and ecological relations of insects, rather than more academic aspects of classification and morphology. Prof. Frost's enthusiasm and knowledge are everywhere evident as he discusses insect associations and specialized habits like leaf-rolling, leaf-mining, and case-making, the gall insects, the boring insects, aquatic insects, etc. He examines all sorts of matters not usually covered in general works, such as: insects as human food, insect music and musicians, insect response to electric and radio waves, use of insects in art and literature. The admirably executed purpose of this book, which covers the middle ground between elementary treatment and scholarly monographs, is to excite the reader to observe for himself. Over 700 illustrations. Extensive bibliography. x + 524pp. 5⅜ x 8.   T517 Paperbound **$2.45**

CATALOGUE OF DOVER BOOKS

COMMON SPIDERS OF THE UNITED STATES, J. H. Emerton. Here is a nature hobby you can pursue right in your own cellar! Only non-technical, but thorough, reliable guide to spiders for the layman. Over 200 spiders from all parts of the country, arranged by scientific classification, are identified by shape and color, number of eyes, habitat and range, habits, etc. Full text, 501 line drawings and photographs, and valuable introduction explain webs, poisons, threads, capturing and preserving spiders, etc. Index. New synoptic key by S. W. Frost. xxiv + 225pp. 5⅜ x 8. **T223 Paperbound $1.45**

THE LIFE STORY OF THE FISH: HIS MANNERS AND MORALS, Brian Curtis. A comprehensive, non-technical survey of just about everything worth knowing about fish. Written for the aquarist, the angler, and the layman with an inquisitive mind, the text covers such topics as evolution, external covering and protective coloration, physics and physiology of vision, maintenance of equilibrium, function of the lateral line canal for auditory and temperature senses, nervous system, function of the air bladder, reproductive system and methods—courtship, mating, spawning, care of young—and many more. Also sections on game fish, the problems of conservation and a fascinating chapter on fish curiosities. "Clear, simple language . . . excellent judgment in choice of subjects . . . delightful sense of humor," New York Times. Revised (1949) edition. Index. Bibliography of 72 items. 6 full-page photographic plates. xii + 284pp. 5⅜ x 8. **T929 Paperbound $1.65**

BATS, Glover Morrill Allen. The most comprehensive study of bats as a life-form by the world's foremost authority. A thorough summary of just about everything known about this fascinating and mysterious flying mammal, including its unique location sense, hibernation and cycles, its habitats and distribution, its wing structure and flying habits, and its relationship to man in the long history of folklore and superstition. Written on a middle-level, the book can be profitably studied by a trained zoologist and thoroughly enjoyed by the layman. "An absorbing text with excellent illustrations. Bats should have more friends and fewer thoughtless detractors as a result of the publication of this volume," William Beebe, Books. Extensive bibliography. 57 photographs and illustrations. x + 368pp. 5⅜ x 8½. **T984 Paperbound $2.00**

BIRDS AND THEIR ATTRIBUTES, Glover Morrill Allen. A fine general introduction to birds as living organisms, especially valuable because of emphasis on structure, physiology, habits, behavior. Discusses relationship of bird to man, early attempts at scientific ornithology, feathers and coloration, skeletal structure including bills, legs and feet, wings. Also food habits, evolution and present distribution, feeding and nest-building, still unsolved questions of migrations and location sense, many more similar topics. Final chapter on classification, nomenclature. A good popular-level summary for the biologist; a first-rate introduction for the layman. Reprint of 1925 edition. References and index. 51 illustrations. viii + 338pp. 5⅜ x 8½. **T957 Paperbound $1.85**

LIFE HISTORIES OF NORTH AMERICAN BIRDS, Arthur Cleveland Bent. Bent's monumental series of books on North American birds, prepared and published under auspices of Smithsonian Institute, is the definitive coverage of the subject, the most-used single source of information. Now the entire set is to be made available by Dover in inexpensive editions. This encyclopedic collection of detailed, specific observations utilizes reports of hundreds of contemporary observers, writings of such naturalists as Audubon, Burroughs, William Brewster, as well as author's own extensive investigations. Contains literally everything known about life history of each bird considered: nesting, eggs, plumage, distribution and migration, voice, enemies, courtship, etc. These not over-technical works are musts for ornithologists, conservationists, amateur naturalists, anyone seriously interested in American birds.

BIRDS OF PREY. More than 100 subspecies of hawks, falcons, eagles, buzzards, condors and owls, from the common barn owl to the extinct caracara of Guadaloupe Island. 400 photographs. Two volume set. Index for each volume. Bibliographies of 403, 520 items. 197 full-page plates. Total of 907pp. 5⅜ x 8½. Vol. I **T931 Paperbound $2.50**
Vol. II **T932 Paperbound $2.50**

WILD FOWL. Ducks, geese, swans, and tree ducks—73 different subspecies. Two volume set. Index for each volume. Bibliographies of 124, 144 items. 106 full-page plates. Total of 685pp. 5⅜ x 8½. Vol. I **T285 Paperbound $2.50**
Vol. II **T286 Paperbound $2.50**

SHORE BIRDS. 81 varieties (sandpipers, woodcocks, plovers, snipes, phalaropes, curlews, oyster catchers, etc.). More than 200 photographs of eggs, nesting sites, adult and young of important species. Two volume set. Index for each volume. Bibliographies of 261, 188 items. 121 full-page plates. Total of 860pp. 5⅜ x 8½. Vol. I **T933 Paperbound $2.35**
Vol. II **T934 Paperbound $2.35**

THE LIFE OF PASTEUR, R. Vallery-Radot. 13th edition of this definitive biography, cited in Encyclopaedia Britannica. Authoritative, scholarly, well-documented with contemporary quotes, observations; gives complete picture of Pasteur's personal life; especially thorough presentation of scientific activities with silkworms, fermentation, hydrophobia, inoculation, etc. Introduction by Sir William Osler. Index. 505pp. 5⅜ x 8. **T632 Paperbound $2.00**

Puzzles, Mathematical Recreations

SYMBOLIC LOGIC and THE GAME OF LOGIC, Lewis Carroll. "Symbolic Logic" is not concerned with modern symbolic logic, but is instead a collection of over 380 problems posed with charm and imagination, using the syllogism, and a fascinating diagrammatic method of drawing conclusions. In "The Game of Logic" Carroll's whimsical imagination devises a logical game played with 2 diagrams and counters (included) to manipulate hundreds of tricky syllogisms. The final section, "Hit or Miss" is a lagniappe of 101 additional puzzles in the delightful Carroll manner. Until this reprint edition, both of these books were rarities costing up to $15 each. Symbolic Logic: Index. xxxi + 199pp. The Game of Logic: 96pp. 2 vols. bound as one. 5⅜ x 8.
T492 Paperbound **$1.50**

PILLOW PROBLEMS and A TANGLED TALE, Lewis Carroll. One of the rarest of all Carroll's works, "Pillow Problems" contains 72 original math puzzles, all typically ingenious. Particularly fascinating are Carroll's answers which remain exactly as he thought them out, reflecting his actual mental process. The problems in "A Tangled Tale" are in story form, originally appearing as a monthly magazine serial. Carroll not only gives the solutions, but uses answers sent in by readers to discuss wrong approaches and misleading paths, and grades them for insight. Both of these books were rarities until this edition, "Pillow Problems" costing up to $25, and "A Tangled Tale" $15. Pillow Problems: Preface and Introduction by Lewis Carroll. xx + 109pp. A Tangled Tale: 6 illustrations. 152pp. Two vols. bound as one. 5⅜ x 8.
T493 Paperbound **$1.50**

AMUSEMENTS IN MATHEMATICS, Henry Ernest Dudeney. The foremost British originator of mathematical puzzles is always intriguing, witty, and paradoxical in this classic, one of the largest collections of mathematical amusements. More than 430 puzzles, problems, and paradoxes. Mazes and games, problems on number manipulation, unicursal and other route problems, puzzles on measuring, weighing, packing, age, kinship, chessboards, joiners', crossing river, plane figure dissection, and many others. Solutions. More than 450 illustrations. vii + 258pp. 5⅜ x 8.
T473 Paperbound **$1.25**

THE CANTERBURY PUZZLES, Henry Dudeney. Chaucer's pilgrims set one another problems in story form. Also Adventures of the Puzzle Club, the Strange Escape of the King's Jester, the Monks of Riddlewell, the Squire's Christmas Puzzle Party, and others. All puzzles are original, based on dissecting plane figures, arithmetic, algebra, elementary calculus and other branches of mathematics, and purely logical ingenuity. "The limit of ingenuity and intricacy," The Observer. Over 110 puzzles. Full Solutions. 150 illustrations. vii + 225pp. 5⅜ x 8.
T474 Paperbound **$1.25**

MATHEMATICAL EXCURSIONS, H. A. Merrill. Even if you hardly remember your high school math, you'll enjoy the 90 stimulating problems contained in this book and you will come to understand a great many mathematical principles with surprisingly little effort. Many useful shortcuts and diversions not generally known are included: division by inspection, Russian peasant multiplication, memory systems for pi, building odd and even magic squares, square roots by geometry, dyadic systems, and many more. Solutions to difficult problems. 50 illustrations. 145pp. 5⅜ x 8.
T350 Paperbound **$1.00**

MAGIC SQUARES AND CUBES, W. S. Andrews. Only book-length treatment in English, a thorough non-technical description and analysis. Here are nasik, overlapping, pandiagonal, serrated squares; magic circles, cubes, spheres, rhombuses. Try your hand at 4-dimensional magical figures! Much unusual folklore and tradition included. High school algebra is sufficient. 754 diagrams and illustrations. viii + 419pp. 5⅜ x 8.
T658 Paperbound **$1.85**

CALIBAN'S PROBLEM BOOK: MATHEMATICAL, INFERENTIAL AND CRYPTOGRAPHIC PUZZLES, H. Phillips (Caliban), S. T. Shovelton, G. S. Marshall. 105 ingenious problems by the greatest living creator of puzzles based on logic and inference. Rigorous, modern, piquant; reflecting their author's unusual personality, these intermediate and advanced puzzles all involve the ability to reason clearly through complex situations; some call for mathematical knowledge, ranging from algebra to number theory. Solutions. xi + 180pp. 5⅜ x 8.
T736 Paperbound **$1.25**

MATHEMATICAL PUZZLES FOR BEGINNERS AND ENTHUSIASTS, G. Mott-Smith. 188 mathematical puzzles based on algebra, dissection of plane figures, permutations, and probability, that will test and improve your powers of inference and interpretation. The Odic Force, The Spider's Cousin, Ellipse Drawing, theory and strategy of card and board games like tit-tat-toe, go moku, salvo, and many others. 100 pages of detailed mathematical explanations. Appendix of primes, square roots, etc. 135 illustrations. 2nd revised edition. 248pp. 5⅜ x 8.
T198 Paperbound **$1.00**

MATHEMAGIC, MAGIC PUZZLES, AND GAMES WITH NUMBERS, R. V. Heath. More than 60 new puzzles and stunts based on the properties of numbers. Easy techniques for multiplying large numbers mentally, revealing hidden numbers magically, finding the date of any day in any year, and dozens more. Over 30 pages devoted to magic squares, triangles, cubes, circles, etc. Edited by J. S. Meyer. 76 illustrations. 128pp. 5⅜ x 8.
T110 Paperbound **$1.00**

CATALOGUE OF DOVER BOOKS

THE BOOK OF MODERN PUZZLES, G. L. Kaufman. A completely new series of puzzles as fascinating as crossword and deduction puzzles but based upon different principles and techniques.
Simple 2-minute teasers, word labyrinths, design and pattern puzzles, logic and observation
puzzles — over 150 braincrackers. Answers to all problems. 116 illustrations. 192pp. 5⅜ x 8.
                                                                T143 Paperbound $1.00

NEW WORD PUZZLES, G. L. Kaufman. 100 ENTIRELY NEW puzzles based on words and their
combinations that will delight crossword puzzle, Scrabble and Jotto fans. Chess words, based
on the moves of the chess king; design-onyms, symmetrical designs made of synonyms; rhymed
double-crostics; syllable sentences; addle letter anagrams; alphagrams; linkograms; and many
others all brand new. Full solutions. Space to work problems. 196 figures. vi + 122pp.
5⅜ x 8.   T344 Paperbound $1.00

MAZES AND LABYRINTHS: A BOOK OF PUZZLES, W. Shepherd. Mazes, formerly associated with
mystery and ritual, are still among the most intriguing of intellectual puzzles. This is a novel
and different collection of 50 amusements that embody the principle of the maze: mazes in
the classical tradition; 3-dimensional, ribbon, and Möbius-strip mazes; hidden messages; spa-
tial arrangements; etc.—almost all built on amusing story situations. 84 illustrations. Essay
on maze psychology. Solutions. xv + 122pp. 5⅜ x 8.   T731 Paperbound $1.00

MAGIC TRICKS & CARD TRICKS, W. Jonson. Two books bound as one. 52 tricks with cards, 37
tricks with coins, bills, eggs, smoke, ribbons, slates, etc. Details on presentation, misdirection,
and routining will help you master such famous tricks as the Changing Card, Card in the
Pocket, Four Aces, Coin Through the Hand, Bill in the Egg, Afghan Bands, and over 75 others.
If you follow the lucid exposition and key diagrams carefully, you will finish these two books
with an astonishing mastery of magic. 106 figures. 224pp. 5⅜ x 8. T909 Paperbound $1.00

PANORAMA OF MAGIC, Milbourne Christopher. A profusely illustrated history of stage magic,
a unique selection of prints and engravings from the author's private collection of magic
memorabilia, the largest of its kind. Apparatus, stage settings and costumes; ingenious ads
distributed by the performers and satiric broadsides passed around in the streets ridiculing
pompous showmen; programs; decorative souvenirs. The lively text, by one of America's
foremost professional magicians, is full of anecdotes about almost legendary wizards: Dede,
the Egyptian; Philadelphia, the wonder-worker; Robert-Houdin, "the father of modern magic;"
Harry Houdini; scores more. Altogether a pleasure package for anyone interested in magic,
stage setting and design, ethnology, psychology, or simply in unusual people. A Dover
original. 295 illustrations; 8 in full color. Index. viii + 216pp. 8⅜ x 11¼.
                                                                T774 Paperbound $2.25

HOUDINI ON MAGIC, Harry Houdini. One of the greatest magicians of modern times explains
his most prized secrets. How locks are picked, with illustrated picks and skeleton keys; how
a girl is sawed into twins; how to walk through a brick wall — Houdini's explanations of 44
stage tricks with many diagrams. Also included is a fascinating discussion of great magicians
of the past and the story of his fight against fraudulent mediums and spiritualists. Edited
by W.B. Gibson and M.N. Young. Bibliography. 155 figures, photos. xv + 280pp. 5⅜ x 8.
                                                                T384 Paperbound $1.35

MATHEMATICS, MAGIC AND MYSTERY, Martin Gardner. Why do card tricks work? How do
magicians perform astonishing mathematical feats? How is stage mind-reading possible? This
is the first book length study explaining the application of probability, set theory, theory of
numbers, topology, etc., to achieve many startling tricks. Non-technical, accurate, detailed!
115 sections discuss tricks with cards, dice, coins, knots, geometrical vanishing illusions, how
a Curry square "demonstrates" that the sum of the parts may be greater than the whole,
and dozens of others. No sleight of hand necessary! 135 illustrations. xii + 174pp. 5⅜ x 8.
                                                                T335 Paperbound $1.00

**EASY-TO-DO ENTERTAINMENTS AND DIVERSIONS WITH COINS, CARDS, STRING, PAPER AND
MATCHES, R. M. Abraham.** Over 300 tricks, games and puzzles will provide young readers
with absorbing fun. Sections on card games; paper-folding; tricks with coins, matches
and pieces of string; games for the agile; toy-making from common household objects;
mathematical recreations; and 50 miscellaneous pastimes. Anyone in charge of groups of
youngsters, including hard-pressed parents, and in need of suggestions on how to keep
children sensibly amused and quietly content will find this book indispensable. Clear,
simple text, copious number of delightful line drawings and illustrative diagrams. Originally
titled "Winter Nights Entertainments." Introduction by Lord Baden Powell. 329 illustrations.
v + 186pp. 5⅜ x 8½.   T921 Paperbound $1.00

STRING FIGURES AND HOW TO MAKE THEM, Caroline Furness Jayne. 107 string figures plus
variations selected from the best primitive and modern examples developed by Navajo,
Apache, pygmies of Africa, Eskimo, in Europe, Australia, China, etc. The most readily under-
standable, easy-to-follow book in English on perennially popular recreation. Crystal-clear
exposition; step-by-step diagrams. Everyone from kindergarten children to adults looking
for unusual diversion will be endlessly amused. Index. Bibliography. Introduction by A. C.
Haddon. 17 full-page plates. 960 illustrations. xxiii + 401pp. 5⅜ x 8½.
                                                                T152 Paperbound $2.00

Entertainments, Humor

ODDITIES AND CURIOSITIES OF WORDS AND LITERATURE, C. Bombaugh, edited by M. Gardner. The largest collection of idiosyncratic prose and poetry techniques in English, a legendary work in the curious and amusing bypaths of literary recreations and the play technique in literature—so important in modern works. Contains alphabetic poetry, acrostics, palindromes, scissors verse, centos, emblematic poetry, famous literary puns, hoaxes, notorious slips of the press, hilarious mistranslations, and much more. Revised and enlarged with modern material by Martin Gardner. 368pp. 5⅜ x 8. T759 Paperbound **$1.75**

A NONSENSE ANTHOLOGY, collected by Carolyn Wells. 245 of the best nonsense verses ever written, including nonsense puns, absurd arguments, mock epics and sagas, nonsense ballads, odes, "sick" verses, dog-Latin verses, French nonsense verses, songs. By Edward Lear, Lewis Carroll, Gelett Burgess, W. S. Gilbert, Hilaire Belloc, Peter Newell, Oliver Herford, etc., 83 writers in all plus over four score anonymous nonsense verses. A special section of limericks, plus famous nonsense such as Carroll's "Jabberwocky" and Lear's "The Jumblies" and much excellent verse virtually impossible to locate elsewhere. For 50 years considered the best anthology available. Index of first lines specially prepared for this edition. Introduction by Carolyn Wells. 3 indexes: Title, Author, First lines. xxxiii + 279pp. T499 Paperbound **$1.35**

THE BAD CHILD'S BOOK OF BEASTS, MORE BEASTS FOR WORSE CHILDREN, and A MORAL ALPHA-BET, H. Belloc. Hardly an anthology of humorous verse has appeared in the last 50 years without at least a couple of these famous nonsense verses. But one must see the entire volumes—with all the delightful original illustrations by Sir Basil Blackwood—to appreciate fully Belloc's charming and witty verses that play so subacidly on the platitudes of life and morals that beset his day—and ours. A great humor classic. Three books in one. Total of 157pp. 5⅜ x 8. T749 Paperbound **$1.00**

THE DEVIL'S DICTIONARY, Ambrose Bierce. Sardonic and irreverent barbs puncturing the pomposities and absurdities of American politics, business, religion, literature, and arts, by the country's greatest satirist in the classic tradition. Epigrammatic as Shaw, piercing as Swift, American as Mark Twain, Will Rogers, and Fred Allen, Bierce will always remain the favorite of a small coterie of enthusiasts, and of writers and speakers whom he supplies with "some of the most gorgeous witticisms of the English language" (H. L. Mencken). Over 1000 entries in alphabetical order. 144pp. 5⅜ x 8. T487 Paperbound **$1.00**

THE PURPLE COW AND OTHER NONSENSE, Gelett Burgess. The best of Burgess's early nonsense, selected from the first edition of the "Burgess Nonsense Book." Contains many of his most unusual and truly awe-inspiring pieces: 36 nonsense quatrains, the Poems of Patagonia, Alphabet of Famous Goops, and the other hilarious (and rare) adult nonsense that place him in the forefront of American humorists. All pieces are accompanied by the original Burgess illustrations. 123 illustrations. xiii + 113pp. 5⅜ x 8. T772 Paperbound **$1.00**

MY PIOUS FRIENDS AND DRUNKEN COMPANIONS and MORE PIOUS FRIENDS AND DRUNKEN COMPANIONS, Frank Shay. Folksingers, amateur and professional, and everyone who loves singing: here, available for the first time in 30 years, is this valued collection of 132 ballads, blues, vaudeville numbers, drinking songs, sea chanties, comedy songs. Songs of pre-Beatnik Bohemia; songs from all over America, England, France, Australia; the great songs of the Naughty Nineties and early twentieth-century America. Over a third with music. Woodcuts by John Held, Jr. convey perfectly the brash insouciance of an era of rollicking unabashed song. 12 illustrations by John Held, Jr. Two indexes (Titles and First lines and Choruses). Introductions by the author. Two volumes bound as one. Total of xvi + 235pp. 5⅜ x 8½. T946 Paperbound **$1.25**

HOW TO TELL THE BIRDS FROM THE FLOWERS, R. W. Wood. How not to confuse a carrot with a parrot, a grape with an ape, a puffin with nuffin. Delightful drawings, clever puns, absurd little poems point out far-fetched resemblances in nature. The author was a leading physicist. Introduction by Margaret Wood White. 106 illus. 60pp. 5⅜ x 8. T523 Paperbound **75¢**

PECK'S BAD BOY AND HIS PA, George W. Peck. The complete edition, containing both volumes, of one of the most widely read American humor books. The endless ingenious pranks played by bad boy "Hennery" on his pa and the grocery man, the outraged pomposity of Pa, the perpetual ridiculing of middle class institutions, are as entertaining today as they were in 1883. No pale sophistications or subtleties, but rather humor vigorous, raw, earthy, imaginative, and, as folk humor often is, sadistic. This peculiarly fascinating book is also valuable to historians and students of American culture as a portrait of an age. 100 original illustrations by True Williams. Introduction by E. F. Bleiler. 347pp. 5⅜ x 8. T497 Paperbound **$1.35**

THE HUMOROUS VERSE OF LEWIS CARROLL. Almost every poem Carroll ever wrote, the largest collection ever published, including much never published elsewhere: 150 parodies, burlesques, riddles, ballads, acrostics, etc., with 130 original illustrations by Tenniel, Carroll, and others. "Addicts will be grateful . . . there is nothing for the faithful to do but sit down and fall to the banquet," N. Y. Times. Index to first lines. xiv + 446pp. 5⅜ x 8.
T654 Paperbound **$2.00**

DIVERSIONS AND DIGRESSIONS OF LEWIS CARROLL. A major new treasure for Carroll fans! Rare privately published humor, fantasy, puzzles, and games by Carroll at his whimsical best, with a new vein of frank satire. Includes many new mathematical amusements and recreations, among them the fragmentary Part III of "Curiosa Mathematica." Contains "The Rectory Umbrella," "The New Belfry," "The Vision of the Three T's," and much more. New 32-page supplement of rare photographs taken by Carroll. x + 375pp. 5⅜ x 8.
T732 Paperbound **$2.00**

THE COMPLETE NONSENSE OF EDWARD LEAR. This is the only complete edition of this master of gentle madness available at a popular price. A BOOK OF NONSENSE, NONSENSE SONGS, MORE NONSENSE SONGS AND STORIES in their entirety with all the old favorites that have delighted children and adults for years. The Dong With A Luminous Nose, The Jumblies, The Owl and the Pussycat, and hundreds of other bits of wonderful nonsense. 214 limericks, 3 sets of Nonsense Botany, 5 Nonsense Alphabets, 546 drawings by Lear himself, and much more. 320pp. 5⅜ x 8.
T167 Paperbound **$1.00**

THE MELANCHOLY LUTE, The Humorous Verse of Franklin P. Adams ("FPA"). The author's own selection of light verse, drawn from thirty years of FPA's column, "The Conning Tower," syndicated all over the English-speaking world. Witty, perceptive, literate, these ninety-six poems range from parodies of other poets, Millay, Longfellow, Edgar Guest, Kipling, Masefield, etc., and free and hilarious translations of Horace and other Latin poets, to satiric comments on fabled American institutions—the New York Subways, preposterous ads, suburbanites, sensational journalism, etc. They reveal with vigor and clarity the humor, integrity and restraint of a wise and gentle American satirist. Introduction by Robert Hutchinson. vi + 122pp. 5⅜ x 8½.
T108 Paperbound **$1.00**

SINGULAR TRAVELS, CAMPAIGNS, AND ADVENTURES OF BARON MUNCHAUSEN, R. E. Raspe, with 90 illustrations by Gustave Doré. The first edition in over 150 years to reestablish the deeds of the Prince of Liars exactly as Raspe first recorded them in 1785—the genuine Baron Munchausen, one of the most popular personalities in English literature. Included also are the best of the many sequels, written by other hands. Introduction on Raspe by J. Carswell. Bibliography of early editions. xliv + 192pp. 5⅜ x 8.
T698 Paperbound **$1.00**

THE WIT AND HUMOR OF OSCAR WILDE, ed. by Alvin Redman. Wilde at his most brilliant, in 1000 epigrams exposing weaknesses and hypocrisies of "civilized" society. Divided into 49 categories—sin, wealth, women, America, etc.—to aid writers, speakers. Includes excerpts from his trials, books, plays, criticism. Formerly "The Epigrams of Oscar Wilde." Introduction by Vyvyan Holland, Wilde's only living son. Introductory essay by editor. 260pp. 5⅜ x 8.
T602 Paperbound **$1.00**

MAX AND MORITZ, Wilhelm Busch. Busch is one of the great humorists of all time, as well as the father of the modern comic strip. This volume, translated by H. A. Klein and other hands, contains the perennial favorite "Max and Moritz" (translated by C. T. Brooks), Plisch and Plum, Das Rabennest, Eispeter, and seven other whimsical, sardonic, jovial, diabolical cartoon and verse stories. Lively English translations parallel the original German. This work has delighted millions since it first appeared in the 19th century, and is guaranteed to please almost anyone. Edited by H. A. Klein, with an afterword. x + 205pp. 5⅝ x 8½.
T181 Paperbound **$1.15**

HYPOCRITICAL HELENA, Wilhelm Busch. A companion volume to "Max and Moritz," with the title piece (Die Fromme Helena) and 10 other highly amusing cartoon and verse stories, all newly translated by H. A. Klein and M. C. Klein: Adventure on New Year's Eve (Abenteuer in der Neujahrsnacht), Hangover on the Morning after New Year's Eve (Der Katzenjammer am Neujahrsmorgen), etc. English and German in parallel columns. Hours of pleasure, also a fine language aid. x + 205pp. 5⅝ x 8½.
T184 Paperbound **$1.00**

THE BEAR THAT WASN'T, Frank Tashlin. What does it mean? Is it simply delightful wry humor, or a charming story of a bear who wakes up in the midst of a factory, or a satire on Big Business, or an existential cartoon-story of the human condition, or a symbolization of the struggle between conformity and the individual? New York Herald Tribune said of the first edition: ". . . a fable for grownups that will be fun for children. Sit down with the book and get your own bearings." Long an underground favorite with readers of all ages and opinions. v + 51pp. Illustrated. 5⅜ x 8½.
T939 Paperbound **75¢**

RUTHLESS RHYMES FOR HEARTLESS HOMES and MORE RUTHLESS RHYMES FOR HEARTLESS HOMES, Harry Graham ("Col. D. Streamer"). Two volumes of Little Willy and 48 other poetic disasters. A bright, new reprint of oft-quoted, never forgotten, devastating humor by a precursor of today's "sick" joke school. For connoisseurs of wicked, wacky humor and all who delight in the comedy of manners. Original drawings are a perfect complement. 61 illustrations. Index. vi + 69pp. Two vols. bound as one. 5⅜ x 8½.
T930 Paperbound **75¢**

Say It language phrase books

These handy phrase books (128 to 196 pages each) make grammatical drills unnecessary for an elementary knowledge of a spoken foreign language. Covering most matters of travel and everyday life each volume contains:

Over 1000 phrases and sentences in immediately useful forms — foreign language plus English.

Modern usage designed for Americans. Specific phrases like, "Give me small change," and "Please call a taxi."

Simplified phonetic transcription you will be able to read at sight.

The only completely indexed phrase books on the market.

Covers scores of important situations: — Greetings, restaurants, sightseeing, useful expressions, etc.

These books are prepared by native linguists who are professors at Columbia, N.Y.U., Fordham and other great universities. Use them independently or with any other book or record course. They provide a supplementary living element that most other courses lack. Individual volumes in:

Russian 75¢	Italian 75¢	Spanish 75¢	German 75¢
Hebrew 75¢	Danish 75¢	Japanese 75¢	Swedish 75¢
Dutch 75¢	Esperanto 75¢	Modern Greek 75¢	Portuguese 75¢
Norwegian 75¢	Polish 75¢	French 75¢	Yiddish 75¢
Turkish 75¢		English for German-speaking people 75¢	
English for Italian-speaking people 75¢		English for Spanish-speaking people 75¢	

Large clear type. 128-196 pages each. 3½ x 5¼. Sturdy paper binding.

Listen and Learn language records

LISTEN & LEARN is the only language record course designed especially to meet your travel and everyday needs. It is available in separate sets for FRENCH, SPANISH, GERMAN, JAPANESE, RUSSIAN, MODERN GREEK, PORTUGUESE, ITALIAN and HEBREW, and each set contains three 33⅓ rpm long-playing records—1½ hours of recorded speech by eminent native speakers who are professors at Columbia, New York University, Queens College.

Check the following special features found only in LISTEN & LEARN:

- **Dual-language recording.** 812 selected phrases and sentences, over 3200 words, spoken first in English, then in their foreign language equivalents. A suitable pause follows each foreign phrase, allowing you time to repeat the expression. You learn by unconscious assimilation.
- **128 to 206-page manual** contains everything on the records, plus a simple phonetic pronunciation guide.
- **Indexed for convenience. The only set on the market** that is completely indexed. No more puzzling over where to find the phrase you need. Just look in the rear of the manual.
- **Practical.** No time wasted on material you can find in any grammar. LISTEN & LEARN covers central core material with phrase approach. Ideal for the person with limited learning time.
- **Living, modern expressions,** not found in other courses. Hygienic products, modern equipment, shopping—expressions used every day, like "nylon" and "air-conditioned."
- **Limited objective.** Everything you learn, no matter where you stop, is immediately useful. You have to finish other courses, wade through grammar and vocabulary drill, before they help you.
- **High-fidelity recording.** LISTEN & LEARN records equal in clarity and surface-silence any record on the market costing up to $6.

"Excellent . . . the spoken records . . . impress me as being among the very best on the market," **Prof. Mario Pei,** Dept. of Romance Languages, Columbia University. "Inexpensive and well-done . . . it would make an ideal present," CHICAGO SUNDAY TRIBUNE. "More genuinely helpful than anything of its kind which I have previously encountered," **Sidney Clark,** well-known author of "ALL THE BEST" travel books.

UNCONDITIONAL GUARANTEE. Try LISTEN & LEARN, then return it within 10 days for full refund if you are not satisfied.

Each set contains three twelve-inch 33⅓ records, manual, and album.

SPANISH	the set $5.95	GERMAN	the set $5.95
FRENCH	the set $5.95	ITALIAN	the set $5.95
RUSSIAN	the set $5.95	JAPANESE	the set $5.95
PORTUGUESE	the set $5.95	MODERN GREEK	the set $5.95
MODERN HEBREW	the set $5.95		

CATALOGUE OF DOVER BOOKS

Americana

THE EYES OF DISCOVERY, J. Bakeless. A vivid reconstruction of how unspoiled America appeared to the first white men. Authentic and enlightening accounts of Hudson's landing in New York, Coronado's trek through the Southwest; scores of explorers, settlers, trappers, soldiers. America's pristine flora, fauna, and Indians in every region and state in fresh and unusual new aspects. "A fascinating view of what the land was like before the first highway went through," Time. 68 contemporary illustrations, 39 newly added in this edition. Index. Bibliography. x + 500pp. 5⅜ x 8. T761 Paperbound $2.00

AUDUBON AND HIS JOURNALS, J. J. Audubon. A collection of fascinating accounts of Europe and America in the early 1800's through Audubon's own eyes. Includes the Missouri River Journals —an eventful trip through America's untouched heartland, the Labrador Journals, the European Journals, the famous "Episodes", and other rare Audubon material, including the descriptive chapters from the original letterpress edition of the "Ornithological Studies", omitted in all later editions. Indispensable for ornithologists, naturalists, and all lovers of Americana and adventure. 70-page biography by Audubon's granddaughter. 38 illustrations. Index. Total of 1106pp. 5⅜ x 8. T675 Vol I Paperbound $2.25
T676 Vol II Paperbound $2.25
The set $4.50

TRAVELS OF WILLIAM BARTRAM, edited by Mark Van Doren. The first inexpensive illustrated edition of one of the 18th century's most delightful books is an excellent source of first-hand material on American geography, anthropology, and natural history. Many descriptions of early Indian tribes are our only source of information on them prior to the infiltration of the white man. "The mind of a scientist with the soul of a poet," John Livingston Lowes. 13 original illustrations and maps. Edited with an introduction by Mark Van Doren. 448pp. 5⅜ x 8. T13 Paperbound $2.00

GARRETS AND PRETENDERS: A HISTORY OF BOHEMIANISM IN AMERICA, A. Parry. The colorful and fantastic history of American Bohemianism from Poe to Kerouac. This is the only complete record of hoboes, cranks, starving poets, and suicides. Here are Pfaff, Whitman, Crane, Bierce, Pound, and many others. New chapters by the author and by H. T. Moore bring this thorough and well-documented history down to the Beatniks. "An excellent account," N. Y. Times. Scores of cartoons, drawings, and caricatures. Bibliography. Index. xxviii + 421pp. 5⅝ x 8⅜. T708 Paperbound $1.95

THE EXPLORATION OF THE COLORADO RIVER AND ITS CANYONS, J. W. Powell. The thrilling first-hand account of the expedition that filled in the last white space on the map of the United States. Rapids, famine, hostile Indians, and mutiny are among the perils encountered as the unknown Colorado Valley reveals its secrets. This is the only uncut version of Major Powell's classic of exploration that has been printed in the last 60 years. Includes later reflections and subsequent expedition. 250 illustrations, new map. 400pp. 5⅝ x 8⅜. T94 Paperbound $2.25

THE JOURNAL OF HENRY D. THOREAU, Edited by Bradford Torrey and Francis H. Allen. Henry Thoreau is not only one of the most important figures in American literature and social thought; his voluminous journals (from which his books emerged as selections and crystallizations) constitute both the longest, most sensitive record of personal internal development and a most penetrating description of a historical moment in American culture. This present set, which was first issued in fourteen volumes, contains Thoreau's entire journals from 1837 to 1862, with the exception of the lost years which were found only recently. We are reissuing it, complete and unabridged, with a new introduction by Walter Harding, Secretary of the Thoreau Society. Foreword by Henry Seidel Canby. Fourteen volumes reissued in two volumes. Total of 1888pp. 8⅜ x 12¼. T312-3 Two volume set, Clothbound $20.00

GAMES AND SONGS OF AMERICAN CHILDREN, collected by William Wells Newell. A remarkable collection of 190 games with songs that accompany many of them; cross references to show similarities, differences among them; variations; musical notation for 38 songs. Textual discussions show relations with folk-drama and other aspects of folk tradition. Grouped into categories for ready comparative study: Love-games, histories, playing at work, human life, bird and beast, mythology, guessing-games, etc. New introduction covers relations of songs and dances to timeless heritage of folklore, biographical sketch of Newell, other pertinent data. A good source of inspiration for those in charge of groups of children and a valuable reference for anthropologists, sociologists, psychiatrists. Introduction by Carl Withers. New indexes of first lines, games. 5⅜ x 8½. xii + 242pp. T354 Paperbound $1.75

Art, History of Art, Antiques, Graphic Arts, Handcrafts

ART STUDENTS' ANATOMY, E. J. Farris. Outstanding art anatomy that uses chiefly living objects for its illustrations. 71 photos of undraped men, women, children are accompanied by carefully labeled matching sketches to illustrate the skeletal system, articulations and movements, bony landmarks, the muscular system, skin, fasciae, fat, etc. 9 x-ray photos show movement of joints. Undraped models are shown in such actions as serving in tennis, drawing a bow in archery, playing football, dancing, preparing to spring and to dive. Also discussed and illustrated are proportions, age and sex differences, the anatomy of the smile, etc. 8 plates by the great early 18th century anatomic illustrator Siegfried Albinus are also included. Glossary. 158 figures, 7 in color. x + 159pp. 5⅝ x 8⅜. T744 Paperbound **$1.50**

AN ATLAS OF ANATOMY FOR ARTISTS, F Schider. A new 3rd edition of this standard text enlarged by 52 new illustrations of hands, anatomical studies by Cloquet, and expressive life studies of the body by Barcsay. 189 clear, detailed plates offer you precise information of impeccable accuracy. 29 plates show all aspects of the skeleton, with closeups of special areas, while 54 full-page plates, mostly in two colors, give human musculature as seen from four different points of view, with cutaways for important portions of the body. 14 full-page plates provide photographs of hand forms, eyelids, female breasts, and indicate the location of muscles upon models. 59 additional plates show how great artists of the past utilized human anatomy. They reproduce sketches and finished work by such artists as Michelangelo, Leonardo da Vinci, Goya, and 15 others. This is a lifetime reference work which will be one of the most important books in any artist's library. "The standard reference tool," AMERICAN LIBRARY ASSOCIATION. "Excellent," AMERICAN ARTIST. Third enlarged edition. 189 plates, 647 illustrations. xxvi + 192pp. 7⅞ x 10⅝. T241 Clothbound **$6.00**

AN ATLAS OF ANIMAL ANATOMY FOR ARTISTS, W. Ellenberger, H. Baum, H. Dittrich. The largest, richest animal anatomy for artists available in English. 99 detailed anatomical plates of such animals as the horse, dog, cat, lion, deer, seal, kangaroo, flying squirrel, cow, bull, goat, monkey, hare, and bat. Surface features are clearly indicated, while progressive beneath-the-skin pictures show musculature, tendons, and bone structure. Rest and action are exhibited in terms of musculature and skeletal structure and detailed cross-sections are given for heads and important features. The animals chosen are representative of specific families so that a study of these anatomies will provide knowledge of hundreds of related species. "Highly recommended as one of the very few books on the subject worthy of being used as an authoritative guide," DESIGN. "Gives a fundamental knowledge," AMERICAN ARTIST. Second revised, enlarged edition with new plates from Cuvier, Stubbs, etc. 288 illustrations. 153pp. 11⅜ x 9. T82 Clothbound **$6.00**

THE HUMAN FIGURE IN MOTION, Eadweard Muybridge. The largest selection in print of Muybridge's famous high-speed action photos of the human figure in motion. 4789 photographs illustrate 162 different actions: men, women, children—mostly undraped—are shown walking, running, carrying various objects, sitting, lying down, climbing, throwing, arising, and performing over 150 other actions. Some actions are shown in as many as 150 photographs each. All in all there are more than 500 action strips in this enormous volume, series shots taken at shutter speeds of as high as 1/6000th of a second! These are not posed shots, but true stopped motion. They show bone and muscle in situations that the human eye is not fast enough to capture. Earlier, smaller editions of these prints have brought $40 and more on the out-of-print market. "A must for artists," ART IN FOCUS. "An unparalleled dictionary of action for all artists," AMERICAN ARTIST. 390 full-page plates, with 4789 photographs. Printed on heavy glossy stock. Reinforced binding with headbands. xxi + 390pp. 7⅞ x 10⅝. T204 Clothbound **$10.00**

ANIMALS IN MOTION, Eadweard Muybridge. This is the largest collection of animal action photos in print. 34 different animals (horses, mules, oxen, goats, camels, pigs, cats, guanacos, lions, gnus, deer, monkeys, eagles—and 21 others) in 132 characteristic actions. The horse alone is shown in more than 40 different actions. All 3919 photographs are taken in series at speeds up to 1/6000th of a second. The secrets of leg motion, spinal patterns, head movements, strains and contortions shown nowhere else are captured. You will see exactly how a lion sets his foot down; how an elephant's knees are like a human's—and how they differ; the position of a kangaroo's legs in mid-leap; how an ostrich's head bobs; details of the flight of birds—and thousands of facets of motion only the fastest cameras can catch. Photographed from domestic animals and animals in the Philadelphia zoo, it contains neither semiposed artificial shots nor distorted telephoto shots taken under adverse conditions. Artists, biologists, decorators, cartoonists, will find this book indispensable for understanding animals in motion. "A really marvelous series of plates," NATURE (London). "The dry plate's most spectacular early use was by Eadweard Muybridge," LIFE. 3919 photographs; 380 full pages of plates. 440pp. Printed on heavy glossy paper. Deluxe binding with headbands. 7⅞ x 10⅝. T203 Clothbound **$10.00**

THE AUTOBIOGRAPHY OF AN IDEA, Louis Sullivan. The pioneer architect whom Frank Lloyd Wright called "the master" reveals an acute sensitivity to social forces and values in this passionately honest account. He records the crystallization of his opinions and theories, the growth of his organic theory of architecture that still influences American designers and architects, contemporary ideas, etc. This volume contains the first appearance of 34 full-page plates of his finest architecture. Unabridged reissue of 1924 edition. New introduction by R. M. Line. Index. xiv + 335pp. 5⅜ x 8. T281 Paperbound **$2.00**

THE DRAWINGS OF HEINRICH KLEY. The first uncut republication of both of Kley's devastating sketchbooks, which first appeared in pre-World War I Germany. One of the greatest cartoonists and social satirists of modern times, his exuberant and iconoclastic fantasy and his extraordinary technique place him in the great tradition of Bosch, Breughel, and Goya, while his subject matter has all the immediacy and tension of our century. 200 drawings. viii + 128pp. 7¾ x 10¾. T24 Paperbound **$1.85**

MORE DRAWINGS BY HEINRICH KLEY. All the sketches from Leut' Und Viecher (1912) and Sammel-Album (1923) not included in the previous Dover edition of Drawings. More of the bizarre, mercilessly iconoclastic sketches that shocked and amused on their original publication. Nothing was too sacred, no one too eminent for satirization by this imaginative, individual and accomplished master cartoonist. A total of 158 illustrations. Iv + 104pp. 7¾ x 10¾. T41 Paperbound **$1.85**

PINE FURNITURE OF EARLY NEW ENGLAND, R. H. Kettell. A rich understanding of one of America's most original folk arts that collectors of antiques, interior decorators, craftsmen, woodworkers, and everyone interested in American history and art will find fascinating and immensely useful. 413 illustrations of more than 300 chairs, benches, racks, beds, cupboards, mirrors, shelves, tables, and other furniture will show all the simple beauty and character of early New England furniture. 55 detailed drawings carefully analyze outstanding pieces. "With its rich store of illustrations, this book emphasizes the individuality and varied design of early American pine furniture. It should be welcomed," ANTIQUES. 413 illustrations and 55 working drawings. 475. 8 x 10¾. T145 Clothbound **$10.00**

THE HUMAN FIGURE, J. H. Vanderpoel. Every important artistic element of the human figure is pointed out in minutely detailed word descriptions in this classic text and illustrated as well in 430 pencil and charcoal drawings. Thus the text of this book directs your attention to all the characteristic features and subtle differences of the male and female (adults, children, and aged persons), as though a master artist were telling you what to look for at each stage. 2nd edition, revised and enlarged by George Bridgman. Foreword. 430 illustrations. 143pp. 6⅛ x 9¼. T432 Paperbound **$1.50**

LETTERING AND ALPHABETS, J. A. Cavanagh. This unabridged reissue of LETTERING offers a full discussion, analysis, illustration of 89 basic hand lettering styles — styles derived from Caslons, Bodonis, Garamonds, Gothic, Black Letter, Oriental, and many others. Upper and lower cases, numerals and common signs pictured. Hundreds of technical hints on make-up, construction, artistic validity, strokes, pens, brushes, white areas, etc. May be reproduced without permission! 89 complete alphabets; 72 lettered specimens. 121pp. 9¾ x 8. T53 Paperbound **$1.35**

STICKS AND STONES, Lewis Mumford. A survey of the forces that have conditioned American architecture and altered its forms. The author discusses the medieval tradition in early New England villages; the Renaissance influence which developed with the rise of the merchant class; the classical influence of Jefferson's time; the "Mechanicsvilles" of Poe's generation; the Brown Decades; the philosophy of the Imperial facade; and finally the modern machine age. "A truly remarkable book," SAT. REV. OF LITERATURE. 2nd revised edition. 21 illustrations. xvii + 228pp. 5⅜ x 8. T202 Paperbound **$1.75**

THE STANDARD BOOK OF QUILT MAKING AND COLLECTING, Marguerite Ickis. A complete easy-to-follow guide with all the information you need to make beautiful, useful quilts. How to plan, design, cut, sew, appliqué, avoid sewing problems, use rag bag, make borders, tuft, every other aspect. Over 100 traditional quilts shown, including over 40 full-size patterns. At-home hobby for fun, profit. Index. 483 illus. 1 color plate. 287pp. 6¾ x 9½. T582 Paperbound **$2.00**

THE BOOK OF SIGNS, Rudolf Koch. Formerly $20 to $25 on the out-of-print market, now only $1.00 in this unabridged new edition! 493 symbols from ancient manuscripts, medieval cathedrals, coins, catacombs, pottery, etc. Crosses, monograms of Roman emperors, astrological, chemical, botanical, runes, housemarks, and 7 other categories. Invaluable for handicraft workers, illustrators, scholars, etc., this material may be reproduced without permission. 493 illustrations by Fritz Kredel. 104pp. 6½ x 9¼. T162 Paperbound **$1.00**

PRIMITIVE ART, Franz Boas. This authoritative and exhaustive work by a great American anthropologist covers the entire gamut of primitive art. Pottery, leatherwork, metal work, stone work, wood, basketry, are treated in detail. Theories of primitive art, historical depth in art history, technical virtuosity, unconscious levels of patterning, symbolism, styles, literature, music, dance, etc. A must book for the interested layman, the anthropologist, artist, handicrafter (hundreds of unusual motifs), and the historian. Over 900 illustrations (50 ceramic vessels, 12 totem poles, etc.). 376pp. 5⅜ x 8. T25 Paperbound **$2.00**

Fiction

FLATLAND, E. A. Abbott. A science-fiction classic of life in a 2-dimensional world that is also a first-rate introduction to such aspects of modern science as relativity and hyperspace. Political, moral, satirical, and humorous overtones have made FLATLAND fascinating reading for thousands. 7th edition. New introduction by Banesh Hoffmann. 16 illustrations. 128pp. 5⅜ x 8. T1 Paperbound **$1.00**

THE WONDERFUL WIZARD OF OZ, L. F. Baum. Only edition in print with all the original W. W. Denslow illustrations in full color—as much a part of "The Wizard" as Tenniel's drawings are of "Alice in Wonderland." "The Wizard" is still America's best-loved fairy tale, in which, as the author expresses it, "The wonderment and joy are retained and the heartaches and nightmares left out." Now today's young readers can enjoy every word and wonderful picture of the original book. New introduction by Martin Gardner. A Baum bibliography. 23 full-page color plates. viii + 268pp. 5⅜ x 8. T691 Paperbound **$1.50**

THE MARVELOUS LAND OF OZ, L. F. Baum. This is the equally enchanting sequel to the "Wizard," continuing the adventures of the Scarecrow and the Tin Woodman. The hero this time is a little boy named Tip, and all the delightful Oz magic is still present. This is the Oz book with the Animated Saw-Horse, the Woggle-Bug, and Jack Pumpkinhead. All the original John R. Neill illustrations, 10 in full color. 287 pp. 5⅜ x 8. T692 Paperbound **$1.50**

28 SCIENCE FICTION STORIES OF H. G. WELLS. Two full unabridged novels, MEN LIKE GODS and STAR BEGOTTEN, plus 26 short stories by the master science-fiction writer of all time! Stories of space, time, invention, exploration, future adventure—an indispensable part of the library of everyone interested in science and adventure. PARTIAL CONTENTS: Men Like Gods, The Country of the Blind, In the Abyss, The Crystal Egg, The Man Who Could Work Miracles, A Story of the Days to Come, The Valley of Spiders, and 21 more! 928pp. 5⅜ x 8. T265 Clothbound **$4.50**

THREE MARTIAN NOVELS, Edgar Rice Burroughs. Contains: Thuvia, Maid of Mars; The Chessmen of Mars; and The Master Mind of Mars. High adventure set in an imaginative and intricate conception of the Red Planet. Mars is peopled with an intelligent, heroic human race which lives in densely populated cities and with fierce barbarians who inhabit dead sea bottoms. Other exciting creatures abound amidst an inventive framework of Martian history and geography. Complete unabridged reprintings of the first edition. 16 illustrations by J. Allen St. John. vi + 499pp. 5⅜ x 8½. T39 Paperbound **$1.85**

SEVEN SCIENCE FICTION NOVELS, H. G. Wells. Full unabridged texts of 7 science-fiction novels of the master. Ranging from biology, physics, chemistry, astronomy to sociology and other studies, Mr. Wells extrapolates whole worlds of strange and intriguing character. "One will have to go far to match this for entertainment, excitement, and sheer pleasure . . . ," NEW YORK TIMES. Contents: The Time Machine, The Island of Dr. Moreau, First Men in the Moon, The Invisible Man, The War of the Worlds, The Food of the Gods, In the Days of the Comet. 1015pp. 5⅜ x 8. T264 Clothbound **$4.50**

THE LAND THAT TIME FORGOT and THE MOON MAID, Edgar Rice Burroughs. In the opinion of many, Burroughs' best work. The first concerns a strange island where evolution is individual rather than phylogenetic. Speechless anthropoids develop into intelligent human beings within a single generation. The second projects the reader far into the future and describes the first voyage to the Moon (in the year 2025), the conquest of the Earth by the Moon, and years of violence and adventure as the enslaved Earthmen try to regain possession of their planet. "An imaginative tour de force that keeps the reader keyed up and expectant," NEW YORK TIMES. Complete, unabridged text of the original two novels (three parts in each). 5 illustrations by J. Allen St. John. vi + 552pp. 5⅜ x 8½.
T1020 Clothbound **$3.75**
T358 Paperbound **$2.00**

3 ADVENTURE NOVELS by H. Rider Haggard. Complete texts of "She," "King Solomon's Mines," "Allan Quatermain." Qualities of discovery; desire for immortality; search for primitive, for what is unadorned by civilization, have kept these novels of African adventure exciting, alive to readers from R. L. Stevenson to George Orwell. 636pp. 5⅜ x 8. T584 Paperbound **$2.00**

A PRINCESS OF MARS and A FIGHTING MAN OF MARS: TWO MARTIAN NOVELS BY EDGAR RICE BURROUGHS. "Princess of Mars" is the very first of the great Martian novels written by Burroughs, and it is probably the best of them all; it set the pattern for all of his later fantasy novels and contains a thrilling cast of strange peoples and creatures and the formula of Olympian heroism amidst ever-fluctuating fortunes which Burroughs carries off so successfully. "Fighting Man" returns to the same scenes and cities—many years later. A mad scientist, a degenerate dictator, and an indomitable defender of the right clash—with the fate of the Red Planet at stake! Complete, unabridged reprinting of original editions. Illustrations by F. E. Schoonover and Hugh Hutton. v + 356pp. 5⅜ x 8½. T1140 Paperbound **$1.75**

Music

A GENERAL HISTORY OF MUSIC, Charles Burney. A detailed coverage of music from the Greeks up to 1789, with full information on all types of music: sacred and secular, vocal and instrumental, operatic and symphonic. Theory, notation, forms, instruments, innovators, composers, performers, typical and important works, and much more in an easy, entertaining style. Burney covered much of Europe and spoke with hundreds of authorities and composers so that this work is more than a compilation of records . . . it is a living work of careful and first-hand scholarship. Its account of thoroughbass (18th century) Italian music is probably still the best introduction on the subject. A recent NEW YORK TIMES review said, "Surprisingly few of Burney's statements have been invalidated by modern research . . . still of great value." Edited and corrected by Frank Mercer. 35 figures. Indices. 1915pp. 5⅜ x 8. 2 volumes.   T36 The Set, Clothbound **$12.50**

A DICTIONARY OF HYMNOLOGY, John Julian. This exhaustive and scholarly work has become known as an invaluable source of hundreds of thousands of important and often difficult to obtain facts on the history and use of hymns in the western world. Everyone interested in hymns will be fascinated by the accounts of famous hymns and hymn writers and amazed by the amount of practical information he will find. More than 30,000 entries on individual hymns, giving authorship, date and circumstances of composition, publication, textual variations, translations, denominational and ritual usage, etc. Biographies of more than 9,000 hymn writers, and essays on important topics such as Christmas carols and children's hymns, and much other unusual and valuable information. A 200 page double-columned index of first lines — the largest in print. Total of 1786 pages in two reinforced clothbound volumes. 6¼ x 9¼.
The set, T333 Clothbound **$17.50**

MUSIC IN MEDIEVAL BRITAIN, F. Ll. Harrison. The most thorough, up-to-date, and accurate treatment of the subject ever published, beautifully illustrated. Complete account of institutions and choirs; carols, masses, and motets; liturgy and plainsong; and polyphonic music from the Norman Conquest to the Reformation. Discusses the various schools of music and their reciprocal influences; the origin and development of new ritual forms; development and use of instruments; and new evidence on many problems of the period. Reproductions of scores, over 200 excerpts from medieval melodies. Rules of harmony and dissonance; influence of Continental styles; great composers (Dunstable, Cornysh, Fairfax, etc.); and much more. Register and index of more than 400 musicians. Index of titles. General Index. 225-item bibliography. 6 Appendices. xix + 491pp. 5⅝ x 8¾.   T705 Clothbound **$10.00**

THE MUSIC OF SPAIN, Gilbert Chase. Only book in English to give concise, comprehensive account of Iberian music; new Chapter covers music since 1941. Victoria, Albéniz, Cabezón, Pedrell, Turina, hundreds of other composers; popular and folk music; the Gypsies; the guitar; dance, theatre, opera, with only extensive discussion in English of the Zarzuela; virtuosi such as Casals; much more. "Distinguished . . . readable," Saturday Review. 400-item bibliography. Index. 27 photos. 383pp. 5⅜ x 8.   T549 Paperbound **$2.00**

ON STUDYING SINGING, Sergius Kagen. An intelligent method of voice-training, which leads you around pitfalls that waste your time, money, and effort. Exposes rigid, mechanical systems, baseless theories, deleterious exercises. "Logical, clear, convincing . . . dead right," Virgil Thomson, N.Y. Herald Tribune. "I recommend this volume highly," Maggie Teyte, Saturday Review. 119pp. 5⅜ x 8.   T622 Paperbound **$1.35**

Prices subject to change without notice.

Dover publishes books on art, music, philosophy, literature, languages, history, social sciences, psychology, handcrafts, orientalia, puzzles and entertainments, chess, pets and gardens, books explaining science, intermediate and higher mathematics, mathematical physics, engineering, biological sciences, earth sciences, classics of science, etc. Write to:

Dept. catrr.
Dover Publications, Inc.
180 Varick Street, N.Y. 14, N.Y.